Homer Laughlin
Decades of Dinnerware

by
Bob Page
Dale Frederiksen
Dean Six

Page/Frederiksen Publications
Greensboro, North Carolina

With Price Guide

ACKNOWLEDGMENTS

Books on collectibles, to be as comprehensive as possible, require the input of a number of people. Some of these people care intensely about the topic and some have worked in and around the product for decades. This project has only been possible with the input and support of a number of these wonderful people. The following people went the extra distance to share knowledge or images and to support our work. Others helped along the way and to each of you, named or unnamed, we sincerely appreciate the kindness shown us.
Please know this book was enriched by the help of:

Joseph Wells, Jr. of the Homer Laughlin China Company
Joseph Wells III of the Homer Laughlin China Company
Judi Noble of the Homer Laughlin China Company
Joe Geisse of the Homer Laughlin China Company
Ann Culler of the Homer Laughlin China Company
The Staff of the Homer Laughlin Outlet
Tom Felt
Mark Peters & Katina Davis
Jacklyn King
Fred Mutchler
James Mitchell, West Virginia State Museum
Jim Zock
Taj Fellion & Joseph Britt of Taj Fellion Antiques
Francis Workman
Venus Wallace and Upstairs Antiques
Steve Hyatt
Gary Geiselman and Grandma's China Closet
Bernice Kolier and Gypsy's Purple Pages of Collectibles
Dustin Michael Maxwell
Armand Shank and Ivy Hills Antiques
Kelly Newsome

Working at Replacements, Ltd. is a wonderful experience in teamwork. We wish to acknowledge all of the Replacements, Ltd. staff whose dedicated work made this book possible. Thanks to each of you for yet another job well done. From the research and production sides, this volume is indeed a team effort. Literally dozens of people have helped in many ways over the long period of development and production, some whose contributions have been most significant include:

Todd Hall, Photographer
Dwayne Whitaker, Photographer
Cindy Allred, Imaging Department Manager
Sherry Blankenship, Graphic Artist
Rob Fisher, Project Specialist
Cora Miller, Pat West, and Chris Kirkman of the Research staff
Sherry Bundy, on line auction purchases and collector contacts
Gay Nell Staley our persistent helper

A special acknowledgment is due Rachael Potts, Replacements, Ltd. art director and designer for this book. Her layout skills and persistent Homer Laughlin sleuthing were invaluable. Her tenacity in seeking backstamps to aid in dating pieces, her skill in drawing all the line drawings from actual pieces, and her desire to maintain a high standard of detail, make this book what it is.
Thank you Rachael.

Published by
Page/Frederiksen Publications
Greensboro, North Carolina

ISBN#: 1-889977-13-6

Copyright © 2003 by Page/Frederiksen Publications
ALL RIGHTS RESERVED
No part of this book may be reproduced without the expressed written permission of the authors and publishers.

Front Cover: Fiesta Medium Green pattern, Dinner Plate; Virginia Rose Tulips in a Basket pattern, Pitcher; Art China, Stein Ewer; Wells Art Glaze Red pattern, Teapot; Harlequin Spruce Green pattern, Fish; and Swing Colonial Kitchen pattern, Demitasse Cup & Saucer Set.
Title page: Harlequin Red, Round Covered Vegetable Bowl.

Additional Copies of this book may be ordered from:

1089 Knox Road, PO Box 26029 Greensboro, North Carolina 27420
1-800-REPLACE (1-800-737-5223) *www.replacements.com*

TABLE OF CONTENTS

Chapter	page #
How To Use This Book	4
Foward	5
History	8
How Big	10
Visual Pattern Index	14
Same Decal on Every Shape	29
Early Shapes	30
American Beauty 1899	34
Colonial 1901	38
The Angelus 1907	41
Hudson 1908	48
Empress 1910	61
Niagara 1910	68
Genesee 1911	71
Republic 1917	81
Kwaker 1920	91
Yellowstone 1926	101
Trellis 1927	110
Newell 1928	113
Wells 1930	120
Century, Riviera 1931	132
Ravenna 1932	149
Jade 1932	153
Orleans 1932	160
Old Roman 1932	164
Virginia Rose 1932	166
OvenServe 1933	184
Chelsea 1933	194
Marigold 1934	196
Craftsman 1934	201
Coronet 1935	205
Fiesta 1935	210
Willow, Americana, Fantasy 1935	238
Nautilus 1936	250
Brittany 1936	260
Harlequin 1936	281
Kitchen Kraft 1937	292
Kraft 1937	299
Tea Rose 1937	304
Tango 1937	306
Eggshell Intro 1937	309
Eggshell Nautilus 1937	310
Eggshell Georgian 1937	335
Eggshell Swing 1938	354
Eggshell Theme 1939	365
Eggshell Andover 1940	373
Eggshell Cavalier 1953	375
Carnival 1938	390
Modern Farmer 1939	393
Serenade 1939	396
Piccadilly 1940	400
Rope Edge 1941	403
Liberty 1942	408
Pastoral, Wild Rose, and Harvest 1944	420
Jubilee, Skytone, Debutante, and Suntone 1948	424
Rhythm 1949	437
Charm House, Duraprint, and Applique 1952	453
Epicure 1955	460
Studio 1957	465
Fashion 1958	468
Triumph 1959	469
Alliance 1960	475
Dover 1960	477
Duratone 1960	481
Saxon 1960	482
Vogue 1963	485
Orbit 1964	487
Victoria 1965	489
Granada 1966	493
Regency 1966	497
Bristol 1970	499
Hearthside 1970	501
International 1970	506
Challenger 1974	509
Tablefair 1980	511
Mixed Shapes	513
Unknown Coupe Patterns	514
Unknown Rim Patterns	517
Toiletries 1800's	520
Children's Sets	523
Giftware	525
World's Fair	529
Mexican Decals	533
How to Read HLC Backstamps	535
Bibliography	536
Authors	537
History of Replacements, Ltd.	538
Other Publications	540
Index	541

HOW TO USE THIS BOOK

The INDEX in this book is as complete as we could make it. If you know the name or pattern number for the piece you are looking for, the quickest way to find your pattern is by looking in the index located at the back of the book, starting on page 141.

If you do not know the pattern name or number, we have created a VISUAL INDEX that allows you to possibly locate your pattern based on the shape of the forms on which it appears. We first show the dinner plate shape — look for one that matches yours. We then show the cup, sugar bowl and creamer to illustrate handles and other forms most commonly found. Simply try to match the shape or form to that of your pattern and follow the directions to the pages indicated. The Visual Index is on pages 14 – 28 of this book.

Thousands of names and pattern numbers are listed in this book. We use the Homer Laughlin Factory or advertised names and pattern numbers when we know them, or have been able to find them. Some of the pieces that might have factory numbers on the bottom of the lids include covered vegetables (casseroles) and round or oval vegetables. Numbers found on pieces generally begin with a letter designating either the shape (such as VR to indicate Virginia Rose) or a private customer for whom the pattern was made (such as MW to indicate Montgomery Ward). Pattern names are found on the bottom of some pieces, but this is very uncommon and generally a more recent practice. We always use factory numbers and names when we can. These appear under the individual plates in the book that illustrate each pattern.

The shape of a pattern (such as Genesee or OvenServe) may be written on the bottom and this will lead you to the chapter where all the patterns we know on that shape will be found. Additionally, we have used period advertisements from magazines and trade journals, catalogs (such as Sears, Montomery Ward, etc.), and other primary source material to determine pattern names and numbers. When other authors or collectors have created or established names that are now used in the collecting world, we have generally used them here too.

In the event that no pattern name or number is known or can be found, Replacements, Ltd. assigns a number to the pattern. This assigned number begins with a code designating Homer Laughlin China, HLC, and then runs serially as they have been identified by Replacements, Ltd. For example, HLC101 is the 101st unknown Homer Lauglin pattern set up and named at Replacements. As we write this, unknown patterns number into the thousands.

Several patterns found at the Homer Laughlin Factory and some from customers have embossed or impressed patterns in the clay. They can be found included in the chapter that contains the basic shape of the plates and hollowware. We have not set them apart.

SIZE VARIANCES may exist when you try to match your piece to the piece type lists in the chapters. A certain amount of variance exists in clay products due to an array of variables. Molds and shapes may have been remade over time creating minor differences. Firing, drying, or actual clay composition may have been slightly different, creating minor size differences. Some pieces are largely hand created, even today, allowing for inherent slight variances. We consider a tolerance of up to ¼th of an inch to be common and greater discrepancies can be found.

Not all Homer Laughlin patterns known to Replacements, Ltd. are in the book. For many we have verbal descriptions, but lack an image. For some patterns, the images we have are not clear enough to use for identification in this book. There clearly are thousands of Homer Laughlin patterns yet to be identified. We hope you enjoy the immense amount of information in this volume. Have fun searching for your patterns and documenting even more patterns than what is represented here.

FOREWORD

The story of Homer Laughlin, the man and the pottery that bears his name, is an amazing tale that spans three centuries.

By some accounts the Homer Laughlin China Company has produced as much as one third of all dinnerware made in America. While such numbers are staggering and impossible to verify, the fact that this upper Ohio Valley company has been so successful for such a long time makes it the subject of many collections and books.

Yet this book aspires to be different. This is the first attempt to identify the expanse and variety of dinnerware patterns the firm has produced. While trying to comprehend the volume of Homer Laughlin production, Joseph Wells, III, a fourth generation factory owner, was asked how many Homer Laughlin patterns had been produced over time. His answer: "Somewhere between 25,000 and 35,000... probably."

The scope of such a project would be encyclopedic, truly requiring volumes, but Homer Laughlin is engaged in producing popular and sellable dinnerware, they are not historians. The company is busy looking forward and ensuring their success in this century.

Above:
Trellis shape,
HLC1345 pattern;
Modernistic, cubist landscape,
photograph taken at the factory.

Above: *Postcard from the Homer Laughlin Factory in Newell, West Virginia.*

Above: *Unknown magazine advertisement from around 1900.*

With their cooperation, Replacements, Ltd. set out to discover, uncover, and document as many Homer Laughlin patterns as possible. This book focuses not on Fiesta or Virginia Rose, patterns about which entire books exist, but about the larger Homer Laughlin product family, including Fiesta and Virginia Rose and many others.

Here is the opportunity for a firm like Replacements, Ltd., engaged in identifying and selling replacement dinnerware and other products, to become involved in and excited about a massive project! When Replacements, Ltd. seeks records and information on many firms we find that the company long ago ceased to exist and no paper, resources, or archives survive. Other companies that are still in business have merged, relocated, or simply cleaned house over the decades. Those companies and their histories are purged of "the old stuff." Homer Laughlin China Company is different.

Homer Laughlin is different because it retains its family-owned, locally-controlled, sense of pride. As we explored the resources at Homer Laughlin we repeatedly met people who told of their family involvement with the company for two and three generations. The employees expressed their sense of identity with Homer Laughlin as a company, and also spoke in terms of the company as an extended family. We too grew to feel this was someplace special.

Above: *Art Glazes on Century and Virginia Rose shaped pitchers; photograph taken at the Homer Laughlin Factory in Newell, West Virginia.*

As we asked questions to uncover the information that would tell the Homer Laughlin China story, friendships and working relationships grew. The Art Department staff shared experiences and the not insignificant records maintained over the decades in their corner of the sprawling complex. The owners allowed us kind and gracious access to people and materials. We hope this account of Homer Laughlin China Company and its impressive production pays tribute to this major American concern, its visionary leadership and its dedicated workers — past and present.

Top left: *Fiesta Shape, Red Older pattern; Disk Pitcher.* **Middle left:** *Fiesta Shape, Cobalt Blue Older pattern; Nesting Bowls.* **Bottom left:** *Fiesta Shape, Light Green Older pattern; Salad Bowl.* **Right:** *Patents for Homer Laughlin China.*

These three design patents, obtained by a New York artist, were assigned to Homer Laughlin in 1928 and reported in a china and glass trade journal along with other patents. The 68,249 design of birds, floras, and urn was used to create Empress pattern 4613, Century pattern 694, Kwaker pattern 4613, and Kwaker pattern Rosewood. 68,250 has been found on Kwaker pattern 4513 and on Hudson pattern 7213. The design patent 68,251 was used on Empress pattern 4713 and on republic pattern 3624. It is likely that other shapes also utilized these designs for patterns not yet identified.

HISTORY

THE HOMER LAUGHLIN CHINA CO.
ESTABLISHED 1871
NEWELL, W.VA. 26050-1299
TEL: 304/387-1300
FAX: 304/387-0593
October 12, 1992

INVOICE
HOMER LAUGHLIN CHINA CO.
MAKERS OF
SEMI-VITREOUS CHINA
NEWELL, W.VA.
Joshua Poole
East Liverpool.O
June 9,1915

The Homer Laughlin China Co.
MAKERS OF
Semi-Vitreous China.
East Liverpool, Ohio.
July 28,1902

THE HOMER LAUGHLIN CHINA CO.
MAKERS OF
HOMER LAUGHLIN CHINA
NEWELL, W.VA.

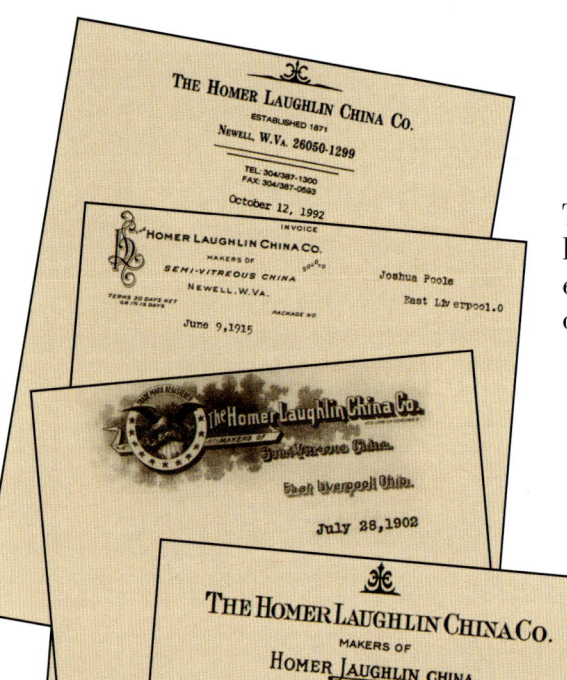

The Laughlin Brothers, Homer and Shakespeare (from an obviously literary family), began making pottery in 1871. A pottery was erected in East Liverpool, Ohio by the brothers and placed in operation as Ohio Valley Pottery.

Shakespeare left the business to pursue other interests in 1877 and in 1897 Homer Laughlin sold his interest in the company that by then bore his name. The new owners were W. E. Wells, Louis I. Aaron and Aaron's sons Marcus and Charles I. Aaron. Today, over a century later, the Wells family continues to own and operate the Homer Laughlin China Company. Several detailed accounts of Homer Laughlin, his family and the early history of the company exist and retelling would not improve or expand on those accounts.

Briefly, the original Homer Laughlin Factory was on River Road in East Liverpool, Ohio.

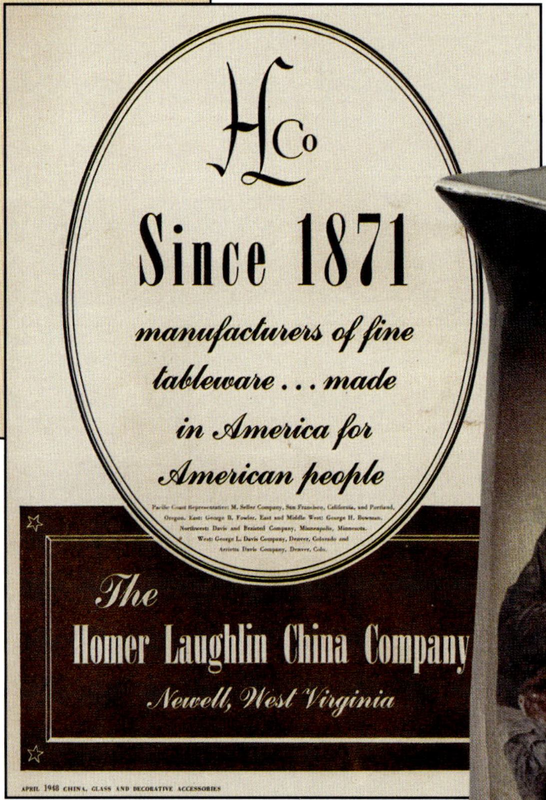

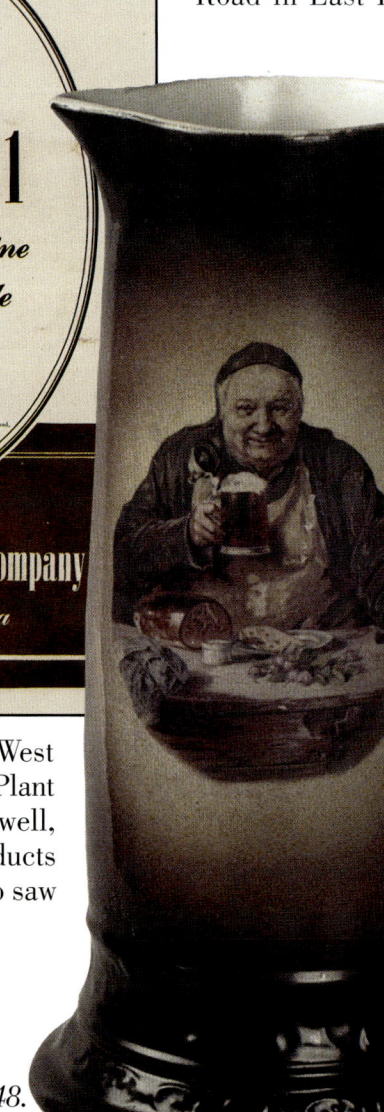

After Homer Laughlin sold his interest in the factory in 1897 he relocated to Los Angeles, CA, but retained a position on the corporate board for several years.

By 1903, the new owners had expanded to operate three factories in East Liverpool. By 1907 a new factory, Plant No. 4, was opened in Newell, West Virginia. Plant No. 5 followed in 1914. 1923 saw the addition of Plant No.'s 6 and 7. Plant No. 8 was built in 1929, all of these in Newell, West Virginia. Plant No. 8 was constructed largely to make products for a single account, the dime store chain Woolworth. 1929 also saw the closure of all production facilities in Ohio.

Above: *Homer Laughlin Letterhead, October 12, 1992.*
Homer Laughlin Letterhead, June 9, 1915.
Homer Laughlin Letterhead, July 28, 1902.
Homer Laughlin Letterhead.
Ad in China, Glass and Decorative Accessories, *April 1948.*
Right: *Monk Stein Ewer.*

The family history of the Aaron and Wells families merit retelling, however briefly, as they illustrate the long and direct involvement of these two families in the success of the company.

William E. Wells (1863-1931) began working at Homer Laughlin in East Liverpool, Ohio as a bookkeeper in 1889. He was one of the four who purchased the factory in 1897. He held various positions at the company, and served as general manager and secretary at the time of his retirement in 1930. His son, Joseph M. Wells, assumed his duties at the factory. Joseph M. Wells (1889-1970) served as general manager and secretary until his retirement in 1959. Joseph M. Wells, Jr. (b. 1915) assumed the duties of general manager from his father in 1959. Joseph M. Wells, III (b. 1941) became the fourth generation of his family to serve as president and general manager of Homer Laughlin, a position he continues to hold today.

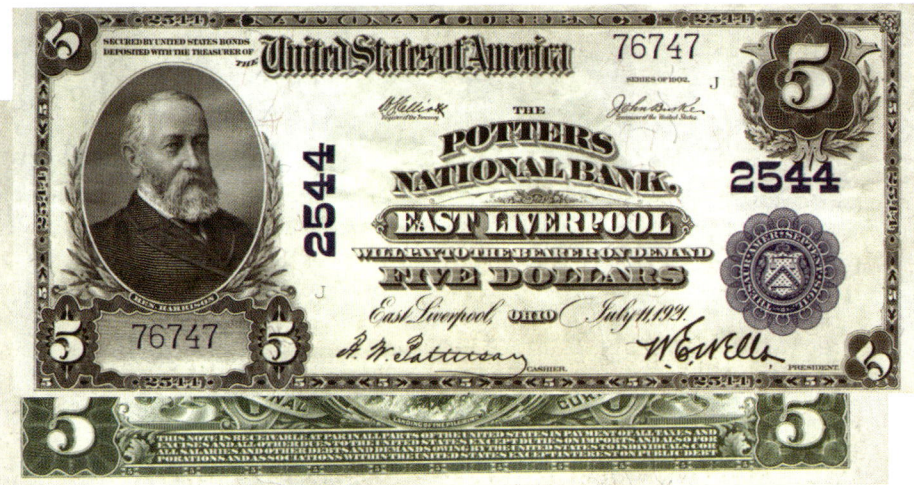

Above: *"The Potters National Bank of East Liverpool, Ohio opened for business in 1881. In this era main street banking began to flourish in many small towns across America. This bank was so named because it serviced the many pottery workers in the area. It was liquidated October 10, 1931, during the great depression. The signers of this note are W. E. Wells, President and H. W. Patterson, Cashier. Mr. Wells became general manager of the Homer Laughlin Company in 1897 and served the company until his death in 1931."*

The Aaron family acquired their interest in Homer Laughlin at the same time as William E. Wells, in 1897. Louis I. Aaron (1857-1919) served as president until 1910. Louis had two sons, Marcus (1869-1954) and Charles I. (1872-1947). Marcus became president upon the retirement of his father in 1910 and served until 1940. Charles I. never married and served as vice president from 1910 until his death. Marcus L. Aaron (1900-1994), son of Marcus Aaron, claimed his father's role as president and continued in the leadership from 1940 until 1989. Marcus Aaron, II (b. 1929) succeeded his father as president in 1989.

In 2002, the near 105 year old two-family partnership ended when, in a friendly acquisition, the Wells family acquired the interest of Aaron family. Both families had actively worked together for over a century and four generations. Amazingly, Joe Wells, III was quoted as saying "Our families have never had an argument, ever, as far as I know." An amazing testimony and perhaps part of the "secret to their success." With this June 2002 transfer, Joe Wells, long the Executive VP and company General Manager, became the new President of Homer Laughlin. With assurances of continued quality, American owned and American manufactured products, The Homer Laughlin China Company is poised for success well into the future!

Above: *Riviera patterns; Light Green Large Pitcher with lid, and Red Syrup with lid.*

How Big Was Homer Laughlin China?

Any single measure, like number of employees, amount of production, etc. is not consistently available over any period of time. Thus only single, isolated figures can be pieced together to convey the size of Homer Laughlin.

In 1908, the company had added a new plant (No. 4) and was operating 62 kilns, 48 decorating kilns, and producing 300,000 pieces of completed pottery each day. Consider that figure again — 300,000 pieces per day. That would be 1.5 million pieces per five-day week, and they were generally working six days a week at that time! Jack Welch, in a history of the company used on its web site today, noted the production capacity at that time was 10% of the "dishes" purchased in the United States. In 1914, another plant and 16 more kilns were added, but by 1920 production could not keep up with demand.

While company literature is uncommon for most periods of Homer Laughlin's history, a 1916 booklet titled *Decorated Ware Descriptions and Prices*, lists hundreds of patterns in production at that time. The possibilities for combining and altering a number of Homer Laughlin decals, gold stamping processes, and other decorative treatments rival Haviland China for complexity and expansiveness.

Decorated Dinnerware Pound Sterling Price List, *May 1937.*

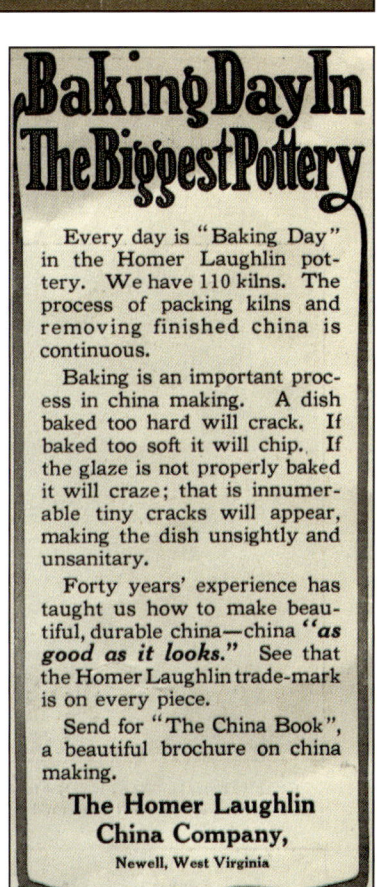

Top Left: The Clay Worker *ad for Ferguson, the company that built Homer Laughlin's largest plant.* **Top Right:** *Postcard showing a section of sample rooms at Homer Laughlin China Co., Newell, W.Va.* **Right:** *Advertisement,* Ladies Home Journal, *July 1912.* **Bottom Left:** *Postcard showing Homer Laughlin China Co., South Front of Plant #2.*

By 1928, Plant 8 had been opened in Newell. At 1,200 feet by 300 feet and multiple-storied, it alone employed 900 people. At this time, the peak employment for Homer Laughlin was reached with about 3,500 people working.

In the company's May 1937 Decorated Dinnerware Pound Sterling Price List, a booklet of 50 plus pages, over 1,100 different patterns were available on 16 different shapes.

Peak production for Homer Laughlin is reported by the company as 1948, when import pottery had not yet fully returned to the American markets after World War II. In that year, Homer Laughlin reports having made 10,128,449 dozen dishes or more than 120 million (120,000,000) dishes.

Homer Laughlin China Co. has been repeatedly cited throughout the 20th century as being the largest pottery in the world. By producing 1.5 million pieces per week and employing 3,500 people it has been a giant, when compared to almost any other pottery! Today the factory complex, with a series of buildings designated individually as Factory #6 and so on, sprawls along the Ohio River for over a mile. At night a huge sign lights the sky. The Homer Laughlin complex covers more than 67 acres. It is impressive. The influence of Homer Laughlin on the world of dinnerware and pottery has been immense by any measure. In 1997 the 500 millionth piece of Fiesta was produced. Fiesta is significant in the Homer Laughlin story, but it is only one pattern among many.

A View of the Jigger Shops on Factory No. 4.

Top: *1908 Postcard; The Homer Laughlin China Co., Largest Pottery of the World, Newell, W.VA.*
Bottom: *Workers at Homer Laughlin from an article in* The Clay Worker *magazine.*

In 1959 Homer Laughlin introduced restaurant wares to the lines offered and in 1970 ceased to offer china as direct sales for home use, focusing full efforts on restaurant ware production. Only the reintroduction of Fiesta returned Homer Laughlin to the home dining table.

Looking back to 1927 and company advertisements, Homer Laughlin declared production in a single shape, Yellowstone, was nearly 10,000 dozen pieces per day! That translates to 2.4 million pieces per month in 1927 in just the Yellowstone shape! And so the story has been for decades. The numbers are staggering, even incomprehensible. What follows is an attempt to give some order to this amazing story.

Top left: *Advertisement;* Crockery and Glass Journal, *May 1940.*
Top right: *Yellowstone advertisement;* The Pottery, Glass & Brass Salesman, *March 31, 1927.* **Above:** *Yellowstone Shape, W127/30 pattern; Round Covered Vegetable Bowl. The decoration uses a common decal of the period.*

VISUAL INDEX
Identify the Shape of Your Pattern

Below are line drawings of the different shapes made by Homer Laughlin. Using these drawings as a "visual index" you may find your pattern based on the shape of the china blanks. Look first for a dinner plate in the form and shape of your pattern. Several shapes are similar. To further help we include some of the more common pieces you might have in your pattern. Looking at a cup for the shape and handle try to find one that best matches your pattern. If you have additional pieces, look at the shape of lids and finials to find more details that best match your pattern. Once you have found the shapes you believe to represent your pattern, go to the pages indicated for more detail on other shapes and on the specific patterns produced on that shape. Be aware that Homer Laughlin in its well over 100 years and tens of thousands of patterns often made the same or very similar decoration/pattern on more than one shape!

Triumph
See Pages 469-474

Charm House
See Pages 453-459

Rhythm
See Pages 437-452

If your pattern has one of these shapes, go to the page indicated.

Studio
See Page 465-467

Fashion
See Page 468

Vogue
See Pages 485-486

Duratone
See Page 481

Bristol
See Pages 499-500

If your pattern has one of these shapes, go to the page indicated.

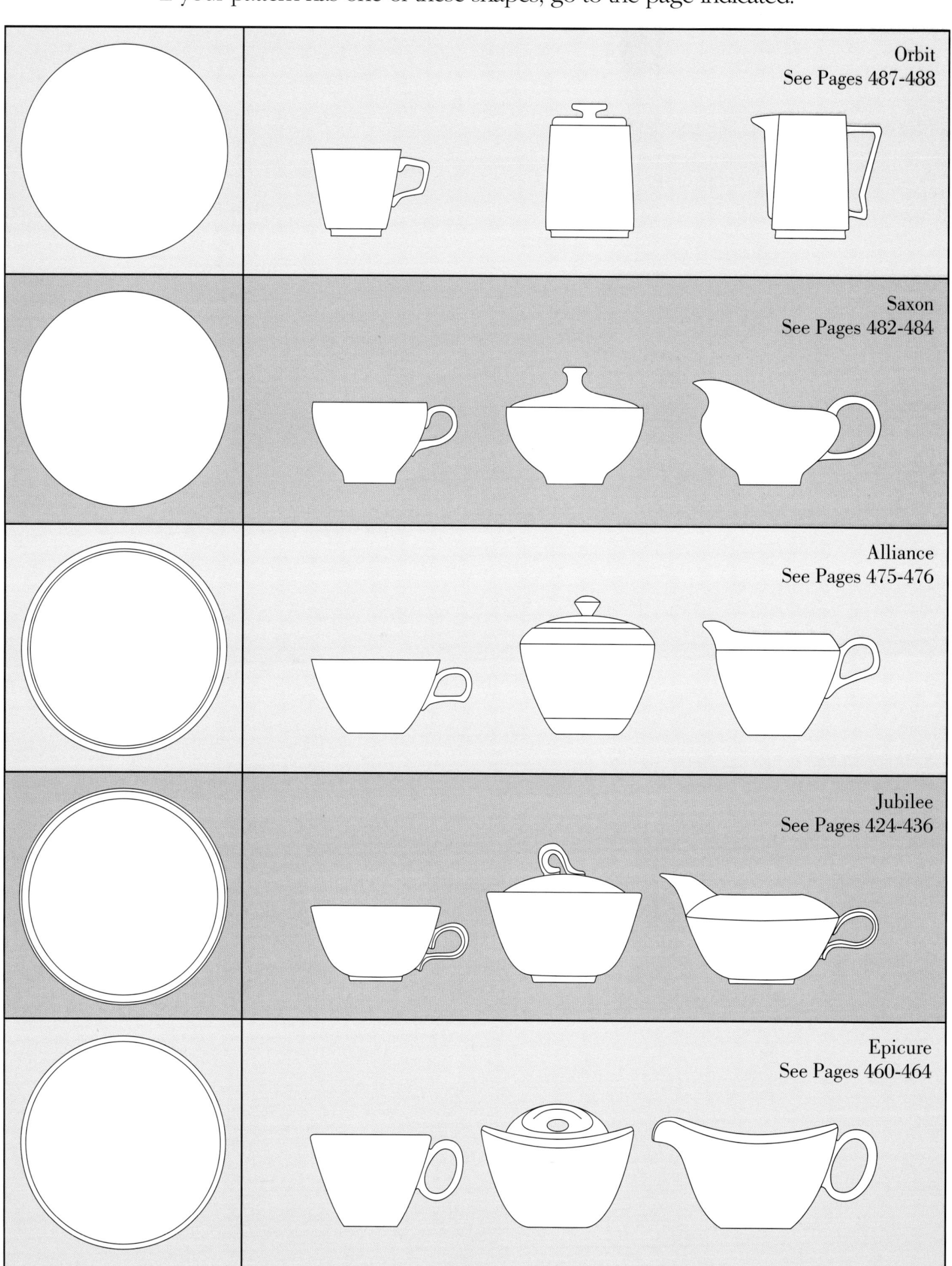

If your pattern has one of these shapes, go to the page indicated.

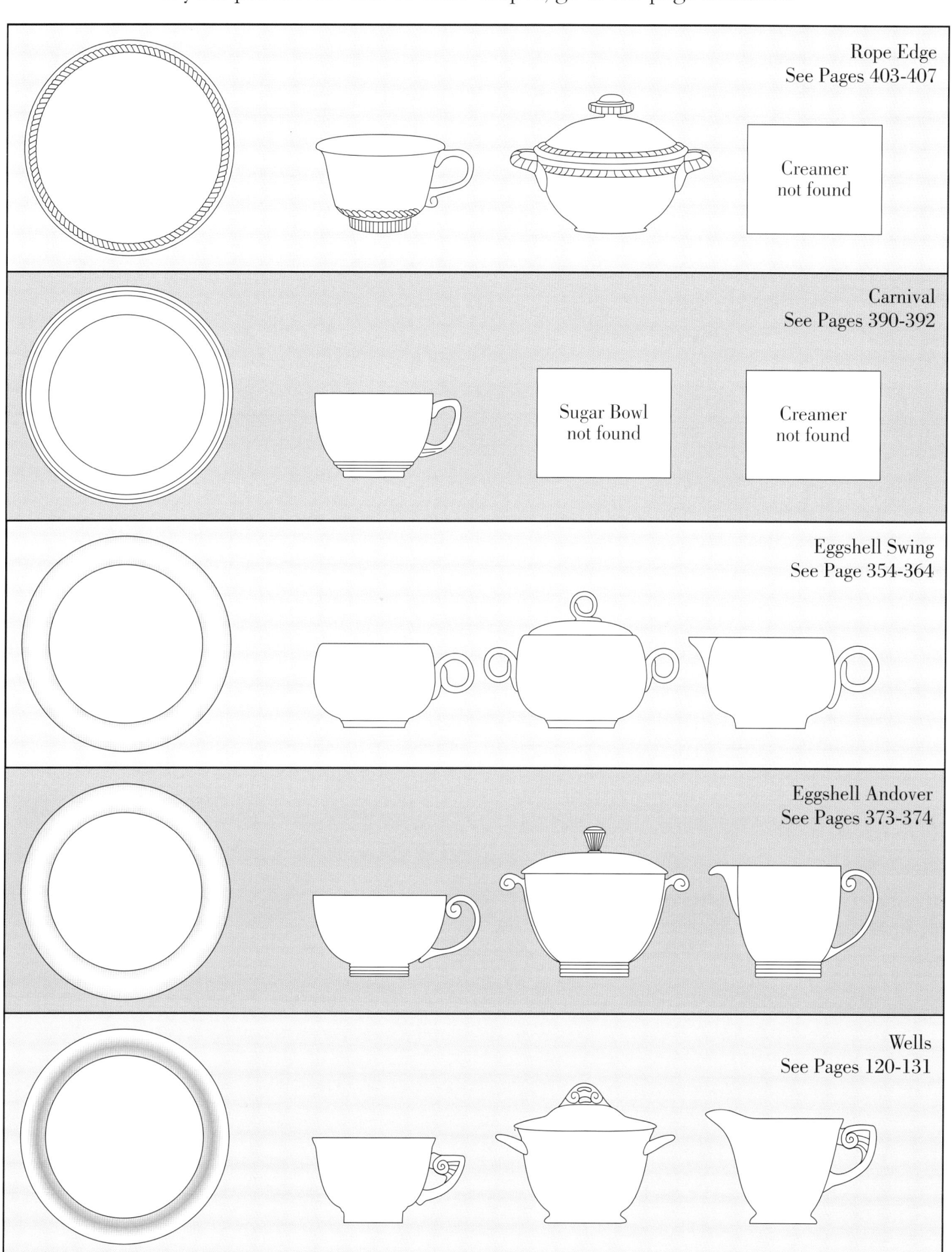

If your pattern has one of these shapes, go to the page indicated.

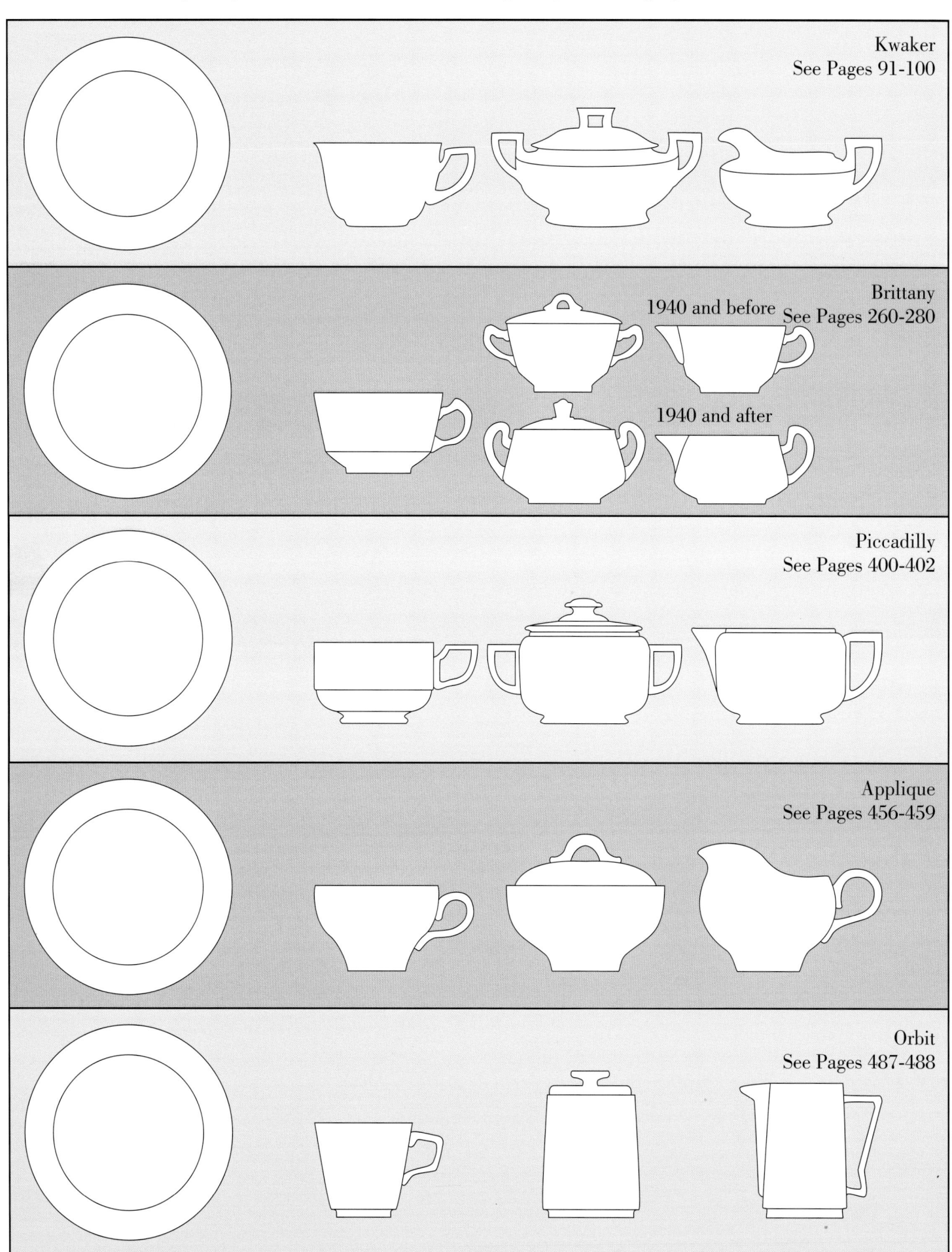

If your pattern has one of these shapes, go to the page indicated.

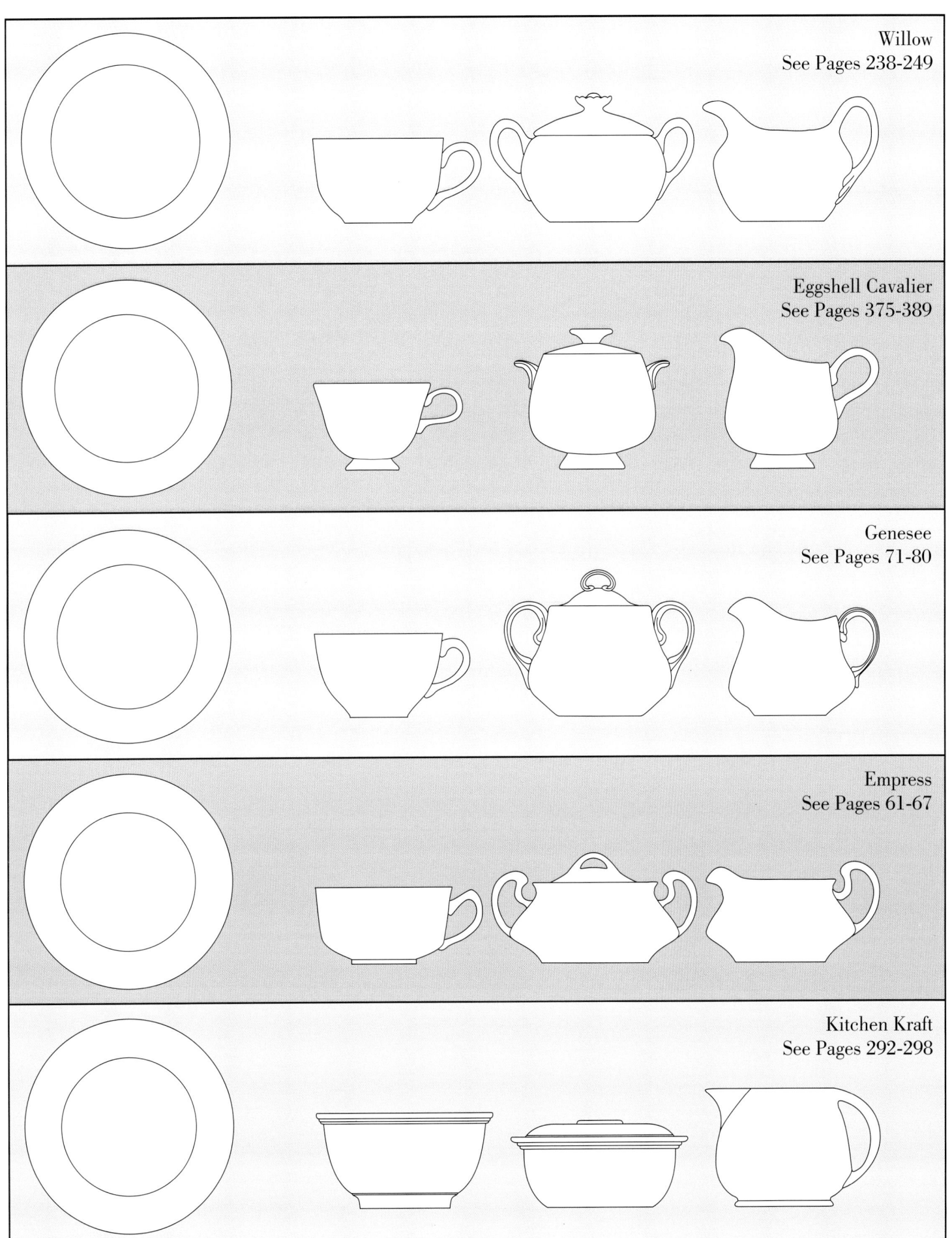

Willow
See Pages 238-249

Eggshell Cavalier
See Pages 375-389

Genesee
See Pages 71-80

Empress
See Pages 61-67

Kitchen Kraft
See Pages 292-298

If your pattern has one of these shapes, go to the page indicated.

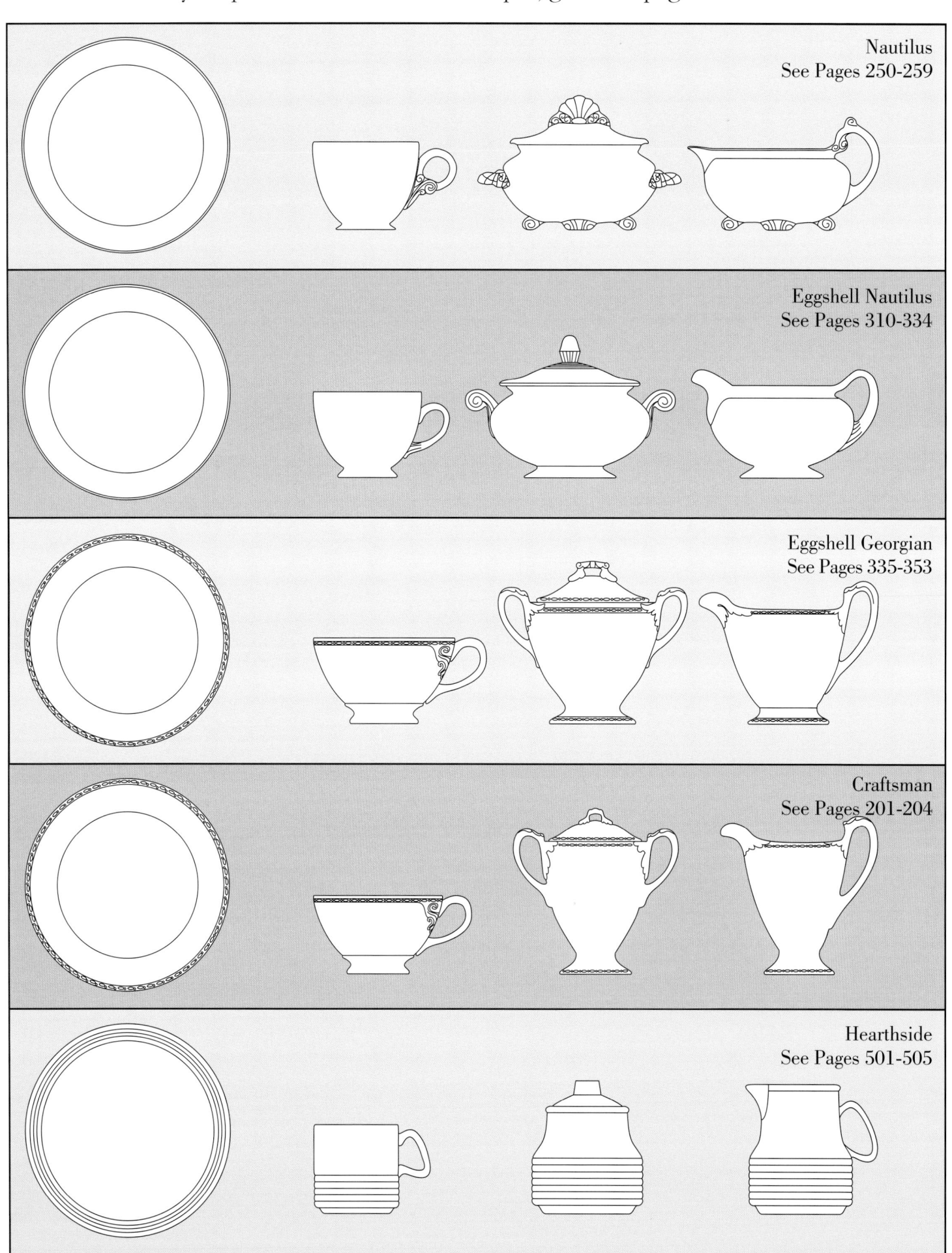

Nautilus
See Pages 250-259

Eggshell Nautilus
See Pages 310-334

Eggshell Georgian
See Pages 335-353

Craftsman
See Pages 201-204

Hearthside
See Pages 501-505

If your pattern has one of these shapes, go to the page indicated.

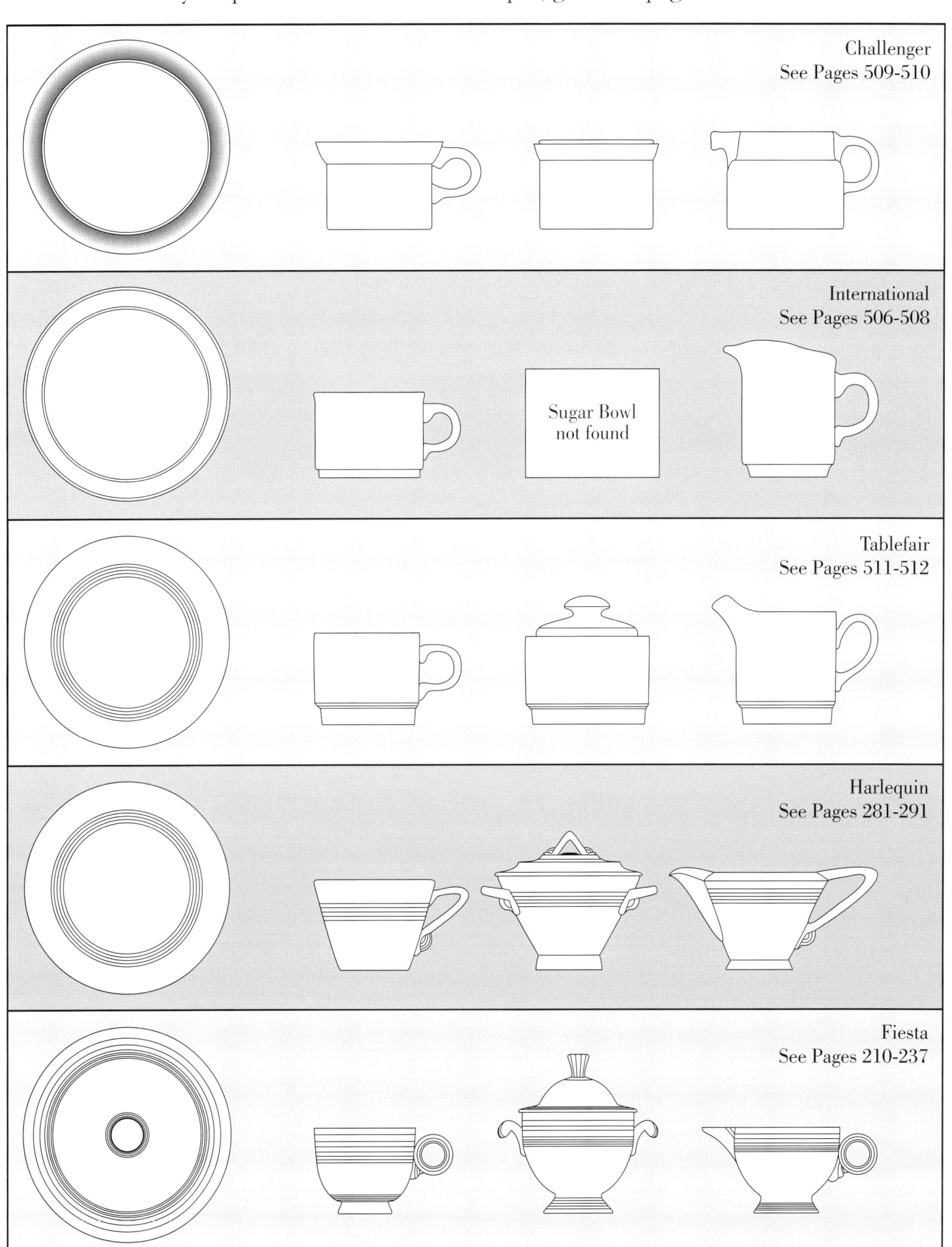

If your pattern has one of these shapes, go to the page indicated.

Modern Farmer
See Pages 393-395

Kraft
See Pages 299-303

Regency
See Pages 497-498

Granada
See Pages 493-496

Serenade
See Pages 396-399

If your pattern has one of these shapes, go to the page indicated.

If your pattern has one of these shapes, go to the page indicated.

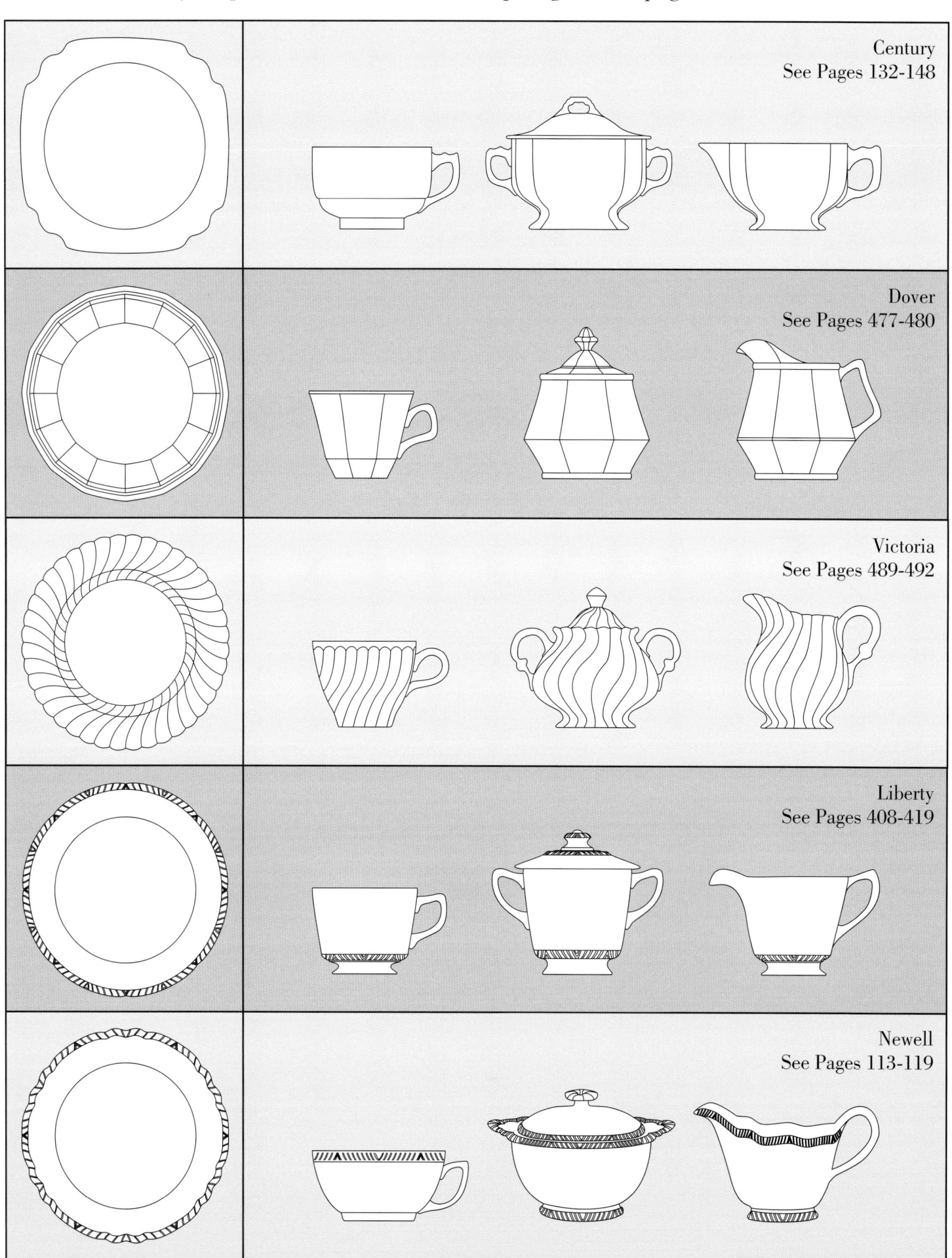

Century
See Pages 132-148

Dover
See Pages 477-480

Victoria
See Pages 489-492

Liberty
See Pages 408-419

Newell
See Pages 113-119

If your pattern has one of these shapes, go to the page indicated.

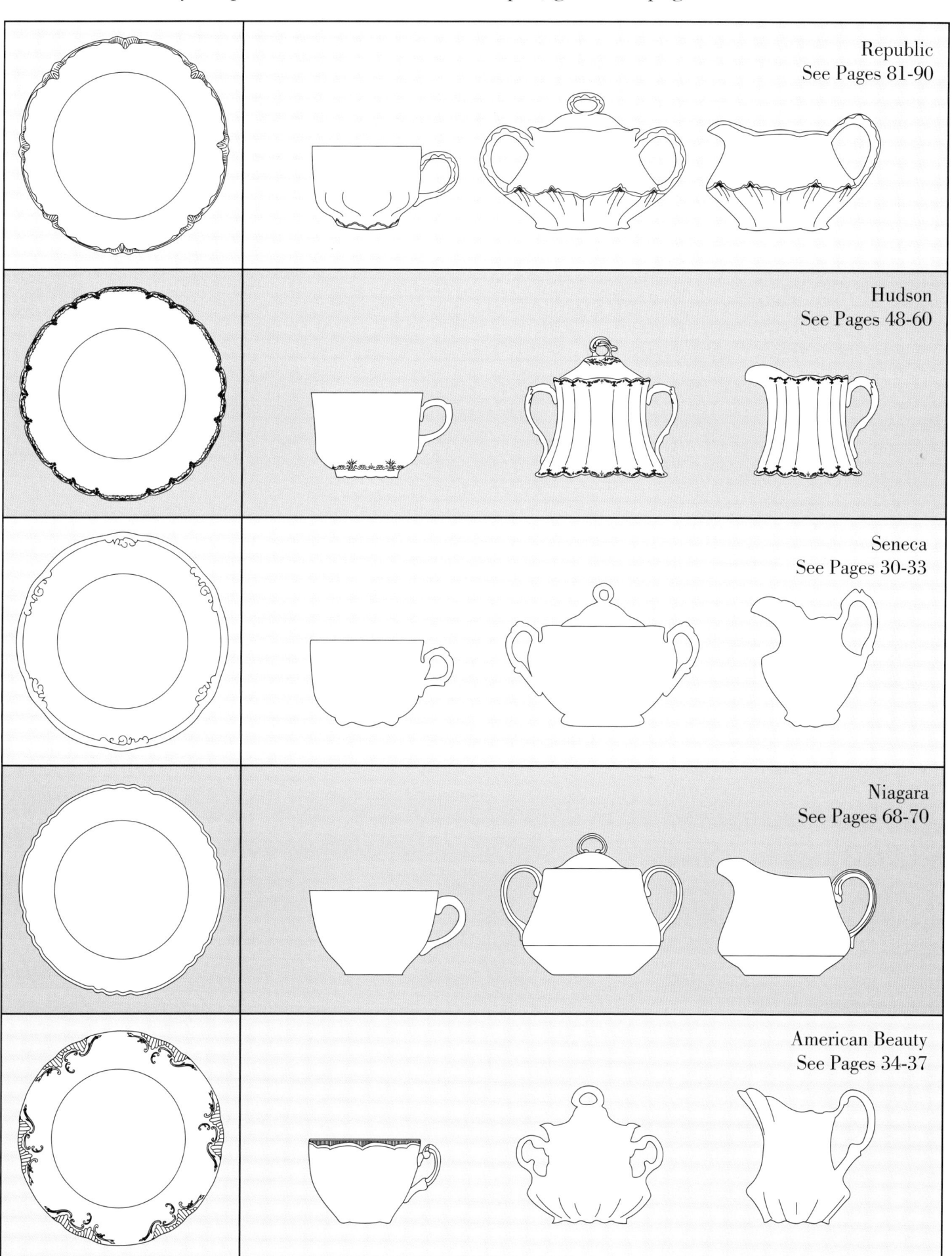

If your pattern has one of these shapes, go to the page indicated.

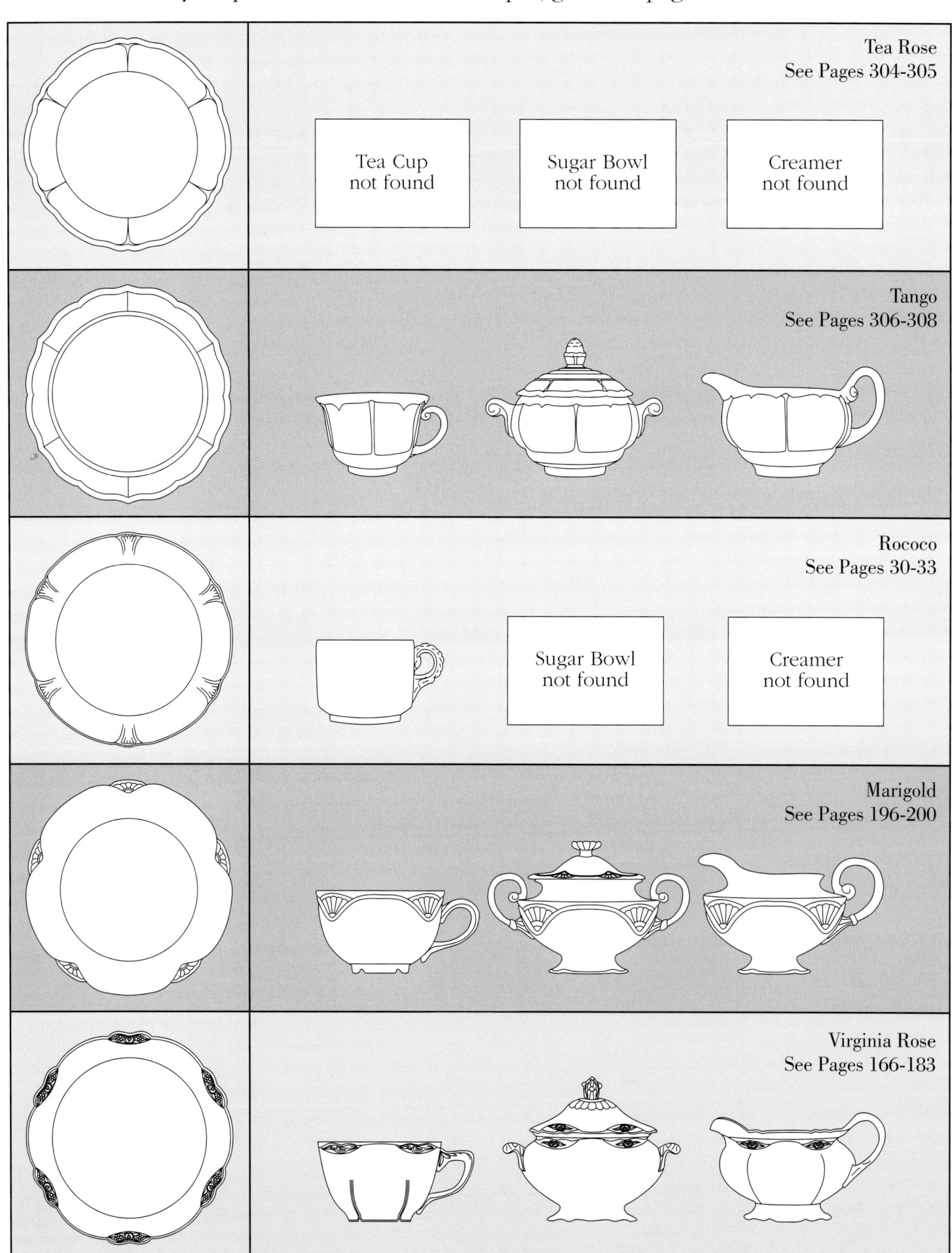

	Tea Rose See Pages 304-305 Tea Cup not found — Sugar Bowl not found — Creamer not found
	Tango See Pages 306-308
	Rococo See Pages 30-33 Sugar Bowl not found — Creamer not found
	Marigold See Pages 196-200
	Virginia Rose See Pages 166-183

If your pattern has one of these shapes, go to the page indicated.

If your pattern has one of these shapes, go to the page indicated.

Old Roman
See Pages 164-165

Ravenna
See Pages 149-152

Sugar Bowl not found

Creamer not found

Orleans
See Pages 160-163

missing lid

Front View of the Newell, W. Va. Plant of The Homer Laughlin China Co.

Same Decal on Many Shapes

It is possible for us to tell you that Homer Laughlin utilized the same decal over and over to create new "patterns." Showing you is much more likely to make our point. Remember that Homer Laughlin believes the company may have produced as many as 35,000 patterns in the over 100 years they have operated! To attain such numbers, common practice included using the same decal/decoration on different shapes and using only a portion of a decal or cutting apart a decal to create a new pattern. Shown here are four excellent examples of these practices. The Colonial Kitchen decal appears as nine different patterns, all variations on the shape or how the decoration around the decal appears. Next is a decoration with small blue flowers on five distinct shapes, one of which further adapts the design and uses only part of the decal. Getting the most variety from a single decal is achieved by cutting the decal apart as seen on two patterns on the Virginia Rose shape. Both of these techniques are demonstrated on the early 20th century blue bird decoration. Here different shapes with the same design/decal are used to create different patterns with four and five bird variations. The use of partial decals for some patterns and rearranging or using partial parts of the decal was a common practice for Homer Laughlin and others.

What does this mean to you as a collector or one seeking a specific pattern? It means there are endless variations on many Homer Laughlin pattern themes. While we have worked diligently to gather hundreds of Homer Laughlin patterns for this book, there are thousands yet to be discovered. In a practical sense it means that you may find your pattern, or what appears to be your pattern, on a shape different from yours or on mixed shapes, a practice common in later years. This does not mean your set is somehow incorrectly assembled, it means you are experiencing one of the multitude of "other" variations on a theme Homer Laughlin devised over the decades. Remember: with Homer Laughlin almost any decoration on almost any shape is potentially out there!

Above: *Applying decals.*

Early Shapes

EARLY SHAPES

The following lines include some of the earliest production for Homer Laughlin. The information available on these lines is brief, as the 100 or so years since their first production has limited the physical samples still available. The illustrations that follow represent some of the listed lines, but are not examples of them all. As the consumer bought and used these early wares, everything associated with living at this time, including the soap available for washing the dishes, eventually took its toll on these products. The early lines were not as resistant to the rigors of daily use as dinnerware that was produced in later years.

ANCHOR	circa 1878
CABLE	circa 1916
DANUBE	pre 1900
GOLDEN GATE	circa 1896
KING CHARLES	circa 1903
LOUIS XVI	circa 1890
ROCOCO	circa 1891
SENECA	circa 1901
SHAKESPEARE	circa 1885
VICTOR	circa 1883

Top right: *Shakespeare Shape, HLC1528 pattern; Oval Covered Vegetable Bowl.* **Top left:** *Typical early Homer Laughlin backstamp.* **Middle left:** *One style of the Golden Gate shape backstamp.* **Bottom left:** *HLC1197 pattern; Premium Stone China backstamp.* **Bottom right:** *HLC1197 pattern; Soup Bowl with rim.*

Early Shapes

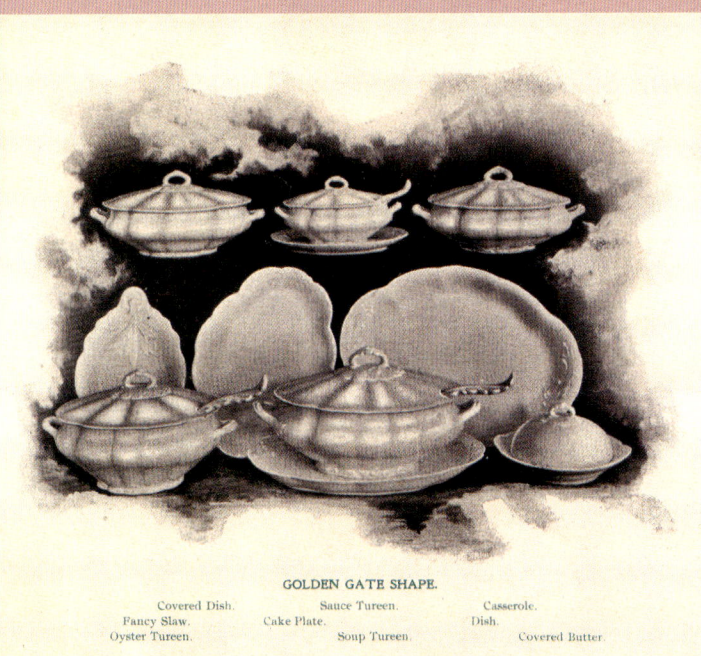

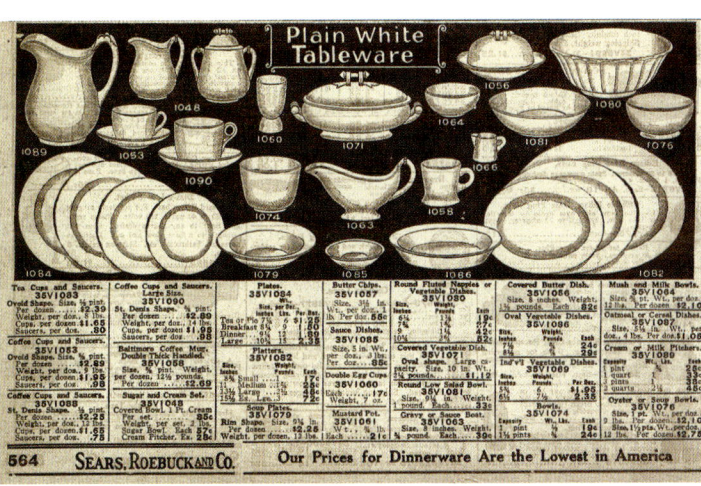

Top left, right, and Middle left: *Golden Gate piece types from the Factory.* **Middle and bottom right:** *Cable and Specialty Items piece types and prices from the Factory.* **Bottom left:** *Cable ad; Sears, Roebuck & Co., 1925.*

Homer Laughlin

Top: *King Charles piece types from the Factory.* **Bottom:** *Seneca piece types from the Factory.*

Early Shapes

Golden Gate Shape

HLC1851
No Trim

HLC1636
Gold Trim

King Charles Shape

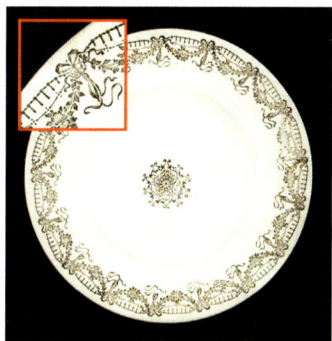
K05
No Trim

Majestic Shape

1107
*Oval Covered Vegetable
Bowl Lid Shown
No Trim*

Rococo Shape

HLC1222
*Salad Plate Shown
Gold Trim*

Shakespeare Shape

HLC1528
*Oval Covered Vegetable
Bowl Shown
Gold Trim*

American Beauty
Piece Types

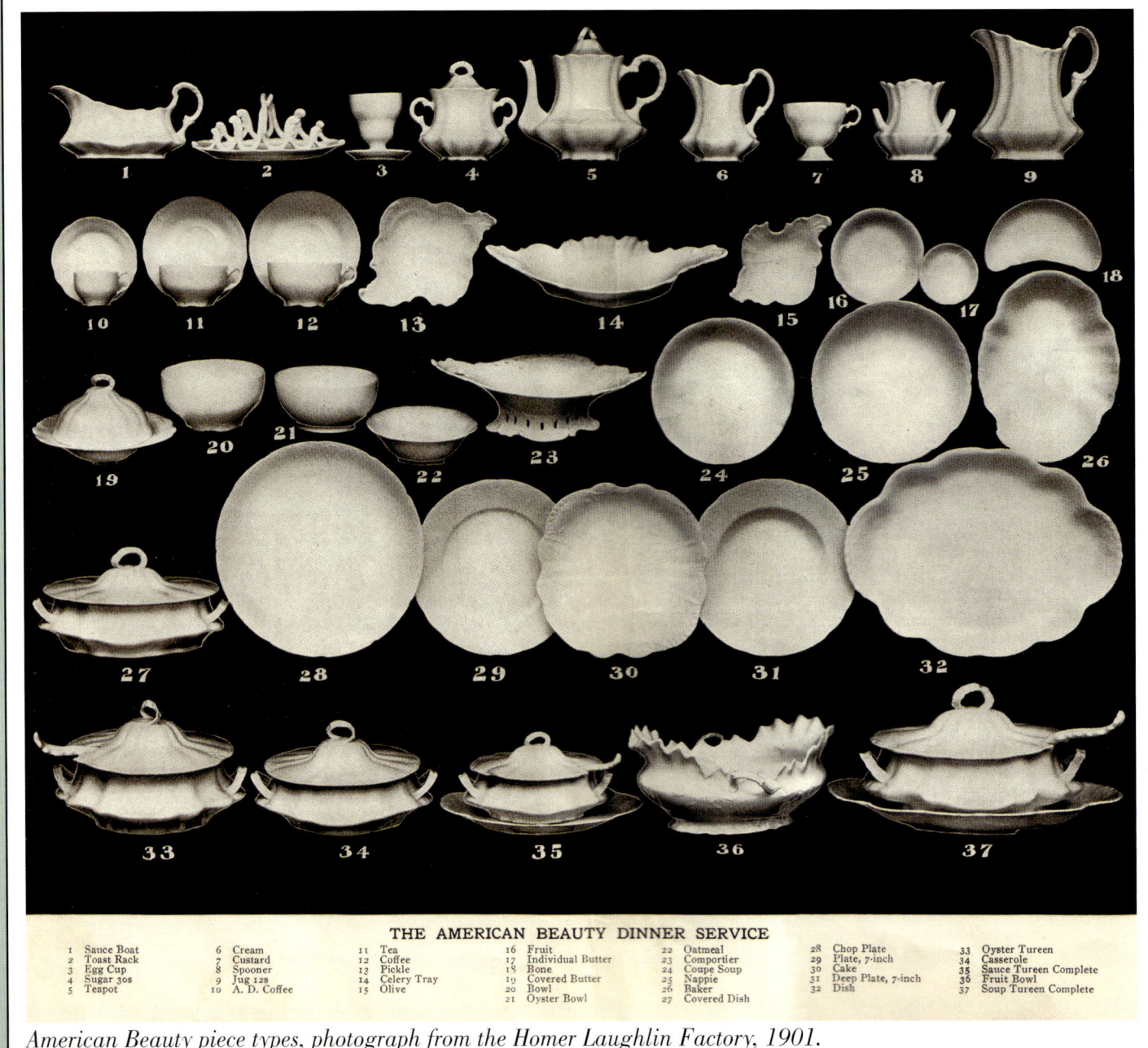

American Beauty piece types, photograph from the Homer Laughlin Factory, 1901.

American Beauty Shape

AMERICAN BEAUTY 1899 – 1908 or later

The line of shapes that constitute American Beauty appear in the 1899 Homer Laughlin Catalog. The 1901 company catalog also shows a number of pieces in the service. American Beauty was an extensive line that included an amazing array of "necessary" forms for Victorian living, such as a comportier, bone dishes, and more. Offered in Sears, Roebuck & Co.'s Catalog of 1908 were the Wood Violet and Gold Stippled patterns. By 1916, the *Homer Laughlin Price List* includes no American Beauty patterns.

American Beauty shapes were used for a line of highly decorated Victorian giftware, marketed as Laughlin Art China, around 1900.

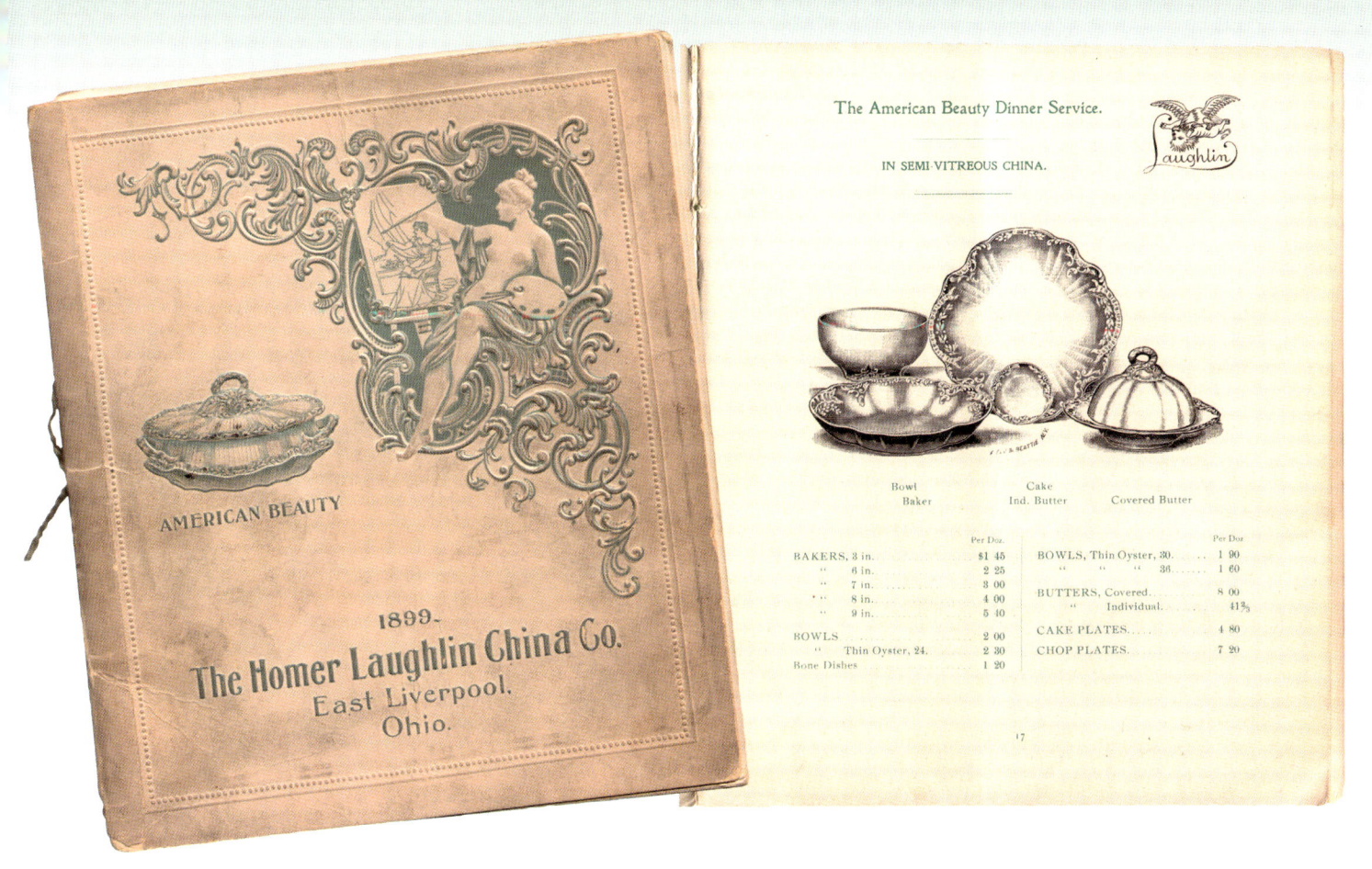

Top: *Wood Violet Gold Stippled pattern; Sears, Roebuck & Co. Catalog, 1908.*
Bottom: *Homer Laughlin American Beauty Catalog, 1899.*

Homer Laughlin

Above: *Homer Laughlin American Beauty Catalog, pages 18-21, 1899.*

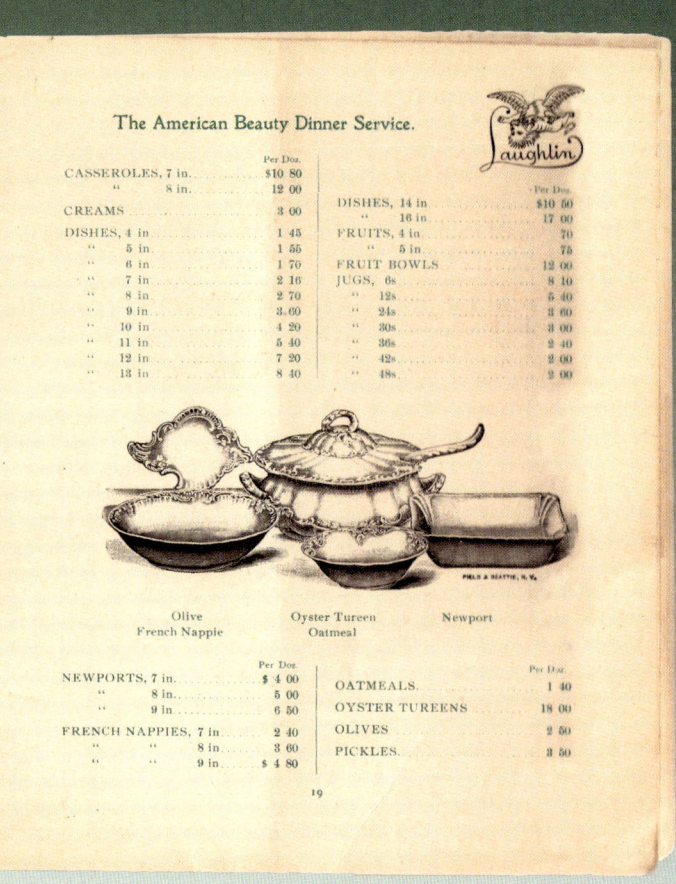

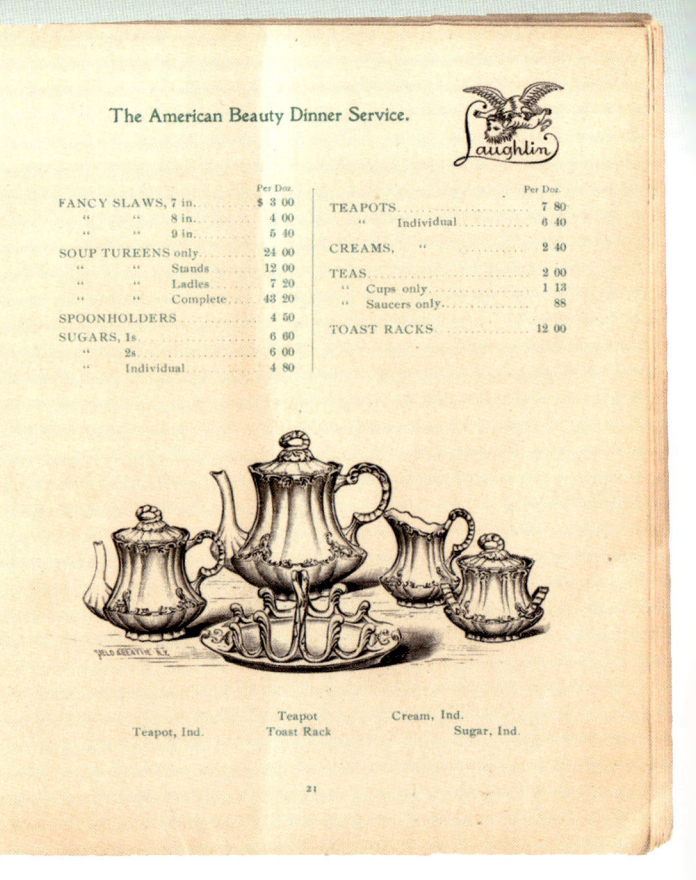

American Beauty Shape

American Beauty Piece Type List

American Beauty piece types appear as given by Homer Laughlin literature.
Measurements are in English Pottery terms, not physical measurements.

Baker, 3 inches	Dish, 7 inches	Newport, 9 inches
Baker, 6 inches	Dish, 8 inches	Oatmeal, 30s
Baker, 7 inches	Dish, 9 inches	Olive
Baker, 8 inches	Dish, 10 inches	Oyster Tureen
Baker, 9 inches	Dish, 11 inches	Pickle
Bone Dish	Dish, 12 inches	Plate, 4 inches
Bowl, 30s	Dish, 13 inches	Plate, 5 inches
Bowl, 36s	Dish, 14 inches	Plate, 6 inches
Bowl, 24s, Oyster, Thin	Dish, 16 inches	Plate, 7 inches
Bowl, 30s, Oyster, Thin	Eggcup	Plate, 8 inches
Bowl, 36s, Oyster, Thin	Fancy Slaw, 7 inches	Plate, Coupe, 6 inches
Butter, Covered	Fancy Slaw, 8 inches	Plate, Coupe, 7 inches
Butter, Individual	Fancy Slaw, 9 inches	Plate, Deep, 7 inches
Cake Plate	French Nappy, 6 inches	Sauce Boat
Casserole, 7 inches	French Nappy, 7 inches	Sauce Boat Stand
Casserole, 8 inches	French Nappy, 8 inches	Sauce Tureen
Celery Tray	French Nappy, 9 inches	Sauce Tureen Ladle
Chop Plate	Fruit, 4 inches	Sauce Tureen Stand
Coffee, Cup & Saucer Set	Fruit, 5 inches	Soup Tureen
Coffee, After Dinner, Cup & Saucer Set	Fruit Bowl	Soup Tureen Ladle
Comportier	Jug, 6s	Soup Tureen Stand
Covered Dish, 7 inches	Jug, 12s	Spoon Holder
Covered Dish, 8 inches	Jug, 24s	Sugar, 24s
Cream	Jug, 30s	Sugar, 30s
Cream, Individual	Jug, 36s	Sugar, Individual
Custard	Jug, 42s	Tea, Cup & Saucer Set
Dish, 4 inches	Jug, 48s	Teapot
Dish, 5 inches	Newport, 7 inches	Teapot, Individual
Dish, 6 inches	Newport, 8 inches	Toast Rack

HLC2112
Gold Trim

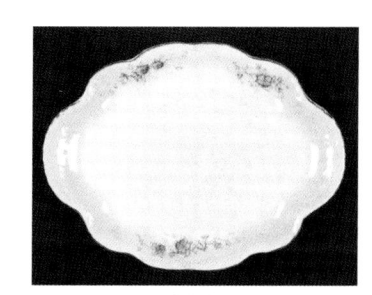

HLC2020
*Oval Platter Shown
Gold Trim*

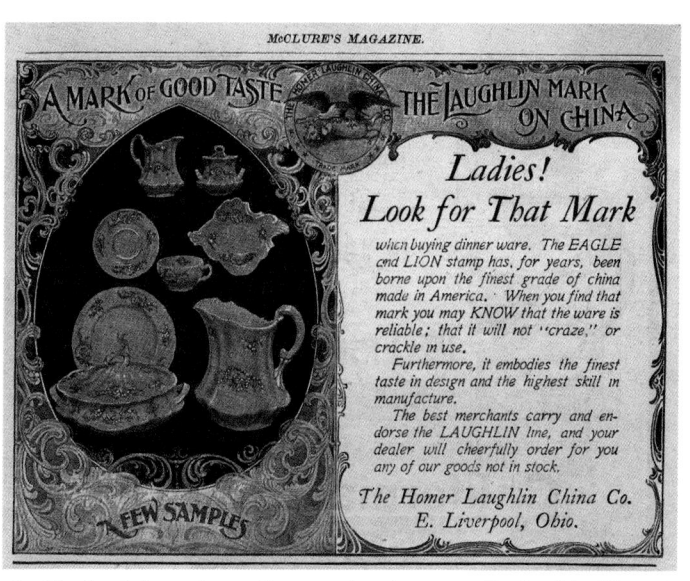

Left: *Typical American Beauty backstamp.* **Right:** McClure's Magazine, *circa 1900.*

Colonial

Piece Types

Colonial piece types, photograph from the Homer Laughlin Factory.

Colonial Shape

COLONIAL 1901

The Colonial patterns produced at the turn of the 20th century appear to have been popular and widely used. However, frequent use of this china took its toll and pieces are not easily found today. Early Colonial was offered in the 1908 Sears, Roebuck & Co. Catalog in the Arbutus Floral pattern. Colonial shaped patterns were discontinued before the issue of the *1916 Homer Laughlin Price List*.

The Homer Laughlin illustrations and piece type list found for Colonial show amazing variety and raise numerous questions. A listing for the "Colonial Dinner Service" includes coffee cups in Colonial, Golden Gate, Ovide and Rococo shapes. There are two distinct lines of jugs, plain Colonial and Geisha. Shapes like Golden Gate were shown in earlier Homer Laughlin Company catalogs as dinnerware lines in their own right. Apparently they had ceased to be popular enough to widely produce but remained in the line, circa 1910, as part of the Colonial listing. This would suggest many things, the least of which is the use of mixed shapes within the line. Such complexities create nightmares for writers, collectors, and historians seeking to understand Homer Laughlin a century later.

Top right: *HLC2120 pattern; Gravy/Sauce Boat.* **Left:** *Colonial Arbutus Floral pattern; 1908 Sears, Roebuck & Co. Catalog.* **Bottom right:** *Typical Colonial backstamp.*

Colonial Piece Type List
From Homer Laughlin Literature with Confirmed Actual Pieces

Bowl, #29	Creamer	Plate, 7 inches
Bowl, Cereal (Oatmeal)	Creamer, Geisha	Plate, Alaska Ice Cream
Bowl, Fruit	Creamer, Individual	Plate, Cake
Bowl, Rectangular, Newport	Cup & Saucer Set, Bouillon	Plate, Dinner
Bowl, Soup Coupe	Cup & Saucer Set, Coffee	Platter, Oval
Bowl, Soup with rim (Deep Plate) 7 inches	Cup & Saucer Set, Demitasse	Spooner
	Cup & Saucer Set, Geisha	Sugar Bowl with lid
Bowl, Vegetable Covered (Casserole/Covered Dish)	Cup & Saucer Set, Ovide	Sugar Bowl with lid, Geisha
	Cup & Saucer Set, Rococo	Sugar Bowl with lid, Individual
Bowl, Vegetable Oval (Baker)	Cup & Saucer Set, Tea	Teapot with lid
Bowl, Vegetable Round (Nappy)	Eggcup	Teapot with lid, Geisha
Bowl, Vegetable Round Covered (Casserole)	Gravy/Sauce Boat	Teapot with lid, Individual
	Pickle	Tureen, Oyster Covered, with Ladle
Butter Dish, Covered	Pitcher/Jug	Tureen, Sauce Covered, with Ladle
Butter Pat, Individual	Pitcher/Jug, Geisha	Tureen, Soup Covered, with Ladle

Colonial Shape

HLC3448
Gold Trim

HLC621
Oval Platter Shown
Gold Trim

4807
Gold Trim

HLC848
Soup Bowl Shown
No Trim

HLC1510
No Trim

HLC2029
Soup Bowl Shown
No Trim

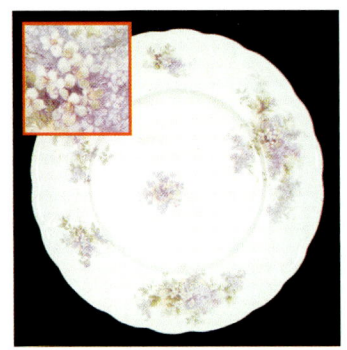

4764
No Trim

HLC997
Salad Plate Shown
Gold Trim

HLC2120
Gravy Boat Shown
Gold Trim

Above left: *Arbutus Green pattern; Teapot with lid.* **Above right:** *Arbutus Green pattern; Creamer. Pictures by Bernice Kolier.*

40

The Angelus
Piece Types

THE HOMER LAUGHLIN CHINA COMPANY, NEWELL, W. VA.

THE ANGELUS DINNER SERVICE.

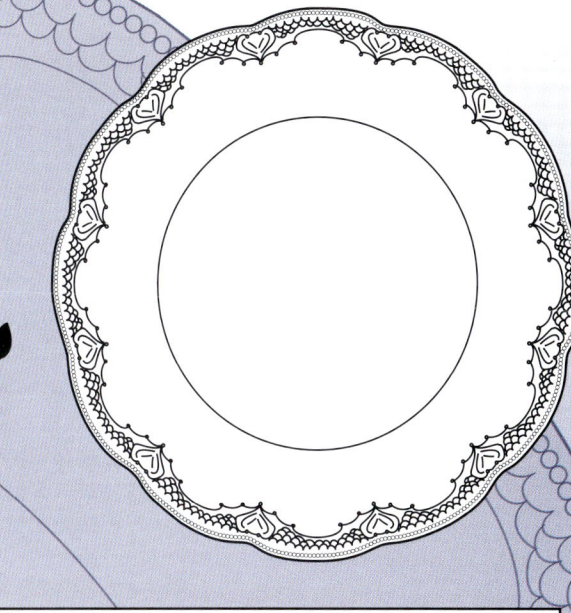

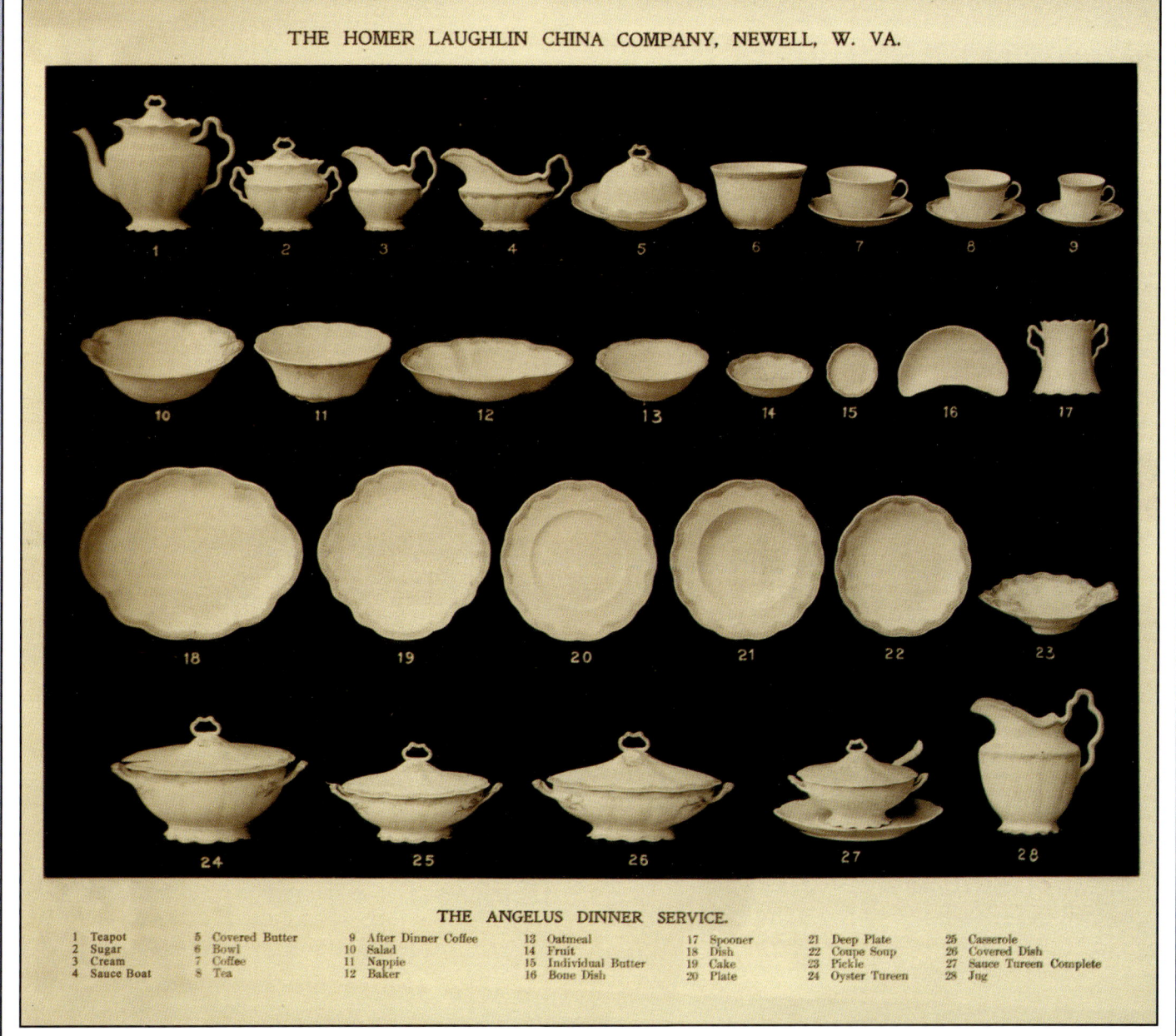

1 Teapot	5 Covered Butter	9 After Dinner Coffee	13 Oatmeal	17 Spooner	21 Deep Plate	25 Casserole
2 Sugar	6 Bowl	10 Salad	14 Fruit	18 Dish	22 Coupe Soup	26 Covered Dish
3 Cream	7 Coffee	11 Nappie	15 Individual Butter	19 Cake	23 Pickle	27 Sauce Tureen Complete
4 Sauce Boat	8 Tea	12 Baker	16 Bone Dish	20 Plate	24 Oyster Tureen	28 Jug

The Angelus piece types, photograph from the Homer Laughlin Factory, 1908.

41

Homer Laughlin

THE ANGELUS 1907 – discontinued between 1916 and 1920

The Angelus shape bears a backstamp proclaiming it to be "The Angelus." From its introduction in 1906-07, the shape remained in production for over ten years. Today The Angelus is not found in abundance, perhaps the result of a century having passed since the peak of its production. This is in contrast to an advertisement purchased by Homer Laughlin in 1908 for *Glass and Pottery World*. Here it was stated that the new Hudson shape being introduced, "is a fitting companion to The Angelus, of which there has been a greater quantity marketed than of any other one shape ever sold in America."

While backstamps include the shape name, these backstamps are not found on the tea, coffee, and demitasse cups. The Angelus has a very Continental look with scalloped edges on flatware shapes and flowing, irregular contoured handles and open finials on serving pieces. The edges of the pieces have a delicate embossed design in the clay.

Reports by other researchers state that both Sears, Roebuck & Co. and Montgomery Ward widely sold patterns on this shape in the early 1900's. The Angelus was first found in a 1908 Sears Catalog where "plain white" and "decorated" patterns were offered. In 1909, Sears had expanded their offerings on The Angelus shape to four patterns. *The 1916 Homer Laughlin Price List* includes a large number of patterns offered on the shape. By 1920, patterns on The Angelus shape were no longer offered in Homer Laughlin catalogs.

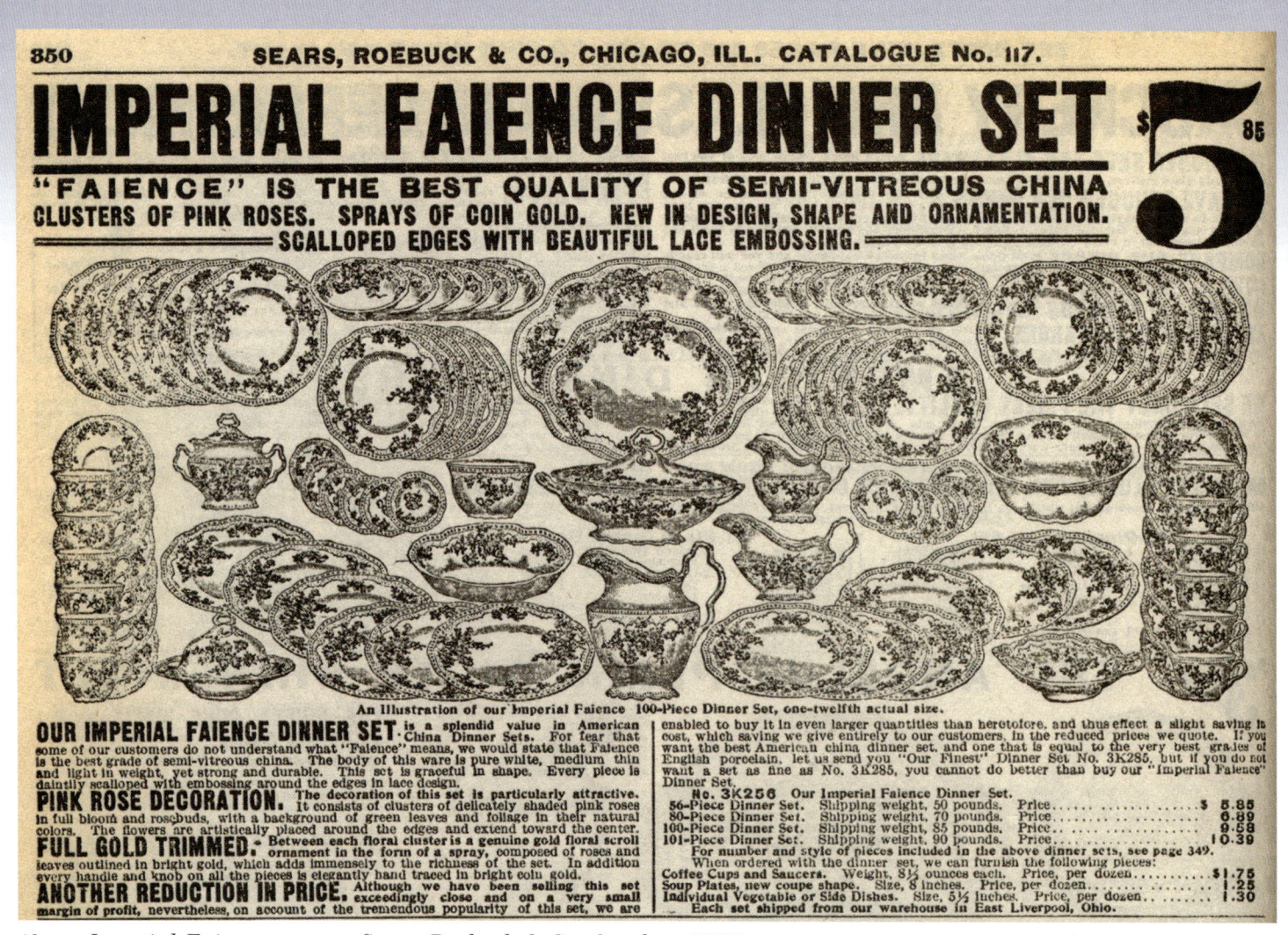

Above: *Imperial Faience pattern; Sears, Roebuck & Co. Catalog, 1908.*

The Angelus Shape

Left: *AX107 pattern; Oval Platter, Oval Vegetable Bowl, Gravy/Sauce Boat, Cup & Saucer Set, Soup Bowl with rim, and Fruit Bowl.* **Middle left:** *Typical Angelus backstamp.* **Middle right:** *AX107 pattern; Round Covered Vegetable Bowl and Oval Covered Vegetable Bowl, both missing lids.* **Bottom:** *The Angelus Plain White pattern; Sears, Roebuck & Co. Catalog, 1908.*

$3.69 THE ANGELUS PLAIN WHITE DINNER SET

THE FINEST PURE WHITE SEMI-VITREOUS CHINA. Our Angelus Dinner Set is the most up to date and best modeled plain white dinner service made. Every piece included in these sets is very richly embossed and artistically modeled, as shown in the illustration. Every piece is very white and thin, and equal to the best grades of English semi-porcelain ware.

ITS WEARING QUALITIES ARE UNSURPASSED, as the body of the ware is composed of the finest grades of clays, fired to a flinty hardness, and covered by a deep, glossy milk white glaze. We guarantee that this set is pure milk white, perfect in selection, without misshapes or small impractical pieces. We formerly sold a cheap, low grade set. Solely on account of our customers we have discontinued it. A low grade plain white set is expensive at any price. It has neither beauty nor quality to recommend it, and anyone who purchases one will never purchase another. At a slight difference in cost we sell you this fine quality high grade set. Shipped direct to our customers from the pottery in East Liverpool, Ohio. Sold only in complete dinner sets as listed.

No. 3K203 Angelus Pure White Semi-Porcelain Dinner Sets.
56-Piece Dinner Set. Shipping weight, 50 pounds. Price $3.69
60-Piece Dinner Set. Shipping weight, 60 pounds. Price 4.45
100-Piece Dinner Set. Shipping weight, 85 pounds. Price 5.89
101-Piece Dinner Set. Shipping weight, 90 pounds. Price 6.45

For number and style of pieces see descriptive matter at the top of this page. When ordered with the regular sets, we can furnish the following pieces:
Coffee Cups and Saucers. Price, per dozen $1.35
Individual Vegetable Dishes. Price, per dozen .... .95
Soup Plates, new coupe shape. Price, per dozen .... .83

Homer Laughlin

The Angelus Piece Type List

(From 1911 Homer Laughlin Price List, sizes given are actual measurements end to end)

Baker, 5½ inches
Baker, 6¼ inches
Baker, 7 inches
Baker, 8 inches
Baker, 9 inches
Baker, 10 inches
Baker, 10½ inches
Baker, 12 inches
Bone Dish
Bouillon Cup, 7¾ ounces
Bowl, 1 pint
Bowl, 1½ pints
Bowl, Oyster, ¾ pints
Bowl, Oyster, 1¼ pints
Bowl, Oyster, 1¾ pints
Butter, Covered
Butter, Individual, 3 inches
Cake, 10 inches
Casserole, 8¼ inches
Casserole, 8¾ inches
Casserole, Notched, 9 inches
Coffee, 9¼ ounces
Coffee, After Dinner, 3¾ ounces
Coffee, K.C., 9½ ounces
Cream, ¾ pint
Dish, 6¼ inches
Dish, 7¼ inches
Dish, 8¼ inches
Dish, 9 inches

Dish, 9¾ inches
Dish, 11 inches
Dish, 11¾ inches
Dish, 13 inches
Dish, 13¾ inches
Dish, 15 inches
Dish, 16 inches
Dish, 17¼ inches
Dish, 19¼ inches
Dish, Covered, 8 inches
Dish, Covered, 9 inches
Dish, Covered, 9¾ inches
Eggcup, Graham, 3 inches
Fruit, 5 inches
Fruit, 5¼ inches
Fruit, Tioga, 5¼ inches
Jug, 1 pint
Jug, 1½ pints
Jug, 2¼ pints
Jug, 3⅛ pints
Jug, 4½ pints
Jug, 6½ pints
Jug, 8 pints
Nappy, 6 inches
Nappy, 6¾ inches
Nappy, 7¾ inches
Nappy, 8¾ inches
Nappy, 9¾ inches
Nappy, 10½ inches

Oatmeal, 5¾ inches
Oatmeal, 6½ inches
Pickle, 8¼ inches
Plate, 6¼ inches
Plate, 7 inches
Plate, 8 inches
Plate, 9 inches
Plate, 9¾ inches
Plate, Chop, 11½ inches
Plate, Coupe, 7¼ inches
Plate, Coupe, 8 inches
Plate, Deep, 9 inches
Salad, 8¼ inches
Salad, 9¼ inches
Salad, 10¼ inches
Sauce Boat, 6 inches
Sauce Boat Stand, 8¾ inches
Sauce Tureen, 6¾ inches
Sauce Tureen Ladle
Sauce Tureen Stand, 10¼ inches
Spooner, 3¼ inches
Sugar, 4¼ inches
Sugar, 4¾ inches
Tea, 7¾ ounces
Tea, K.C., 7½ ounces
Teapot with lid
Tureen, Oyster, 9¼ inches

The Angelus Piece Type List

Piece Type List of Confirmed Actual Pieces Known to Replacements

Bone Dish
Bowl, Cereal (Oatmeal)
Bowl, Cranberry
Bowl, Fruit
Bowl, Soup Coupe
Bowl, Soup with rim
Bowl, Vegetable Oval (Baker)
Bowl, Vegetable Oval Covered
 (Covered Dish)
Bowl, Vegetable Round Covered
 (Casserole)
Bowl, Vegetable Round (Nappy)

Bowl, Vegetable Round (Salad)
Butter, Round Covered
Butter Pat
Creamer
Cup & Saucer Set
Cup & Saucer Set, Bouillon
Cup & Saucer Set, Coffee
Cup & Saucer Set, Demitasse
Gravy/Sauce Boat (one handle)
Gravy/Sauce Boat with Underplate
 and lid (two handles)
Pickle

Pitcher/Jug
Plate, Cake
Plate, Dinner
Platter, Oval
Spooner
Sugar Bowl with lid
Teapot with lid
Tureen, Oyster with lid
Tureen, Sauce with lid,
 Underplate, and Ladle

The Angelus Shape

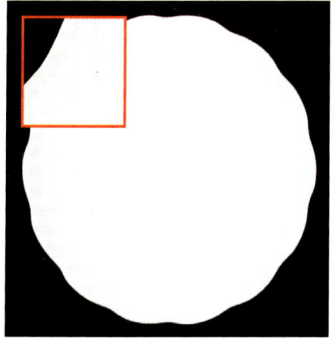

The Angelus
Salad Plate Shown
No Trim

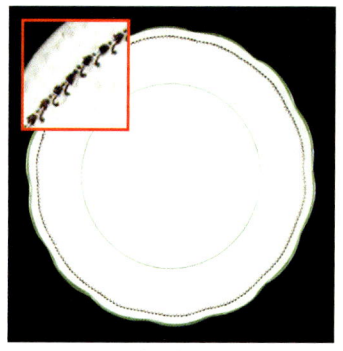

AX26
Green Trim

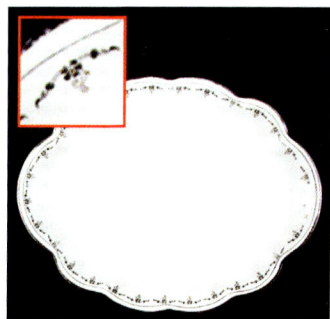

HLC851
Oval Platter Shown
Gold Trim

AX55
Gold Trim

AX60
Gold Trim

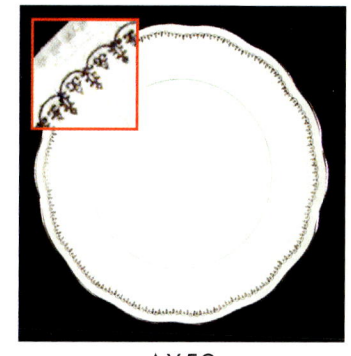

AX59
Gold Trim

AX30
Blue Trim

AX32
Gold Trim

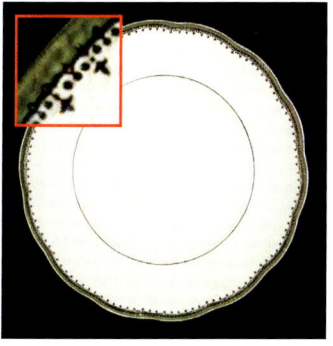

AX56
Green Band
No Trim

AX27
Green Band
Gold Trim

AX57
Yellow Band
No Trim

AX85
Yellow Band
Gold Trim

HLC1143
Oval Platter Shown
Copper Band
Gold Trim

AX86
Red Band
Gold Trim

1140
No Trim

HLC1042
Gold Trim

45

The Angelus Shape

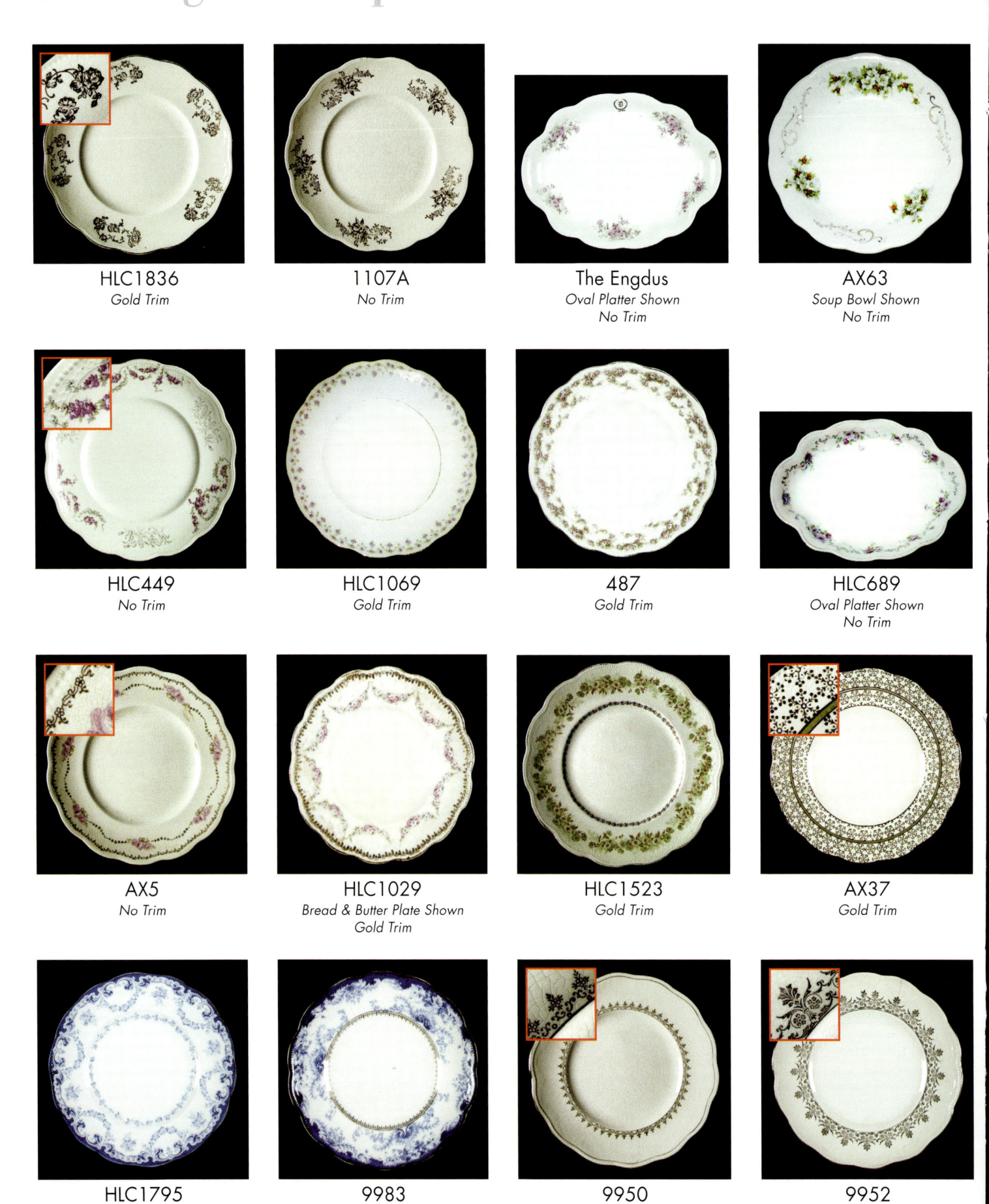

HLC1836
Gold Trim

1107A
No Trim

The Engdus
Oval Platter Shown
No Trim

AX63
Soup Bowl Shown
No Trim

HLC449
No Trim

HLC1069
Gold Trim

487
Gold Trim

HLC689
Oval Platter Shown
No Trim

AX5
No Trim

HLC1029
Bread & Butter Plate Shown
Gold Trim

HLC1523
Gold Trim

AX37
Gold Trim

HLC1795
No Trim

9983
Gold Trim

9950
Gold Trim

9952
Gold Trim

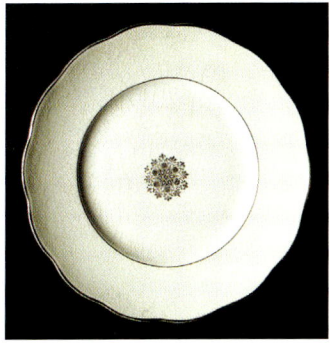

The Angelus Shape

AX107
Gold Trim

HLC2183
*Luncheon Plate Shown
No Trim*

W7S
No Trim

W9S
No Trim

HLC1692
No Trim

HLC1377
No Trim

HLC1835
No Trim

HLC1275
*Salad Plate Shown
No Trim*

DOLLY! THESE ARE AMERICAN BEAUTIES TOO.

A MARK OF GOOD TASTE

For there are two Kinds

—"the roses of the rich, and the delightful china table service called **An American Beauty**, bearing the Laughlin Eagle & Lion hall-mark, and kept by the best dealers of America."

There are other Laughlin services of equal beauty—the classic **Colonial** and the exquisitely modeled **Golden Gate**, all of a richness and grace in shape and decoration and of a lightness never before attempted by American china makers. Yet they may be had at a small cost— a luxury for a little, and

"All that beauty, all that wealth e'er gave."

The Homer Laughlin China Co.,
East Liverpool, Ohio.

Above: *Unknown magazine advertisement from around 1900.*

47

Hudson

Piece Types

THE HOMER LAUGHLIN CHINA COMPANY, NEWELL, W. VA.

THE HUDSON DINNER SERVICE.

1 Teapot	8 Coffee	14 Oatmeal, 30s	20 Dish, 10 inch	26 Oyster Tureen
2 Sugar, 30s	9 Tea	15 Fruit, 4 inch	21 Cake	27 Covered Dish, 7 inch
3 Cream	10 After Dinner Coffee	16 Individual Butter	22 Covered Butter	28 Casserole, 7 inch
4 Individual Sugar	11 Salad, 7 inch	17 Bone	23 Deep Plate, 7 inch	29 Sauce Tureen Complete
5 Individual Cream	12 Nappy, 7 inch	18 Pickle	24 Plate, 7 inch	30 Celery Tray
6 Sauce Boat	13 Baker, 7 inch	19 Spooner	25 Coupe Soup, 7 inch	21 Jug, 24s
7 Bowl, 30s				

Hudson piece types, photograph from the Homer Laughlin Factory, 1908.

48

Hudson Shape

HUDSON 1908 – 1928

The trade journal *Glass and Pottery World* reported the introduction of the Hudson shape, January 1, 1908, in a full-page advertisement from Homer Laughlin. It was a shape that would in time include almost 70 different piece types and be decorated with dozens of patterns. As with many of the decorations made by Homer Laughlin through the years, many of the names and pattern numbers remain a mystery.

A 1912 booklet, *The China Book*, featured several attractive Hudson shaped patterns. *The Homer Laughlin Price List* of January 1, 1916, included several hundred design options on the Hudson shape. This was indeed a popular and widely used shape for Homer Laughlin in the early 1900's and was one of the six Homer Laughlin shapes listed in *The Pottery, Glass & Brass Salesman* of February 2, 1928. Hudson shapes are shown in the Homer Laughlin catalogs of 1922 and 1926, but have ceased appearing by the 1929 catalog. Most Hudson shaped pieces will include the word Hudson as part of its backstamp.

$7.48 WHITE AND GOLD DINNER SET

FINEST QUALITY OF CHINA—HAVILAND SHAPE
FULL GOLD DECORATIONS. A SOLID BURNISHED EDGE AND LACE BORDER
A REFINED SET IN PERFECT STYLE AND EXQUISITE TASTE

Illustration of our White and Gold 100-Piece Dinner Set, one-twelfth actual size.

WHITE AND GOLD is considered to be the most artistic and refined decoration used in dinner ware. It is always in the very best of taste; it has always a rich appearance on the table. Flower decorations may change and go out of style, but a white and gold dinner set is always fashionable and always in style.

SPECIAL SELECTED QUALITY. The ware from which this dinner set is made, is of the highest grade of pure white American porcelain, specially selected. This means that our White and Gold Dinner Set is equal to the best grade of English porcelain ware and is absolutely perfect in every respect.

NEW HAVILAND SHAPE. The shape of this set is the same as that of "Our Finest" Decorated American China Dinner Set, No. 3K285. It is a copy of the newest Haviland shape. Each piece is the acme of gracefulness and beauty, and is light and thin, yet very strong and durable. Each piece is elaborately embossed in ornamental design and the shape of the handles gives an appearance of extra lightness to the covered ware. It is a set that appeals to people of refined taste.

DECORATED WITH BURNISHED COIN GOLD. The exquisite gold decoration of this set makes it, without question of a doubt, the handsomest white and gold American china dinner set ever sold. The edge of every piece is decorated with a broad band of burnished coin gold, supplemented with an inside lace border of coin gold, which follows the outline of the rich embossing. All the handles are elaborately hand traced with gold. In ordering, please mention the number of pieces desired. Shipped from the pottery in East Liverpool, Ohio.

No. 3K280   White and Gold Dinner Set.
56-Piece Dinner Set. Shipping weight, 50 pounds. Price............$ 7.48
80-Piece Dinner Set. Shipping weight, 60 pounds. Price............ 8.75
100-Piece Dinner Set. Shipping weight, 84 pounds. Price............ 10.95
101-Piece Dinner Set. Shipping weight, 90 pounds. Price............ 11.75
For number and style of pieces included in the sets quoted above, see page 349.
When ordered with regular sets, we can furnish the following pieces:
Coffee Cups and Saucers. Price, per dozen.................$1.98
Individual Vegetable Dishes. Price, per dozen................1.65
Soup Plates, new coupe shape. Price, per dozen..............1.48

Top right: *One of several styles of the Hudson backstamp.* **Above:** *White and Gold pattern; Sears, Roebuck & Co. Catalog, 1908.*

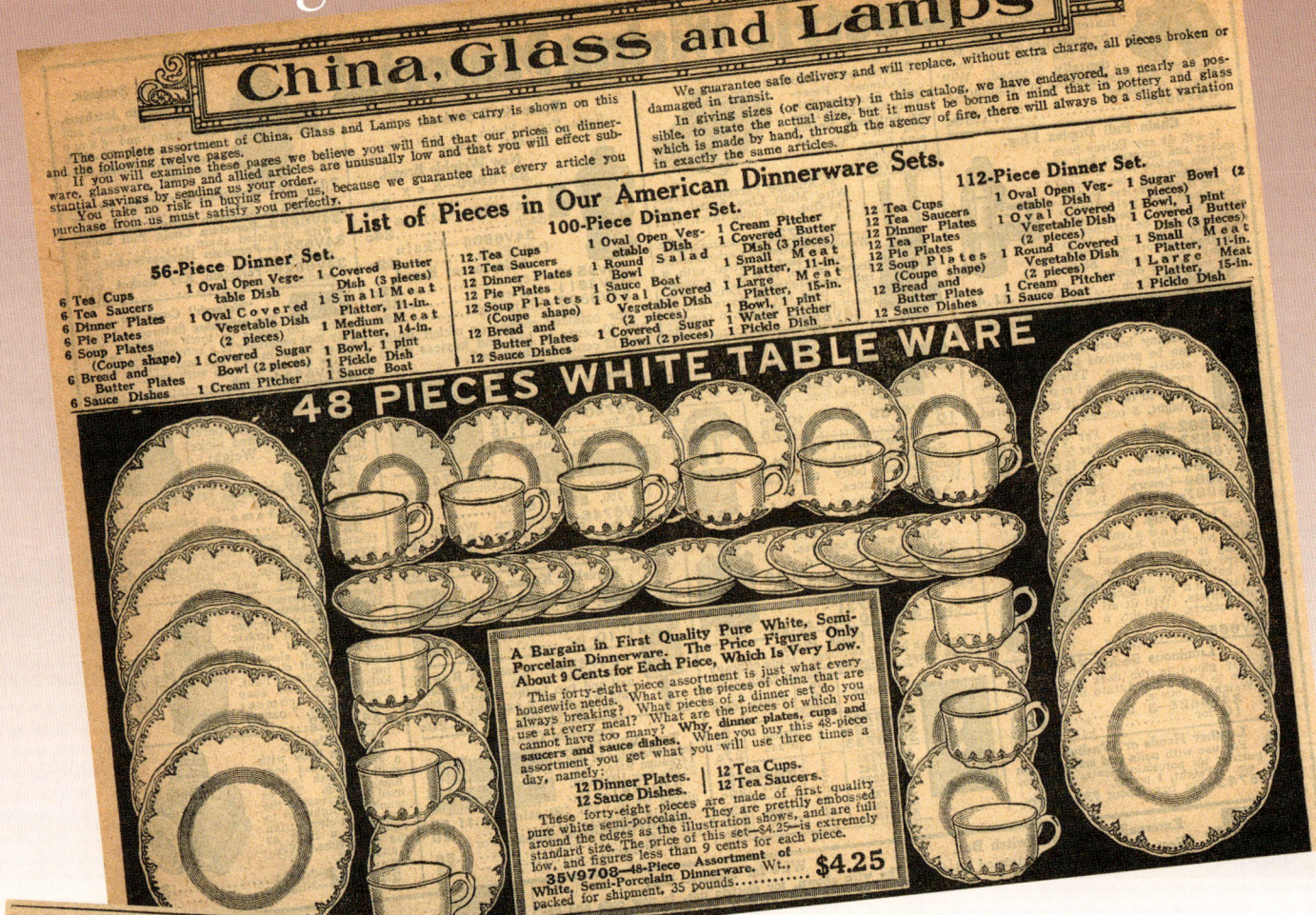

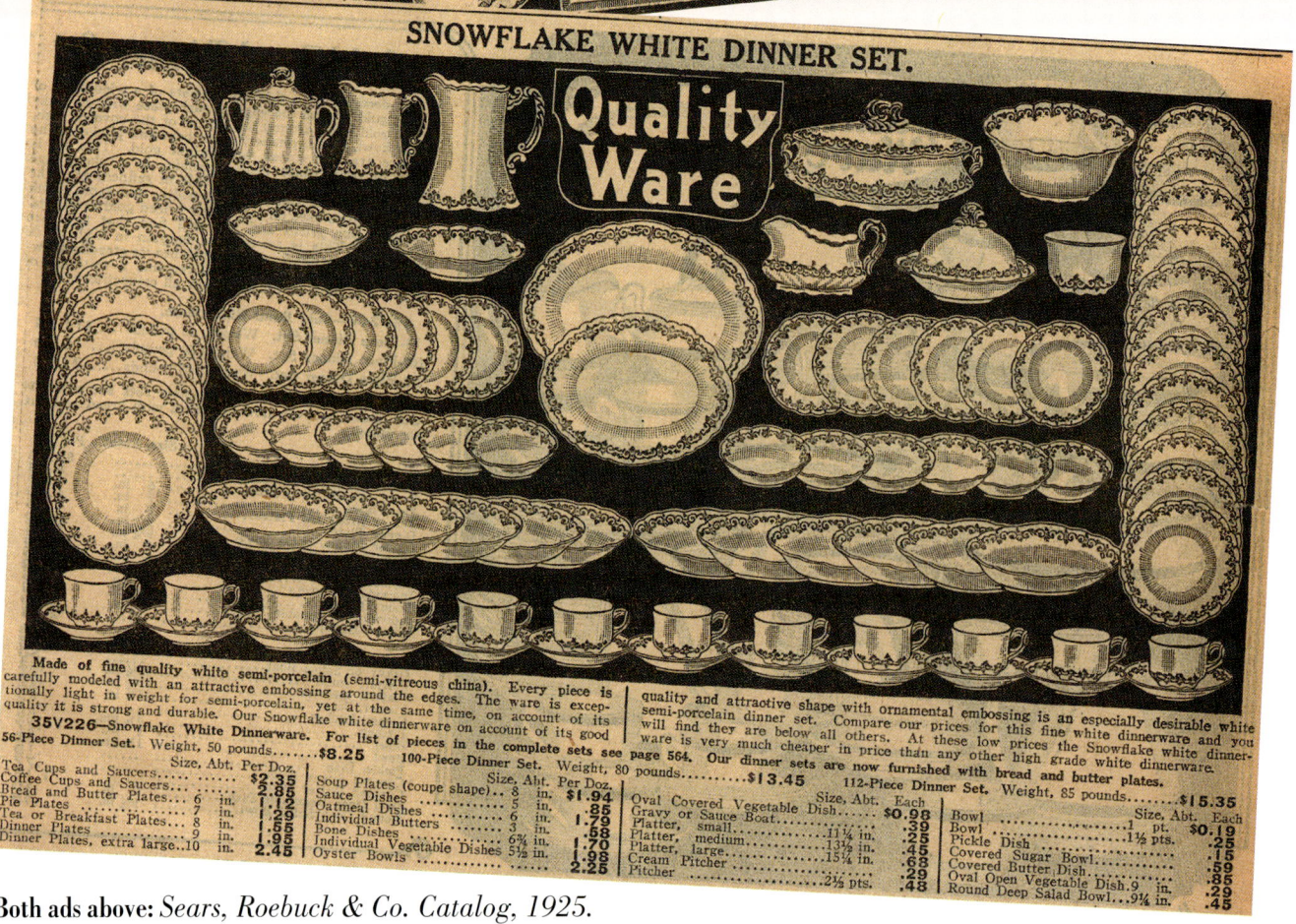

Homer Laughlin

Both ads above: *Sears, Roebuck & Co. Catalog, 1925.*

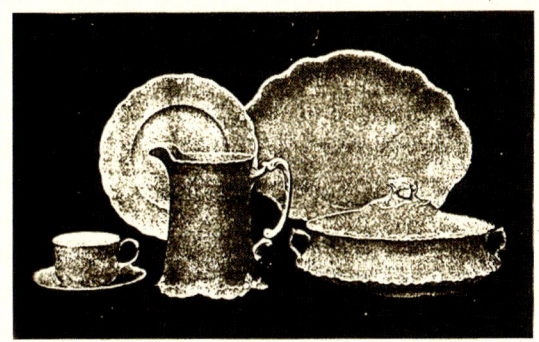

Hudson Shape

Top left: *Hudson advertisement;* Glass and Pottery World, *1908.*
Top right and bottom: *Hudson pages from* The China Book, *Homer Laughlin promotional booklet.*

Homer Laughlin

Top: *H111 pattern; Postcard for Hudson, front and back.* **Bottom left:** *HLC3112 pattern; Individual Creamer.* **Bottom right:** *Magazine advertisement for Hudson.*

Hudson Shape

Top: *H135 pattern; Oval Platter, Soup Coupe Bowl, Pickle, Fruit Bowl, Cup & Saucer Set, and Oval Vegetable Bowl.*
Bottom left: *H135 pattern; Round Covered Vegetable Bowl, and Oval Covered Vegetable Bowl.* **Bottom right:** *H111 pattern; Sugar Bowl with lid, and Gravy/Sauce Boat with unattached Underplate.*

Homer Laughlin

Hudson Piece Type List

From Homer Laughlin Literature

Bone Dish
Bowl, 1 pint*
Bowl, 1½ pints
Bowl, 2 pints
Bowl, Fruit, 5 inches
Bowl, Fruit, 5¼ inches
Bowl, Fruit, 6 inches
Bowl, Oatmeal, 5¾ inches
Bowl, Oatmeal, 6¼ inches
Bowl, Oyster Thin, ¾ pint
Bowl, Oyster Thin, 1¼ pints
Bowl, Oyster Thin, 1¾ pints
Bowl, Soup (Deep Plate), 9¾ inches
Bowl, Soup Coupe (Plate), 7⅛ inches
Bowl, Soup Coupe (Plate), 8 inches
Bowl, Vegetable Oval (Baker), 5¼ inches
Bowl, Vegetable Oval (Baker), 6¼ inches
Bowl, Vegetable Oval (Baker), 6⅞ inches
Bowl, Vegetable Oval (Baker), 8 inches
Bowl, Vegetable Oval (Baker), 9 inches
Bowl, Vegetable Oval (Baker), 10 inches
Bowl, Vegetable Oval (Baker), 10¾ inches
Bowl, Vegetable Oval (Baker), 11¾ inches
Bowl, Vegetable Round (Nappy), 6 inches
Bowl, Vegetable Round (Nappy), 7 inches
Bowl, Vegetable Round (Nappy), 7⅞ inches
Bowl, Vegetable Round (Nappy), 8⅞ inches
Bowl, Vegetable Round (Nappy), 10 inches

Butter, Individual
Butter with lid
Casserole, 7 inches
Casserole, 7⅞ inches
Casserole Notched, 7⅞ inches
Celery, 12½ inches
Cream, ⅝ pint
Cream, Individual, ½ pint
Cup & Saucer Set, After Dinner, 3½ ounces
Cup, Bouillon Hudson
Cup, Bouillon Ovide
Cup & Saucer Set, Coffee Hudson 10¼ ounce
Cup & Saucer Set, Coffee Ovide 10¼ ounces
Cup & Saucer Set, Tea Hudson, 8 ounces
Cup & Saucer Set, Tea Ovide, 8¼ ounces
Dish, Covered, 7¼ inches
Dish, Covered, 8 inches
Dish, Covered, 9 inches
Eggcup, Boston, 4 inches
Gravy/Sauce Boat with unattached Underplate
Horseradish
Jug, ½ pint
Jug, ¾ pint
Jug, 1⅛ pints
Jug, 1¾ pints
Jug, 2½ pints
Jug, 3½ pints
Jug, 5 pints
Jug, 6 pints
Pickle, 8¼ inches
Plate, 6 inches
Plate, 7⅛ inches
Plate, 8 inches

Plate, 9 inches
Plate, 9¾ inches
Plate, Cake
Plate, Chop, 11½ inches
Plate, Fruit, 6¼ inches
Plate, Fruit, 7 inches
Plate, Fruit, 8 inches
Plate, Fruit, 9 inches
Platter (Dish), 6¼ inches
Platter (Dish), 7¼ inches
Platter (Dish), 8 inches
Platter (Dish), 9½ inches
Platter (Dish), 10½ inches
Platter (Dish), 11½ inches
Platter (Dish), 12½ inches
Platter (Dish), 13½ inches
Platter (Dish), 14½ inches
Platter (Dish), 15¼ inches
Platter (Dish), 17½ inches
Platter (Dish), 19¾ inches
Salad, 8 inches
Salad, 9 inches
Salad, 9¾ inches
Salad Tioga, 8 inches
Salad Tioga, 9 inches
Salad Tioga, 10 inches
Spooner, two handles
Sugar, 3¾ inches
Sugar, 4 inches
Sugar, Individual, 3¼ inches
Teapot with lid
Tureen, Oyster, 8¼ inches
Tureen, Sauce with Ladle and attached Underplate
Tureen, Sauce with Ladle and unattached Underplate
*Reported but not confirmed.

Hudson Known Piece Types

Piece Types known to Replacements

Bone Dish, 6¾ inches
Bowl, Fruit, 5 inches
Bowl, Soup Coupe, 8 inches
Bowl, Vegetable Oval, 8¾ inches
Bowl, Vegetable Oval Covered, 10 inches
Bowl, Vegetable Round, 8½ inches
Bowl, Vegetable Round Covered, 9 inches

Bowl, Vegetable Round Covered, 10 inches
Butter Dish, Round, 7⅜ inches
Creamer
Cup & Saucer Set
 Cup, 2½ inches
 Saucer, 5⅞ inches
Nut Dish, 5⅜ inches
Pitcher, Small

Plate, Luncheon, 9⅛ inches
Plate, Salad, 7¼ inches
Platter, Oval, 13⅜ inches
Platter, Oval, 14¾ inches
Relish, 7¼ inches
Relish, 8⅝ inches
Sugar Bowl with lid

Hudson Shape

HLC558
No Trim

H232
Green Band
No Trim

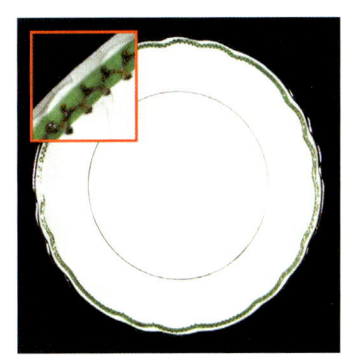

H27
Green Band
Gold Trim

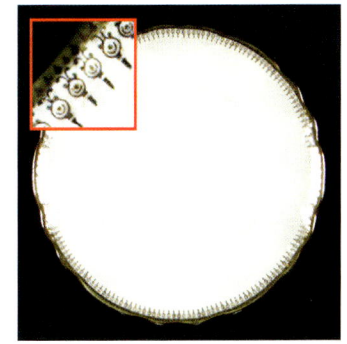

H152
Green Band
Gold Trim

H154
Red Band
Gold Trim

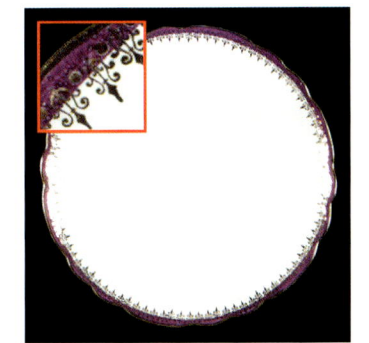

H153
Red Band
Gold Trim

HLC743
Soup Bowl Shown
Red Band
Gold Trim

HLC3112
Creamer Shown
Green Band
Gold Trim

149
Green Band
No Trim

H157
Green Band
Gold Trim

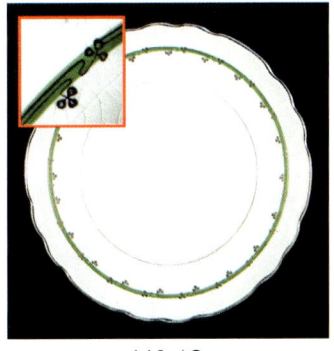

H149
Green Band
Gold Trim

H150
Red Band
Gold Trim

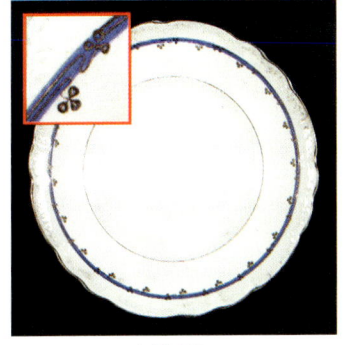

H151
Blue Band
Gold Trim

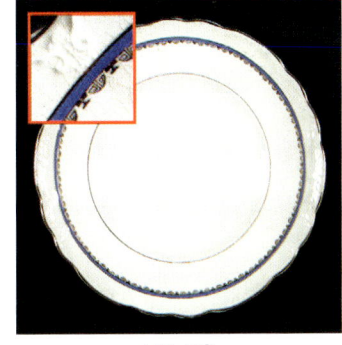

H158
Blue Band
Gold Trim

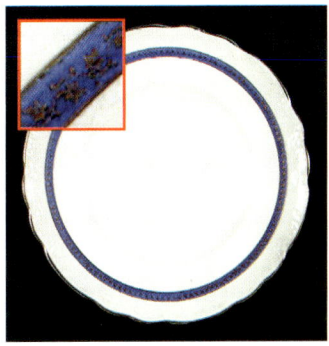

H160
Blue Band
Gold Trim

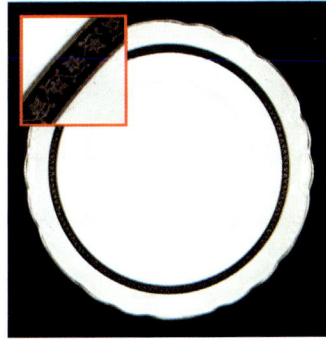

H159
Black Band
Gold Trim

Hudson Shape

HLC1381
Gold Trim

HLC959
*Salad Plate Shown
Gold Trim*

HLC1015
*Luncheon Plate Shown
Gold Trim*

H111
Gold Trim

H110
Gold Trim

H4101
Gold Trim

HLC2054
*Soup Bowl Shown
Gold Trim*

H129
Gold Trim

HLC1259
Gold Trim

H216
Gold Trim

HLC1186
*Luncheon Plate Shown
No Trim*

H225
Gold Trim

HLC1263
Green Trim

H230
Gold Trim

HLC1380
Gold Trim

H314
No Trim

Hudson Shape

HLC1842 No Trim	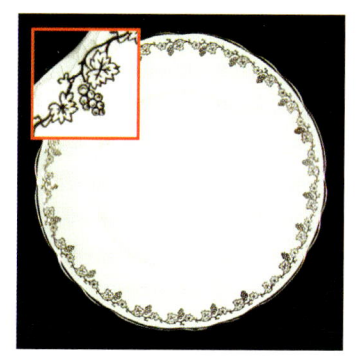 **H315** Gold Trim	 **H2100** No Trim	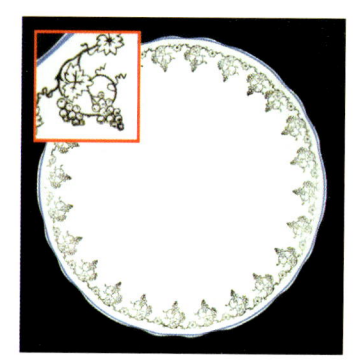 **6201** Blue Trim
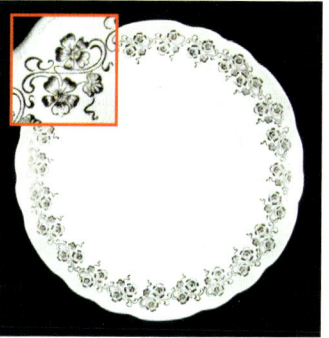 **BT1/M1** No Trim	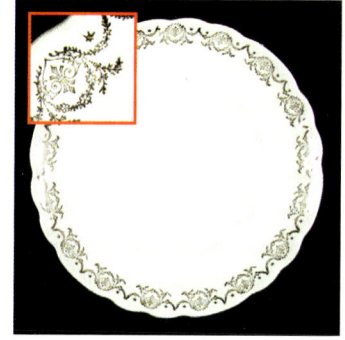 **H2400** No Trim	 **H2500** No Trim	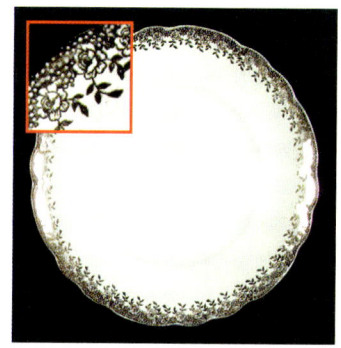 **M6S** No Trim
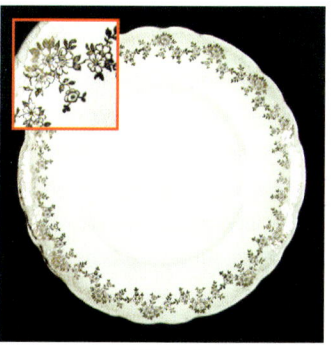 **WMS3** No Trim	 **GH1500** No Trim	 **HLC1047** No Trim	 **HLC1382** No Trim
 **W3S** No Trim	 **6830** Gold Trim	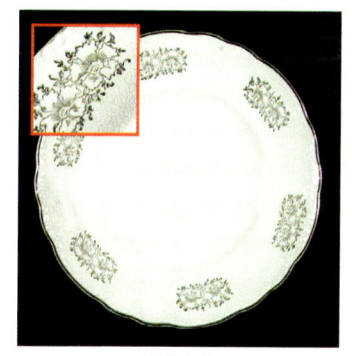 **6865** Gold Trim	 **863** Gold Trim

Hudson Shape

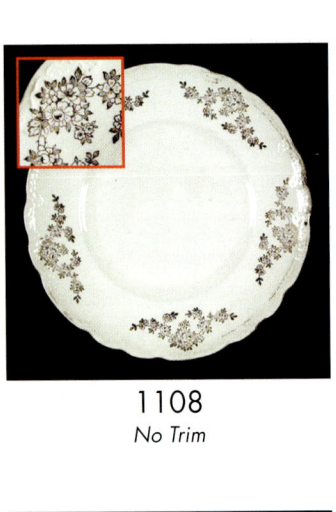

1108 No Trim	**G1100** No Trim	**X2S** No Trim	**K7673** No Trim
4806 Gold Band No Trim	**HLC989** Oval Platter Shown Gold Trim	**H420** Gold Trim	**W5S** No Trim
H3000 No Trim	**3017** No Trim	**E155** No Trim	**B4S/W4S** No Trim
HLC2100 No Trim	**H107** Gold Trim	**H7213** Blue Trim	**HLC1841** No Trim

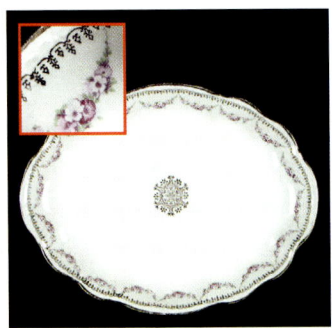

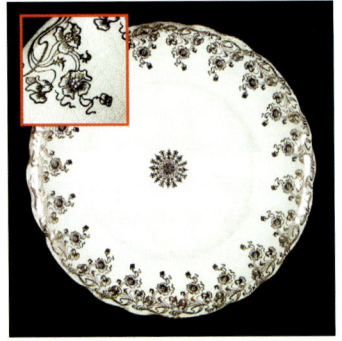

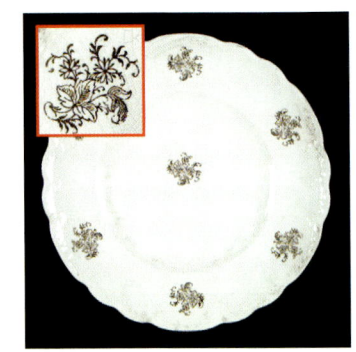

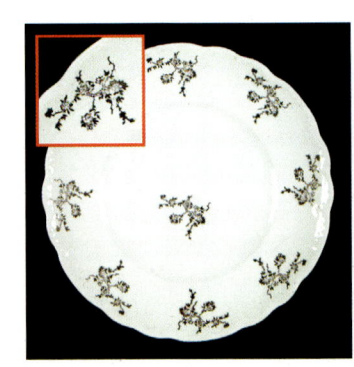

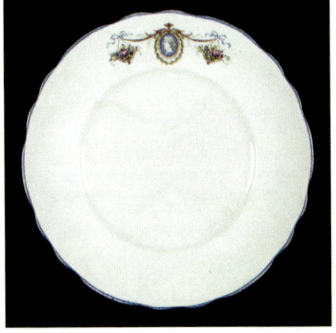

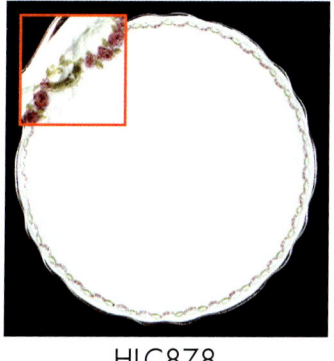

Hudson Shape

HLC878
Gold Trim

HLC950
Bread & Butter Plate Shown
Gold Trim

HLC600
Oval Platter Shown
Gold Trim

HLC887
Saucer Shown
Gold Trim

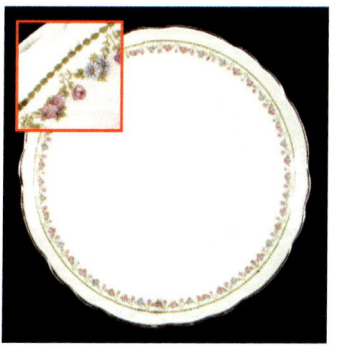

W35
Gold Trim

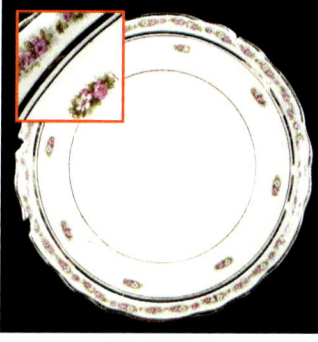

HLC899
Gold Trim

4304
No Trim

HLC1188
No Trim

HLC1100
Oval Platter Shown
Gold Trim

W817
No Trim

HLC1840
Gold Trim

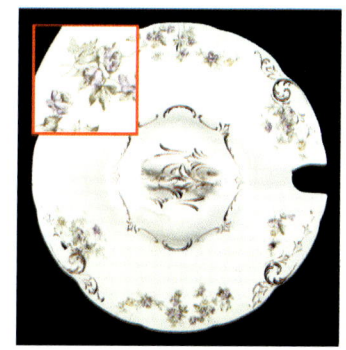

HLC749
Round Covered Vegetable
Bowl Lid Shown
No Trim

1699
No Trim

K24
No Trim

HLC2190
Oval Platter Shown
No Trim

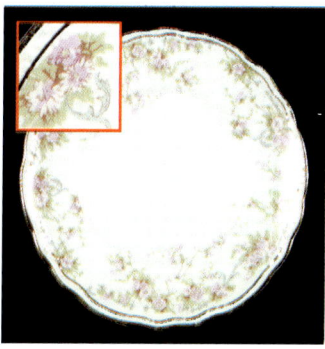

H135
Bread & Butter Plate Shown
Gold Trim

Hudson Shape

HLC1110
Luncheon Plate Shown
Gold Trim

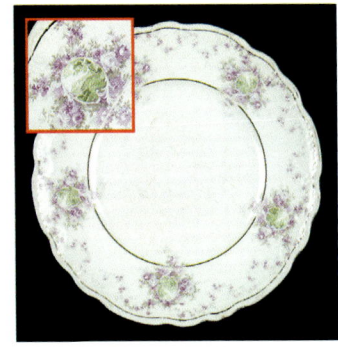

HLC960
Luncheon Plate Shown
Gold Trim

H1804
Gold Trim

W30
Gold Trim

W114
Gold Trim

HLC916
Luncheon Plate Shown
No Trim

HLC2035
Gold Trim

HLC2070
No Trim

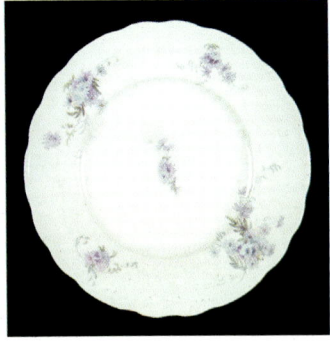

HLC1852
No Trim

HLC1199
Gold Trim

HLC564
No Trim

EMPRESS

Piece Types

THE HOMER LAUGHLIN CHINA COMPANY, NEWELL, W. VA.

THE EMPRESS DINNER SERVICE.

1 Teapot	8 After Dinner Coffee	15 Nappie, 7 inch	22 Boston Egg Cup	29 Sauce Boat and Stand
2 Sugar	9 Covered Butter	16 Coupe Soup, 7 inch	23 Spoon Holder	30 Oyster Tureen only
3 Cream	10 Double Handle Sauce Boat	17 Oatmeal, 36s	24 Dish, 10 inch	31 Casserole, 7 inch
4 Individual Sugar	11 Fast Stand Sauce Boat	18 Fruit, 4 inch	25 Cake Plate	32 Covered Dish, 7 inch
5 Individual Cream	12 Cream Soup and Stand	19 Individual Butter	26 Plate, 7 inch	33 Sauce Tureen Complete
6 Coffee	13 Bouillon Cup and Saucer	20 Bone Dish	27 Baker, 7 inch	34 Jug, 24s
7 Tea	14 Ramekin and Stand	21 Bowl, 36s	28 Pickle	

Page Seven

Empress piece types, photograph from the Homer Laughlin Factory.

Homer Laughlin

EMPRESS — 1910 – circa 1937 or later

The Empress shape has been found with backstamps dated as early as 1915. *The Ladies Home Journal* featured Empress in a Homer Laughlin Christmas ad in its December 1914 issue. *The 1916 Homer Laughlin Price List* includes dozens of patterns on the shape. Empress shapes are illustrated in the Homer Laughlin catalogs of 1920, 1922, 1926, and 1929. It was one of only six shapes in production in 1928 (*Pottery, Glass & Brass Salesman*, February 2, 1928). The Sears, Roebuck & Co. Catalog included patterns on the Empress shape from 1929 through 1932.

By 1930, the Butler Brothers Catalog offered the Capitol pattern on the Empress shape. As late as 1937, over three decades after it was introduced, *The Homer Laughlin Pound Sterling Price Booklet* shows Empress still offered with 67 different decorations/patterns!

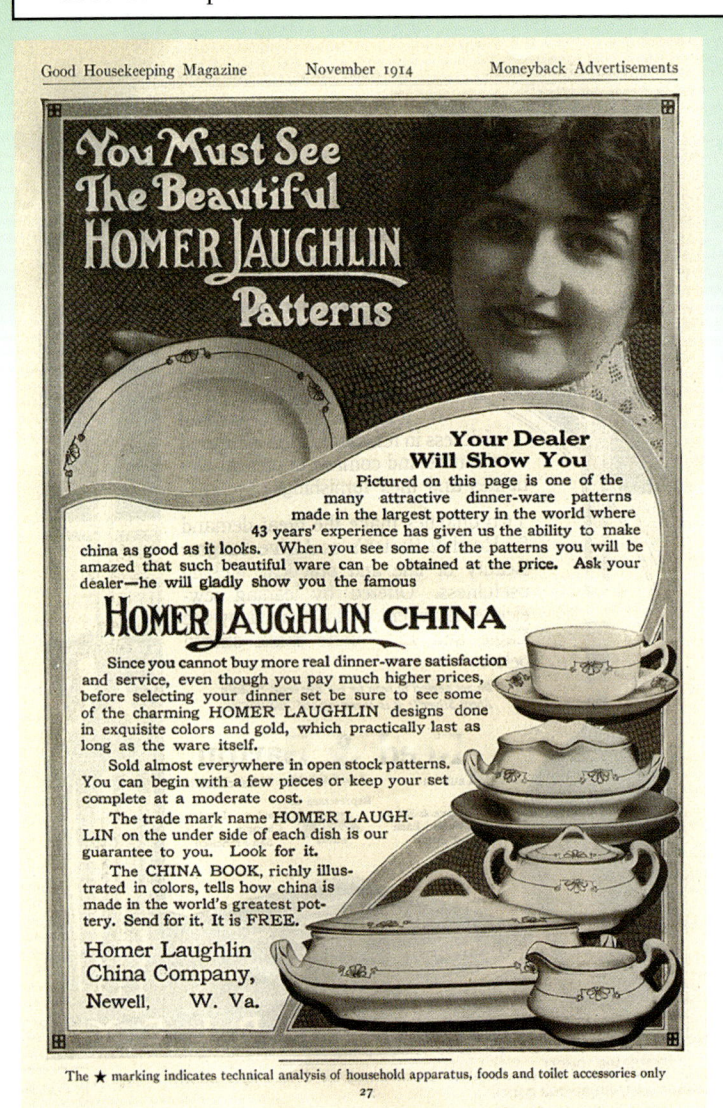

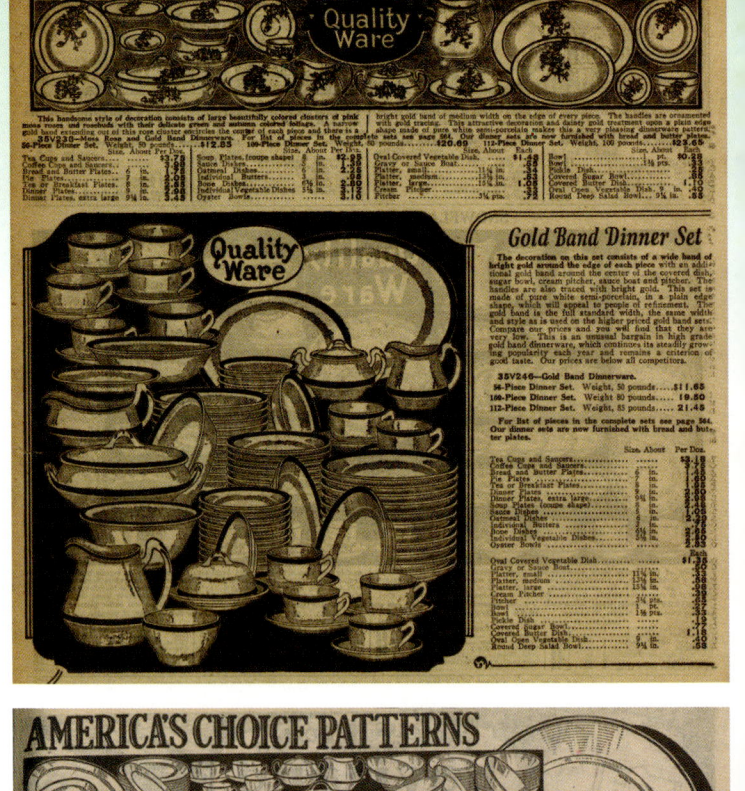

Top right: HLC1176 pattern; Teapot with lid. **Left:** E8703 pattern; Good Housekeeping Magazine, *1914*. **Second down on right:** Typical Empress backstamp. **Third down on right:** Pink Moss Rose E4904 (top) and Gold Band (bottom) patterns; Sears, Roebuck & Co. Catalog, 1925. **Bottom right:** Bright and Matte Gold trim patterns; Sears, Roebuck & Co. Catalog, 1929. Note, in some Empress ads the small jug is pictured in place of the creamer.

Empress Shape

Empress Piece Type List

From Homer Laughlin Literature with Confirmed Actual Pieces

Bone Dish
Bowl, 1¼ pints
Bowl, Cereal, 4½ inches
Bowl, Cranberry
Bowl, Cream Soup & Saucer Set
Bowl, Fruit, 5⅛ inches
Bowl, Fruit, 5⅝ inches
Bowl, Oyster, ¾ pints
Bowl, Oyster, 1¼ pints
Bowl, Soup Coupe, 7⅛ inches
Bowl, Soup Coupe, 7⅞ inches
Bowl, Soup with rim, 9⅛ inches
Bowl, Vegetable Oval, 5½ inches
Bowl, Vegetable Oval, 7⅛ inches
Bowl, Vegetable Oval, 8 inches
Bowl, Vegetable Oval, 8⅞ inches
Bowl, Vegetable Oval, 9⅞ inches
Bowl, Vegetable Oval, 11 inches
Bowl, Vegetable Oval Covered, 8 inches
Bowl, Vegetable Round, 6½ inches
Bowl, Vegetable Round, 7⅝ inches
Bowl, Vegetable Round, 8½ inches
Bowl, Vegetable Round, 9½ inches
Bowl, Vegetable Round, 10½ inches

Bowl, Vegetable Round Covered, 6¼ inches
Butter Dish, Round with lid
Butter Pat, Individual, 3 inches
Creamer
Creamer, Individual
Cup & Saucer Set, 2 inches
Cup & Saucer Set, Bouillon
Cup & Saucer Set, Coffee, 8 oz.
Cup & Saucer Set, Demitasse, 1⅝ inches
Eggcup, Boston/Sherbet, 4 inches
Gravy/Sauce Boat, one handle
Gravy/Sauce Boat with attached Underplate, no handles, 5¾ inches
Gravy/Sauce Boat with attached Underplate, two handles
Jug, ½ pints
Jug, ⅞ pints
Jug, 1⅜ pints
Jug, 2¼ pints
Jug, 3⅜ pints
Jug, 4¾ pints
Jug, 6¼ pints
Pickle, 8½ inches
Plate, Bread & Butter, 6 inches
Plate, Cake, 10¼ inches

Plate, Dessert, 7 inches
Plate, Dinner, 9⅝ inches
Plate, Luncheon, 9 inches
Plate, Salad, 8 inches
Platter, 6¼ inches
Platter, 7⅛ inches
Platter, 8⅜ inches
Platter, 9⅛ inches
Platter, 10¼ inches
Platter, 11⅜ inches
Platter, 12½ inches
Platter, 13⅝ inches
Platter, 14¼ inches
Platter, 15⅝ inches
Platter, 17¼ inches
Ramekin and Stand
Spooner
Sugar Bowl with lid, 3⅞ inches
Sugar Bowl with lid, Individual, 3¼ inches
Teapot with lid
Tray, Celery, 11 inches
Tureen, Oyster with notched lid, 7¾ inches
Tureen, Sauce with Ladle and Stand

Top left: *HLC3014 pattern;* Gravy/Sauce Boat with attached Underplate. **Middle left:** *HLC1960 pattern;* Creamer, and Sugar Bowl with lid. **Bottom left:** *Rose & Lattice pattern;* Round Covered Vegetable Bowl. **Bottom Right:** *Rose & Lattice pattern;* Platters, Salad Plate, Bread & Butter Plate, Luncheon Plate, Cup & Saucer Set, and Fruit Bowl.

Empress Shape

E2202
Gold Trim

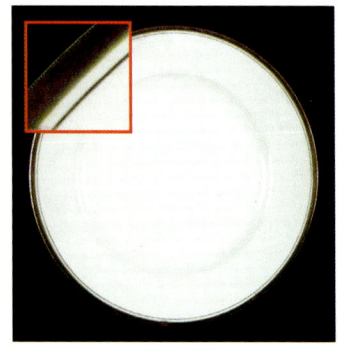

E2002
Gold Trim

Gold Band
Bread & Butter Plate Shown
Gold Trim

E4102
Gold Trim

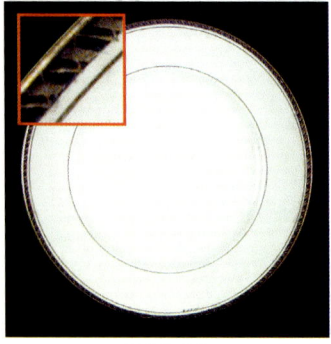

E5203
Gold Trim

HLC1176
Teapot Shown
Gold Trim

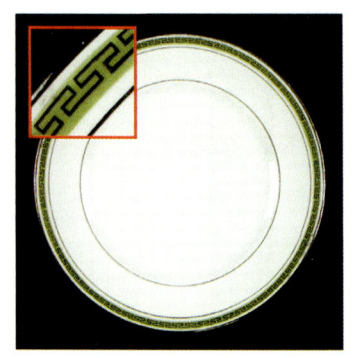

E187
Gold Trim

E272
Oval Covered Vegetable Bowl Shown
Gold Trim

E3903
Gold Trim

HLC235
Bone Dish Shown
Gold Trim

E3406
Gold Trim

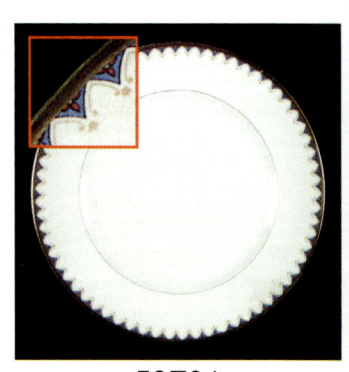

E2706
Gold Trim

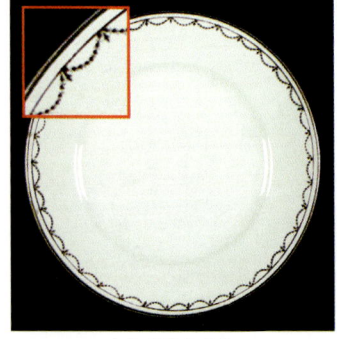

HLC2069
Gold Trim

HLC2015
Gold Trim

HLC2075
Gold Trim

HLC2017
Oval Platter Shown
Black Trim

Empress Shape

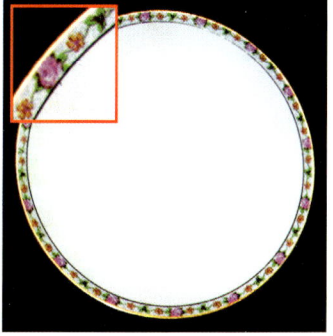

E7505
Gold Trim

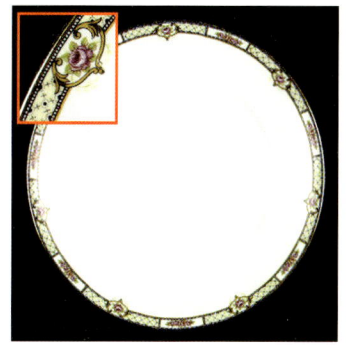

Rose & Lattice
Gold Trim

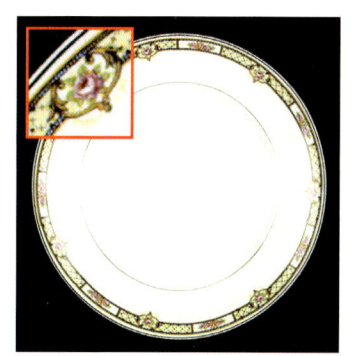

HLC176
Black Trim

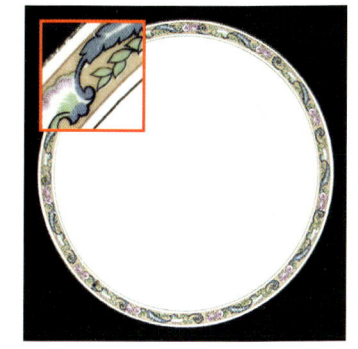

HLC1016
Luncheon Plate Shown
Gold Trim

W530
Gold Trim

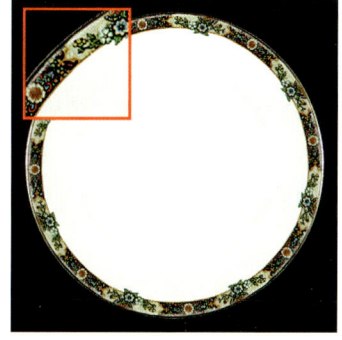

HLC905
Gold Trim

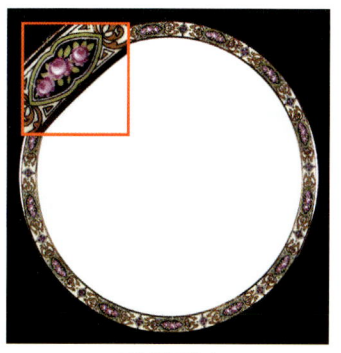

HLC726
Luncheon Plate Shown
Gold Trim

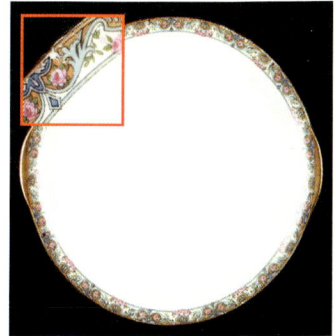

HLC498
Handled Cake Plate Shown
Gold Trim

HLC1960
Creamer & Sugar Bowl Shown
Gold Trim

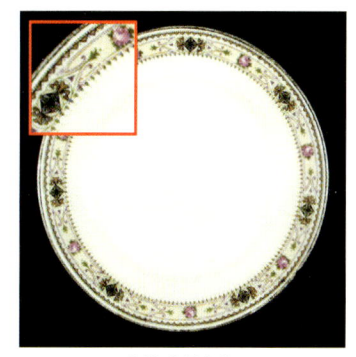

HLC510
Salad Plate Shown
Gold Trim

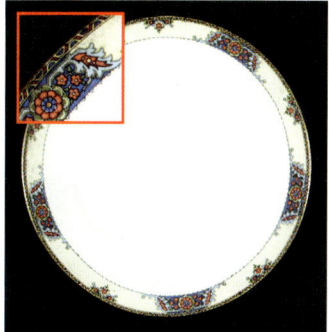

E8115
Gold Trim

HLC3014
Gravy Boat Shown
Gold Trim

HLC3003
Relish Shown
No Trim

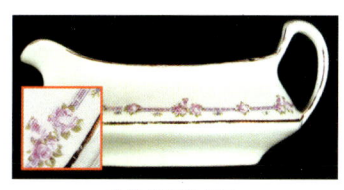

HLC2132
Gravy Boat Shown
Gold Trim

E3006
Gold Trim

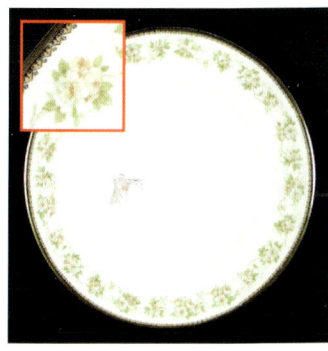

E3806
Gold Trim

65

Empress Shape

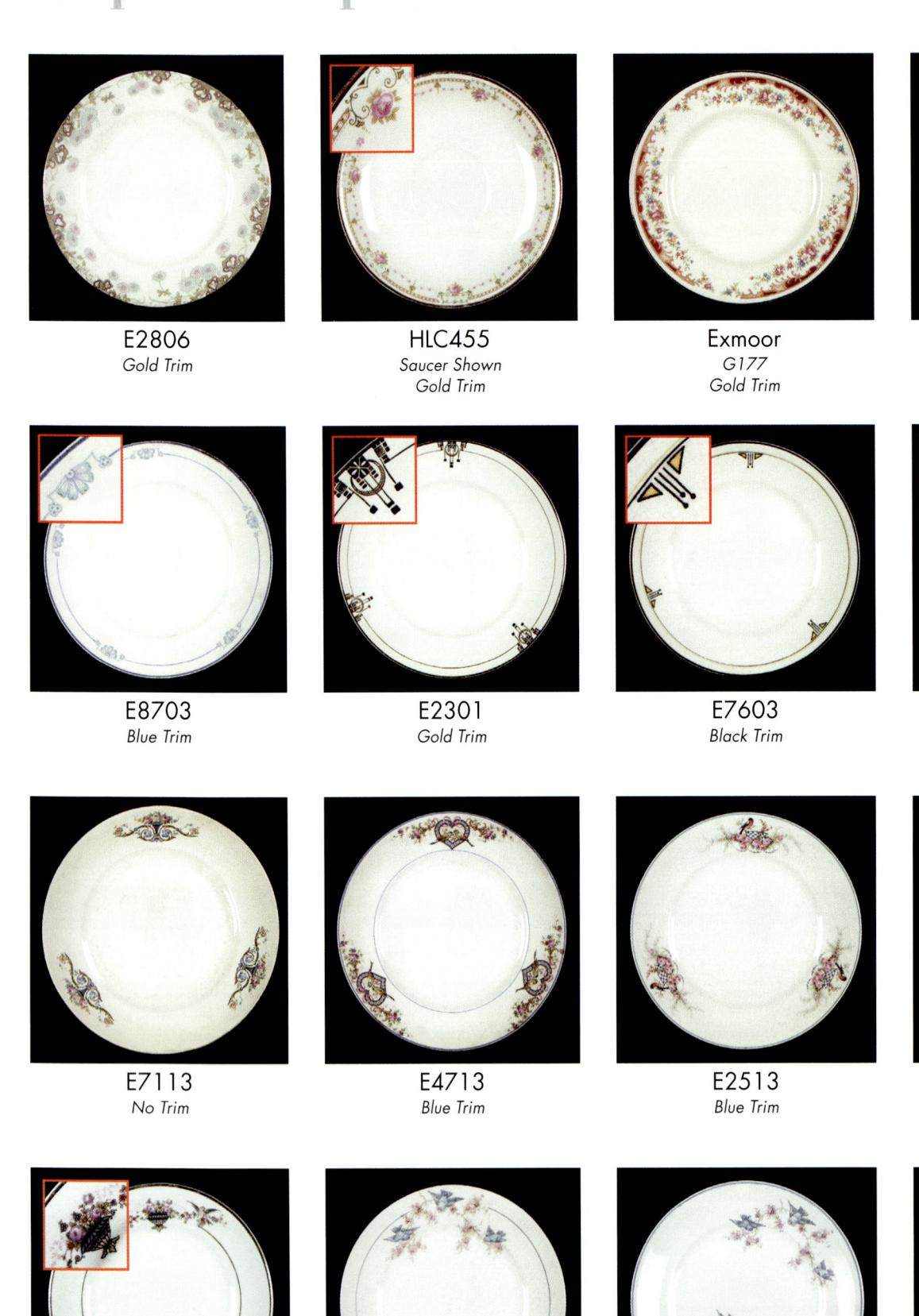

E2806 *Gold Trim*	**HLC455** *Saucer Shown Gold Trim*	**Exmoor** *G177 Gold Trim*	 **E7504B** *Gold Trim*
E8703 *Blue Trim*	**E2301** *Gold Trim*	**E7603** *Black Trim*	 **HLC2108** *Blue Trim*
E7113 *No Trim*	**E4713** *Blue Trim*	**E2513** *Blue Trim*	 **HLC2125** *Gold Trim*
E4613 *Bread & Butter Plate Shown Gold Trim*	 **E7413** *No Trim*	 **Flying Bluebird** *Blue Trim*	 **E7104** *Gold Trim*

Empress Shape

E4904
Gold Trim

HLC746
*Oval Platter Shown
No Trim*

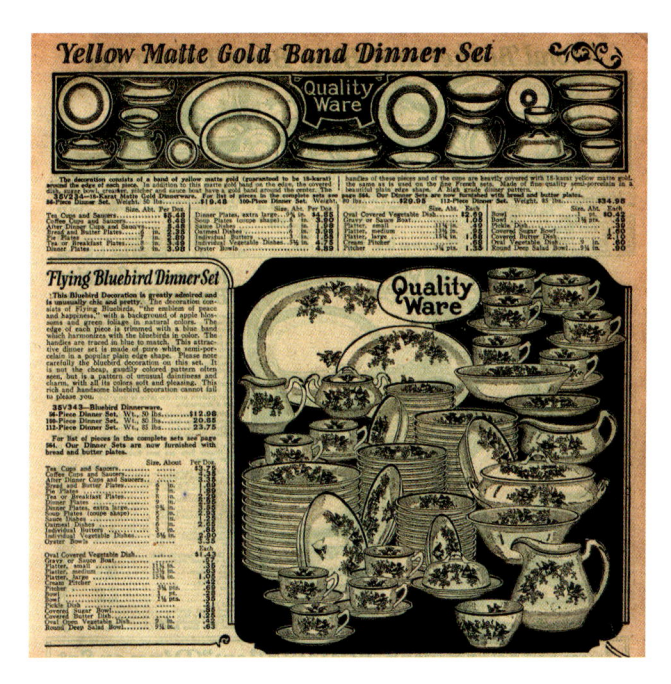

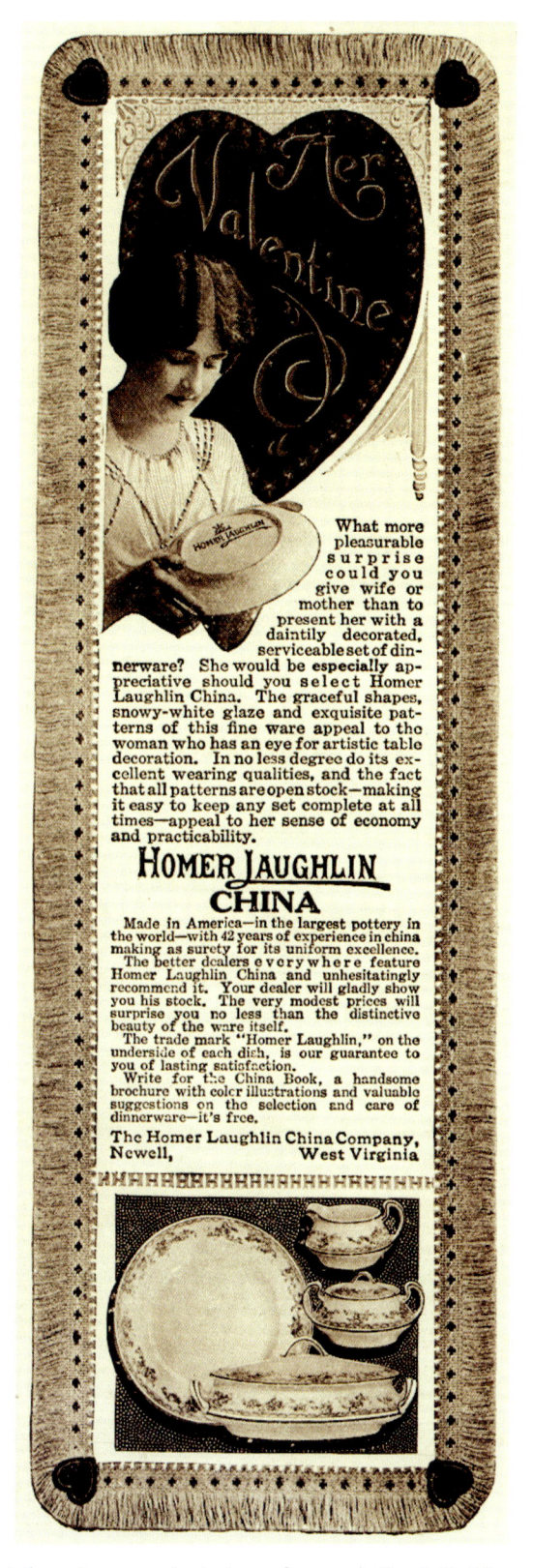

Above: *Advertisement (origin unknown).* **Top left:** *Matte Gold Band (top) and Flying Bluebird patterns; Sears, Roebuck & Co. Catalog, 1925.* **Bottom left:** *Floral Basket with Blue Band (top), and Rose & Lattice patterns; Sears, Roebuck & Co. Catalog, 1925.*

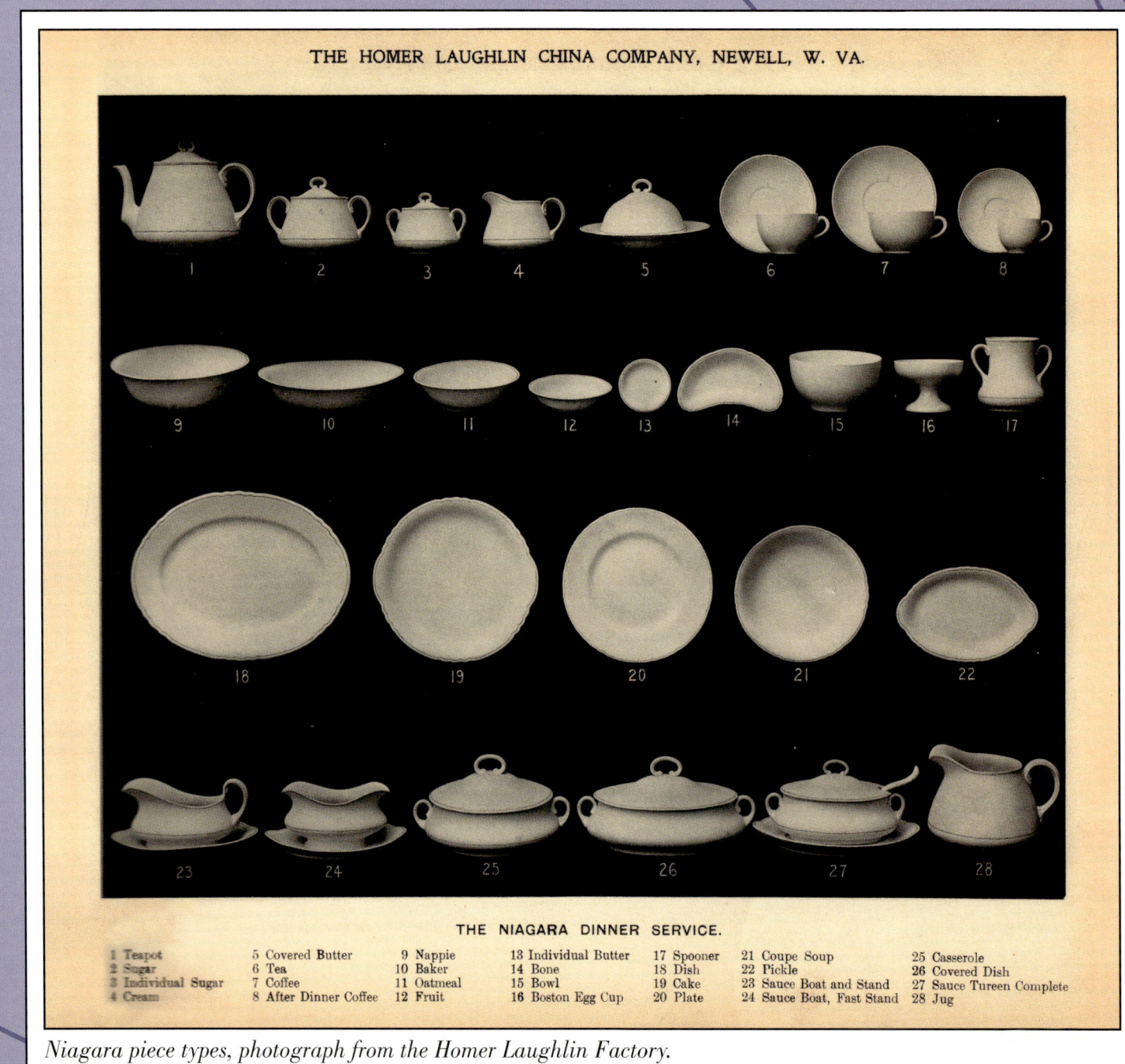

Niagara

Piece Types

THE HOMER LAUGHLIN CHINA COMPANY, NEWELL, W. VA.

THE NIAGARA DINNER SERVICE.

1 Teapot	5 Covered Butter	9 Nappie	13 Individual Butter	17 Spooner	21 Coupe Soup	25 Casserole
2 Sugar	6 Tea	10 Baker	14 Bone	18 Dish	22 Pickle	26 Covered Dish
3 Individual Sugar	7 Coffee	11 Oatmeal	15 Bowl	19 Cake	23 Sauce Boat and Stand	27 Sauce Tureen Complete
4 Cream	8 After Dinner Coffee	12 Fruit	16 Boston Egg Cup	20 Plate	24 Sauce Boat, Fast Stand	28 Jug

Niagara piece types, photograph from the Homer Laughlin Factory.

Niagara Shape

NIAGARA   circa 1910

Niagara resembles another Homer Laughlin shape, Genesee. Both have open looping handles, fluid graceful forms and are, at a glance, strikingly similar. Niagara has faint embossing into the clay which Genesee does not have. On a Niagara plate, the embossing is a gentle scalloped line near the edge. A similar, and often faint embossed scallop, rings the hollowware at the object's widest point. Look for these faint embossings by touch as much as by sight. A final distinguishing point is the backstamp. Most pieces in both shapes have a distinctive backstamp naming their shape.

The Niagara dinner service is illustrated and pieces are listed in the May 1, 1910 Homer Laughlin Catalog. This is the earliest reference to the shape found. It has ceased to be offered by the time the 1916 price list appears.

Niagara Piece Type List

From Homer Laughlin Literature with Confirmed Actual Pieces

Bone Dish	Butter Pat, Individual	Plate, Cake
Bowl, Cereal (Oatmeal)	Creamer	Plate, Dinner
Bowl, Cranberry	Cup & Saucer Set, Coffee	Platter, Oval
Bowl, Fruit	Cup & Saucer Set, Demitasse	Spooner
Bowl, Soup Coupe	Cup & Saucer Set, Tea	Sugar Bowl with lid
Bowl, Vegetable Oval (Baker)	Eggcup, Boston	Sugar Bowl with lid, Individual
Bowl, Vegetable Oval Covered (Covered Dish)	Gravy/Sauce Boat	Teapot with lid
Bowl, Vegetable Round (Nappy)	Gravy/Sauce Boat Underplate/Relish/Pickle	Tureen, Sauce with lid, Underplate and Ladle
Bowl, Vegetable Round Covered (Casserole)	Gravy/Sauce Boat with attached Underplate	
Butter Dish with lid	Pitcher/Jug	

Top right: *Typical Niagara backstamp.* **Left:** *HLC1299 pattern; Gravy/Sauce Boat.* **Right:** *HLC2157 pattern; Oval Covered Vegetable Bowl.*

Niagara Shape

HLC3029 Oval Platter Shown Gold Trim	**N224** Gold Trim	**N164** Gold Trim	**N199** Gold Trim
N552 Gold Trim	**N212** Gold Trim	**N213** Gold Trim	**K16** Gold Trim
HLC2099 Oval Platter Shown Gold Trim	**HLC1299** Gravy Boat Shown Gold Trim	**HLC2157** Oval Covered Vegetable Bowl Shown No Trim	**K7673N** No Trim

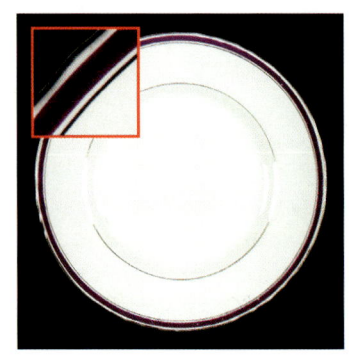

Genesee

Piece Types

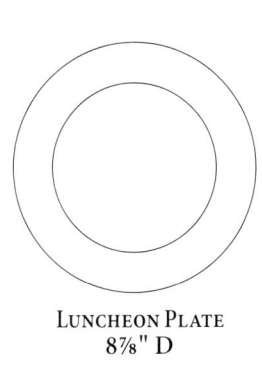

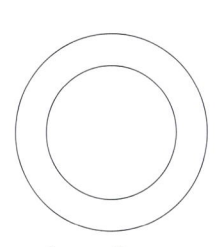

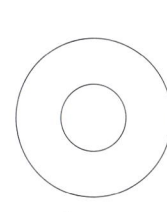

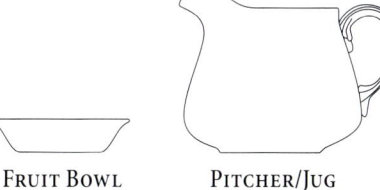

These drawings were made from actual stock at Replacements, Ltd. Check the piece type list for all known piece types in this shape.

Luncheon Plate
8⅞" D

Salad Plate
7" D

Saucer
5⅝" D

Cup
4⅜" W
2¼" H

Fruit Bowl
5⅛" W
1⅛" H

Pitcher/Jug
8⅛" W
5⅞" H

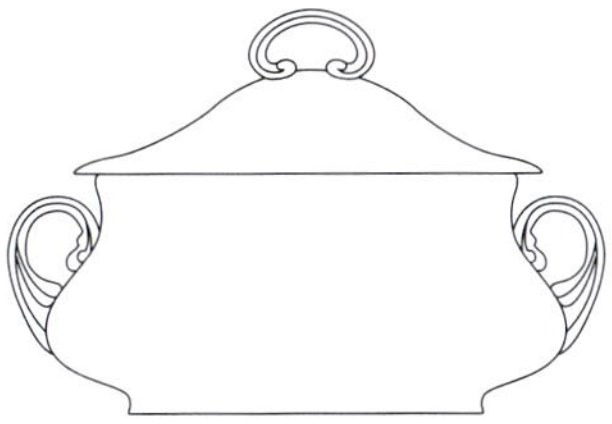

Oyster Tureen with lid
10⅞" W
7⅛" H

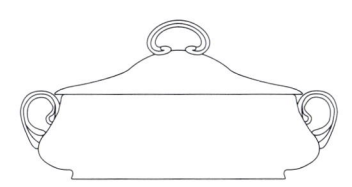

Oval Covered Vegetable Bowl
11½" W
5⅝" H

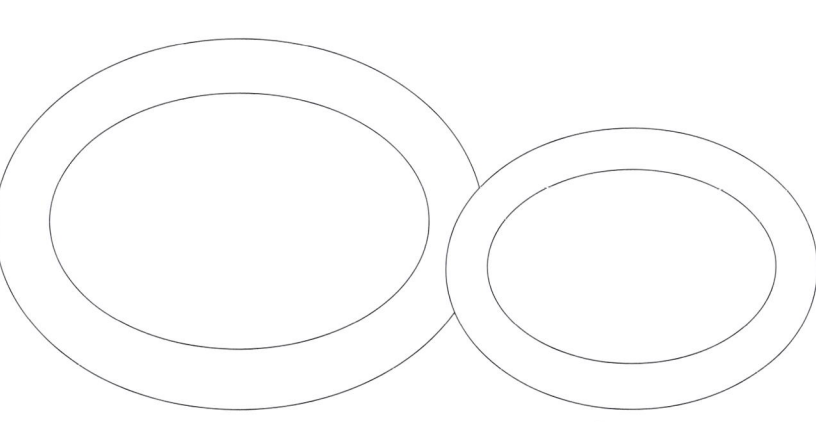

17" Platter
17⅞" W
13⅛" H

13" Platter
13¾" W
10" H

Above: *Good Housekeeping Magazine, November 1913.*

71

Homer Laughlin

GENESEE 1911 – discontinued between 1916 & 1920

Genesee is found in a 1911 Homer Laughlin Company price list on "fine white ware." It has been reported that Sperry & Hutchinson, producers of S&H green stamps, marketed Genesee shaped patterns in 1911, and S.H. Kress (today's K-Mart) marketed the patterns in 1912.

Genesee appears in the 1912 Homer Laughlin promotional booklet, *The China Book*. Genesee was one of the most popular shapes of its day; well over 400 patterns were offered on the shape. *The 1916 Homer Laughlin Price List* included more patterns on Genesee than on any other shape. Genesee was discontinued sometime prior to 1920. The shape did not appear in the *1920 Catalog and Price List for Plain White Ware* (a catalog of undecorated blanks, where Republic, Empress, Kwaker, etc. shapes did appear in 1920).

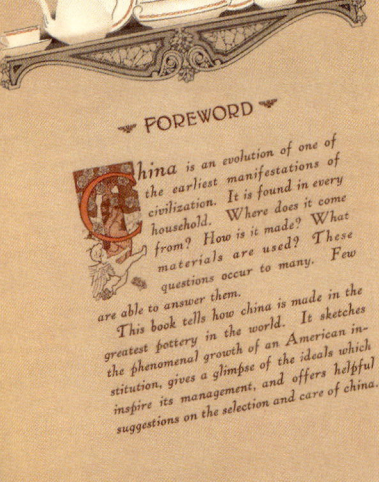

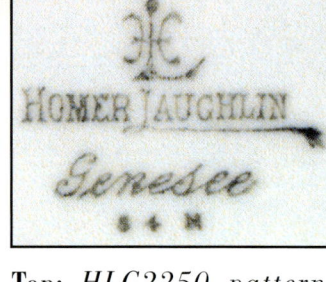

Top: *HLC2250 pattern; Pitcher/Jug.* **Bottom left:** The China Book, *cover.* **Bottom middle:** The China Book, *inside cover.* **Bottom right:** *Typical Genesee backstamp.*

Genesee Shape

The China Book *inside pages.* **Top left:** *G-1305 pattern.* **Top right:** *G-1705 pattern.*
Bottom left: *G-302 pattern.* **Bottom right:** *G-1601 pattern.*

Homer Laughlin

Genesee Piece Type List

From 1911 Homer Laughlin Literature (English measurements)

Bone Dish, 6½ inches
Bowl, 1⅝ pints
Bowl, 11¼ inches
Bowl, Cereal, 5⅞ inches
Bowl, Cereal, 6½ inches
Bowl, Cranberry
Bowl, Fruit, 5⅛ inches
Bowl, Fruit, 5⅝ inches
Bowl, Fruit, 6 inches
Bowl, Soup Coupe
Bowl, Soup with rim, 9⅛ inches
Bowl, Vegetable Oval, 5½ inches
Bowl, Vegetable Oval, 8¼ inches
Bowl, Vegetable Oval, 9 inches
Bowl, Vegetable Oval, 10 inches
Bowl, Vegetable Oval, 11¼ inches
Bowl, Vegetable Oval Covered, 8¼ inches
Bowl, Vegetable Oval Covered, 8¾ inches
Bowl, Vegetable Round, 6½ inches
Bowl, Vegetable Round, 7⅝ inches
Bowl, Vegetable Round, 8½ inches
Bowl, Vegetable Round, 9½ inches
Bowl, Vegetable Round, 10½ inches
Bowl, Vegetable Round, 11½ inches
Bowl, Vegetable Round Covered, 7⅜ inches

Bowl, Vegetable Round Covered, 8¼ inches
Butter Dish, Round Covered
Butter Pat, Individual, 3⅛ inches
Creamer, ⅞ Pint
Creamer, Individual, ½ pint
Cup & Saucer Set, Bouillon, 10½ oz.
Cup & Saucer Set, Coffee, 10½ oz.
Cup & Saucer Set, Demitasse, 3½ oz.
Cup & Saucer Set, Tea, 8¼ oz.
Dish, 6⅜ inches
Dish, 7⅜ inches
Dish, 8⅛ inches
Dish, 9½ inches
Dish, 10½ inches
Eggcup, Boston, 4 inches
Gravy/Sauce Boat, 6 inches
Gravy/Sauce Boat Fast Stand, 9⅛ inches
Gravy/Sauce Boat Underplate, 9⅛ inches
Pickle/Relish
Pitcher/Jug, ½ pint
Pitcher/Jug, ⅞ pint
Pitcher/Jug, 1½ pints
Pitcher/Jug, 2⅜ pints
Pitcher/Jug, 4 pints
Pitcher/Jug, 4⅞ pints
Pitcher/Jug, 7⅝ pint

Plate, Bread & Butter, 6⅝ inches
Plate, Cake
Plate, Coupe, 7⅛ inches
Plate, Coupe, 7⅞ inches
Plate, Dessert, 7¼ inches
Plate, Dinner, 9⅞ inches
Plate, Luncheon, 9⅛ inches
Plate, Salad, 8¼ inches
Platter, 11½ inches
Platter, 12⅜ inches
Platter, 13¾ inches
Platter, 14¾ inches
Platter, 15½ inches
Platter, 17⅞ inches
Platter, 19⅞ inches
Spooner, 3¼ inches
Sugar Bowl with lid, 24s, 3½ inches
Sugar Bowl with lid, 30s, 3½ inches
Sugar Bowl with lid, Individual, 2⅞ inches
Teapot with lid, 3¼ pint
Tray, Celery
Tureen, Oyster, 8¼ inches
Tureen, Sauce, 6¼ inches
Tureen, Sauce Ladle
Tureen, Sauce Stand, 10¼ inches

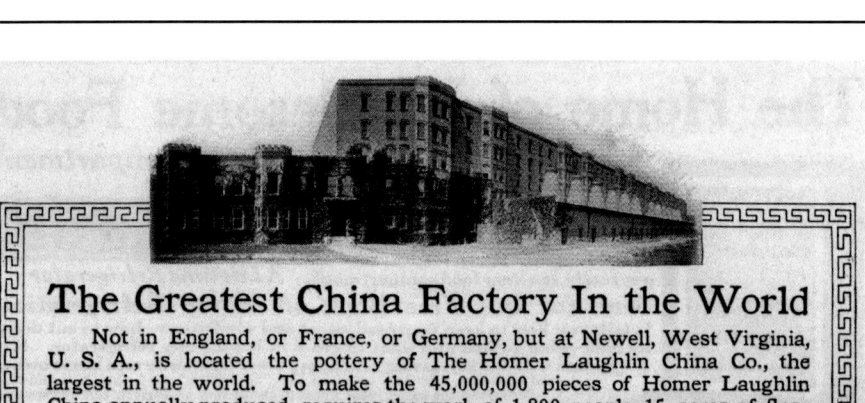

The Greatest China Factory In the World

Not in England, or France, or Germany, but at Newell, West Virginia, U. S. A., is located the pottery of The Homer Laughlin China Co., the largest in the world. To make the 45,000,000 pieces of Homer Laughlin China annually produced, requires the work of 1,800 people; 15 acres of floor space is necessary; and for decorating, $60,000 worth of gold alone is used annually. These figures indicate the popularity of Homer Laughlin China.

In addition to its beauty and refinement of design and decoration, Homer Laughlin China gives splendid service. It is *"as good as it looks."* In buying see that the trade-mark name "Homer Laughlin" appears on the under side of each piece of sufficient size.

The Homer Laughlin China Co.,
Newell, West Virginia

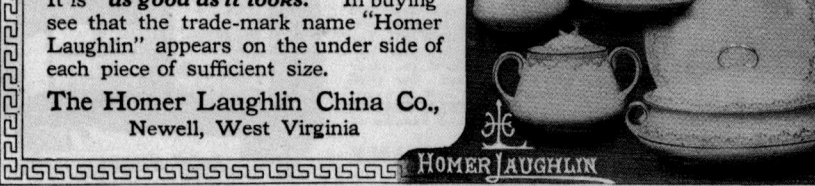

Left: *Unknown magazine ad from 1912.* **Top right:** *HLC1175 pattern; Fruit Bowl, Dinner Plate, Salad Plate, and Cup & Saucer Set.* **Bottom right:** *G2003 pattern; Oyster Tureen with lid, and Oval Covered Vegetable Bowl.*

Genesee Shape

G312 Gold Trim	**G2802** Black Line, Gold Trim	**G2606** Gold Trim	**G1402** Black & Gold Band, Gold Trim
G3803 Black & Gold Edge Design, Gold Trim	**HLC1671** Gold Trim	**HLC2140** Tureen Shown, Gold Trim	**HLC1355** Gold Trim
HLC1674 Gold Trim	**W117** No Trim	**G1600** No Trim	**HLC1673** Gold Trim
G300 Gold Trim	**G286** Gold Trim	**G1301** Gold Trim	**G1701** Gold Trim

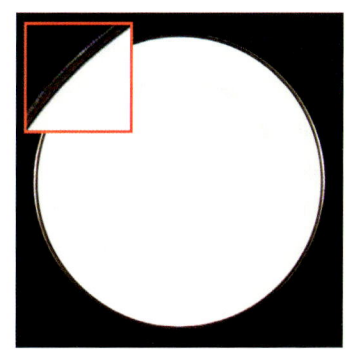

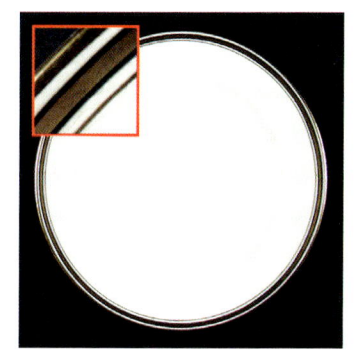

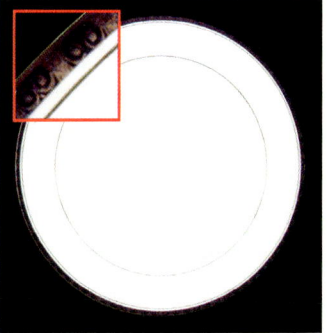

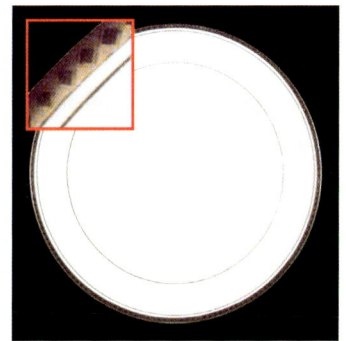

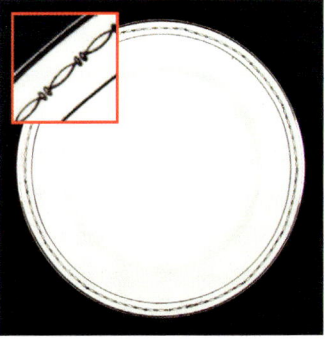

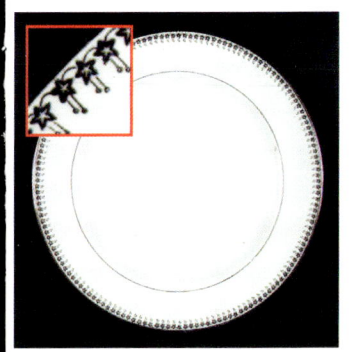

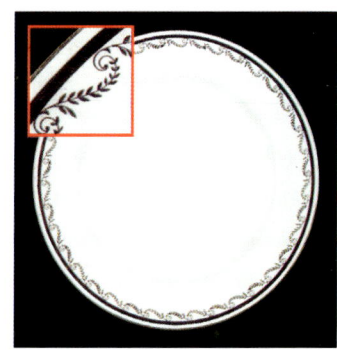

Genesee Shape

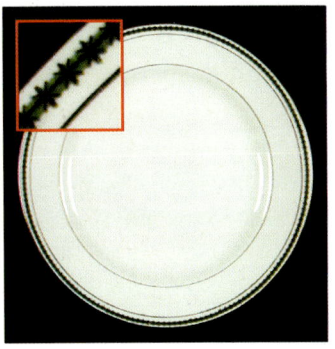

G4103 Green Band Gold Trim	**1203** Green Band No Trim	**PK16** Pink (Mauve) Band No Trim	**G1201** Gold Trim
K26 No Trim	**G220** Gold Trim	**G295** Gold Trim	**HLC1450** Blue Band Gold Trim
W213 No Trim	**G4003** Green Band Gold Trim	**G2801** Gold Trim	**HLC1107** Luncheon Plate Shown Green Band Gold Trim
RAY2 Pink Band No Trim	**G291** Green Band Gold Trim	**G3303G** Black Band No Verge Gold Trim	**G2203** Black Band Gold Trim

Genesee Shape

G271
Green Band
Gold Trim

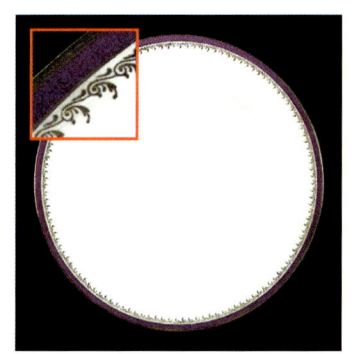

G2103
Red Band
Gold Trim

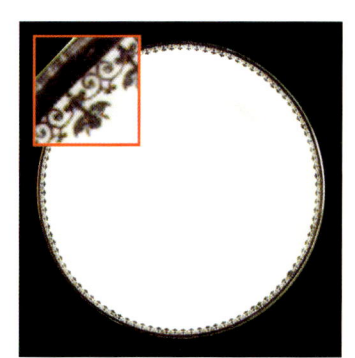

G2601
Rust Band
Gold Trim

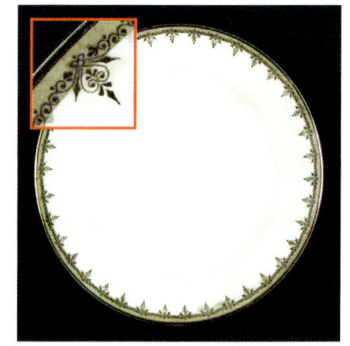

HLC1691
Tan Band
Gold Trim

W215
Tan Band
Gold Trim

W33
Red Band
No Trim

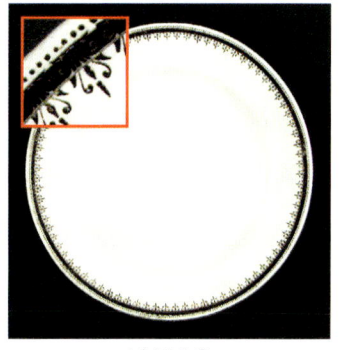

W113
Black Band
No Trim

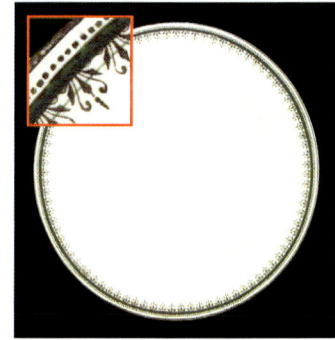

G2303
Green Band
Gold Trim

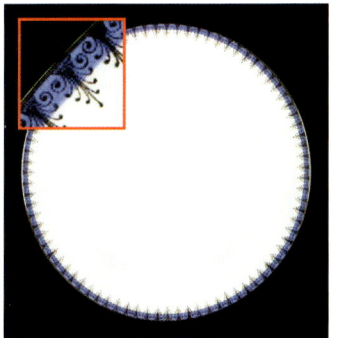

G2003
Blue Band
Gold Trim

HLC886
Vegetable Bowl Missing Lid Shown
Black Band
Gold Trim

G2406
Gold Band & Trim

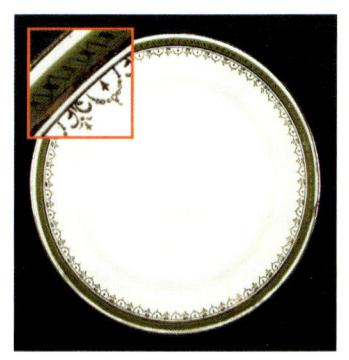

G2503
Green Band
Gold Trim

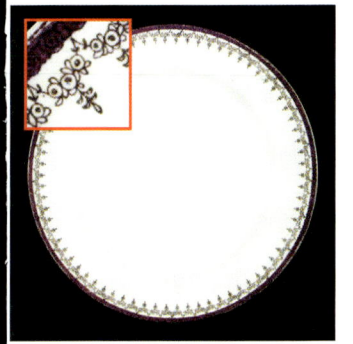

W11
Red Band
Gold Trim

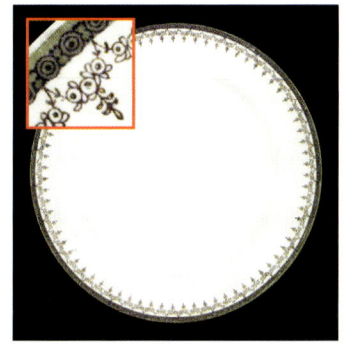

HLC196
Green Band
No Trim

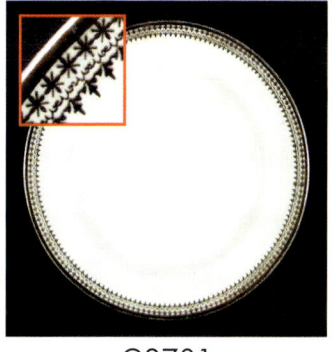

G2701
Gold Band & Trim

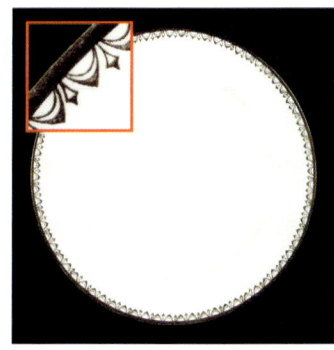

G1401
Gold Band & Trim

Genesee Shape

HLC1672 *Green Band Gold Trim*	**G1506** *Gold Band & Trim*	**W613** *No Trim*	**G4105** *Green Band Gold Trim*
G4605 *Turquoise Band Gold Trim*	**W713** *No Trim*	**K1413** *Green Band Gold Trim*	**G4205** *Gold Trim*
G3905 *Black Band Gold Trim*	**HLC1072** *Gold Trim*	**G3805** *Gold Band & Trim*	**G4805** *Gold Trim*
G1106 *Gold Trim*	**HLC477** *Gold Trim*	**G1206** *Gold Trim*	**HLC1522** *Oval Vegetable Bowl Shown No Trim*

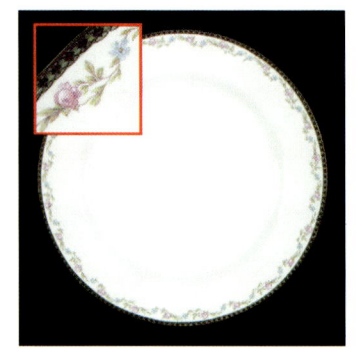

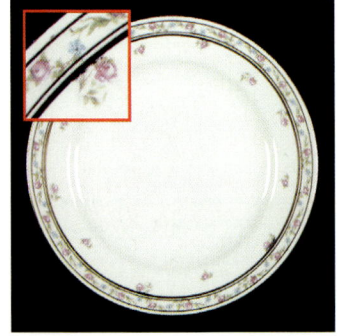

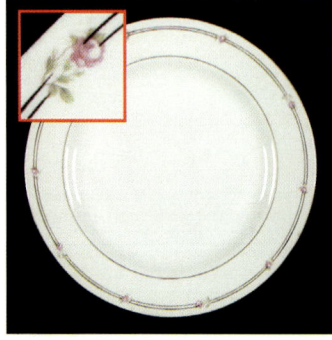

Genesee Shape

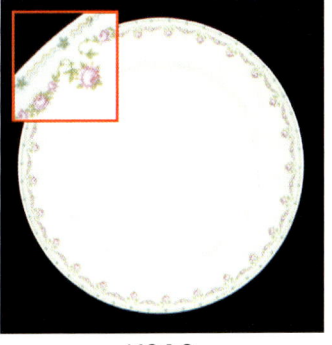

K913
No Trim

K3314
No Trim

K35
No Trim

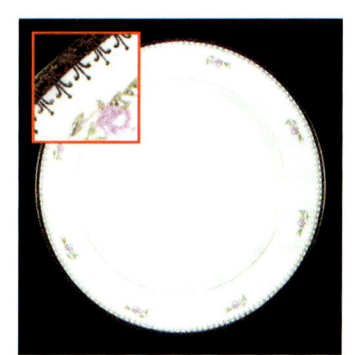

G2106
Black Band
Gold Trim

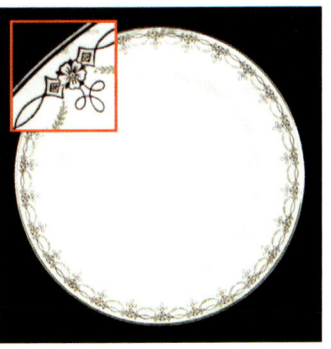

RAY1
Gold Trim

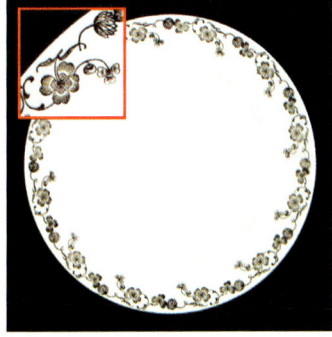

1200
No Trim

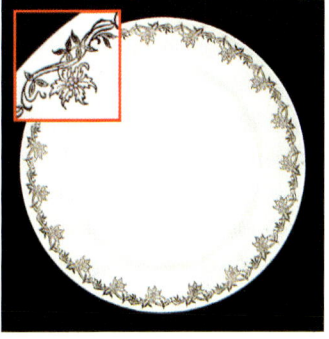

G1300
No Trim

1400
No Trim

HLC1509
Oval Platter Shown
Gold Trim

HLC3013
Oval Platter Shown
No Trim

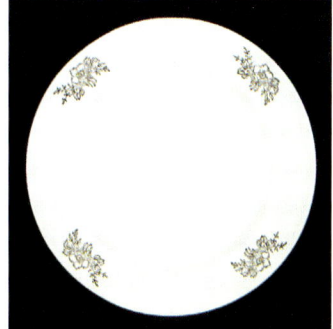

G1700
No Trim

HLC3002
Creamer Shown
No Trim

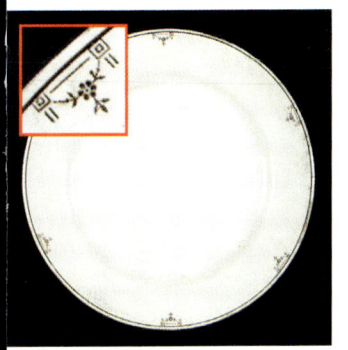

G275
Gold Trim

G278
No Trim

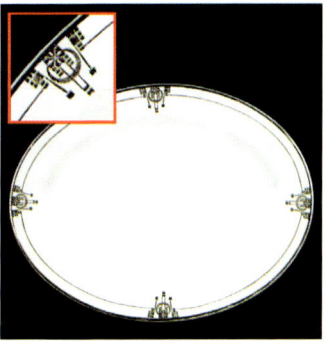

G2301
Oval Platter Shown
Gold Trim

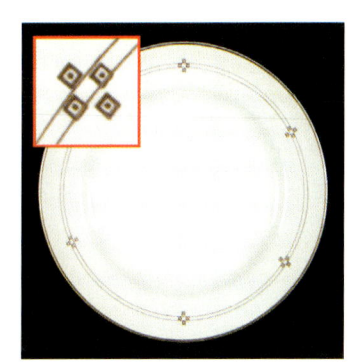

G270
Gold Trim

Genesee Shape

HLC292 *Blue Trim*	**HLC438** *Blue Trim*	**HLC205** *Salad Plate Shown Blue Trim*	**W813** *Gold Trim*
K1013 *Gold Trim*	**HLC1109** *Oval Platter Shown Gold Trim*	**HLC1270** *Red Trim*	**HLC1269** *Purple Trim*
HLC1175 *Luncheon Plate Shown Gold Trim*	**Butler Brothers** *BB7 Gold Trim*	**HLC1046** *Gold Band No Trim*	

REPUBLIC

Piece Types

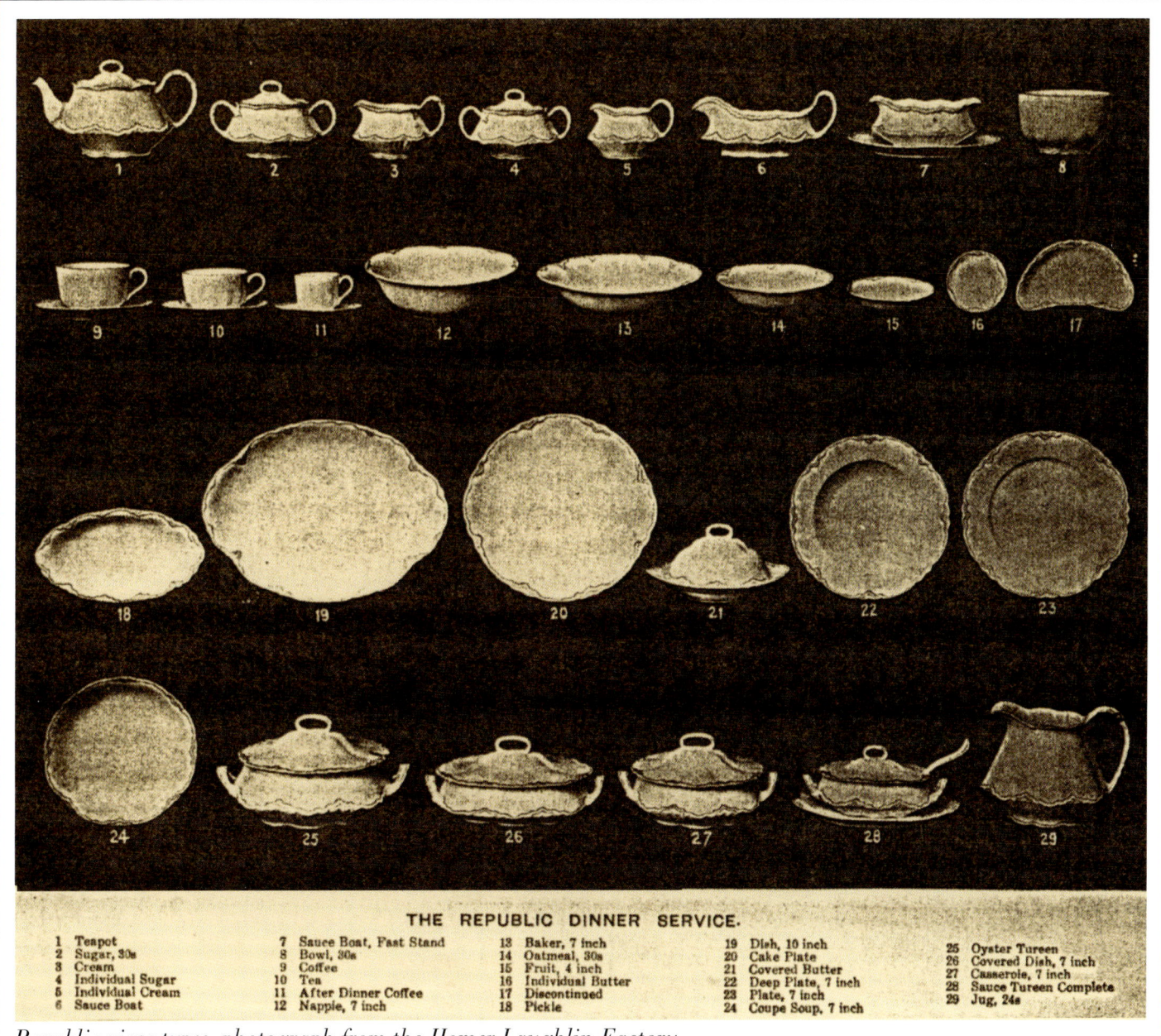

THE REPUBLIC DINNER SERVICE.

1	Teapot	7	Sauce Boat, Fast Stand	13	Baker, 7 inch	19	Dish, 10 inch	25	Oyster Tureen
2	Sugar, 30s	8	Bowl, 30s	14	Oatmeal, 30s	20	Cake Plate	26	Covered Dish, 7 inch
3	Cream	9	Coffee	15	Fruit, 4 inch	21	Covered Butter	27	Casserole, 7 inch
4	Individual Sugar	10	Tea	16	Individual Butter	22	Deep Plate, 7 inch	28	Sauce Tureen Complete
5	Individual Cream	11	After Dinner Coffee	17	Discontinued	23	Plate, 7 inch	29	Jug, 24s
6	Sauce Boat	12	Nappie, 7 inch	18	Pickle	24	Coupe Soup, 7 inch		

Republic piece types, photograph from the Homer Laughlin Factory.

Homer Laughlin

REPUBLIC 1917 – 1959

The Republic shape was featured in the company catalogs for 1920, 1922, 1926, and 1929. In the *Homer Laughlin Pound Sterling Price Booklet of 1937* the shape was offered with 20 different decorations/patterns. Pottery wizard Harvey Duke has described Republic as Homer Laughlin's version of Haviland China's Ranson shape and indeed it is very similar in form. The Republic shape emulates a number of successful European china lines. A memorable feature of Republic is its looped ribbon style handles, again reminiscent of Haviland. The shape has a very old style, classic Victorian look, and is found in white and ivory glazes.

Republic shapes were decorated with gold border treatments in the earliest years and floral and other decals in later years. Pieces bear the common Homer Laughlin backstamps of the period. At Replacements, Ltd., pieces of Republic have been seen with backstamp dates as early as 1917, and as late as 1959.

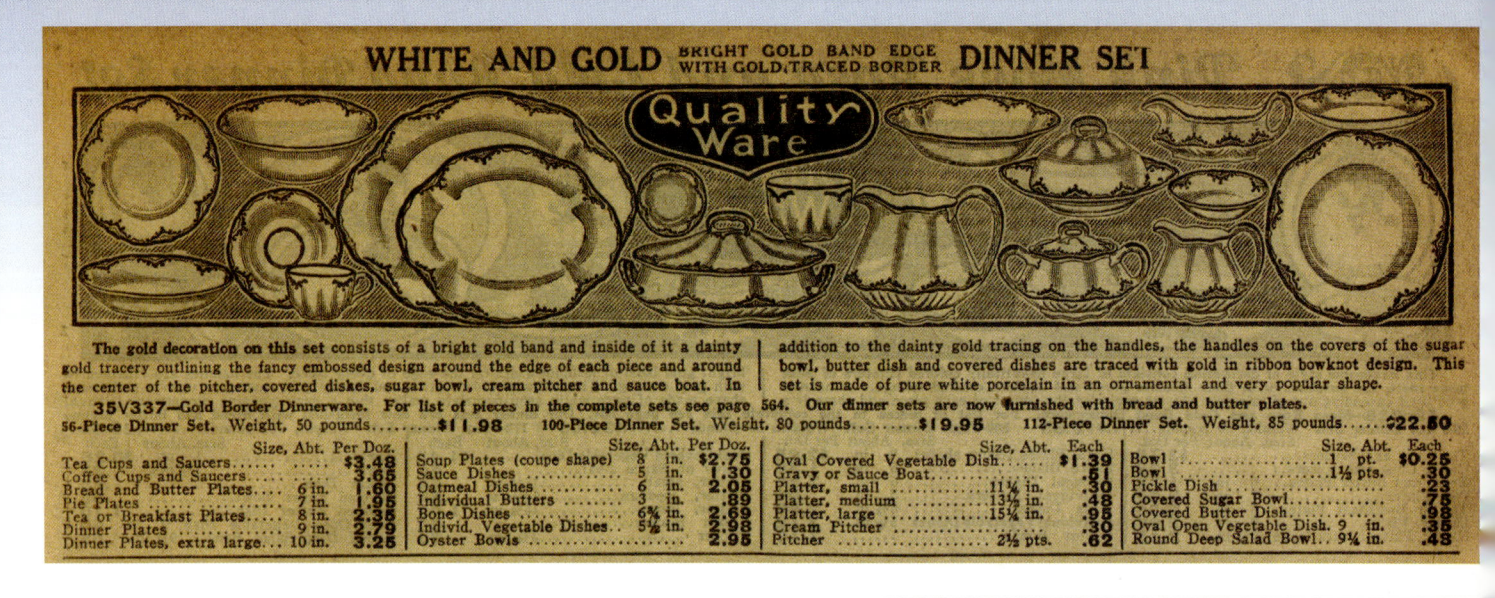

Top right: *Republic pattern; Teapot with lid.* **Middle:** *White and Gold pattern; Sears, Roebuck & Co. Catalog, 1925.* **Bottom Left:** *Century pattern; Butler Brothers Catalog, 1925.* **Bottom right:** *Jean pattern; Creamer with gold spray on handle, and Creamer with stripe on handle.*

Republic Shape

Top left: *HLC110 pattern; Dinner Plate, Salad Plate, Bread & Butter Plate, Cup & Saucer Set, Fruit Bowl, Creamer, and Sugar Bowl with lid.* **Top right:** *HLC110 pattern; Two Oval Platters, Soup Bowl with rim, Round Covered Vegetable Bowl, and Gravy/Sauce Boat Underplate/Relish.* **Middle left:** *Jean pattern; Dinner Plate, Luncheon Plate, Salad Plate, Bread & Butter Plate, Creamer, Sugar Bowl with lid, Cup & Saucer Set, and Soup Coupe Bowl.* **Middle right:** *Jean pattern; Oval Vegetable Bowl, Cereal Bowl, Soup Coupe Bowl, and Fruit Bowl.* **Bottom left:** *Jean pattern; Handled Oval Platter, Oval Platter, Handled Oval Platter, and Gravy/Sauce Boat.*

Homer Laughlin

Republic Piece Type List

From Homer Laughlin Literature with Confirmed Actual Pieces

- Bone Dish
- Bowl, Cranberry
- Bowl, Fruit
- Bowl, Cereal
- Bowl, Soup Coupe
- Bowl, Soup with rim
- Bowl, Vegetable Oval
- Bowl, Vegetable Oval Covered
- Bowl, Vegetable Round
- Bowl, Vegetable Round Covered
- Butter Dish, Round with lid
- Butter Pat
- Creamer
- Creamer, Individual

- Cup & Saucer Set
- Cup & Saucer Set, Coffee
- Cup & Saucer Set, Demitasse
- Gravy/Sauce Boat
- Gravy/Sauce Boat with attached Underplate
- Gravy/Sauce Boat Underplate/Relish
- Pitcher/Jug
- Plate, Bread & Butter
- Plate, Cake
- Plate, Dessert
- Plate, Dinner
- Plate, Luncheon
- Plate, Salad

- Platter, Oval, 11¾ inches
- Platter, Oval, 13⅝ inches
- Platter, Oval, 15⅜ inches
- Platter, Oval Handled, 11 inches
- Platter, Oval Handled, 13⅛ inches
- Platter, Oval Handled, 15 inches
- Sugar Bowl with lid
- Sugar Bowl with lid, Individual
- Teapot with lid
- Tureen, Oyster
- Tureen, Sauce with lid, Ladle, and Underplate

Above right: *Jean pattern; Round Covered Vegetable Bowl.* **Top left:** *Earliest Republic backstamp we have seen, 1917.* **Bottom left:** *Unknown magazine advertisement from 1900.* **Bottom right:** *Latest Republic backstamp we have seen, 1959.*

Republic Shape

Republic — *No Trim*

W617 — *Gold Trim*

R5106 — *Gold Accents / Gold Trim*

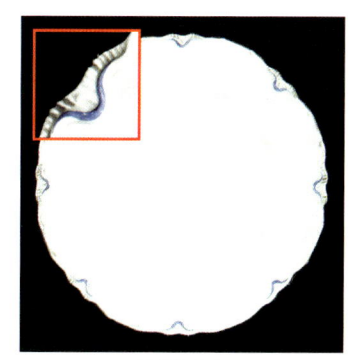

R5206 — *Blue Accents / Gold Trim*

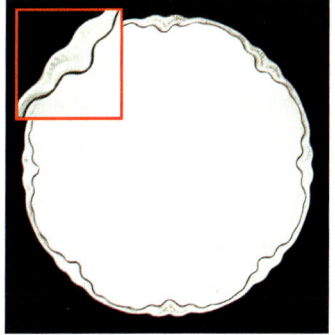

R4806 — *Gold Band / No Trim*

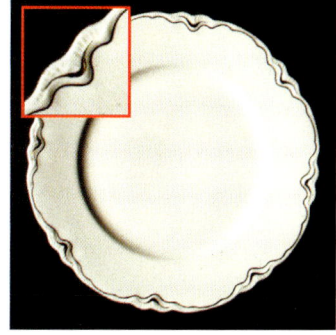

R5006 — *Gold Accents & Band / No Trim*

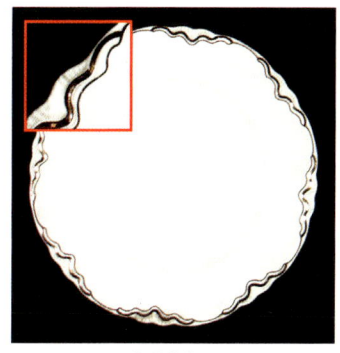

R5306 — *Gold Accents & Band / No Trim*

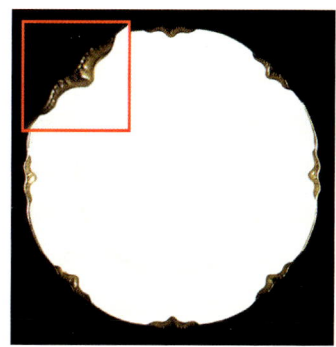

HLC3118 — *Gold Trim*

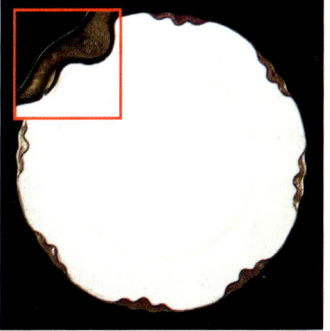

R3202 — *Gold Accent / Black Trim*

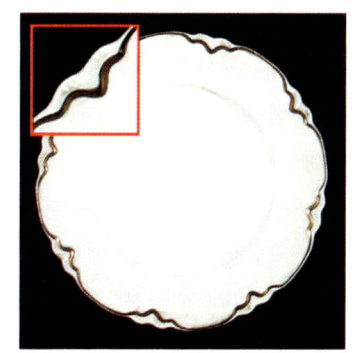

HLC2178 — *Gold Band / No Trim*

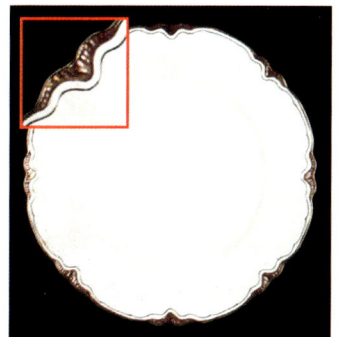

HLC1112 — *Black Band / Gold Trim*

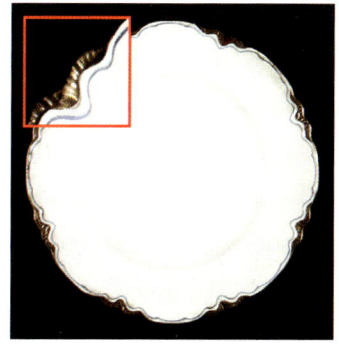

R3302 — *Blue Band / Gold Trim*

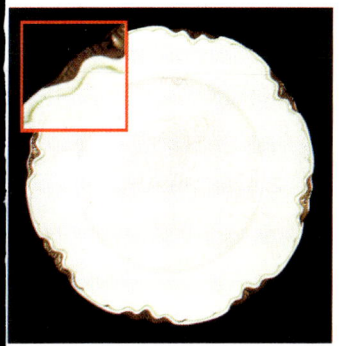

R3102 — *Green Band / Gold Trim*

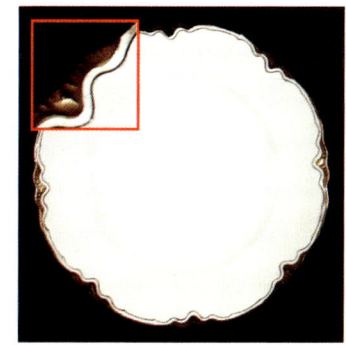

R3402 — *Black Band / Gold Trim*

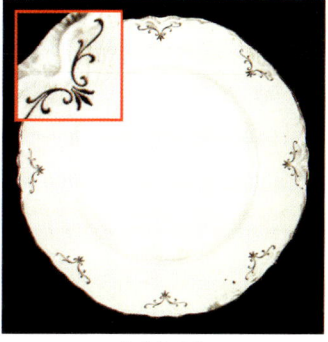

R5101 — *Gold Trim*

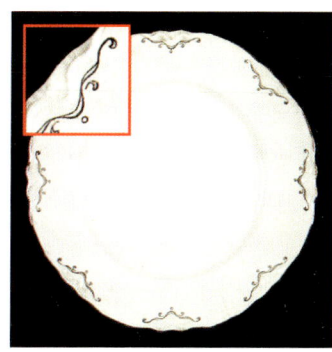

R5001 — *Gold Trim*

Republic Shape

R4901 *Gold Trim*	**HLC1665** *No Trim*	**HLC1670** *No Trim*	**HLC850** *Gold Trim*
R3300 *No Trim*	**R2700** *No Trim*	**E783** *No Trim*	**5801** *Gold Trim*
R6401 *Gold Trim*	**HLC1193** *Bread & Butter Plate Shown No Trim*	**HLC991** *Bread & Butter Plate Shown Gold Trim*	**4862** *Gold Trim*
Golden Rose *Gold Trim*	**6001** *Gold Trim*	**HLC343** *Salad Plate Shown Gold Trim*	**HLC2044** *Bread & Butter Plate Shown Gold Trim*

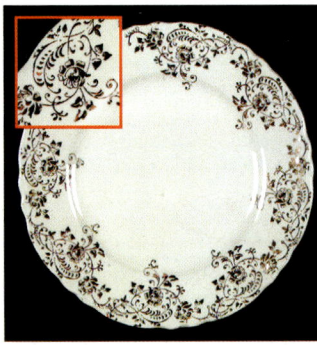

Republic Shape

HLC3110 *Gold Trim*	**HLC785** *Salad Plate Shown No Trim*	**HLC874** *Gold Trim*	**HLC142** *Gold Trim*
HLC172 *Bread & Butter Plate Shown Gold Trim*	**HLC470** *Gold Trim*	**HLC468** *Gold Trim*	**R3624** *Gold Trim*
HLC128 *No Trim*	**CC8** *Gold Trim*	**CC5** *Gold Trim*	**HLS53** *No Trim*
HLS52 *Platinum Trim*	**HLC1893** *Gold Trim*	**HLC1891** *Gold Trim*	**HLC1892** *No Trim*

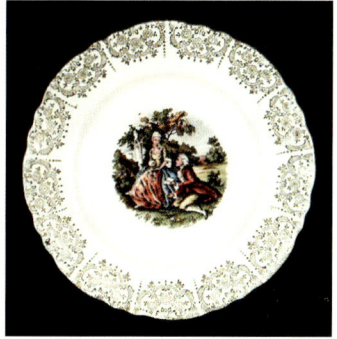

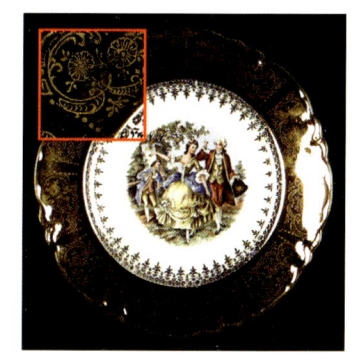

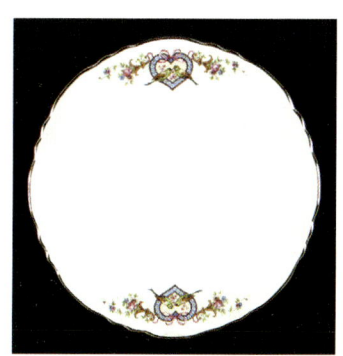

Republic Shape

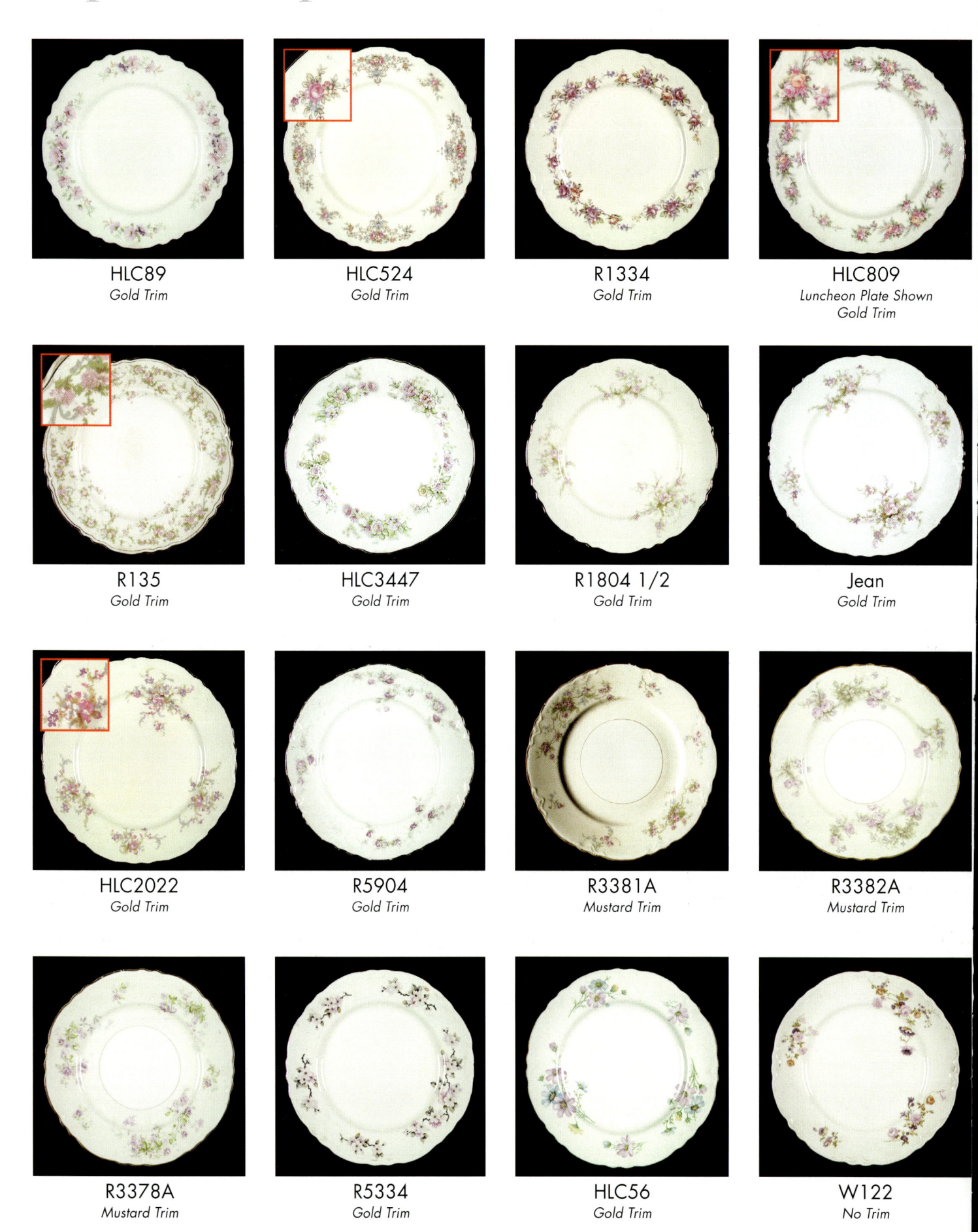

HLC89 *Gold Trim*	**HLC524** *Gold Trim*	**R1334** *Gold Trim*	**HLC809** *Luncheon Plate Shown* *Gold Trim*
R135 *Gold Trim*	**HLC3447** *Gold Trim*	**R1804 1/2** *Gold Trim*	**Jean** *Gold Trim*
HLC2022 *Gold Trim*	**R5904** *Gold Trim*	**R3381A** *Mustard Trim*	**R3382A** *Mustard Trim*
R3378A *Mustard Trim*	**R5334** *Gold Trim*	**HLC56** *Gold Trim*	**W122** *No Trim*

Republic Shape

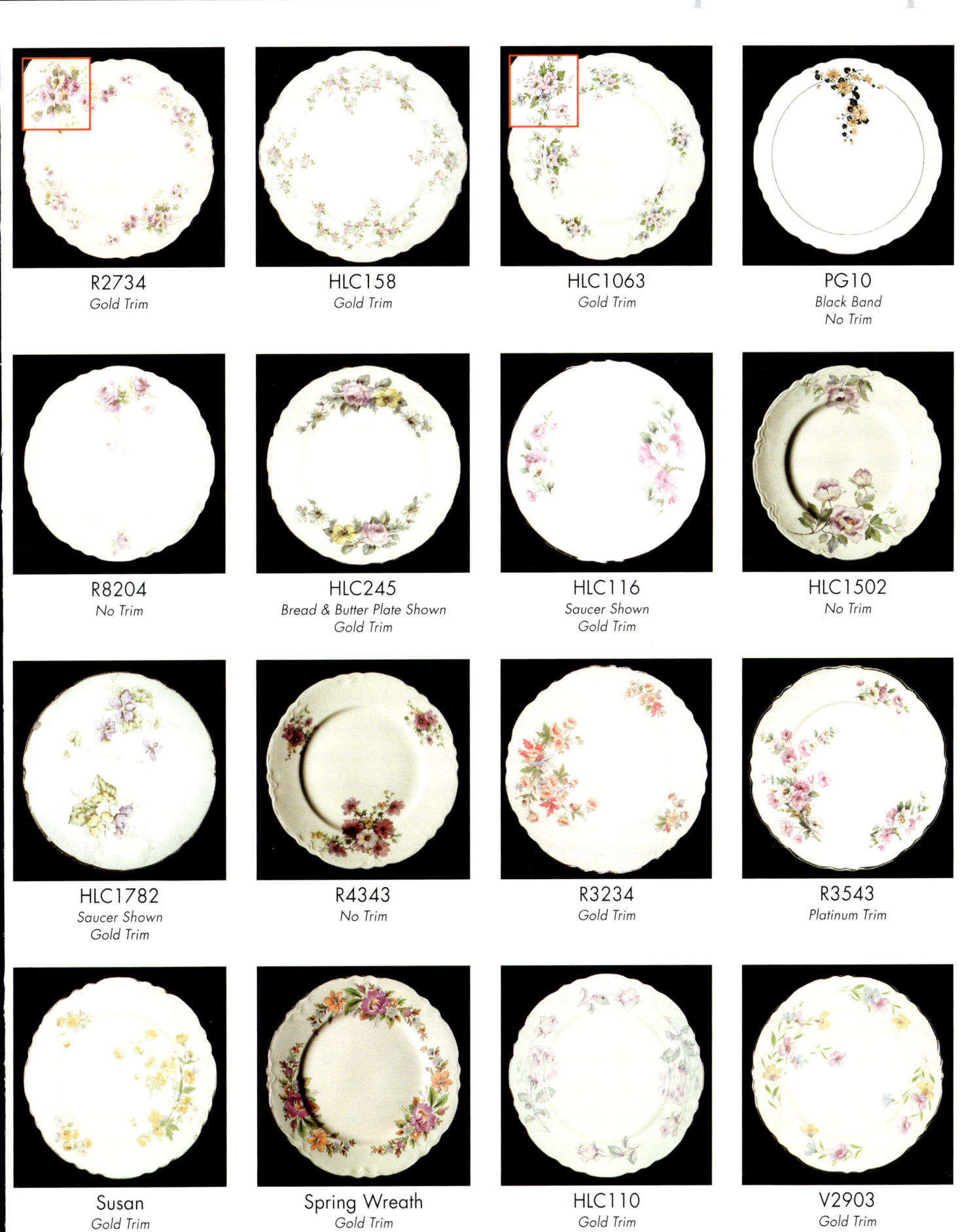

R2734 Gold Trim	**HLC158** Gold Trim	**HLC1063** Gold Trim	**PG10** Black Band No Trim
R8204 No Trim	**HLC245** Bread & Butter Plate Shown Gold Trim	**HLC116** Saucer Shown Gold Trim	**HLC1502** No Trim
HLC1782 Saucer Shown Gold Trim	**R4343** No Trim	**R3234** Gold Trim	**R3543** Platinum Trim
Susan Gold Trim	**Spring Wreath** Gold Trim	**HLC110** Gold Trim	**V2903** Gold Trim

Republic Shape

Avon
by Cunningham & Pickett
Gold Trim

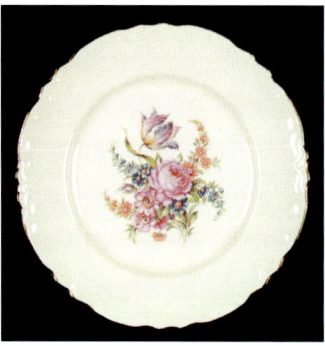

Wayside
by Cunningham & Pickett
Luncheon Plate Shown
Gold Trim

HLC856
Gold Trim

Colonial Kitchen
Gold Trim

HLC3105
No Trim

Maple Leaf
R9524
Gold Trim

HLC435
Gold Trim

Priscilla
by Household Institute
Gold Trim

HLC2025
Gold Trim

HLC310
Gold Trim

R1294
Gold Trim

W1726
No Trim

K93
Blue Trim

Kwaker

Piece Types

THE HOMER LAUGHLIN CHINA COMPANY, NEWELL, W. VA.

THE KWAKER DINNER SERVICE.

1 Sugar	6 Tea	11 Covered Butter	16 Dish, 12 inch	21 Handled Salad
2 Cream	7 Coffee	12 Fast Stand Sauce Boat	17 Cake Plate	22 Casserole, 7 inch
3 Teapot	8 Bowl, 36s	13 Sauce Boat	18 Plate, 7 inch	23 Covered Salad
4 After Dinner Coffee	9 Fruit, 4 inch	14 Coupe Soup, 7 inch	19 Pickle	24 Covered Dish, 7 inch
5 Bouillon Cup and Saucer	10 Oatmeal, 36s	15 Nappie, 7 inch	20 Baker, 7 inch	25 Jug, 24s

Kwaker piece types, photograph from the Homer Laughlin Factory.

Homer Laughlin

KWAKER
1920 – circa 1948 or later

The Kwaker shape was successful for Homer Laughlin. It is listed in the company catalogs of 1920, 1922, 1926, and 1929. Ads for the shape appear in the *Pottery, Glass & Brass Salesman* of December 10, 1925 (decoration K 5315 M) and August 6, 1925 (decoration K 5615 M). The most distinguishable feature of Kwaker is the Sheraton styled handles that protrude above the tops of most hollowware pieces.

The Butler Brothers wholesale catalog of 1930 features the Kwaker shape, Presidential pattern. In the *Homer Laughlin Pound Sterling Price Booklet of 1937*, the Kwaker shape was offered with 103 different decorations/patterns. It was one of the most used Homer Laughlin shapes at that time.

Kwaker shaped lines are found in Sears catalogs from at least the 1925 catalog through the 1948 catalog, an impressive twenty-three years.

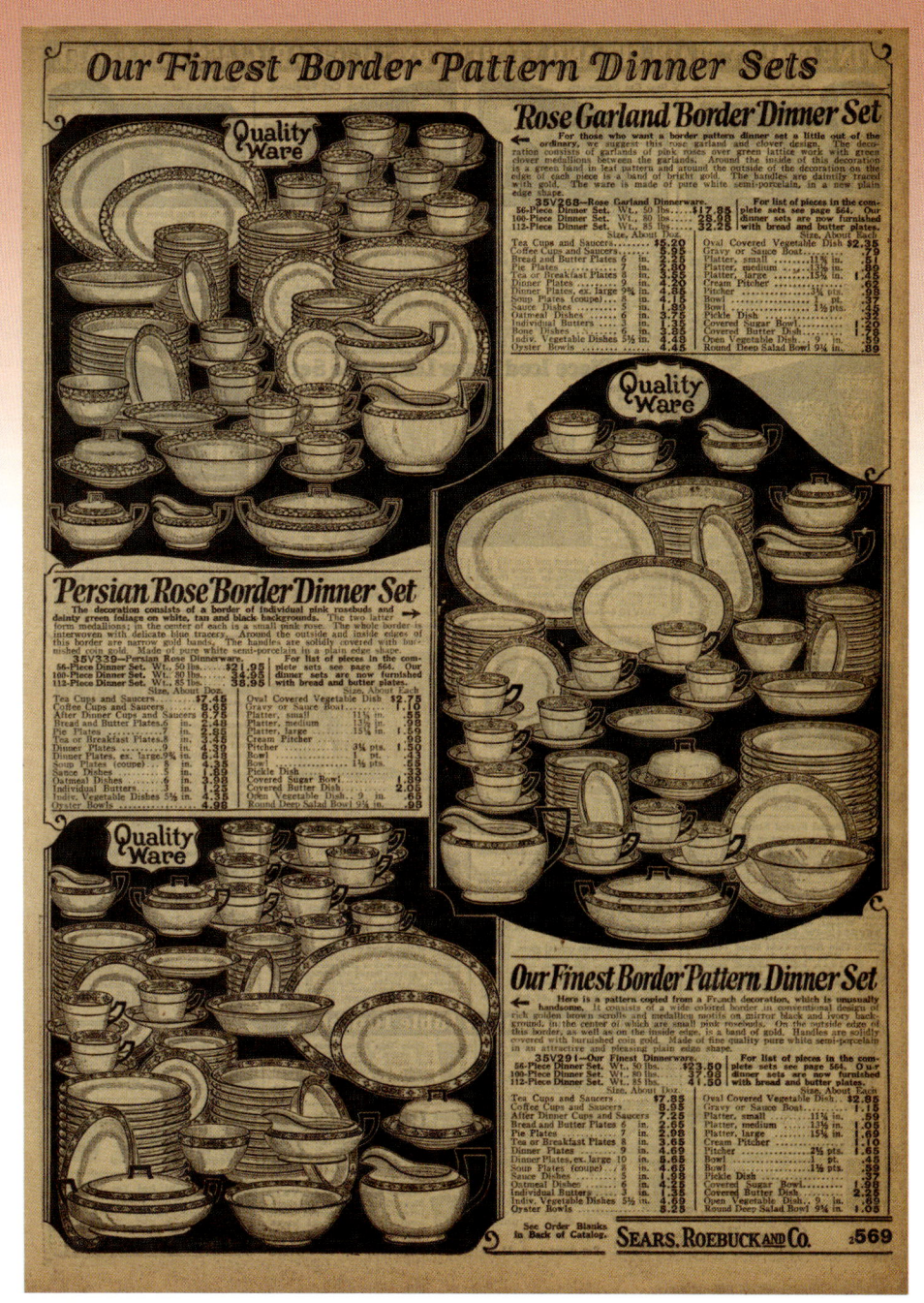

Top left: *Rose Garland, Persian Rose, and "our finest border decoration" patterns; Sears, Roebuck & Co. Catalog, 1925.*
Top right: *Darcy pattern; Sears, Roebuck & Co. Catalog, 1941.*

Kwaker Shape

Gold Bowknot and Gold Band Dinner Set

There is nothing that appeals in a gold decorated dinner set as quickly and strongly as a decoration which combines beauty with daintiness. That is just what this set does. The decoration consists of bright gold bowknots connected together with a thin line of blue, with a bright gold band around outside edge of each piece and around center of the hollow pieces. Handles are traced with gold. This gold and blue treatment upon a new popular plain edge is a pleasing combination. Made of pure white semi-porcelain. Our Dinner Sets are now furnished with bread and butter plates.

35V245—Gold Bowknot and Band Dinnerware. For list of pieces in the complete sets see page 564.

56-Piece Dinner Set. Weight, 50 pounds.....$14.50
100-Piece Dinner Set. Weight, 80 pounds.....$23.75
112-Piece Dinner Set. Weight, 85 pounds.....$26.35

	Size, Abt.	Per Doz.
Tea Cups and Saucers		$4.25
Coffee Cups and Saucers		4.45
Bread and Butter Plates	6 in.	1.98
Pie Plates	7 in.	2.25
Tea or Breakfast Plates	8 in.	2.85
Dinner Plates	9 in.	3.65
Dinner Plates, extra large	9¾ in.	3.98
Soup Plates (coupe shape)	8 in.	3.42
Sauce Dishes	5 in.	1.60
Oatmeal Dishes	6 in.	2.59
Individual Butters	3 in.	1.08
Bone Dishes	6½ in.	3.15
Individual Vegetable Dishes	5½ in.	3.50
Oyster Bowls		3.65

	Size, Abt.	Each
Oval Covered Vegetable Dish		$1.65
Gravy or Sauce Boat		.62
Platter, small	11½ in.	.35
Platter, medium	13½ in.	.59
Platter, large	15¼ in.	1.18
Cream Pitcher		.48
Pitcher	3¼ pts.	.79
Bowl	1 pt.	$0.30
Bowl	1½ pts.	.35
Pickle Dish		.29
Covered Sugar Bowl		$0.95
Covered Butter Dish		1.18
Oval Open Vegetable Dish	9 in.	.45
Round Deep Salad Bowl	9¼ in.	.59

Sears, Roebuck and Co. 2567

"Gold Bowknot"—"Homer Laughlin" trademarked, fine quality thin pure white semi-porcelain, rich bright glaze, gold "Bowknot" border decoration with connecting blue verge line, bright gold decorated edges, gold traced handles and knobs.

E971—50 piece set. Shipping weight about 50 lbs. SET (50 pcs) **$9.50**
E972—100 piece set. Shipping weight about 90 lbs. SET (100 pcs) **$18.50**

"Vandemere"—"Homer Laughlin" trademarked, "Kwaker" shape, fine quality thin pure white light weight semi-porcelain, ⅜ in. border decoration with tan and pale green over ivory background, interspersed with delicate pink rosebuds, in medallion border effect, gold band edges and inner gold border, solid burnished coin gold handles and knobs, upright pieces with gold band base.

E990—50 piece set. Shipping weight about 50 lbs. SET (50 pcs) **$14.25**
E991—100 Piece Set. Shipping weight about 90 lbs. SET (100 pcs) **$28.50**

NOW! SEARS New BUDGET PLAN
Only $5.00 Down
Puts This SELECT DINNERWARE in Your Home on EASY MONTHLY PAYMENTS

NOW comes the Sears Budget Plan on dinnerware sets, by far the most liberal, economical, convenient we have ever offered! Low down payments and small monthly payments! The easiest, simplest way you can imagine to put these high quality dinner sets on your table, enabling you to enjoy them while paying for them. Fine quality dinnerware on easy monthly payments in less than cash prices elsewhere—that is in a nutshell—is the Sears Budget Plan on dinnerware. Note the beauty of these fine American and imported patterns—the fact that Sears immense buying power can command. Then think! Only $5.00 puts them on your table.

AMERICAN SUNRISE PORCELAIN 100-Pc. Set $30.75 $4.00 Monthly Payments

$5.00 Down $4.00 Per Month
The "Garland" Pattern
Our finest American china (semi-porcelain). A delightful 100-piece service in ivory body with a pleasing and dainty decoration. Border is of blue and ivory paneled with artistic design of pink roses and blue forget-me-nots, with green leaves. The shoulder of each piece has gold hairline and all handles are covered with rich matte gold. Shipping wt. 95 lbs. Shipped Prepaid.

35T364—100-Piece set **$27.95**
35T364—55-Piece set **$30.75**
Use Time Payment Order Blank in Back of Catalog.

Neville

Top left: *Gold Bowknot and Gold Band patterns; Sears, Roebuck & Co. Catalog, 1925.* **Middle left:** *Gold Bowknot pattern; Butler Brothers Catalog, 1925.* **Middle right:** *Vandemere pattern; Butler Brothers Catalog, 1925.* **Bottom left:** *Garland pattern; Sears, Roebuck & Co. Catalog, 1929.* **Bottom right:** *Neville pattern; Sears, Roebuck & Co. Catalog, 1943.*

Homer Laughlin

Kwaker Piece Type List

From Homer Laughlin Literature with Confirmed Actual Pieces

- Bowl, Cereal
- Bowl, Cranberry
- Bowl, Cream Soup & Saucer Set
- Bowl, Fruit
- Bowl, Salad Covered
- Bowl, Salad Handled
- Bowl, Soup Coupe
- Bowl, Vegetable Oval
- Bowl, Vegetable Oval Covered
- Bowl, Vegetable Round
- Bowl, Vegetable Round Covered
- Butter Dish Round with lid

- Creamer
- Cup & Saucer Set, Bouillion*
- Cup & Saucer Set, Coffee
- Cup & Saucer Set, Demitasse
- Cup & Saucer Set, Tea
- Gravy/Sauce Boat
- Gravy/Sauce Boat with attached Underplate
- Gravy/Sauce Boat Underplate/Relish
- Plate, Bread & Butter
- Plate, Cake
- Plate, Dessert

- Plate, Dinner
- Plate, Luncheon
- Plate, Salad
- Platter, Oval, 11 3/8 inches
- Platter, Oval, 13 1/4 inches
- Platter, Oval, 15 5/8 inches
- Pitcher/Jug (Ivora Shape)
- Pitcher/Jug (round body)
- Pitcher/Jug (square body)
- Sugar Bowl with lid
- Teapot with lid

*Reported but not confirmed.

Top left: Neville pattern; Dinner Plate, Cup & Saucer Set, Salad Plate, Bread & Butter Plate, and Fruit Bowl. **Top middle:** Neville pattern; Two Oval Platters, Round Vegetable Bowl, Oval Vegetable Bowl, and Soup Coupe Bowl. **Top right:** Rose & Lattice pattern; Dinner Plate, Oval Platter, Gravy/Sauce Boat, Oval Vegetable Bowl, Fruit Bowl, Creamer, and Bread & Butter Plate. **Middle left:** HLC54 pattern; Sugar Bowl with lid, and Creamer. **Middle:** HLC54 pattern; Ivora Shape Pitcher. **Middle right:** HLC54 pattern; Square Body Pitcher. **Left:** K61 pattern; Oval Covered Vegetable Bowl.

Kwaker Shape

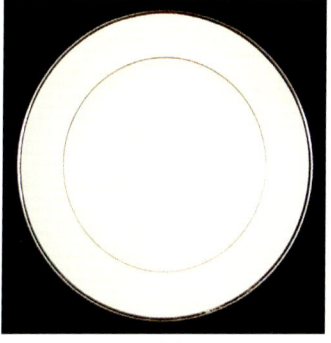

K6906
Bread & Butter Plate Shown
Gold Trim

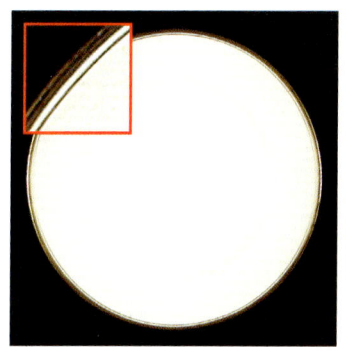

K5602
Gold Trim

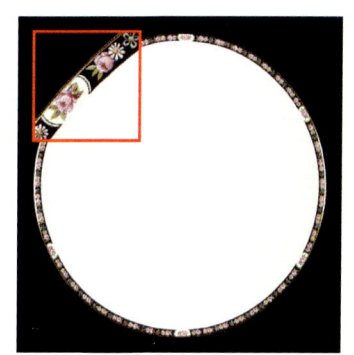

K8415
No Verge
Gold Trim

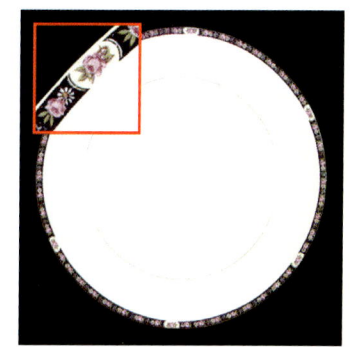

K8477
No Trim

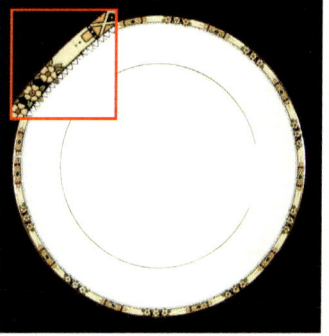

K1027
Gold Trim

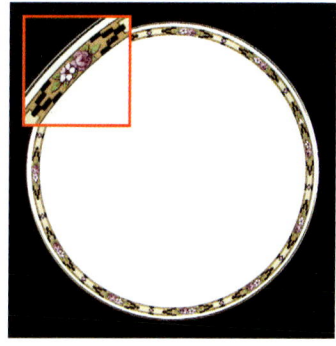

JJ647
No Verge
Gold Trim

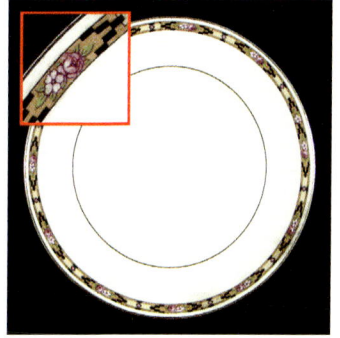

HLC615
Gold Trim

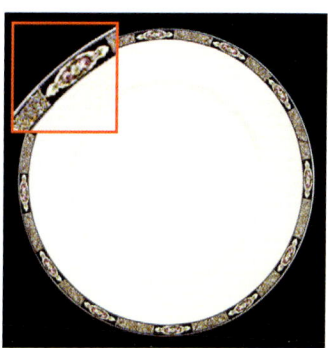

HLC106
No Verge
Blue Trim

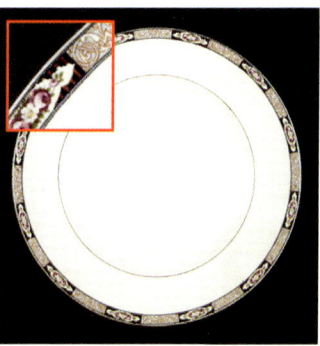

K5677M
Blue Trim

HLC358
Salad Plate Shown
No Verge
Gold Trim

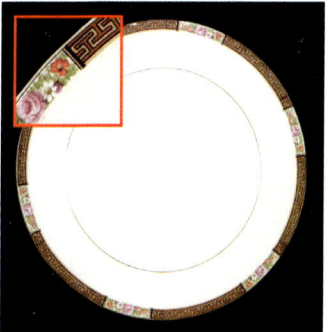

K3177M
No Trim

HLC2171
Gold Trim

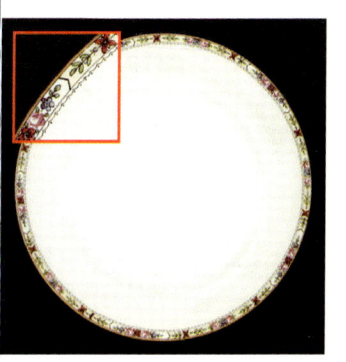

HLC812
No Verge
Gold Trim

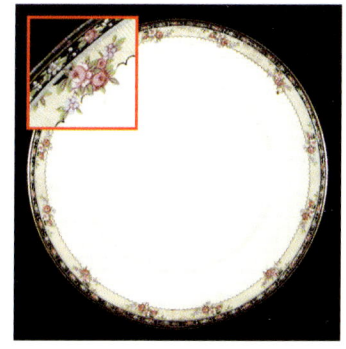

HLC614
No Verge
Gold Trim

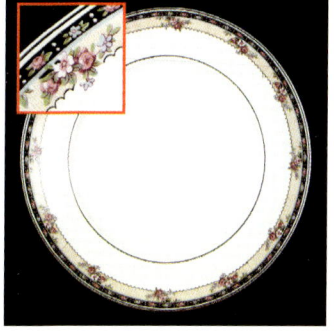

K61
Black Trim

K6177M
No Trim

Kwaker Shape

K4315M *Gold Band & Trim*	**K8317** *Blue Band Gold Trim*	**Rose & Lattice** *Gold Trim*	**JJ63** *Gold Trim*
K8677 *Mustard Trim*	**K6877** *Blue Trim*	**HLC801** *Oval Platter Shown Gold Trim*	**K7877** *No Trim*
K3577M *Luncheon Plate Shown Gold Trim*	**K9277M** *Gold Trim*	**K9477** *No Trim*	**K9177M** *No Trim*
K1077M *No Trim*	**LK1** *Gold Trim*	**Neville** *K2253 No Trim*	**K4424** *Salad Plate Shown Gold Trim*

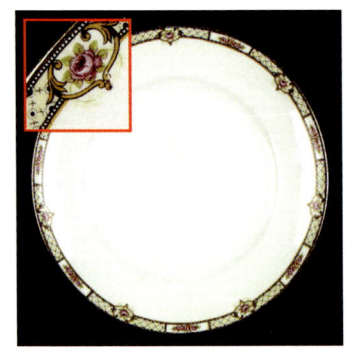

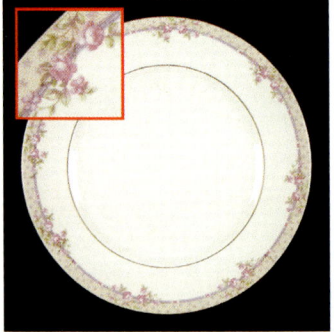

Kwaker Shape

K8077M
No Trim

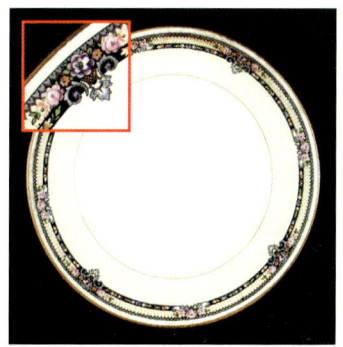

K7817
Mustard Trim

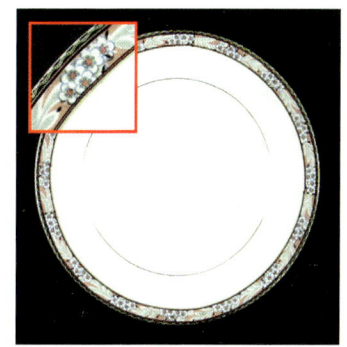

K3477M
No Trim

K8177M
No Trim

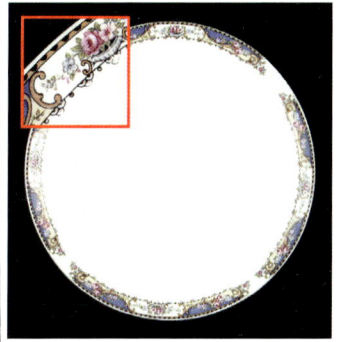

HLC779
*Luncheon Plate Shown
No Verge or Trim*

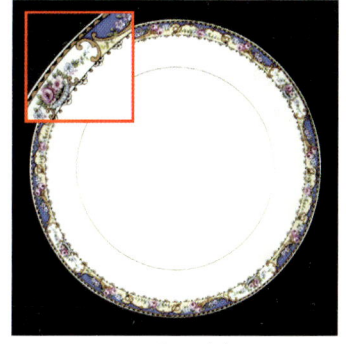

K7077M
No Trim

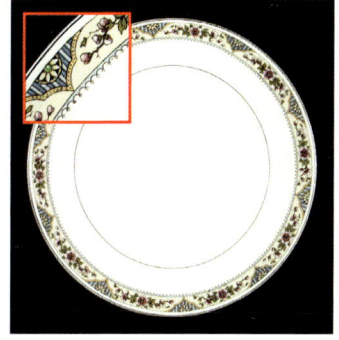

K655
Gold Trim

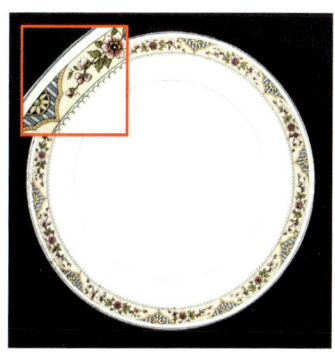

K657
Blue Verge & Trim

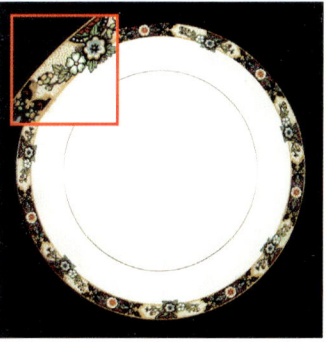

HR20
Black Trim

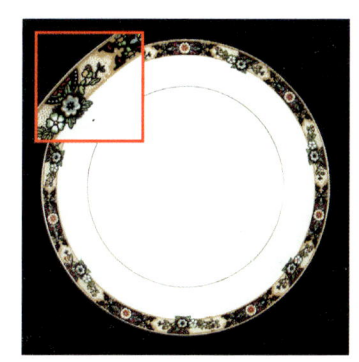

K1877M
Tan Trim

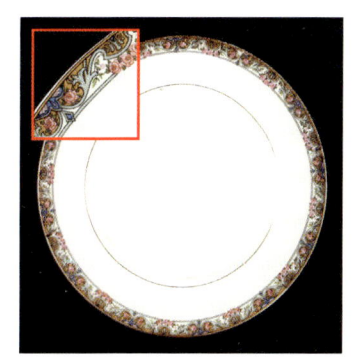

K2277M
Mustard Trim

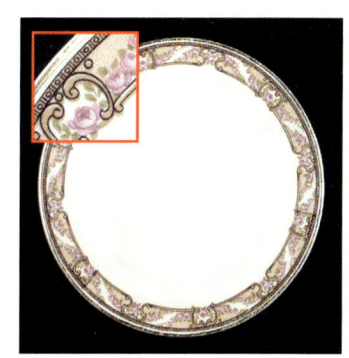

E1315M
*Bread & Butter Plate Shown
No Verge
Gold Trim*

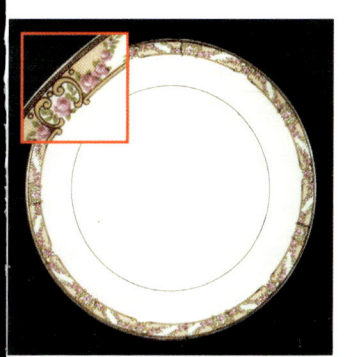

K1377M
Gold Trim

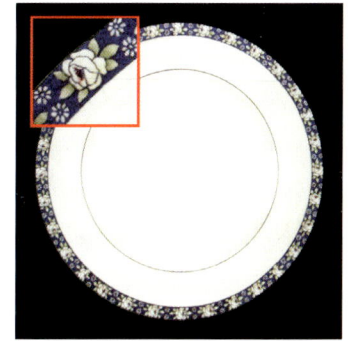

K3377
No Trim

HLC1411
Red Verge & Trim

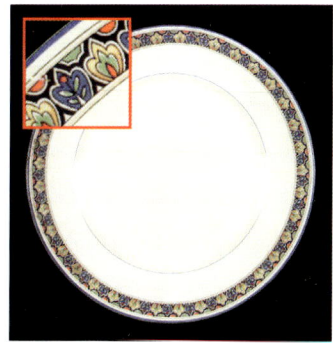

HLC1412
Blue Verge & Trim

Kwaker Shape

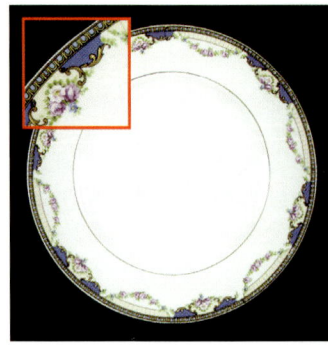

7103-2
Mustard Trim

7103-3
Mustard Trim

K671-7
Saucer Shown
Gold Trim

K8655
Tan Trim

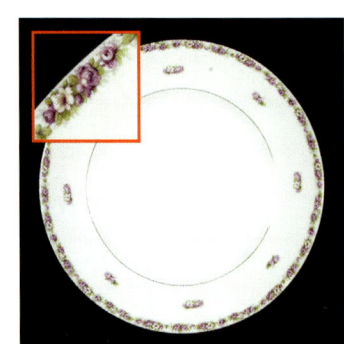

K8917M
No Trim

K6137
No Trim

K1477M
No Trim

K3677M
No Trim

K7517
Mustard Trim

K7254
No Trim

K9104B
Gold Trim

HLC1359
Gold Trim

Darcy
K8124
Gold Trim

K5913
Blue Trim

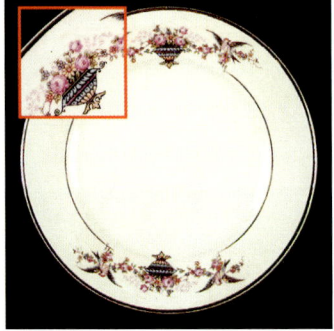

Rosewood
Gold Trim

Rosewood
K9504
Gold Trim

Kwaker Shape

K4613	K5713	K7313	HLC735
Blue Trim	Green Verge Red Trim	Blue Verge & Trim	Salad Plate Shown No Verge Blue Trim

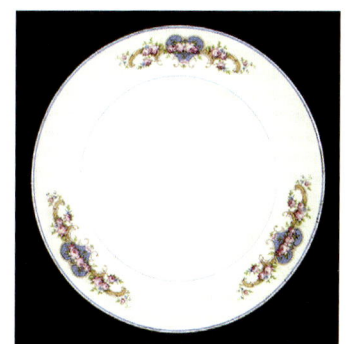

HLC890	K4513	K8623	K8723
Covered Vegetable Bowl Shown Gold Trim	Blue Trim	Green Trim	Green Trim

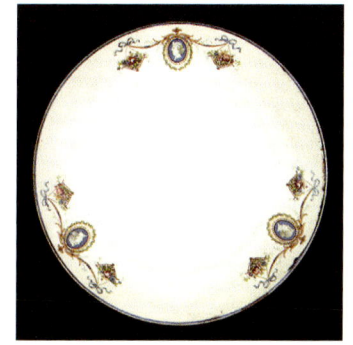

K4124	K14	Nasturtium	HLC1384
No Trim	No Trim	K8904B Gold Trim	Red Trim

K3443	K3623	K2713	K9577M
Gold Trim	Mustard Trim	Blue Trim	No Trim

Kwaker Shape

HLC1137
Oval Platter Shown
No Trim

G190
No Trim

7090
Black Trim

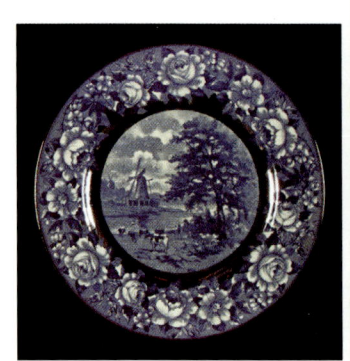

G118
Platinum Trim

K2413
Blue Trim

HLC1284
Bread & Butter Plate Shown
No Trim

Right: *Cardboard advertisement for Homer Laughlin China, free with Octagon soap coupons, 1936.*

YELLOWSTONE

Piece Types

These drawings were made from actual stock or literature at Replacements, Ltd. Check the piece type list for all known piece types in this shape.

Dinner Plate
9¾" D

Luncheon Plate
9" D

Salad Plate
8" D

Dessert Plate
7⅛" D

Bread & Butter Plate
6¼" D

Saucer
6" D

Cup
2⅜" H

Bouillon Saucer
6" D

Bouillon Cup
2¼" H

Oval Vegetable Bowl
11" W
2¼" H

Oval Vegetable Bowl
9" W

Fruit Bowl
5" W

Round Vegetable Bowl
9⅜" W
3" H

Round Vegetable Bowl
8⅜" W

Soup Bowl with Rim
9⅛" W

Soup Coupe Bowl, Large
8¼" W

Soup Coupe Bowl, Small
7¼" W

Cereal Coupe Bowl
5⅝" W

Round Vegetable Bowl
9⅞" W
3" H

Round Covered Vegetable Bowl   9⅝" W x 4⅜" H

Sugar Bowl with lid, Large
4"

Sugar Bowl with lid, Small
3½"

Creamer
2¾"

Covered Butter Dish
7¾" W
3¼" H

Pitcher
5¼"

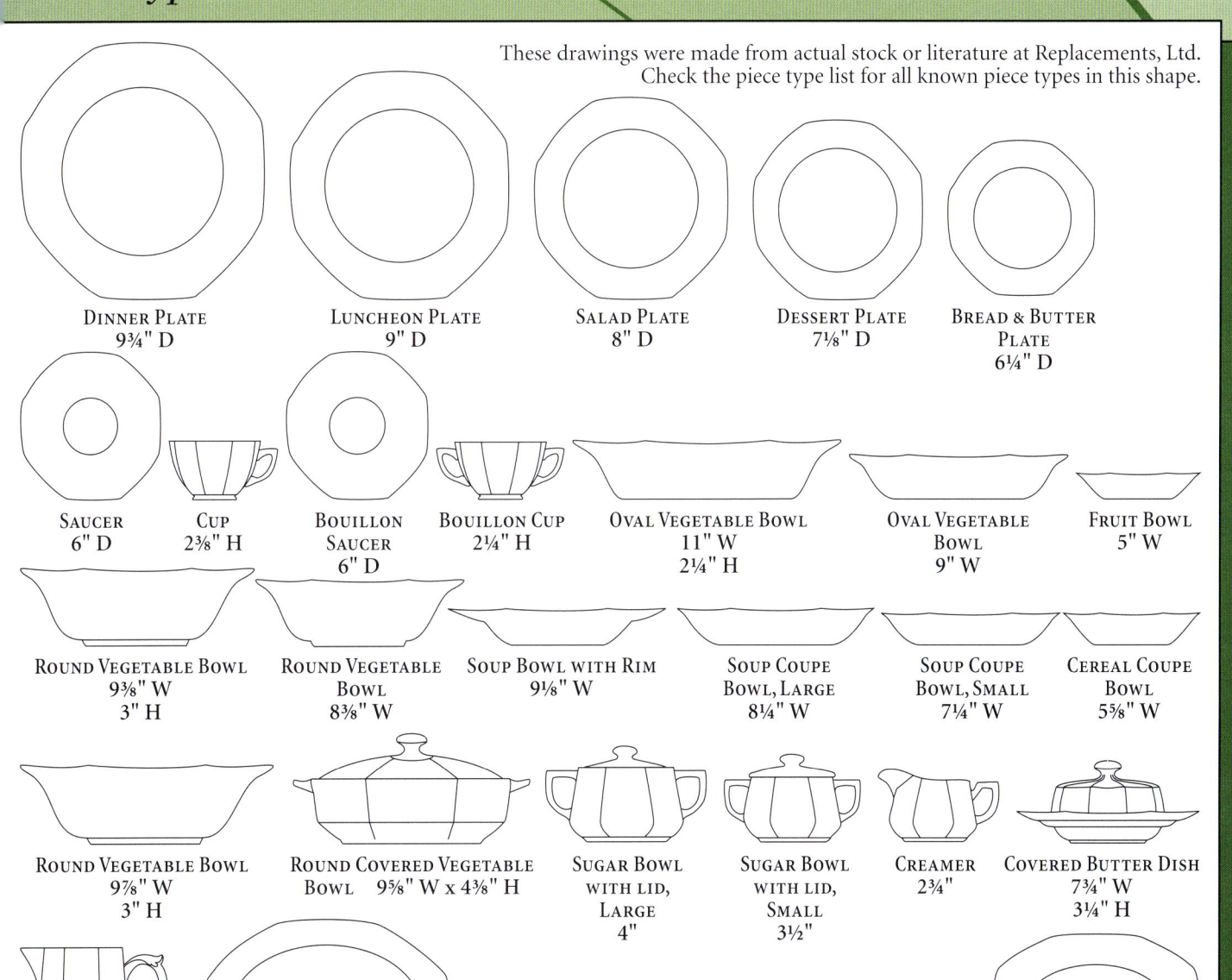

Platter
10" W

Cranberry Bowl
4⅞" H

Sherbet
3⅛" H

Gravy/Sauce Boat
8½" W

Gravy/Sauce Boat Underplate/Relish
8½" W x 5⅝" H

Homer Laughlin

YELLOWSTONE 1926 – 1937 or later

The octagonal Yellowstone shape first appears in the *Homer Laughlin Catalog of 1926*. It was heavily touted in full-page national advertisements by 1927. Homer Laughlin wrote some very upbeat, almost boastful advertisement copy about the success of Yellowstone: "If popularity of a line is to be measured by the volume and promptness of reorders, the Yellowstone decorations have achieved a degree of success that has never been equaled and probably never approached by any other dinnerware line from anywhere at any time" (*China, Glass & Lamps*, January 1927). Two months later, in March 1927, further advertisement copy reads: "The Laughlin establishment operates six plants, with a total capacity equivalent to one hundred kilns. Three of these plants… are devoted almost exclusively to the production of Yellowstone. The distribution of that shape alone for the last half of 1926 approached ten thousand dozens per day, all decorated. The daily production of Yellowstone, if placed in line, would stretch from the Battery in New York to the Harlem River and three miles beyond, and you may have some idea of the daily sales of Yellowstone. There must be a reason."

In 1928, there were only six shapes being offered by Homer Laughlin and Yellowstone was one of them (*The Pottery, Glass & Brass Salesman*, February 2, 1928). Sears offered "Autumn Ivory," a Yellowstone shaped pattern as early as 1929. In *The Homer Laughlin Pound Sterling Price Booklet of 1937*, 81 Yellowstone patterns were offered.

Above: *W127, W426, and W428 patterns; Ladies Home Journal, October 1929.*

Piece Types

15" PLATTER
15⅛" W x 10⅞" H

13" PLATTER
13⅝" W x 9½" H

11" PLATTER
11¼" W x 8⅛" H

Yellowstone Shape

No. 8—Pattern Y-1 Single Column Newspaper Cut	No. 11—Pattern Y-17 Single Column Newspaper Cut	No. 14—Pattern Y-39 Single Column Newspaper Cut	No. 17—Pattern N-75 Single Column Newspaper Cut
No. 9—Pattern Y-12 Single Column Newspaper Cut	No. 12—Pattern Y-18 Single Column Newspaper Cut	No. 15—Pattern Y-60 Single Column Newspaper Cut	No. 18—Pattern N-80 Single Column Newspaper Cut
No. 10—Pattern Y-16 Single Column Newspaper Cut	No. 13—Pattern Y-36 Single Column Newspaper Cut	No. 16—Pattern Y-79 Single Column Newspaper Cut	No. 19—Burley Spittoon

CHINA, GLASS & LAMPS — January 10, 1927

THE YELLOWSTONE DINNER SERVICE

Ivory Body Exclusively.   *Octagon Model*

The Yellowstone is striking in simplicity. There is no relief work, embossing, or irregular surface to compete with, or to detract from, the decorative effects. The soft ivory shade, reproducing the exquisite color tone of Belleek, and the plain octagon outlines, provide the ideal frame and background for the fine variety of original decorations especially designed for this model.

If the popularity of a line is to be measured by the volume and promptness of reorders, the Yellowstone decorations have achieved a degree of success that has never been equalled and probably never approached by any other dinner line from anywhere at any time.

The prices are an agreeable surprise.

THE PRESENT LINE-UP IS—
- YELLOWSTONE SHAPE IN IVORY BODY ONLY
- REPUBLIC AND KWAKER SHAPES IN BOTH IVORY AND WHITE BODIES
- EMPRESS AND HUDSON SHAPES IN WHITE BODY ONLY
- COMPLETE LINE OF CABLE STAPLES IN WHITE BODY ONLY
- COMPLETE LINE OF HOTEL WARE, DOUBLE THICK, WHITE BODY
- COMPLETE LINE OF HOTEL WARE, HALF THICK, WHITE BODY
- A GOOD ASSORTMENT OF TOILET SHAPES

The Kwaker has previously been our leading shape in border, medallion, and gold and white treatments. All of these patterns may now be had on the Kwaker in either the white or ivory body.

Production—The equivalent of forty kilns on Ivory. The equivalent of sixty kilns on white.

The Homer Laughlin China Co.
Newell, W. Va., and East Liverpool, Ohio

Autumn Ivory Pattern

$4.68 32-Pc. Set Postpaid

Autumn's gay coloring has been captured for this delightful service. It's fashioned in the modish octagon pattern with conventional floral design of yellow flowers with burnt orange centers and slate color stems and leaves touched with black. Strictly first selection semi-porcelain.

35T338¼—Complete Sets. For lists of pieces in sets see page 731.

32-Piece Set. We Pay Postage.....**$4.68**
59-Piece Set. Weight, 52 lbs.
Shipped Prepaid..................**$13.25**
96-Piece Set. Weight, 75 lbs.
Shipped Prepaid..................**$18.79**

35T338	Size, About	Set of six, Postpaid
Tea Cups and Saucers		$1.68
Coffee Cups and Saucers		1.85
Bread and Butter Plates	6 in.	.85
Pie Plates	7 in.	.98
Tea or Breakfast Plates	8 in.	1.18
Dinner Plates	9 in.	1.56
Dinner Plates, extra large	9¾ in.	1.69
Soup Plates (coupe shape)	8 in.	1.53
Sauce Dishes	5 in.	.62
Oatmeal Dishes	6 in.	1.08
Oyster Bowls		1.42

35T338	Size, Abt.	Each, Postpaid
Covered Vegetable Dish		$1.42
Gravy or Sauce Boat		.53
Platter, small	11¼ in.	.52
Platter, medium	13½ in.	.75
Platter, large	15¼ in.	1.18
Cream Pitcher		.43
Pitcher	3½ pts	.80
Bowl	1 pt.	.37
Covered Sugar Bowl		.72
Pickle Dish		.43
Covered Butter Dish		1.03
Oval Open Veg. Dish	9 in.	.46
Round Deep Salad Bowl	9¼ in.	.78

Top: *Newspaper cuts sent to retailers by the factory for use in advertisements.* **Bottom left:** *Advertisement; China, Glass & Lamps, January 10, 1927.* **Bottom right:** *Autumn Ivory pattern; Sears, Roebuck & Co. Catalog, 1929.*

Homer Laughlin

Top left: JJ45 pattern; Round Vegetable Bowl, Oval Platter, Dinner Plate, Salad Plate, Bread & Butter Plate, and Soup Bowl. **Top right:** HLC420 pattern; Bouillon Cup & Saucer Set, Dinner Plate, and Cup. **Middle left:** W132 pattern; Small Pitcher, Dinner Plate, Salad Plate, Cereal Bowl, and Oval Platter. **Middle right:** Y14 pattern; Soup Bowl with rim, Creamer, and Sugar Bowl with lid. **Bottom left:** W426 pattern; Round Covered Vegetable Bowl, Oval Vegetable Bowl, Fruit Bowl, Gravy/Sauce Boat, Cup, and Sugar Bowl missing lid.

Yellowstone Shape

Yellowstone Piece Type List

From 1929 Homer Laughlin Catalog with Confirmed Actual Pieces

Bowl, Cereal Coupe, 5⅝ inches
Bowl, Cranberry, 4⅞ inches
Bowl, Fruit, 5 inches
Bowl, Soup Coupe Large, 8¼ inches
Bowl, Soup Coupe Small, 7¼ inches
Bowl, Soup with rim, 9⅛ inches
Bowl, Vegetable Oval, 9 inches
Bowl, Vegetable Oval, 11 inches
Bowl, Vegetable Round, 8⅜ inches
Bowl, Vegetable Round, 9⅜ inches
Bowl, Vegetable Round, 9⅞ inches
Bowl, Vegetable Round Covered, 9⅝ inches
Butter Dish, Round Covered
Creamer, 2¾ inches

Cup & Saucer Set
   Cup, 2⅜ inches
   Saucer, 6 inches
Cup & Saucer Set, Bouillon
   Cup, 2¼ inches
   Saucer, 6 inches
Cup & Saucer Set, Coffee
Gravy/Sauce Boat
Gravy/Sauce Boat Underplate/Relish
   8½ inches
Pitcher, Large Open
Pitcher, Large with lid
Pitcher, Small Open, 5¼ inches
Pitcher, Small with lid
Plate, Bread & Butter, 6¼ inches

Plate, Dessert, 7⅛ inches
Plate, Dinner, 9¾ inches
Plate, Luncheon, 9 inches
Plate, Salad, 8 inches
Platter, 10 inches
Platter, 11¼ inches
Platter, 13⅝ inches
Platter, 15⅛ inches
Relish, Lugged
Sherbet, 3⅛ inches
Sugar Bowl with lid, Large, 4 inches
Sugar Bowl with lid, Small, 3½ inches
Teapot with lid

Top left: W132 pattern; Small Pitcher. **Middle left:** Y43 pattern; Dinner Plate, Salad Plate, Cup & Saucer Set, and Bread & Butter Plate. **Middle:** Y43 pattern; Oval Vegetable Bowl, Round Vegetable Bowl, Fruit Bowl, and Soup Bowl. **Middle right:** Y43 pattern; Gravy/Sauce Boat with attached Underplate, Round Covered Vegetable Bowl, and Round Butter Dish with lid. **Bottom left:** W127/30 pattern; Salad Plate, Dinner Plate, Oval Platter, Cranberry Bowl, Round Vegetable Bowl, Cereal Bowl, Creamer, Fruit Bowl, and Sherbet. **Bottom right:** Golden Rose pattern; Dinner Plate, Salad Plate, Fruit Bowl, Gravy/Sauce Boat, Sugar Bowl with lid, Cup & Saucer Set, and Round Vegetable Bowl.

Yellowstone Shape

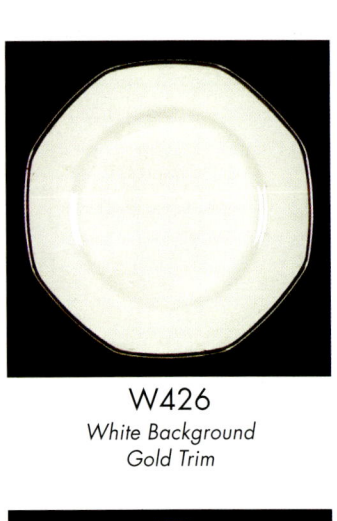

W426 *White Background Gold Trim*	 **Y14** *Cream Background Gold Trim*	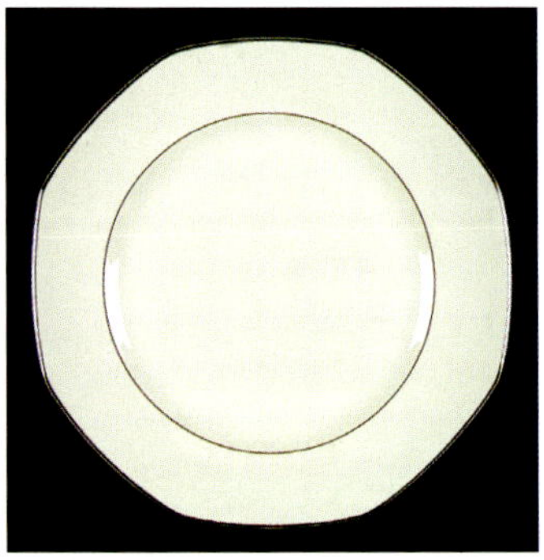 **HLC595** *Gold Trim*	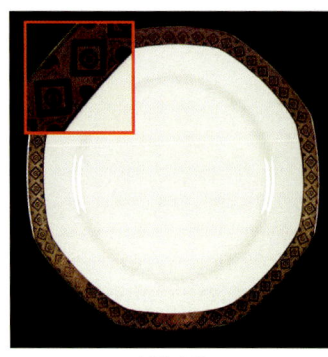 **Y162** *Gold Trim*
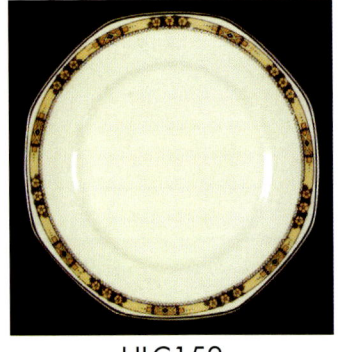 **HLC152** *Bread & Butter Plate Shown Black Trim*	 **AJS26** *No Trim*	 **Y40** *Mustard Trim*	 **HLC1116** *Oval Platter Shown Rust Trim*
 **HLC576** *Black Trim*	 **Y795** *Black Trim*	 **HLC1371** *Blue Trim*	 **Y24** *Gold Trim*
 **HLC420** *Platinum Trim*	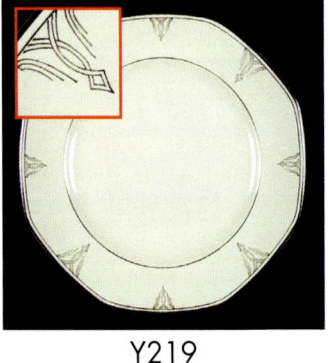 **Y219** *Platinum Trim*	 **CAC84** *Gold Trim*	 **Y137** *No Trim*

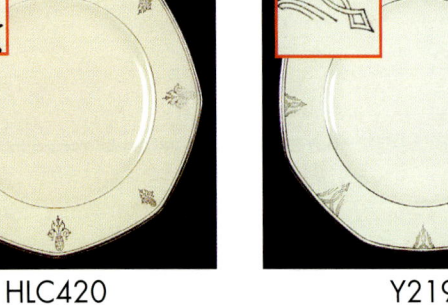

Yellowstone Shape

Y137G
Green Trim

HLC3107
*Oval Vegetable Bowl Shown
No Trim*

HLC1266
No Trim

A335
No Trim

JJ45
Gold Trim

HLC1020
Platinum Trim

W132
Platinum Trim

HLC702
Platinum Trim

HLC2110
*Handled Cake Plate Shown
Gold Trim*

Y43
Black Trim

HLC375
*Salad Plate Shown
No Trim*

Golden Rose
Black Trim

W127/30
Black Trim

HLC3016
*Round Covered Vegetable Bowl
Missing Lid Shown
Black Trim*

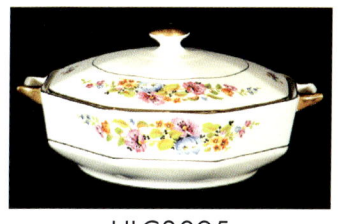

HLC3095
*Round Covered Vegetable
Bowl Shown
Gold Trim*

Wild Rose
Y220
Gold Trim

Yellowstone Shape

Y222
Platinum Trim

HLC3080
Platinum Trim

HLC190
Platinum Trim

HLC181
Luncheon Plate Shown
Black Trim

HLC836
Luncheon Plate Shown
No Trim

HLC2027
Red Trim

HLC877
Gold Trim

HLC3023
No Trim

HLC518
No Trim

HLC2085
No Trim

Maxicana
W440
Red Trim

HLC151
Bread & Butter Plate Shown
Gold Trim

HLC2037
Black Band
No Trim

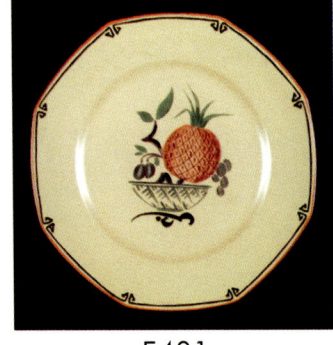

E481
Orange Trim

HLC697
Soup Bowl Shown
No Trim

HLC1134
Red Trim

Yellowstone Shape

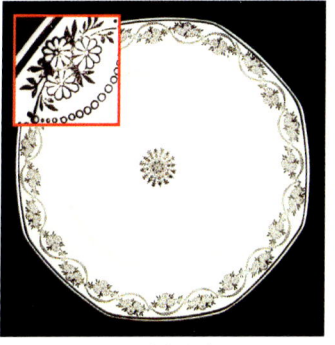

HLC364
Gold Trim

YELLOWSTONE DINNER SERVICE

1 Tea	4 Jug. 24s	8 Baker, 7 inch	12 Pickle	16 Fruit, 4 inch
2 Coffee	5 Cream	9 Grape Fruit	13 Relish	17 Dish, 8 inch

Above: *Yellowstone piece types, photograph from the Homer Laughlin Factory.*

109

TRELLIS

Piece Types

Cup 4⅝" W 2½" H

Dinner Plate

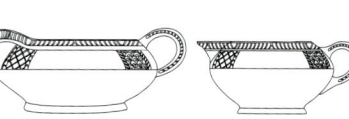

Gravy/Sauce Boat

Creamer 5⅜" W 2½" H

Sugar Bowl with lid

Jug, Small

Round Covered Vegetable Bowl

These drawings were made from actual stock or literature at Replacements, Ltd. Check the piece type list for all known piece types in this shape.

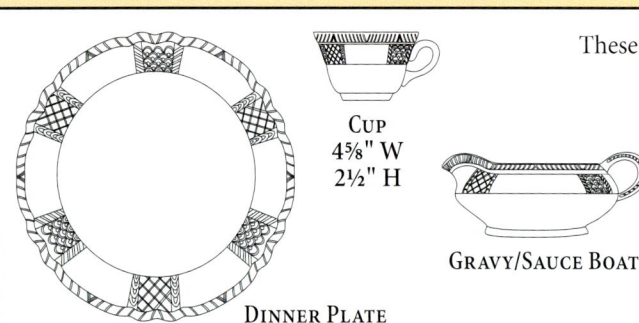

TRELLIS 1927 – 1931 or later

The Trellis line was introduced around 1927 and produced through at least 1931. Trellis and the Newell line (introduced a year later) were probably modeled together, as the rope-edged shape is the same for both lines, the difference being that Trellis has extra embossing dividing the rim into six sections. The Trellis line was one shape available for promotional use to specific customers. A January 1930 ad for Mother's Oats, in *Holland's The Magazine of the South*, features the Trellis line. Many decorations were available on this line, with several patterns featuring floral decals on the six rim panels. Although pieces may be marked with the Homer Laughlin name, more commonly found marks would only include the name "Trellis," not signifying the origin of the piece at all.

Top right: *QO10 pattern; Cup.* **Bottom right:** *HLC2078 pattern; Creamer.*

Trellis Piece Type List

From Homer Laughlin Literature with Confirmed Actual Pieces

Bowl, Cereal, 6 inches
Bowl, Fruit, 5 inches
Bowl, Soup Coupe, 7½ inches
Bowl, Soup Coupe, 8 inches
Bowl, Soup with rim, 9 inches
Bowl, Vegetable Oval, 8 inches
Bowl, Vegetable Round Covered

Creamer
Cup & Saucer Set
   Cup, 2½ inches
Gravy/Sauce Boat
Jug, Small
Plate, Bread & Butter, 6 inches
Plate, Dessert, 7 inches

Plate, Dinner, 10 inches
Plate, Luncheon, 9 inches
Plate, Salad, 8 inches
Platter, 10 inches
Platter, 11¼ inches
Platter, 13 inches
Sugar Bowl with lid

Trellis Shape

HLC674 *No Trim*	**HLC1978** *No Trim*	**HLC786** *Gold Trim*	**HLC2078** *Green Trim*
T2 *No Trim*	**QO10** *No Trim*	**T26** *No Trim*	**T91** *Platinum Trim*
T35 *Green Trim*	**T27** *Green Trim*	**T24** *Green Trim*	**T8028** *Platinum Trim*
KD5 *Platinum Trim*	**T92** *Gold Trim*	**T7** *No Trim*	**T93** *Gold Trim*

Trellis Shape

T95
Platinum Trim

T46
No Trim

T48
No Trim

T50
No Trim

HLC2019
*Luncheon Plate Shown
No Trim*

HLC1867
Platinum Trim

Right: *HLC674 pattern; Dinner Plate, and Cup.* **Bottom left:** Holland's The Magazine of the South *advertisement, 1930.* **Bottom right:** *Larkin Co. Premium Catalog, 1930.*

Trellis Pattern

Proof that an undecorated pattern may also have beauty is found in this lovely new set, so appropriately called the "Trellis" because of the embossed design. You will delight in its value, too. The ideal every-day dinnerware. Strong and durable. Ivory body. Scalloped edges.

Size of Set	32-pc.	41-pc.
Number	3472	3487
With Purchase	$7	$11
Shpg. wt.	18 lbs.	22 lbs.

China—for you

in every package of Mother's China Oats
—A premium coupon, too

t's the oats *themselves* and the way they're milled

that makes Mother's Oats so much better

Mother's Oats—China Brand

Mother's Oats comes in 2 styles: the Regular, and Quick Mother's that cooks in 2½ minutes

NEWELL

Piece Types

Newell piece types, photograph from the Homer Laughlin Factory.

Homer Laughlin

NEWELL 1928 – circa 1940

The first notice of the Newell shape is found in a full-page advertisement in *The Pottery, Glass & Brass Salesman* of February 2, 1928. The copy reads: "The tendency toward graceful lines and delicate modeling promises to be a feature of the popular taste for 1928…" and shown there is a selection of Newell with decoration N2023. Homer Laughlin ads in January 1927 list the lines then available and Newell is not included (*Crockery, Glass & Lamps,* January 10, 1927). Newell does appear in the 1929 Homer Laughlin Catalog.

Newell is reportedly a Frederick Rhead design and incorporates a gadroon edge, reminiscent of English tableware. Sears appears to have offered it for only one year, 1929, where it was featured with the Yellowstone Glaze. Homer Laughlin historian Jack Welch noted, the Newell design "was not a spectacular success, although it sold modestly for more than a decade." Newell was redesigned to become the Liberty shape.

Top left: *N3128 pattern; Round Covered Vegetable Bowl, Oval Platter, and Gravy/Sauce Boat with unattached Underplate.*
Bottom left: *HLC1090 pattern; Customer supplied photograph.*
Right: *Hawthorn pattern; Larkin Catalog, 1933.*

Newell Shape

Newell Piece Type List

From Homer Laughlin Literature with Confirmed Actual Pieces

Bowl, 1⅛ pints
Bowl, 1⅝ pints
Bowl, Fruit, 5 inches
Bowl, Fruit, 5½ inches
Bowl, Oatmeal
Bowl, Oyster, 1¼ pints
Bowl, Oyster, 5¾ pints
Bowl, Soup Coupe, 7¼ inches
Bowl, Soup Coupe, 8 inches
Bowl, Vegetable Oval, 5½ inches
Bowl, Vegetable Oval, 7⅛ inches
Bowl, Vegetable Oval, 8⅛ inches
Bowl, Vegetable Oval, 9¼ inches
Bowl, Vegetable Oval, 10¼ inches
Bowl, Vegetable Round, 7 inches
Butter with lid
Butter, Individual, 3 inches

Casserole with lid, 10 inches
Creamer
Cup & Saucer Set, After Dinner, 4 ounces
Cup & Saucer Set, Bouillon, 8 ounces
Cup & Saucer Set, Coffee, 10 ounces
Cup & Saucer Set, Tea, 8½ ounces
Gravy/Sauce Boat
Gravy/Sauce Boat with attached Underplate, no handle
Gravy/Sauce Boat Underplate/Relish
Pitcher/Jug
Plate, 6¼ inches
Plate, 7¼ inches

Plate, 8½ inches
Plate, 9⅛ inches
Plate, 10 inches
Plate, Cake, 10¾ inches
Plate, Deep, 9⅛ inches
Platter, 8⅜ inches
Platter, 9¼ inches
Platter, 10½ inches
Platter, 11½ inches
Platter, 12½ inches
Platter, 13¼ inches
Platter, 15¼ inches
Platter, 17¼ inches
Sugar Bowl with lid
Teapot with lid

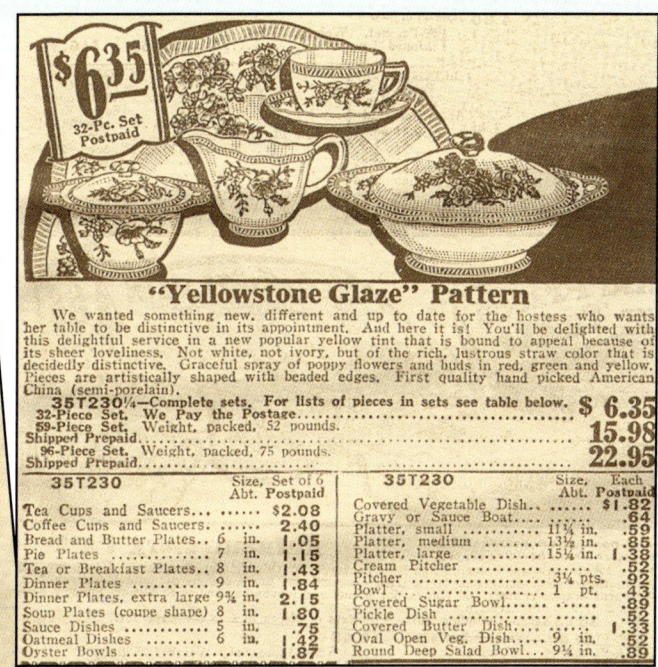

Left: *N2023 pattern;* The Pottery Glass & Brass Salesman, 1928. **Right:** *"Yellowstone Glaze" pattern;* Sears, Roebuck & Co. Catalog, 1929.

115

Newell Shape

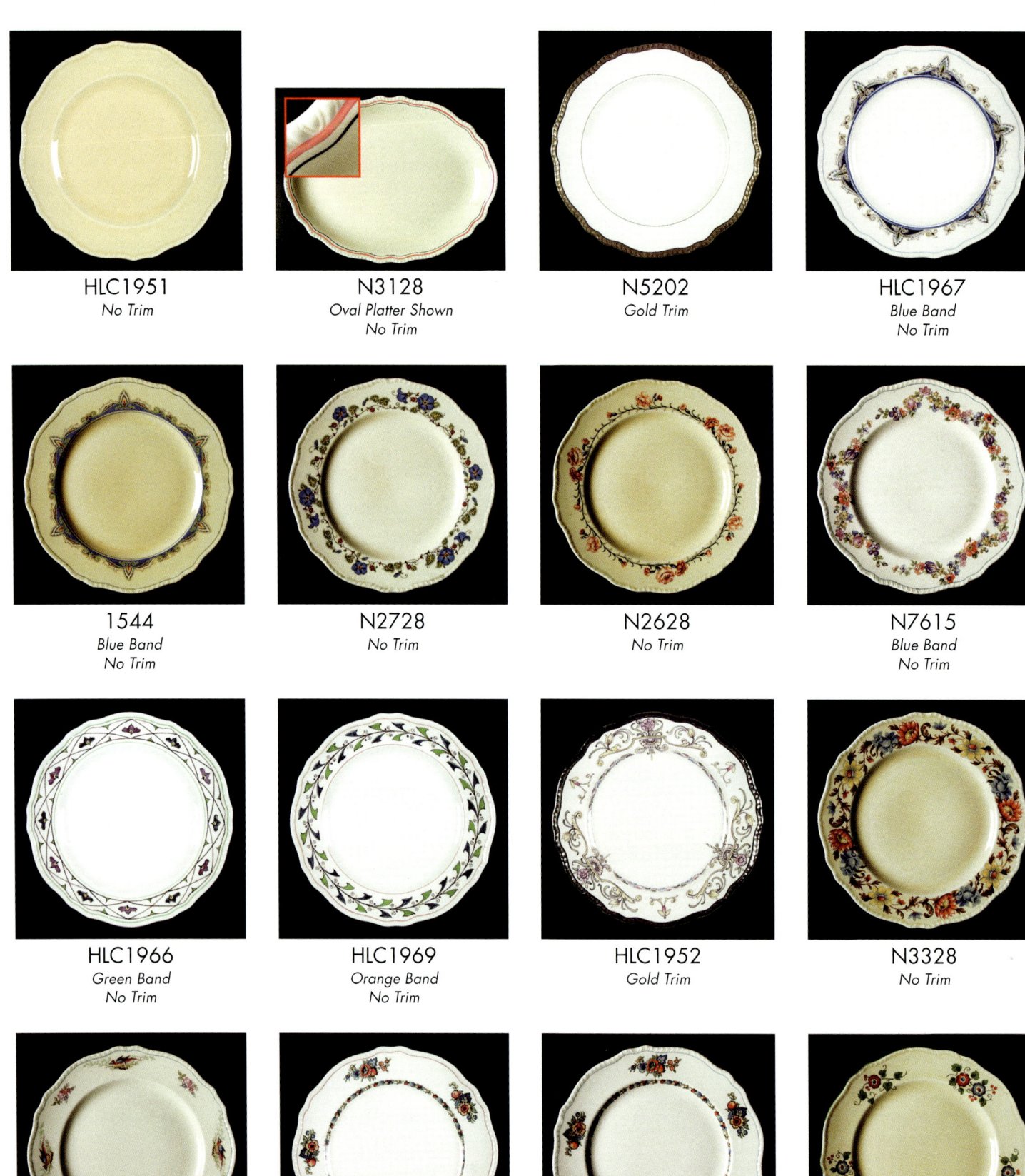

HLC1951	N3128	N5202	HLC1967
No Trim	Oval Platter Shown No Trim	Gold Trim	Blue Band No Trim

1544	N2728	N2628	N7615
Blue Band No Trim	No Trim	No Trim	Blue Band No Trim

HLC1966	HLC1969	HLC1952	N3328
Green Band No Trim	Orange Band No Trim	Gold Trim	No Trim

N2723	N7715	N7415	W42930
Blue Band No Trim	Orange Band No Trim	Blue Band No Trim	Green Trim

116

Newell Shape

N2928
Blue Band
No Trim

N2423
Orange Band
No Trim

N4143
Platinum Trim

XN6
No Trim

N6828
Platinum Trim

N6928
Platinum Trim

N3943
Platinum Trim

N7028
Platinum Trim

HLC868
Platinum Trim

HLC2004
Green Band
No Trim

N6528
Black Band
No Trim

N7128
Platinum Trim

N2123
Black Band
No Trim

HLC1639
Orange Band
No Trim

N2124
No Trim

N80
No Trim

Newell Shape

N3928 No Trim	**N1728** No Trim	**N3023** Black Band No Trim	**N5728** Green Band No Trim
Song of Spring No Trim	**Hawthorn** No Trim	**N2228** Black Band No Trim	**HLC1997** Black Band No Trim
71002 Orange Band No Trim	**N5428** Black Band No Trim	**HLC1090** No Trim	**N3123** Red Band No Trim
N3923 Blue Trim	**HLC3452** Green Trim	**N8228** Platinum Trim	**HLC2206** No Trim

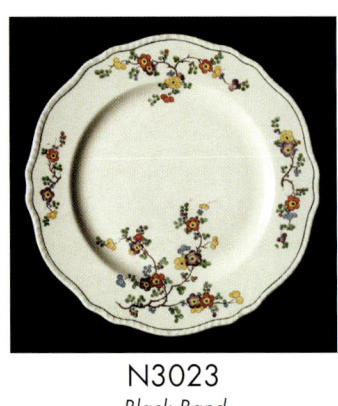

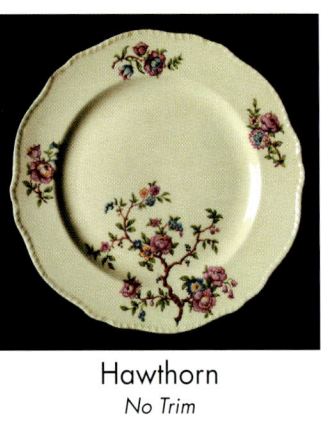

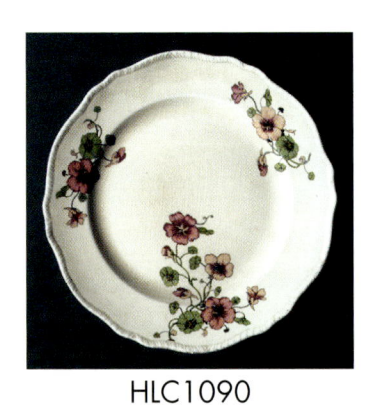

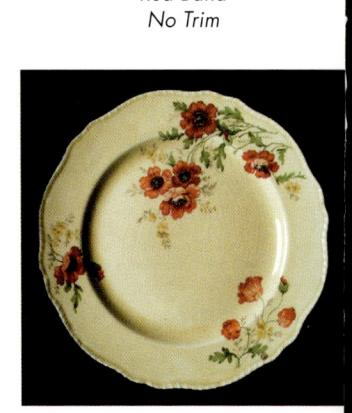

Newell Shape

HLC1104
No Trim

N3628
No Trim

N2023
Saucer Shown
Black Band
No Trim

N2823
Red Band
No Trim

HLC1968
No Trim

Above: *Hawthorn pattern; Larkin Catalog, 1939.*

119

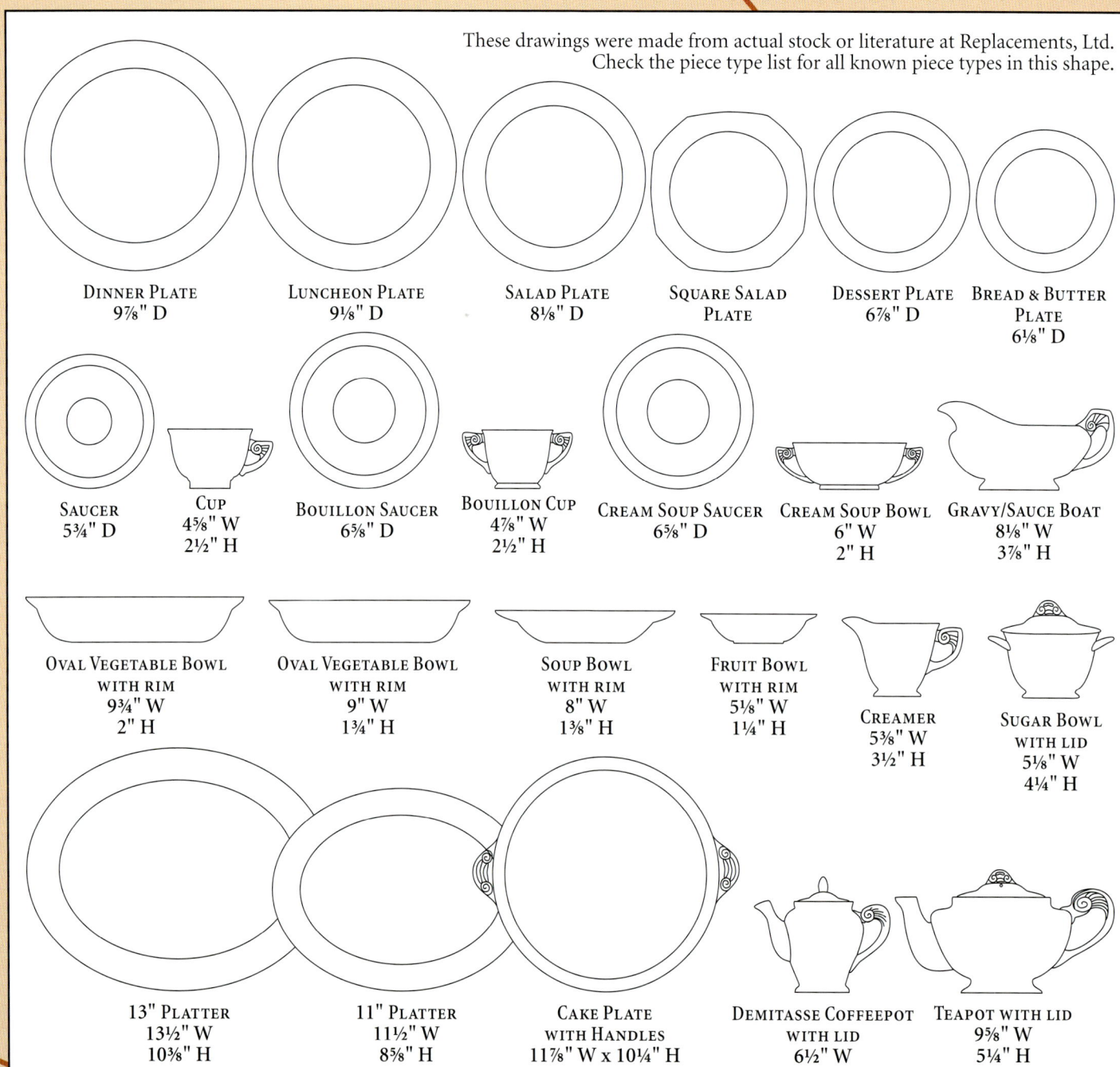

Wells

Piece Types

These drawings were made from actual stock or literature at Replacements, Ltd. Check the piece type list for all known piece types in this shape.

Dinner Plate	9⅞" D
Luncheon Plate	9⅛" D
Salad Plate	8⅛" D
Square Salad Plate	
Dessert Plate	6⅞" D
Bread & Butter Plate	6⅛" D
Saucer	5¾" D
Cup	4⅝" W, 2½" H
Bouillon Saucer	6⅝" D
Bouillon Cup	4⅞" W, 2½" H
Cream Soup Saucer	6⅝" D
Cream Soup Bowl	6" W, 2" H
Gravy/Sauce Boat	8⅛" W, 3⅞" H
Oval Vegetable Bowl with Rim	9¾" W, 2" H
Oval Vegetable Bowl with Rim	9" W, 1¾" H
Soup Bowl with Rim	8" W, 1⅜" H
Fruit Bowl with Rim	5⅛" W, 1¼" H
Creamer	5⅜" W, 3½" H
Sugar Bowl with Lid	5⅛" W, 4¼" H
13" Platter	13½" W, 10⅜" H
11" Platter	11½" W, 8⅝" H
Cake Plate with Handles	11⅞" W x 10¼" H
Demitasse Coffeepot with Lid	6½" W
Teapot with Lid	9⅝" W, 5¼" H

Wells Shape

WELLS circa 1930 – 1945 or later

The Wells shape was designed by Frederick Rhead and is reminiscent of art pottery. Open work embossed handles are a distinctive feature of the Wells shape.

Some of the most interesting glazes Homer Laughlin ever produced were used on the Wells shape. Solid color patterns are marked with a "Wells Art Glazes" backstamp. The solid colors utilized for Wells art glazes include: Rust, Red, Peach, Yellow, Green, and Ivory. Examples of a Blue pattern exist but are infrequently found.

Decal decorations were also used on the Wells shape. Patterns with these decorations often have the multicolored peacock decal backstamp. A silver/platinum peacock backstamp was also used.

Montgomery Ward must have had considerable success with patterns on this shape. Between 1930 and 1945 Wells shaped patterns were frequently offered in the catalog. The most successful pattern offered was Gold Stripe, as the name implies, a simple striped pattern. Gold Stripe was offered from 1938 to 1945. This long run makes the Wells shape one of the most popular produced by Homer Laughlin, a longevity far surpassing the likes of the more recognized Virginia Rose and others.

The December 1936 *Crockery and Glass Journal* lists the Wells Art Glazes in its 1937 previews. The *Homer Laughlin Pound Sterling Price Booklet of 1937* has listings for Wells Ivory Body (a glossy surface) and Wells Vellum Glaze (a matte surface) patterns. There were 62 different Wells decorations/patterns available from Homer Laughlin in 1937.

The Wells peacock backstamp was used on some Century, Jade, and even Orleans shaped pieces during this same mid-1930's to 1940 era. The reason for using this backstamp on these other shapes is unknown to the authors.

Flight of the Swallows, Wells Art Glazes, and Flowers of the Dell patterns; Montgomery Ward, 1931.

SPECIAL OFFER!

76 PIECE MATCHED TABLE SERVICE $8.98 Complete

"MODERN LAUREL" COMPLETE SERVICE FOR SIX

32-Pc. Dinner Set

6 ea. of Teacups, Saucers, Bread and Butter Plates, Dinner Plates, Sauce Dishes; 1 Small Platter and 1 Open Vegetable Dish. Ship. wt. 24 lbs. **Shipped from** Chicago, Baltimore or Atlanta. Send order to nearest House.
A486 C 6301—32-Piece Set if purchased separately....$3.98

18-Pc. Glassware Set

586 C 6750—6 Goblets. Ship. wt. 5 lbs....................$1.44
586 C 6751—6 Sherbets. Ship. wt. 4 lbs....................$1.44
586 C 6752—6 Salad Plates. Ship. wt. 7 lbs. 8 oz.............$1.74
486 C 6749—18 Pieces above if bought separately. Ship. wt. 16 lbs....................$4.62

26-Pc. Silverware Set

Silver-plated over nickel-silver base to last 10 years! Service includes: 6 Teaspoons, 6 Soup Spoons, 6 Dinner Forks, 6 Dinner Knives, 1 Butter Knife and 1 Sugar Shell. Shipping weight 3 lbs.
86 C 2901—26 Pieces if purchased separately.....$2.25

Just See What You Save..... Wards Regular Price $10.85!

"At last—everything to match!" writes an enthusiastic customer. "My table is the envy of my guests." Fashion-wise women know that a matching table service is important. The *actual photograph* above tells you this more eloquently than words. The "Modern Laurel" border of the dishes is repeated by the silver gray cutting of the glassware and again in the pattern of the silverware.

But let's have PROOF! Let's shop through Wards own Catalog and see what you save. For dinnerware look on these two pages. "Modern Laurel" is a jade green border—smart and tasteful on ivory-white glazed American semi-porcelain of first quality . . . each piece hand selected. Similar patterns, you will note, sell for $4.79. Turn to Page 385 to see Wards regular glassware prices—27c to 33c each for goblets, sherbets and salad plates of the same thin blown, clear crystal glass. The silverware is identically the same quality and pattern Wards sell for $2.25 (see Page 397 for extra pieces). Silver-plated to last ten years, with the same nickel-silver alloy base used in finest silver plate. Handles are satin finished with highly polished bowls, blades and tines.

A386 C 6300—Complete 76-Piece Service for 6. Ship. wt. 43 lbs. **Shipped from** Chicago, Baltimore or Atlanta. Send Order to nearest House. *Mailable*....................$8.98
586 C 6305—**Open Dinnerware Stock** — See table bottom of opposite page.

FOR WARDS FINER SILVERWARE PATTERNS — See Pages 431 to 434

GOLD STRIPE

Always a Best Seller

$3.49 32-Pc. Set

"Our Ladies' Aid bought Gold Stripe for church suppers," writes one customer, "we couldn't equal Wards quality at $4.00 for the 32-piece set." And so practical because its trim gold and white severity combines nicely with dinnerware patterns you already have. Pleasant round shapes of first quality American semi-porcelain, glazed ivory-white and double lined with bright gold . . . a fine inner line and wider outside edge. 32 and 53-piece sets **shipped from** Chicago, Baltimore or Atlanta. Send Order to nearest House. *Mailable.* 95-Pc. set shipped in 2 packages. *See opposite page for list of pieces in each set.*

A486 C 6041—32-Pc. Set. Ship. wt. 23 lbs..$3.49
586 C 6045—Creamer and Sugar. Wt. 4 lbs..75c
A486 C 6042—53-Pc. Set. Ship. wt. 42 lbs.. 6.49
386 C 6044—95-Pc. Set. Ship. wt. 76 lbs.. 12.49
586 C 6045—**Open Stock**—See table opposite page.

Gold Border

$5.49 32-piece Set — $9.98 53-piece Set — $18.95 95-piece Set

Look how Wards Bureau of Design has improved the popular gold border style of dinnerware! Gold has always been an ideal dinnerware decoration and now it achieves greater beauty than ever before in this smart, modern pattern. See it in color on back cover. The shapes of the pieces are also new and modern.

Patterns are in bright gold on clear domestic semi-porcelain. Oven proof casserole and Pie plate to match on Page 330.

486 A 6081—32-Pc. Set. Ship. wt. 20 lbs....$ 5.49
486 A 6082—53-Pc. Set. Ship. wt. 44 lbs.... 9.98
386 A 6084—95-Pc. Set. Ship. wt. 85 lbs.... 18.95

586 A 6085—INDIVIDUAL PIECES.

Article (Average sizes given)	Ship. Wt.	Price
Teacups, 7-oz	10 oz.	23c
Tea Saucers	10 oz.	15c
Bread and Butter Plates, 6¼-in.	12 oz.	17c
Pie or Salad Plates, 7⅛-in	13 oz.	19c
Dinner Plates, 9-in	1 lb.	31c
Soup Dishes, 7½-in	1 lb.	29c
Sauce Dishes, 5-in	10 oz.	15c
Covered Sugar Bowl	2 lbs.	89c
Creamer	2 lbs.	49c
Covered Vegetable Dish	5 lbs.	$1.79
Gravy, Sauce Boat, No stand.	2 lbs.	69c
Platter, small, about 11-in	4 lbs.	45c
Platter, medium about 13-in	5 lbs.	79c
Platter, large, about 15¼-in	6 lbs.	$1.39
Round Salad Bowl, 8¾-in	4 lbs.	55c
Oval Open Vegetable Dish, 9 in.	4 lbs.	55c

Top left: *Modern Laurel pattern; Montgomery Ward, 1936-1937.* **Top middle:** *Gold Stripe pattern; Montgomery Ward, 1936-1937.* **Top right:** *Gold Border pattern; Montgomery Ward, 1935.* **Middle left:** *Wells Art Glaze–Rust pattern; Platters, and Saucer. Note variations in color.* **Middle second from left:** *Typical Wells Art Glaze backstamp.* **Middle third from left:** *Less common Wells backstamp.* **Middle right:** *Most common Wells silver peacock backstamp.* **Bottom left:** *Wells Art Glaze–Rust pattern; Dinner Plate, Cake Plate, Cup & Saucer Set, Sugar Bowl with lid, Demitasse Coffeepot missing lid, Oval Vegetable Bowl with rim, and Creamer.* **Third down on right:** *Wells color peacock backstamp, vellum mark, and pattern number.* **Bottom right:** *Wells metallic silver peacock backstamp.*

Wells Shape

Wells Piece Type List

From Homer Laughlin Literature with Confirmed Actual Pieces

Bowl, Cream Soup & Saucer Set
   Bowl, 2 inches
   Saucer, 6⅝ inches
Bowl, Fruit with rim, 5⅛ inches
Bowl, Soup with rim, 8 inches
Bowl, Vegetable Oval with rim, 9 inches
Bowl, Vegetable Oval with rim, 9¾ inches
Bowl, Vegetable Round*
Bowl, Vegetable Round Covered
Coffeepot with lid, Demitasse
Creamer
Creamer, Demitasse
Cup & Saucer Set
   Cup, 2½ inches
   Saucer, 5¾ inches

Cup & Saucer Set, Bouillon
   Cup, 2½ inches, vertical handles
   Saucer, 6⅝ inches
Cup & Saucer Set, Demitasse
Eggcup, Double
Gravy/Sauce Boat
Gravy/Sauce Boat Underplate/Relish
Muffin/Butter Dish with lid
Pitcher with lid, Batter
Pitcher with lid, Syrup
Plate, Bread & Butter, 6⅛ inches
Plate, Cake, 11⅞ inches
Plate, Dessert, 6⅞ inches
Plate, Dinner, 9⅞ inches
Plate, Luncheon, 9⅛ inches
Plate, Salad, 8⅛ inches

Plate, Salad Square
Platter, Oval, 11½ inches
Platter, Oval, 13½ inches
Platter, Oval, 15½ inches*
Sugar Bowl with lid
Sugar Bowl with lid, Demitasse, horizontal handles
Teapot with lid
Tray, Serving, Embossed
Tumbler with handle
*Reported but not confirmed.

Top left: *Wells Art Glaze–Red pattern; Teapot with lid.* **Middle left:** *Wells Art Glaze–Red pattern; Luncheon Plate, Dinner Plate, Oval Platter, Teapot with lid, Sugar Bowl missing lid, Oval Vegetable Bowl with rim, Fruit Bowl with rim, Cream Soup Bowl Saucer, and Bread & Butter Plate.* **Middle right:** *Wells Art Glaze–Green pattern; Oval Platter, Bouillon Cup, and Dinner Plate.* **Bottom left:** *Wells Art Glaze–Red pattern; Cream Soup & Saucer Set.* **Bottom middle:** *Wells Art Glaze–Peach pattern; Oval Platter, Dinner Plate, Luncheon Plate, Salad Plate, Sugar Bowl with lid, Fruit Bowl with rim, Soup Bowl with rim, and Bread & Butter Plate.* **Bottom right:** *Wells Art Glaze–Green pattern; Embossed Serving Tray.*

Wells Shape

Wells Art Glaze–Yellow *Bread & Butter Plate Shown* *No Trim*	**2039** *Turquoise* *No Trim*	**Wells Art Glaze–Green** *Bread & Butter Plate Shown* *No Trim*	**Wells Art Glaze–Blue** *Bread & Butter Plate Shown* *No Trim*
Wells Art Glaze–Peach *No Trim*	**Wells Art Glaze–Rust** *No Trim*	**Wells Art Glaze–Red** *No Trim*	**W4743** *Blue Trim*
HLC1559 *Square Salad Plate Shown* *No Trim*	**HLC1560** *Square Salad Plate Shown* *No Trim*	**MAW4** *Platinum Trim & Band*	**W5502** *Gold Trim*
W5833 *Platinum Trim*	**W7506** *Gold Trim*	**FW14** *Gold Trim*	**W7806** *Platinum Trim*

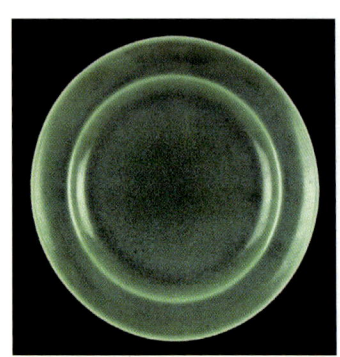

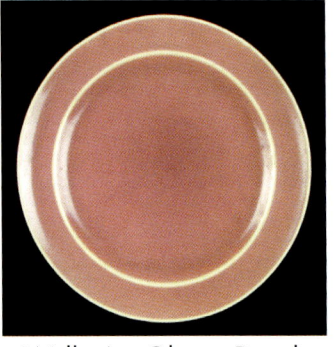

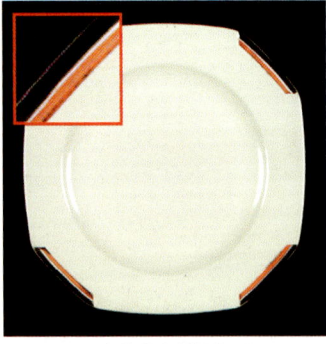

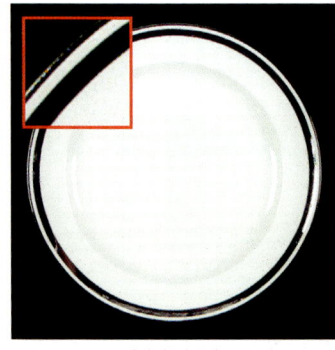

Wells Shape

W6833 Platinum Trim	**533** Platinum Trim	**D533** Square Salad Plate Shown Green Trim	**W1970** Gold Trim
W4970 Gold Trim	**W8377** No Trim	**W6470** Gold Trim	**W5670** Gold Trim
W5270 Gold Trim	**W9480M** No Trim	**W6170** Gold Trim	**W6180M** No Trim
W6580M No Trim	**W4324** No Trim	**W9570** Gold Trim	**FW13** No Trim

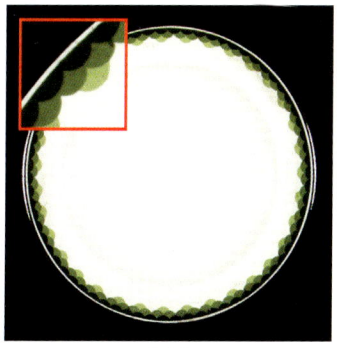

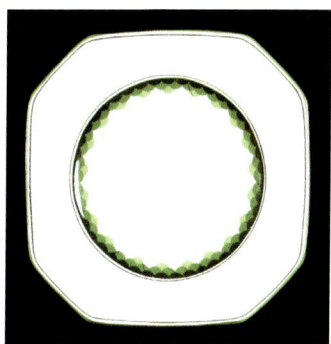

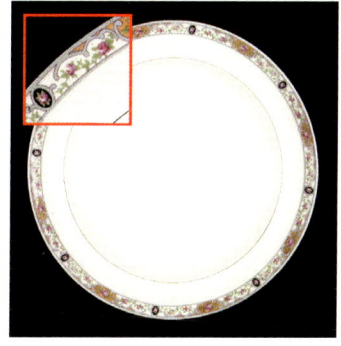

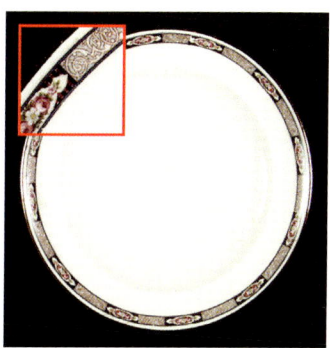

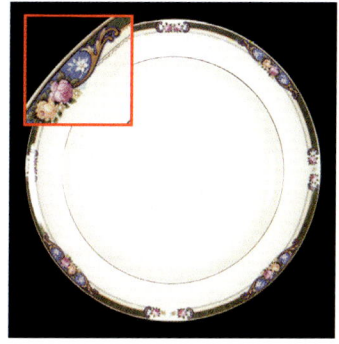

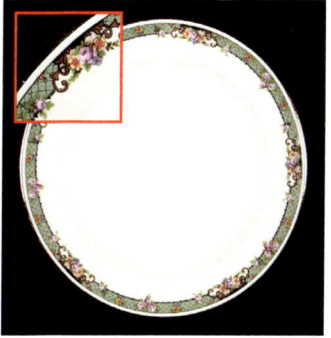

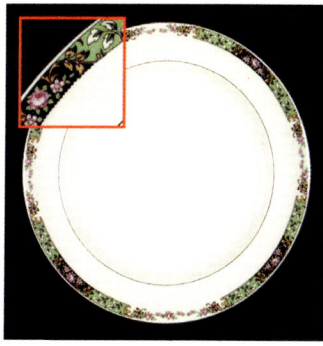

125

Wells Shape

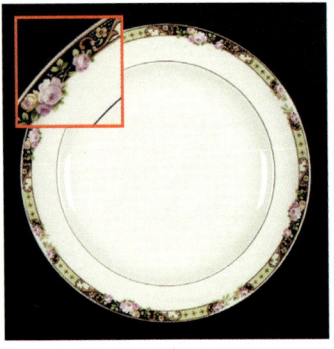

W3924/W4224
No Trim

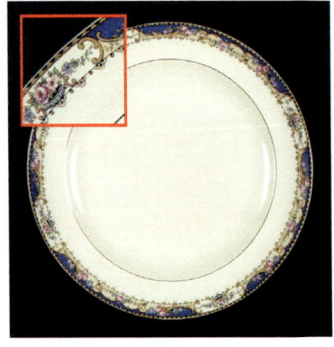

W7080M
No Trim

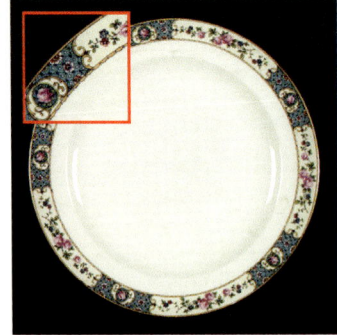

HLC1048
Gold Trim

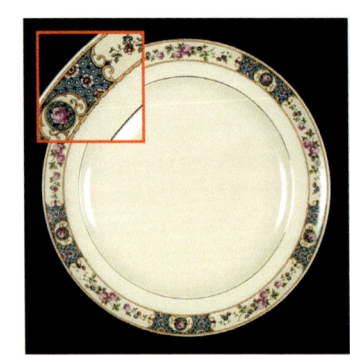

W6780M
No Trim

4740A
Brown/Blue Scrolls
Cream Body
No Trim

4740E
Brown/Blue Scrolls
White Body
No Trim

4740D
Green/Brown Scrolls
No Trim

4740H
Green/Orange Scrolls
No Trim

4740B
Brown/Red Scrolls
No Trim

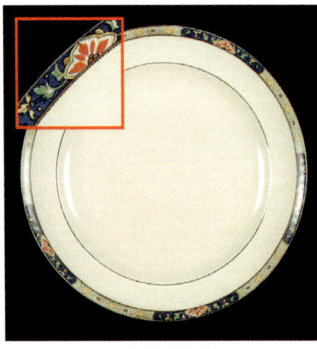

W8980
No Trim

W9980M
No Trim

8487A
Orange Trim

HLC1363
Luncheon Plate Shown
Gold Trim

HLC1464
Platinum Trim

HLC1463
Platinum Trim

HLC1763
Red Trim

Wells Shape

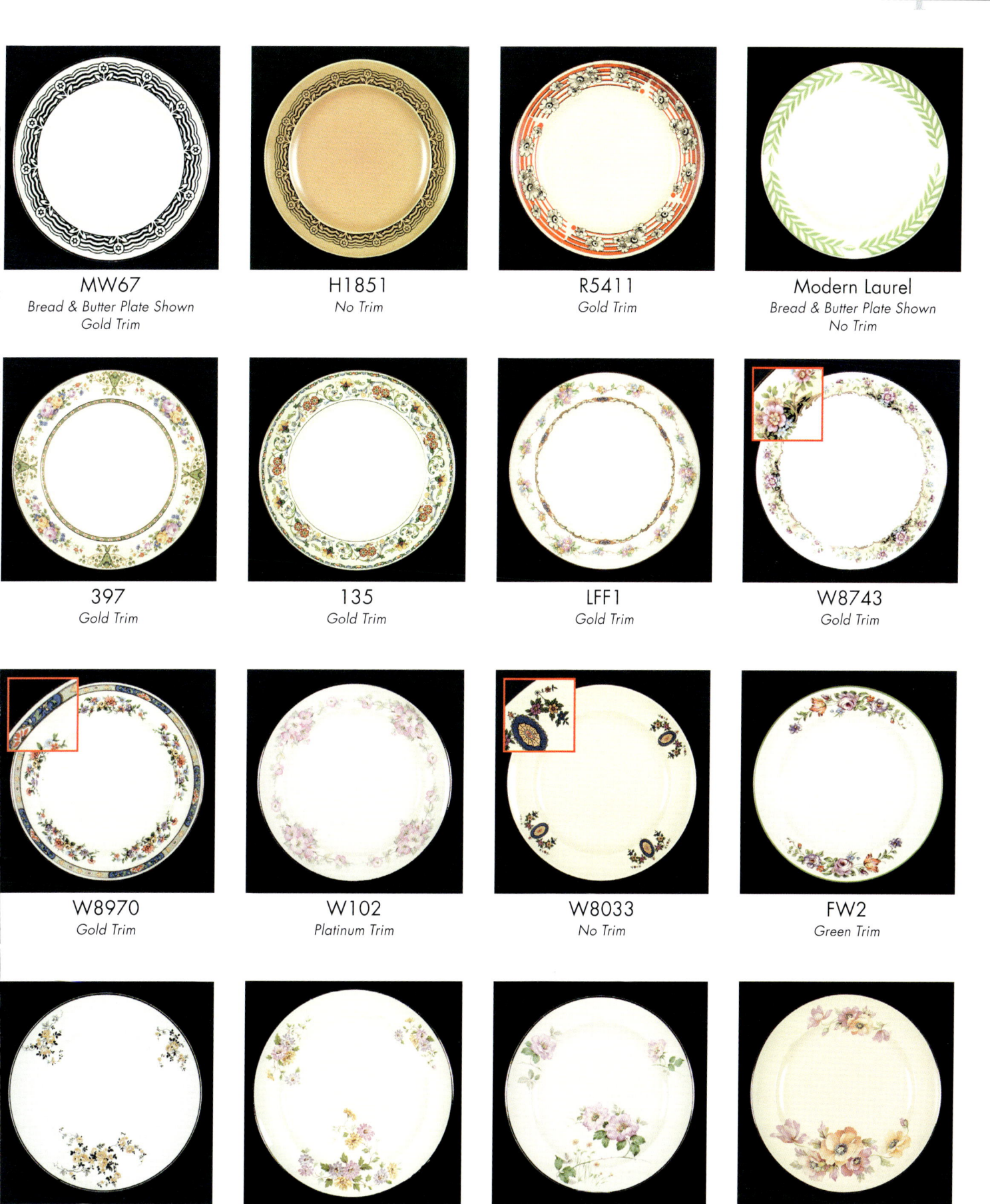

MW67 *Bread & Butter Plate Shown* *Gold Trim*	**H1851** *No Trim*	**R5411** *Gold Trim*	**Modern Laurel** *Bread & Butter Plate Shown* *No Trim*
397 *Gold Trim*	**135** *Gold Trim*	**LFF1** *Gold Trim*	**W8743** *Gold Trim*
W8970 *Gold Trim*	**W102** *Platinum Trim*	**W8033** *No Trim*	**FW2** *Green Trim*
W226 *Black Trim*	**HLC1345** *Platinum Trim*	**W6033/W6933** *Platinum Trim*	**W6433** *Platinum Trim*

Wells Shape

W6233
Platinum Trim

W6333
Green Trim

W1133
Platinum Trim

RG4508
Green Trim

W6733
Platinum Trim

RGC24
Black Trim

4523
Square Salad Plate Shown
No Trim

Flight Of The Swallows
Gravy Boat Shown
Green Trim

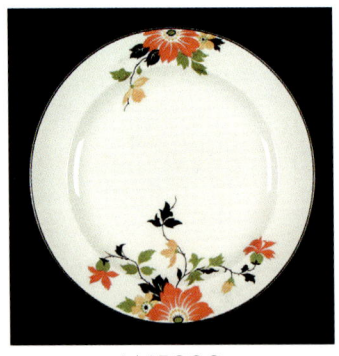

W5923
Black Trim

W8523
Black Trim

W7933
Gold Trim

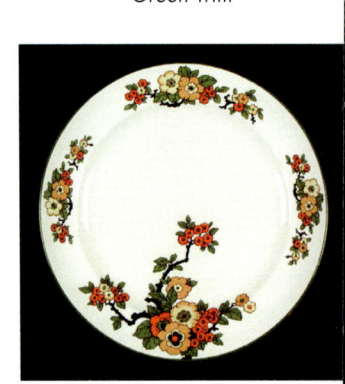

W9423
Green Trim

W7733
Platinum Trim

W104
Platinum Trim

W106
Platinum Trim

W2543
Platinum Trim

Wells Shape

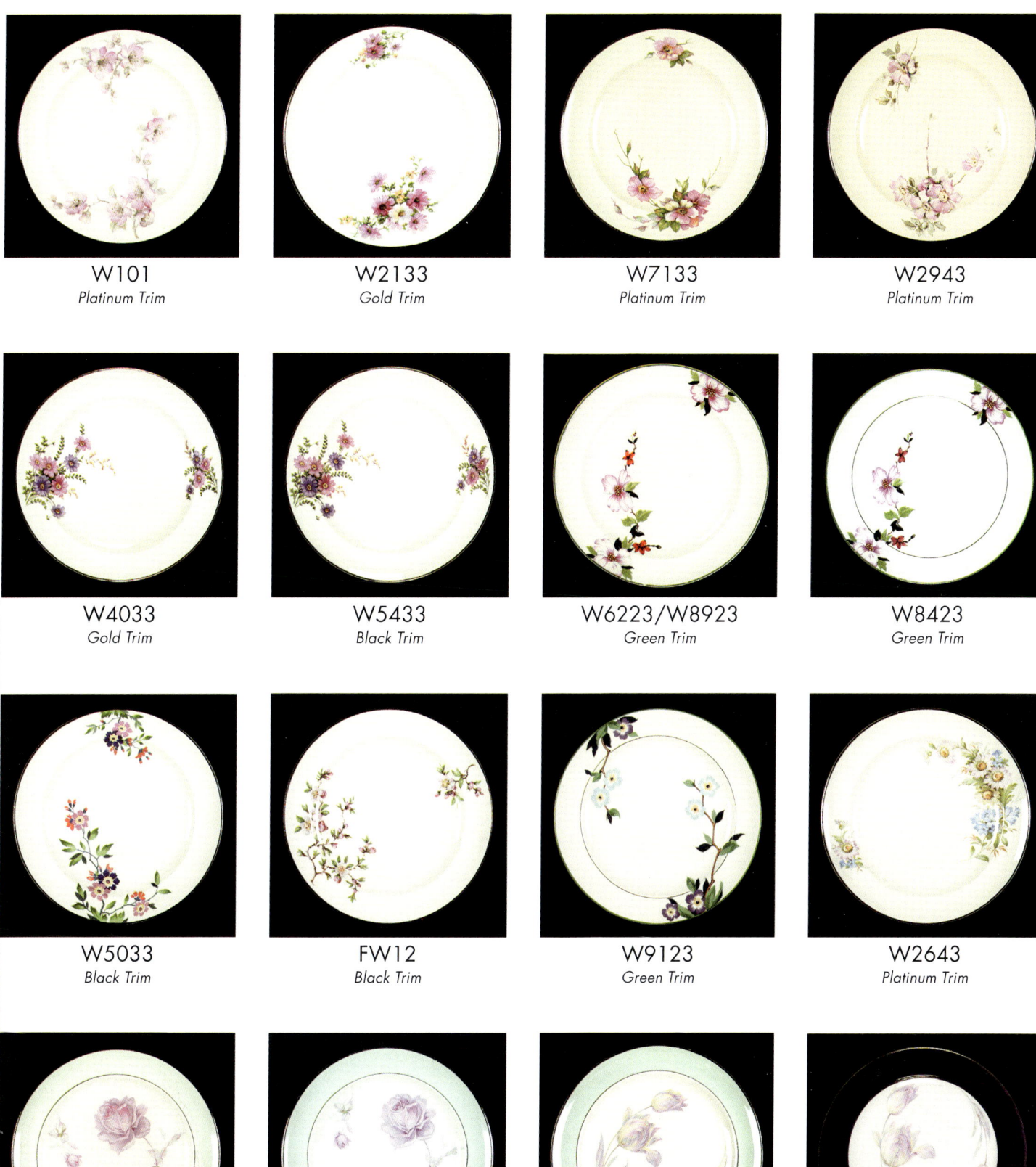

W101 *Platinum Trim*	**W2133** *Gold Trim*	**W7133** *Platinum Trim*	**W2943** *Platinum Trim*
W4033 *Gold Trim*	**W5433** *Black Trim*	**W6223/W8923** *Green Trim*	**W8423** *Green Trim*
W5033 *Black Trim*	**FW12** *Black Trim*	**W9123** *Green Trim*	**W2643** *Platinum Trim*
W2633 *Pale Green Rim* *Platinum Trim*	**W3733** *Light Blue Rim* *Platinum Trim*	**W9823** *Blue/Green Rim* *Platinum Trim*	**W4633** *Platinum Trim*

Wells Shape

HLC1791
Bread & Butter Plate Shown
Platinum Trim

W2733
Pale Green Rim
Platinum Trim

W2338
Pink Rim
Platinum Trim

W6023
Green Trim

HLC722
Green Trim

W7633
Platinum Trim

W2833
Pale Green Rim
Platinum Trim

W2533
Platinum Trim

W3133
Pale Green Rim
Gold Trim

W6123
Green Trim

W9223
Platinum Trim

W4923
Green Trim

W7923
Platinum Trim

HLC1512
Black Trim

718DPBR
Platinum Trim

718DP
Salad Plate Shown
Green Trim

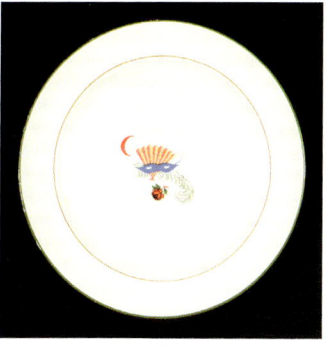

Wells Shape

586 Green Trim	**585** Square Salad Plate Shown Platinum Trim	**HUC2** Green Trim	**W5333** Gold Trim
HLC776 Luncheon Plate Shown Yellow Rim No Trim	**HLC776** Luncheon Plate Shown Blue Rim No Trim	**HLC776** Luncheon Plate Shown Lime Green Rim No Trim	**W2333** Gold Trim
Wally Yellow Trim	**704RG** Gold Trim	**4113** Gold Trim	**HLC1786** Light Blue Design No Trim
HLC1783 Dark Blue Design No Trim	**HLC1784** Pink Design No Trim	**HLC1785** Plum Design No Trim	**HLC1787** Red Design No Trim

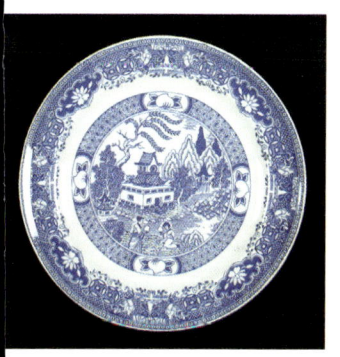

Century

Piece Types

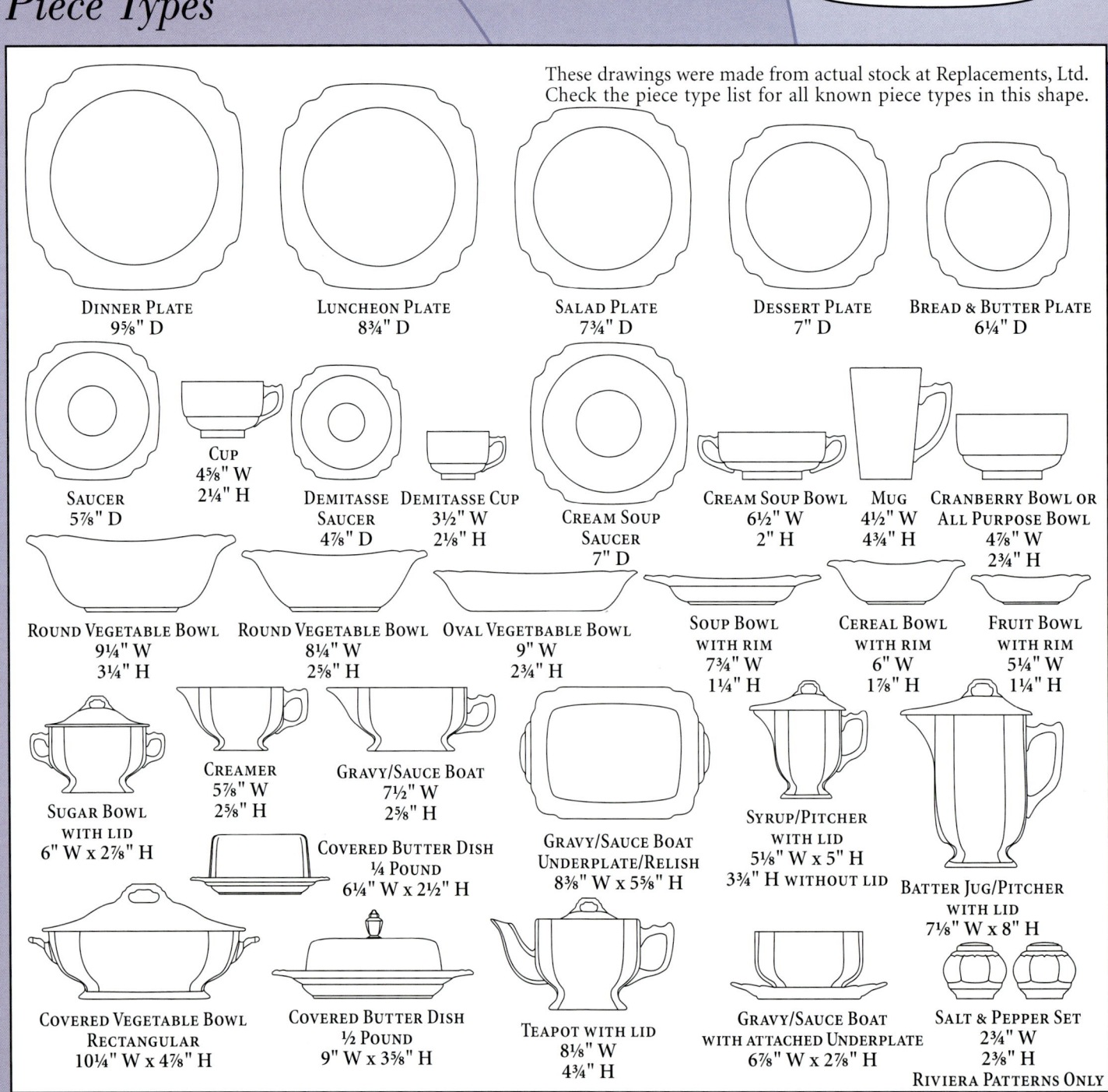

These drawings were made from actual stock at Replacements, Ltd. Check the piece type list for all known piece types in this shape.

Dinner Plate 9⅝" D	**Luncheon Plate** 8¾" D	**Salad Plate** 7¾" D	**Dessert Plate** 7" D	**Bread & Butter Plate** 6¼" D
Saucer 5⅞" D	**Cup** 4⅝" W, 2¼" H	**Demitasse Saucer** 4⅞" D	**Demitasse Cup** 3½" W, 2⅛" H / **Cream Soup Saucer** 7" D	**Cream Soup Bowl** 6½" W, 2" H / **Mug** 4½" W, 4¾" H / **Cranberry Bowl or All Purpose Bowl** 4⅞" W, 2¾" H
Round Vegetable Bowl 9¼" W, 3¼" H	**Round Vegetable Bowl** 8¼" W, 2⅝" H	**Oval Vegetable Bowl** 9" W, 2¾" H	**Soup Bowl with Rim** 7¾" W, 1¼" H	**Cereal Bowl with Rim** 6" W, 1⅞" H / **Fruit Bowl with Rim** 5¼" W, 1¼" H
Sugar Bowl with Lid 6" W x 2⅞" H	**Creamer** 5⅞" W, 2⅝" H / **Covered Butter Dish ¼ Pound** 6¼" W x 2½" H	**Gravy/Sauce Boat** 7½" W, 2⅝" H	**Gravy/Sauce Boat Underplate/Relish** 8⅜" W x 5⅝" H	**Syrup/Pitcher with Lid** 5⅛" W x 5" H, 3¾" H without lid / **Batter Jug/Pitcher with Lid** 7⅛" W x 8" H
Covered Vegetable Bowl Rectangular 10¼" W x 4⅞" H	**Covered Butter Dish ½ Pound** 9" W x 3⅝" H	**Teapot with Lid** 8⅛" W, 4¾" H	**Gravy/Sauce Boat with Attached Underplate** 6⅞" W x 2⅞" H	**Salt & Pepper Set** 2¾" W, 2⅜" H RIVIERA PATTERNS ONLY

132

Century Shape

CENTURY 1931 – 1951 or later

Homer Laughlin introduced its new Century shape during the Great Depression in 1931. The square shape, with scalloped corners, taunted classic round dinnerware and was less formal and more playful than most European (and American) table settings at that time. It was a time in history when playfulness was welcomed and needed in the midst of bleakness. The Century shape is found with a great variety of decorations; with color bands, silver and gold applications, or assorted color decals. In the *Homer Laughlin Price Booklet of 1937*, the Century shape was offered with 94 different decorations/patterns.

It was also in 1931 that glass giant Fostoria, just a few short miles down the Ohio River in West Virginia, introduced a similarly shaped line of square dinnerware very much like Homer Laughlin's Century. Fostoria called their square shape Mayfair, and like Homer Laughlin's Century, it was the basis for several decorated patterns.

The Century shape, with the Vellum glaze, was listed in *Crockery and Glass Journal* (December, 1936) as a "1937 Preview" for the Pittsburgh show. Author Harvey Duke reports Century Vellum was introduced in 1931, with the inception of the shape. While traditional Century has a glossy surface glaze, Century Vellum has a soft matte finish described as being like "old polished ivory." Century typically will have a common "Homer Laughlin" backstamp, but might also be found with one of the "Wells" backstamps. This shape was widely produced into the 1940's, but production was limited for several years after that.

Century was widely distributed by consumer catalog. Butler Brothers, a wholesale distributor, offered three decorations on the Century shape in their November-December 1935 catalog. We see ads in the Montgomery Ward catalog starting with the 1936-37 Fall & Winter edition. Included at this time was the Briar Rose pattern which remained in the Montgomery Ward line through at least 1940. The 1951 Sears catalog shows a "Dick Tracy" child's set featuring a Century shaped plate as part of the set.

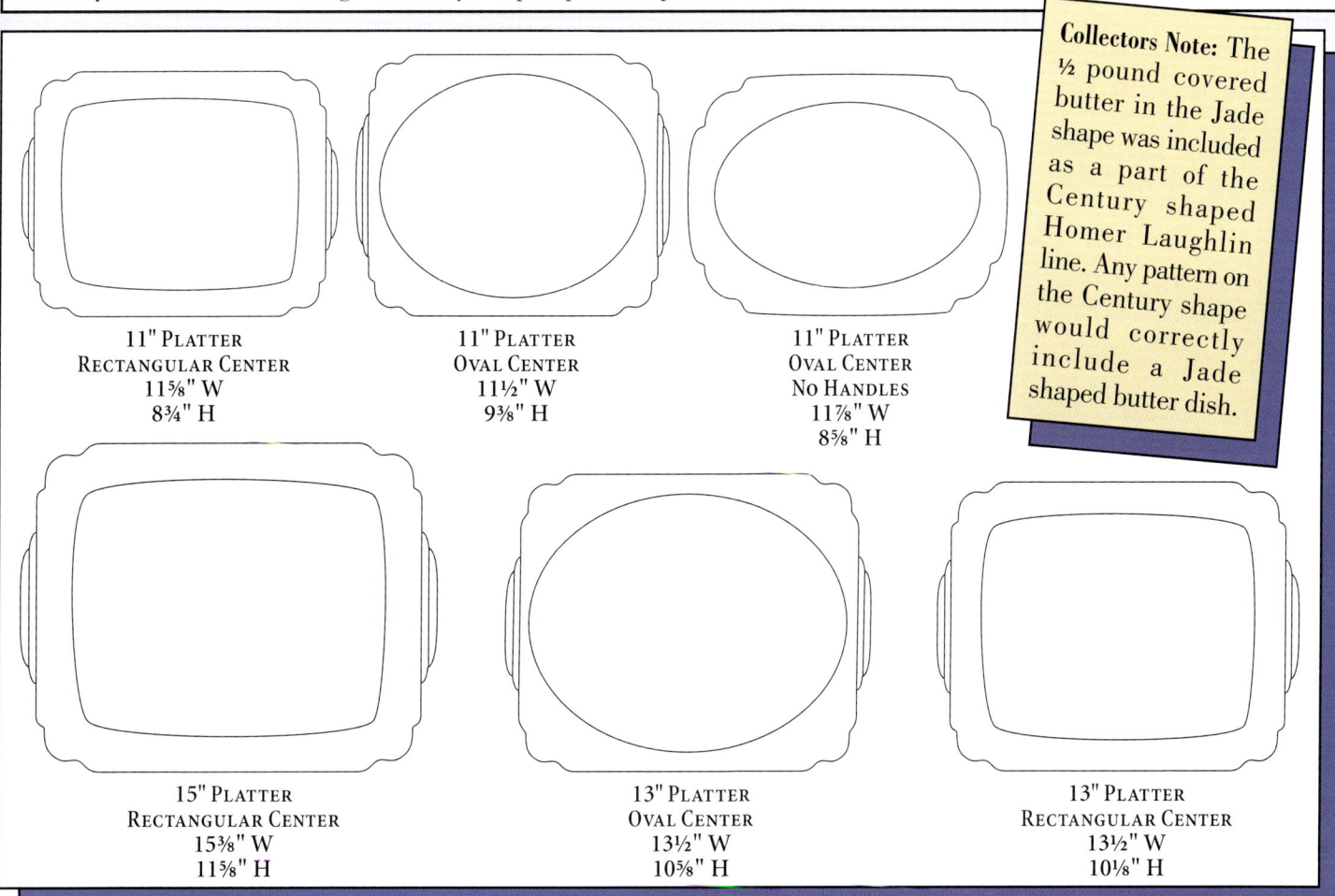

Collectors Note: The ½ pound covered butter in the Jade shape was included as a part of the Century shaped Homer Laughlin line. Any pattern on the Century shape would correctly include a Jade shaped butter dish.

| 11" Platter Rectangular Center 11⅝" W 8¾" H | 11" Platter Oval Center 11½" W 9⅜" H | 11" Platter Oval Center No Handles 11⅞" W 8⅝" H |

| 15" Platter Rectangular Center 15⅜" W 11⅝" H | 13" Platter Oval Center 13½" W 10⅝" H | 13" Platter Rectangular Center 13½" W 10⅛" H |

Homer Laughlin

VELLUM WARE

VELLUM WARE is the name of a non-reflecting texture developed to meet present day requirements for a dull finish tableware.

This tableware possesses the color and surface of old polished ivory and is the correct answer to the demand for an entirely new decorative effect.

The trend of design and texture of furniture, draperies, wall papers, rugs and glass has been towards the elimination of shining and glaring surfaces, but to date, existing tablewares have retained their glassy and highly reflective appearance.

The soft tone of the Vellum background is achieved through the combination of a rich old ivory and the sheen and glow of a satin-like glaze.

To emphasize the beauty of this new glaze, the Century square shape of pleasing simplicity and softly rounded angles was created.

A wide variety of modern naturalistic floral arrangements in delicate and warm colors complete a beautiful ensemble.

The charm and quality of this new Vellum Ware lends itself perfectly to delightful tablesettings. It is cheerful and bright at breakfast time, friendly and restful for luncheon, gay and intimate at teatime and under the candleglow of the dinner table it is a masterpiece of loveliness.

Top left: *Century Shape; Vellum Ware pamphlet, cover and inside, c. 1930's.*
Middle left: *Mexicana pattern; "Larkin China" by Walter Ayars, p163.*
Middle right: *HLC336 pattern; "Larkin China" by Walter Ayars, p130, 1933.*
Bottom left: *HLC895 pattern; Butler Brothers Catalog, 1935.*
Bottom right: *JJ50 pattern (left), unknown pattern (right); Butler Brothers Catalog, 1935.*

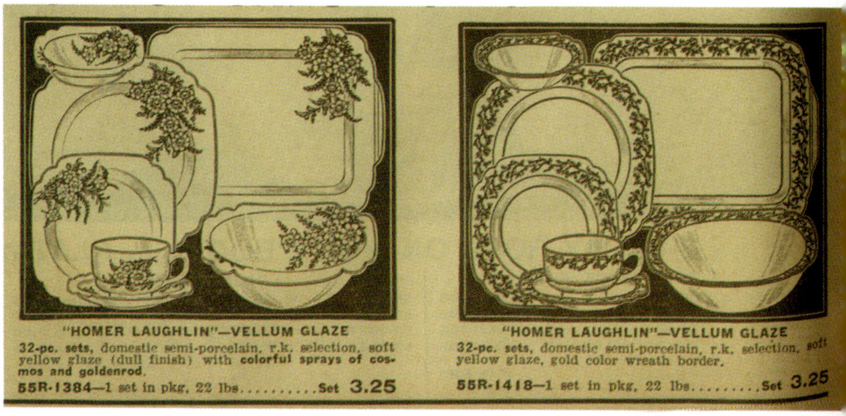

Century Shape

Briar Rose $5.79
USUAL $8.98 VALUE 32-Pc.

The special "vellum" glaze gives an unusual deep Ivory satin finish that harmonizes perfectly with the Wild Rose sprays of delicate pink and gray-green. Actually costs more to make than most Dinnerware because of its special glaze—yet Wards price for the 32-piece set is $3.19 less than you would usually pay.

Smart square plates. Gleaming platinum color line traces all edges. First quality, Triple-Selected American Semi-Porcelain. *All sets Mailable.* 95-pc. set shipped in 2 packages. For composition of sets see Page 319.

486 B 6291—32-Piece.
Service for 6. Ship. wt. 23 lbs. **$5.79**

586 B 6295—Creamer and Sugar. Ship. wt. 2 lbs. 8 oz **$1.60**

486 B 6292—53-Piece.
Service for 8. Ship. wt. 42 lbs. **$10.95**

386 B 6294—95-Piece.
Service for 12. Ship. wt. 76 lbs. **$19.95**

586 B6295—Open Stock. See Page 319.

Top left: *Briar Rose pattern; Montgomery Ward, 1936-37 Fall & Winter.* **Top right:** *Briar Rose pattern; Luncheon Plate, Bread & Butter Plate, and Cup & Saucer Set.* **Middle right:** *Briar Rose pattern; Platter with oval center, and Platter with rectangular center.* **Bottom left:** *C24 pattern; Soup Bowl with rim, and Cranberry Bowl.* **Bottom middle:** *C24 pattern; Gravy/Sauce Boat with attached Underplate.* **Bottom right:** *C24 pattern; Dinner Plate, Luncheon Plate, Bread & Butter Plate, and Cup & Saucer Set.*

Homer Laughlin

Top left: *C8 pattern; Oval Vegetable Bowl, Platter with rectangular center, Gravy/Sauce Boat, and Creamer.* **Top right:** *C33 pattern; 13" Platter with rectangular center, 11" Platter with rectangular center, and Covered Vegetable Bowl.* **Middle left:** *English Garden pattern; Cup & Saucer Set, Luncheon Plate, Salad Plate, and Bread & Butter Plate.* **Middle right:** *English Garden pattern; Round Vegetable Bowl, Platter with rectangular center, Fruit Bowl with rim, and in HLC2254 pattern, Soup Bowl with rim.* **Bottom left:** *English Garden pattern; Cup & Saucer Set, and Demitasse Cup & Saucer Set.* **Bottom right:** *English Garden pattern; Sugar Bowl with lid, and Creamer.*

RIVIERA

Century Shape
Riviera Line

CENTURY SHAPE – RIVIERA LINE   1938

The Century shape, when produced with a solid colored glaze, becomes the "Riviera" line. Riviera patterns were first made in 1938 and do not have backstamps. The colors considered to be Riviera are: Harlequin Yellow, Ivory, Light Green, Mauve Blue, and Red. Riviera pieces can also been found in Fiesta colors made for Fiesta Ensembles.

Above: Mauve Blue Oval Covered Vegetable Bowl, Red Syrup with lid, Light Green Pitcher with lid, Ivory Sugar Bowl with lid, and Yellow Teapot with lid.

Homer Laughlin

Top: *Yellow, Light Green, Red, and Mauve Blue Cup & Saucer Sets.* **Bottom:** *Yellow Cup, Light Green Saucer, Red Oval Vegetable Bowl, Yellow Platter with oval center, Mauve Blue Salad Plate, Red Syrup Pitcher with lid, Yellow Creamer, Light Green Mug, Red Pepper Shaker, Light Green Salt Shaker, and Mauve Blue Creamer.*

Century Shape
Riviera Line

Top left to bottom right: *Yellow Teapot with lid, Light Green Large Pitcher with lid, Red Syrup Pitcher with lid, Red Mug, Mauve Blue Sugar Bowl with lid and Creamer, Light Green Covered Vegetable Bowl, Ivory Cream Soup & Saucer Set, Yellow Platter with oval center, and Yellow Platter with rectangular center.*

139

Homer Laughlin

Above: Salt & Pepper Shakers in Ivory, Light Green, Mauve Blue, Yellow, and Red. **Top right:** Ivory Pattern; Platter oval center, Platter rectangular center, Soup Bowl with rim, Round Vegetable Bowl, Cup & Saucer Set, Cereal Bowl with rim, Salt Shaker, and Fruit Bowl with rim. **Bottom left:** Red ½ pound and ¼ pound Butter Dishes. **Bottom right:** Luncheon Plate, Salad Plate, and Cup & Saucer Set in Red, Ivory, Yellow, Light Green, and Mauve Blue; Yellow Teapot with lid.

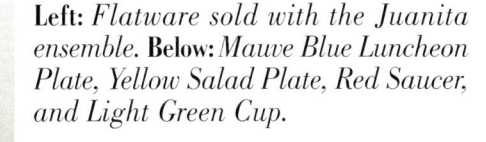

Century Shape
Riviera Line

Century/Riviera Piece Type List

From Homer Laughlin Catalog with Confirmed Actual Pieces

Bowl, Cereal (Oatmeal), 6 inches
Bowl, Cranberry (Deep, 1 pint), 4⅞ inches
Bowl, Cream Soup & Saucer Set
   Bowl, 6½ inches
   Saucer, 7 inches
Bowl, Fruit with rim, 5¼ inches
Bowl, (Onion Soup Lugged)*
Bowl, Oyster, 1 pint*
Bowl, Soup with rim (Plate), 7¾ inches
Bowl, Vegetable Oval (Baker), 8¼ inches
Bowl, Vegetable Oval (Baker), 9 inches
Bowl, Vegetable Oval Covered (Casserole), 10¼ inches
Bowl, Vegetable Round (Nappy), 7 inches
Bowl, Vegetable Round (Nappy), 8 inches
Bowl, Vegetable Round (Nappy), 9¼ inches
Butter Dish with lid, ¼ pound

Butter Dish with lid, ½ pound
Creamer
Cup & Saucer Set
   Cup, 2¼ inches
   Saucer, 5⅞ inches
Cup & Saucer Set, Coffee*
Cup & Saucer Set, Demitasse
   Cup, 2⅛ inches
   Saucer, 4⅞ inches
Eggcup, Double
Gravy/Sauce Boat
Gravy/Sauce Boat Underplate/Relish, 8⅜ inches
Gravy/Sauce Boat with attached Underplate
Muffin Cover
Mug, 4¾ inches
Pitcher, ⅝ pints*
Pitcher, Batter Jug with lid, 8 inches
Pitcher, Juice
Pitcher, Syrup with lid, ⅝ pints
Plate, Bread & Butter, 6¼ inches
Plate, Cake, 11½ inches

Plate, Dessert, 7 inches
Plate, Dinner, 9⅝ inches
Plate, Dinner Large, 10 inches
Plate, Grill, 9¾ inches
Plate, Luncheon, 8¾ inches
Plate, Salad, 7¾ inches
Platter, 10 inches*
Platter, oval well, 11½ inches
Platter, oval well, no handles, 11⅞ inches
Platter, oval well, 13½ inches
Platter, rectangular well, 11⅝ inches
Platter, rectangular well, 13½ inches
Platter, rectangular well, 15⅜ inches
Platter Square, rectangular well, bigger handles, 11½ inches
Salt & Pepper Set
Sugar Bowl with lid
Teapot with lid
Tumbler, Juice

*Reported but not confirmed.

Juanita Dinnerware Service

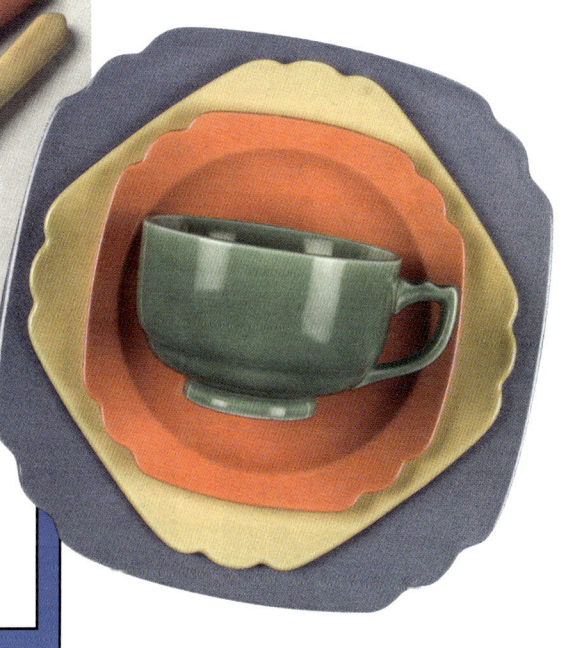

The Juanita Dinnerware Service was marketed much like the Fiesta Ensemble, primarily by furniture companies as a promotion. It was a 119 piece set made up of a 48-piece dinnerware set of Riviera (complete service for 8), a 26-piece flatware set imaged above, and a 48-piece glassware set of clear glasses with solid colored bands. The glassware and flatware were made by other companies for Homer Laughlin. In the late 1930's, this service could be purchased with a payment plan of $1.00 down and 50¢ per month.

Left: *Flatware sold with the Juanita ensemble.* **Below:** *Mauve Blue Luncheon Plate, Yellow Salad Plate, Red Saucer, and Light Green Cup.*

Century Shape (No Trim)

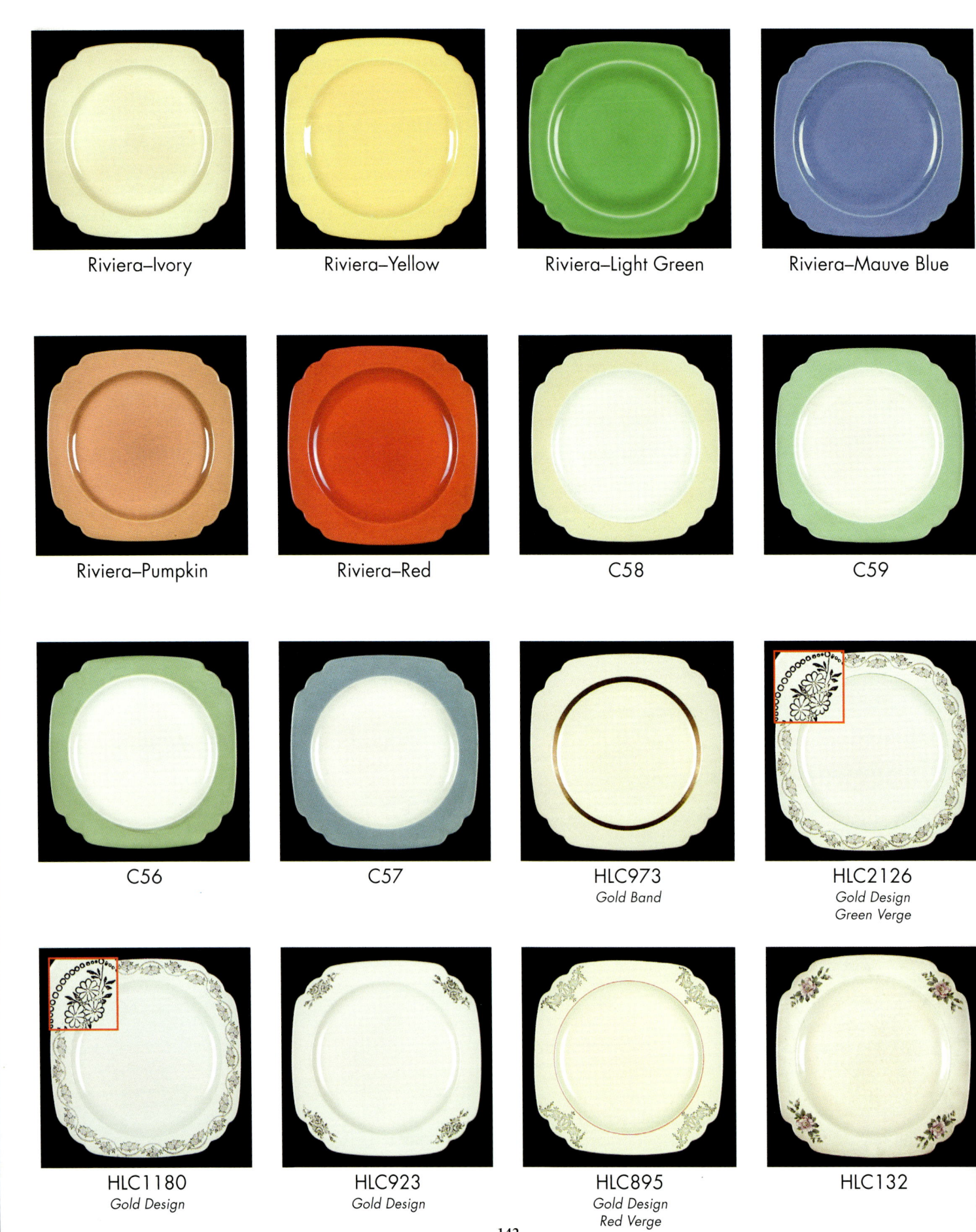

Riviera–Ivory	Riviera–Yellow	Riviera–Light Green	Riviera–Mauve Blue
Riviera–Pumpkin	Riviera–Red	C58	C59
C56	C57	HLC973 *Gold Band*	HLC2126 *Gold Design* *Green Verge*
HLC1180 *Gold Design*	HLC923 *Gold Design*	HLC895 *Gold Design* *Red Verge*	HLC132

Century Shape (No Trim)

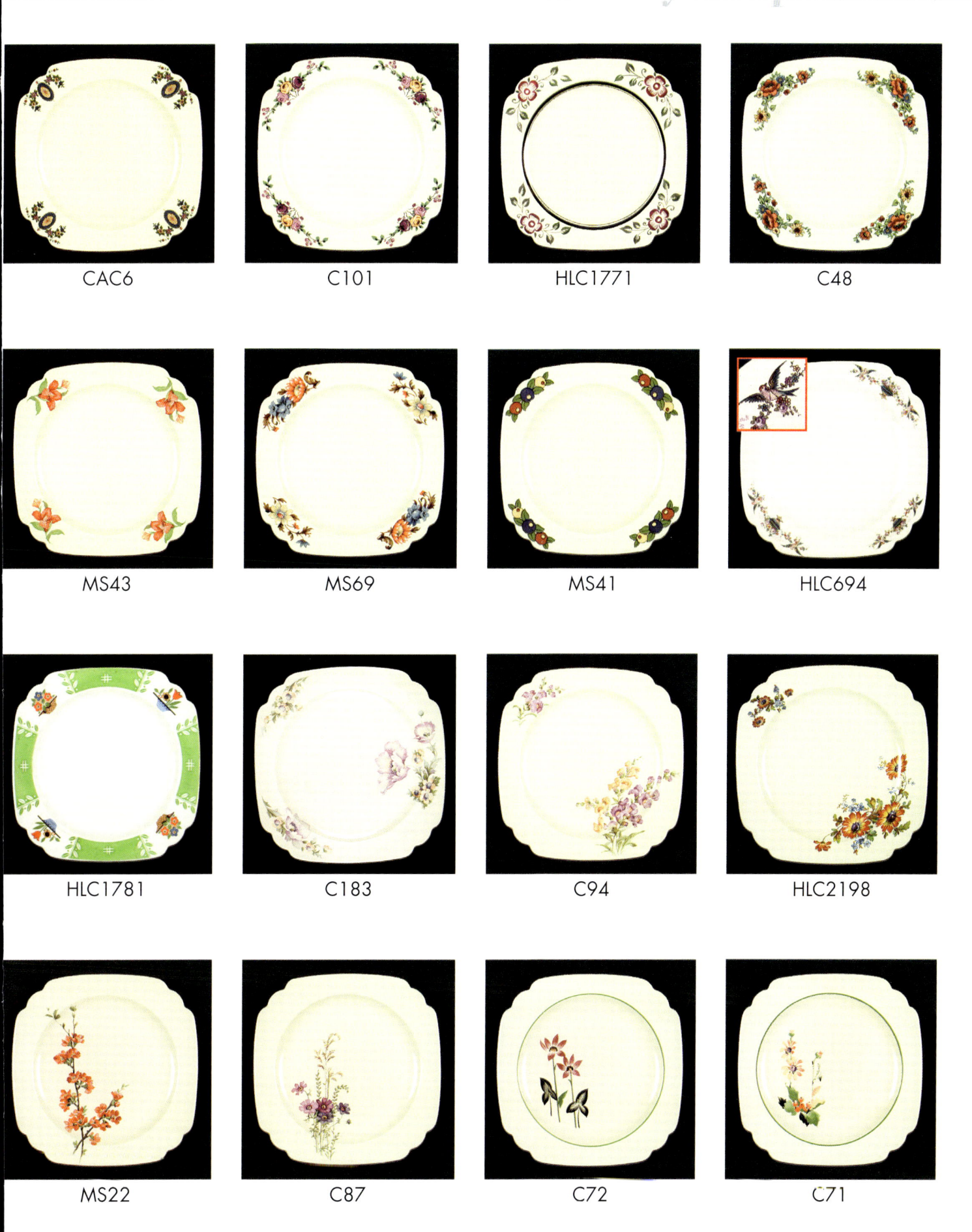

CAC6	C101	HLC1771	C48
MS43	MS69	MS41	HLC694
HLC1781	C183	C94	HLC2198
MS22	C87	C72	C71

143

Century Shape (No Trim)

TS2	MS146	Columbine	C65
C64	Conchita	Mexicana	Hacienda
Old English Scene	C99	CAC55	C73
HLC2040	HLC2134 *Platter Shown*	HLC1247	HLC1125

Century Shape (With Trim)

HLC2128 *Platinum Trim*	**C96** *Black Verge Platinum Trim*	**C15** *Gold Trim*	**HLC724** *Platinum Trim*
C14 *Gold Trim*	**HLC2124** *Green Trim*	**C7** *Green Trim*	**HLC569** *Blue Trim*
HLC2131 *also known as "Royal Gold" by Pearl China Gold Trim*	**HLC718** *Bread & Butter Plate Shown Gold Trim*	**HLC1504** *Gold Trim*	**Rose Medallion** *C114 Platinum Trim*
HLC1071 *Platinum Trim*	**HLC495** *Platinum Trim*	**C43** *Gold Trim*	**C106** *Platinum Trim*

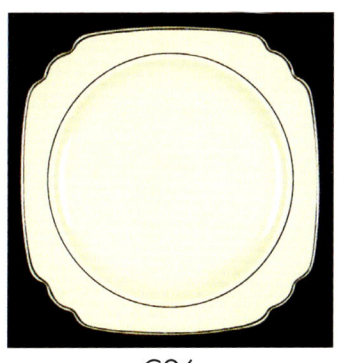

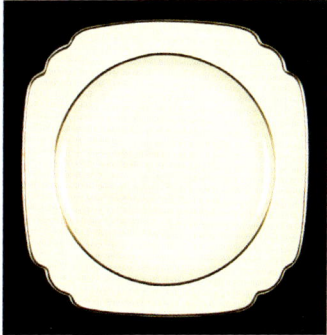

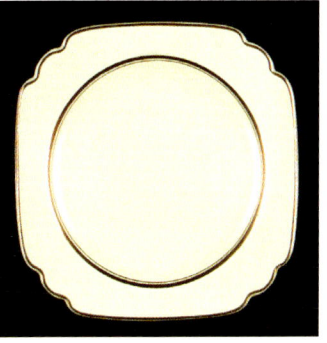

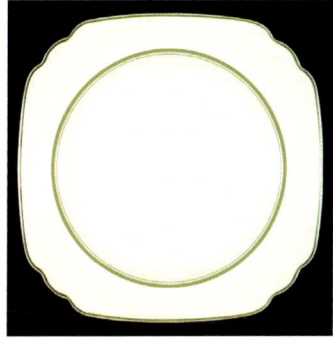

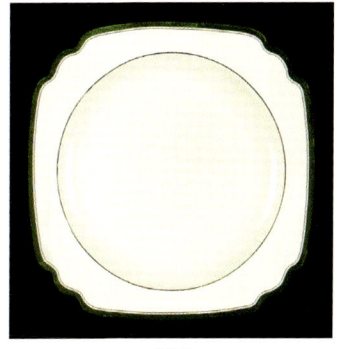

Century Shape (With Trim)

C207 *Gold Trim*	**C110** *Platinum Trim*	**1180C** *Green Trim*	**C116** *Platinum Trim*
HLC182 *Bread & Butter Plate Shown Platinum Trim*	**JJ50** *Gold Trim*	**HLC336** *also known as "Ohio" by Pearl China Platinum Trim*	**C205** *Gold Trim*
C107 *Platinum Trim*	**C82** *Gold Trim*	**Briar Rose** *Platinum Trim*	**C84** *Gold Trim*
HLC2197 *Platinum Trim*	**C3** *Platinum Trim*	**R1275** *Gold Trim*	**C17** *Gold Trim*

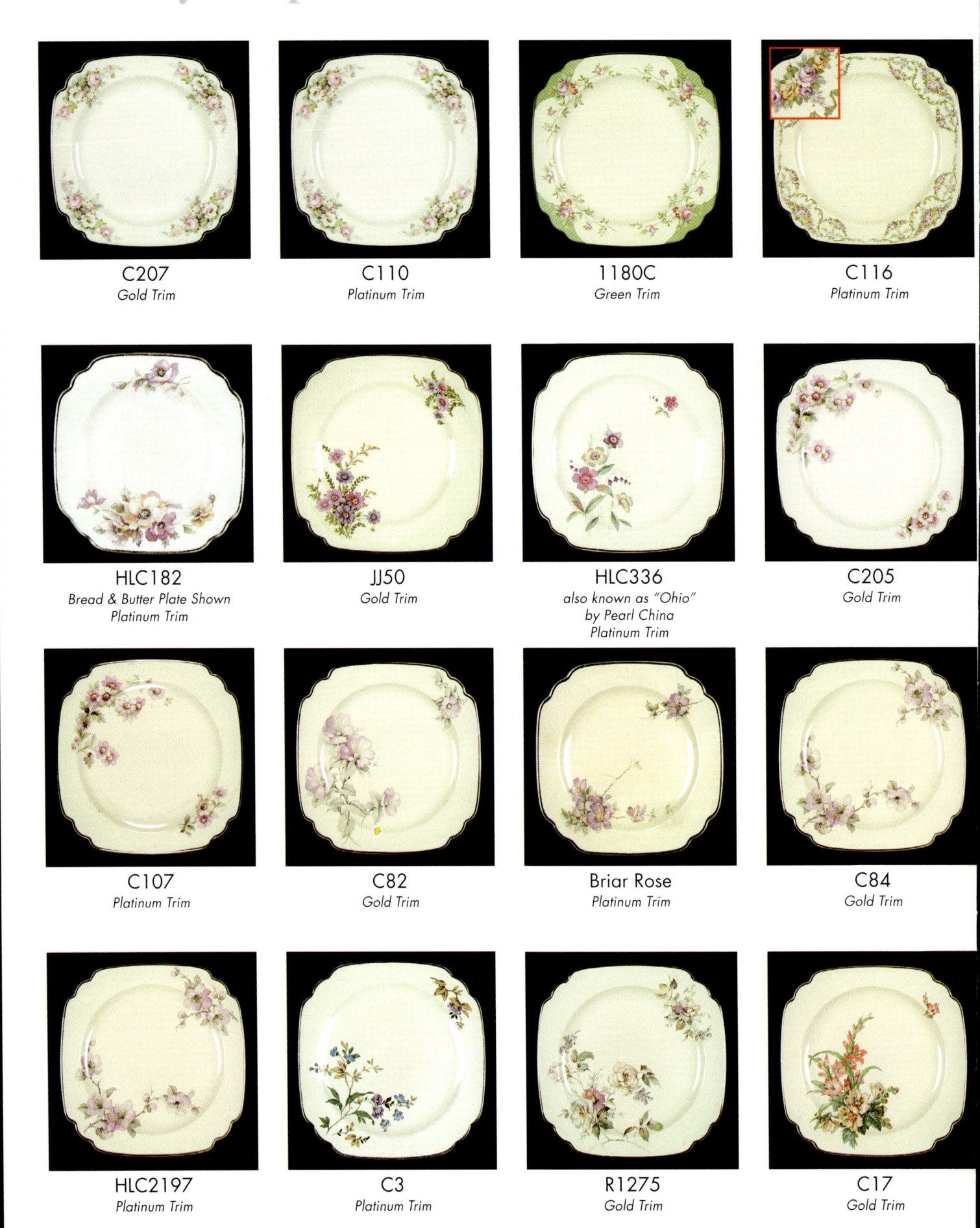

Century Shape (With Trim)

C79/C124 *Green Trim*	**C204** *Gold Trim*	**C33** *Platinum Trim*	**C29** *Gold Trim*
HLC2021 *Vegetable Bowl Shown Platinum Trim*	**C28** *Orange Trim*	**C129** *Gold Trim*	**C41** *Gold Trim*
C61 *Gold Trim*	**HLC1629** *Gold Trim*	**C121** *Platinum Trim*	**C108** *Platinum Trim*
C6 *Gold Trim*	**C206** *Blue Trim*	**C77** *Gold Trim*	**C202** *Gold Trim*

Century Shape (With Trim)

C21 *Gold Trim*	 **C203** *Platinum Trim*	 **C8** *Platinum Trim*	 **C95** *Gold Trim*
 **C24** *Platinum Trim*	 **C23** *Green Trim*	 **English Garden** *Green Trim*	 **HLC2254** *Soup Bowl Shown Green Trim*
 **HLC3086** *Platter Shown Orange Trim*	 **C97** *Gold Trim*	 **HLC1144** *Gold Trim*	 **HLC892** *Gold Trim*
 **Garland** *C45, C132 Gold Trim*			

Ravenna

Left: *Unknown pattern; Sears, Roebuck & Co., 1932-1933.*
Right: *Typical Ravenna backstamp.*

RAVENNA 1932 – 1933 or later

Similar to Orleans, Ravenna was designed in the early 1930's when Homer Laughlin was experimenting with embossed dinnerware. English ceramist Frederick Rhead had joined Homer Laughlin in 1927, and the English influence is evident in both the Ravenna and Orleans lines. Ravenna, like other embossed shapes, was short-lived. Possibly the success of Virginia Rose, an embossed line reportedly introduced in 1929, led Homer Laughlin to try other embossed shapes? Ravenna patterns were usually created by applying decal decorations on white ware, no solid color Ravenna is known.

The Sears mail order catalogs of 1932 and 1933 feature three Ravenna shaped patterns. Ravenna is often an overlooked Homer Laughlin shape because pieces may not have a backstamp. Other times pieces may be marked "Ravenna," making no mention of Homer Laughlin, or they may have a traditional Homer Laughlin backstamp. It is not uncommon for variances in backstamps to be found within a single Ravenna pattern.

Ravenna Piece Type List

From Homer Laughlin Literature with Confirmed Actual Pieces

- Bowl, Fruit, 5½ inches
- Bowl, Vegetable Oval, 9¼ inches
- Bowl, Vegetable Round, 8¼ inches
- Creamer, ½ pint
- Cup & Saucer Set
- Gravy/Sauce Boat
- Plate, Bread & Butter, 7 inches
- Plate, Dinner, 10 inches
- Plate, Luncheon/Salad, 9 inches
- Platter, 11⅛ inches
- Platter, 13¼ inches
- Sugar Bowl with lid

Ravenna Shape

R3734 Platinum Trim	**RV1043** No Trim	**RV28** Black Verge No Trim	**RV34** No Trim
RV27 Green Verge No Trim	**RV1143** No Trim	**RV9233** No Trim	**RV45** No Trim
RV1343 No Trim	**RV9533** Green Verge No Trim	**RV49** No Trim	**RV31** No Trim
RV44 No Trim	**4812B** Black Verge No Trim	**RV25** Black Verge No Trim	**RV12** Green Verge No Trim

Ravenna Shape

RV20 Black Verge No Trim	**RV23** No Trim	**RV5** Black Verge No Trim	**RV36** No Trim
RV7 Green Verge No Trim	**RV43** No Trim	**RV47/RV52** No Trim	**RV39** No Trim
RV41 Platinum Trim	**RV50** Gold Trim	**RV19** Green Verge No Trim	**CAC24** No Trim
HLC1014 Salad Plate Shown No Trim	**RV48** No Trim	**R8533** No Trim	**R8733** No Trim

Ravenna Shape

HLC1157
No Trim

R8333
No Trim

RV4
No Trim

RV3
Green Verge
No Trim

RV46
No Trim

Left: *Rosemary, Wind-Blown, and Springtime patterns; Sears, Roebuck & Co. Catalog, 1932-1933.*

JADE

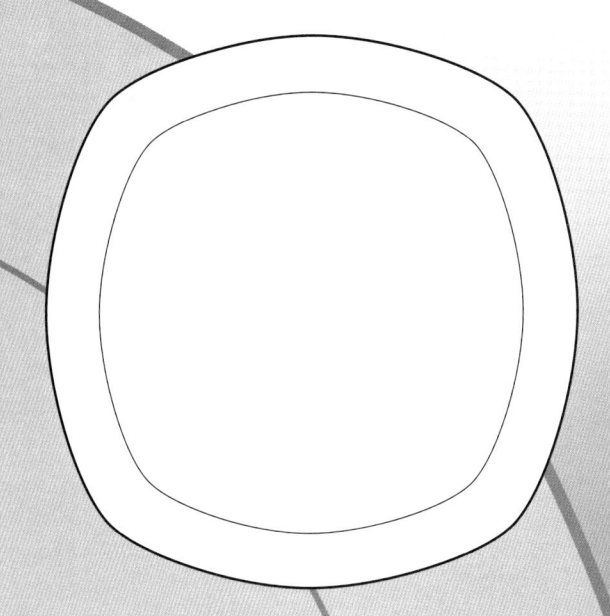

Piece Types

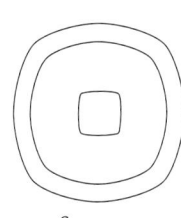

These drawings were made from actual stock at Replacements, Ltd. Check the piece type list for all known piece types in this shape.

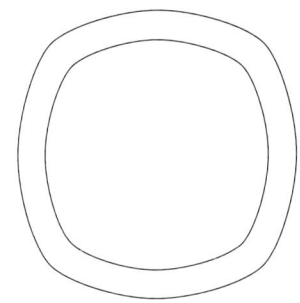

Dinner Plate	Salad Plate	Dessert Plate	Bread & Butter Plate	Saucer	Cup
9⅞" D	8" D	7" D	6" D	6" D	5¾" W, 2¼" H

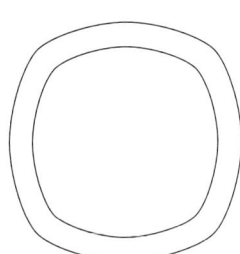

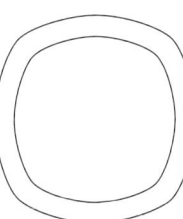

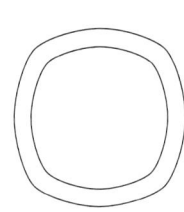

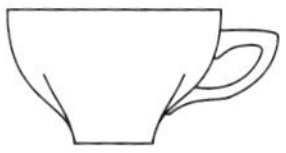

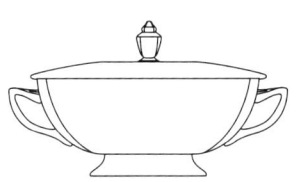

Square Covered Vegetable Bowl	Gravy Boat with attached Underplate	Gravy/Sauce Boat	Sugar Bowl with lid	Creamer	Cranberry Bowl
9¾" W x 5¼" H	8⅛" W, 2¾" H	7⅞" W, 3" H	5⅛" W, 4⅜" H	5⅜" W, 4" H	5⅛" W, 2¾" H

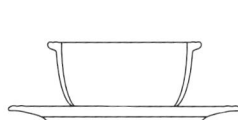

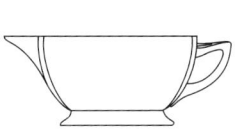

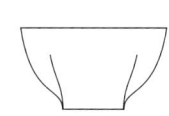

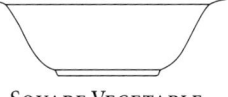

Square Vegetable Bowl	Square Vegetable Bowl	Rectangular Vegetable Bowl	Cereal Bowl	Soup Bowl with Rim
8¼" W, 2¾" H	7⅜" W, 2½" H	8⅞" W, 1¾" H	6⅛" W, 1¾" H	8" W x 1⅜" H

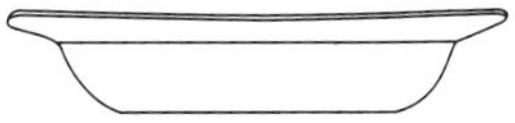

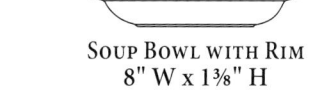

13" Platter	11" Platter	Cake/Chop Plate	Gravy/Sauce Boat Underplate/Relish	Covered Butter Dish Rectangular
13¼" W, 10" H	11⅝" W, 8⅞" H	10½" W, 11⅜" H	8⅞" W x 5¾" H	9" W x 3⅝" H

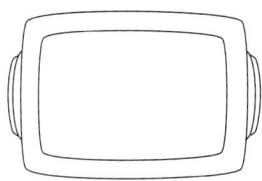

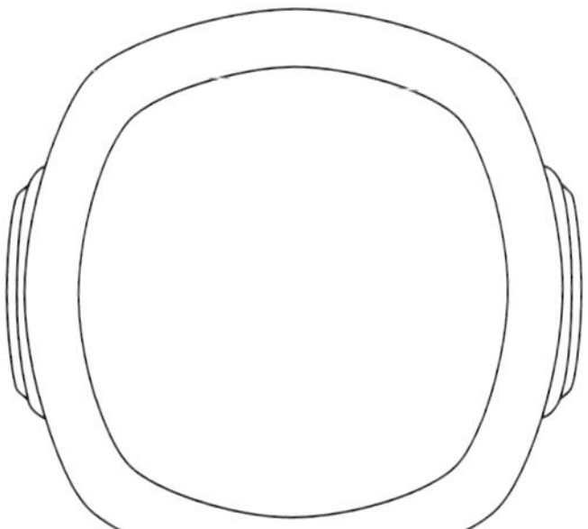

153

Homer Laughlin

JADE 1932 – circa 1936

Jade was introduced in 1932. Sears offered a pattern, "The Romance" on the Jade shape in their 1932 catalog, but had no offerings on the Jade shape in their 1933 catalog. During the Great Depression the "modern" rounded square shapes of Jade were a pleasant diversion from tradition, but perhaps too much of a diversion? It appears to have been in production a relatively short time. An original art mock-up for a 1933 Homer Laughlin catalog, found at the factory, included the Jade shape. The latest backstamp found by the authors was a Homer Laughlin 1934 traditional mark. Jade does not appear in any Homer Laughlin offerings after 1937.

A wonderful art quality glaze called Clair de Lune by Homer Laughlin was utilized on the Jade shape to create a soft "moonlight" colored body of a pale blue/green. Clair de Lune glazed pieces have gained a collector following. Jade pieces often bear no backstamp, making them difficult to identify as Homer Laughlin. Some Jade pieces have the multicolored, elaborate Wells peacock backstamp. This is thought to indicate the vellum or matte yellow glaze and not denote the pattern or shape.

Above left: The Romance pattern; Sears, Roebuck & Co. Catalog, 1932–33 Fall & Winter. Above right: Multi-Colored peacock Jade backstamp. Right: The Romance pattern; Soup Bowl with rim, Bread & Butter Plate, Platter, Creamer, Cup & Saucer Set, and Sugar Bowl with lid.

Jade Shape

Top left: J62 pattern; Dinner Plate, Salad Plate, Bread & Butter Plate, Oval Vegetable Bowl, Round Vegetable Bowl, Cup & Saucer Set, and Soup Bowl with rim. **Top right:** J62 pattern; Platter, Cake/Chop Plate, Gravy/Sauce Boat, Creamer, Covered Vegetable Bowl, and Covered Butter Dish. **Middle right:** HLC541 pattern; Sugar Bowl missing lid, Dinner Plate, Salad Plate, Covered Butter Dish, Gravy/Sauce Boat with attached Underplate, Pickle Dish, Cup & Saucer Set, and Cranberry Bowl. **Bottom left:** HLC541 pattern; Cereal Bowl, Round Vegetable Bowl, and Soup Bowl with rim. **Bottom right:** J213 pattern; Platter, Oval Vegetable Bowl, and Bread & Butter Plate.

Homer Laughlin

Jade Piece Type List

From 1933 Homer Laughlin Catalog Supplemented with Confirmed Actual Pieces

Bowl, Cereal, 6⅛ inches
Bowl, Cranberry, 5⅛ inches
Bowl, Cream Soup & Saucer Set
Bowl, Fruit*
Bowl, Soup with rim, 8 inches
Bowl, Vegetable Rectangular, 8⅞ inches
Bowl, Vegetable Rectangular, 9⅞ inches
Bowl, Vegetable Square, 7⅜ inches
Bowl, Vegetable Square, 8¼ inches
Bowl, Vegetable Square Covered, 9¾ inches
Butter Dish, Rectangular with lid
Coffeepot with lid
Creamer

Cup & Saucer Set
   Cup, 2¼ inches, 7 ounces
   Saucer, 6 inches
Cup & Saucer Set, Boullion*
Cup & Saucer Set, Coffee*
Cup & Saucer Set, Demitasse*
Gravy/Sauce Boat, one handle
Gravy/Sauce Boat with attached Underplate, handleless
Gravy/Sauce Boat Underplate/Relish, 8⅞ inches
Pitcher, Batter with lid
Pitcher, Batter without lid
Pitcher, Syrup with lid

Pitcher, Syrup without lid
Plate, Bread & Butter, 6 inches
Plate, Cake/Chop, 10½ inches
Plate, Dessert, 7 inches
Plate, Dinner, 9⅞ inches
Plate, Luncheon
Plate, Salad, 8 inches
Platter, 11⅝ inches
Platter, 13¼ inches
Platter, 15⅛ inches
Sugar Bowl with lid
*Reported but not confirmed.

Collectors Note: The Gravy/Sauce Boat with unattached Underplate is rectangular, the Gravy/Sauce with attached Underplate is handleless and square.

Collectors Note: The butter dish originally designed for Jade is the same shape as the butter dish for Virginia Rose and Riviera shaped patterns.

Above: *Original artwork for a Jade, Clair de Lune Glaze pamphlet.* **Left:** *Clair de Lune backstamps.*

Jade Shape

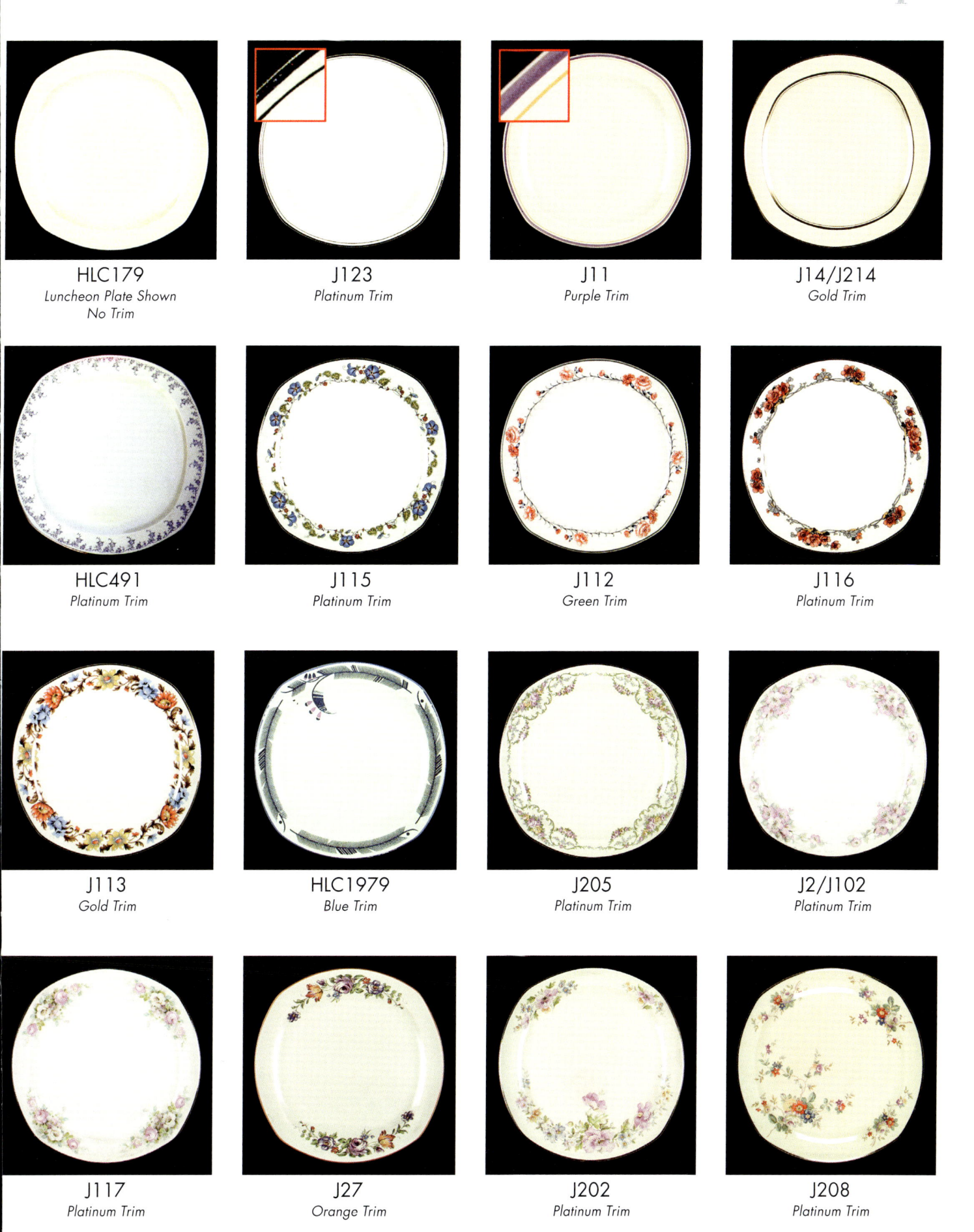

HLC179 *Luncheon Plate Shown No Trim*	**J123** *Platinum Trim*	**J11** *Purple Trim*	**J14/J214** *Gold Trim*
HLC491 *Platinum Trim*	**J115** *Platinum Trim*	**J112** *Green Trim*	**J116** *Platinum Trim*
J113 *Gold Trim*	**HLC1979** *Blue Trim*	**J205** *Platinum Trim*	**J2/J102** *Platinum Trim*
J117 *Platinum Trim*	**J27** *Orange Trim*	**J202** *Platinum Trim*	**J208** *Platinum Trim*

Jade Shape

J4 *Platinum Trim*	**J5/J105** *Platinum Trim*	**J209** *Platinum Trim*	**J6/J106** *Platinum Trim*
J201 *Platinum Trim*	**The Romance** *Platinum Trim*	**HLC2091** *Platinum Trim*	**J62** *Platinum Trim*
J212 *Platinum Trim*	**J41** *Platinum Trim*	**J37** *Platinum Trim*	**J9** *Platinum Trim*
J3 *Platinum Trim*	**J30** *Green Trim*	**J44** *Platinum Trim*	**J224** *Platinum Trim*

Jade Shape

HLC541	J43	1121RG	J213
Green Trim	Platinum Trim	Platinum Trim	Orange Trim

J36	J7/J207	HLC3103	HLC1975
Yellow Trim	Green Trim	Blue Trim	Luncheon Plate Shown Platinum Trim

Rear View of Plant No. 4, Homer Laughlin China Co., Newell, W. Va.

Above: *Plant rear view, photograph from the Factory.*

159

Orleans

Piece Types

These drawings were made from actual stock or literature at Replacements, Ltd. Check the piece type list for all known piece types in this shape.

Luncheon Plate
9¼" D

Bread & Butter Plate
6½" D

Saucer
5⅞" D

Cup
2⅜" W

Creamer

Sugar Bowl
MISSING LID

11" Platter
11½" W
9" H

Round Vegetable Bowl
9¾" W
3⅛" H

Round Vegetable Bowl
8⅞" W
3" H

Oval Vegetable Bowl
9¼" W
1¾" H

Fruit Bowl
5⅝" W
1½" H

Right: W232 pattern; Round Vegetable Bowl.

Orleans Shape

ORLEANS
1932 – until after 1941 (Harvey Duke)

Orleans is another of the Homer Laughlin early 1930's shapes with a heavily embossed border. Authors have noted its resemblance to Ovenserve and Ravenna. Orleans is found predominately as white ware with decal decoration; however, some solid colored pieces are reported. The art glazed pieces may bear a backstamp of "Antique Orleans," while decorated pieces bear a Homer Laughlin backstamp.

In *The Homer Laughlin Company Pound Sterling Price Booklet of 1937*, Orleans is listed with 15 different decorations/patterns offered.

Orleans Piece Type List
From Homer Laughlin Literature with Confirmed Actual Pieces

Bowl, Cereal (Oatmeal)*
Bowl, Fruit, 5⅝ inches
Bowl, Soup Coupe, 7 inches*
Bowl, Soup with rim
Bowl, Vegetable Oval, 8¼ inches*
Bowl, Vegetable Oval, 9¼ inches
Bowl, Vegetable Rectangular Covered
Bowl, Vegetable Round, 8⅞ inches
Bowl, Vegetable Round, 9¾ inches

Creamer
Cup & Saucer Set
   Cup, 2⅜ inches
   Saucer, 5⅞ inches
Gravy/Sauce Boat
Pickle*
Pitcher/Jug
Plate, Bread & Butter, 6½ inches
Plate, Dessert, 7½ inches*

Plate, Dinner, 10¼ inches*
Plate, Luncheon, 9¼ inches
Plate, Salad, 8⅜ inches*
Platter, 10½ inches*
Platter, 11½ inches
Platter, 13 inches*
Sugar Bowl, Open
Sugar Bowl with lid
*Reported but not confirmed.

Collectors Note: There are two sugar bowls in the Orleans shape. The first sugar bowl was designed without a lid and has handles that rise above the opening of the bowl. Later, a second sugar bowl was designed with a lid and handles that are much lower.

Left: *O12 pattern; Oval Platter, Dinner Plate, Bread & Butter Plate, Cup & Saucer Set, Oval Vegetable Bowl, and Fruit Bowl.*

Orleans Shape

Antique–Burnt Orange
Bread & Butter Plate Shown
No Trim

HLC3092
Platinum Trim

O45
Platinum Trim

O43
No Trim

O34
No Trim

O60
No Trim

O32
No Trim

O63
No Trim

O10
No Trim

O19
No Trim

O35
Platinum Trim

O31
No Trim

O27
No Trim

W232
No Trim

O25
No Trim

O12
Luncheon Plate Shown
No Trim

162

Orleans Shape

HLC2181 *Platinum Trim*	**O65** *Gold Trim*	**O28** *Platinum Trim*	**O52** *No Trim*
O37 *No Trim*	**O79** *No Trim*	**O16** *No Trim*	**O56** *Platinum Trim*
O39 *No Trim*	**W142** *No Trim*		

Right: *Slip filler, photograph found at the Factory.*

Old Roman

Piece Types

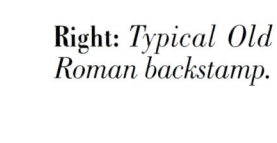

These drawings were made from actual stock or literature at Replacements, Ltd. Check the piece type list for all known piece types in this shape.

Right: *Typical Old Roman backstamp.*

| Dinner Plate | Square Salad Plate | Saucer 6" D | Cup 4⅝" W 2½" H | Sugar Bowl Open | Creamer |

OLD ROMAN
circa 1932 (H. Duke)

The creation of the Old Roman line was likely influenced by the ancient art and architecture of the Roman Empire. The classical design of plants and urns within the embossed rim is reminiscent of other more popular lines produced by companies in America and England. The rope edge outlining the scalloped shape enhances the embossing, creating a very elegant line. Whether decorated by a pinstripe or heavier coloration, Old Roman is a mastery of design in its own right.

Above: *HLC2038 pattern; Cup & Saucer Set.*

Old Roman Piece Type List

From Homer Laughlin Literature with Confirmed Actual Pieces

Bowl, Fruit
Bowl, Soup with rim
Bowl, Vegetable Oval
Creamer

Cup & Saucer Set
Cup, 2½" H
Saucer, 6 inches
Plate, Bread & Butter

Plate, Dinner
Plate, Salad Square
Platter, Oval
Sugar Bowl, Open

Old Roman Shape

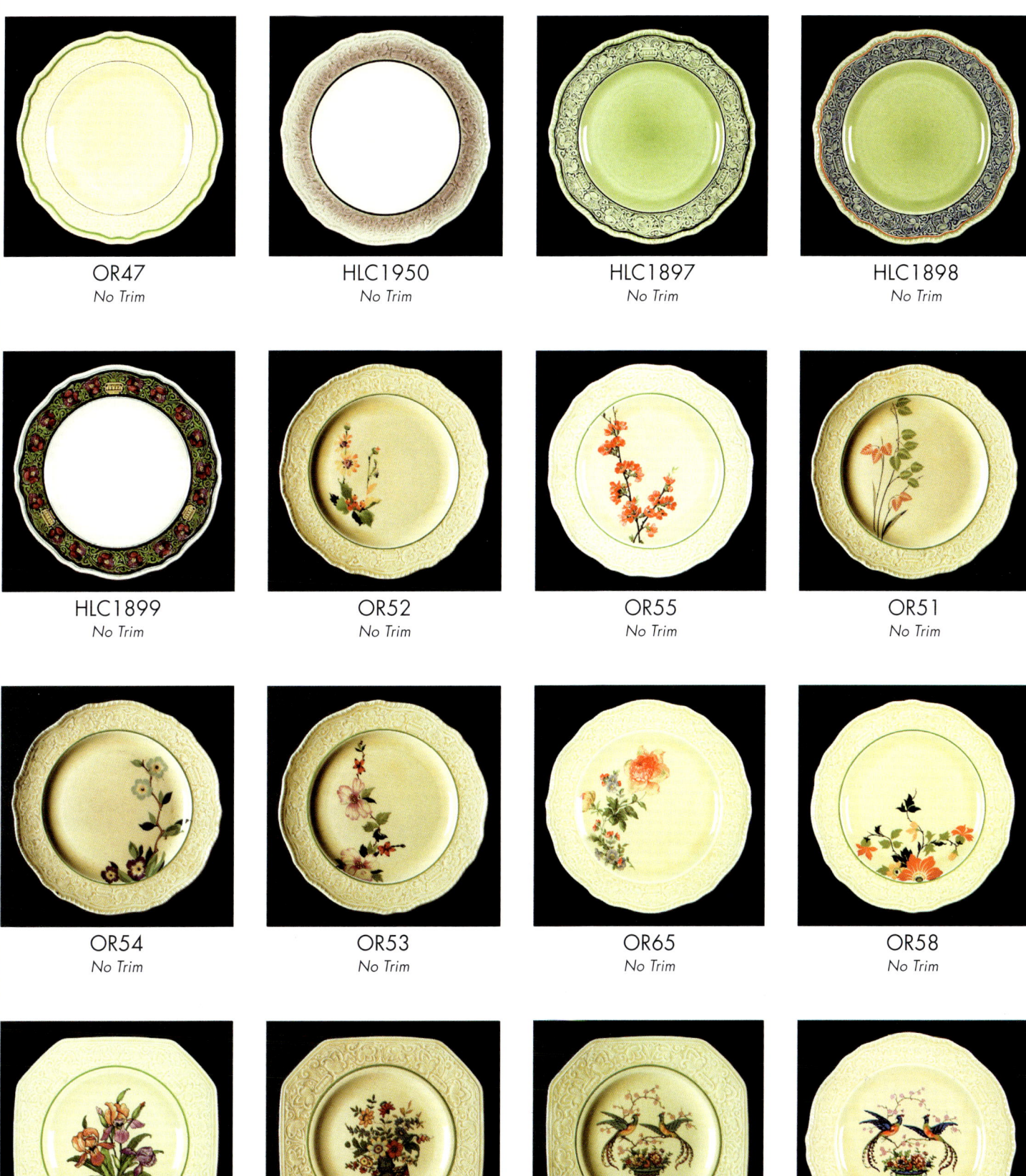

OR47	HLC1950	HLC1897	HLC1898
No Trim	No Trim	No Trim	No Trim

HLC1899	OR52	OR55	OR51
No Trim	No Trim	No Trim	No Trim

OR54	OR53	OR65	OR58
No Trim	No Trim	No Trim	No Trim

OR72	OR73	OR78	HLC2161
Square Salad Plate Shown No Trim	Square Salad Plate Shown No Trim	Square Salad Plate Shown No Trim	No Trim

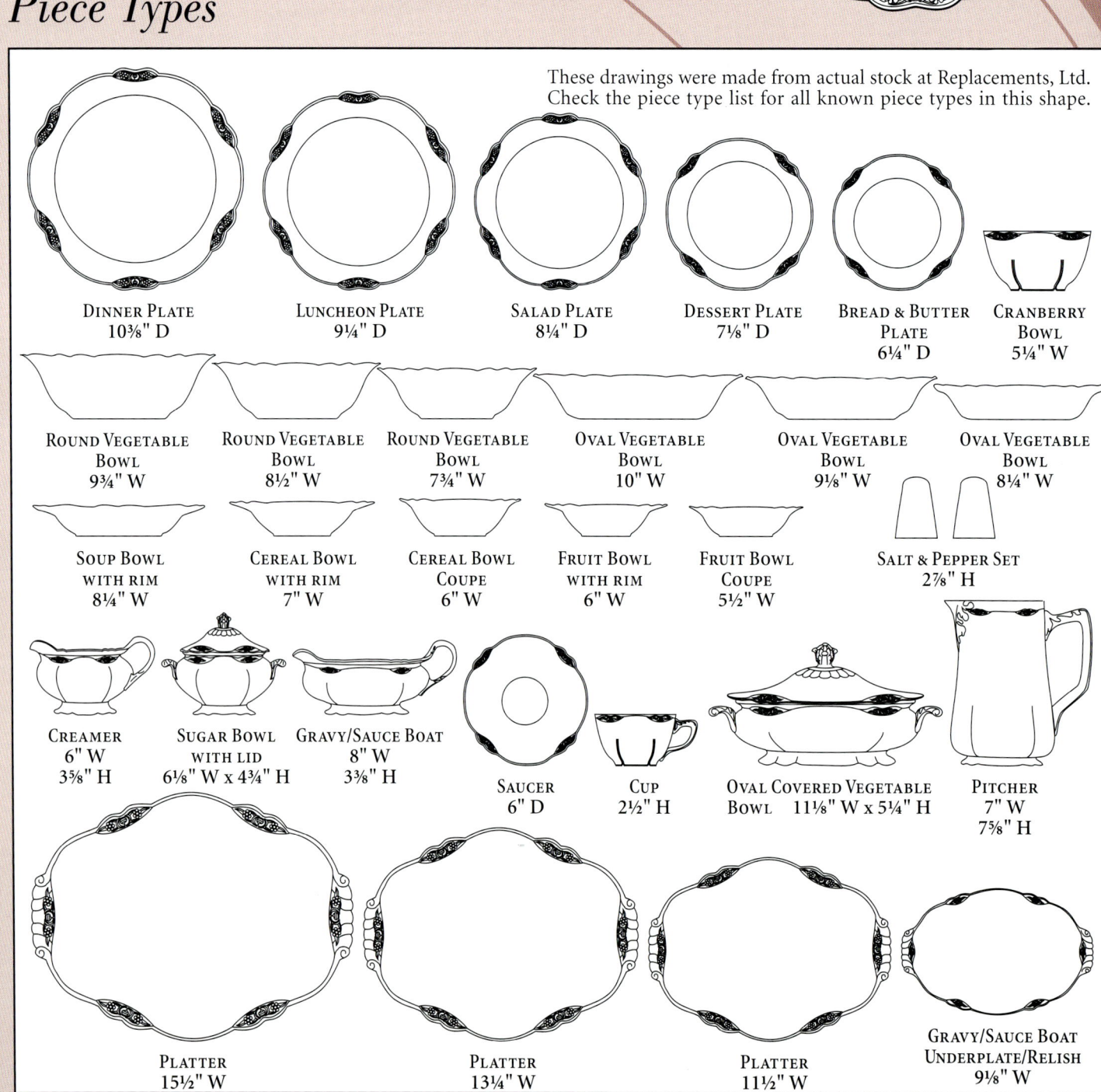

VIRGINIA ROSE

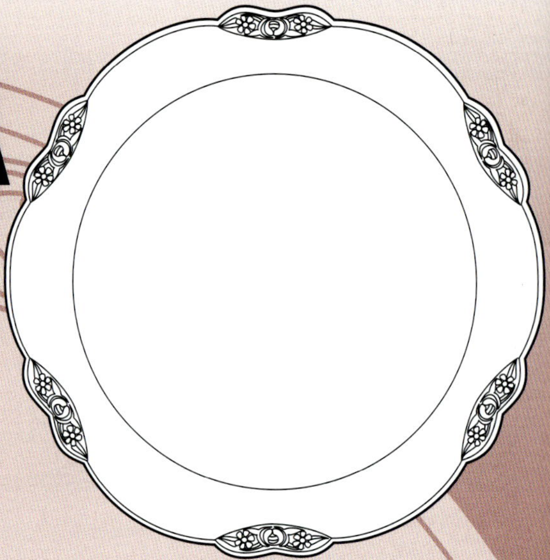

Piece Types

These drawings were made from actual stock at Replacements, Ltd. Check the piece type list for all known piece types in this shape.

Dinner Plate 10⅜" D	**Luncheon Plate** 9¼" D	**Salad Plate** 8¼" D	**Dessert Plate** 7⅛" D	**Bread & Butter Plate** 6¼" D	**Cranberry Bowl** 5¼" W
Round Vegetable Bowl 9¾" W	**Round Vegetable Bowl** 8½" W	**Round Vegetable Bowl** 7¾" W	**Oval Vegetable Bowl** 10" W	**Oval Vegetable Bowl** 9⅛" W	**Oval Vegetable Bowl** 8¼" W
Soup Bowl with Rim 8¼" W	**Cereal Bowl with Rim** 7" W	**Cereal Bowl Coupe** 6" W	**Fruit Bowl with Rim** 6" W	**Fruit Bowl Coupe** 5½" W	**Salt & Pepper Set** 2⅞" H

Creamer 6" W 3⅝" H
Sugar Bowl with Lid 6⅛" W x 4¾" H
Gravy/Sauce Boat 8" W 3⅜" H
Saucer 6" D
Cup 2½" H
Oval Covered Vegetable Bowl 11⅛" W x 5¼" H
Pitcher 7" W 7⅝" H

Platter 15½" W
Platter 13¼" W
Platter 11½" W
Gravy/Sauce Boat Underplate/Relish 9⅛" W

Virginia Rose Shape

VIRGINIA ROSE 1932 – 1966

The first thing that beginning collectors should know about Virginia Rose is that it is foremost a shape — one that features many patterns. Author Harvey Duke has reported over 450 patterns on the Virginia Rose shape!

China, Glass & Lamps in February 1933 featured a picture of Virginia Rose shaped tableware in a photo essay called, "new wares for 1933 seen at the Pittsburgh exhibit." The caption under Virginia Rose reads: "The new Virginia Rose shape from the Homer Laughlin China Co., early American in spirit." If Virginia Rose was introduced at a trade show in 1933, production on the shape would have likely begun in 1932. Author Richard Racheter reports in his book on Virginia Rose finding numerous pieces with backstamps indicating production in 1932, but none earlier. Racheter notes the shape was in production as late as 1966.

In the *Homer Laughlin Company Pound Sterling Price Booklet of 1937,* Virginia Rose appears with 138 patterns/decorations in production at that time alone. Homer Laughlin historian, Jack Welch, notes on the company web site that Virginia Rose was for many years the main line produced at Plant 8. "It sold well for decades, with 625,701 dozen pieces produced in 1933 and 643,056 dozen produced in 1951." That would indicate a possible production of over 7 million pieces per year for almost 20 years. In 1940-1941, Virginia Rose appeared in the Sears catalog, the only time we found it offered by Sears. Montgomery Ward sold Virginia Rose shaped patterns in 1934.

Some pieces in Virginia Rose were made exclusively for certain customers. J.J. Newberry was reportedly the only account to be sold Virginia Rose cream soups or shakers. Because only a small number of patterns were produced for J.J. Newberry, as opposed to the overall total production, collecting some of these pieces will be difficult at best.

Two Virginia Rose shape patterns are far more commonly found and collected than others, JJ59 and VR128. The JJ denotes it was an exclusive pattern for the J.J. Newberry account.

Tulips in a Basket pattern; Covered Batter Jug.

These piece types are only found in the Sheffield Dresden pattern.

Chop Plate
12½" W

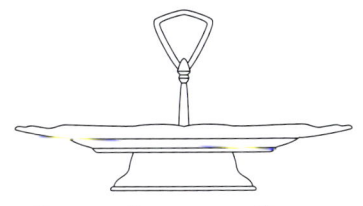

Serving Plate with Handle
12½" W
6½" H

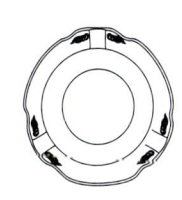

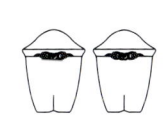

Ashtray
5¾" W

Salt & Pepper Set
2⅜" W
3" H

Homer Laughlin

Top left: *JJ59 pattern; Covered Butter Dish.* **Top right:** *JJ59 pattern; Salt & Pepper Set.* **Middle left:** *Fluffy Rose #1 pattern; Cereal Coupe Bowl, Round Vegetable Bowl, and Fruit Bowl.* **Second down on right:** *Fluffy Rose #1 pattern; Soup Bowl with Rim, Cranberry Bowl, and Fruit Bowl.* **Third down on right:** *Fluffy Rose #1 pattern; Three Oval Platters, Oval Vegetable Bowl, Gravy/Sauce Boat, and Oval Covered Vegetable Bowl.* **Bottom left:** *Fluffy Rose #1 pattern; Cereal Coupe Bowl, Cake Plate, Round Vegetable Bowl, and Fruit Bowl.* **Bottom right:** *Fluffy Rose #1 pattern; Dinner Plate, Salad Plate, Bread & Butter Plate, Cup & Saucer Set, Creamer, and Sugar Bowl with lid.*

Virginia Rose Shape

MATCHED OVENWARE & DINNERWARE
"HOMER LAUGHLIN"—Domestic semi-porcelain, ivory body with 3 spray floral decoration, platinum color lines. This is our exclusive decoration! For a complete list of this pattern on a factory shipment basis, write—Mgr. Dinnerware Dept.

OVENWARE—WITHSTANDS HEAT OR COLD
6 STYLE ASSORTMENT

Asst. consists of 2 each of the following sets: 10¾ in. cake plate & server, 10 in. mixing bowl and spoon, 8½ in. casserole, 7½ in. casserole & 9 in. plate, 8½ in. baking dish & 9 in. plate, and two pie plates & server.
55R-591—1 doz sets in carton, 50 lbs. .... Doz sets 7.35

PIE PLATE SETS
55R-597—10½ in. plate, server. ½ doz sets in carton, 18 lbs. .... Doz sets 5.50

CASSEROLE
55R-592—8½ in. ½ doz in pkg, 20 lbs. .... Doz 7.20

CAKE PLATE SETS
55R-596—10¾ in. plate, server. ½ doz sets in pkg, 18 lbs. .... Doz sets 6.00

MIXING BOWL SETS
55R-593—10 in. bowl, spoon. ½ doz sets in pkg, 20 lbs. .... Doz sets 7.50

BAKING DISHES
55R-595—8½ in. dish, 9 in. plate. ½ doz sets in carton, 22 lbs. .... Doz sets 7.20

ROYAL CASSEROLES
55R-594—7½ in., 9 in. plate. ½ doz sets in carton, 25 lbs. .... Doz sets 7.75

OPEN STOCK DINNERWARE...AND SETS

OPEN STOCK
55-3000—Cups & saucers, cup 2⅜ in. high, saucer 5⅞ in. .... Doz 2.20
55-3002—7 in. plates. .... Doz 1.20
55-3004—9¼ in. plates. .... Doz 1.65
55-3006—8⅜ in. coupe soups. ... Doz 1.72
55-3012—5½ in. Fruit Dishes. .. Doz .82
55-3013—6 in. Fruit Dishes. ... Doz 1.08
55-3011—8¼ in. Nappies. .... Doz 2.75
55-3008—11¼ in. Platters. ..... Doz 2.65

LUNCHEON & DINNER SETS
1 set in pkg.
55R-3019—32-Pc. Set. 22 lbs. Set 3.75
55R-3024—54-Pc. Set. 45 lbs. Set 7.50
55R-3025—66-Pc. Set. 50 lbs. Set 9.95
55R-3026—95-Pc. Set. 95 lbs. Set 13.95

FOR COMPOSITION OF SETS SEE NEARBY PAGE

206   BUTLER BROTHERS, BALTIMORE   O▲9-354

Collectors Note: The Cable shape Eggcup, Jade shape Covered Butter, Swing shape Salt & Pepper, and miscellaneous mugs were decorated and sold with some Virginia Rose sets.

Top: *Ovenserve pieces decorated to match Virginia Rose dinner set VR351 pattern; Butler Brothers Catalog, November-December, 1935.* **Bottom left:** *VR128 pattern, Ovenserve Shape; Round Covered Vegetable Bowl decorated to match Virginia Rose dinner set Fluffy Rose #1 pattern.* **Bottom right:** *JJ59 Kitchen Kraft Round Covered Vegetable Bowl, and Pie Plate; decorated to match Virginia Rose dinner set.*

169

Homer Laughlin

Top left: *Bouquet pattern;* Dinner Plate, Salad Plate, Bread & Butter Plate, Cup & Saucer Set, and Creamer. **Top middle:** *Bouquet pattern;* Two Round Vegetable Bowls, Fruit Bowl, and Oval Vegetable Bowl. **Top right:** *Nosegay pattern;* Sears & Roebuck Catalog, 1941. **Middle left:** *Patrician pattern;* Sugar Bowl with lid, and Creamer. **Middle:** *Colonial Kitchen pattern;* Soup Bowl with rim, Bread & Butter Plate, and Fruit Bowl. **Bottom left:** *Patrician pattern;* Larkin Catalog, 1934-35. **Bottom right:** *Armand pattern;* Cup & Saucer Set, Dinner Plate, Oval Vegetable Bowl, and Bread & Butter Plate.

170

Virginia Rose Shape

Top left: *Dresden pattern; Dinner Plate, Salad Plate, Bread & Butter Plate, and Cup & Saucer Set.* **Top right:** *Dresden pattern; Serving Plate.* **Bottom left:** *Dresden Pattern; Homer Laughlin Factory photograph.* **Middle right:** *Dresden pattern; Salt & Pepper Set.* **Bottom right:** *Typical Dresden pattern backstamps.*

Homer Laughlin

Virginia Rose Piece Type List

From Homer Laughlin Literature with Confirmed Actual Pieces

Ashtray (Dresden only)
Bowl, Cereal Coupe, 6 inches
Bowl, Cereal with rim, 7 inches
Bowl, Cranberry, 5¼ inches
Bowl, Cream Soup & Saucer Set
Bowl, Fruit Coupe, 5½ inches
Bowl, Fruit with rim, 6 inches
Bowl, Lugged*
Bowl, Soup with rim, 8¼ inches
Bowl, Vegetable Oval, 8¼ inches
Bowl, Vegetable Oval, 9⅛ inches
Bowl, Vegetable Oval, 10 inches
Bowl, Vegetable Oval Covered, 11⅛ inches
Bowl, Vegetable Round, 7¾ inches
Bowl, Vegetable Round, 8½ inches
Bowl, Vegetable Round, 9¾ inches
Butter, ¼ lb. with lid (Dresden only)
Butter, ½ lb. with lid (Jade Shape)
Butter Dish, Round with lid

Coffeepot with lid (Dresden only)
Creamer
Cup & Saucer Set
　Cup, 2½ inches
　Saucer, 6 inches
Cup & Saucer Set, Demitasse*
Cup & Saucer Set, St. Denis
　Cup, 3¼ inches
　Saucer, 5⅞ inches
Eggcup, Double (Cable Shape)
Gravy/Sauce Boat
Gravy/Sauce Boat with attached Underplate
Gravy/Sauce Boat Underplate/Relish, 9⅛ inches
Mug (Cable Shape)
Mug (Dresden only)
Pitcher, 7⅝ inches
Pitcher with lid, 7⅝ inches
Pitcher, Syrup, 5 inches

Pitcher, Syrup with lid, 5 inches
Plate, Bread*
Plate, Bread & Butter, 6¼ inches
Plate, Cake with handles*
Plate, Chop (Dresden only)
Plate, Dessert, 7⅛ inches
Plate, Dinner, 10⅜ inches
Plate, Luncheon, 9¼ inches
Plate, Salad, 8¼ inches
Platter, Oval, 11½ inches
Platter, Oval, 13¼ inches
Platter, Oval, 15½ inches
Salt & Pepper Set (Dresden only)
Salt & Pepper Set (Jubilee Shape)
Salt & Pepper Set (Swing Shape)
Serving Plate with handle (Dresden only)
Sugar Bowl with lid
Teapot with lid (Dresden only)
*Reported but not confirmed.

Differences in confusing Fluffy Rose patterns

Fluffy Rose #2
1 Decal
Platinum Trim

Fluffy Rose #5
2 Decals
No Trim

Fluffy Rose #1
2 Decals
Platinum Trim

Bottom left: *Louise pattern; Sears, Roebuck & Co. Catalog, 1941.* Bottom second from left: *Patrician pattern; Butler Brothers Catalog, 1935.* Bottom third from left: *Colorful Virginia Rose Spray; Butler Brothers Catalog, 1935.* Bottom right: *Silver Colored Rose Design; Butler Brothers Catalog, 1935.*

Virginia Rose Shape

HLC450 *No Trim*	**Double Gold Band** *Gold Trim*	**Red Ring** *Red Trim*	**HLC1037** *No Trim*
VR114 *Gold Trim*	**Gold Rose** *VR115* *Gold Trim*	**Silver Rose** *VR124* *Platinum Trim*	**Silver Scrolls** *VR172* *Platinum Trim*
HLC1189 *Platinum Trim*	**HLC655** *Platinum Trim*	**VR120** *Gold Trim*	**VR121** *Platinum Trim*
VR122 *Platinum Trim*	**HLC3047** *Platinum Design* *No Trim*	**Woodland Gold** *Gold Trim*	**HLC3010** *Oval Platter Shown* *Gold Trim*

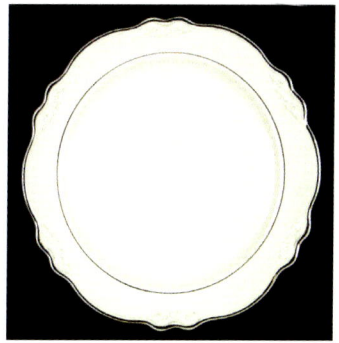

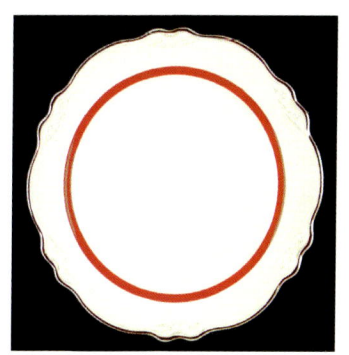

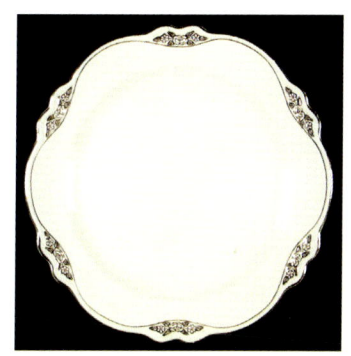

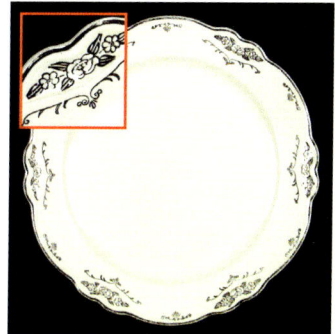

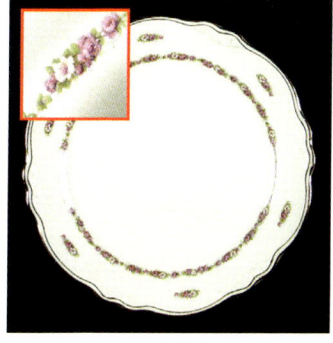

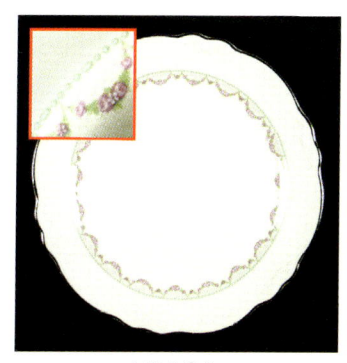

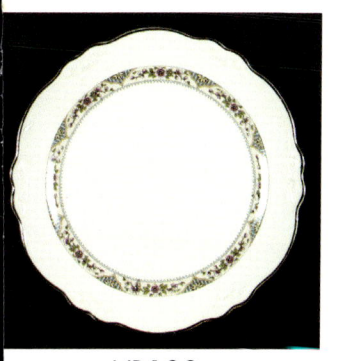

Virginia Rose Shape

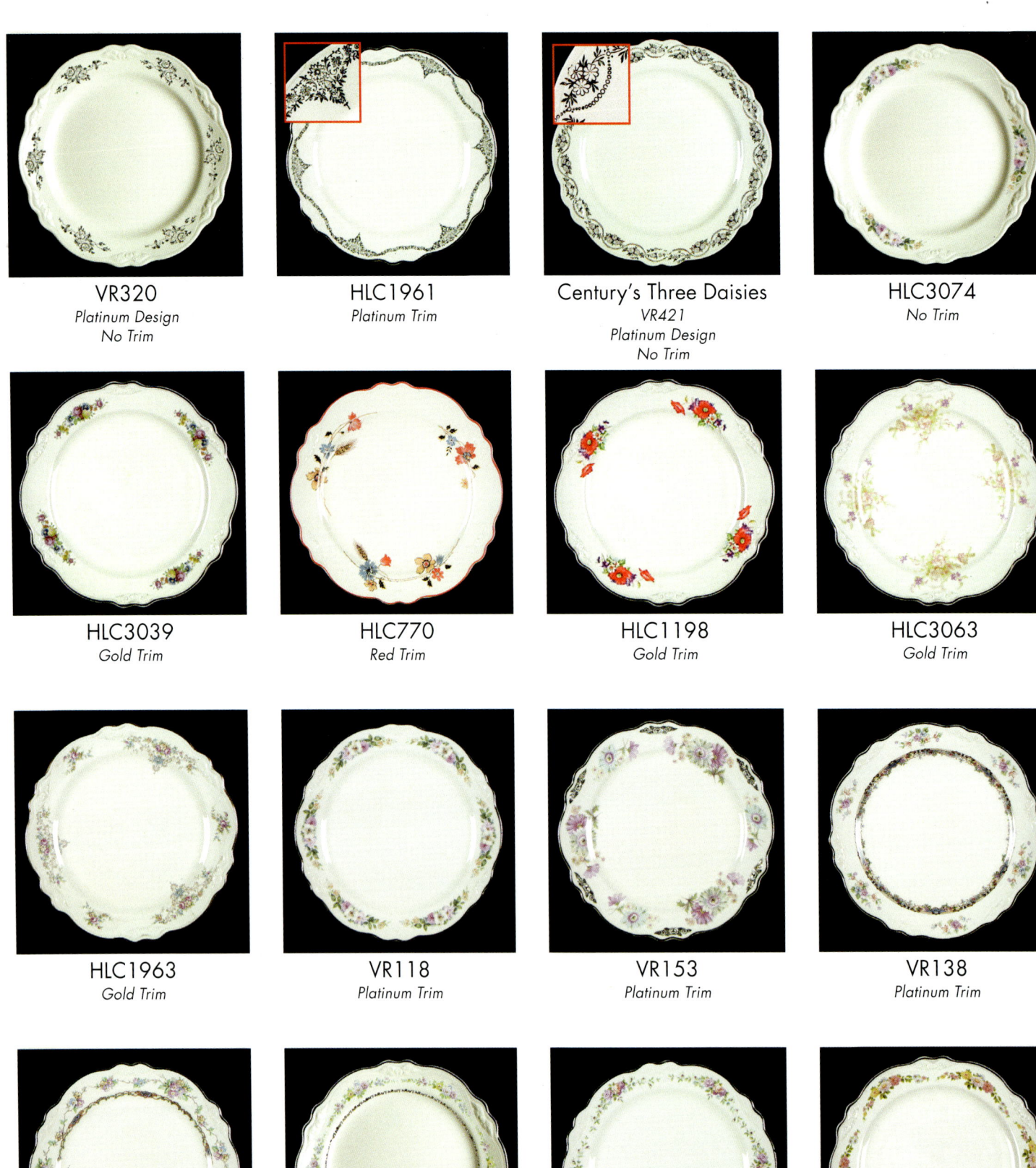

VR320
Platinum Design
No Trim

HLC1961
Platinum Trim

Century's Three Daisies
VR421
Platinum Design
No Trim

HLC3074
No Trim

HLC3039
Gold Trim

HLC770
Red Trim

HLC1198
Gold Trim

HLC3063
Gold Trim

HLC1963
Gold Trim

VR118
Platinum Trim

VR153
Platinum Trim

VR138
Platinum Trim

Maude
VR108
Platinum Trim

HLC3049
Platinum Trim

Rose Melody
VR109
Platinum Trim

HLC3053
Platinum Trim

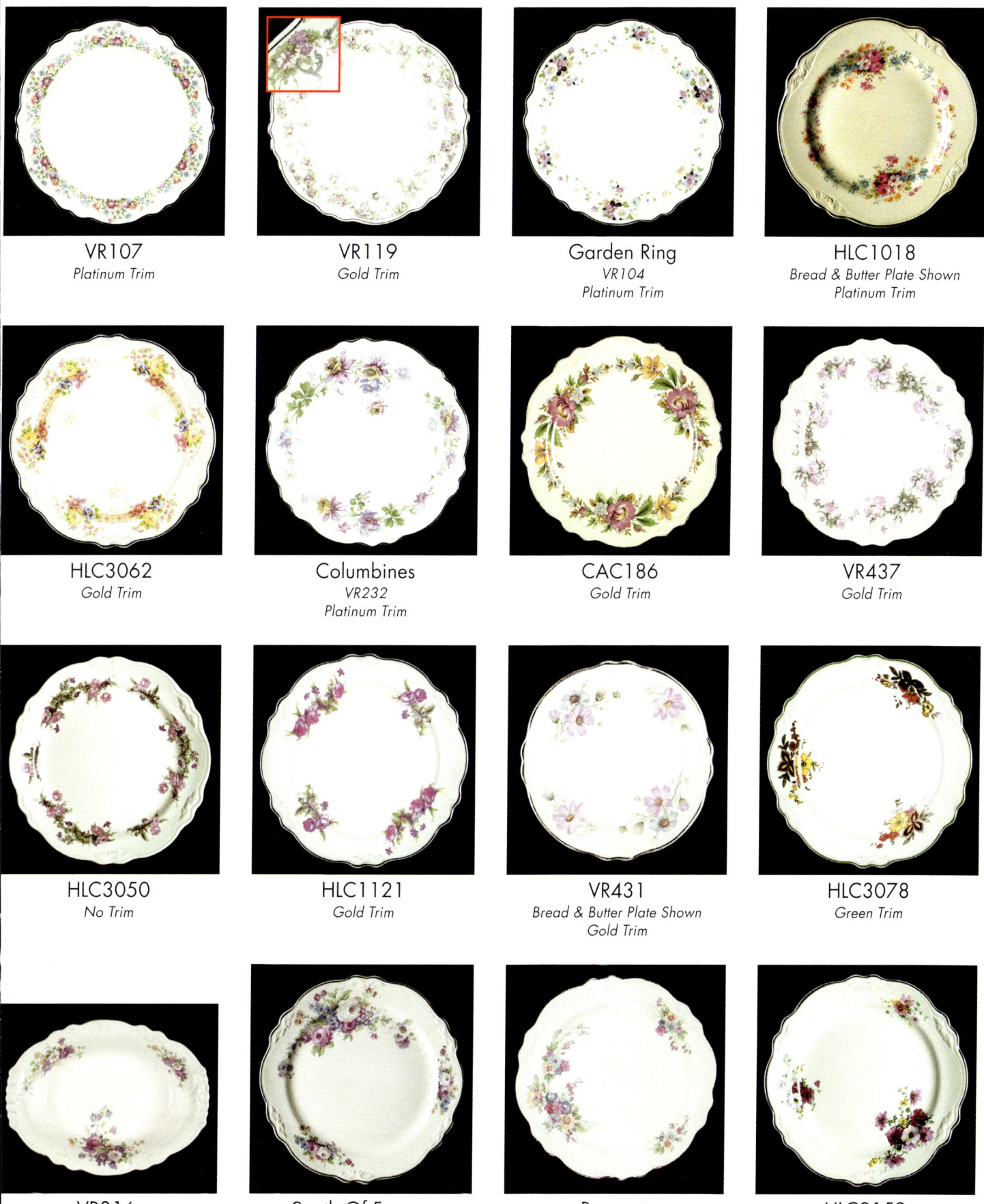

Virginia Rose Shape

VR107
Platinum Trim

VR119
Gold Trim

Garden Ring
VR104
Platinum Trim

HLC1018
Bread & Butter Plate Shown
Platinum Trim

HLC3062
Gold Trim

Columbines
VR232
Platinum Trim

CAC186
Gold Trim

VR437
Gold Trim

HLC3050
No Trim

HLC1121
Gold Trim

VR431
Bread & Butter Plate Shown
Gold Trim

HLC3078
Green Trim

VR316
Oval Vegetable Bowl Shown
No Trim

South Of France
VR387
Luncheon Plate Shown
Platinum Trim

Bouquet
W137
Platinum Trim

HLC2152
Platinum Trim

Virginia Rose Shape

HLC1142
Luncheon Plate Shown
Platinum Trim

HLC2153
Platinum Trim

HLC2151
Platinum Trim

HLC3075
Platinum Trim

Liza
VR351
Platinum Trim

Armand
No Trim

Armand
Gold Trim

Armand
VR235
Platinum Trim

HLC1962
No Trim

JJ59
Platinum Trim

VR152
Gold Trim

R2256
Platinum Trim

VR162
Green Trim

HLC1599
Platinum Trim

A740
Platinum Trim

VR141
Platinum Trim

Virginia Rose Shape

Louise
R5766, VR390
Platinum Trim

R5745
Platinum Trim

HLC1373
Platinum Trim

VR142
Platinum Trim

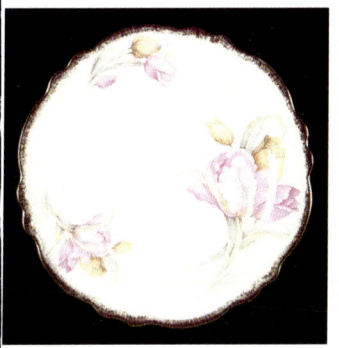

VR151
Gold Trim

VR134
No Trim

HLC675
Gold Trim

Wild Rose 1
VR269
Platinum Trim

VR135
No Trim

HLC704
Gold Trim

VR175
Platinum Trim

HLC3044
Platinum Trim

VR266
Platinum Trim

HLC3077
*Oval Vegetable Bowl Shown
Platinum Trim*

HLC352
Gold Trim

HLC2101
*Bread & Butter Plate Shown
Gold Trim*

177

Virginia Rose Shape

HLC3056 *No Trim*	**Head Of Class** *VR101* *Platinum Trim*	**HLC3038** *Gold Trim*	**VR155** *Platinum Trim*
HLC276 *No Trim*	**Wild Pink Rose** *VR233* *Platinum Trim*	**R5671** *Gold Trim*	**HLC2163** *Platinum Trim*
VR132 *No Trim*	**Red Beauty** *Oval Platter Shown* *No Trim*	**Red Beauty** *Platinum Trim*	**HLC1965** *Platinum Trim*
Pastel Wood Rose *VRD220* *Platinum Trim*	**HLC3060** *No Trim*	**HLC3061** *No Trim*	**HLC2186** *Platinum Trim*

Virginia Rose Shape

Fluffy Rose 5
Luncheon Plate Shown
No Trim

Fluffy Rose 1
VR128
Platinum Trim

Fluffy Rose 2
VR178
Luncheon Plate Shown
Platinum Trim

VR133
No Trim

Meadow Goldenrod
VR411
Platinum Trim

HLC3079
Oval Platter Shown
Gold Trim

HLC3011
Oval Platter Shown
No Trim

HLC3041
Platinum Trim

HLC2150
Gold Trim

HLC3076
Platinum Trim

HLC3059
Gold Trim

HLC3068
Gold Trim

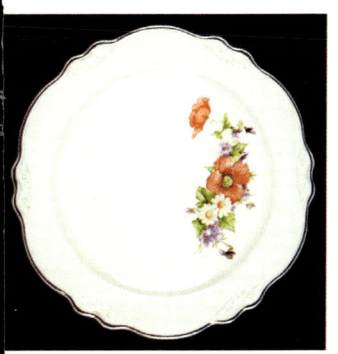

HLC3066
Platinum Trim

VR143
Gold Trim

Nosegay
VR423
No Trim

HLC103
Luncheon Plate Shown
Platinum Trim

Virginia Rose Shape

HLC3032
Platinum Trim

HLC399
Platinum Trim

Blue Bonnet
VR420
Gold Trim

HLC3057
Platinum Trim

Tulips In A Basket
VR396
Platinum Trim

Tulips In A Basket
VR412
Gold Trim

Tulips In A Basket
Red Trim

Water Lily
VR398
Platinum Trim

HLC3054
Gold Trim

HLC1364
Bread & Butter Plate Shown
Gold Trim

HLC2039
Gravy Boat Shown
Platinum Trim

HLC3035
Gravy Boat Shown
No Trim

HLC3048
No Trim

HLC3046
Creamer Shown
No Trim

HLC2182
Oval Platter Shown
No Trim

HLC3031
Oval Platter Shown
No Trim

Virginia Rose Shape

HLC783
Oval Platter Shown
No Trim

HLC1155
Oval Covered Vegetable Bowl Shown
No Trim

HLC3072
Sugar Bowl Shown
No Trim

HLC2154
Sugar Bowl Shown
No Trim

HLC3052
No Trim

Petipoint
CP95
by Cunningham & Pickett
Gold Trim

HLC3033
Gold Trim

HLC3034
Gold Trim

HLC155
Luncheon Plate Shown
Gold Trim

HLC3083
Round Vegetable Bowl Shown
No Trim

HLC897
Cake Plate Shown
No Trim

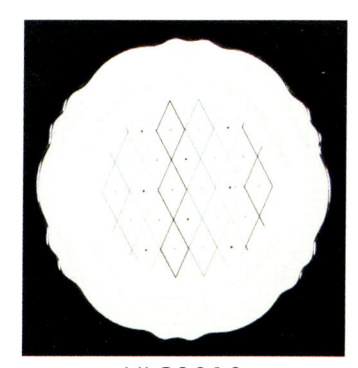

HLC2010
Platinum Trim

HLC987
No Trim

HLC3042
No Trim

Colonial Kitchen
Gold Trim

Golden Rose 2
Luncheon Plate Shown
Gold Trim

Virginia Rose Shape

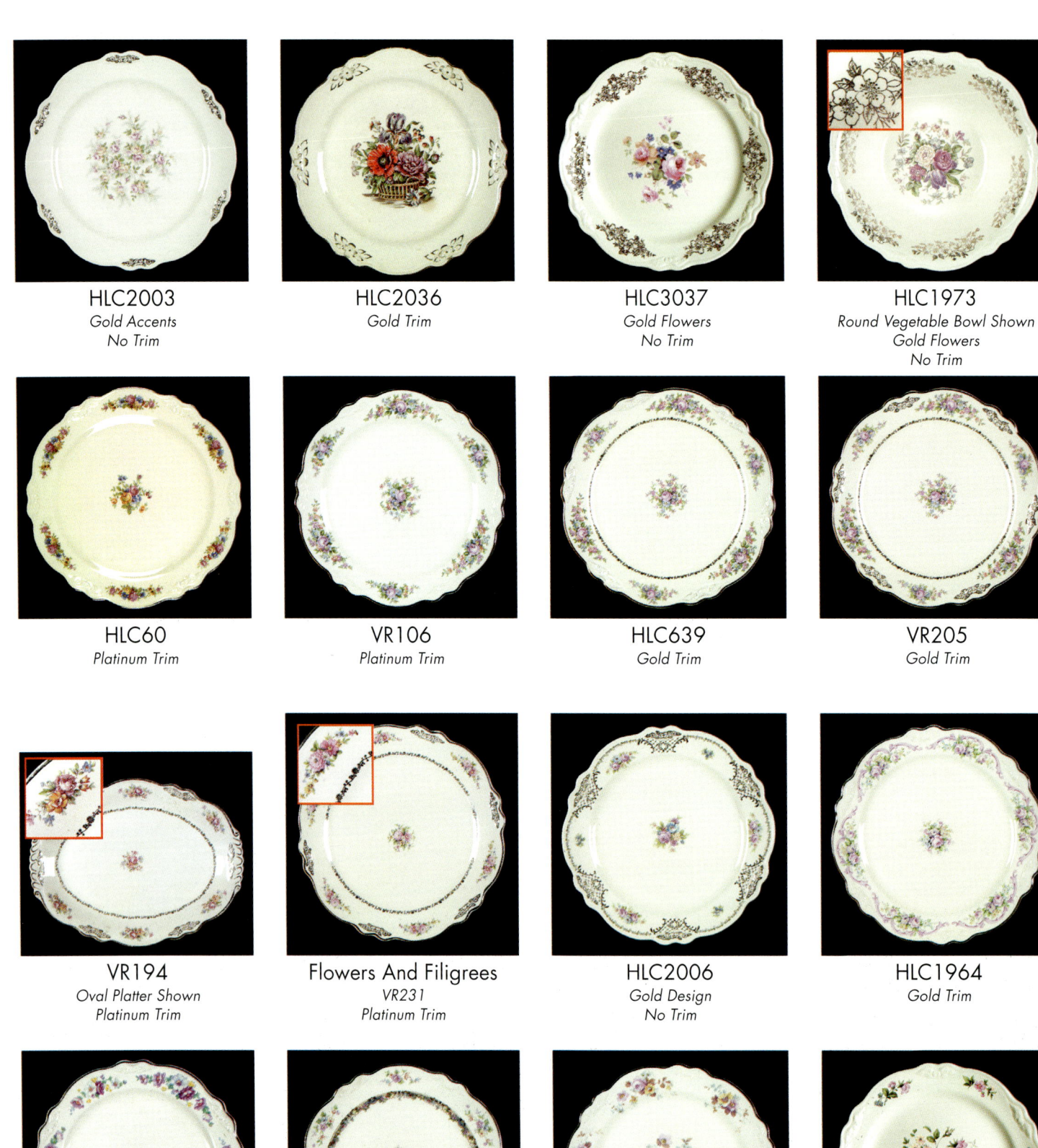

HLC2003 *Gold Accents* *No Trim*	**HLC2036** *Gold Trim*	**HLC3037** *Gold Flowers* *No Trim*	**HLC1973** *Round Vegetable Bowl Shown* *Gold Flowers* *No Trim*
HLC60 *Platinum Trim*	**VR106** *Platinum Trim*	**HLC639** *Gold Trim*	**VR205** *Gold Trim*
VR194 *Oval Platter Shown* *Platinum Trim*	**Flowers And Filigrees** *VR231* *Platinum Trim*	**HLC2006** *Gold Design* *No Trim*	**HLC1964** *Gold Trim*
HLC1073 *Platinum Trim*	**VR136** *Platinum Trim*	**VR105** *Platinum Trim*	**HLC3040** *No Trim*

Virginia Rose Shape

Springtime
W245
Gold Trim

M212V
Platinum Trim

Dresden
No Trim

HLC3067
Yellow Trim

HLC3071
Gold Design
No Trim

Century's Three Daisies
Gold Design
No Trim

Century's Three Daisies
VR261
Platinum Design
No Trim

HLC125
Bread & Butter Plate Shown
Gold Design
No Trim

HLC664
Gold Filigree
No Trim

HLC1001
Round Vegetable Bowl Shown
Gold Filigree, Green Band
No Trim

HLC668
Round Vegetable Bowl Shown
Gold Filigree, Green Band
No Trim

HLC3070
Gold Filigree
No Trim

HLC2121
Gold Filigree
No Trim

HLC161
Gold Trim

HLC977
Luncheon Plate Shown
Gold Flowers
No Trim

HLC3045
Oval Platter Shown
Gold Design
Red Trim

183

OVENSERVE

Piece Types

These drawings were made from actual stock or literature at Replacements, Ltd. Check the piece type list for all known piece types in this shape.

Dinner Plate 10" D

Luncheon Plate 9¼" D

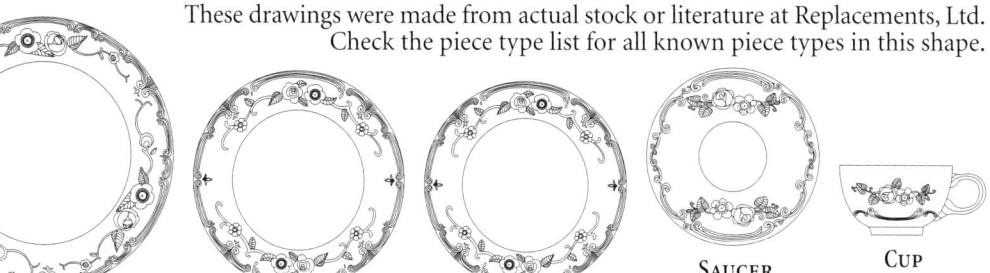

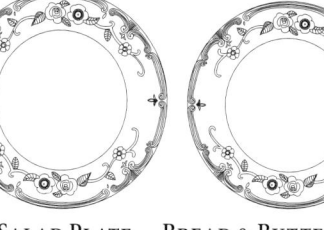

Salad Plate 7" D

Bread & Butter Plate 6½" D

Saucer 5¾" D

Cup 4⅞" W 2¼" H

Oval Baker, Medium 8¼" W

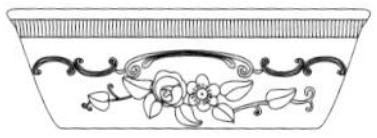

Oval Baker, Small 6¼" W 2" H

Creamer

Sugar Bowl with Lid

Baked Apple Bowl 4¾" W 2¾" H

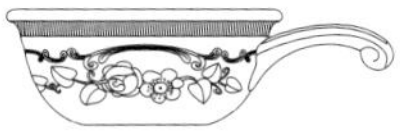

French Casserole 6½" W 1¾" H

Custard 3½" W 2½" H

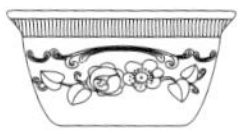

Ramekin 3¾" W 1⅞" H

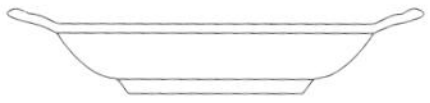

Shirred Egg Dish 6⅞" W 1⅜" H

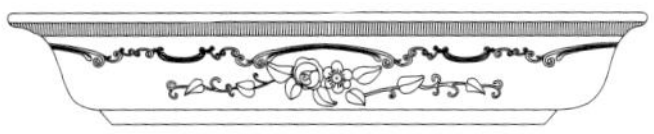

Pie Plate 10¾" W 1⅞" H

Fruit Bowl/Individual Pie Plate 5⅝" W 1⅝" H

Round Covered Casserole 8½" W x 3⅝" H

Top right: *Typical OvenServe backstamp.*
Bottom right: *Larkin Catalog, 1936.*

OVENSERVE BAKING SET

Bake and serve food piping hot in these dishes dainty enough and pretty enough to grace any table. Or use them for desserts, salads, etc., that require freezing in the refrigerator. Ivory semi-porcelain ware hand decorated with brightly colored flowers.

The set is positively proof against breakage due to oven heat. Set consists of: 8½-in. covered casserole; 9-in. plate; 10½-in. pie plate; four round baking dishes, 4½, 5½, 7 and 8½-in. in diameter; 6 3-in. custard cups. Mlg. wt. 15 lbs.

1718 Given for **$6.50** in Coupons

OvenServe Shape

OVENSERVE
1933 – 1947 or later

OvenServe was filed for registration as a trademark July 31, 1933. Use of the mark was claimed since July 1, 1933. The OvenServe shapes are predominately kitchen and bake ware, but cups, saucers, and plates were also produced.

Identical OvenServe pieces were marked with either a Homer Laughlin or Taylor, Smith & Taylor backstamp. The smaller pieces, made to fit inside Quaker Oats boxes, were made at both factories. Homer Laughlin's production of the larger pieces are more plentiful in yellow, pumpkin, and ivory with handpainted green details. Other OvenServe colors are reported infrequently. Taylor, Smith & Taylor did not produce the larger pieces and their manufacturing of the smaller shapes included colors not in the Homer Laughlin color pallet. Decorations applied to Homer Laughlin OvenServe include handpainted highlights on the embossed pattern and a variety of decals (which at times seem to flow obliviously over the existing relief pottery).

In the *Homer Laughlin Pound Sterling Price Booklet of 1937*, OvenServe is listed as available with 71 different decorations/patterns. Also noted were OvenServe patterns produced expressly for Royal Metal Manufacturing Co., M. Seller (the Hoosier-like cabinet manufacturer), and Butler Brothers, the wholesale catalog business.

In 1935, Montgomery Ward and the wholesale firm Butler Brothers both illustrate OvenServe shapes. By 1936, Larkin, the mail order soap company, illustrates Homer Laughlin OvenServe in its catalog.

As late as December 1947, the trade journal *China, Glass and Decorative Accessory* features Homer Laughlin ads touting OvenServe.

Two pieces which bear an OvenServe backstamp are actually the Daisy Chain shape. The name is a reference to the obvious chains of flowers/daisies that encircle the pieces. The two shapes, a pie plate and covered casserole, were marked and marketed by Homer Laughlin as part of the OvenServe line and thus seem rightly included here, despite their design variances from other OvenServe pieces.

Top left: *Pumpkin pattern; Luncheon Plate, Salad Plate, Cup & Saucer Set, and Small Oval Baker.* **Top middle:** *Pumpkin pattern; Bean Pot missing lid, Ramekin, Custard, Baked Apple, and Small Round Baking Dish.* **Top right:** *Turquoise pattern; Ramekin, Custard, and Fruit Bowl.* **Bottom left:** *HLC896 pattern; Bean Pot with lid, Luncheon Plate, Oval Baker, Round Baking Dish, and Small Pie Plate.* **Bottom right:** *HLC896 pattern; Long Handled Spoon, and Large Pie Plate.*

Homer Laughlin

OvenServe
"The oven ware for table service"

OVENSERVE is the newest development in cuisine and dining table wares. It consists of a comprehensive series of shapes designed for baking, broiling, chilling, freezing, and otherwise preparing meats, vegetables, desserts, and other foods.

This series includes various types of casseroles in different sizes, meat and fish platters, pie plates, dessert dishes, and baking dishes for vegetables. And, in order to provide a perfect table setting for these wares, cups and saucers and three sizes of serving plates have been made in the same style and decorative treatment.

You will enjoy the new experience of preparing your food, baking it in the oven, chilling it in the refrigerator when desirable, and finally serving it on the table—all in the same dish.

There is no possibility that the change in temperature between the hot oven and cold refrigerator will damage an OVENSERVE piece in any way. Moreover, OVENSERVE dishes can be taken directly from the oven and placed upon wet and cold surfaces with safety.

The beauty and style of this new utility ware, together with its practical features, assure OVENSERVE a ready place in every home. It decorates the kitchen, inspires the housewife in the preparation of superlative dishes, harmonizes with any table arrangement, and assists in awakening the appetite of the most indifferent diner.

The inexpensiveness of OVENSERVE is in no way a measure of its worth. OVENSERVE is a quality product manufactured to sell at popular prices.

ROUND BAKING DISH

NO.	SIZE	CAPACITY
104	4½ in.	8 oz.
105	5½ in.	12 oz.
106	7 in.	1½ pt.
107	8½ in.	2½ pt.

FROM the individual to the family size, the round baking dish is a valuable aid for baking appetizing dishes such as spaghetti, macaroni, scalloped potatoes, and other vegetables. In fact, to obtain a thoroughly baked food, OVENSERVE baking dishes excel, because the heat is retained so well and distributed so evenly. When not in use for baking, each size has its own special table use. The smaller sizes are perfect for serving cereals and sliced or stewed fruits.

Cover, number 302, is available for the 5½ inch round baking dish.

CASSEROLE WITH COVER

NO.	SIZE	CAPACITY
301	6 in.	1 pt.
303	8½ in.	2½ pt.

WHO does not like delicious chicken dishes, cooked with vegetables, and those popular scalloped and au gratin combinations? All of these favorite recipes, when baked in the OVENSERVE casserole, will come from the oven done to a turn. The sunken handle of the cover permits the placing of one casserole upon another in the refrigerator for storage purposes. In this dish food may be kept as a left-over, reheated, and served again. Also suitable for gelatin, aspics, and frozen puddings. This dish is the Jack-of-all-trades of the OVENSERVE line. Its uses are manifold.

CUSTARDS AND RAMEKINS

NO.	SIZE	CAPACITY
501 (custard)	3½ in.	6 oz.
203 (ind. bean)	4 in.	8 oz.
504 (ramekin)	3¾ in.	5 oz.

CUSTARDS and ramekins are individual baking dishes extraordinary—"extraordinary" because they can be used for so many different baking and serving purposes. Actually, they are indispensable items of OVENSERVE ware. Custards; junkets; baked beans; crabmeat, oyster, and fruit cocktails are only a few of the possible uses. It is an ideal egg cup. You will find it just the right size and mold for individual portions of cranberry jelly, or for snow pudding, Spanish and Bavarian cream, and similar desserts.

SHIRRED EGG DISH

NO.	SIZE
801	6 in.
802 (Welsh rarebit)	7 in.

ONE of the aristocrats of the OVENSERVE line. This appealing and useful shape comes in two sizes. It is a low-rimmed, circular platterette with two ornamental lugs or lips. Primarily designed for baked egg combinations, this shape may also be used for preparing many other dishes. A well-known chef recommends its use for chicken a la king, noodles au gratin, apple dumplings, mushrooms on toast, chicken and calf's liver, and bacon or ham and eggs. It is the one and only shape for Welsh rarebit. But its use does not end with baking. It is an ideal dish for serving stewed fruits, berries, and desserts.

Above: *Factory retail pamphlet about OvenServe.*

OvenServe Shape

PIE PLATE

NO.	SIZE
600	5½ in.
601	9 in.
602	10½ in.

THE OVENSERVE pie plate is beautifully fashioned. Because it is so attractive, you will always want to have the pie served at the table in the same dish in which it has been baked. Then, too, by avoiding transferring or cutting the pie before serving, you insure an unbroken crust and the retention of all filling. It will be a delight to find how uniformly browned the crust is when baked in the OVENSERVE pie plate.

Who does not enjoy delectable, deep dish pies? The smallest size pie plate is designed especially for baking individual, deep dish fruit pies.

OVENSERVE is truly a friend in the kitchen. It is efficient for baking; it is handy for warming left-overs; and it reduces dish-washing to a minimum. OVENSERVE is easily kept spotlessly clean.

At the Table

In the Kitchen

OVENSERVE entices jaded appetites. It is cheerful at breakfast; it is inviting at luncheon; and for the evening meal, its refreshing beauty strikes a new style note. OVENSERVE is the SMART new TABLEWARE.

OVENSERVE is a trusty handmaid in the pantry. It molds tasty salads and desserts; it chills creams and puddings; and it stores left-overs in the refrigerator. OVENSERVE may be taken directly from icebox to oven.

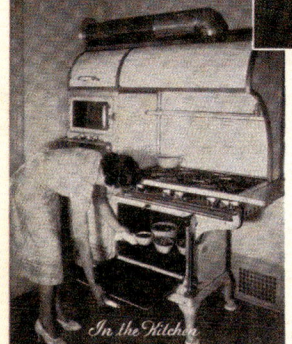

In the Pantry

FRENCH CASSEROLE

NO.	SIZE	CAPACITY
304	4½ in.	8 oz.
305	5½ in.	12 oz.

A CHARMING little handled casserole, commonly used in Continental homes and rapidly becoming popular in this country. One of the most convenient dishes for baking and serving baked and poached eggs, spaghetti and macaroni combinations, onion soup, baked beans, and stuffed green peppers. The French casserole is a delightful shape that is as efficient in the kitchen as it is distinctive on the dining-table. When half its possibilities are recognized, this piece will be as indispensable in the home as the every day cup and saucer.

The larger size may be used with or without a cover.

PLATES .. CUP AND SAUCER

NO.	SIZE
403	7 in. (actual measurement)
404	9 in. (actual measurement)
405	10 in. (actual measurement)
401 (cup)	8 oz. 402 (saucer)

THE plates, cups, and saucers have the same pattern and design as the other OVENSERVE articles. When these are used together, they create a harmonious ensemble on the dining-table; and when the plates, cups, and saucers are used alone as tableware, they are extremely attractive and distinctive in appearance.

All OVENSERVE ware is made of exactly the same materials, and consequently the plates, cups, and saucers will withstand the same temperature changes as all the other pieces. This fact makes it possible to use the plates as a tray for the baking dishes in the oven. The plates are also splendid for warming up left-overs—and for actual baking, if desired.

OVAL BAKING DISH

NO.	SIZE	CAPACITY
101	6 in.	½ pt.
102	8 in.	1 pt.
103	11 in.	2½ pt.

THREE graceful oval dishes: individual, kitchenette, and family size. Splendid for making tasty, deep dish meat pies. Suitable for baked onions, baked tomatoes, stuffed peppers, and all baked desserts.

PLATTER

NO.	SIZE
702	11½ in. (actual measurement)
703	13½ in. (actual measurement)

EVERY housewife will enjoy the sensation of serving a sizzling hot steak on the same platter on which it has been broiled, with the assurance that the meat will remain hot on the table. The platter can also be used for broiling, baking, and serving sausages, pork, veal, and mutton chops.

Above: *Factory retail pamphlet about OvenServe.*

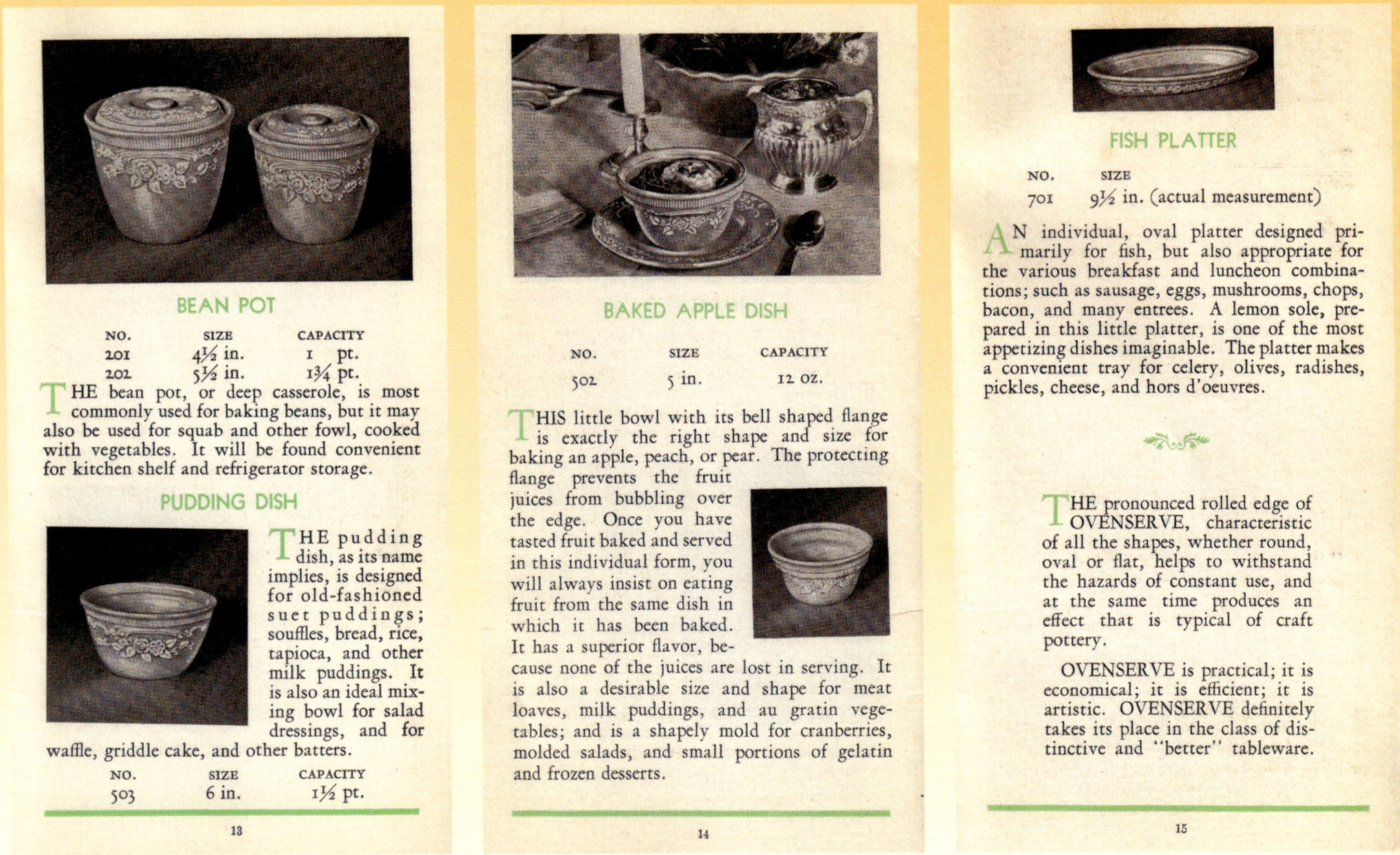

Homer Laughlin

BEAN POT

NO.	SIZE	CAPACITY
201	4½ in.	1 pt.
202	5½ in.	1¾ pt.

THE bean pot, or deep casserole, is most commonly used for baking beans, but it may also be used for squab and other fowl, cooked with vegetables. It will be found convenient for kitchen shelf and refrigerator storage.

PUDDING DISH

THE pudding dish, as its name implies, is designed for old-fashioned suet puddings; souffles, bread, rice, tapioca, and other milk puddings. It is also an ideal mixing bowl for salad dressings, and for waffle, griddle cake, and other batters.

NO.	SIZE	CAPACITY
503	6 in.	1½ pt.

BAKED APPLE DISH

NO.	SIZE	CAPACITY
502	5 in.	12 oz.

THIS little bowl with its bell shaped flange is exactly the right shape and size for baking an apple, peach, or pear. The protecting flange prevents the fruit juices from bubbling over the edge. Once you have tasted fruit baked and served in this individual form, you will always insist on eating fruit from the same dish in which it has been baked. It has a superior flavor, because none of the juices are lost in serving. It is also a desirable size and shape for meat loaves, milk puddings, and au gratin vegetables; and is a shapely mold for cranberries, molded salads, and small portions of gelatin and frozen desserts.

FISH PLATTER

NO.	SIZE
701	9½ in. (actual measurement)

AN individual, oval platter designed primarily for fish, but also appropriate for the various breakfast and luncheon combinations; such as sausage, eggs, mushrooms, chops, bacon, and many entrees. A lemon sole, prepared in this little platter, is one of the most appetizing dishes imaginable. The platter makes a convenient tray for celery, olives, radishes, pickles, cheese, and hors d'oeuvres.

THE pronounced rolled edge of OVENSERVE, characteristic of all the shapes, whether round, oval or flat, helps to withstand the hazards of constant use, and at the same time produces an effect that is typical of craft pottery.

OVENSERVE is practical; it is economical; it is efficient; it is artistic. OVENSERVE definitely takes its place in the class of distinctive and "better" tableware.

Top: *Factory retail pamphlet about OvenServe.* **Middle left:** *HLC1278 pattern; Shirred Egg Dish, Saucer, Salad Plate, Round Covered Vegetable Bowl, and Ramekin.* **Middle right:** *HLC1044 pattern; Luncheon Plate with original OvenServe sticker.* **Bottom left:** *Yellow pattern; Custard, Oval Platter, and Large Pie Plate.* **Bottom middle:** *Yellow pattern; Small Oval Baker, Fruit Bowl, and French Casserole.* **Bottom right:** *Brown pattern; Small Oval Baker, and French Casserole.*

OvenServe Shape

Top left: *Pumpkin pattern backstamp compared to Taylor, Smith & Taylor's backstamp on Yellow pattern.*
Top right: *Yellow Taylor, Smith & Taylor, Brown Homer Laughlin, Pink Taylor, Smith & Taylor, Forest Green Taylor, Smith & Taylor, and Pumpkin Homer Laughlin Oval Bakers.* **Right:** *Homer Laughlin's Pink Custard, Yellow Small French Casserole, and Turquoise Fruit Bowl.* **Bottom:** *Side view and top view of Pink pattern Small French Casserole by Taylor, Smith & Taylor compared to Homer Laughlin Pumpkin pattern Small French Casserole.*

Homer Laughlin

OvenServe Piece Type List

From Homer Laughlin Literature with Confirmed Actual Pieces (Sizes from Literature)

Ashtray
Baked Apple, 4¾ inches, 12 oz., #502
Bean Pot, 4½ inches, 1 pt., #201
Bean Pot, 5½ inches, 1¾ pt., #202
Bean Pot, Individual, 4 inches, 8 oz., #203
Bowl, Fruit (Individual Pie Plate), 5½ inches, #600
Bowl, Mixing (footed, not oven-proof) 7¾ inches, 2 pt.
Bowl, Mixing (footed, not oven-proof) 8⅞ inches, 3 pt.
Bowl, Mixing (footed, not oven-proof) 9¾ inches, 5 pt.
Bowl, Mixing (footed, not oven-proof) 11 inches
Bowl, Mixing (footed, not oven-proof) 12¼ inches, 12 pt.
Bowl, Oval Baking Small, 6 inches, ½ pt., #101
Bowl, Oval Baking Medium, 8 inches, 1 pt., #102
Bowl, Oval Baking Large, 11 inches, 2½ pt., #103
Bowl, Round Baking, 4½ inches, 8 oz., #104
Bowl, Round Baking, 5½ inches, 12 oz., #105
    Cover, #302
Bowl, Round Baking, 7 inches, 1½ pt., #106
Bowl, Round Baking, 8½ inches, 2½ pt., #107
Casserole, French, 4½ inches, 8 oz., #304
Casserole, French (can use cover),
    5½ inches, 12 oz., # 305
Casserole, Round Covered, 6 inches, 1 pt., #301
Casserole, Round Covered, 8½ inches, 2½ pt., #303
Creamer
Cup & Saucer Set
    Cup, 2¼ inches, 8 oz., #401
    Saucer, 5¾ inches, #402

Custard, 3½ inches, 6 oz., #501
    sold with Tinned Baking Rack, holds six
Dish, Pudding Bowl, 6 inches, 1½ pt., #503
Dish, Shirred Egg, 6 inches, #801
Dish, Shirred Egg, 7 inches, #802
Fork, Salad, #842
Knife, Cake, #270
Pitcher, Large (Batter Jug)
Pitcher, Small (Milk Pitcher/Measuring Cup)
Plate, Bread & Butter, 6½ inches
Plate, Dinner, 10 inches, #405
Plate, Luncheon, 9¼ inches, #404
    underplate for 8½ inch Round Covered Casserole
Plate, Pie, 9 inches, #601
Plate, Pie, 10½ inches, #602
Plate, Salad, 7 inches, #403
    underplate for 6 inch Round Covered Casserole
Platter, 9½ inches, #701
Platter, 11½ inches, #702
Platter, 13½ inches, #703
Ramekin, 3¾ inches, 5 oz., #504
Spoon, #267
Spoon, Long Handle, #274
Sugar Bowl, Open
Sugar Bowl with lid
Teapot with lid, #271*

*Reported but not confirmed.

Top left: *Yellow* pattern; French Casserole. **Top right:** *Fluffy Rose 1* pattern; Covered Casserole. **Middle right:** *Turquoise* pattern; Custard. **Bottom:** Montgomery Ward, 1936–1937.

DAISY CHAIN

DAISY CHAIN circa 1937

In *The Homer Laughlin Pound Sterling Price Booklet of 1937*, Daisy Chain is listed. There were 16 decorations or patterns available on the Daisy Chain shape; However, the price list clearly notes at the page top: "3 Piece Daisy Chain Set (1 Casserole Covered 8" and Pie Plate 9½")." Daisy Chain, as a shape, consists of a casserole with lid and pie plate. Nothing more than these three pieces.

Daisy Chain was cited as having an "Old Ivory Glaze" and was not offered in solid colors.

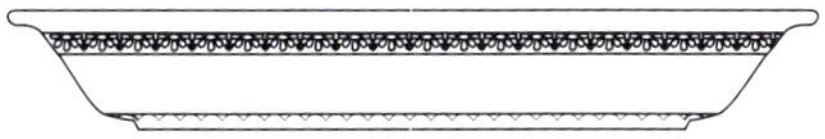

PIE PLATE
10⅝" W
1½" H

Top right: *Mexicana pattern; Pie Plate top.* **Bottom right:** *Mexicana pattern; Pie Plate bottom.* **Bottom left:** *Unknown catalog advertisement.*

Decorated Earthenware
Here's a really pretty ovenware that makes every meal seem like a party! Heat-proof . . . yet decorated like fine china! Creamy ivory glaze, with delicate sprays of pink flowers and green leaves. Chromium-plated metal frames won't rust or tarnish or stain permanently.
586 C 6804—8½-in. Casserole and Frame. Ship. wt. 6 lbs. $1.19
586 C 6805—Casserole Only. Ship. wt. 5 lbs. 79c
586 C 6806—Two 9-in. Pie Plates and Frame. Ship. wt. 5 lbs. 95c
586 C 6807—Pie Plate Only. Ship. wt. 3 lbs. 8 oz. ....Each 32c
586 C 6809—10⅝-in. Cake Tray and 9½ in. Server. Ship. wt. 3 lbs. 79c

191

OvenServe Shape

OvenServe–Cream
Oval Baker Shown
No Trim

HLC1278
Bread & Butter Plate Shown
Platinum Trim

OvenServe–Yellow
Oval Baker Shown
No Trim

OvenServe–Turquoise
Fruit Bowl Shown
No Trim

OvenServe–Pumpkin
Bread & Butter Plate Shown
No Trim

OvenServe–Pink
Custard Cup Shown
No Trim

OvenServe–Brown
Oval Baker Shown
No Trim

HLC594
Salad Plate Shown
No Trim

OS81
Red Trim

HLC896
No Trim

HLC3100
No Trim

HLC3101
Oval Baker Shown
Platinum Trim

Armand
Pie Serving Plate Shown
Platinum Trim

HLC1277
Pie Serving Plate Shown
No Trim

HLC3017
Round Covered Casserole
Lid Shown
No Trim

HLC2018
Luncheon Plate Shown
Platinum Trim

OvenServe Shape

HLC1276
Platinum Trim

HLC1044
*Luncheon Plate Shown
Red Trim*

HLC3001
Red Trim

Mexicana
*Daisy Chain Shape
Pie Serving Plate Shown
No Trim*

Above: *Factory workers at Homer Laughlin.*

Chelsea

Piece Types

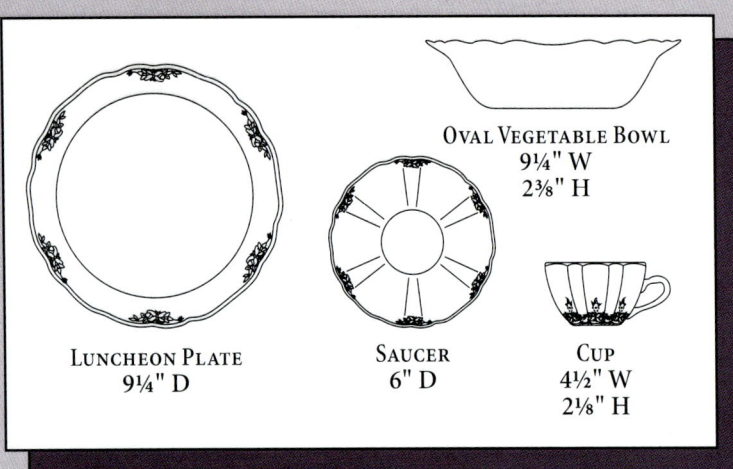

Luncheon Plate 9¼" D

Oval Vegetable Bowl 9¼" W, 2⅜" H

Saucer 6" D

Cup 4½" W, 2⅛" H

CHELSEA   circa 1933

Chelsea has some of the visual design elements of Virginia Rose and was made by both Homer Laughlin and Taylor, Smith & Taylor. It was Taylor, Smith & Taylor who produced the shapes in a more extensive tableware line, with their backstamp predominately displayed. Chelsea was made by both manufacturers for use by Quaker Oats. It is a short-lived shape with only a few pieces.

Chelsea Piece Type List

From Homer Laughlin Literature with Confirmed Actual Pieces

Bowl, Cereal*
Bowl, Vegetable Oval, 9¼ inches
Cup & Saucer Set
    Cup, 2⅛ inches
    Saucer, 6 inches

Plate, Luncheon, 9¼ inches
Plate, Salad*
Platter, Oval*
*Reported but not confirmed.

Top right: *CH31 pattern; Cup & Saucer Set, Luncheon Plate, and Oval Vegetable Bowl.*

Chelsea Shape

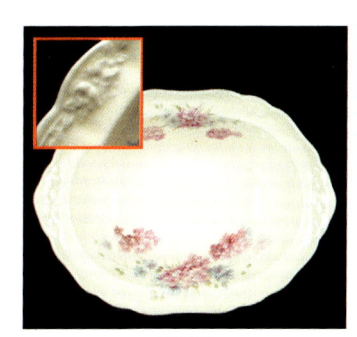

HLC1600	HLC1996	CH5	CH31
No Trim	Luncheon Plate Shown No Trim	Oval Vegetable Bowl Shown No Trim	Luncheon Plate Shown No Trim

Above: *Kenmore pattern; Larkin Catalog, 1936.*
Right: *Blue Bells pattern; Larkin Catalog, 1928.*

195

Marigold

Piece Types

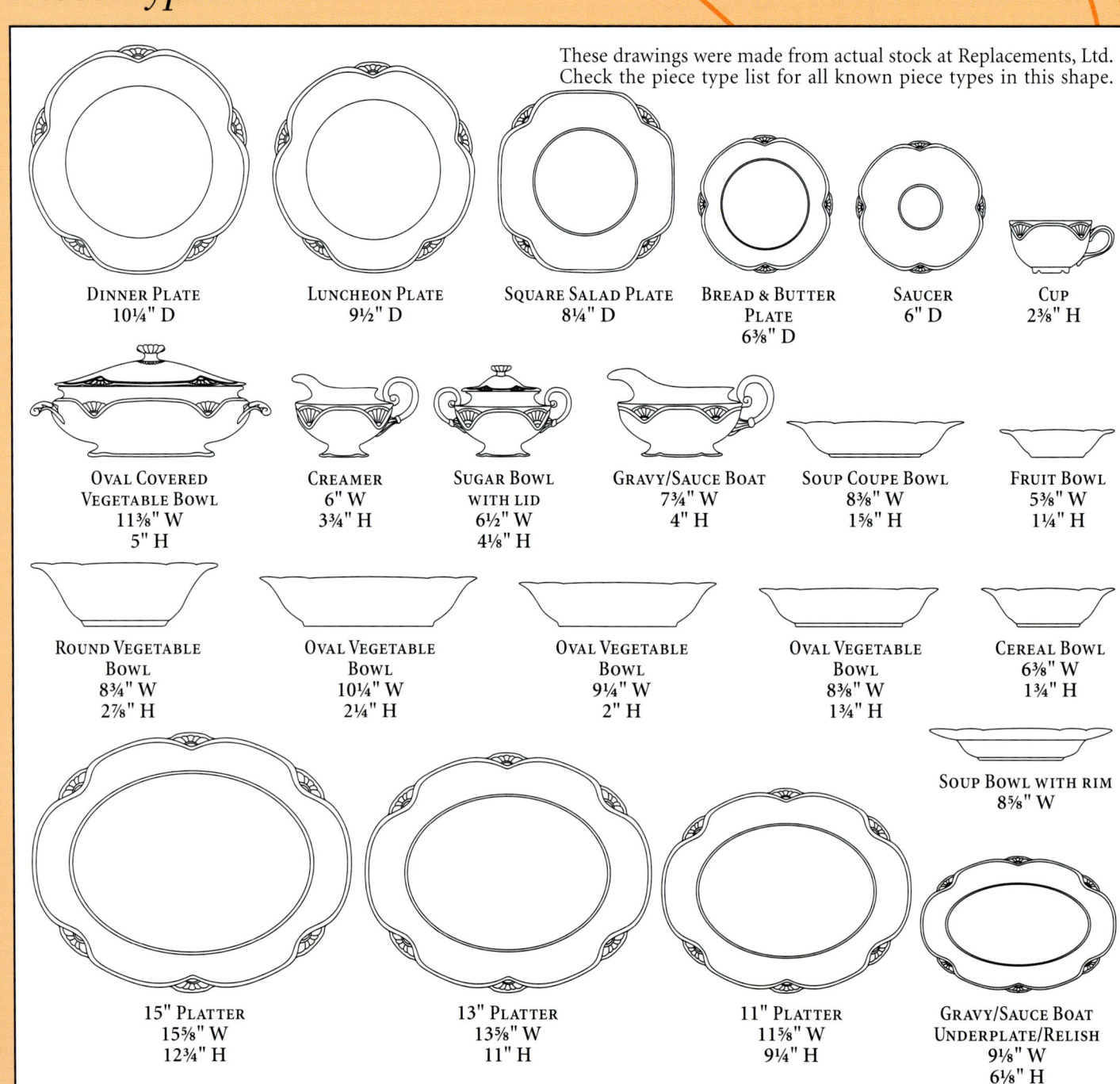

These drawings were made from actual stock at Replacements, Ltd. Check the piece type list for all known piece types in this shape.

Dinner Plate 10¼" D	**Luncheon Plate** 9½" D	**Square Salad Plate** 8¼" D	**Bread & Butter Plate** 6⅜" D	**Saucer** 6" D	**Cup** 2⅜" H
Oval Covered Vegetable Bowl 11⅜" W 5" H	**Creamer** 6" W 3¾" H	**Sugar Bowl with lid** 6½" W 4⅛" H	**Gravy/Sauce Boat** 7¾" W 4" H	**Soup Coupe Bowl** 8⅜" W 1⅝" H	**Fruit Bowl** 5⅜" W 1¼" H
Round Vegetable Bowl 8¾" W 2⅞" H	**Oval Vegetable Bowl** 10¼" W 2¼" H	**Oval Vegetable Bowl** 9¼" W 2" H	**Oval Vegetable Bowl** 8⅜" W 1¾" H	**Cereal Bowl** 6⅜" W 1¾" H	
				Soup Bowl with rim 8⅝" W	
15" Platter 15⅝" W 12¾" H	**13" Platter** 13⅝" W 11" H	**11" Platter** 11⅝" W 9¼" H	**Gravy/Sauce Boat Underplate/Relish** 9⅛" W 6⅛" H		

Marigold Shape

MARIGOLD 1934 – 1937 or later

Marigold was new, circa 1934, when an article in *The Pottery, Glass & Brass Salesman* (August 16, 1934) detailed the decorative treatments offered on the shape. In 1935, Marigold shaped lines were offered in the catalog of the nationwide wholesaler Butler Brothers. In *The Homer Laughlin Pound Sterling Price Booklet of 1937*, Marigold appeared with 47 different decorations/patterns.

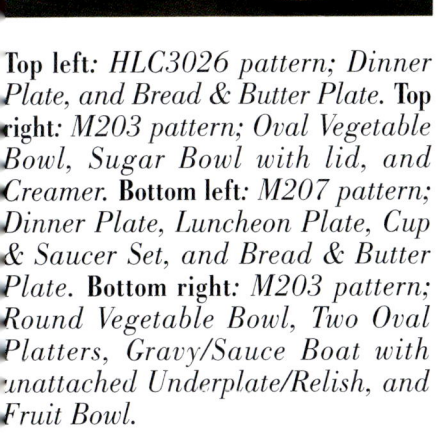

Top left: HLC3026 pattern; Dinner Plate, and Bread & Butter Plate. **Top right**: M203 pattern; Oval Vegetable Bowl, Sugar Bowl with lid, and Creamer. **Bottom left**: M207 pattern; Dinner Plate, Luncheon Plate, Cup & Saucer Set, and Bread & Butter Plate. **Bottom right**: M203 pattern; Round Vegetable Bowl, Two Oval Platters, Gravy/Sauce Boat with unattached Underplate/Relish, and Fruit Bowl.

Homer Laughlin

"HOMER LAUGHLIN"—IVORY—SILVER COLOR TRIM
32-pc. sets, domestic semi-porcelain, r.k. selection, silver color embossed design.
55R-1353—1 set in pkg. 22 lbs..........Set 2.50

Top left: *W134 pattern; Two Oval Platters, and Square Salad Plate.* **Top right:** *W134 pattern; Oval Covered Vegetable Bowl.*
Middle left: *W134 pattern; Butler Brothers Catalog, 1935.* **Middle right:** *HLC3043 pattern; Small Pitcher.*

Marigold Piece Type List

From Homer Laughlin Literature with Confirmed Actual Pieces

Bowl, Cereal, 6⅜ inches
Bowl, Fruit, 5⅜ inches
Bowl, Soup Coupe, 8⅜ inches
Bowl, Soup with rim, 8⅝ inches
Bowl, Vegetable Oval, 8⅜ inches
Bowl, Vegetable Oval, 9¼ inches
Bowl, Vegetable Oval, 10¼ inches
Bowl, Vegetable Oval Covered, 11⅜ inches

Bowl, Vegetable Round, 8¾ inches
Creamer
Cup & Saucer Set
   Cup, 2⅜ inches
   Saucer, 6 inches
Gravy/Sauce Boat
Gravy/Sauce Boat Underplate/Relish, 9⅛ inches
Plate, Bread & Butter, 6⅜ inches

Plate, Dinner, 10¼ inches
Plate, Luncheon, 9½ inches
Plate, Salad Square, 8¼ inches
Platter, Oval, 11⅝ inches
Platter, Oval, 13⅝ inches
Platter, Oval, 15⅝ inches
Sugar Bowl with lid

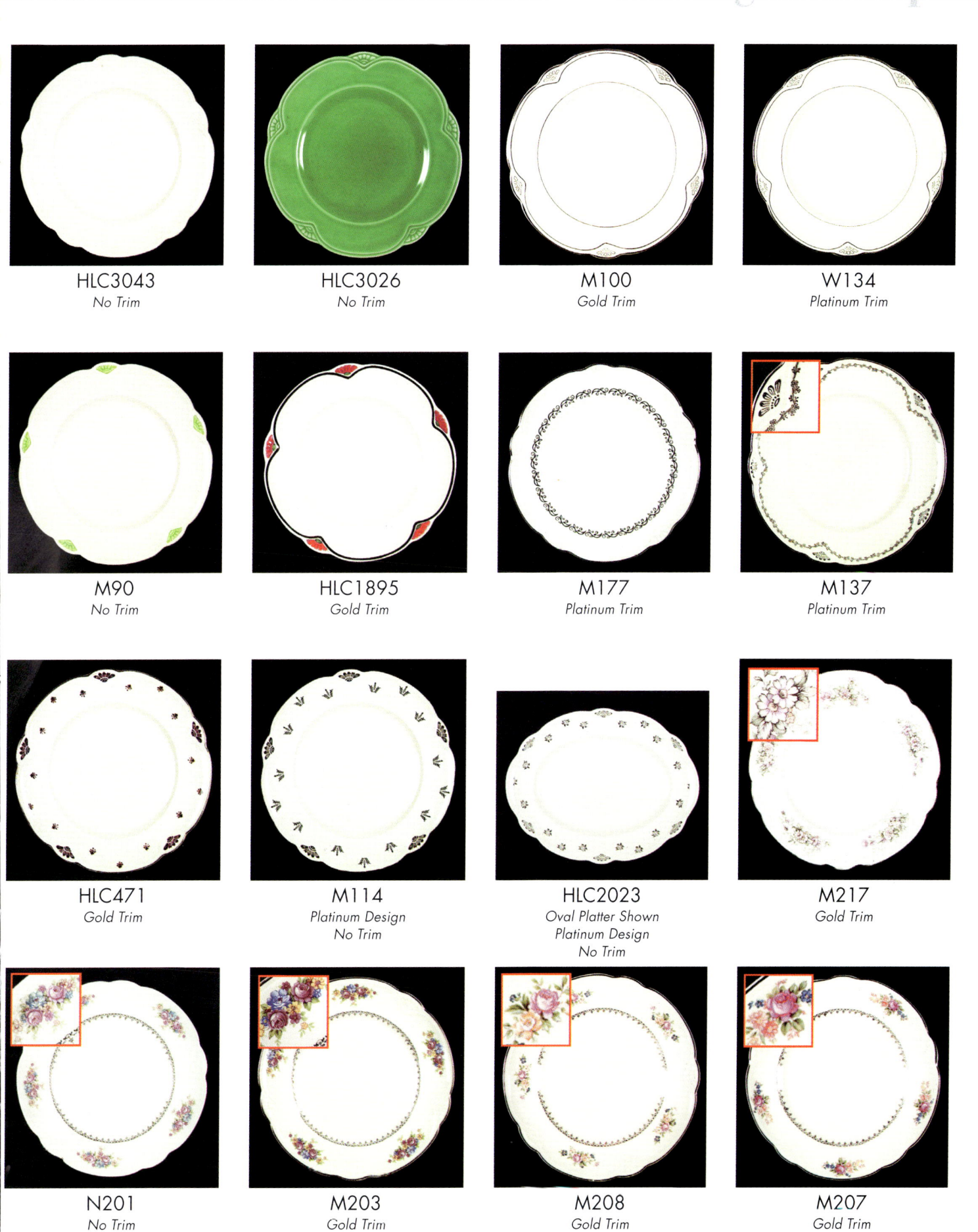

Marigold Shape

HLC3043 No Trim	**HLC3026** No Trim	**M100** Gold Trim	**W134** Platinum Trim
M90 No Trim	**HLC1895** Gold Trim	**M177** Platinum Trim	**M137** Platinum Trim
HLC471 Gold Trim	**M114** Platinum Design No Trim	**HLC2023** Oval Platter Shown Platinum Design No Trim	**M217** Gold Trim
N201 No Trim	**M203** Gold Trim	**M208** Gold Trim	**M207** Gold Trim

Marigold Shape

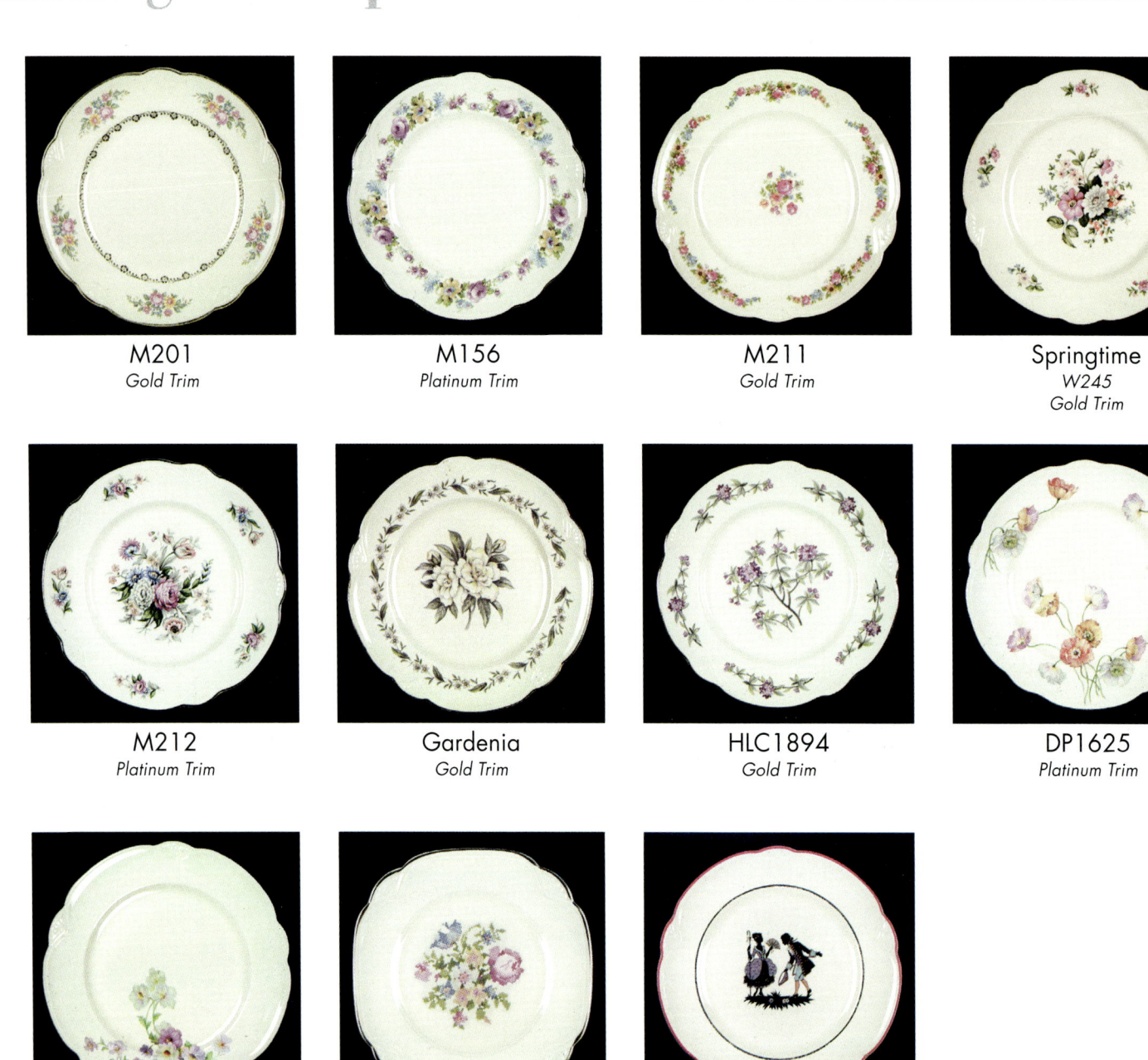

M201 *Gold Trim*	**M156** *Platinum Trim*	**M211** *Gold Trim*	**Springtime** *W245* *Gold Trim*
M212 *Platinum Trim*	**Gardenia** *Gold Trim*	**HLC1894** *Gold Trim*	**DP1625** *Platinum Trim*
HLC3081 *No Trim*	**Petipoint** by Cunningham & Pickett Square Salad Plate Shown *Gold Trim*	**HLC866** *Multi-Motif* *Red Trim*	

CRAFTSMAN

Piece Types

These drawings were made from actual stock at Replacements, Ltd. Check the piece type list for all known piece types in this shape.

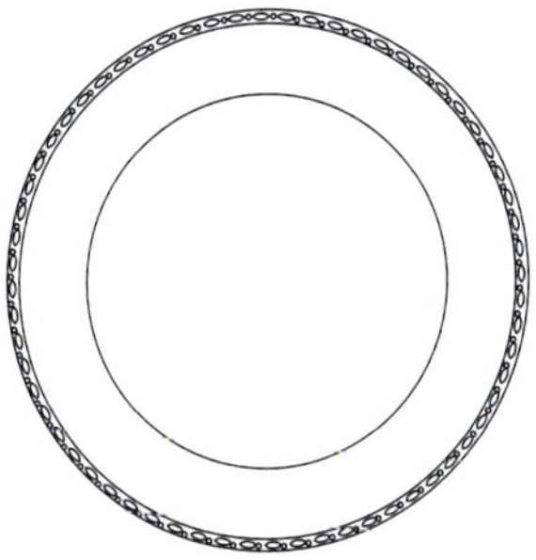

Dinner Plate
10⅛" D

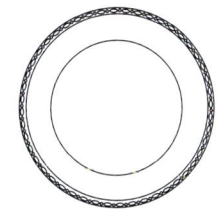

Dessert Plate
7" D

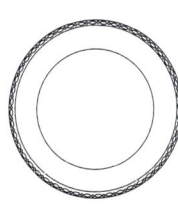

Bread & Butter Plate
6¼" D

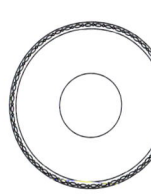

Saucer
5⅞" D

Cup
4¾" W
2¼" H

Sugar Bowl with lid
5¼" W
5⅛" H

Creamer
5" W
4⅞" H

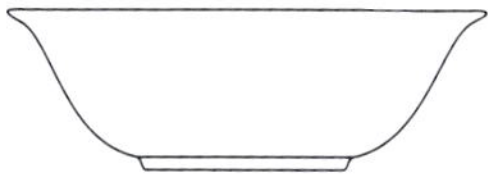

Round Vegetable Bowl
8⅝" W
2⅞" H

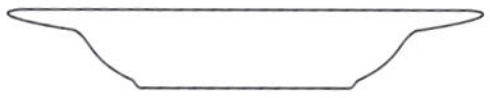

Soup Bowl with rim
8⅝" W
1⅜" H

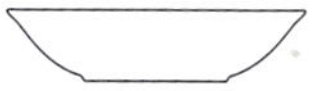

Fruit Bowl
5½" W
1¼" H

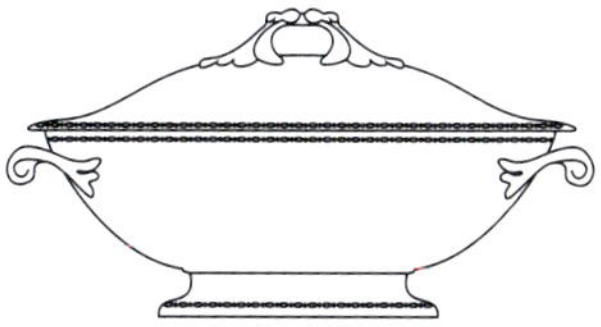

Oval Covered Vegetable Bowl
10⅝" W
5⅝" H

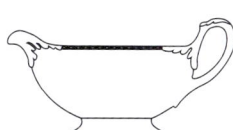

Gravy/Sauce Boat
8¼" W
4¼" H

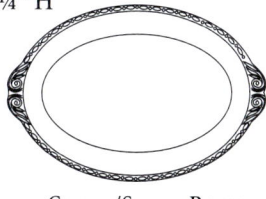

Gravy/Sauce Boat Underplate/Relish
9¼" W
6⅛" H

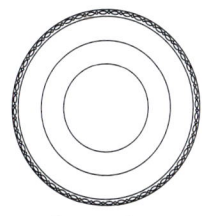

Cream Soup Bowl Saucer
6⅞" D

Cream Soup Bowl
6⅜" W
2⅛" H

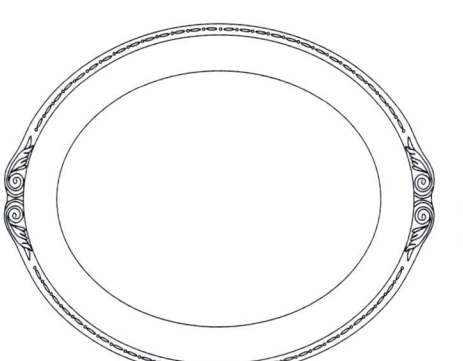

15" Oval Platter
15⅝" W
12⅜" H

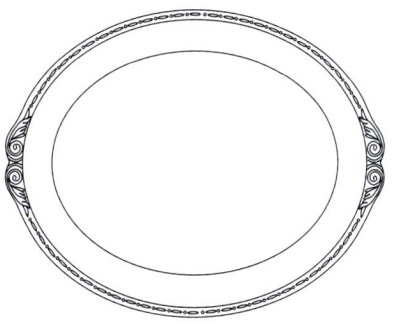

13" Oval Platter
13¾" W
10⅞" H

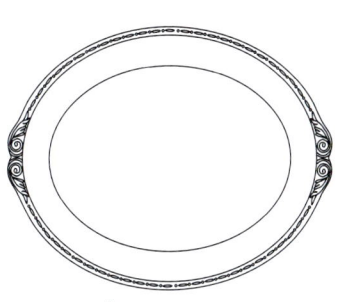

11" Oval Platter
11¾" W
9⅛" H

Homer Laughlin

CRAFTSMAN
1934 – 1936 or later

In her *Lehner's Encyclopedia of U.S. Marks on Pottery, Porcelain & Clay*, author Lois Lehner noted that "Craftsman Dinnerware was filed for registration" as a trademark on December 20, 1933, and Homer Laughlin claimed use of it from that date. Homer Laughlin placed a full-page ad for Craftsman dinnerware in *Pottery, Glass and Brass Salesman*, August 16, 1934. In promoting the Gobelin pattern, this ad said: "Here is another Craftsman development…with its delicate border, its dainty beaded edges, its rich brilliant texture…it is the service that thousands of women have been waiting to purchase…" An advertisement in *Crockery & Glass Journal*, December 1936, mentions Craftsman dinnerware and is the last mention of the shape found.

It is noteworthy that the shapes of Craftsman are identical to Eggshell Georgian except for a restyled creamer and sugar bowl. Perhaps the success and introduction of the Homer Laughlin Eggshell lines deemed a new name to fit with the new clay body used on the Eggshell Georgian patterns?

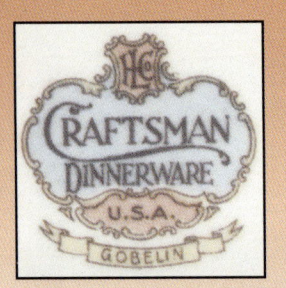

Top left: *Gobelin pattern; backstamp.*
Top middle: *Formal Red pattern; backstamp.*
Middle left: *Gobelin pattern; Sugar Bowl with lid, and Creamer.* **Right:** *Gobelin pattern; Magazine advertisement.* **Bottom left:** *Gobelin pattern; Cup & Saucer Set.*

Craftsman Shape

Craftsman Piece Type List

From Homer Laughlin Literature with Confirmed Actual Pieces

Bowl, Cream Soup & Saucer Set
   Bowl, 6⅜ inches
   Saucer, 6⅞ inches
Bowl, Fruit, 5½ inches
Bowl, Soup with rim, 8⅝ inches
Bowl, Vegetable Oval Covered
   (Casserole), 10⅝ inches
Bowl, Vegetable Round (Nappy),
   8⅝ inches

Creamer
Cup & Saucer Set
   Cup, 2¼ inches
   Saucer, 5⅞ inches
Gravy/Sauce Boat
Gravy/Sauce Boat Underplate/Relish,
   9¼ inches
Plate, Bread & Butter, 6¼ inches
Plate, Dessert, 7 inches

Plate, Dinner, 10⅛ inches
Platter, Oval, 11¾ inches
Platter, Oval, 13¾ inches
Platter, Oval, 15⅝ inches
Sugar Bowl with lid

Collectors Note: Formal can also be found with a Pearl China backstamp.

Formal $7.49
USUAL $10.95 VALUE   32-Pc.

Imitated by many—but never equalled! Rich, elegant—the wide Gold edged border of rich Mandarin Red is decorated with a Rich Gold floral pattern as fine as filigree. Inside edge of border is a lacy pattern of Gold. Outside edge is narrow embossed band edged with Gold. Triple-Selected first quality Ivory-White American Semi-Porcelain.
All handles Gold traced. *All sets Mailable*. 95-pc. shipped in 2 packages. For set composition see Page 319.
486 B 6261—32-Piece.
Service for 6. Ship. wt. 25 lbs.   **$7.49**
586 B 6265—Creamer, Sugar. Shipping weight 3 pounds   **$2.00**
486 B 6262—53-Piece. Service for 8. Wt. 42 lbs. $17.95 Value   **$14.95**
386 B 6264—95-Piece. Service for 12. Wt. 80 lbs. $32.50 Value   **$25.95**
586 B 6265—Open Stock—see Page 319.

WARDS 317

$7.49
32-Pc.

Formal... Like Imported China

Actually this is Triple-Selected First Quality American Semi-Porcelain—but everyone who sees it thinks it is real imported China! That's because the rich pattern is like the lovely formal service plates of fine imported wares. "I use these plates as service plates with my other dinnerware," writes one delighted customer. Wide Gold-edged border of rich Mandarin Red, decorated with a 22-K Gold floral pattern as fine as filigree. Inside edge of border is a lacy pattern of Gold. Outside edge is a narrow embossed band edged with Gold. All handles are Gold traced. 32-piece set is at least a $10.95 value—larger sets bring you even greater savings! The glassware and cutlery shown in the table setting are sold on Pages 394 and 395. *All sets Mailable*. Sets shipped from Chicago, Baltimore, Albany or Pittsburgh. Mail order to nearest House. 95 piece set shipped in 2 packages. See Page 393 for Set Composition.
P486 A 6261—32-Piece Set. Service for Six. Ship. wt. 25 pounds   **$7.49**
586 A 6265—Creamer and Sugar. Shipping weight 3 pounds   **$1.98**
P486 A 6262—53-Piece. Service for Eight. Ship. wt. 42 lbs. Usual $17.95 value   **$13.95**
P386 A 6264—95-Piece. Service for 12. Ship. wt. 80 lbs. Usual $32.50 value   **$24.95**
586 A 6265—Open Stock. State pattern and articles. Price table, Pg. 393.

Left: Formal pattern; Montgomery Ward, 1939.
Right: Formal pattern; Montgomery Ward, 1938-39.

203

Craftsman Shape

Aurelia
G13
Luncheon Plate Shown
Gold Trim

G22
Gold Band
No Trim

HLC968
Gold Trim

HLC503
Soup Bowl Shown
Gold Trim

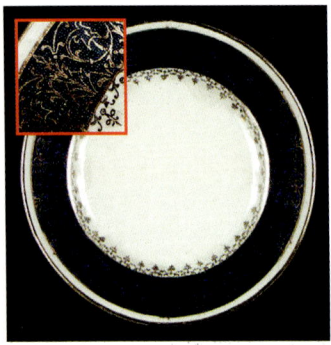

HLC2165
Bread & Butter Plate Shown
Gold Trim

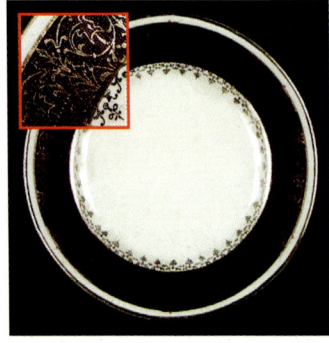

HLC906
Bread & Butter Plate Shown
Gold Trim

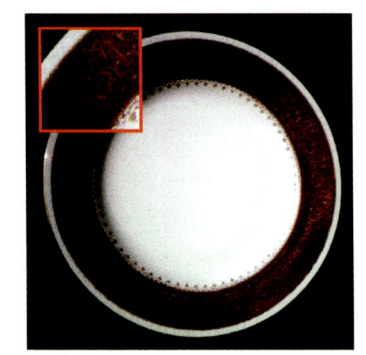

HLC707
Gold Trim

Formal
also known as "G150"
by Pearl China
Gold Trim

Sienna
Saucer Shown
Gold Trim

Gobelin
Gold Trim

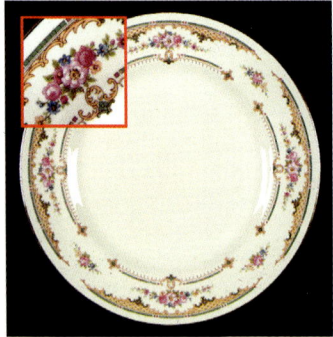

Chartreuse
Gold Trim

Primuline
Gold Trim

Elaine
Dessert Plate Shown
Gold Trim

Cynthia
Oval Platter Shown
Platinum Trim

CORONET

Piece Types

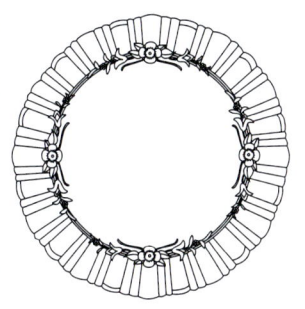

These drawings were made from actual stock or literature at Replacements, Ltd. Check the piece type list for all known piece types in this shape.

Dinner Plate
9⅞" D

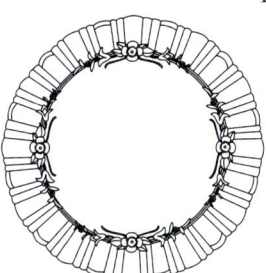

Luncheon Plate
9¼" D

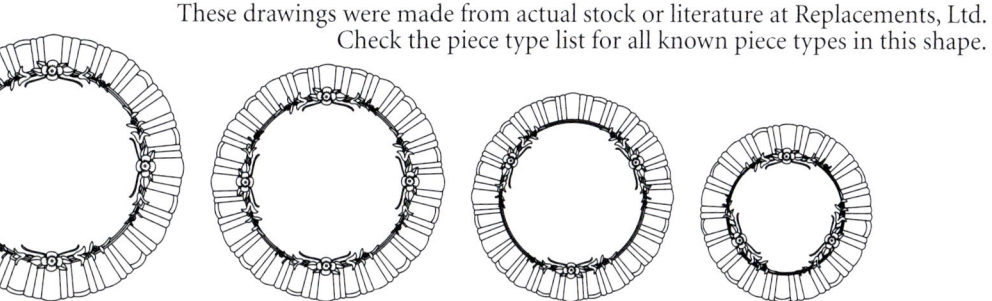

Salad Plate
8¼" D

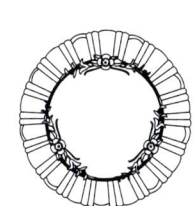

Dessert Plate
7¼" D

Bread & Butter Plate
6⅛" D

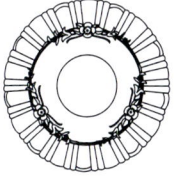

Saucer
6" D

Cup
2¾" H

Creamer
5½" W
4" H

Sugar Bowl
with lid

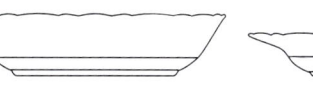

Oval Vegetable Bowl
9¼" W
2⅛" H

Soup Bowl with rim
8⅜" W

Cereal Bowl, Lugged
6⅛" W

Cereal Coupe Bowl
6⅛" W

Fruit Bowl
5¼" W
1¼" H

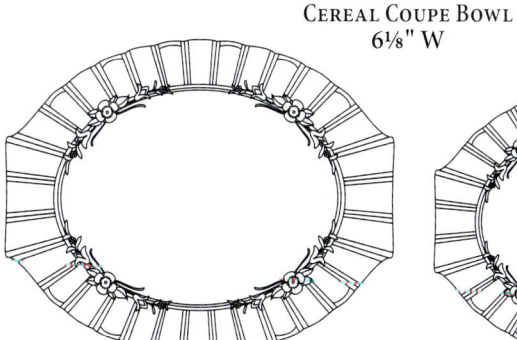

13" Platter
13⅝" W x 10¾" H

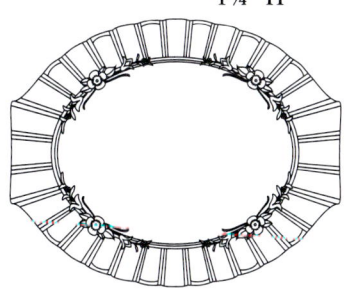

11" Platter
11⅝" W x 9⅛" H

DINNERWARE SETS
Service for 6, 8 or 12

Regular R.K. quality domestic semi-porcelain, beautifully worked designs in attractive colors.

PLATINUM WREATH

"Homer Laughlin" Ware—Ivory body, unique flaring shape, embossed wreath and border.
55R-4748—32-pc. set, "Service for 6"
1 set in pkg, 23 lbs............Set 3.25
55R-4754—66-pc. set, "Service for 8"
1 set in pkg, 50 lbs............Set 8.75
55R-4755—95-pc. set, "Service for 12"
1 set in pkg, 95 lbs............Set 11.50

FLORAL MEDALLIONS

Ivory body, embossed border with floral & gold medallions, gold edge line.
55R-6065—32-pc. set, "Service for 6"
1 set in carton, 20 lbs.........Set 4.75
55R-6066—62-pc. set, "Service for 8"—standard 54-pc. set except with jug soups and 10 in. dinner plates plus 8 B & B plates.
1 set in carton, 50 lbs..........Set 10.50
55R-6067—95-pc. set, "Service for 12"—with jug soups and 10 in. dinner plates.
1 set in carton, 95 lbs..........Set 17.00

Above: *Platinum Wreath and Floral Medallions patterns; Butler Brothers Catalog, 1935.*

Homer Laughlin

CORONET
1935 – 1937 or later

Coronet debuted in 1935 in the Montgomery Ward catalog with the initial offering of the Pink Print pattern. In the *Homer Laughlin Pound Sterling Price Booklet of 1937*, the Coronet shape is offered with 82 different patterns or decorations. It was one of the products touted in a December 1936 ad in the *China & Glass Journal*, where Homer Laughlin listed their "1937 Previews" for the Pittsburgh trade show.

Coronet shape, with its floral embossing at the edge of the well, accented by lines protruding to the scalloped edge, was a perfect design for various decorations. The embossing accents the patterns, whose decorations only appear in the plate's center, as well as making a perfect pallet for decorating the embossed design itself with a single or multiple color scheme. The pieces are commonly marked with a crown, "Coronet," a Homer Laughlin monogram, and "U.S.A."

Top right: *Typical Coronet backstamp.* **Above left:** *June Rose pattern; Larkin Catalog, 1935-36.* **Right:** *Pink Print pattern; Montgomery Ward Catalog, 1935.* **Bottom left:** *HLC1019 pattern; Oval Platter, Salad Plate, Cereal Bowl, Bread & Butter Plate, and Dinner Plate.* **Bottom middle:** *Platinum Wreath pattern; Oval Platter, Dinner Plate, Salad Plate, Fruit Bowl, Cereal Bowl, Creamer, and Soup Bowl with rim.*

Coronet Shape

CORONET (LIGHT YELLOW GLAZE)

Pattern	Sel.	S	D.S.	Unc.	Mat.	Description
CO-100	Sch.	$7.75	$8.25	$8.75	$9.75	1 sprig, 953, no line
CO-101	Sch.	7.75	8.25	8.75	9.75	1 sprig, 4125, no line
CO-102	Sch.	9.25	9.75	10.25	11.25	6 sprigs, 1238, silver edge
CO-103	Sch.	8.25	8.75	9.25	10.25	1 sprig (CO-100) gold edge
CO-104	Sch.	8.25	8.75	9.25	10.25	1 sprig (CO-101) gold edge
CO-105	Sch.	8.25	8.75	9.25	10.25	1 sprig, 1456, green edge
CO-107	Sch.	8.00	8.50	9.00	10.00	Gold stamp verge embossing & edge
CO-108	Sch.	7.25	7.75	8.00	9.25	Silver stamp verge embossing
CO-109	Sch.	7.75	8.25	8.75	9.75	Silver stamp verge embossing & edge
CO-110	Sch.	9.25	9.75	10.25	11.25	6 sprigs, 4195, gold edge
CO-111	Sch.	9.25	9.75	10.25	11.25	5 sprigs, 4048, asst'd gold stamps
CO-112	Sch.	10.00	10.50	11.25	12.00	5 sprigs, 1356, gold edge
CO-113	Sch.	7.75	8.25	8.75	9.75	1 sprig, (CO-105) no line
CO-114	Sch.	7.75	8.25	8.75	9.75	1 sprig, 1612, no line
CO-115	Sch.	7.75	8.25	8.75	9.75	1 sprig, 585, no line
CO-117	Sch.	9.25	9.75	10.25	11.25	3 sprigs, 819, gold edge
CO-118	Sch.	8.75	9.25	9.75	10.75	3 sprigs, 926, silver edge
CO-119	Sch.	9.00	9.50	10.00	11.00	3 sprigs, 729, gold edge
CO-121	Sch.	10.00	10.50	11.25	12.00	5 sprigs, (CO-111) gold edge & asst'd stamp
CO-122	Sch.	7.75	8.25	8.75	9.75	Asst'd silver stamp, no line
CO-524	Sch.	8.00	8.50	9.00	10.00	Gold ornament border stamp, gold edge
CO-526	Sch.	8.00	8.50	9.00	10.00	Gold ornament border stamp, gold edge
CO-527	Sch.	8.75	9.25	9.75	10.75	3 sprigs, D-1625, gold edge
CO-529	Sch.	10.00	10.50	11.25	12.00	4 sprigs, 1334, pink edge, silver handles
CO-532	Sch.	7.75	8.25	8.75	9.75	1 sprig, 1318, no line
CO-535	Sch.	8.25	8.75	9.25	10.25	3 sprigs (CO-527) no line
CO-537	Sch.	7.75	8.25	8.75	9.75	1 sprig, 1121, no line
CO-543	Sch.	8.75	9.25	9.75	10.75	2 sprigs (J-6) silver edge
CO-546	Sch.	8.25	8.75	9.25	10.25	1 sprig (CO-532) green edge
CO-547	Sch.	8.25	8.75	9.25	10.25	1 sprig (CO-114) green edge
CO-549	Sch.	7.50	8.00	8.25	9.50	1 sprig (RV-1) no line
CO-550	Sch.	10.00	10.50	11.25	12.00	4 sprigs (CO-111) gold edge & stamps
CO-551	Sch.	7.00	7.50	7.75	9.00	1 sprig (Y-137) no line
CO-552	Sch.	8.00	8.50	9.00	10.00	1 sprig (RV-1) silver stamp
CO-553	Sch.	9.00	9.50	10.00	11.00	4 sprigs (CO-111) gold edge
CO-555	3rds	6.00	6.25	6.75	8.00	1 sprig (RV-8133) no line
CO-556	3rds	6.00	6.25	6.75	8.00	1 sprig (RV-1843) no line
CO-557	Sch.	8.25	8.75	9.25	10.25	1 sprig (CO-115) silver edge
CO-558	Sch.	8.75	9.25	9.75	10.75	3 sprigs (OS-81) red edge
CO-559	Sch.	7.25	7.75	8.00	9.25	16 asst'd silver stamps only
CO-562	3rds	6.50	7.00	7.25	8.50	3 sprigs (W-129) no line
CO-563	3rds	6.50	7.00	7.25	8.50	3 sprigs (W-227) no line
CO-564	J. J. Newberry					1 sprig, 5005, no line
CO-565	Sch.	7.00	7.50	7.75	9.00	1 sprig (J.J.54) no line
CO-567	3rds	7.00	7.50	7.75	9.00	3 sprigs (W-129) silver edge

Pattern	Sel.	S	D.S.	Unc.	Mat.	Description
CO-569	3rds	$7.00	$7.50	$7.75	$9.00	1 sprig (W-1733) silver edge
CO-570	3rds	6.00	6.25	6.75	8.00	1 sprig (J.J.54) no line
CO-572	Sch.	8.75	9.25	9.75	10.75	3 sprigs (OS-111) silver edge
CO-573	Sch.	7.00	7.50	7.75	9.00	1 sprig (RV-1843) no line
CO-574	Sch.	7.00	7.50	7.75	9.00	1 sprig (RV-7833) no line
CO-578	Sch.	7.75	8.25	8.75	9.75	Silver border stamp and edge line
CO-579	Sch.	7.25	7.75	8.00	9.25	Silver border stamp only
CO-582	Sch.	7.50	8.00	8.25	9.50	1 sprig (RV-1) silver stamps, no line
CO-583	Sch.	7.50	8.00	8.25	9.50	1 sprig (RV-7833) silver stamps, no line
CO-584	Sch.	7.50	8.00	8.25	9.50	1 sprig (W-1733) silver stamps, no line
CO-586	Sch.	7.50	8.00	8.25	9.50	1 sprig (Y-135) silver stamps, no line
CO-588	Sch.	8.25	8.75	9.25	10.25	1 sprig, (CO-100) silver edge
CO-589	Sch.	8.25	8.75	9.25	10.25	3 sprigs (CO-118) no line
CO-590	Sch.	8.75	9.25	9.75	10.75	3 sprigs (VR-235) silver edge
CO-591	Sch.	8.75	9.25	9.75	10.75	2 sprigs (VR-128) silver edge
CO-593	Sch.	8.75	9.25	9.75	10.75	3 sprigs (VR-232) silver edge
CO-594	Sch.	8.75	9.25	9.75	10.75	3 sprigs (CO-117) no line
CO-595	3rds	6.50	7.00	7.25	8.50	1 sprig (J.J.54) silver edge
CO-597	Sch.	7.50	8.00	8.25	9.50	Gold edge line only
CO-600	Sch.	7.75	8.25	8.75	9.75	1 sprig, 1375, no line
CO-601	Sch.	7.50	8.00	8.25	9.50	1 sprig, 1388, no line
CO-602	Sch.	7.75	8.25	8.75	9.75	1 sprig, 797, no line
CO-603	Sch.	8.75	9.25	9.75	10.75	6 sprigs (CO-110) no line
CO-604	Sch.	7.50	8.00	8.25	9.50	1 sprig, 1423, no line
CO-605	Sch.	8.25	8.75	9.25	10.25	1 sprig (CO-600) silver edge
CO-606	Sch.	7.00	7.50	7.75	9.00	1 sprig, (C-211) no line
CO-607	Sch.	7.75	8.25	8.75	9.75	1 sprig, (C-211) 12 silver stamps, no line
CO-608	Sch.	7.00	7.50	7.75	9.00	1 sprig (RV-8133) no line
CO-609	Sch.	8.25	8.75	9.25	10.25	1 sprig (CO-604) 12 silver stamps, no line
CO-610	Sch.	8.25	8.75	9.25	10.25	1 sprig (CO-105) gold edge line
CO-611	Sch.	8.25	8.75	9.25	10.25	1 sprig (CO-114) gold edge line
CO-612	Sch.	8.25	8.75	9.25	10.25	1 sprig (CO-537) gold edge line
CO-613	Sch.	8.25	8.75	9.25	10.25	1 sprig (CO-532) gold edge line

Above: *Coronet shaped patterns offered in the* **Decorated Dinner Ware Pound Sterling Prices, May 1st, Nineteen Hundred Thirty-Seven, Homer Laughlin China Company.** *Note: pattern CO-564 was exclusively for J.J. Newberry, a common practice for larger Homer Laughlin clients.* **Below:** *HLC1998 pattern; Bread & Butter Plate and Lugged Cereal Bowl.*

Coronet Piece Type List

From Homer Laughlin Literature with Confirmed Actual Pieces

- Bowl, Cereal, 6⅛ inches
- Bowl, Cereal Lugged, 6⅛ inches
- Bowl, Fruit, 5¼ inches
- Bowl, Soup with rim, 8⅜ inches
- Bowl, Vegetable Oval, 9¼ inches
- Bowl, Vegetable Round, 8¾ inches
- Bowl, Vegetable Round Covered, 8¾ inches
- Creamer
- Cup & Saucer Set
  - Cup, 2¾ inches
  - Saucer, 6 inches
- Gravy/Sauce Boat
- Gravy/Sauce Boat Underplate/Relish
- Plate, Bread & Butter, 6⅛ inches
- Plate, Dessert, 7¼ inches
- Plate, Dinner, 9⅞ inches
- Plate, Luncheon, 9¼ inches
- Plate, Salad, 8¼ inches
- Platter, Oval, 11⅝ inches
- Platter, Oval, 13⅝ inches
- Platter, Oval, 15¼ inches
- Sugar Bowl with lid

Coronet Shape

HLC1896
No Trim

HLC1052
Gold Trim

HLC1693
Gold Trim

HLC247
Platinum Trim

CO110
Gold Trim

HLC1034
Luncheon Plate Shown
Platinum Decoration
No Trim

Platinum Wreath
CO109
Luncheon Plate Shown
Platinum Trim

CO57
No Trim

CO58
No Trim

CO63
No Trim

HLC1051
Gold Trim

HLC1683
Oval Platter Shown
Platinum Trim

HLC1174
Oval Platter Shown
Gold Trim

CO574
No Trim

CO604
No Trim

HLC949
Fruit Bowl Shown
Gold Trim

208

Coronet Shape

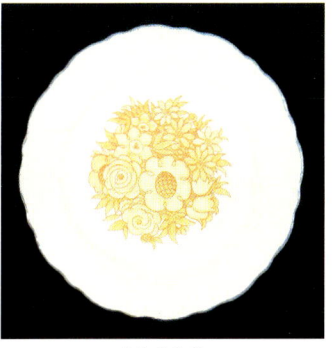

R1810
Blue Trim

R1808
Red Trim

CO532
No Trim

CO118
No Trim

HLC1998
*Bread & Butter Plate Shown
No Trim*

Pink Print
No Trim

HLC2081
*Luncheon Plate Shown
No Trim*

CO553
*Bread & Butter Plate Shown
Gold Trim*

HLC1019
Pink Trim

HLC104
*Bread & Butter Plate Shown
Gold Trim*

Fiesta

Piece Types

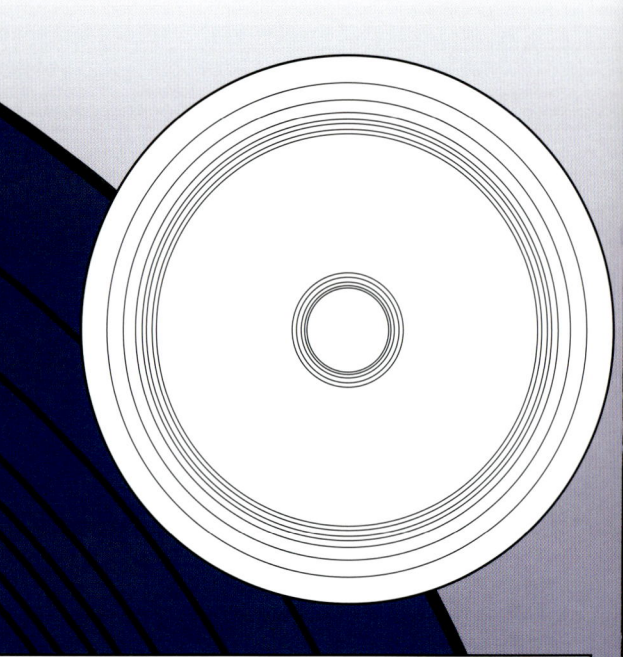

Row 1 (piece labels): FLOWER VASE 10" · COFFEE POT REG. · TEA POT LARGE · TEA POT MEDIUM · COFFEE POT A. D. · CARAFE · ICE PITCHER · JUG (2 PTS.) · COVERED SUGAR · CREAMER · BUD VASE · CANDLE HOLDER TRIPOD · CANDLE HOLDER BULB · SALT & PEPPER SHAKERS · MARMALADE · MUSTARD

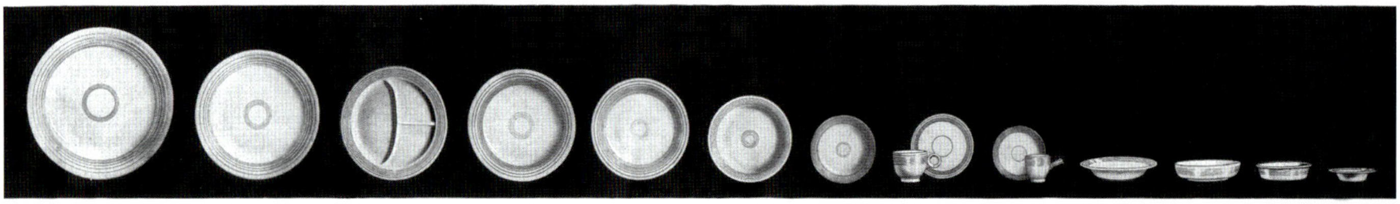

Row 2 (piece labels): CHOP PLATE 15" · CHOP PLATE 13" · COMPARTMENT PLATE 10½" · PLATE 10" · PLATE 9" · PLATE 7" · PLATE 6" · TEA CUP & SAUCER · COFFEE CUP & SAUCER A. D. · DEEP PLATE 8" · DESSERT 6" · FRUIT 5" · ASH TRAY

Row 3 (piece labels): FOOTED SALAD BOWL · NESTED BOWLS 11½" TO 5" · COVERED CASSEROLE · CREAM SOUP CUP · COVERED ONION SOUP · RELISH TRAY · COMPORT 12" · SWEETS COMPORT · NAPPIE 9½" · NAPPIE 8½" · EGG CUP · TUMBLER · TOM & JERRY MUG · UTILITY TRAY

COLOR! That's the trend today . . . a trend that has gained momentum steadily in every department of design and decoration, in every room of our homes. Emphasis is withdrawn from the drab, uninteresting monotones . . . and placed heavily upon brightness, gayety . . . color! It is in this spirit of gayety and color that we offer you Fiesta . . . a new ware that provides endless possibilities for interesting, tasteful and eye-catching color effects in dressing the modern table.

Fiesta comes in five lovely colors . . . Green, Yellow, Blue, Old Ivory and Red . . . all brilliant, all cheerful, all endowed with a pleasant feeling of good fellowship, informality and gracious living. Whether used for serving breakfast, luncheon, informal supper, or buffet, Fiesta makes the meal a truly gay occasion. It gives the hostess an opportunity to create her own table effects by combining, according to her tastes or the occasion, any colors in any way she desires. Plates of one color, cream soups of another, contrasting cups and saucers . . . it's fun to set a table with Fiesta !

Fiesta is superbly shaped, is of high quality both in material and texture, is designed and executed with artistic skill of the first order. It offers a wide variety of items, increasing the possibilities of creating a table ensemble of true color harmony. And although pleasantly reminiscent of the lovely Faience tradition, it is thoroughly modern and different. Best of all, Fiesta is extremely reasonable in price, may be bought by the piece, and thus affords the purchaser a chance to build up a set not only of whatever items, but of whatever colors, she desires.

PRICE LIST
(Per Piece)

ITEM	BLUE YELLOW GREEN OLD IVORY	RED
Tea Cups	.45	.55
Tea Saucers	.25	.40
Plates, 10 inch	.70	1.00
Plates, 9 inch	.65	.90
Plates, 7 inch	.55	.70
Plates, 6 inch	.35	.55
Deep Plates, 8 inch	.55	.70
Cream Soup Cups	.90	1.15
Onion Soups, Covered	1.35	1.80
Fruits, 5 inch	.25	.40
Desserts, 6 inch	.65	.80
Coffee Cups, A.D.	.40	.45
Coffee Saucers, A.D.	.25	.40
Chop Plates, 15 inch	2.00	2.75
Chop Plates, 13 inch	1.40	2.25
Nappies, 9½ inch	1.60	1.50
Nappies, 8½ inch	.80	1.10
Casseroles, Covered	2.70	3.75
Comports, 12 inch	2.75	4.50
Comports, Sweets, 5½ inch	1.15	1.60
Compartment Plates, 10½ inch	1.15	1.60
Salad Bowls, Footed, 12 inch	4.25	5.00
Sugars, Covered	1.35	1.80
Creams	.80	1.10
Coffee Pots, A.D.	2.00	2.75
Coffee Pots, Regular	2.50	3.10
Tea Pots, Large, 8 Cup	2.50	3.10
Tea Pots, Medium, 6 Cup	2.25	3.15
Ice Pitchers, 2 Quarts	2.65	4.00
Jugs, 2 Pint	1.50	2.25
Carafes, 3 Pints	2.85	3.85
Salt Shakers	.55	.80
Pepper Shakers	.55	.80
Mustards, Covered	.80	1.15
Marmalade Jars, Covered	1.25	1.65
Utility Trays	.80	1.10
Relish Trays, Complete	2.90	4.50
Egg Cups	.55	.70
Tom and Jerry Mugs	.55	.70
Tumblers, 10 oz.	.55	.70
Candle Holders, Tripod	1.30	1.60
Candle Holders, Bulb	.80	1.00
Ash Trays	.25	.35
Bud Vases	.80	1.10
Flower Vases, 8 inch	1.15	2.00
Flower Vases, 10 inch	2.00	3.30
Flower Vases, 12 inch	3.10	4.30
Bowls, 11½ inch	2.25	2.95
Bowls, 10 inch	1.75	2.50
Bowls, 8 inch	1.00	1.40
Bowls, 7 inch	.80	1.15
Bowls, 6 inch	.70	1.00
Bowls, 5 inch	.45	.70
Bowls, 5 inch	.35	.65

Canadian Representative—
THE J. H. WEIR COMPANY
51 Wellington Street West · Toronto, Ontario

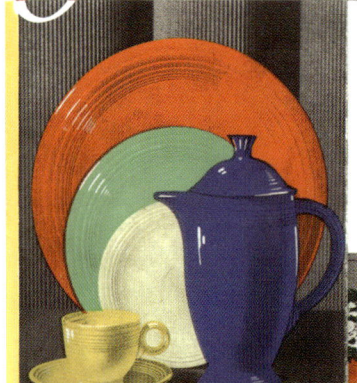

THE HOMER LAUGHLIN CHINA CO., NEWELL, W. VA.

Fiesta Shape

FIESTA   1935 – currently in production

Fiesta is the best selling dinnerware in America. In 1997, Homer Laughlin celebrated the production of 500 million pieces of Fiesta. Created in 1935, by then Homer Laughlin art director Frederic Rhead, the line is by far the most successful and sought after of all Homer Laughlin lines. Entire books have been dedicated to just Fiesta alone.

A special shape was commissioned to commemorate the production of the 500 millionth piece of Fiesta. The Presentation Bowl is a low, classic form modeled by senior Homer Laughlin designer Jope Geisse and completed August 21, 1997. The creation of this special piece is a highlight in the Fiesta line's long history. Prior to this event, the line had been discontinued and reintroduced. The Fiesta story is complex. There are sixteen periods, groupings, or types of product that relate to the Fiesta name and style:

1935	Old/Original/Vintage Fiesta
1935	Old Fiesta with Decals
1930's–1940's	Fiesta with Stripes
1936	Fiesta Harmony Line *Fiesta and Nautilus combination*
1937	Fiesta Kitchen Kraft *Kitchen Kraft shapes dipped in Fiesta colors*
1939	Fiesta Ensembles *Fiesta sold as a set with glassware and flatware*
1954-5	Calendar Plates
1962	Fiesta Casuals *Solid Fiesta with stenciled Fiesta*
1967	Sheffield Amberstone
1969	Fiesta Ironstone
1970	Coventry Casualtone
1986	New Fiesta
	New Fiesta with Decals
	Children's Fiesta
	Fiesta Mates *Restaurant shapes dipped in Fiesta colors*
	Go-Alongs *Fiesta products made by other companies*

Top: *Raspberry Presentation Bowl; Created to commemorate the 500 millionth piece of Fiesta.* **Bottom:** *Turquoise Daffy Duck Cup, Red Large Flower Vase, Lilac Covered Butter Dish, Medium Green Dinner Plate, Yellow with Maroon Stripes Luncheon Plate, Christmas Small Disk Pitcher, Light Green Cake Lifter, Amberstone Coffeepot with lid, Chartreuse Dots Tumbler, Red Small Casserole with lid, Turquoise Carafe with lid, and Casualstone Gravy/Sauce Boat.*

Fiesta Glaze Colors

Color	Years	Color	Years	Color	Years
Red	1936–1943 & 1959–1972	Antique Gold (Ironstone)	1969–1972	Sea Mist Green	1991–
Cobalt Blue	1936–1951	Turf Green (Ironstone)	1969–1972	Lilac	1993–1995
Light Green	1936–1951	Mango Red (Ironstone)	1969–1972	Persimmon	1995–
Yellow (old)	1936–1969	White	1986–	Sapphire	1996–1997
Ivory (old)	1936–1951	Black	1986–	Chartreuse (new)	1997–1999
Turquoise (old)	1937–1969	Rose (new)	1986–	Pearl Gray	1999–2001
Forest Green	1951–1959	Apricot	1986–1998	Juniper	1999–2001
Rose (old)	1951–1959	Cobalt Blue (new)	1986–	Cinnabar	2000–
Chartreuse (old)	1951–1959	Yellow (new)	1987–2002	Sunflower	2001–
Gray (old)	1951–1959	Turquoise (new)	1988–	Plum	2002–
Medium Green	1959–1969	Periwinkle Blue	1989–	Shamrock	2003–

Fiesta Shape

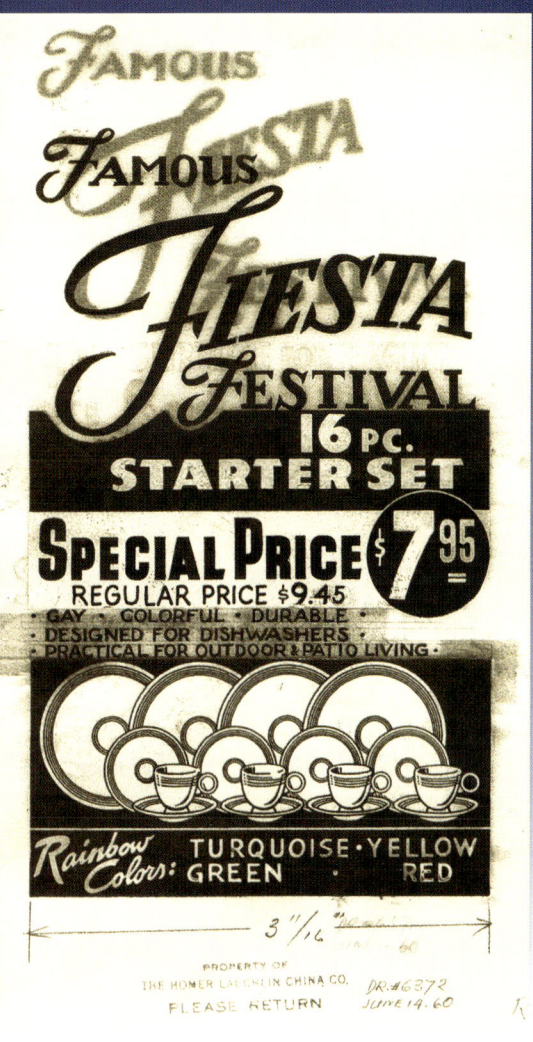

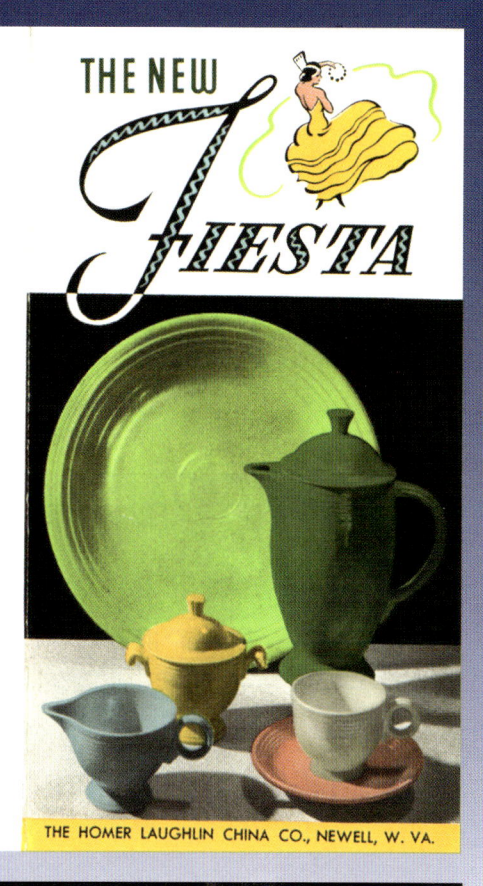

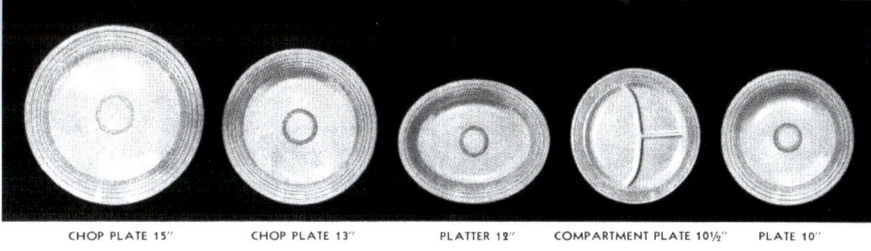

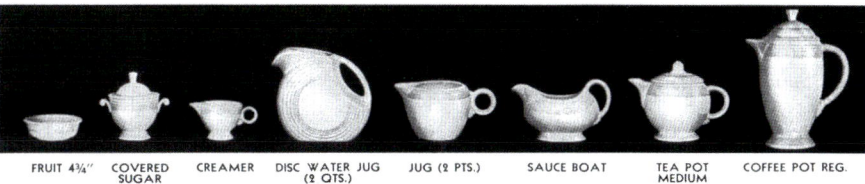

Top left: *Mock-up for a Fiesta ad.*
Right: *1951 Fiesta retail pamphlet.*
Bottom left: *All Fiesta dinner plates new and old through 2001.*

Fiesta Shape

MATCH OR MIX COLORS

Fiesta Juice Set   2514 $1   Cash or Certificates

Seven-piece beverage set of genuine Fiesta pottery. One-quart pitcher of distinctive style and six tumblers in green, blue, yellow, and red—all in assorted colors. All pieces have the quality, grace, smartness of line and characteristic texture for which this genuine Fiesta pottery is famous.

Height of pitcher, 5¾ in.; tumblers, 3½ in. Ideal for serving fruit juices and beverages. Mailing weight 4 lbs.

Colorful Fiesta Ware

Color comes to the dining table—gay, bright, cheerful colors that help make every meal a gala occasion. It is decidedly smart and great fun to use this new Fiesta pottery, which, with its brilliant green, yellow, blue and red pieces, adds a delightful informality and good fellowship. It gives the hostess the opportunity to create a wide variety of table effects that contribute to gracious living. Perfect for the informal supper, buffet or luncheon, and, for breakfast, helps to start the day right.

Fiesta pottery is of decidedly high quality, famous for its design, material and texture, and the artistic skill with which it is fashioned. Only in genuine, nationally-advertised Fiesta ware can you get such craftsmanship and value.

The set, offering service for four, consists of:
- 4 Cups—1 each green, blue, yellow, red
- 4 Saucers—1 each, green, blue, yellow, red
- 4 9-in. Plates—1 each, green, blue, yellow, red
- 4 7-in. Plates—1 each, green, blue, yellow, red
- 4 5-in. Fruit Saucers—1 each, green, blue, yellow, red
- 1 13-in Chop Plate in blue
- 1 8½-in. Nappy in yellow
- 1 Covered Sugar Bowl in green
- 1 Cream Pitcher in red

25-Pc. Set, 2566   Coupon Price $14   Cash Price $7   Mlg. wt. 24 lbs.

Fiesta Ware

Color on the table is the order of the day! Gay, bright, cheerful colors that help make every meal a gala occasion. It is not only good style, but also great fun to use this Fiesta pottery; its brilliant colors add a delightful informality which promotes good fellowship.

It gives the hostess the opportunity to create a wide variety of table effects that contribute to gracious living. Perfect for the informal supper, buffet, or luncheon; used for breakfast, helps to start the day right.

Fiesta pottery is of decidedly high quality, famous for its design, material, and texture, and the artistic skill with which it is fashioned. Only in this *genuine, nationally-advertised* Fiesta ware can you get such craftsmanship and value.

Choice of:

25-piece Service — The 25-piece set provides a service for four. Consists of one green, one blue, one yellow, and one red of each of the following pieces: 9-in. dinner plates, 7-in. plates, fruit saucers, teacups, and saucers. There is also an 8½-in. nappy in yellow, a covered sugar bowl in green, and the cream pitcher is red. Match your service for each person or mix your colors as much as you wish. Either way is exciting. Mailing weight 24 lbs.
2566 $7.75   Cash or Certificates

50-piece Service — The 50-piece set provides a service for eight. Consists of two green, two blue, two yellow, and two red of each of the following pieces: 9-in. dinner plates, 7-in. plates, fruit saucers, teacups, and saucers. Also included is a 13-in. chop plate in green and another in red, a covered sugar bowl in yellow, a cream pitcher in blue, salt shaker in turquoise, pepper shaker in red, ash tray in turquoise, and another in red. Mailing weight 45 lbs.
3445 $13.25   Cash or Certificates

Fiesta Ware Drip-Cut Server

Now you can get the famous Drip-Cut Server in Fiesta Ware! The patented drip-cut top cuts the flow and contents positively cannot drip when closed and are kept sanitary. Perfect for serving syrup, honey, cream, salad dressing, etc.

Base of this gracefully-shaped, new pitcher is of genuine Fiesta pottery in soft-green color. Capacity, 13 oz. Height, 5¾ in. Mailing weight 1 lb.

2311 $1   Cash or Certificates

Top left: *Juice Set in a metal rack.* **Top right:** *1940 Larkin ad; Walter Ayars book,* Larkin China. **Middle left:** *1938 Larkin ad; Walter Ayars book,* Larkin China. **Bottom right:** *1940 Larkin ad; Walter Ayars book,* Larkin China. **Middle right:** *Fiesta–Red pattern; Drip-Cut Syrup.* **Bottom right:** *Larkin ad; Walter Ayars book,* Larkin China.

Original Fiesta

ORIGINAL FIESTA (30's)

Original Fiesta, called Vintage Fiesta by some collectors, are the colors and shapes introduced originally or added in subsequent years to the initial 1936-1969 offering. There were six original introductory Fiesta colors. Five "50's" colors were later added.

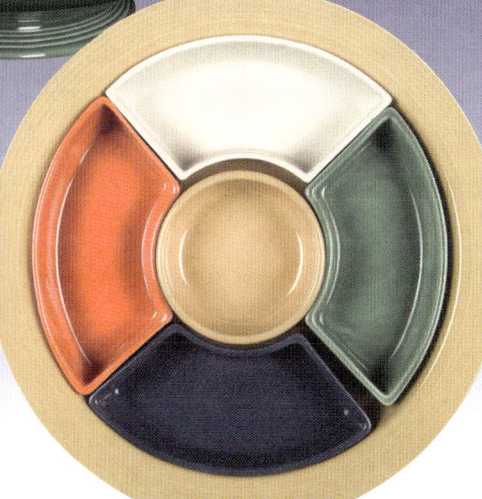

Top right: Light Green Salad Bowl, and Red Nested Mixing Bowls. **Middle left:** *Yellow Coffeepot with lid, Red Dinner Plate, Cobalt Blue Luncheon Plate, Light Green Salad Plate, Yellow Bread & Butter Plate, Ivory Demitasse Cup & Saucer Set, Turquoise Cup & Saucer Set, Light Green Creamer, Red Sugar Bowl with lid, and Cobalt Blue Salt & Pepper Set.* **Middle right:** *Relish Tray with inserts.* **Bottom left:** *Red Comport.* **Bottom right:** *Light Green Disk Water Pitcher, and Water Tumblers in each of the 30's colors.*

Original Fiesta

Top left: *Yellow Large Chop Plate, Cobalt Blue Chop Plate, Red Gravy/Sauce Boat, Turquoise Eggcup, Ivory Drip-Cut Syrup, and Light Green Jug.* **Top right:** *Light Green Carafe with lid, Ivory Demitasse Coffeepot with lid, Turquoise Juice Cup, and Cobalt Blue Demitasse Cup & Saucer Set.* **Middle left:** *Yellow Salt Shaker, Red Marmalade with lid, and Cobalt Blue Mustard with lid.* **Middle right:** *Light Green Tray, Ivory Grill Plate, Yellow Small Disk Pitcher, Turquoise Tom & Jerry Mug, Red Ashtray, and Cobalt Blue Lugged Cream Soup Bowl.* **Bottom left:** *Red Bud Vase, Cobalt Blue Bulb Candleholder, and Yellow Tripod Candleholder.* **Bottom right:** *Yellow Sugar Bowl with lid, Turquoise Round Covered Vegetable Bowl, and Ivory Onion Soup Bowl with lid.*

Original Fiesta

ORIGINAL FIESTA (50's)

Five "50's" colors added later to Original Fiesta: Forest Green, Rose, Chartreuse, Gray, and Medium Green.

Top left: *Gray Large Teapot with lid, Chartreuse Round Covered Vegetable Bowl, Forest Green Medium Teapot with lid, Medium Green Creamer, and Rose Gravy/Sauce Boat.* **Top right:** *Medium Green Dinner Plate, Gray Luncheon Plate, Chartreuse Salad Plate, Forest Green Bread & Butter Plate, and Rose Demitasse Cup & Saucer Set.* **Middle left:** *Gray Cup & Saucer Set, Chartreuse Coffeepot with lid, Rose Ashtray, Forest Green Creamer, and Medium Green Sugar Bowl with lid.* **Middle right:** *Medium Green Soup Bowl, Rose Oval Platter, Gray Grill Plate, Forest Green Disk Pitcher, and Chartreuse Cream Soup Bowl.* **Bottom left:** *Chartreuse, Medium Green, Gray, Forest Green, and Rose Mugs.* **Bottom right:** *Rose Dessert Bowl, Gray Round Vegetable Bowl, Forest Green Fruit Bowl, Chartreuse Fruit Bowl, and Medium Green Bowl.*

Fiesta Casuals

FIESTA CASUALS

These are the only known patterns made for the Fiesta Casuals Line. Only the dinner plate, salad plate, platter, and the saucer for the cup were made with the flower stencil. The solid colored pieces sold with this line were the nappie, fruit bowl, creamer, sugar bowl with lid, and cup.

Top: *Yellow Carnation pattern; Oval Platter, Dinner Plate, Salad Plate, Nappie, Fruit Bowl, Sugar Bowl with lid, Creamer, and Cup & Saucer Set.*
Bottom: *Hawaiian 12-Point Daisy pattern; Dinner Plate, Salad Plate, Nappie, Sugar Bowl with lid, Fruit Bowl, Cup & Saucer Set, and Creamer.*

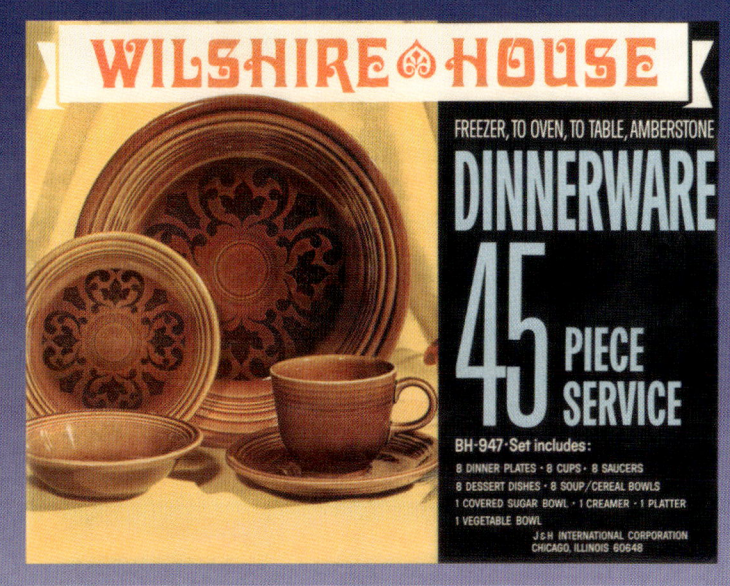

Fiesta Amberstone

SHEFFIELD AMBERSTONE

Sheffield Amberstone was a promotional line produced by Homer Laughlin. It includes shapes from Original Fiesta and new shapes made specifically for Amberstone. The line was predominately marketed in grocery stores as a "purchase the shape of the week" line. Produced with a brown glaze, some pieces have a black silk screen decoration. It was made circa 1967.

Top left: *Literature from the Factory.* **Top right:** *Box label.* **Bottom left:** *Sheffield Amberstone pattern; Bowl, Coffeepot with lid, Mug, Cup & Saucer Set, Sugar Bowl with Lid, Plate, Butter Dish with lid, and Creamer.* **Middle right:** *Dinner Plate, Oval Platter, Round Covered Vegetable Bowl, Salt & Pepper Set, and Gravy/Sauce Boat with unattached Underplate.* **Bottom right:** *Fruit Bowl, Cereal Bowl, Soup Bowl with rim and Round Vegetable Bowl.*

219

Fiesta Casualtone

FIESTA CASUALSTONE

Fiesta Casualstone was a similar promotional line as Amberstone, except the color was a warm gold and the silk screen design was more delicate. Literature refers to the line as Coventry Casualstone. It was produced circa 1970. Both Amberstone and Casualstone use shapes and colors that not all collectors accept as "true" Fiesta.

Bottom: *Casualstone* pattern; Box label from the Homer Laughlin Factory.
Bottom: *Casualstone* pattern; Round Covered Vegetable bowl, Gravy/Sauce Boat with unattached Underplate, Dinner Plate, Luncheon Plate, Soup Bowl with Rim, Sugar Bowl with lid, Creamer, Fruit Bowl, Bread & Butter Plate, and Cup & Saucer Set.

Fiesta Ironstone

FIESTA IRONSTONE

Fiesta Ironstone used forms created for Amberstone in the traditional solid colors of Antique Gold, Turf Green, and Mango Red. Mango Red uses the same red glaze as original Fiesta Red. Turf Green is a very 70's avocado green that would have matched kitchen appliances of that time. Antique Gold went with all the other 1970's colored appliances. This 1969 incarnation of Fiesta was produced until 1972. None of the Ironstone pieces have the Fiesta backstamps. There are only three piece types with slight differences between original Fiesta and Ironstone pieces: The gravy boat, 12½" platter, and disk water pitcher used the old molds, but the Fiesta backstamp was removed. The sugar bowl, teapot, and coffeepot lids have been redesigned. Old Fiesta did not have any flared bowls. In Ironstone they created the following flared bowls: fruit, cereal, salad, round vegetable, and round covered casserole. Other new pieces include a mug and gravy underplate. The coffeepot, teapot, round covered vegetable bowl, salad bowl, and disk water pitcher were only made in Antique Gold and Amberstone. The cup and creamer have a redesigned, "C" handle. The pepper has one less hole and they both have slightly larger holes than in the original line. The following pieces were made in all three colors: dinner plate, salad plate, 12½" platter, salt & pepper set, gravy boat & underplate, fruit bowl, soup bowl, round covered vegetable bowl, round vegetable bowl, cup & saucer set, sugar bowl, and creamer.

Top left: *Mango Red Oval Platter, Dinner Plate, Salad Plate, Gravy/Sauce Boat, Fruit Bowl, and Sugar Bowl with lid.* **Top middle:** *Mango Red pattern; Back of a Dinner Plate (no rings at edge).* **Bottom left:** *Photograph of Fiesta Ironstone at a trade show.* **Top right:** *Turf Green Oval Platter, Soup Bowl, Gravy/Sauce Boat, Cup, Fruit Bowl, and Salt Shaker.* **Second down on right:** *Antique Gold Sugar Bowl with lid, and Creamer.* **Third down on right:** *Antique Gold Dinner Plate, Mug, and Cup & Saucer Set.* **Bottom right:** *Antique Gold Round Vegetable Bowl, Fruit Bowl, and Salt & Pepper Set.*

New Fiesta

NEW FIESTA

New Fiesta was first available February 28, 1986 at the Culture Center Complex gift shop in the West Virginia State Museum, Charleston, West Virginia. This was coupled with a celebration of the centennial of Homer Laughlin, a museum exhibition, and an article on the company in the state cultural museum. New Fiesta, with additions of new colors and shapes, continues in production today.

Top left: Chartreuse pattern; Fiesta sign. **Top right:** Sunflower Demitasse Cup & Saucer Set, Turquoise Cappaccino Mug, and Yellow Pedestal Mug. **Middle:** Persimmon Pizza Tray, Yellow Chop Plate, Shamrock Green Dinner Plate, Lilac Luncheon Plate, Sapphire Salad Plate, Pearl Gray Bread & Butter Plate, and Cinnabar Demitasse Saucer. **Bottom left:** Cinnabar Denver Mug, Persimmon Embossed Tom & Jerry Mug, Chartreuse Tom & Jerry Mug, and White Tower Mug. **Bottom left:** Apricot Cup & Saucer Set, Rose Jumbo Cup & Saucer Set, and Turquoise Demitasse Cup & Saucer Set.

New Fiesta

Top left: *Yellow, Pearl Gray, and Rose Mixing Bowls Set.* **Top right:** *Yellow, Pearl Gray, and Rose Mixing Bowls Set, stacked.* **Second down on left:** *Sunflower Snack Set Plate with Turquoise Cup.* **Second down on right:** *Sea Mist Green Snack Set with Bouillon Cup.* **Third down on left:** *Plum Gusto Bowl.* **Third down right:** *Sunflower Chili/Jumbo Bowl & Saucer Set.* **Bottom left:** *Yellow Serving Bowl, Lilac Round Vegetable Bowl, Sea Mist Green Cereal Bowl, and Apricot Soup Bowl.* **Bottom right:** *Napkin Rings in new Fiesta colors: Persimmon, Rose, Yellow, Sunflower, Cobalt Blue, Turquoise Blue, Cinnabar, White, Periwinkle Blue, Sea Mist Green, and Pearl Gray.*

New Fiesta

Top left: *Black Sugar Bowl with lid, Cinnabar Creamer, Cobalt Blue Teapot with lid, and Juniper Cup & Saucer Set.* **Top right:** *Perssimon Mini Disk Pitcher, Sea Mist Green Disk Juice Pitcher, and Lilac Disk Water Pitcher.* **Middle left:** *Cinnabar Large Pie Plate, White Medium Pie Plate, and Plum Small Pie Plate.* **Middle right:** *Cinnabar Demitasse Cup & Saucer Set, Rose Small Teapot with lid, and Periwinkle Blue Coffeepot with lid.* **Bottom left:** *Black Relish/Utility Tray, and Cinnabar Bread Tray.* **Bottom right:** *Periwinkle Blue Oval Vegetable Bowl, Lilac Gravy/Sauce Boat, Turquoise Tripod Bowl, and White Range Salt & Pepper Set.*

New Fiesta

Top left: *Sea Mist Green Hostess Tray, and White Cereal Bowl.* **Top right:** *Sea Mist Green 9" Oval Platter, Yellow 11" Oval Platter, Persimmon 13" Oval Platter, Persimmon Bouillon Cup, and Yellow Denver Mug.* **Middle left:** *Pearl Gray Pasta Bowl with rim, Sea Mist Green Soup Bowl with rim, and Periwinkle Fruit Bowl.* **Middle:** *Cobalt Blue, Cinnabar, Persimmon, and Juniper Trivets.* **Middle right:** *Yellow Handled Serving Tray, Periwinkle Blue Sugar Caddy, and Persimmon Footed Bowl.* **Bottom left:** *Persimmon Disk Water Pitcher, and Tumblers.* **Bottom right:** *Turquoise Crock.*

New Fiesta

Top left: *Persimmon, Periwinkle Blue, Rose, White, Cobalt Blue, Yellow, Sea Mist Green, and Turquoise Blue Bud Vases.* **Top right:** *Rose Tripod Candlestick, and Pearl Gray Bulb Candleholder.* **Middle left:** *8" Flower Vases.* **Middle right:** *Turquoise Clock.* **Bottom right:** *Pink Millennium I Vase, Sea Mist Green Millennium II Vase, Chartreuse Millennium III Vase, and Pearl Gray Millennium Tapered Candlestick.*

New Fiesta

Top left: *Cinnabar Spoon Rest, Lilac Salt & Peppr Set, White Round Covered Vegetable Bowl, and Chartreuse Covered Butter Dish.* **Top right:** *Cinnabar Tumbler, and Chartreuse Carafe.* **Middle left:** *Chartreuse Goblet.* **Middle right:** *Chartreuse Anniversary Disk Pitcher.* **Bottom left:** *Lilac Figure Eight Tray with Sugar Bowl with lid, and Creamer.* **Bottom right:** *Chartreuse Disk Pitcher backstamp with a raised H. If a Disk Water Pitcher has a raised H it is definitely a new piece. If it does not have a raised H it can be either a new piece or old piece.*

New Fiesta with Decals and Children's Fiesta

NEW FIESTA WITH DECALS

Many new Fiesta patterns are being made with decals. Most are sold through the Factory, but Betty Crocker and Mega China are two companies that have exclusive rights to also sell patterns with decals. The Looney Tunes pattern below was sold in Warner Brothers Stores.

CHILDREN'S FIESTA

There are several small sets made for children from Fiesta molds. This tea set is the most popular. Other sets usually consist of a tumbler, luncheon plate, and bowl.

Top left: *Stars and Stripes pattern; Bud Vase.* **Top midle:** *Looney Tunes Sylvester on Yellow pattern; Soup Bowl with rim, Dinner Plate, and Cup & Saucer Set.* **Top right:** *Looney Tunes Christmas pattern; Teapot with lid.* **Bottom left:** *Christmas pattern; Disk Pitcher, Chop Plate, Dinner Plate, Salad Plate, Disk Juice Pitcher, Bud Vase, Cup & Saucer Set, Sugar Bowl with lid, Creamer, Tree Ornament, and Salt & Pepper Set.* **Bottom right:** *My First Fiesta® Children's Set*

New Fiesta with decals:
Triple Hearts (Valentine's Day)
Easter Eggs (Easter)
Shamrock (St. Patrick's Day)
  (also the name of a Fiesta color)
Stars and Stripes (4th of July)
Fireworks (4th of July)
Mardi Gras (with stripes)
Happy Pumpkin (Halloween)
Turkey Day (Thanksgiving)
Tis The Season (Christmas)
Cookies for Santa (Christmas Snack Set)
Christmas Fiesta (Christmas)
Sugar Plum Fairy (Christmas)
Hawaiian Ware

Children's Sets:
Just Ducky (Small Children's Set)
Some Bunny for Easter (Children's Set)
Baby's First Fiesta (2 Piece Set)
#8494 of fish and water (3 Piece Set)
#8490 of a cat, dog, & duck (3 Piece Set)
#8491 Cruisin' (Noah's Arc) (3 Piece Set)
Hometown Heroes (3 Piece Set)

Made by Homer Laughlin for Warner Brothers:
Bugs Bunny on Periwinkle Blue
Daffy Duck on Turquoise New
Porky Pig on Rose New
Scooby Doo on Sea Mist Green
Scooby Doo on White
Sylvester on Yellow New
Tweety Bird on White

Made by Homer Laughlin for Mega China:
Champagne
Mystique
Moonshine

Made by Homer Laughlin for Betty Crocker:
Holiday Collection (Christmas)

Many specialty items were also made. This is an incomplete list.

The Fiesta Ensembles and Go-Alongs

FIESTA ENSEMBLE

The Fiesta Ensemble was a set of over 100 pieces of Fiesta consisting of flatware, glasses, and Riviera serving pieces that could create place settings for eight. This ensemble was used in store promotions, especially furniture stores. In the 1939 newspaper advertisement for Davidsons, reproduced by Gr8plates, a 109 piece Fiesta Ensemble is offered for $14.95. This service for eight included:
Eight, five piece place settings in Red, Yellow, Cobalt Blue, and Light Green;
Glass ashtray made by another manufacturer;
24 glasses as shown to the right;
A serving set of Riviera, including a rectangular platter, round vegetable bowl, sugar bowl with lid, and creamer; and Eight place settings of flatware.

FIESTA GO-ALONGS

Go-Alongs were made by other maufacturers to "go along" with Fiesta dinnerware. Below are some examples, like the metal handles and serving holders, produced by Royal Metal.

Top right: *Glassware made for Homer Laughlin to be sold with the Fiesta Ensemble.* **Middle right:** *Several Riviera serving pieces were sold with the Fiesta Ensemble. Shown are the Yellow Rectangular Platter, Red Round Vegetable Bowl, Light Green Creamer and Sugar Bowl with lid. Other colors were also made and many people believe that Cobalt Riviera pieces were produced as serving pieces for the Ensemble.* **Middle left:** *Medium Green Luncheon Plate with metal handle.* **Bottom left:** *Flatware sold with new Fiesta.* **Bottom middle:** *Turquoise Bowl in a Royal Metal serving dish.* **Bottom right:** *Hankscraft Eggcups.*

Fiesta Piece Type Lists

Fiesta Piece Type Lists

Original Fiesta Line Piece Type List
Ashtray, 6½ inches
Bowl, Cream Soup, 6⅝ inches
Bowl, Dessert/Fruit, 6¼ inches
Bowl, Fruit, 4¾ inches
Bowl, Fruit, 5½ inches
Bowl, Fruit, 11¾ inches
Bowl, Mixing with lid #1
    Bowl, 3½ H inches
    Lid, 5 W inches
Bowl, Mixing with lid #2
    Bowl, 4 H inches
    Lid, 6 W inches
Bowl, Mixing with lid #3
    Bowl, 4½ H inches
    Lid, 6¾ W inches
Bowl, Mixing with lid #4
    Bowl, 5 H inches
    Lid, 7¾ W inches
Bowl, Mixing #5
    Bowl, 5¾ H inches
Bowl, Mixing #6
    Bowl, 6⅜ H inches
Bowl, Mixing #7
    Bowl, 7⅛ H inches
Bowl, Onion Soup with lid, 6⅛ inches
Bowl, Salad Footed, 11⅜ inches
Bowl, Salad Individual, 7⅝ inches
Bowl, Salad Promotional, 9¾ inches
Bowl, Soup with rim, 8⅜ inches
Bowl, Vegetable Round/Nappy, 8½ inches
Bowl, Vegetable Round/Nappy, 9½ inches
Bowl, Vegetable Round Covered, Casserole 9¾ inches
Candleholder, Bulb, 3¾ inches
Candleholder, Tripod, 3½ inches
Carafe with lid, 9¼ inches
Coffeepot with lid, Demitasse, 7⅝ inches
Coffeepot with lid, Regular, 10⅜ inches
Comport, 12⅜ inches
Comport, Sweets, 5⅛ inches
Creamer, Individual, 4⅞ W inches
Creamer, Ring Handle, 5⅞ W inches
Creamer, Stick Handle, 4⅝ W inches
Cup & Saucer Set, Demitasse
    Cup, 2½ inches
    Saucer, 5¼ inches
Cup & Saucer Set, Regular
    Cup, 2⅞ inches
    Saucer, 6 inches
Eggcup, 3⅛ inches
French Casserole, 11⅞ inches
Gravy/Sauce Boat, 8 inches
Jug, 2 pint, 4¼ inches
Marmalade Jar with lid, 4½ inches
Mug, Tom & Jerry, 3⅛ inches
Mustard with lid, 3 inches
Pitcher, Disk Juice, 6 inches
Pitcher, Disk Water, 7½ inches
Pitcher, Ice, 6⅜ inches
Plate, Bread & Butter, 6⅜ inches
Plate, Cake, 10⅜ inches
Plate, Chop, 12⅜ inches
Plate, Chop, 14¼ inches
Plate, Dinner, 10½ inches
Plate, Grill, 10½ inches
Plate, Grill, 11¾ inches
Plate, Luncheon, 9½ inches
Plate, Salad, 7½ inches
Platter, Oval, 12⅝ inches
Salt & Pepper Set, 2¾ inches
Sugar Bowl with lid, 5 H inches
Sugar Bowl with lid, Individual, 3½ H inches
Syrup, Drip-Cut, 5¾ inches
Teapot with lid, Large, 6¾ inches
Teapot with lid, Medium, 5⅛ inches
Tray, Figure 8, 10⅜ inches for Individual Sugar and Creamer
Tray, Relish with 5 inserts, 10⅞ inches
Tray, Utility, 10½ inches
Tumbler, Juice, 3½ inches
Tumbler, Juice, 3¾ inches
Tumbler, Water, 4½ inches
Vase, Bud, 6⅜ inches
Vase, Flower, 8 inches
Vase, Flower, 10 inches
Vase, Flower, 11¾ inches

Fiesta Harmony Line Piece Type List
Fiesta Pieces:
Candlesticks, Bulb, one pair
Comport, 12⅜ inches
Creamer
Plate, Bread & Butter, 6 inches
Plate, Chop, 15 inches
Plate, Dinner, 10½ inches
Plate, Salad, 7½ inches
Salt & Pepper Set
Sugar Bowl with lid
Nautilus Pieces:
Baker, 10 inches
Bowl, Fruit, 5¾ inches
Bowl, Vegetable Round, 8⅝ inches
Cup & Saucer Set
    Cup, 2⅝ inches
    Saucer, 5⅝ inches
Plate, Bread & Butter, 6⅜ inches
Plate, Luncheon, 9⅛ inches

Top: *Yellow Individual Sugar Bowl with lid and Creamer and Cobalt Blue Figure 8 Tray.*

Fiesta Amberstone and Casualstone Piece Type List
Ashtray
Bowl, Cereal
Bowl, Fruit/Dessert
Bowl, Salad
Bowl, Soup, stenciled
Bowl, Vegetable
Bowl, Vegetable Round Covered
Butter Dish with lid, stenciled
Coffeepot with lid
Creamer
Cup & Saucer Set
    Cup
    Saucer, stenciled
Gravy/Sauce Boat
Marmalade with notched lid
Mug
Pitcher, Disk Water
Plate, Bread & Butter
Plate, Chop
Plate, Dinner, stenciled
Plate, Pie, stenciled, 9 inches
Plate, Salad, stenciled
Platter, Oval, stenciled, 13 inches
Salt & Pepper Set
Sugar Bowl with lid
Teapot with lid
Tray, Serving with handle, stenciled

Ironstone Piece Type List
Bowl, Cereal, 6½ inches
Bowl, Fruit/Dessert, 5½ inches
Bowl, Vegetable Round, 8⅞ inches
Bowl, Vegetable Round Covered, 9¾ inches, Antique Gold only
Bowl, Salad, 10½ inches, Antique Gold only
Coffeepot with lid, 10¾ inches Antique Gold only
Creamer, 6 inches
Cup & Saucer Set
    Cup, 2¾ inches
    Saucer, 6¼ inches
Gravy/Sauce Boat, 8 inches
Gravy/Sauce Boat Underplate, 9⅛ inches
Mug, 2⅞ inches
Pitcher, Disk Water, 7½ inches Antique Gold only
Plate, Dinner, 10⅛ inches
Plate, Salad, 7½ inches
Platter, Oval, 12⅝ inches
Salt & Pepper Set, 2¾ inches
Sugar Bowl with lid, 5⅛ inches
Teapot with lid, 5 inches Antique Gold only

Fiesta Piece Type Lists

Fiesta Casuals Line Piece Type List
Bowl, Fruit, 5½ inches
Bowl, Vegetable Round, 8½ inches
Creamer
Cup & Saucer Set
  Cup, 2⅞ inches
  Saucer, 6 inches
Plate, Dinner, 10½ inches
Plate, Salad, 7½ inches
Platter, Oval, 12⅝ inches
Sugar Bowl with lid

Fiesta New Piece Type List
Beverage Set, 60th Anniversary,
  Pitcher, Disk Water
  Tumblers, 4
Bowl, Betty Crocker
Bowl, Cereal, 5⅝ inches
Bowl, Cereal Stacking, 6½ inches
Bowl, Chili, 3½ H x 4⅝ W inches
Bowl, Fruit, 5⅜ inches
Bowl, Gusto, 6 inches
Bowl, Hostess
Bowl, Mixing Small, 7½ inches
Bowl, Mixing Medium, 8½ inches
Bowl, Mixing Large, 9½ inches
Bowl, Pasta Individual, 12 inches
Bowl, Pedestal, 9⅝ inches
Bowl, Presentation (tri-footed),
  11⅝ inches
Bowl, Serving/Salad, 10½ inches, 39oz.
Bowl, Soup Coupe, 6⅞ inches
Bowl, Soup with rim, 9 inches
Bowl, Tripod, 3⅝ inches
Bowl, Vegetable Oval, 12 inches
Bowl, Vegetable Round, 8¼ inches
Bowl, Vegetable Round Covered,
  9⅜ W inches
Butter Dish with lid
Candleholder, Bulb, 3⅝ inches
Candleholder, Millenium/Tapered,
  6⅛ inches
Candleholder, Tripod/Pyramid,
  3½ inches
Carafe, Open with handle, 7⅝ inches
Clock
Clock, 60th Anniversary
Coffeepot with lid, 7½ inches, 4 cups
Creamer
Creamer, Individual, Figure 8,
  4¾ W inches
Cup, Bouillon, 4 inches
Cup & Saucer Set
  Cup, 2¾ inches
  Saucer, 5⅞ inches
Cup & Saucer Set, Demitasse
  Cup (Ring handle), 2⅜ inches
  Saucer, 4⅞ inches
Cup & Saucer Set, Demitasse
  Cup (Stick handle), 2⅜ inches
  Saucer, 4⅞ inches
Cup & Saucer Set, Jumbo
  Cup, 3½ inches
  Saucer, 6¾ inches
Goblet
Gravy/Sauce Boat
Mug, Capuccino, 6⅛ inches
Mug, Denver, 3⅞ inches
Mug, Fan (Tom & Jerry Embossed),
  3½ inches
Mug, Pedestal, 6⅛ inches
Mug, Tom & Jerry, 3½ inches
Mug, Tower, 3½ inches
Napkin Ring
Pie, Baker/Plate, 6¼ inches
Pie, Baker/Plate, 8 inches
Pie, Baker/Plate, 10¼ inches
Pitcher, Disk Water, 7⅛ inches, 67¼ oz.
Pitcher, Disk Water, with woman decal
Pitcher, Disk Juice, 5¾ inches, 28 oz.
Pitcher, Disk Mini, 3¼ inches, 5 oz.
Plate, Bread & Butter, 6⅛ inches
Plate, Chop, 11¾ inches
Plate, Dinner, 10½ inches
Plate, Luncheon, 9 inches
Plate, Salad, 7¼ inches
Plate, Snack with well, 10½ inches
Platter, Oval, 9⅝ inches
Platter, Oval, 11⅝ inches
Platter, Oval, 13⅝ inches
Salt & Pepper Set
Salt & Pepper Set, Rangetop
Spoon Rest, 8 inches
Sugar Bowl with lid, Individual,
  Figure 8, 3¾ H inches
Sugar Bowl with lid, no handles,
  4¼ H inches
Sugar Caddy, 3¼ inches
Teapot with lid, 2 Cups, 5 inches
Teapot with lid, 4 Cups, 7¼ inches
Tray, Bread, 12 inches
Tray, Chip & Dip/Hostess
  Tray, 12¼ inches
Tray, Figure 8, 10 inches
Tray, Pizza, 15 inches
Tray, Relish/Utility/Corn with handles,
  9½ inches
Tray, Serving/Cake with handles,
  12 inches
Tray, Tidbit, 1 Tier
Tray, Tidbit, 2 Tier
Tray, Tidbit, 3 Tier
Trivet, 6 inches
Tumbler, 3¾ inches

Utensil Crock/Holder, 6⅝ inches
Vase, Bud, 6¼ inches
Vase, Flower Small, 7¾ inches
Vase, Flower Medium, 9⅝ inches
Vase, Millenium I (2 handle)
Vase, Millenium II (no handle, disk)
Vase, Millenium III (no handle, tall)
Vase, Monarch
Vase, Royalty
More piece types are added every year.

Fiesta Mates Piece Type List
Baker
Bowl, Pedestal
Creamer, Individual, Small
Cup & Saucer Set, Demitasse
Cup & Saucer Set, Jumbo
Mug, Denver, 3⅞ inches
Mug, Tower, 3½ inches
Ramekin
Skillet
Sugar Caddy
Teapot with lid, Colonial, Individual

Fiesta for Mega China
Bowl, Soup Coupe, 6⅞ inches
Bowl, Soup with rim, 9 inches
Carafe, Open, 7⅝ inches
Coffeepot with lid, 7½ inches, 4 cups
Mug, Tom & Jerry, 3½ inches
Pitcher, Disk Water
Plate, Dinner, 10½ inches
Plate, Salad, 7½ inches
Tumbler

Old Fiesta Colors: Red, Yellow, Cobalt Blue, Ivory, Light Green Nested Mixing Bowls.

Fiesta Shape

Fiesta–White *Newer, 1986–Active* No Trim	**Fiesta–Gray** *Older, 1951–1959* No Trim	**Fiesta–Pearl Gray** *Newer, 1999–2001* No Trim	**Fiesta–Ivory (Cream)** *Older, 1936–1951* No Trim
Fiesta–Yellow *Older, 1936–1969* No Trim	**Fiesta–Yellow** *Newer, 1987–2002* No Trim	**Fiesta–Sunflower** *Newer, 2001–Active* No Trim	**Fiesta–Antique Gold** *Ironstone, 1969–72* No Trim
Fiesta–Apricot *Newer, 1986–1998* No Trim	**Fiesta–Rose** *Newer, 1986–Active* No Trim	**Fiesta–Rose** *Older, 1951–1959* No Trim	**Fiesta–Persimmon** *Newer, 1995–Active* No Trim
Fiesta–Periwinkle Blue *Newer, 1989–Active* No Trim	**Fiesta–Turquoise** *Older, 1937–1969* No Trim	**Fiesta–Turquoise** *Newer, 1988–Active* No Trim	**Fiesta–Sea Mist Green** *Newer, 1991–Active* No Trim

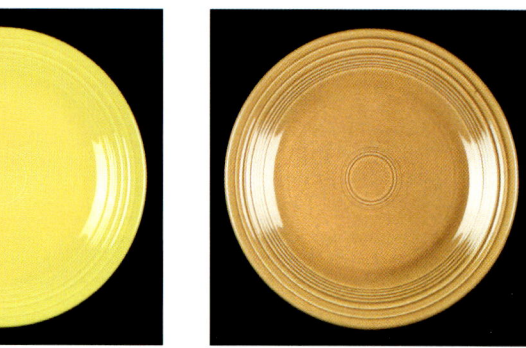

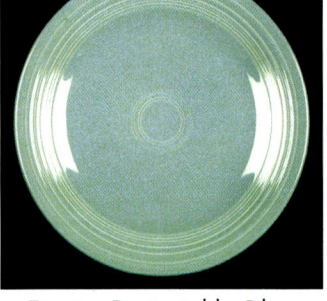

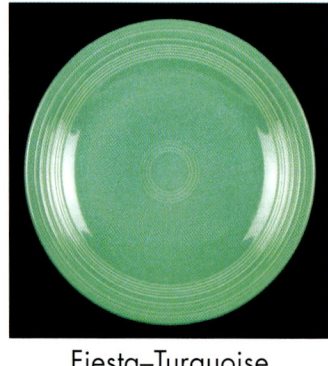

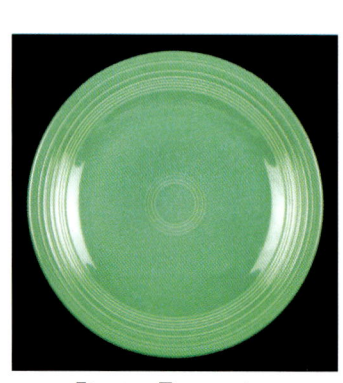

Fiesta Shape

Fiesta–Medium Green
Older, 1959–1969
No Trim

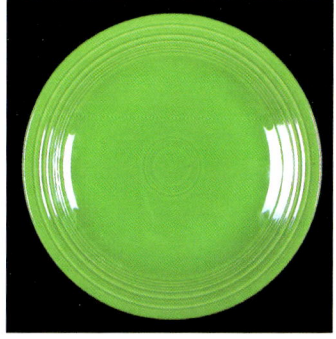

Fiesta–Shamrock Green
Newer, 2003–Active
No Trim

Fiesta–Light Green
Older, 1936–1951
No Trim

Fiesta–Chartreuse
Older, 1951–1959
No Trim

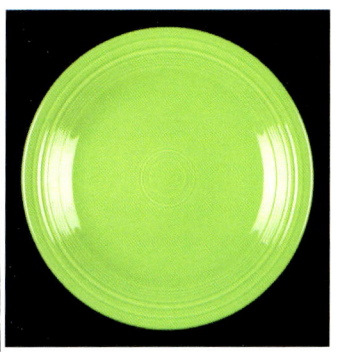

Fiesta–Chartreuse
Newer, 1997–1999
No Trim

Fiesta–Turf Green
Ironstone, 1969–72
No Trim

Fiesta–Forest Green
Older, 1951–1959
No Trim

Fiesta–Juniper
Newer, 1999–2001
No Trim

Fiesta–Sapphire Blue
Newer, 1996–1997
Bloomingdale's Exclusive
No Trim

Fiesta–Lilac
Newer, 1993–1995
No Trim

Fiesta–Plum
Newer, 2002–Active
No Trim

Fiesta–Cobalt Blue
Older, 1936–1951
No Trim

Fiesta–Cobalt Blue
Newer, 1986–Active
No Trim

Fiesta–Cinnabar (Maroon)
Newer, 2000–Active
No Trim

Fiesta–Mango Red (Orange)
Ironstone, 1969–72
No Trim

Fiesta–Red (Orange)
Older, 1936–1943 & 1959–1972
No Trim

Fiesta Shape

Fiesta–Black
Newer, 1986–Active
No Trim

HLC1987
Green Trim

Fiesta–Red Stripe (Yellow)
Red Trim

HLC1287
No Trim

HLC3088
Gold Trim

HLC3012
Chop Plate Shown
Red Trim

Yellow Carnation
F107
No Trim

Hawaiian Daisy
F108
No Trim

Castilian
by Coventry
No Trim

Amberstone
by Sheffield
No Trim

Fiesta–Loony Tunes (Yellow)
Warner Brothers Exclusive
No Trim

Fiesta–Loony Tunes Christmas
Warner Brothers Exclusive
Teapot Shown
No Trim

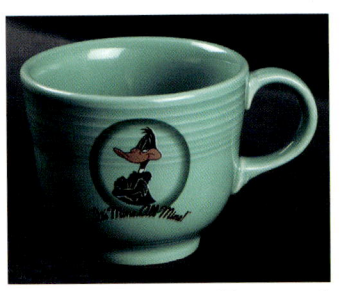

Fiesta–Loony Tunes (Turquoise)
Warner Brothers Exclusive
Cup Shown
No Trim

Fiesta–Scooby Doo (Sea Mist Green)
Warner Brothers Exclusive
No Trim

Fiesta–Christmas
No Trim

"Old" Fiesta Colors

Empty boxes are pieces that we believe were not made.

Piece	Red	Cobalt Blue	Light Green	Yellow (Old)	Ivory (Old)	Turquoise (Old)	Forest Green	Rose (Old)	Chartreuse (Old)	Gray (Old)	Medium Green
Ashtray, 6 1/2"	●	●	●	●	●	●					
Bowl, Cream Soup, 6 5/8"	●	●	●	●	●	●	●	●	●	●	●
Bowl, Dessert/Fruit, 6 1/4"	●	●	●	●	●	●	●	●	●	●	
Bowl, Fruit, 4 3/4"	●	●	●	●	●	●		●	●	●	
Bowl, Fruit, 5 1/2"	●	●	●	●	●	●	●	●	●	●	●
Bowl, Fruit, 11 3/4"	●	●	●	●	●	●					
Bowl, Mixing with lid #1, 5"	●	●	●	●	●	no lid					
Bowl, Mixing with lid #2, 6"	●	●	●	●	●	no lid					
Bowl, Mixing with lid #3, 6 3/4"	●	●	●	●	●	no lid					
Bowl, Mixing with lid #4, 7 3/4"	●	●	●	●	●	no lid					
Bowl, Mixing #5, 8 1/2"	●	●	●	●	●	●					
Bowl, Mixing #6, 9 3/4"	●	●	●	●	●	●					
Bowl, Mixing #7, 11"	●	●	●	●	●	●					
Bowl, Onion Soup with lid, 6 1/8"	●	●	●	●	●	●					
Bowl, Salad Footed, 11 3/8"	●	●	●	●	●	●					
Bowl, Salad Individual, 7 5/8"	●			●		●					●
Bowl, Salad Promotional, 9 3/4"		●		●	●						
Bowl, Soup with rim, 8 3/8"	●	●	●	●	●	●	●	●	●	●	●
Bowl, Vegetable Round/Nappy, 8 1/2"	●	●	●	●	●	●	●	●	●	●	●
Bowl, Vegetable Round/Nappy, 9 1/2"	●	●	●	●	●	●					
Bowl, Vegetable Round Covered, Casserole, 9 3/4"	●	●	●	●	●	●	●	●	●	●	●
Candleholder, Bulb, 3 3/4"	●	●	●	●	●	●					
Candleholder, Tripod, 3 1/2"	●	●	●	●	●						
Carafe with lid, 9 1/4"	●	●	●	●	●	●					
Coffeepot with lid, Demitasse, 7 5/8"	●	●	●	●	●	●					
Coffeepot with lid, Regular, 10 3/8"	●	●	●	●	●	●	●	●	●	●	
Comport, 12 3/8"	●	●	●	●	●	●					
Comport, Sweets, 5 1/8"	●	●	●	●	●	●					
Creamer Individual, 4 7/8"	●			●		●					
Creamer, Ring Handle, 5 7/8"	●	●	●	●	●	●	●	●	●	●	●
Creamer, Stick Handle, 4 5/8"	●	●	●	●	●	●					
Cup & Saucer Set, Demitasse	●	●	●	●	●	●	●	●	●	●	
Cup & Saucer Set, Regular	●	●	●	●	●	●	●	●	●	●	●
Eggcup, 3 1/8"	●	●	●	●	●	●					
French Casserole, 11 7/8"				●							
Gravy/Sauce Boat, 8"	●	●	●	●	●	●	●	●	●	●	●
Jug, 2 pint, 4 1/4"	●	●	●	●	●	●					
Marmalade Jar with lid, 4 1/2"	●	●	●	●	●	●					
Mug, Tom & Jerry, 3 1/8"	●	●	●	●	●	●	●	●	●	●	
Mustard with lid, 3"	●	●	●	●	●	●					
Pitcher, Disk Juice, 6"	●		●	●						●	
Pitcher, Disk Water, 7 1/2"	●	●	●	●	●	●					
Pitcher, Ice, 6 3/8"	●	●	●	●	●	●					
Plate, Bread & Butter, 6 3/8"	●	●	●	●	●	●	●	●	●	●	●
Plate, Cake, 10 3/8"	●	●	●	●	●						
Plate, Chop, 12 3/8"	●	●	●	●	●	●	●	●	●	●	●
Plate, Chop, 14 1/4"	●	●	●	●	●	●	●	●	●	●	
Plate, Dinner, 10 1/2"	●	●	●	●	●	●	●	●	●	●	●
Plate, Grill, 10 1/2"	●	●	●	●	●	●					
Plate, Grill, 11 3/4"	●	●	●	●	●	●					
Plate, Luncheon, 9 1/2"	●	●	●	●	●	●	●	●	●	●	●
Plate, Salad, 7 1/2"	●	●	●	●	●	●	●	●	●	●	●
Platter, Oval, 12 5/8"	●	●	●	●	●	●	●	●	●	●	●
Salt & Pepper Set, 2 3/4"	●	●	●	●	●	●					
Sugar Bowl with lid, Individual, 3 1/2"		●		●		●					
Sugar Bowl with Lid, Regular, 5"	●	●	●	●	●	●	●	●	●	●	
Syrup, Drip-Cut, 5 3/4"	●	●	●	●	●	●					
Teapot with lid, Large, 6 3/4"	●	●	●	●	●	●					
Teapot with lid, Medium, 5 1/8"	●	●	●	●	●	●	●	●	●	●	●
Tray, Figure 8, 10 3/8"		●		●		●					
Tray, Relish with 5 inserts, Base	●	●	●	●	●	●					
Tray, Relish with 5 inserts, Side Inserts	●	●	●	●	●	●					
Tray, Relish with 5 inserts, Center Insert	●	●	●	●	●	●					
Tray, Utility, 10 1/2"	●	●	●	●	●	●					
Tumbler, Juice, 3 1/2" or 3 3/4"	●	●	●	●	●	●	●	●	●	●	
Tumbler, Water, 4 1/2	●	●	●	●	●	●					
Vase, Bud, 6 3/8"	●	●	●	●	●	●					
Vase, Flower, 8"	●	●	●	●	●	●					
Vase, Flower, 10"	●	●	●	●	●	●					
Vase, Flower, 11 3/4"	●	●	●	●	●	●					

"New" Fiesta Colors

Empty boxes are pieces that we believe were not made or we have not seen.

Item	White	Black	Rose (New)	Apricot	Cobalt Blue (New)	Yellow (New)	Turquoise (New)	Periwinkle Blue	Sea Mist Green	Lilac	Persimmon	Sapphire	Chartreuse (New)	Pearl Gray	Juniper	Cinnabar	Sunflower	Plum	Shamrock
Beverage Set, 60th Anniversary																			
Bowl, Cereal, 5 5/8" #460	■	■	■	■	■	■	■	■	■	■	■	■	■	■	■	■	■	■	■
Bowl, Cereal Stacking, 6 1/2"	■		■	■	■	■	■	■	■	■	■		■	■	■	■	■	■	■
Bowl, Chili, 4 5/8"	■	■	■	■	■	■	■	■	■	■	■		■	■	■	■	■	■	■
Bowl, Fruit, 5 3/8" 6 1/4oz. #459	■	■	■	■	■	■	■	■	■	■	■	■	■	■	■	■	■	■	■
Bowl, Gusto, 6" 23oz. #723	■	■	■	■	■	■	■	■	■	■	■		■	■	■	■	■	■	■
Bowl, Hostess	■		■								■					■			
Bowl, Mixing Small, 7 1/2" 44 oz. #421	■		■	■	■	■	■				■		■	■	■	■	■	■	■
Bowl, Mixing Medium, 8 1/2" 60oz. #422	■		■	■	■	■	■				■		■	■	■	■	■	■	■
Bowl, Mixing Large, 9 1/2" 70oz. #482	■		■	■	■	■	■				■		■	■	■	■	■	■	■
Bowl, Pasta Individual, 12" 21oz. #462	■	■	■	■	■	■	■	■	■	■	■		■	■	■	■	■	■	■
Bowl, Pedestal, 9 5/8" 64oz. #765	■	■	■		■	■	■				■		■	■	■	■	■	■	■
Bowl, Presentation, (tri-footed), 11 5/8"	■	■	■		■	■	■				■		■	■	■	■			
Bowl, Serving/Salad, 10 1/2" 2qt. #455	■	■	■	■	■	■	■	■	■	■	■		■	■	■	■	■	■	■
Bowl, Soup Coupe, 6 7/8" 19oz. #461	■	■	■	■	■	■	■	■	■	■	■	■	■	■	■	■	■	■	■
Bowl, Soup with rim, 9" #451	■	■	■	■	■	■	■	■	■	■	■	■	■	■	■	■	■	■	■
Bowl, Tripod, 3 5/8" #766	■	■	■		■	■	■				■		■	■	■	■	■		
Bowl, Vegetable Oval, 12" #409	■		■	■	■	■	■				■		■	■	■	■	■	■	
Bowl, Vegetable Round/Nappy, 8 1/4" #471	■	■	■	■	■	■	■	■	■	■	■	■	■	■	■	■	■	■	■
Bowl, Vegetable, Round Covered Cass. #495	■	■	■	■	■	■	■	■	■	■	■		■	■	■	■	■	■	■
Butter Dish with lid 7 1/8" #494	■	■	■	■	■	■	■	■	■	■	■		■	■	■	■	■	■	■
Candleholder, Bulb, 3 5/8" #488	■	■	■	■	■	■	■	■	■	■	■		■	■	■	■	■	■	
Candleholder, Millenium/Tapered, 6 1/8"	■	■	■		■	■	■				■		■	■	■	■	■		
Candleholder, Tripod/Pyramid	■	■	■	■	■	■	■	■	■	■	■		■	■	■				
Carafe, Open with handle, 7 5/8" 60oz. #448	■	■	■	■	■	■	■				■	■	■	■	■	■	■		
Clock #473																			
Clock, 60th Anniversary																			
Coffeepot with lid, 7 1/2" 4 cups #493	■	■	■	■	■	■	■	■	■	■	■		■	■	■	■	■	■	■
Creamer, Individual, Figure 8, 4 3/4"	■	■	■	■	■	■	■				■		■	■	■	■	■		
Creamer, Regular 7oz. #492	■	■	■	■	■	■	■	■	■	■	■	■	■	■	■	■	■	■	■
Cup, Bouillon, 4" 6 3/4oz. #450	■	■	■	■	■	■	■	■	■	■	■		■	■	■	■	■	■	■
Cup & Saucer Set, Cup #452 Saucer #470	■	■	■	■	■	■	■	■	■	■	■	■	■	■	■	■	■	■	■
Cup & Saucer Set, Demitasse, Ring Handle	■		■	■	■	■	■				■		■	■	■	■	■		
Cup & Saucer Set, Demitasse, Stick Handle	■	■	■	■	■	■	■				■		■	■	■	■	■		
Cup & Saucer Set, Jumbo, Cup#149 Sau.#293	■	■	■	■	■	■	■	■	■	■	■		■	■	■	■	■	■	■
Goblet #429	■		■	■	■	■	■	■	■	■	■		■	■	■				
Gravy/Sauce Boat 18 1/2oz. #486	■	■	■	■	■	■	■	■	■	■	■	■	■	■	■	■	■	■	■
Mug, Cappuccino, 6 1/8" 21oz. #418	■	■	■	■	■	■	■				■		■	■	■	■	■		
Mug, Denver, 3 7/8"	■	■	■	■	■	■	■	■	■	■	■	■	■	■	■	■	■	■	■
Mug, Pedestal, 6 1/8" 18oz. #424	■	■	■	■	■	■	■				■		■	■	■	■	■		
Mug, Tom & Jerry, 3 1/2" 10 1/4oz. #453	■	■	■	■	■	■	■	■	■	■	■		■	■	■	■	■	■	■
Mug, Tom & Jerry Embossed/Fan	■		■		■	■	■				■		■	■	■	■	■		
Mug, Tower, 3 1/2"	■	■	■	■	■	■	■				■		■	■	■	■	■		
Napkin Ring #469	■	■	■	■	■	■	■	■	■	■	■		■	■	■	■	■		
Pie, Baker/Plate, 6 1/4"	■	■	■		■	■	■				■		■	■	■	■	■		
Pie, Baker/Plate, 8"	■	■	■	■	■	■	■				■		■	■	■	■	■		
Pie, Baker/Plate, 10 1/4" #487	■	■	■	■	■	■	■	■	■	■	■		■	■	■	■	■	■	■
Pitcher, Disk Water, 7 1/8" 67 1/4 oz. #484	■	■	■	■	■	■	■	■	■	■	■	■	■	■	■	■	■	■	■
Pitcher, Disk Water with woman decal																			
Pitcher, Disk Juice, 5 3/4" 28 oz. #485	■	■	■	■	■	■	■	■	■	■	■		■	■	■	■	■	■	■
Pitcher, Disk Mini, 3 1/4" 5 oz. #475	■	■	■	■	■	■	■	■	■	■	■		■	■	■	■	■	■	■
Plate, Bread & Butter, 6 1/8" #463	■	■	■	■	■	■	■	■	■	■	■	■	■	■	■	■	■	■	■
Plate, Chop, 11 3/4" #467	■	■	■	■	■	■	■	■	■	■	■	■	■	■	■	■	■	■	■
Plate, Dinner, 10 1/2" #466	■	■	■	■	■	■	■	■	■	■	■	■	■	■	■	■	■	■	■
Plate, Luncheon, 9" #465	■	■	■	■	■	■	■	■	■	■	■	■	■	■	■	■	■	■	■
Plate, Salad, 7 1/4" #464	■	■	■	■	■	■	■	■	■	■	■	■	■	■	■	■	■	■	■
Plate, Snack, with cup well, 10 1/2" #760	■	■	■	■	■	■	■				■		■	■	■	■	■		
Platter, Oval, 9 5/8" #456	■	■	■	■	■	■	■		■		■		■	■	■	■	■		
Platter, Oval, 11 5/8" #457	■	■	■	■	■	■	■	■	■	■	■	■	■	■	■	■	■	■	■
Platter, Oval, 13 5/8" #458	■	■	■	■	■	■	■				■		■	■	■	■	■		
Salt & Pepper Set #497	■	■	■	■	■	■	■	■	■	■	■	■	■	■	■	■	■	■	■
Salt & Pepper Set, Rangetop	■	■	■		■	■	■				■		■	■	■	■	■		
Spoon Rest, 8"	■	■	■		■	■	■				■		■	■	■	■	■		
Sugar Bowl with lid, Individual Figure 8	■	■	■	■	■	■	■				■		■	■	■	■	■		
Sugar Bowl with lid, Regular no handles #498	■	■	■	■	■	■	■	■	■	■	■	■	■	■	■	■	■	■	■
Sugar Caddy, 3 1/2" #479	■	■	■	■	■	■	■				■		■	■	■	■	■		
Teapot with lid, 2 Cups, 5" #764	■	■	■		■	■	■				■		■	■	■	■	■		
Teapot with lid, 4 Cups, 7 1/4" 44oz. #496	■	■	■	■	■	■	■	■	■	■	■	■	■	■	■	■	■	■	■
Tray, Bread, 12" #412	■	■	■	■	■	■	■				■		■	■	■	■	■		
Tray, Chip & Dip/Hostess, 12 1/4" #753	■	■	■	■	■	■	■				■		■	■	■	■	■		

"New" Fiesta Colors

Empty boxes are pieces that we believe were not made or we have not seen.

	White	Black	Rose (New)	Apricot	Cobalt Blue (New)	Yellow (New)	Turquoise (New)	Periwinkle Blue	Sea Mist Green	Lilac	Persimmon	Sapphire	Chartreuse (New)	Pearl Gray	Juniper	Cinnabar	Sunflower	Plum	Shamrock
Tray, Figure 8, 10"																			
Tray, Pizza, 15" #505																			
Tray, Relish/Utility w/ Handles, 9 1/2"#499																			
Tray, Serving/Cake with Handles, 12"																			
Trivet, 6"																			
Tumbler, 3 3/4" 6 1/2oz. #446																			
Utensil Crock/Holder, 6 5/8"																			
Vase, Bud, 6 1/4" #490																			
Vase, Flower Small, 7 3/4" #440																			
Vase, Flower Medium, 9 5/8" #491																			
Vase, Millenium I (2 handle)																			
Vase, Millenium II (no handle, disk)																			
Vase, Millenium III (no handle tall)																			
Vase, Monarch #566																			
Vase, Royalty #565																			

Willow Shapes

WILLOW SHAPES 1935 – 1964

In this chapter, three pattern designs share one common set of shapes. Willow (Blue and Pink), Fantasy (Blue and Rose), and Americana–Currier & Ives patterns all have in common the basic Willow shapes. As a result, this chapter is configured differently from most in this book. Because all three patterns share the same shape of sugar, creamer, cup and saucer, and gravy or sauce boat, they are presented together.

Blue Willow
No Trim

Pink Willow
No Trim

Blue Fantasy
No Trim

Rose Fantasy
Oval Platter Shown
No Trim

Americana–Currier & Ives
No Trim

WILLOW SHAPED PIECES COMMON TO ALL HOMER LAUGHLIN WILLOW SHAPED PATTERNS

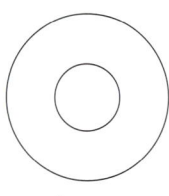

SUGAR BOWL WITH LID	CREAMER	SAUCER	CUP	GRAVY/SAUCE BOAT
6⅛" W	5½" W	5¾" D	4⅞" W	7¼" W
3⅞" H	3¾" H		2⅜" H	4⅛" H

238

Blue Willow

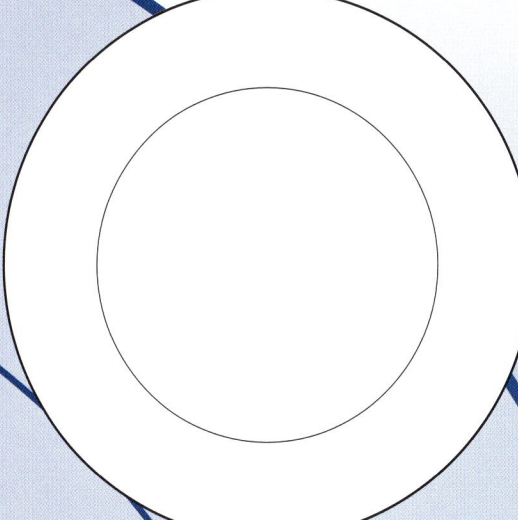

Piece Types

Willow Shaped Pieces Common To All Homer Laughlin Willow Shaped Patterns

These drawings were made from actual stock at Replacements, Ltd. Check the piece type list for all known piece types in this shape.

Sugar Bowl with lid	Creamer	Saucer	Cup	Gravy/Sauce Boat
6⅛" W 3⅞" H	5½" W 3¾" H	5¾" D	4⅞" W 2⅜" H	7¼" W 4⅛" H

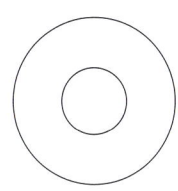

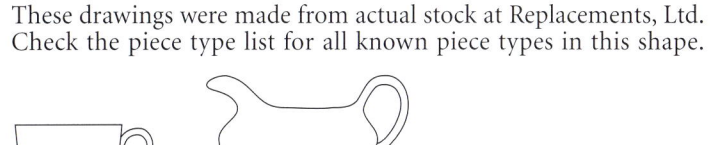

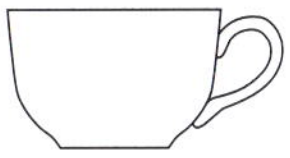

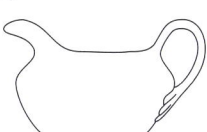

Blue Willow Variances Over Time

Empress Shaped Bowls (approximately 1935–1958)

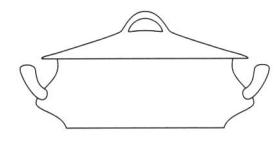

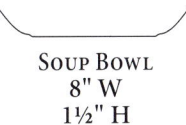

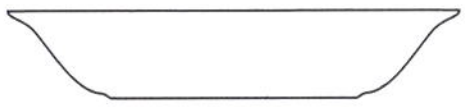

Round Covered Vegetable Bowl
8⅞" W
4" H

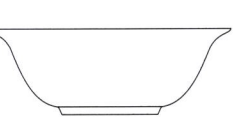

Round Vegetable Bowl	Oval Vegetable Bowl	Soup Bowl	Soup Bowl	Cereal Bowl	Fruit Bowl
8⅝" W 2⅞" H	9⅜" W 2¼" H	8" W 1½" H	7⅛" W 1½" H	5⅞" W 1⅞" H	5⅛" W 1¼" H

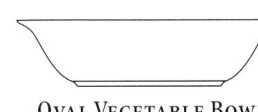

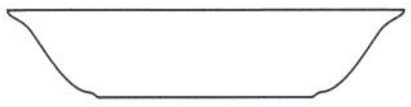

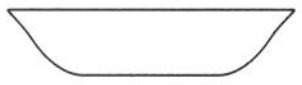

Wells Shaped Pieces (approximately 1941–1944)

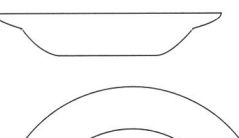

Soup Bowl with rim
8⅛" W
1½" H

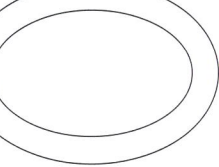

Gravy/Sauce Boat Underplate/Relish
9" W

Teapot with lid
9¾" W
5¼" H

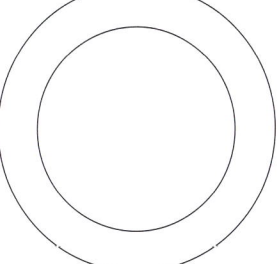

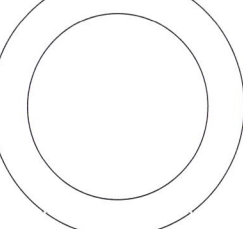

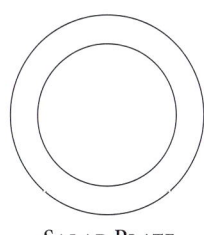

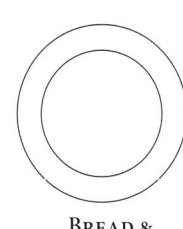

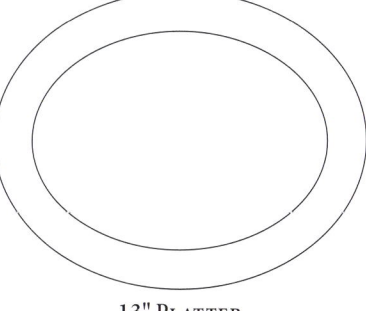

Dinner Plate	Luncheon Plate	Salad Plate	Bread & Butter Plate	13" Platter
9⅞" D	9" D	7⅞" D	6⅛" D	13⅜" W x 10¼" H

Blue Willow Pattern

BLUE WILLOW   1935 – 1964

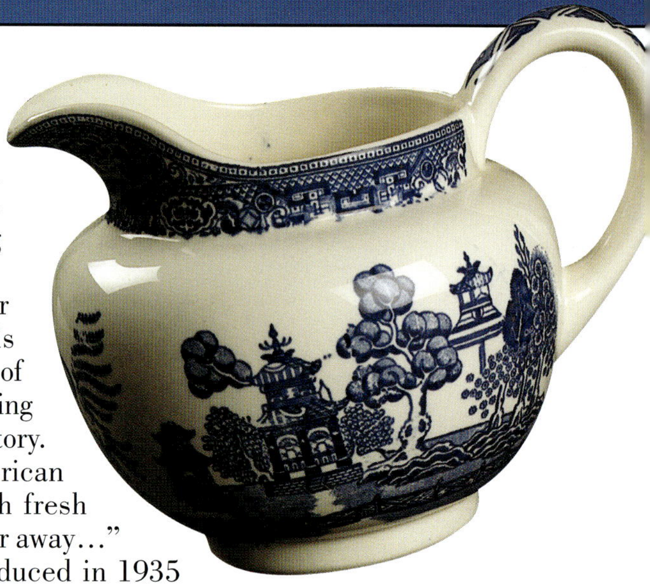

Blue Willow is a famous, old pattern commonly recognized and widely produced. Homer Laughlin developed new shapes for this pattern which were used in combination with existing shapes. These new shapes were known as Willow.

A Montgomery Ward mail-order catalog, one of Homer Laughlin's best customers for this pattern, describes this legendary decoration as follows: "The ancient Chinese tale of two lovers who were changed into white doves related in charming detail. Originally made in 1782 by a famous old English factory. It was brought to this country by clipper ship. Modern American methods of dinnerware manufacturing bring it to you with fresh vividness. Design applied under glaze; cannot wash off or wear away…"

Blue Willow, as created by Homer Laughlin, was introduced in 1935 and produced until 1964. It sold well in a number of catalogs and evolved over time. One set of hollowware shapes was used consistently. This hollowware is what defines the Willow shape. To suit changing customer tastes, flatware shapes for Blue Willow were changed over time. Extensive examination suggests these rough time frames for the various flatware shapes: Empress shape, 1935-1958; Wells shape, 1941-1944; Brittany shape, 1941-1964; and Rhythm shape, 1954-1964. During World War II, the always popular Blue Willow produced by English, Japanese, and other potters was no longer available; as a result, Homer Laughlin experienced a surge in Blue Willow sales from the early to mid 1940's.

Note that Pink Willow was also produced by Homer Laughlin between 1937 and 1942, using both Empress and Wells shapes to supplement the otherwise unique Willow forms.

Brittany Shaped Pieces (approximately 1941–1964)

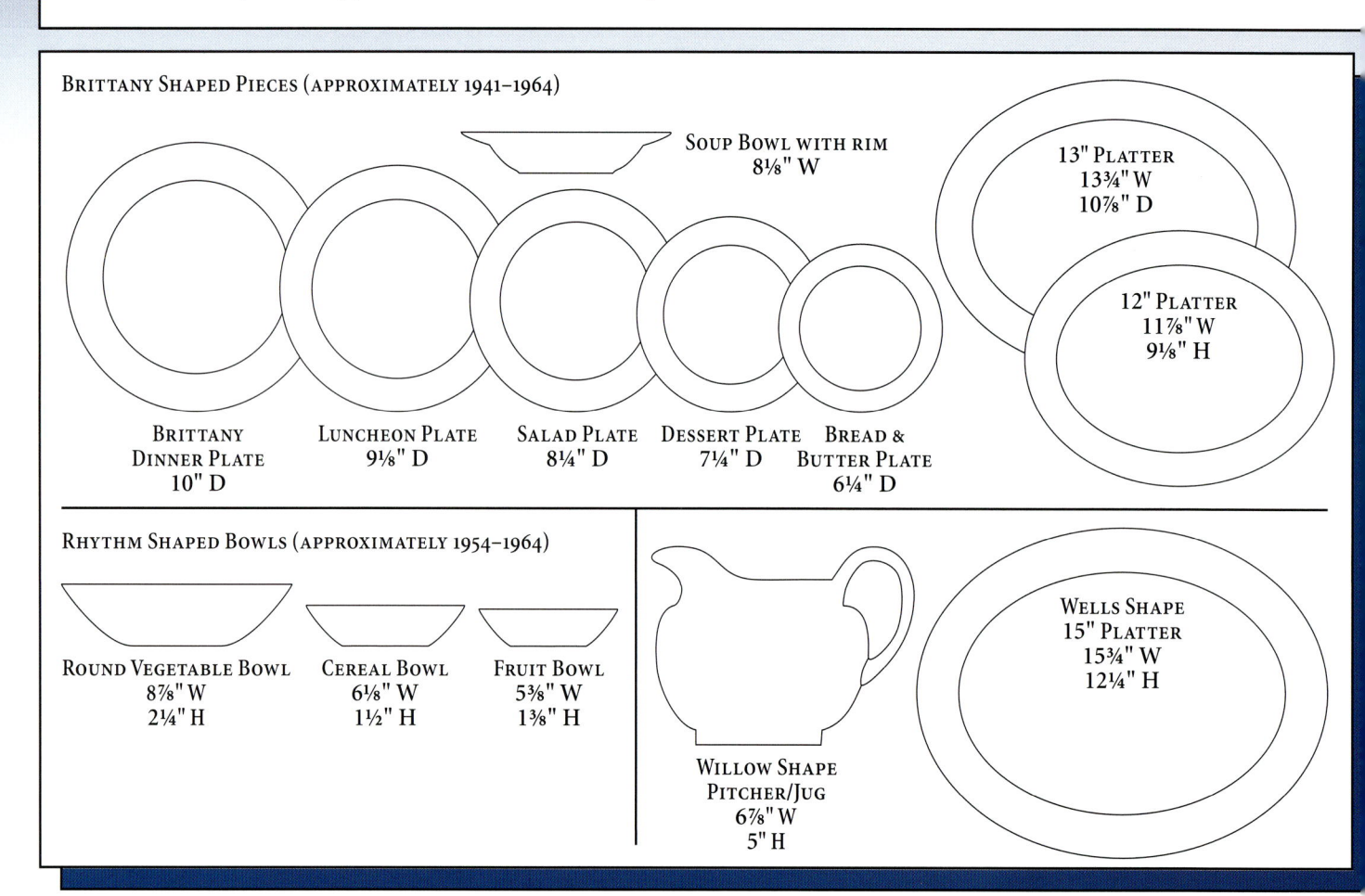

- Brittany Dinner Plate 10" D
- Luncheon Plate 9⅛" D
- Salad Plate 8¼" D
- Dessert Plate 7¼" D
- Bread & Butter Plate 6¼" D
- Soup Bowl with rim 8⅛" W
- 13" Platter 13¾" W 10⅞" D
- 12" Platter 11⅞" W 9⅛" H

Rhythm Shaped Bowls (approximately 1954–1964)

- Round Vegetable Bowl 8⅞" W 2¼" H
- Cereal Bowl 6⅛" W 1½" H
- Fruit Bowl 5⅜" W 1⅜" H

- Willow Shape Pitcher/Jug 6⅞" W 5" H
- Wells Shape 15" Platter 15¾" W 12¼" H

Blue Willow Pattern

Ever Popular "Blue Willow" $5.98

The ancient Chinese tale of two lovers who were changed into white doves related in charming detail. Originally made in 1782 by a famous old English factory, it was brought to this country by clipper ship. Modern American methods of dinnerware manufacture bring it to you with fresh vividness. Design applied under glaze; cannot wash off or wear away. Four times selected American semi-porcelain; glaze will not crack. Sugar and Creamer included only in 35-piece, 53-piece and 95-piece sets.

35 E 04425—State size of set. Mailable.
20-piece set—service for four. Shipping weight, 15 pounds......$3.49
32-piece set—standard service for six. Shpg. wt., 20 lbs........ 5.98
35-piece set—complete service for six. Same as 32-pc. set with sugar and creamer instead of sauce dishes. Shpg. wt., 22 lbs.$7.98
53-piece set—service for eight. Shipping weight, 40 pounds..... 11.59
35 EM 4425—Not mailable.
95-piece set—service for twelve. Shipping weight, 70 pounds..... 21.50

Blue Willow $5.69 32-Pc.

A famous pattern designed over two hundred years ago from an ancient Chinese legend. The rich all-over design is applied under the glaze—can't wear off. You'll find this pattern an excellent choice for your Early American dining room. Set Pieces, Page 570. Ship. wts. sets, 12 lbs.; 20 lbs.; 38 lbs.; 69 lbs.
486 A 6363—20-Piece Set. Serves Four..$3.29
P486 A 6361—32-Pc. Set. Serves Six.... 5.69
P486 A 6362—53-Pc. Set. Serves Eight.. 10.95
P386 A 6364—95-Pc. Set. Serves Twelve.19.95
586 A 6365—Milk Pitcher. 28 oz. capacity. 4¼ inches high. Ship. wt. 2 lbs..........59c
586A6365—Open Stock. State Pcs. See Pg. 570.

Blue Willow—MADE IN AMERICA $3.98 32-Pc.
LOWEST PRICE IN YEARS FOR THIS POPULAR PATTERN

Quaint charming Blue Willow—the authentic age-old design that has appealed to American women for hundreds of years! Everyone loves this picturesque all-over design, inspired by an ancient Chinese legend of young love.
Wards Blue Willow is Triple-selected First Quality American Semi-Porcelain. It has a brighter, clearer design than some cheaper imported types of Blue Willow. The design on Wards Blue Willow is applied under the glaze—can never wear off. It is check-proof and crazeproof. Buy American-made Blue Willow for the biggest value. American pattern varies only slightly from import pattern previously carried.
See Composition of Sets and Open Stock listings above. *All sets Mailable.* 95-piece set shipped in two packages. Sets shipped from Chicago, Baltimore, Albany or Pittsburgh. Mail order to nearest house.

586 A 6365—Creamer and Sugar. Shipping weight 3 pounds........$1.32
586 A 6365—Milk Pitcher. 4¾ in. high. Shipping weight 2 pounds........59c
P486 A 6362—53-Pc. Service for Eight. Shipping weight 42 pounds.......$8.49
P486 A 6364—95-Pc. Service for Twelve. Shipping weight 76 pounds.....$17.49
586 A 6365—Open Stock. State Blue Willow and name of art. See Table above.
586 A 6600—Blue Willow Glasses. Tall, 9½-oz. Chip-proof edge. Match Blue Willow dish design. Shipping weight 3 lbs. 8 oz. 6 for...............98c
86 A 7757—12-Piece Blue Handle Cutlery Set. Stainless steel blades and tines—never need polishing. 5-in. semi-ground blades. Non-inflammable Blue Catalin handles harmonize perfectly with Blue Willow dinnerware and glassware. 86 A 7757—12-Pc. Set. 6 Knives, 6 Forks. Ship. wt. set 1 lb. 8 oz.......27c

P486 A 6361—32-Pc. Service for Six. Ship. wt. 23 pounds...........$3.98

BA WARDS 393

Top left: *Blue Willow pattern; Montgomery Ward Catalog, 1943.* **Top right:** *Blue Willow pattern; Sears, Roebuck & Co. Catalog, 1943.* **Middle right:** *Blue Willow pattern, Brittany shaped plates; Dinner Plate, Luncheon Plate, Salad Plate, Bread & Butter Plate, and Saucer.* **Bottom left:** *Blue Willow pattern; Montgomery Ward Catalog, 1938-1939 Fall & Winter.* **Bottom right:** *Blue Willow pattern, Wells shaped plates; Dinner Plate, Luncheon Plate, Salad Plate, Bread & Butter Plate, and Cup & Saucer Set.*

Homer Laughlin

Top left: *Blue Willow pattern, Empress shaped bowls; Round Vegetable Bowl, Oval Vegetable Bowl, Soup Bowl, Fruit Bowl and Cereal Bowl.* **Middle left:** *Blue Willow pattern, coupe shaped bowls; Round Vegetable Bowl, Cereal Bowl, and Fruit Bowl.* **Top right:** *Blue Willow pattern; Wells shaped Oval Platter, Sugar Bowl with lid, and Creamer.* **Middle right:** *Blue Willow pattern; Round Covered Vegetable Bowl.* **Bottom:** *Blue Willow pattern; Three of the four bowl shapes we have found Shown are Soup Bowls; Empress shape, Wells shape, and Kwaker shape. Not shown is a coupe shaped bowl.*

Blue Willow Pattern

Blue Willow Piece Type List

From Homer Laughlin Literature with Confirmed Actual Pieces

Bowl, Cereal Empress, 5⅞ inches
Bowl, Cereal Rhythm, 6⅛ inches
Bowl, Cranberry
Bowl, Fruit Empress, 5⅛ inches
Bowl, Fruit Rhythm, 5⅜ inches
Bowl, Soup Empress, 7⅛ inches
Bowl, Soup Empress, 8 inches
Bowl, Soup with rim Brittany, 8⅛ inches
Bowl, Soup with rim Wells, 8⅛ inches
Bowl, Vegetable Oval Empress, 9⅜ inches
Bowl, Vegetable Round Empress, 8⅝ inches
Bowl, Vegetable Round Rhythm, 8⅞ inches

Bowl, Vegetable Round Covered Empress, 8⅞ inches
Creamer, Willow
Cup & Saucer Set Willow
   Cup, 2⅜ inches
   Saucer, 5¾ inches
Cup & Saucer Set Willow, Jumbo
Eggcup
Gravy/Sauce Boat Willow
Gravy/Sauce Boat Underplate/Relish Wells, 9 inches
Pitcher/Jug, Willow
Plate, Bread & Butter Brittany, 6¼ inches
Plate, Bread & Butter Wells, 6⅛ inches
Plate, Dessert Brittany, 7¼ inches

Plate, Dinner Brittany, 10 inches
Plate, Dinner Wells, 9⅞ inches
Plate, Luncheon Brittany, 9⅛ inches
Plate, Luncheon Wells, 9 inches
Plate, Salad Brittany, 8¼ inches
Plate, Salad Wells, 7⅞ inches
Platter, Oval Brittany, 11⅞ inches
Platter, Oval Brittany, 13¾ inches
Platter, Oval Wells, 11½ inches
Platter, Oval Wells, 13⅜ inches
Platter, Oval Wells, 15¾ inches
Sugar Bowl with lid, Willow
Teapot with lid, Wells/Willow
   body is Wells
   lid is Willow

Pink Willow Piece Type List

From Homer Laughlin Literature with Confirmed Actual Pieces

Bowl, Fruit Empress, 5⅛ inches
Bowl, Vegetable Oval Empress, 9⅜ inches
Bowl, Vegetable Round Empress, 8⅝ inches

Cup & Saucer Set Willow
   Cup, 2⅜ inches
   Saucer, 5¾ inches
Gravy/Sauce Boat Underplate/Relish Wells, 9 inches
Plate, Bread & Butter Wells, 6⅛ inches

Plate, Dinner Wells, 9⅞ inches
Plate, Luncheon Wells, 9 inches
Plate, Salad Wells, 7⅞ inches
Platter, Oval Wells, 11½ inches
Platter, Oval Wells, 13⅜ inches
Platter, Oval Wells, 15¾ inches

Top right: Blue Willow pattern; Teapot with lid. Body is Wells shape, lid is Willow shape. **Bottom left:** *Pink Willow pattern; Three Oval Platters, and Oval Vegetable Bowl.* **Bottom right:** *Pink Willow pattern; Round Vegetable Bowl, Dinner Plate, Cup, and Fruit Bowl.*

Fantasy

Bottom left: *Montgomery Ward Catalog, 1939.*
Bottom right: *Montgomery Ward Catalog, 1938-1939.*

FANTASY 1938 – 1939

Fantasy patterns use the same basic shapes as the Blue Willow and Americana patterns. Fantasy and Americana were made expressly for Montgomery Ward. Perhaps this shape, regardless of decoration, was a Montgomery Ward exclusive? Fantasy appeared in a few issues of the Montgomery Ward catalog for a short time around 1938-1939. The round covered vegetable bowl in Fantasy appears unique to this pattern. The handles, foot, and other elements are different from those used for the similar Blue Willow and Americana patterns.

Fantasy
USUAL $9 TO $12 VALUE $4.98 32-Pc.

Smart English style print. An imported pattern of this same quality usually sells for $9 to $12 for a 32-piece set. Wards produced it in America to save one-half. The lovely all-over pattern is applied under the glaze for permanent lasting beauty—it can't wear off. Your choice of deep Blue or soft Rose on Cream-White. First quality Triple-Selected American Semi-Porcelain. *All sets Mailable.* 95-piece set shipped in 2 packages. Set Composition, Page 319.

Fantasy—Smart English Style Print
$4.98 32-Pc.

An imported pattern of this same quality usually sells for $9 to $12 for a 32-Pc. Set. Wards produced it in America to save you one-half. Your choice of Blue or Rose on First Quality triple-selected American Dinnerware. The pattern is applied under the glaze—can't wear off.
All sets Mailable. Sets shipped from Chicago, Baltimore, Albany or Pittsburgh. Mail order to nearest House. Ship. wts.: 32-Pc., 23 lbs.; 53-Pc., 42 lbs.; 95-Pc., 76 lbs.; Sugar, Creamers 3 lbs.
For Composition of Sets, see Page 393.

Rose Fantasy
P486 A 6336—32-Pc. Service for 6..$4.98
586 A 6340—Sugar and Creamer.....1.44
P486 A 6337—53-Pc. Service for 8...9.98
P386 A 6339—95-Pc. Serv. for 12...17.95
586 A 6340—Open Stock. See Page 393.

Blue Fantasy
P486 A 6326—32-Pc. Service for 6..$4.98
586 A 6330—Sugar and Creamer.....1.44
P486 A 6327—53-Pc. Service for 8...9.98
P386 A 6329—95-Pc. Serv. for 12...17.95
586 A 6330—Open Stock. See Page 393.

244

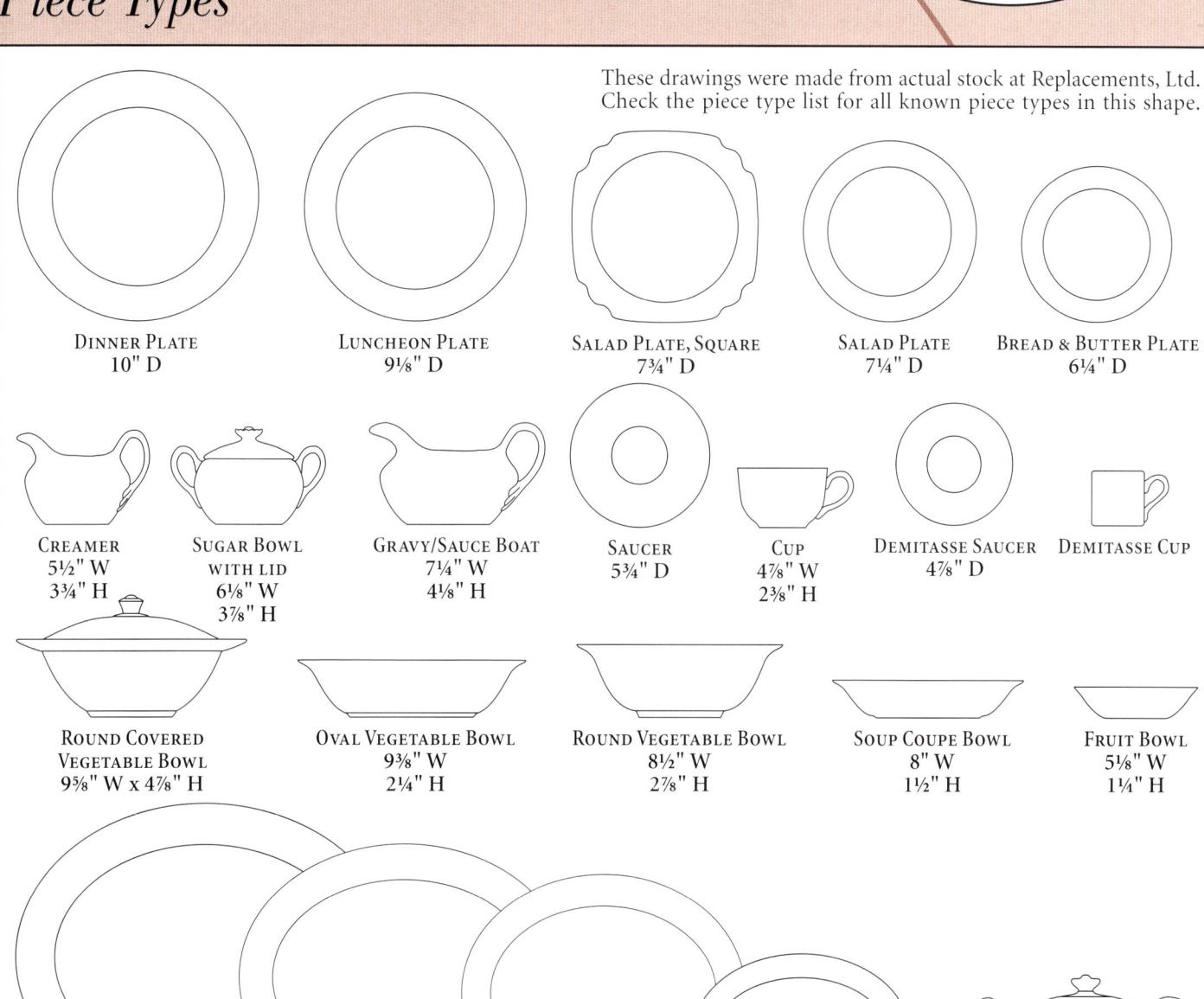

AMERICANA
An American Subject from
CURRIER & IVES PRINTS

Piece Types

These drawings were made from actual stock at Replacements, Ltd. Check the piece type list for all known piece types in this shape.

Dinner Plate
10" D

Luncheon Plate
9⅛" D

Salad Plate, Square
7¾" D

Salad Plate
7¼" D

Bread & Butter Plate
6¼" D

Creamer
5½" W
3¾" H

Sugar Bowl with lid
6⅛" W
3⅞" H

Gravy/Sauce Boat
7¼" W
4⅛" H

Saucer
5¾" D

Cup
4⅞" W
2⅜" H

Demitasse Saucer
4⅞" D

Demitasse Cup

Round Covered Vegetable Bowl
9⅝" W x 4⅞" H

Oval Vegetable Bowl
9⅜" W
2¼" H

Round Vegetable Bowl
8½" W
2⅞" H

Soup Coupe Bowl
8" W
1½" H

Fruit Bowl
5⅛" W
1¼" H

15" Platter
15¾" W

13" Platter
13⅝" W
10⅜" H

11" Platter
11¾" W
9½" H

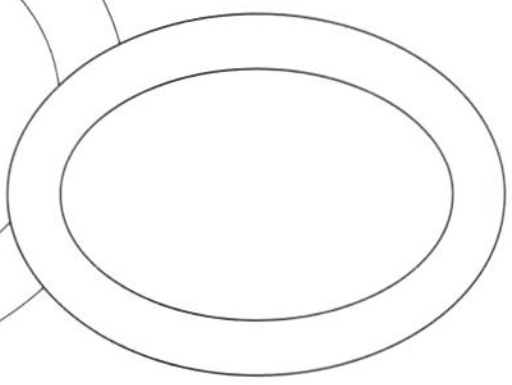

Gravy/Sauce Boat Underplate/Relish
9" W

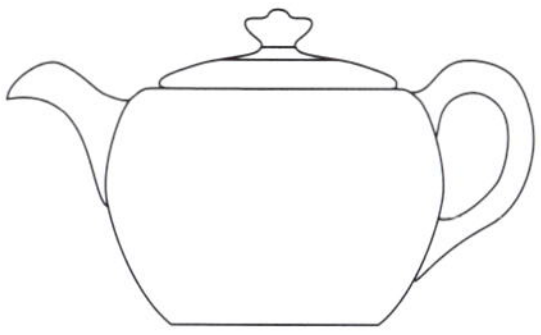

Teapot with lid
9⅝" W
5½" H

Americana Pattern

AMERICANA: CURRIER & IVES

circa 1942 – 1956

Americana was an exclusive pattern for Montgomery Ward. We first found this pattern in their 1942 catalog and it remained in production as late as 1956.

The backstamp never mentions the line as "Americana," but Montgomery Ward labeled it that way in its catalogs, and authors have adopted the name. The backstamp cites the Currier & Ives prints used to develop the numerous designs. Americana is one of several Homer Laughlin patterns influenced by English styled tableware. Historic scenes or prints were transferred onto the dinnerware to create the pattern.

The plates and a few other pieces are on the Brittany shape, but the pattern includes pieces in the Empress and Willow shapes as well. The teapot and after dinner coffee shapes seem distinct to this pattern.

Two other red "historic scenes" patterns were made by Homer Laughlin during this same period: see Early American Homes for J. C. Penney and Historical America for Woolworths. Not surprisingly, Montgomery Ward, J. C. Penney, and Woolworths were competitors in the marketplace.

Above left: *Montgomery Ward Catalog, 1942-43 Fall & Winter.* **Right:** *Montgomery Ward Catalog, 1944.*

Americana Pattern

Top: *Americana set from c. 1930 factory photograph. Note, not all pieces are completely decorated!*
Middle left: *Demitasse Cup & Saucer Set.*
Bottom: *Demitasse Cup; Original drawing dated 1930, compliments Homer Laughlin China Company.*

"VIEW OF SAN FRANCISCO, CALIFORNIA" CURRIER & IVES   DRNO. 2101 AUG. 30.
A. D. CUP   ROLL NO. 5.

Homer Laughlin

Top: *Fruit Bowl, Bread & Butter Plate, Dinner Plate, Soup Coupe Bowl, Cream Soup Bowl, and Cup & Saucer Set.*
Bottom left: *Luncheon Plate backstamp.* **Bottom right:** *Round Covered Vegetable Bowl, Chop Plate, Oval Platter, and Creamer.*

Americana Pattern

Americana Piece Type List

From Homer Laughlin Literature with Confirmed Actual Pieces

Bowl, Fruit, 5⅛ inches ....On The Mississippi
Bowl, Soup Coupe, 8 inches ....Fox Hunting, Full Cry
Bowl, Vegetable Round, 8½ inches ....The Road, Winter
Bowl, Vegetable Round Covered, 9⅝ inches................Partridge Shooting (on lid); Husking (inside bowl)
Bowl, Vegetable Oval, 9⅜ inches ....Maple Sugaring
Creamer...Surrender of Burgoyne 1777 (one side)
  Declaration of Independence (other side)
Cup & Saucer Set ....View of New York
    Cup, 2⅜ inches
    Saucer, 5¾ inches
Cup & Saucer Set, Demitasse ....View of San Francisco
    Cup
    Saucer, 4⅞ inches
Eggcup...Across the Continent
Gravy/Sauce Boat...Preparing for Market & Harvest
Gravy/Sauce Boat Underplate/Relish, 9 inches ....Winter in the Country
Plate, Bread & Butter, 6¼ inches ....Hudson River–Crows Nest
Plate, Chop Round, 13 inches ....The Rocky Mountains
Plate, Dinner, 10 inches ....Home Sweet Home
Plate, Luncheon, 9⅛ inches...Western Farmer's Home
Plate, Salad, 7¼ inches ....Clipper Ship Great Republic
Plate, Salad Square, 7¾ inches ....Landing of the Pilgrims 1620
Platter, 11¾ inches...View of Harpers Ferry (W.) VA.
Platter, 13⅝ inches...Suspension Bridge, Niagara Falls
Platter, 15¾ inches...Home to Thanksgiving
Sugar Bowl with lid...Birthplace of Washington (one side)
  Franklin Experiment (other side)
  Patterned print only on lid
Teapot with lid ....Washington Family at Mt. Vernon
  Patterned print only on lid

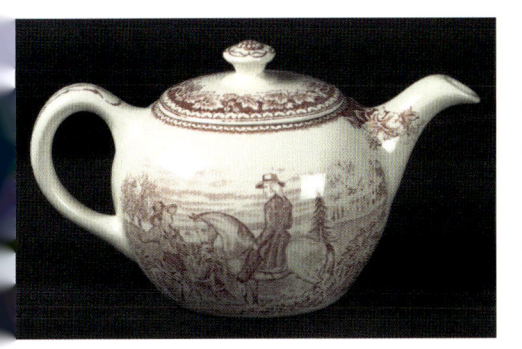

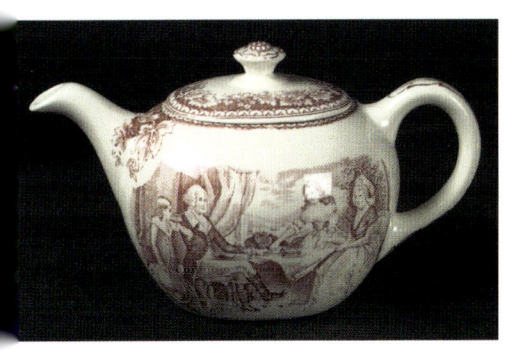

Left: *Teapot with lid, both sides; "Washington at Mt. Vernon" (top), and "Washington Family" (bottom).* **Right:** *Sugar Bowl with lid; "Franklin's Experiment" shown and "Birthplace of Washington" on reverse side. Creamer; "Surrender of Burgoyne 1777" shown, and "Declaration of Independence" on reverse side.*

Nautilus

Piece Types

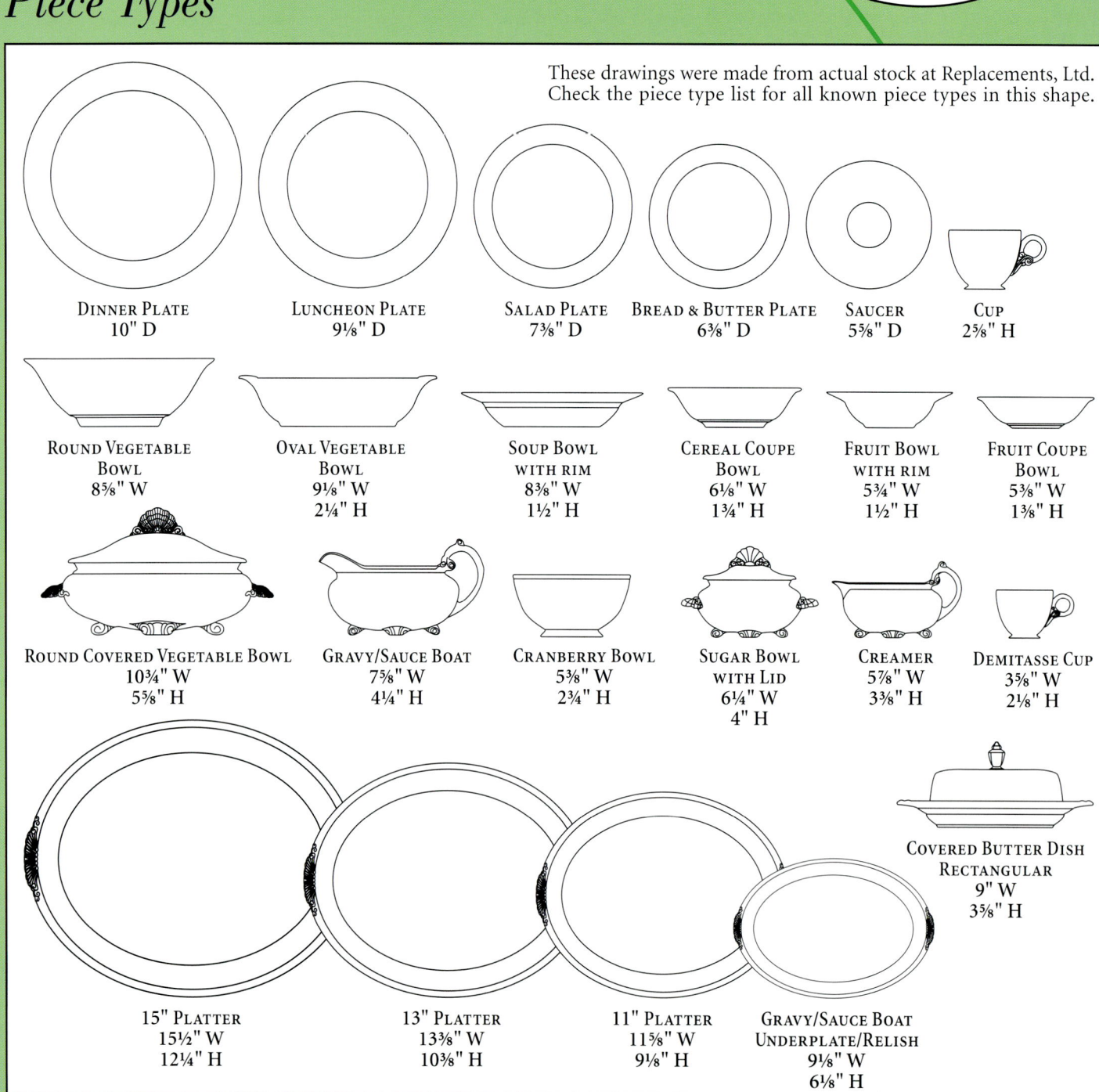

These drawings were made from actual stock at Replacements, Ltd.
Check the piece type list for all known piece types in this shape.

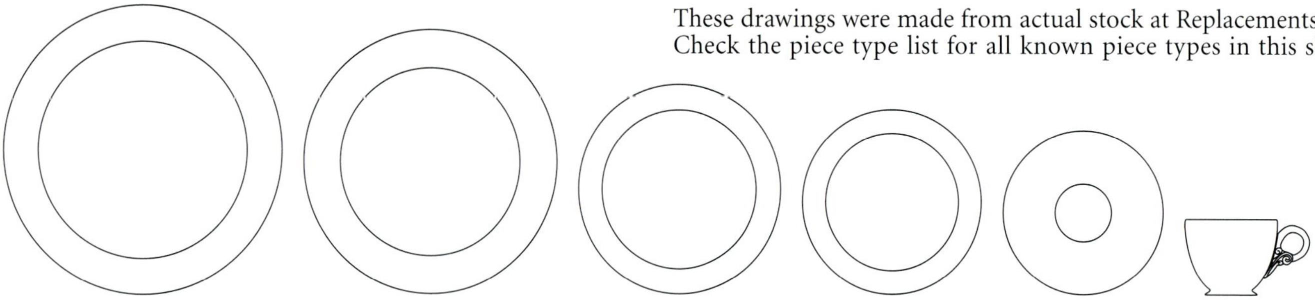

Dinner Plate 10" D | Luncheon Plate 9⅛" D | Salad Plate 7⅜" D | Bread & Butter Plate 6⅜" D | Saucer 5⅝" D | Cup 2⅝" H

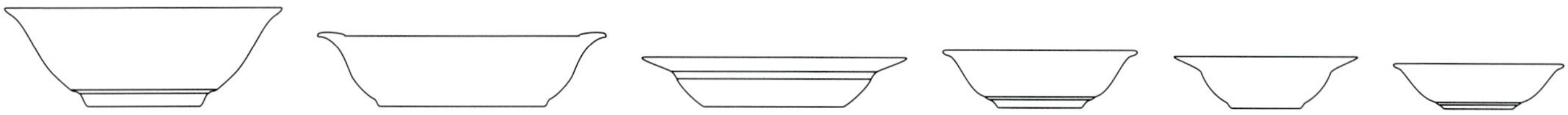

Round Vegetable Bowl 8⅝" W | Oval Vegetable Bowl 9⅛" W 2¼" H | Soup Bowl with Rim 8⅜" W 1½" H | Cereal Coupe Bowl 6⅛" W 1¾" H | Fruit Bowl with Rim 5¾" W 1½" H | Fruit Coupe Bowl 5⅜" W 1⅜" H

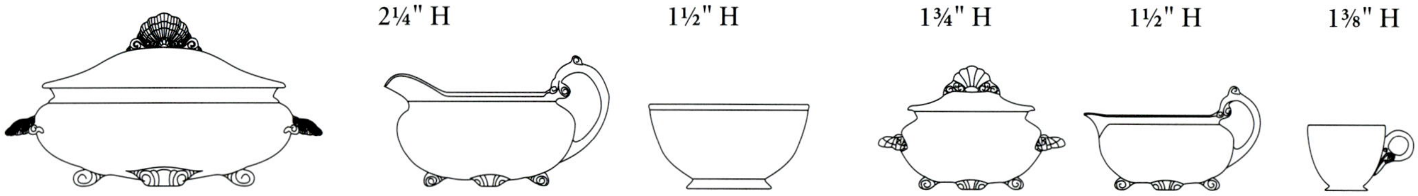

Round Covered Vegetable Bowl 10¾" W 5⅝" H | Gravy/Sauce Boat 7⅝" W 4¼" H | Cranberry Bowl 5⅜" W 2¾" H | Sugar Bowl with Lid 6¼" W 4" H | Creamer 5⅞" W 3⅜" H | Demitasse Cup 3⅝" W 2⅛" H

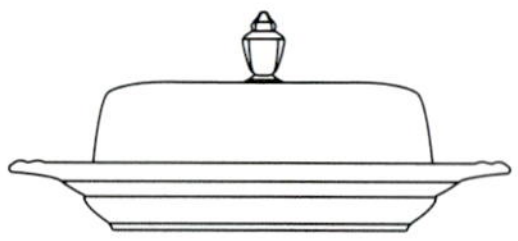

Covered Butter Dish Rectangular 9" W 3⅝" H

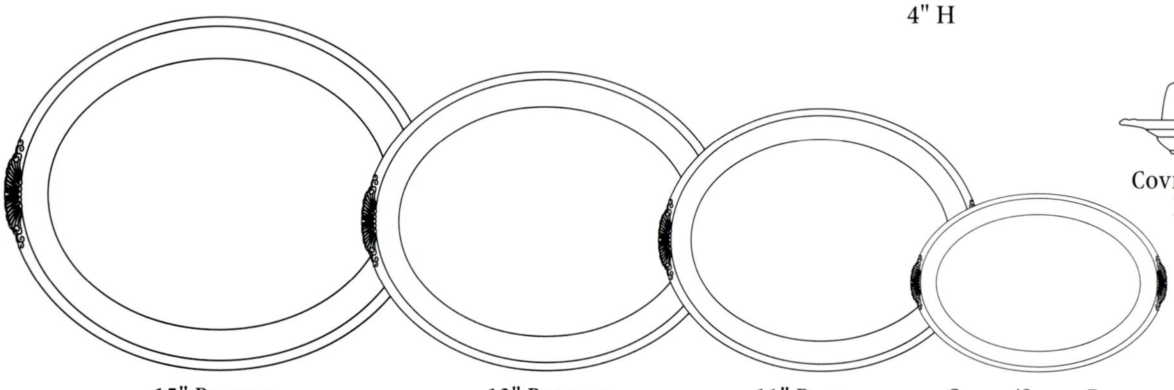

15" Platter 15½" W 12¼" H | 13" Platter 13⅜" W 10⅜" H | 11" Platter 11⅝" W 9⅛" H | Gravy/Sauce Boat Underplate/Relish 9⅛" W 6⅛" H

Nautilus Shape

NAUTILUS 1936 –

The Nautilus shape was in production before Eggshell Nautilus was introduced. The Nautilus name was inspired by the ocean related elements of the design; finials are shell-like as are some handles and the feet on pieces. In the *1937 Homer Laughlin Pound Sterling Prices* book, Nautilus was available in over 100 patterns.

Nautilus appears in the Sears, Roebuck & Co. Catalog in 1936. The Rosebud Wreath pattern was the first offering found in the Montgomery Ward Catalog, Fall & Winter, 1936-37.

The wonderfully graphic Early America pattern on Nautilus was promoted in a full-page illustrated ad in October 1936. The sudden appearance of the shape in both national catalogs and the full-page national ad, all in 1936, suggests that Nautilus was introduced that year.

Eggshell Nautilus was introduced a short time after Nautilus and has distinctly different shapes.

Left: Original art for Newell pattern, from the Homer Laughlin Factory.
Right: Rosebud Wreath pattern; Montgomery Ward Catalog, 1936-37.

251

Homer Laughlin

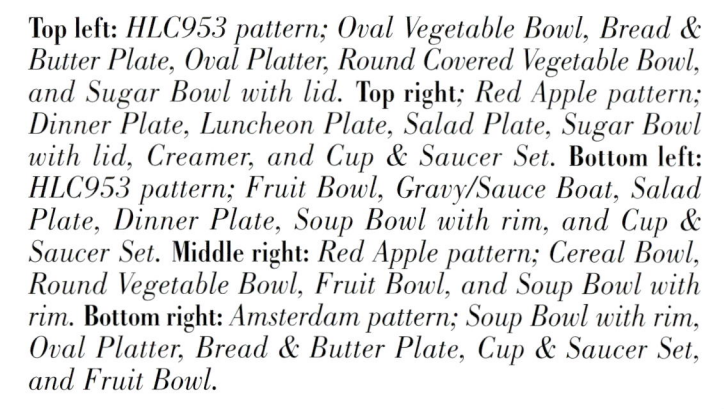

Top left: *HLC953 pattern; Oval Vegetable Bowl, Bread & Butter Plate, Oval Platter, Round Covered Vegetable Bowl, and Sugar Bowl with lid.* **Top right;** *Red Apple pattern; Dinner Plate, Luncheon Plate, Salad Plate, Sugar Bowl with lid, Creamer, and Cup & Saucer Set.* **Bottom left:** *HLC953 pattern; Fruit Bowl, Gravy/Sauce Boat, Salad Plate, Dinner Plate, Soup Bowl with rim, and Cup & Saucer Set.* **Middle right:** *Red Apple pattern; Cereal Bowl, Round Vegetable Bowl, Fruit Bowl, and Soup Bowl with rim.* **Bottom right:** *Amsterdam pattern; Soup Bowl with rim, Oval Platter, Bread & Butter Plate, Cup & Saucer Set, and Fruit Bowl.*

Nautilus Shape

Nautilus Piece Type List

From Homer Laughlin Literature with Confirmed Actual Pieces

Bowl, Cereal Coupe, 6⅛ inches
Bowl, Cranberry, 5⅜ inches
Bowl, Fruit Coupe, 5⅜ inches
Bowl, Fruit with rim, 5¾ inches
Bowl, Soup Onion
Bowl, Soup with rim, 8⅜ inches
Bowl, Vegetable Oval, 9⅛ inches
Bowl, Vegetable Round, 8⅝ inches
Bowl, Vegetable Round Covered, 10¾ inches
Butter Dish with lid, ¼ lb.

Creamer
Cup & Saucer Set
   Cup, 2⅝ inches
   Saucer, 5⅝ inches
Cup & Saucer Set, Demitasse
   Cup, 2⅛ inches
   Saucer
Eggcup, Double
Gravy/Sauce Boat
Gravy/Sauce Boat Underplate/Relish, 9⅛ inches

Mug, Baltimore Coffee
Plate, Bread & Butter, 6⅜ inches
Plate, Dinner, 10 inches
Plate, Luncheon, 9⅛ inches
Plate, Salad, 7⅜ inches
Platter, Oval, 11⅝ inches
Platter, Oval, 13⅜ inches
Platter, Oval, 15½ inches
Sugar Bowl with lid

Above: *W-138 pattern; undated Homer Laughlin Factory Catalog illustrations.*

Nautilus Shape

HLC1620
No Trim

HLC1621
No Trim

HLC1622
No Trim

HLC1700
No Trim

HLC1991
No Trim

HLC1990
No Trim

HLC2160
Oval Platter Shown
No Trim

Early America
Oval Platter Shown
Multi-Motif
No Trim

R2134B
No Trim

R2134A
No Trim

R2140A
No Trim

R2140B
No Trim

R2526
No Trim

N277
No Trim

Hacienda
N363
No Trim

R4703
No Trim

Nautilus Shape

W138A No Trim	 **HLC3097** No Trim	 **R2519** No Trim	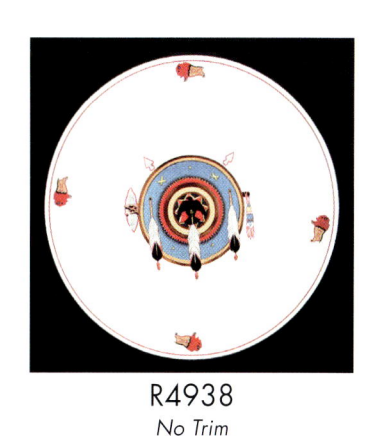 **R4938** No Trim
 **R4939** No Trim	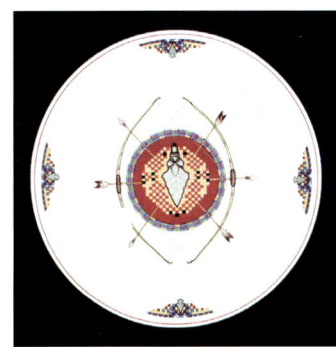 **Cheyenne** R4937 No Trim	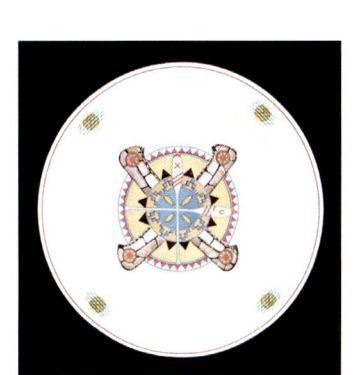 **R4941** No Trim	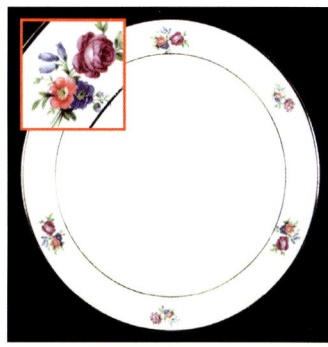 **Dresden** *CP14* by Cunningham & Pickett Luncheon Plate Shown Gold Trim
 **W239** Gold Trim	 **N388** Gold Trim	 **HLC925** Gold Trim	 **Colonial** by Cunningham & Pickett Gold Trim
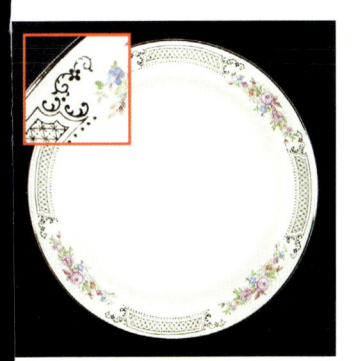 **HLC1362** Gold Trim	 **HLC1357** Gold Trim	 **N300** Gold Trim	 **N301** Gold Trim

Nautilus Shape

N318 *Gold Trim*	**HLC183** *Bread & Butter Plate Shown* *Gold Trim*	**N200** *Gold Trim*	**HLC910** *Gold Trim*
HLC1255 *Gold Trim*	**HLC953** *Gold Trim*	**HLC1501** *Gold Trim*	**HLC907** *No Trim*
HLC1346 *No Trim*	**N291** *Bread & Butter Plate Shown* *No Trim*	**R2168** *No Trim*	**Red Apple** *JJ150* *Green Trim*
HLC1385 *Soup Bowl Shown* *Gold Trim*	**HLC204** *Gold Trim*	**Magnolia** *by Cunningham & Pickett* *Gold Trim*	**W150** *No Trim*

256

Nautilus Shape

Coronation Rose
Gold Trim

Heirloom
*by Cunningham & Pickett
Luncheon Plate Shown
Gold Trim*

N334
No Trim

HLC756
No Trim

Cardinal
*by Cunningham & Pickett
Gold Trim*

Cardinal
*N211
Gold Trim*

Chintz
*by Cunningham & Pickett
Gold Trim*

Bouquet
*by Cunningham & Pickett
Luncheon Plate Shown
Gold Trim*

HLC1457
Gold Trim

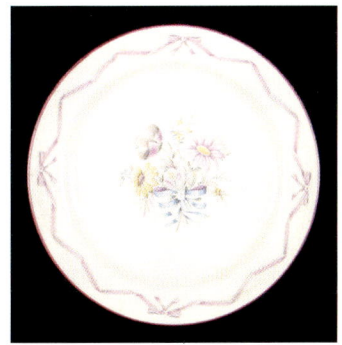

HLC1368
Pink Trim

N419
Gold Trim

ML4
Gold Trim

N428
No Trim

HLC625
*Luncheon Plate Shown
No Trim*

HLC1237
Gold Trim

N429
No Trim

257

Nautilus Shape

HLC622
Gold Trim

HLC3019
Multi-Motif
Gold Trim

Currier & Ives–Green
Multi-Motif
Gold Trim

Amsterdam
Multi-Motif
Gold Trim

HLC3022
Luncheon Plate Shown
Gold Filigree
No Trim

FC125
Gold Trim

HLC1347
Gold Trim

Newell
Gold Trim

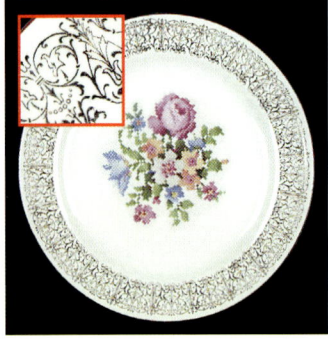

HLC1178
Gold Trim

HLC1356
Gold Filigree
No Trim

HLC1366
Gold Filigree
No Trim

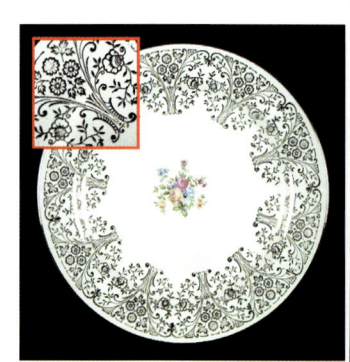

HLC1648
Gold Trim

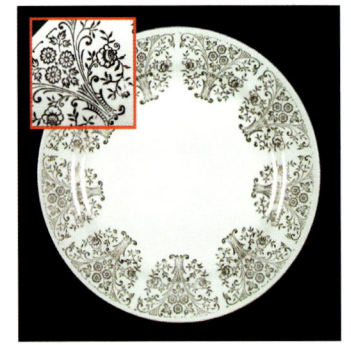

HLC1654
Gold Filigree
No Trim

WHC1
Gold Trim

HLC448
Gold Trim

HLC473
Gold Trim

Nautilus Shape with Charm House, Eggshell Nautilus & Rhythm Hollowware

Lady Stratford
Gold Trim

Lady Greenbriar
*AS1
Gold Trim*

Above: *Workers at the Homer Laughlin Factory.*

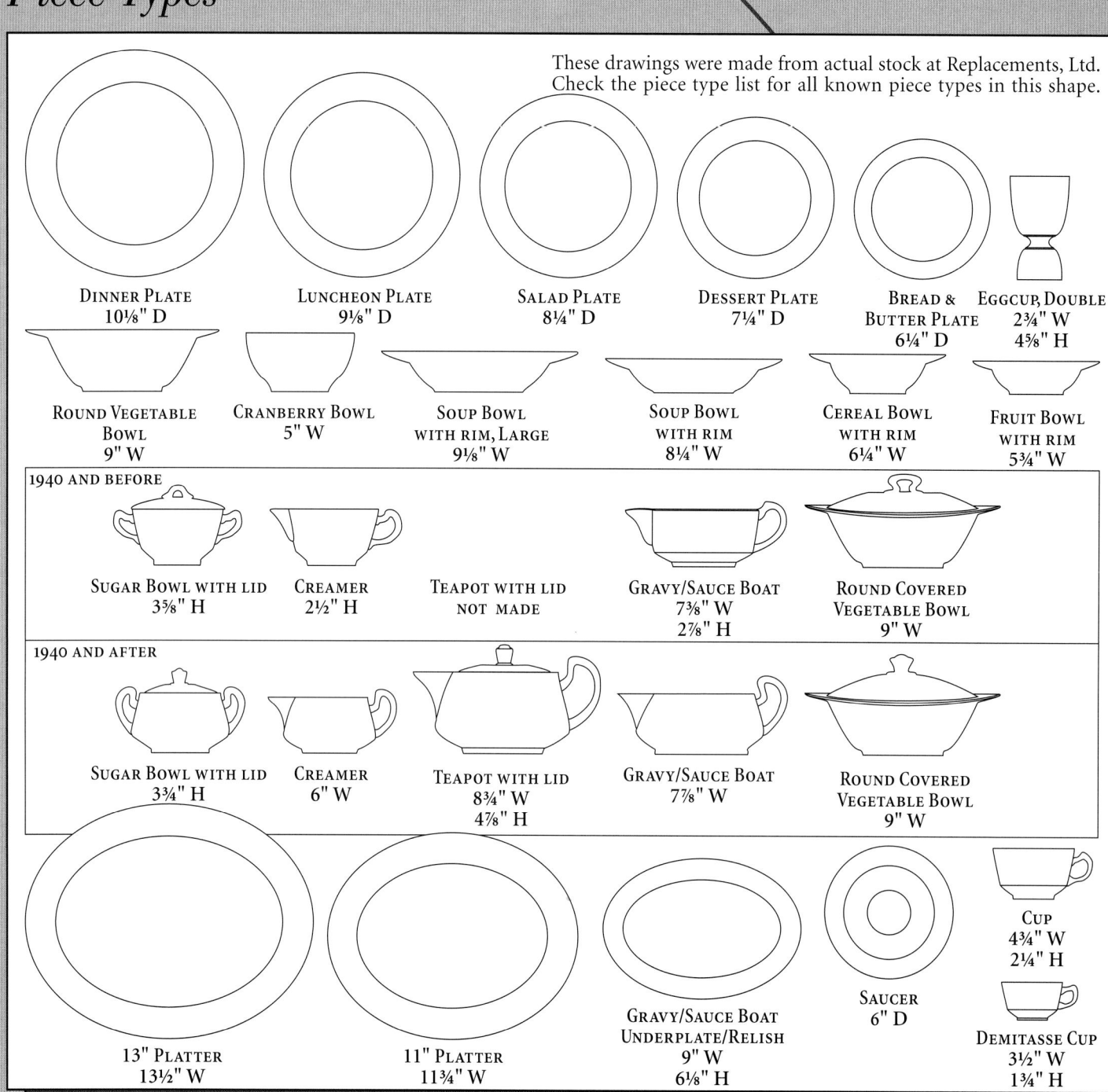

Brittany

Piece Types

These drawings were made from actual stock at Replacements, Ltd. Check the piece type list for all known piece types in this shape.

Piece	Dimensions
Dinner Plate	10⅛" D
Luncheon Plate	9⅛" D
Salad Plate	8¼" D
Dessert Plate	7¼" D
Bread & Butter Plate	6¼" D
Eggcup, Double	2¾" W, 4⅝" H
Round Vegetable Bowl	9" W
Cranberry Bowl	5" W
Soup Bowl with rim, Large	9⅛" W
Soup Bowl with rim	8¼" W
Cereal Bowl with rim	6¼" W
Fruit Bowl with rim	5¾" W

1940 and Before

Sugar Bowl with lid	3⅝" H
Creamer	2½" H
Teapot with lid	not made
Gravy/Sauce Boat	7⅜" W, 2⅞" H
Round Covered Vegetable Bowl	9" W

1940 and After

Piece	Dimensions
Sugar Bowl with lid	3¾" H
Creamer	6" W
Teapot with lid	8¾" W, 4⅞" H
Gravy/Sauce Boat	7⅞" W
Round Covered Vegetable Bowl	9" W

Piece	Dimensions
13" Platter	13½" W
11" Platter	11¾" W
Gravy/Sauce Boat Underplate/Relish	9" W, 6⅛" H
Saucer	6" D
Cup	4¾" W, 2¼" H
Demitasse Cup	3½" W, 1¾" H

Brittany Shape

BRITTANY 1936 – 1958 or later

Reported by various authors as a new Homer Laughlin line in 1936, we found the Brittany shape first appeared in advertisements in September 1936 (*Crockery, Glass & Lamps*). Shown were four variations of a two-tone plaid border decoration.

The Brittany shape was featured in several illustrated ads in 1937. The shape included numerous patterns. In the *Homer Laughlin Company Pound Sterling Price Booklet of 1937*, Brittany shapes were featured with 40 decorations/patterns, indicating the expansive use of the shape shortly after its introduction.

Both Sears and Montgomery Ward sold patterns on Brittany for extended times. Sears illustrations of Brittany patterns were found in catalogs from 1940 through 1955; while Montgomery Ward offered Brittany patterns from 1936 until at least 1958.

New patterns were introduced on the Brittany shape as late as 1958. *China, Glass & Tableware* featured advertisements promoting Sugar Pine and Florence that year.

Shakespeare Country on the Brittany shape was made exclusively for Laughlin International, a marketing company based in Alliance, Ohio.

Even today, Homer Laughlin produces heavy-bodied restaurant lines that are an adaptation of the Brittany shape called Diplomat (gold edge and verge lines) and Sterling (platinum edge and verge lines).

Top left: *Brittany 1940 and before shape, Shamrock pattern; Montgomery Ward, 1936-1937.* **Top middle:** *Brittany 1940 and before shape, Lady Alice pattern; Montgomery Ward, 1939-1940.* **Top right:** *Majestic pattern; Brittany piece types from the factory.* **Bottom left:** *Brittany 1940 and after shape, Clive pattern; Sears 1940.* **Bottom middle:** *Brittany 1940 and after shape, Hemlock pattern; Sears 1941.*

Homer Laughlin

Top left: *Florence* pattern; China, Glass & Tableware, February 1958. **Top middle:** *True Love* pattern; China, Glass & Tableware, June 1957. **Top right:** *Sugar Pine* pattern; China, Glass & Tableware, July 1958. **Second down on left:** Brittany 1940 and after shape, HLC109 pattern; Creamer, Teapot with lid, and Sugar Bowl with lid. **Second down on right:** Brittany 1940 and before shape on left, and 1940 and after shape on right, B1323 pattern; Round Covered Vegetable Bowls. **Third down on left:** Brittany 1940 and before shape, B1323 pattern; Sugar Bowl with lid, and Creamer. **Third down on right:** Brittany 1940 and after shape, B1323 pattern; Sugar Bowl with lid and Creamer. **Bottom left:** Brittany 1940 and before shape, B1345 pattern Gravy/Sauce Boat. **Bottom right:** Brittany 1940 and after shape, HLC3015 pattern; Gravy/Sauce Boat.

262

Brittany Shape

Brittany Piece Type List

From Homer Laughlin Literature with Confirmed Actual Pieces

Bowl, Cereal with rim, 6¼ inches
Bowl, Cranberry, 5 inches
Bowl, Cream Soup & Saucer Set
Bowl, Fruit with rim, 5¾ inches
Bowl, Soup with rim, 8¼ inches
Bowl, Soup Large with rim, 9⅛ inches
Bowl, Vegetable Round, 9 inches
Bowl, Vegetable Round Covered, 9 inches (after 1940)
Bowl, Vegetable Round Covered, 9 inches (before 1940)
Creamer (after 1940)

Creamer (before 1940)
Cup & Saucer Set
  Cup, 2¼ inches
  Saucer, 6 inches
Cup & Saucer Set, Demitasse
  Cup, 1¾ inches
  Saucer
Eggcup, Double
Gravy/Sauce Boat (after 1940)
Gravy/Sauce Boat (before 1940)
Gravy/Sauce Boat Underplate/Relish, 9 inches

Plate, Bread & Butter, 6¼ inches
Plate, Dessert, 7¼ inches
Plate, Dinner, 10⅛ inches
Plate, Luncheon, 9⅛ inches
Plate, Salad, 8¼ inches
Platter, Oval, 11¾ inches
Platter, Oval, 13½ inches
Sugar Bowl with lid (after 1940)
Sugar Bowl with lid (before 1940)
Teapot with lid (after 1940)

Top left: *Majestic pattern; Round Vegetable Bowl, Luncheon Plate, Salad Plate, Bread & Butter Plate, Fruit Bowl with rim, Soup Bowl with rim, and Cup & Saucer Set.* **Top right:** *Majestic pattern; Oval Platter, Sugar Bowl with lid, and Creamer.* **Bottom left:** *Shakespeare Country–Blue pattern; Round Vegetable Bowl, Chop Plate, Cereal Bowl with rim, and Fruit Bowl with rim.* **Bottom right:** *Shakespeare Country–Blue pattern; Dinner Plate, Salad Plate, Creamer, Sugar Bowl with lid, and Cup & Saucer Set.*

Brittany Shape (No Trim)

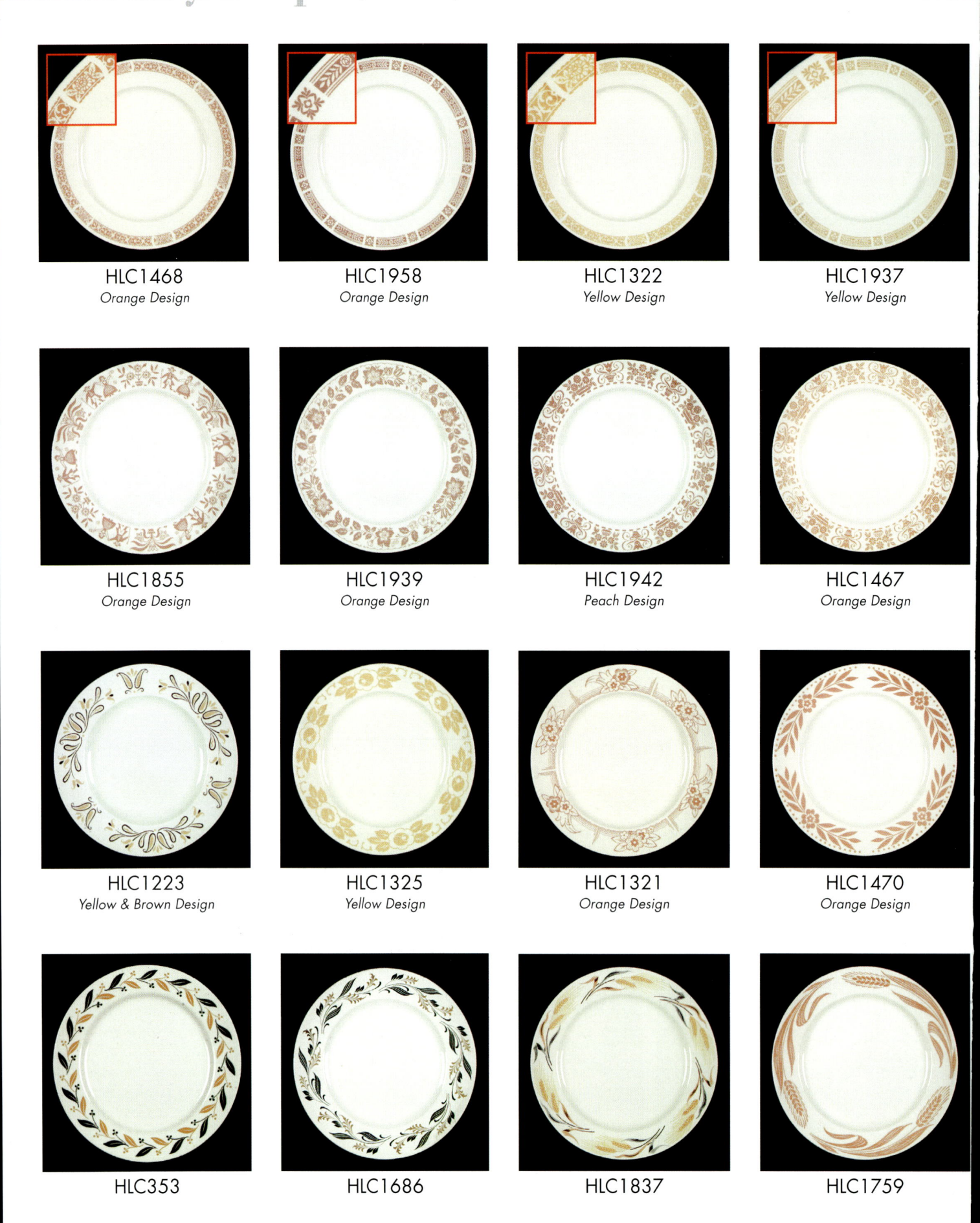

HLC1468 *Orange Design*	**HLC1958** *Orange Design*	**HLC1322** *Yellow Design*	**HLC1937** *Yellow Design*
HLC1855 *Orange Design*	**HLC1939** *Orange Design*	**HLC1942** *Peach Design*	**HLC1467** *Orange Design*
HLC1223 *Yellow & Brown Design*	**HLC1325** *Yellow Design*	**HLC1321** *Orange Design*	**HLC1470** *Orange Design*
HLC353	**HLC1686**	**HLC1837**	**HLC1759**

Brittany Shape (No Trim)

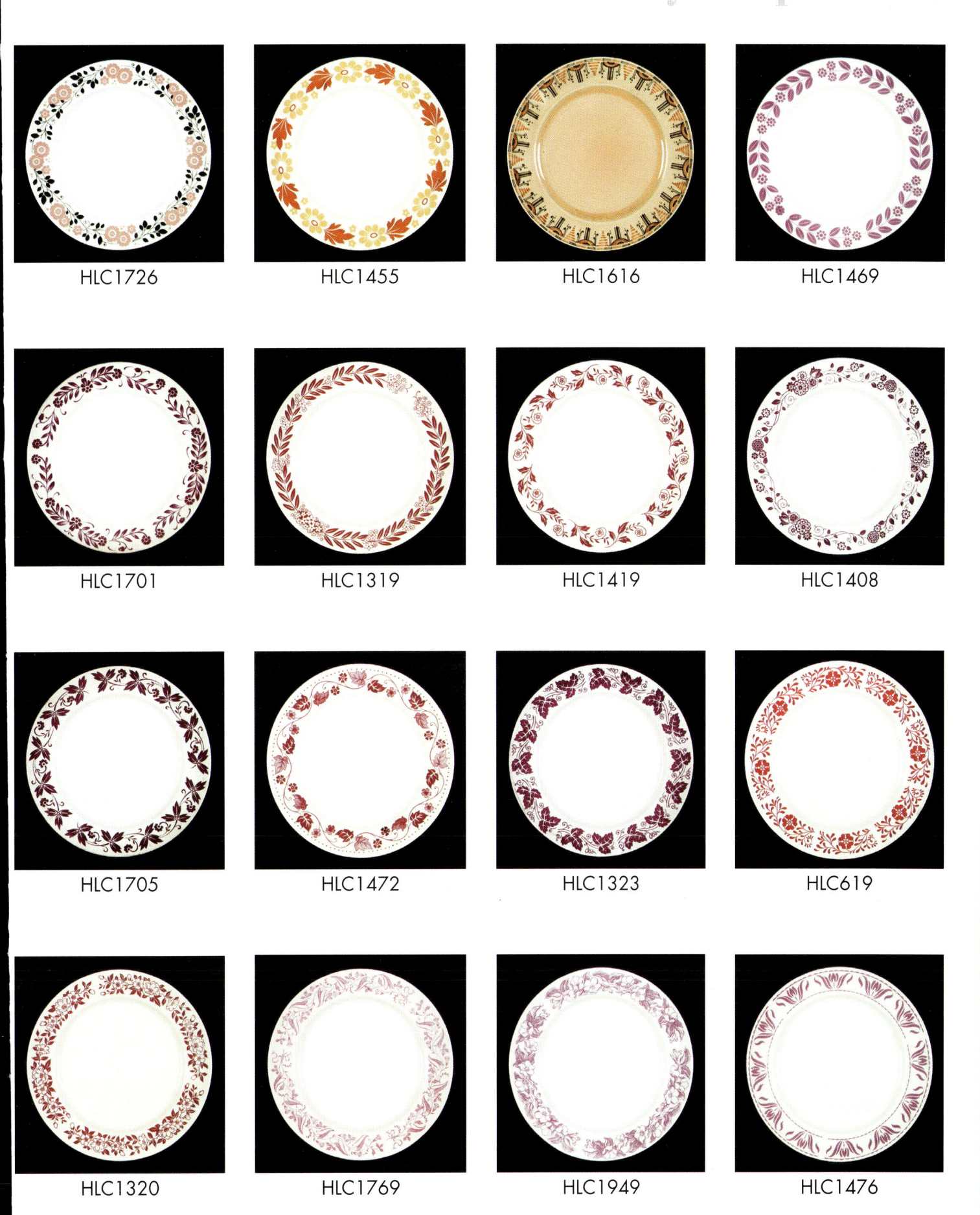

HLC1726	HLC1455	HLC1616	HLC1469
HLC1701	HLC1319	HLC1419	HLC1408
HLC1705	HLC1472	HLC1323	HLC619
HLC1320	HLC1769	HLC1949	HLC1476

Brittany Shape (No Trim)

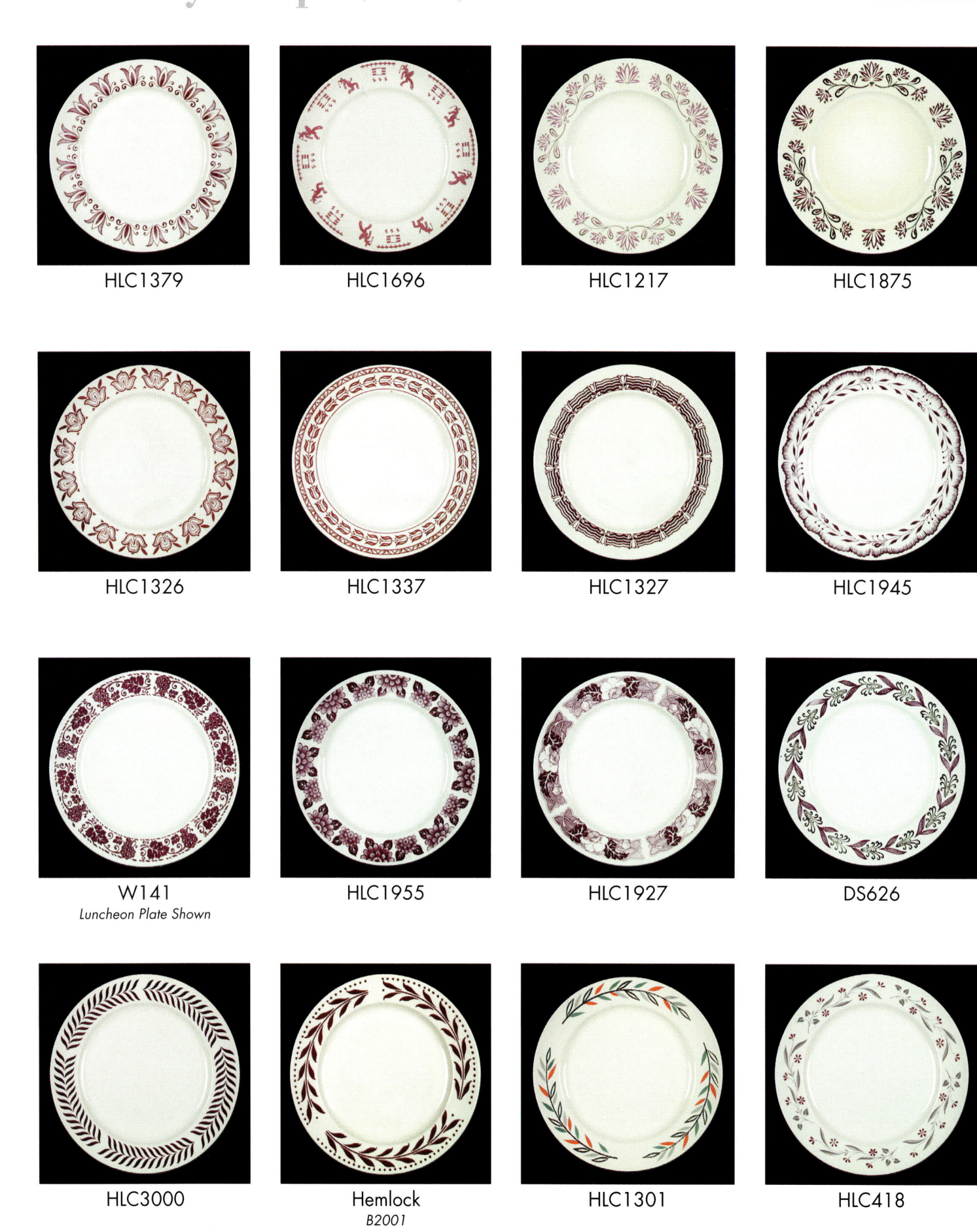

HLC1379	HLC1696	HLC1217	HLC1875
HLC1326	HLC1337	HLC1327	HLC1945
W141 *Luncheon Plate Shown*	HLC1955	HLC1927	DS626
HLC3000	Hemlock *B2001*	HLC1301	HLC418

Brittany Shape (No Trim)

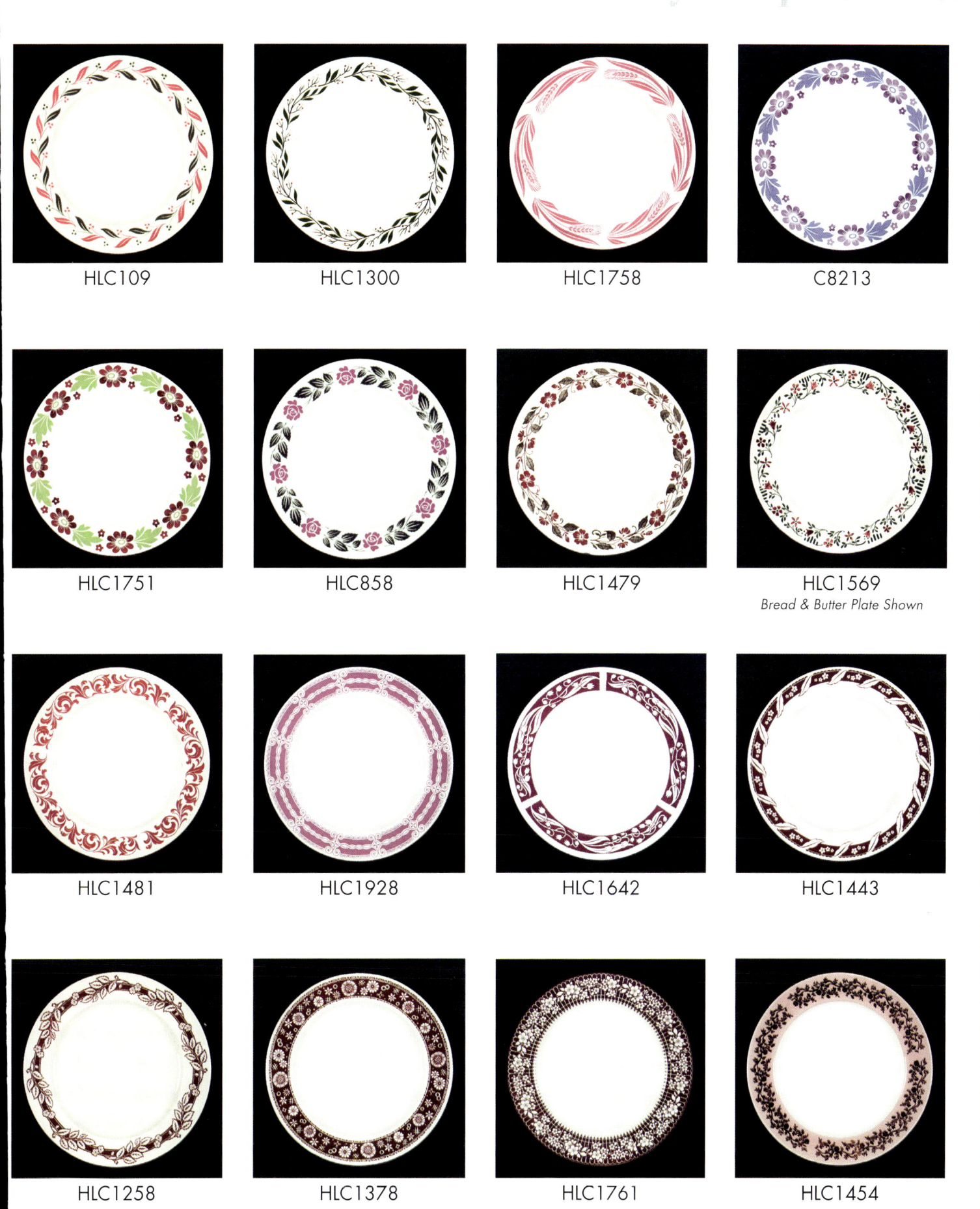

HLC109	HLC1300	HLC1758	C8213
HLC1751	HLC858	HLC1479	HLC1569 *Bread & Butter Plate Shown*
HLC1481	HLC1928	HLC1642	HLC1443
HLC1258	HLC1378	HLC1761	HLC1454

Brittany Shape (No Trim)

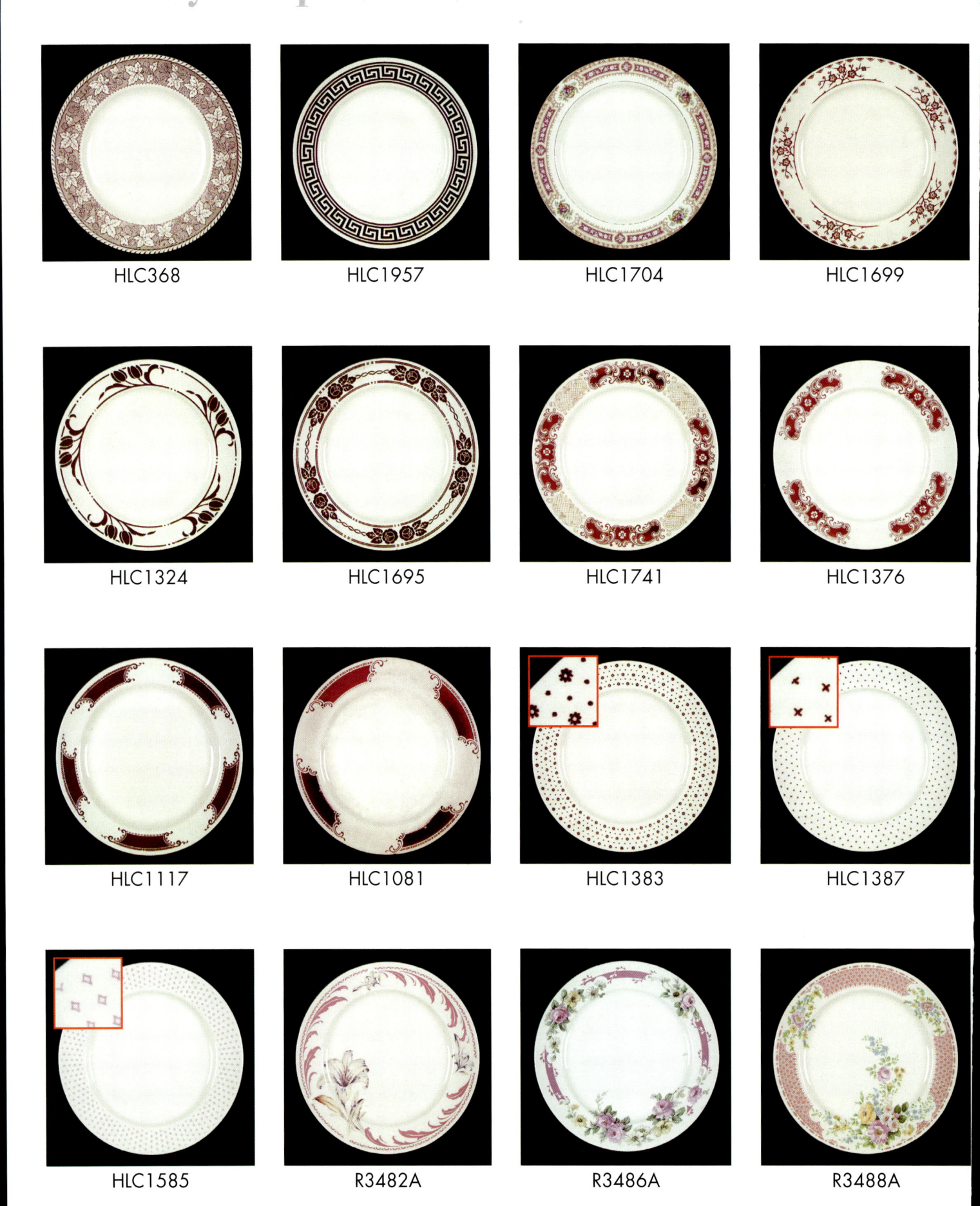

HLC368	HLC1957	HLC1704	HLC1699
HLC1324	HLC1695	HLC1741	HLC1376
HLC1117	HLC1081	HLC1383	HLC1387
HLC1585	R3482A	R3486A	R3488A

Brittany Shape (No Trim)

HLC1614	HLC1615	HLC1415	R3562A
R8412	HLC1060	HLC1766	R3597A
R3453A	R3446A	R3435A	English Scenes–Brown
HLC1798 *Oval Platter Shown*	HLC1919	 HLC1471	 HLC1936

269

Brittany Shape (No Trim)

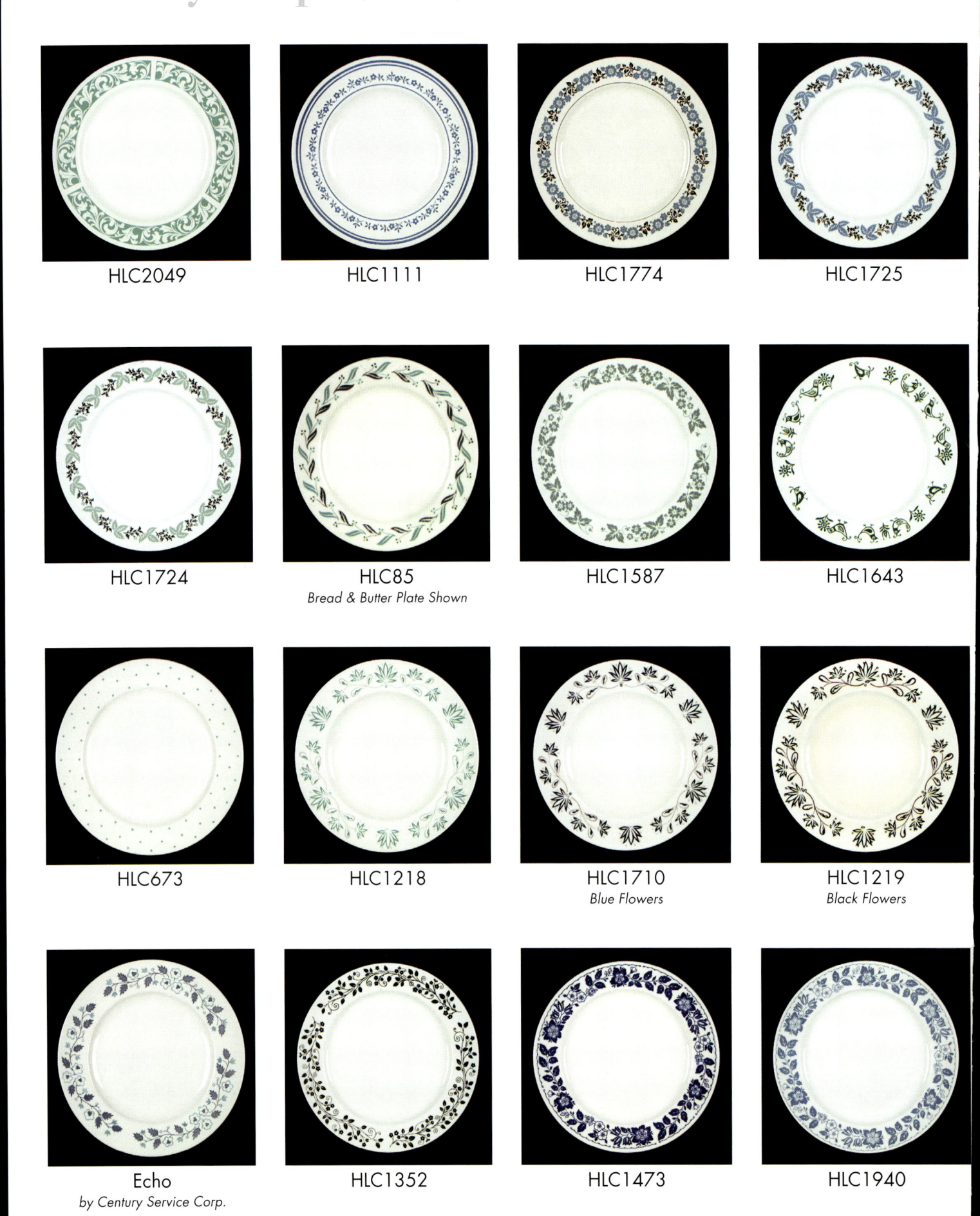

| HLC2049 | HLC1111 | HLC1774 | HLC1725 |

| HLC1724 | HLC85
Bread & Butter Plate Shown | HLC1587 | HLC1643 |

| HLC673 | HLC1218 | HLC1710
Blue Flowers | HLC1219
Black Flowers |

| Echo
by Century Service Corp. | HLC1352 | HLC1473 | HLC1940 |

Brittany Shape (No Trim)

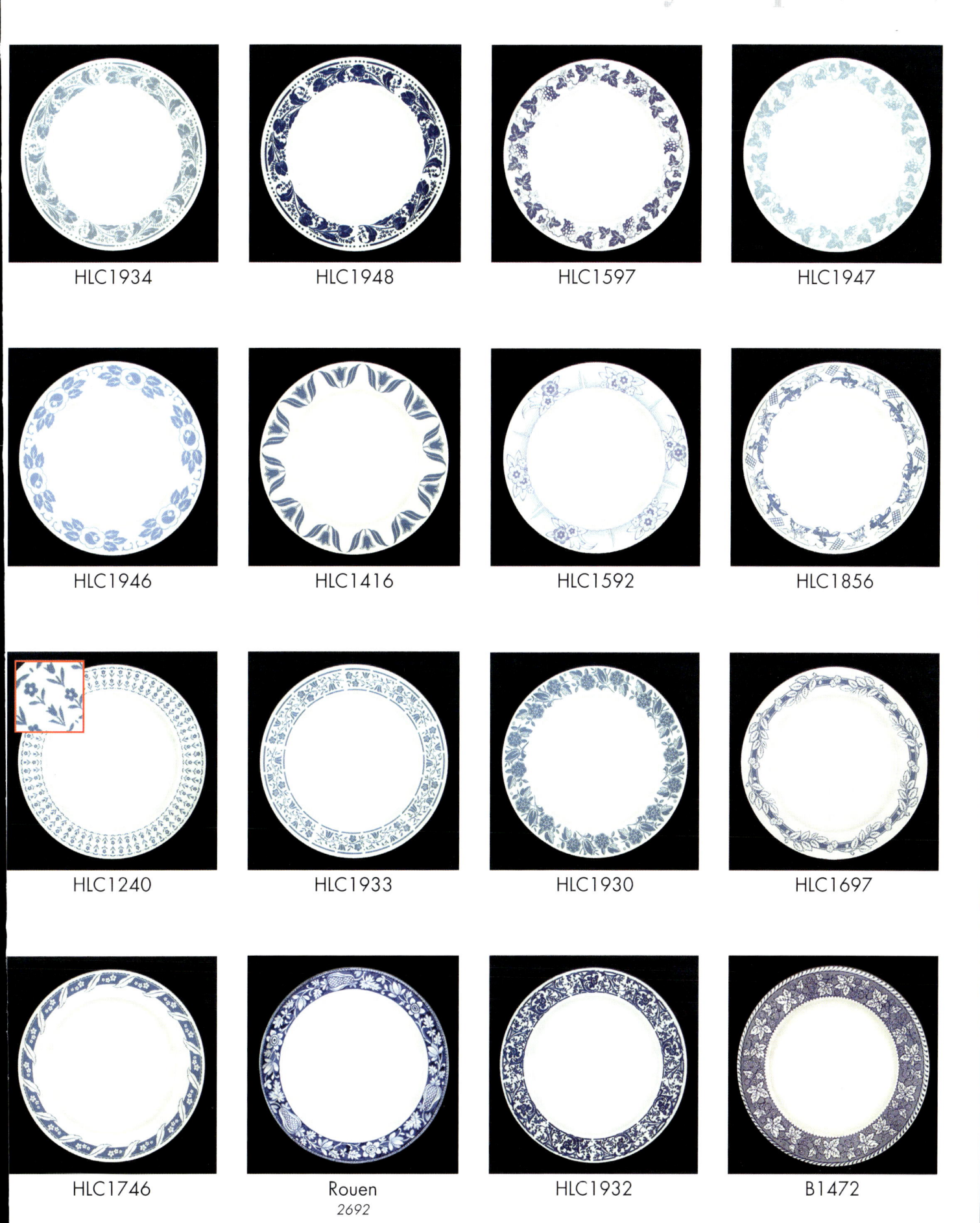

HLC1934	HLC1948	HLC1597	HLC1947
HLC1946	HLC1416	HLC1592	HLC1856
HLC1240	HLC1933	HLC1930	HLC1697
HLC1746	Rouen 2692	HLC1932	B1472

Brittany Shape (No Trim)

HLC1938	HLC1756	HLC1593	HLC860 *Bread & Butter Plate Shown*
HLC107	Sylvan	HLC1089 *Fruit Bowl Shown*	HLC1475
HLC258	D5626	HLC1480	HLC1956
R3455A	R3449A	R3483A	R3448A

Brittany Shape (No Trim)

R3459A	 Sturbridge	 HLC1861	 HLC1203
 R152588	 Shakespeare Country–Blue	 Shakespeare Country-Blue	 American Subjects–Blue
 HLC243	 The Constellation–Blue *Salad Plate Shown*	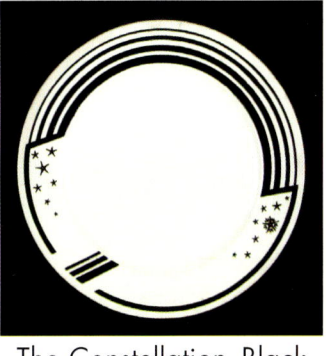 The Constellation–Black *Salad Plate Shown*	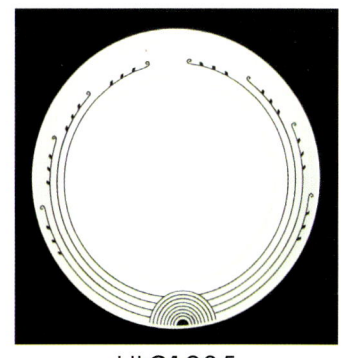 HLC1935
 HLC1465			

Brittany Shape (With Trim)

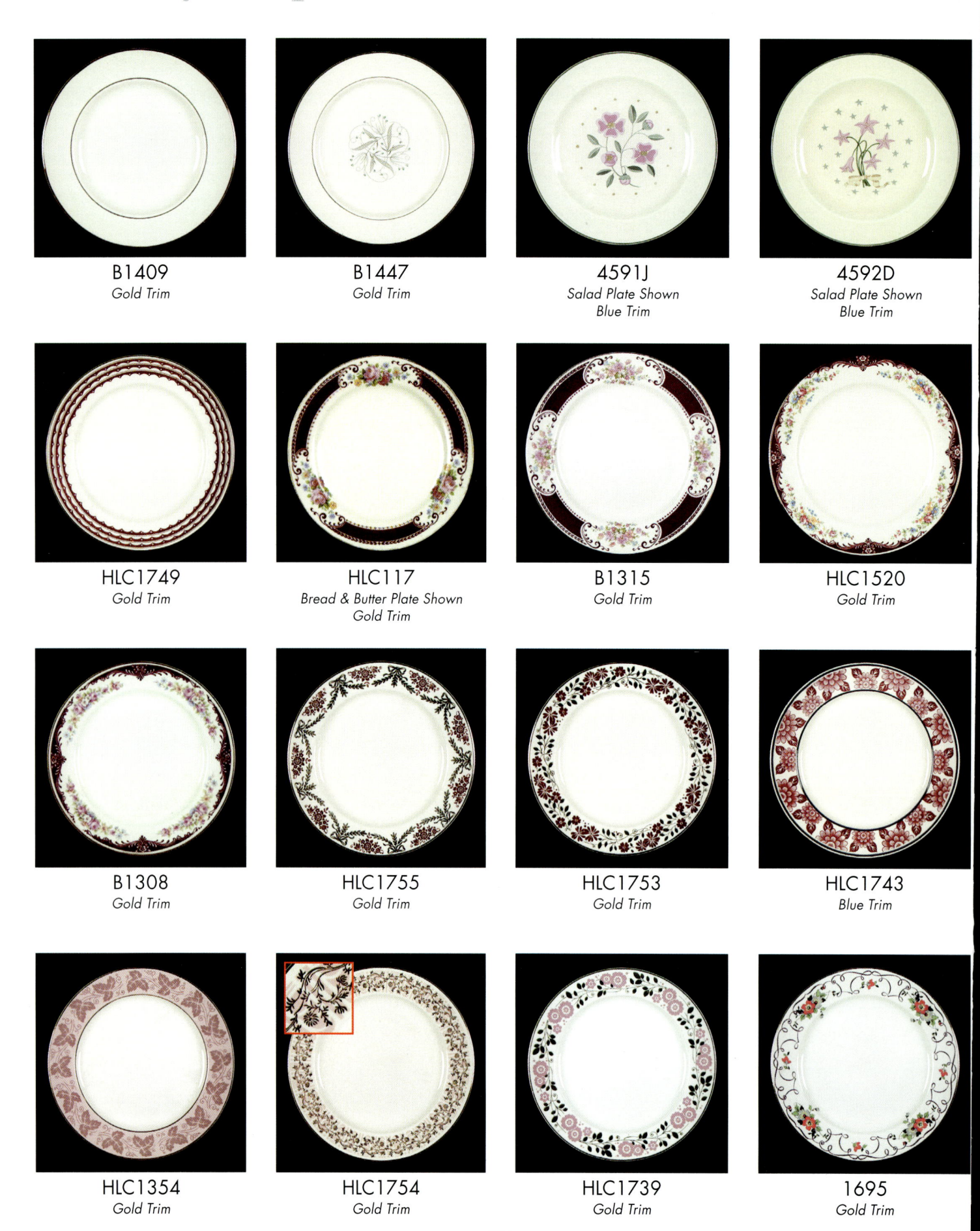

B1409 *Gold Trim*	**B1447** *Gold Trim*	**4591J** *Salad Plate Shown Blue Trim*	**4592D** *Salad Plate Shown Blue Trim*
HLC1749 *Gold Trim*	**HLC117** *Bread & Butter Plate Shown Gold Trim*	**B1315** *Gold Trim*	**HLC1520** *Gold Trim*
B1308 *Gold Trim*	**HLC1755** *Gold Trim*	**HLC1753** *Gold Trim*	**HLC1743** *Blue Trim*
HLC1354 *Gold Trim*	**HLC1754** *Gold Trim*	**HLC1739** *Gold Trim*	**1695** *Gold Trim*

Brittany Shape (With Trim)

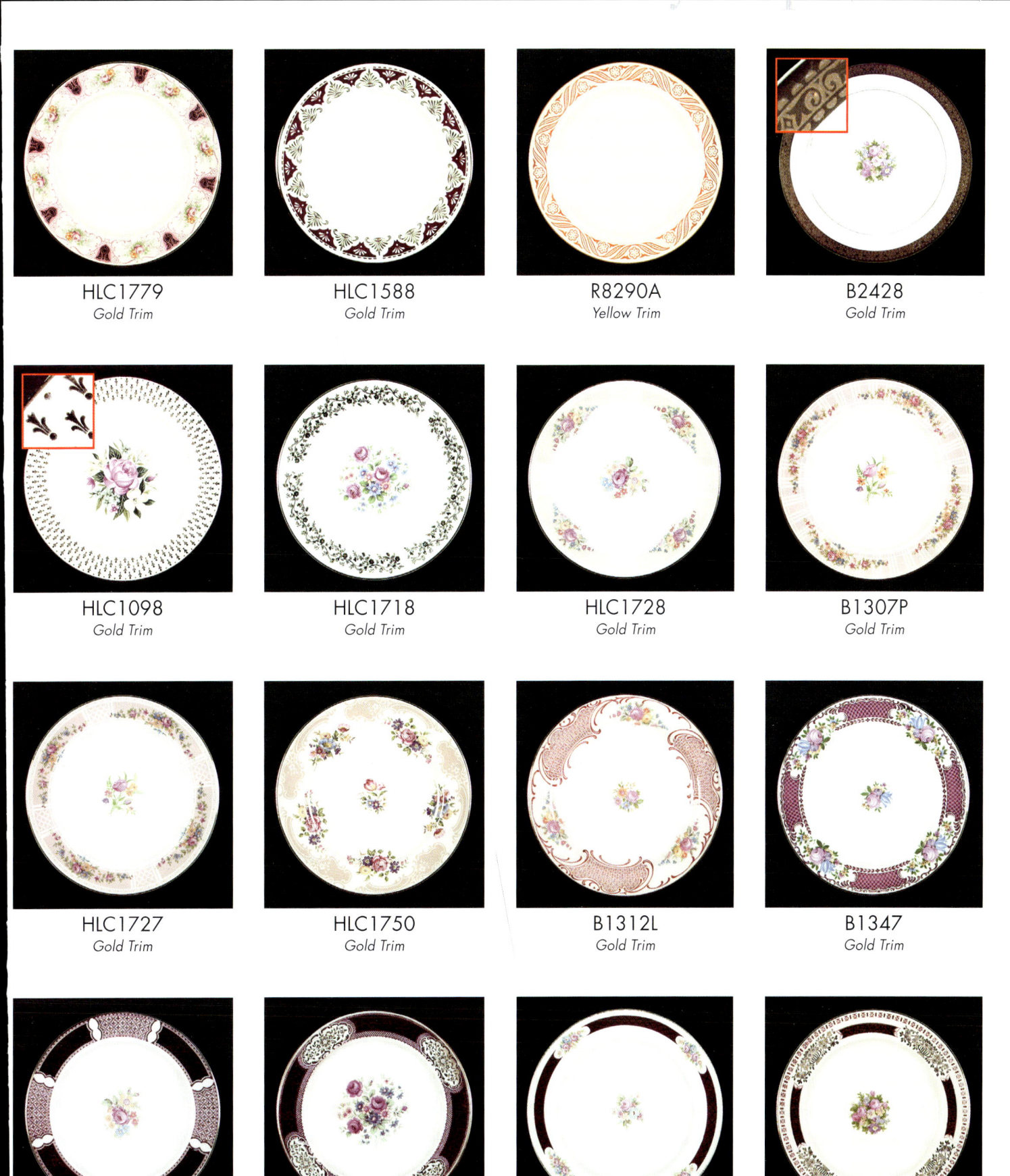

HLC1779 *Gold Trim*	HLC1588 *Gold Trim*	R8290A *Yellow Trim*	B2428 *Gold Trim*
HLC1098 *Gold Trim*	HLC1718 *Gold Trim*	HLC1728 *Gold Trim*	B1307P *Gold Trim*
HLC1727 *Gold Trim*	HLC1750 *Gold Trim*	B1312L *Gold Trim*	B1347 *Gold Trim*
HLC1729 *Gold Trim*	HLC1582 *Gold Trim*	HLC972 *Luncheon Plate Shown Gold Trim*	HLC1410 *Gold Trim*

275

Brittany Shape (With Trim)

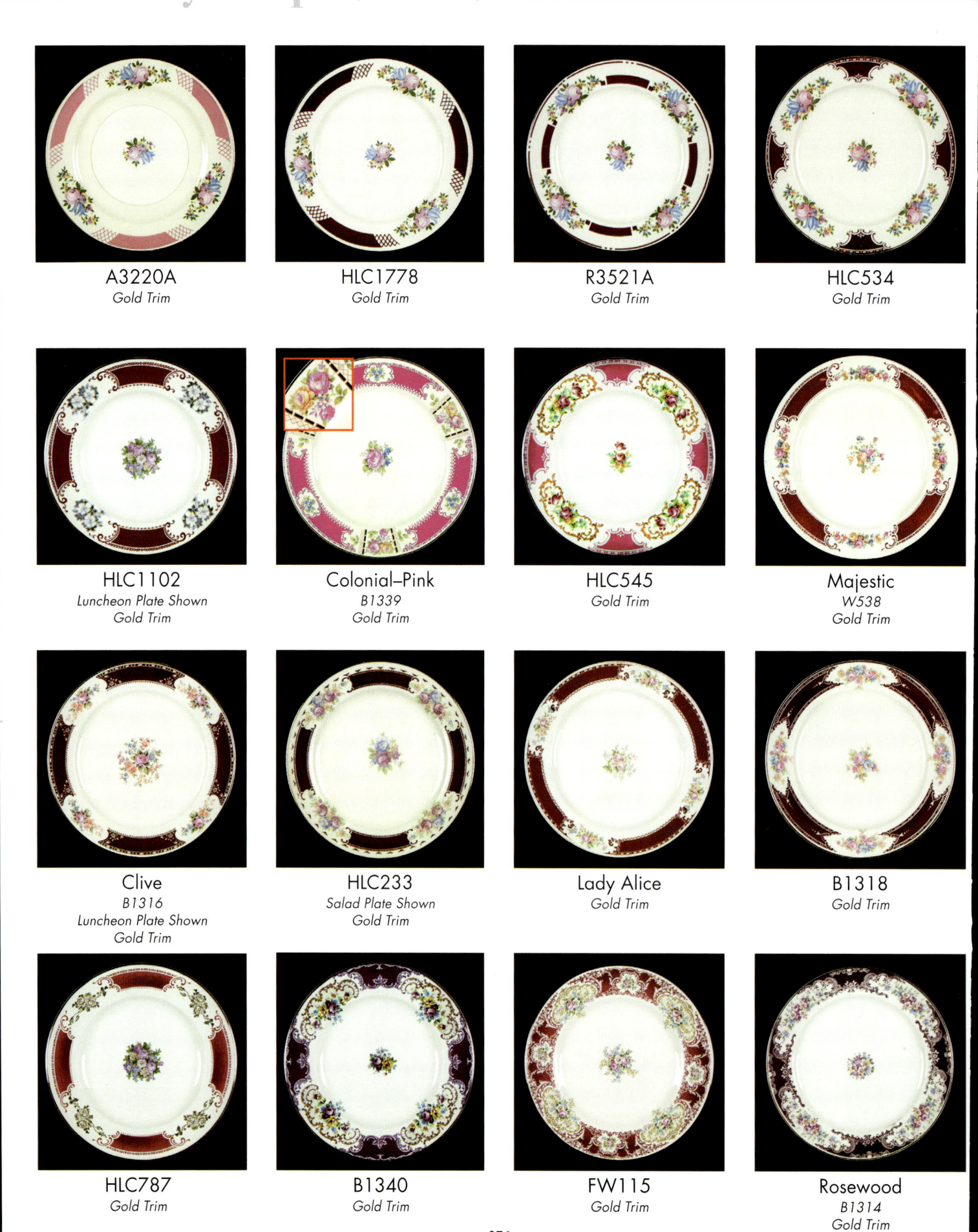

A3220A *Gold Trim*	**HLC1778** *Gold Trim*	**R3521A** *Gold Trim*	**HLC534** *Gold Trim*
HLC1102 *Luncheon Plate Shown* *Gold Trim*	**Colonial–Pink** *B1339* *Gold Trim*	**HLC545** *Gold Trim*	**Majestic** *W538* *Gold Trim*
Clive *B1316* *Luncheon Plate Shown* *Gold Trim*	**HLC233** *Salad Plate Shown* *Gold Trim*	**Lady Alice** *Gold Trim*	**B1318** *Gold Trim*
HLC787 *Gold Trim*	**B1340** *Gold Trim*	**FW115** *Gold Trim*	**Rosewood** *B1314* *Gold Trim*

Brittany Shape (With Trim)

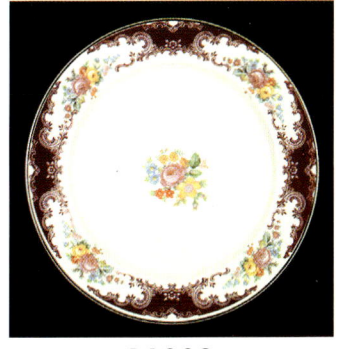

B1309 *Gold Trim*	**B1319** *Gold Trim*	**B1312** *Gold Trim*	**B1350** *also called "JCP86"* *Gold Trim*
B1355 *Gold Trim*	**HLS9** *Gold Trim*	**6402** *Black Trim*	**HLC1909** *Platinum Trim*
R3235A *Gold Trim*	**The Shrewsbury** *Green Trim*	**HLC1775** *Gold Trim*	**HLC1770** *Gold Trim*
HLC1764 *Gold Trim*	**HLC1773** *Gold Trim*	**HLC1748** *Blue Trim*	**HLC1747** *Green Trim*

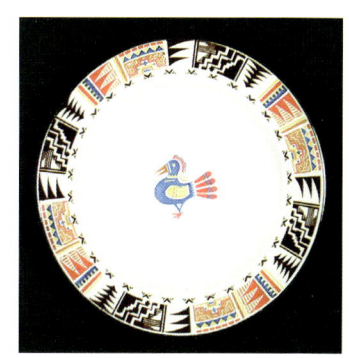

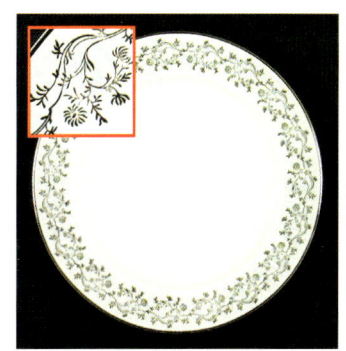

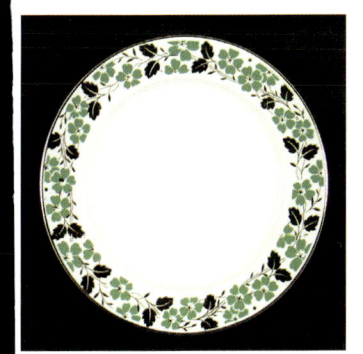

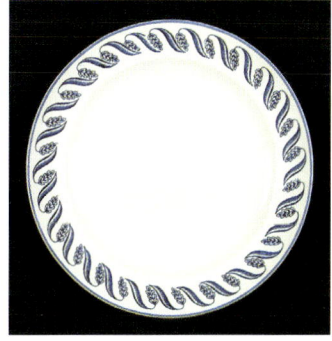

277

Brittany Shape (With Trim)

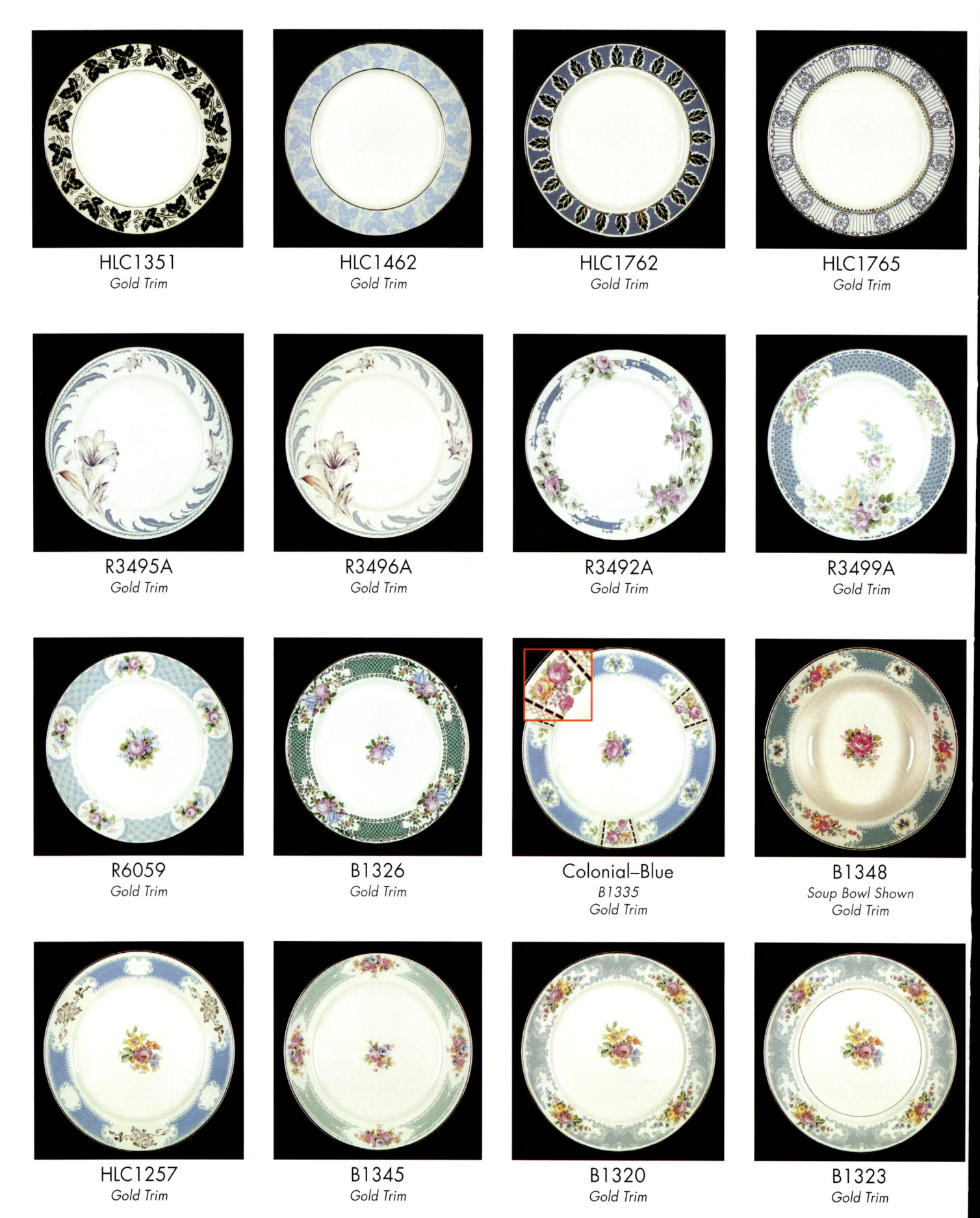

HLC1351 *Gold Trim*	**HLC1462** *Gold Trim*	**HLC1762** *Gold Trim*	**HLC1765** *Gold Trim*
R3495A *Gold Trim*	**R3496A** *Gold Trim*	**R3492A** *Gold Trim*	**R3499A** *Gold Trim*
R6059 *Gold Trim*	**B1326** *Gold Trim*	**Colonial–Blue** *B1335* *Gold Trim*	**B1348** *Soup Bowl Shown* *Gold Trim*
HLC1257 *Gold Trim*	**B1345** *Gold Trim*	**B1320** *Gold Trim*	**B1323** *Gold Trim*

Brittany Shape (With Trim)

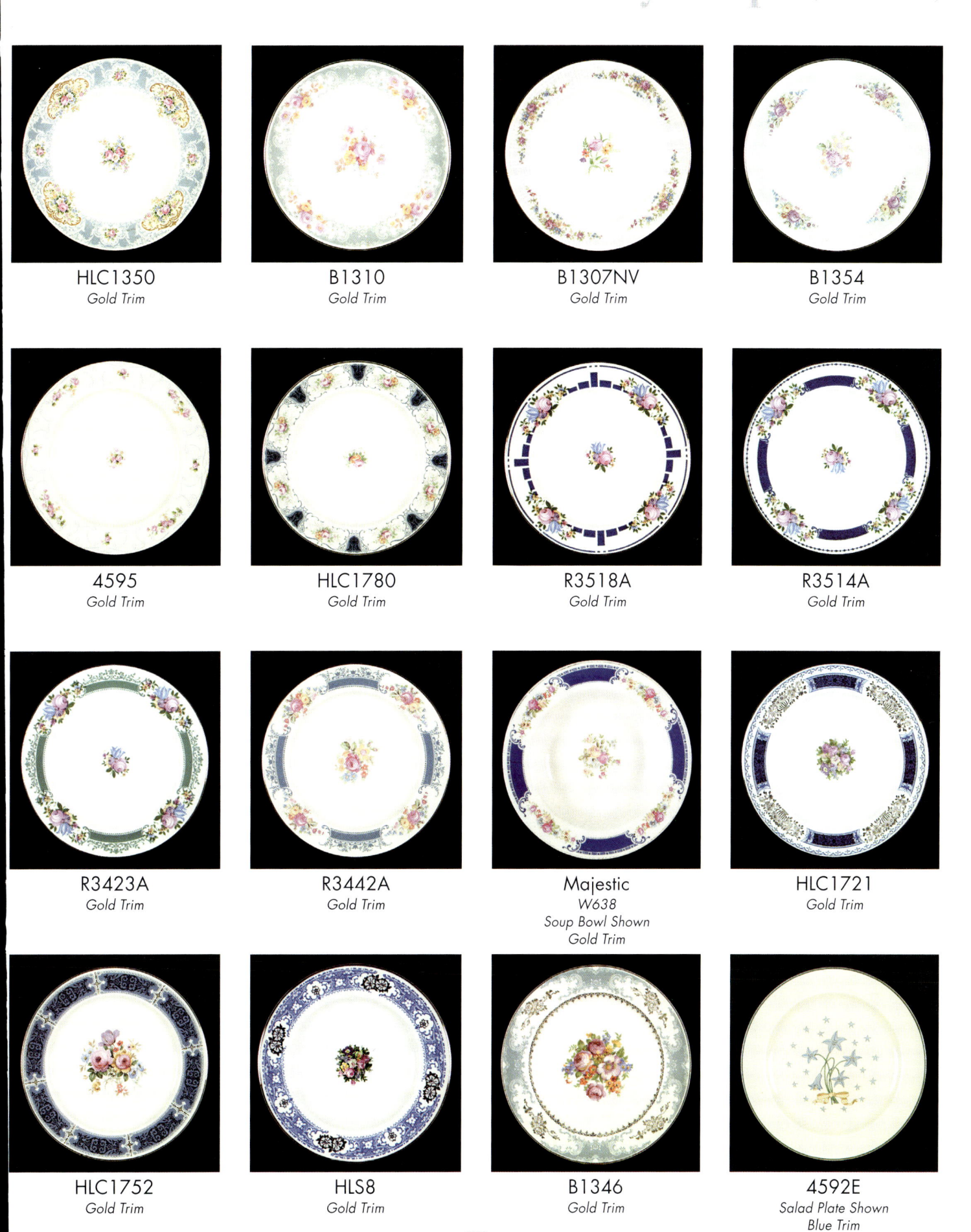

HLC1350
Gold Trim

B1310
Gold Trim

B1307NV
Gold Trim

B1354
Gold Trim

4595
Gold Trim

HLC1780
Gold Trim

R3518A
Gold Trim

R3514A
Gold Trim

R3423A
Gold Trim

R3442A
Gold Trim

Majestic
W638
Soup Bowl Shown
Gold Trim

HLC1721
Gold Trim

HLC1752
Gold Trim

HLS8
Gold Trim

B1346
Gold Trim

4592E
Salad Plate Shown
Blue Trim

Brittany Shape (With Trim)

4592A
Salad Plate Shown
Blue Trim

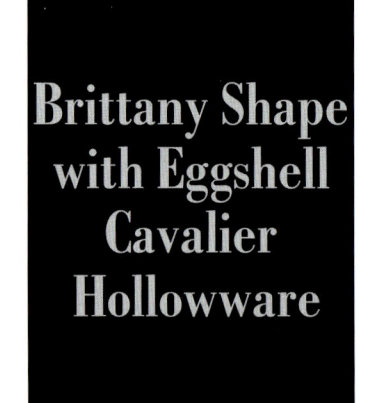

Brittany Shape with Eggshell Cavalier Hollowware

CV55
Platinum Trim

Eggshell Cavalier Shape with Brittany Cups

Imperial
by Lifetime China
Gold Trim

HLC342
Platinum Trim

Above: *Original drawings for Brittany patterns.*

HARLEQUIN

Piece Types

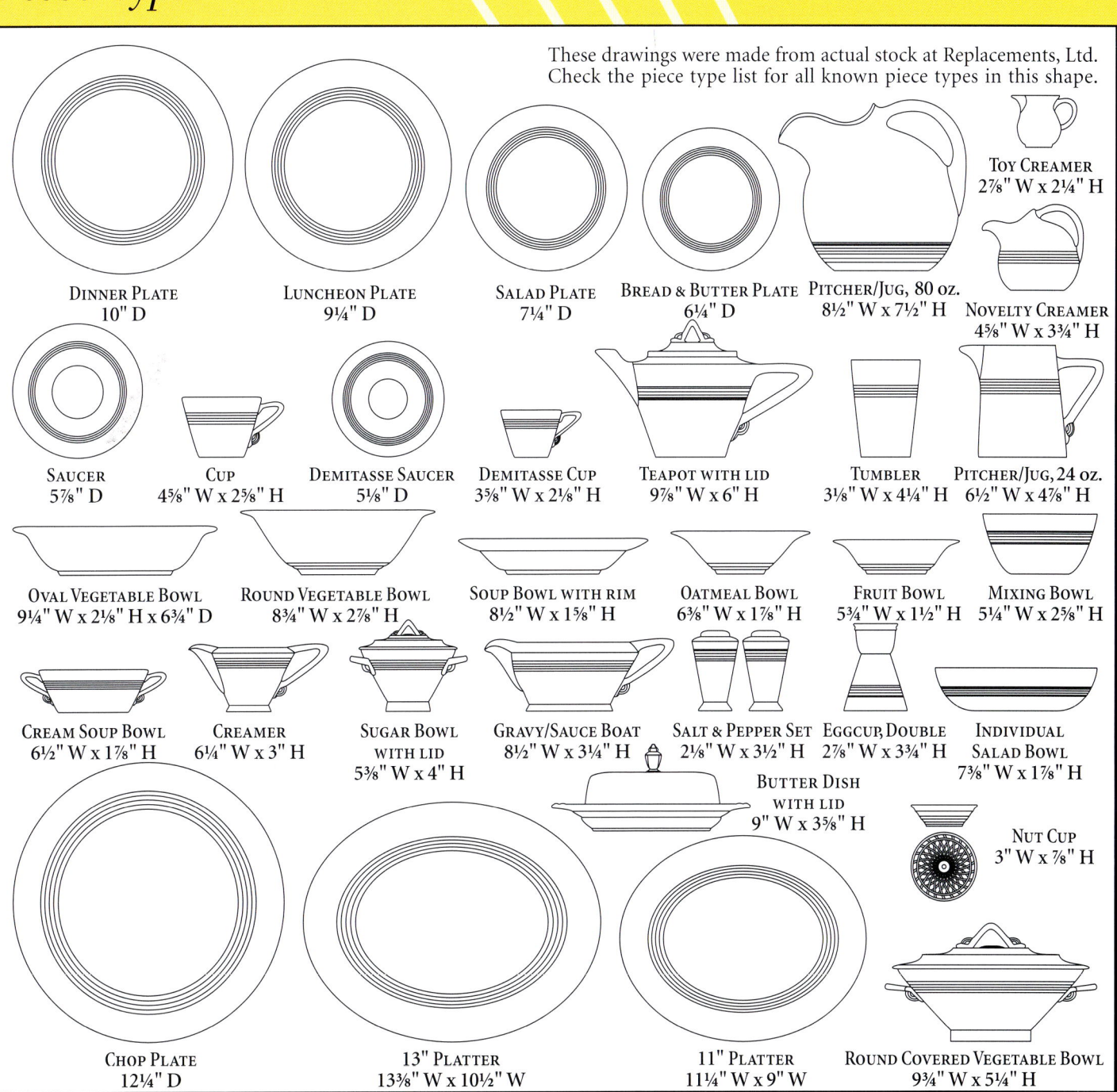

These drawings were made from actual stock at Replacements, Ltd. Check the piece type list for all known piece types in this shape.

Dinner Plate
10" D

Luncheon Plate
9¼" D

Salad Plate
7¼" D

Bread & Butter Plate
6¼" D

Pitcher/Jug, 80 oz.
8½" W x 7½" H

Toy Creamer
2⅞" W x 2¼" H

Novelty Creamer
4⅝" W x 3¾" H

Saucer
5⅞" D

Cup
4⅝" W x 2⅝" H

Demitasse Saucer
5⅛" D

Demitasse Cup
3⅝" W x 2⅛" H

Teapot with lid
9⅞" W x 6" H

Tumbler
3⅛" W x 4¼" H

Pitcher/Jug, 24 oz.
6½" W x 4⅞" H

Oval Vegetable Bowl
9¼" W x 2⅛" H x 6¾" D

Round Vegetable Bowl
8¾" W x 2⅞" H

Soup Bowl with rim
8½" W x 1⅝" H

Oatmeal Bowl
6⅜" W x 1⅞" H

Fruit Bowl
5¾" W x 1½" H

Mixing Bowl
5¼" W x 2⅝" H

Cream Soup Bowl
6½" W x 1⅞" H

Creamer
6¼" W x 3" H

Sugar Bowl with lid
5⅜" W x 4" H

Gravy/Sauce Boat
8½" W x 3¼" H

Salt & Pepper Set
2⅛" W x 3½" H

Eggcup, Double
2⅞" W x 3¾" H

Individual Salad Bowl
7⅜" W x 1⅞" H

Butter Dish with lid
9" W x 3⅝" H

Nut Cup
3" W x ⅞" H

Chop Plate
12¼" D

13" Platter
13⅜" W x 10½" W

11" Platter
11¼" W x 9" W

Round Covered Vegetable Bowl
9¾" W x 5¼" H

Homer Laughlin

HARLEQUIN 1936 – 1964; 1979 – 1982

Harlequin was produced by Homer Laughlin China exclusively for the dime store chain F. W. Woolworth. It is reported to have been in active production until 1964.

To beginning collectors, distinguishing between Harlequin and Fiesta (both single color, ringed patterns) may be confusing. A major difference is the shape of the flatware. Fiesta flatware is coupe shaped with rings near the edge and center. Harlequin flatware is rim shaped with rings near the inside of the rim.

Original introductory colors for Harlequin include: Mauve Blue, Yellow, Spruce Green, and Maroon. During the 1940's, Red, Rose, Turquoise, and Light Green were introduced. During the 1950's, Forest Green, Chartreuse, Medium Green, and Gray were added and some of the original colors were discontinued. Ivory and Cobalt pieces in Harlequin are reported by author Mark Gonzalez.

A reissue of Harlequin was offered by Woolworth from 1979 until 1982. Turquoise, Coral, a slightly varied Medium Green, and Yellow were produced in the newer issue. Harlequin pieces never had backstamps until its 1979 reintroduction.

Top right: *Maroon, Turquoise, Rose, Forest Green, and Yellow; Teapots with lids.* **Bottom left:** *Red; Cup, and Ashtray Saucer.*
Bottom right: *Mauve Blue, Red, Spruce Green, Maroon, Medium Green, and Yellow; Nut Cups.*

1930's Harlequin

1930's HARLEQUIN

Harlequin original introductory colors in the 1930's include: Mauve Blue, Yellow, Spruce Green, and Maroon.

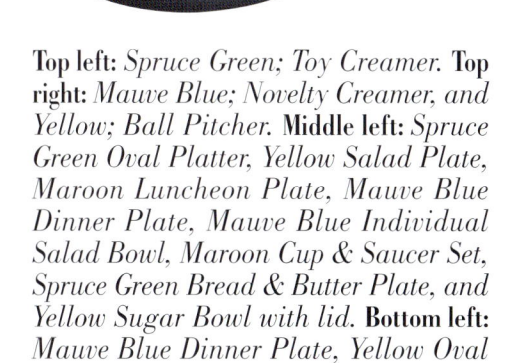

Top left: *Spruce Green; Toy Creamer.* **Top right:** *Mauve Blue; Novelty Creamer, and Yellow; Ball Pitcher.* **Middle left:** *Spruce Green Oval Platter, Yellow Salad Plate, Maroon Luncheon Plate, Mauve Blue Dinner Plate, Mauve Blue Individual Salad Bowl, Maroon Cup & Saucer Set, Spruce Green Bread & Butter Plate, and Yellow Sugar Bowl with lid.* **Bottom left:** *Mauve Blue Dinner Plate, Yellow Oval Platter, Spruce Green Cup & Saucer Set, and Maroon Teapot with lid.* **Bottom right:** *Mauve Blue Oatmeal Bowl, Yellow Round Vegetable Bowl, Spruce Green Oval Vegetable Bowl, and Maroon Fruit Bowl.*

1940's Harlequin

1940's HARLEQUIN

In the 1940's, the colors added to Harlequin were: Red, Rose, Turquoise, and Light Green.

Top right: *Red Tumbler.* **Middle:** *Rose Salt & Pepper Set, Light Green Pitcher, Turquoise Oval Platter, Light Green Dinner Plate, Red Covered Vegetable Bowl, Rose Teapot with lid, Light Green Cream Soup Bowl, Turquoise Demitasse Cup & Saucer Set, and Red Creamer.* **Bottom left:** *Red Gravy/Sauce Boat, Rose Luncheon Plate, Light Green Cup & Saucer Set, and Turquoise Demitasse Cup & Saucer Set.* **Bottom right:** *Turquoise Butter Dish with lid.*

1950's Harlequin

1950's HARLEQUIN

In the early 1950's Chartreuse, Forest Green, and Gray were added. At the end of the 50's, Medium Green (the same as old Fiesta Medium Green) was introduced.

Top: *Forest Green Teapot with lid.* **Middle left:** *Gray Dinner Plate, Chartreuse Salad Plate, Forest Green Bread & Butter Plate, and Medium Green Saucer.* **Middle right:** *Chartreuse Ashtray with basketweave pattern.* **Bottom left:** *Gray Oval Platter, Chartreuse Dinner Plate, Forest Green Salad Bowl with rim, and Medium Green Cup & Saucer Set.* **Bottom right:** *Chartreuse Salad Plate, Gray Luncheon Plate, Forest Green Bread & Butter Plate, Medium Green Dinner Plate, Forest Green Creamer, Gray Sugar Bowl with lid, and Chartreuse Cranberry Bowl.*

1970's Harlequin

1970's Harlequin 1979 – 1982

From 1979 through 1982, Woolworth sold a reissue of Harlequin. These colors included: Coral, Medium Green, Yellow, and Turquoise. Coral is more vibrant than the muddy Rose color of the 1940's. Medium Green is difficult to distinguish from the late 1950's version. The 1950's Medium Green is a cleaner, brighter green. The 1970's Medium Green is a little muddy. There is a noticeable difference between the Medium Green pieces of the 1970's and 1950's only when you place them side by side. It is very difficult to tell the difference between the Yellow and Turquoise pieces of the older and newer. The newer pieces have a more consistent glaze color. Look for a backstamp on the backs of pieces from the 1970's. There are also slight size differences between a few pieces which are illustrated near the end of this section. The 1970's reissue was limited to a 45 piece set with service for eight. Serving pieces were limited. The following pieces were made in all four colors: dinner plate, salad plate, oatmeal bowl, and cup and saucer. The sugar bowl was only made in yellow and has a closed finial, unlike the older one. The creamer was only made in Turquoise. The round vegetable bowl was only made in Medium Green. The chop plate was a new piece type that was not produced in earlier colors, it was made in Coral and Yellow. There were no other piece types made for the 1970's set. The only pieces that are indistinguishable between the old and new are the creamers and cup and saucer sets in Turquoise and Yellow.

Top left: *Yellow, Medium Green, Coral, and Turquoise Dinner Plates.* **Top right:** *Coral Chop Plate, Yellow Dinner Plate, Medium Green Salad Plate, and Turquoise Saucer.* **Middle right:** *Turquoise Dinner Plate, Yellow Salad Plate, Coral Cup & Saucer Set, and Medium Green Oatmeal Bowl.* **Bottom right:** *Medium Green Round Vegetable Bowl, Coral Chop Plate, Turquoise Creamer, and Yellow Sugar Bowl with lid.*

Harlequin Cup & Saucer Sets in All 16 Colors

Homer Laughlin

Old
Dinner Plate
Never has backstamp.
9-15/16" Width
5-3/8" Bottom Ring

New
Dinner Plate
May have backstamp.
10-1/16" Width
5-7/8" Bottom Ring

Old
Oatmeal Bowl
Never has backstamp.
6-3/8" Width
2-9/16" Bottom Ring
1-3/4" Height

New
Oatmeal Bowl
May have backstamp.
6-3/8" Width
2-1/4" Bottom Ring
1-15/16" Height

Above: *Rose Dinner Plate.*

Above: *Coral Dinner Plate.*

Above: *Turquoise Older Oatmeal Bowl.*

Above: *Turquoise Newer Oatmeal Bowl.*

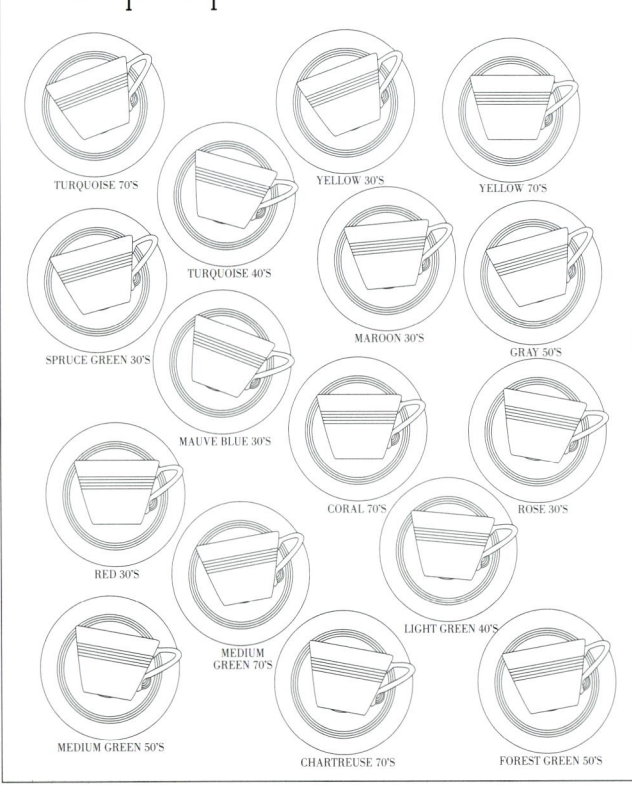

Harlequin Cup & Saucer Sets in All 16 Colors

TURQUOISE 70'S, YELLOW 30'S, YELLOW 70'S, TURQUOISE 40'S, MAROON 30'S, GRAY 50'S, SPRUCE GREEN 30'S, MAUVE BLUE 30'S, CORAL 70'S, ROSE 30'S, RED 30'S, MEDIUM GREEN 70'S, LIGHT GREEN 40'S, MEDIUM GREEN 50'S, CHARTREUSE 70'S, FOREST GREEN 50'S

Above: *Harlequin Cup & Saucer Sets, labeled.*

Old
Salad Plate
Never has backstamp.
7-1/4" Width
4-1/16" Bottom Ring

New
Salad Plate
May have backstamp.
7-3/8" Width
4-1/2" Bottom Ring

Above: *Yellow Older Salad Plate.*

Above: *Yellow Newer Salad Plate.*

Left: *Medium Green Newer backstamp. Although Medium Green Newer wasn't introduced until 1979, this backstamp is dated 1976.*

288

Harlequin Shape

Harlequin Piece Type List

From Homer Laughlin Literature with Confirmed Actual Pieces

Ashtray, basketweave,
  three cigarette rests, 4½ inches
Ashtray, plain rim with rings,
  three cigarette rests, 5½ inches
Ashtray/Saucer,
  one cigarette rest, 6¼ inches
Bowl, Cream Soup, 6½ inches
Bowl, Fruit, 5¾ inches
Bowl, Mixing, 5¼ inches
Bowl, Oatmeal, 6⅜ inches
Bowl, Salad Individual, 7⅜ inches
Bowl, Soup with rim, 8½ inches
Bowl, Vegetable Oval, 9¼ inches
Bowl, Vegetable Round, 8¾ inches
Bowl, Vegetable Round Covered,
  9¾ inches
Butter Dish with lid, ½ pound
  (Jade shape)
Candlestick, 1⅞ inches
Creamer, regular
Creamer, with high spout 1
Creamer, with high spout 2
Creamer, Novelty, with rings
Creamer, Toy, no rings
Cup & Saucer Set
  Cup, 2⅝ inches
  Saucer, 5⅞ inches

Cup & Saucer Set, Demitasse
  Cup, 2⅛ inches
  Saucer, 5⅛ inches
Cup & Saucer, Large (no rings)
  Cup, 3 inches
  Saucer, 6 inches
Eggcup, Double, 3¾ inches
Eggcup, Single, 2½ inches
Gravy/Sauce Boat
Marmalade with notched lid
Nut Cup, basketweave
Nut Cup, individual with basketweave
Pitcher/Jug, Ball, 80 oz., rings at base
Pitcher/Jug, Tankard, 24 oz.
Plate, Bread & Butter, 6¼ inches
Plate, Dinner, 10 inches
Plate, Luncheon, 9¼ inches
Plate, Salad, 7¼ inches
Platter, Oval, 11¼ inches
Platter, Oval, 13⅜ inches
Salt & Pepper Set
Sugar Bowl with lid, open handles
  and finial
Teapot with lid
Tray, Relish with four inserts,
  10⅞ inches
Tumbler, 4¼ inches

Reissue Piece Type List

Bowl, Oatmeal, 6⅜ inches
Bowl, Vegetable Round, 12⅞ inches
  only in Medium Green
Creamer
  only in Turquoise
Cup & Saucer Set
  Cup, 2⅝ inches
  Saucer, 5⅞ inches
Plate, Chop, 12¼ inches
  only in Yellow and Coral
Plate, Dinner, 10⅛ inches
Plate, Salad, 7⅜ inches
Sugar Bowl with lid,
  closed handles and finial,
  only in Yellow
Syrup, drip-cut, 5⅞ inches

Harlequin Animals

Cat
Donkey
Duck
Fish
Lamb
Penguin

Top left: *Gold Duck, and Spruce Green Fish.* **Top right:** *Toy Creamers.* **Bottom left:** *Mauve Blue Ashtray.* **Bottom middle:** *Yellow Double Eggcup.* **Bottom right:** *Turquoise Single Eggcup.*

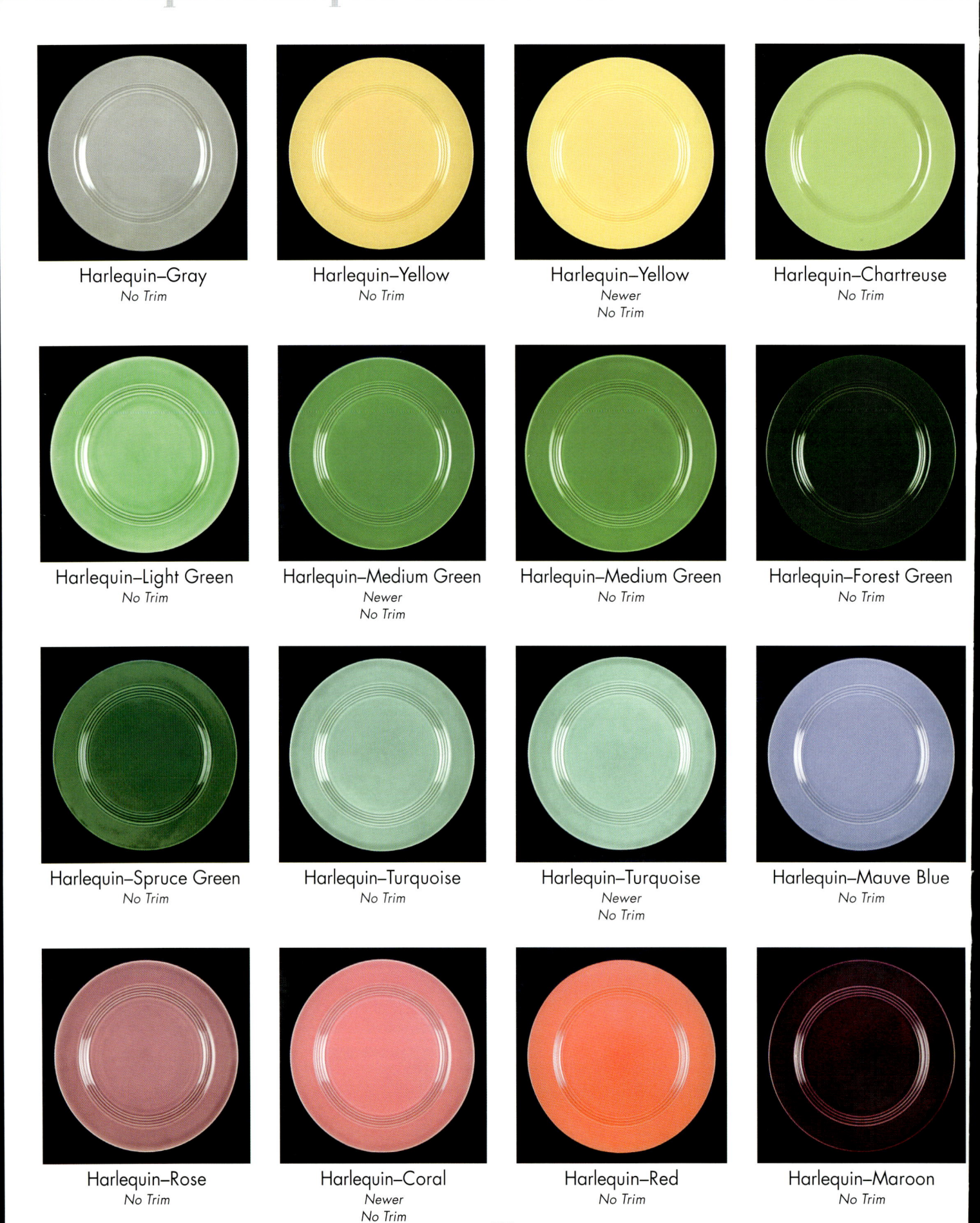

Harlequin Shape

Harlequin–Gray *No Trim*	**Harlequin–Yellow** *No Trim*	**Harlequin–Yellow** *Newer* *No Trim*	**Harlequin–Chartreuse** *No Trim*
Harlequin–Light Green *No Trim*	**Harlequin–Medium Green** *Newer* *No Trim*	**Harlequin–Medium Green** *No Trim*	**Harlequin–Forest Green** *No Trim*
Harlequin–Spruce Green *No Trim*	**Harlequin–Turquoise** *No Trim*	**Harlequin–Turquoise** *Newer* *No Trim*	**Harlequin–Mauve Blue** *No Trim*
Harlequin–Rose *No Trim*	**Harlequin–Coral** *Newer* *No Trim*	**Harlequin–Red** *No Trim*	**Harlequin–Maroon** *No Trim*

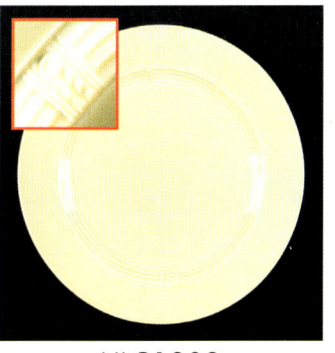

Harlequin Shape

HLC1989 *No Trim*	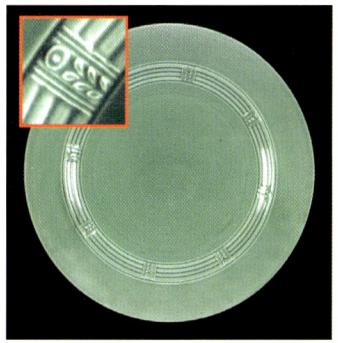 **2337-A** *No Trim*	 **2337A** *No Trim*	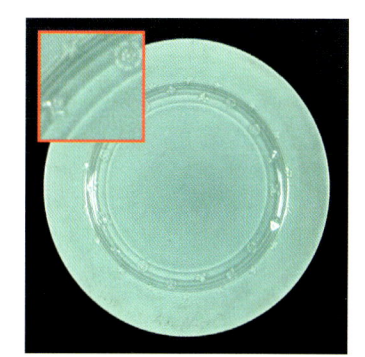 **HLC2012** *No Trim*
 **HLC1534** *No Trim*	 **B1141** *Handpainted* *No Trim*	 **HLC1610** *Handpainted* *No Trim*	 **HLC1612** *Handpainted* *No Trim*
 **HLC1860** *Handpainted* *No Trim*	 **HLC1609** *Handpainted* *No Trim*	 **HLC1611** *Handpainted* *No Trim*	 **HLC1859** *Handpainted* *No Trim*

KITCHEN KRAFT

Piece Types

These drawings were made from actual stock or literature at Replacements, Ltd. Check the piece type list for all known piece types in this shape.

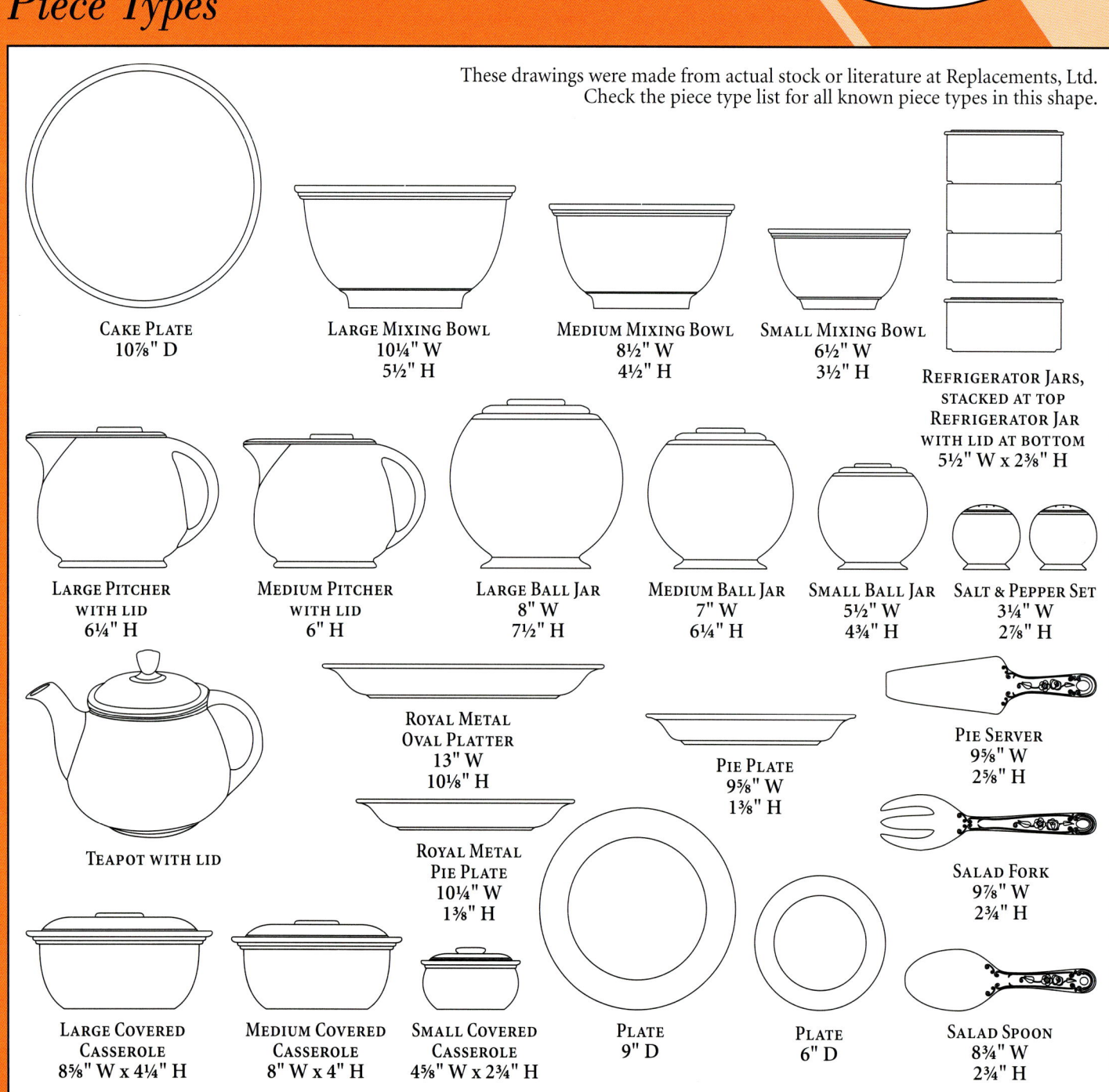

Cake Plate
10⅞" D

Large Mixing Bowl
10¼" W
5½" H

Medium Mixing Bowl
8½" W
4½" H

Small Mixing Bowl
6½" W
3½" H

**Refrigerator Jars, stacked at top
Refrigerator Jar with lid at bottom**
5½" W x 2⅜" H

Large Pitcher
with lid
6¼" H

Medium Pitcher
with lid
6" H

Large Ball Jar
8" W
7½" H

Medium Ball Jar
7" W
6¼" H

Small Ball Jar
5½" W
4¾" H

Salt & Pepper Set
3¼" W
2⅞" H

Teapot with lid

Royal Metal Oval Platter
13" W
10⅛" H

Royal Metal Pie Plate
10¼" W
1⅜" H

Pie Plate
9⅝" W
1⅜" H

Pie Server
9⅝" W
2⅝" H

Salad Fork
9⅞" W
2¾" H

Large Covered Casserole
8⅝" W x 4¼" H

Medium Covered Casserole
8" W x 4" H

Small Covered Casserole
4⅝" W x 2¾" H

Plate
9" D

Plate
6" D

Salad Spoon
8¾" W
2¾" H

Kitchen Kraft Shape

KITCHEN KRAFT 1937 – 1960's or later

Kitchen Kraft is a line of kitchenware. Many, but not all, Kitchen Kraft patterns were decorated to supplement existing Homer Laughlin tableware patterns. A pie plate, covered casserole, or mixing bowl might have the same decal or design as a tableware pattern on another Homer Laughlin shape. Ads were found as early as July 1937 in *China, Glass and Lamps,* and as late as 1947 in *China, Glass and Decorative Accessories,* promoting Kitchen Kraft.

Fiesta Kitchen Kraft is the Kitchen Kraft shape with a solid color Fiesta glaze, just one example of the line supplementing other existing patterns.

Royal Metal Manufacturing produced metal frames to hold a number of Kitchen Kraft shapes. These kitchen and after-oven or stove use pieces are collectible in their own right. Homer Laughlin china in Royal Metal frames were marketed as Royal products.

Some Kitchen Kraft shapes have backstamps marked Kitchen Kraft OvenServe. This indicated the object's ability to be used in the oven and is not related to the OvenServe shape. See the OvenServe chapter to learn more about OvenServe shapes.

Left: *Magazine advertisement; China, Glass & Lamps, July 1937.* **Top right:** *N1581 pattern; Teapot with lid.* **Bottom right:** *Typical Kitchen Kraft backstamp.*

Homer Laughlin

KITCHEN KRAFT OVENWARE

This smart, new, matching, colorful, distinctively-styled pottery brings the usefulness of ovenware to pieces designed for other purposes. All pieces are in ivory with a colorful decoration in red, blue, orange, and green, set off by a red border-line, bringing harmony and beauty to your kitchen. All will stand oven heat.

Casserole Set
Consists of 8½-in. covered casserole that holds about 2 qts. and 9½-in. pie plate that can be used as a service plate under the casserole.
Mailing weight 4½ lbs.
Coupon
1990   Price $2.60
Cash Price $1.30

Covered Jar
Can be used for cookies, pretzels, crackers, sugar, or as bean pot. 6⅞ in. high; capacity, 4 qts. Mlg. wt. 4½ lbs.
Coupon
1882   Price $2.60
Cash Price $1.30

Mixing Bowl Set
Three dandy, deep bowls just the right shape and having rim that allows good grip. And you can bake in them! 6 in., 8 in. and 10 in. in diam. Mailing weight 8 lbs.
Coupon
1889   Price $2.70
Cash Price $1.35

Top left: *Advertisement from a Larkin Catalog found in* Larkin China, *page 164, Walter Ayars book.* **Top right:** *Sun Porch pattern; Pie Server, and Cake Plate.* **Middle right:** *Priscilla pattern, made by Homer Laughlin, sold by Household Institute; Pie Plate, Pitcher, Cake Plate, and Large Covered Casserole.* **Bottom:** *Rhythm Rose pattern, made by Homer Laughlin, sold by Household Institute; Mixing Bowls Set.*

Kitchen Kraft Shape

Top left: *Fiesta Kitchen Kraft patterns; Red Pie Plate, Cobalt Blue Cake Plate, Yellow Pie Plate, and Light Green Oval Platter.* **Top right:** *Fiesta Kitchen Kraft patterns; Red Medium Covered Casserole, Yellow Large Covered Casserole, and Red Small Covered Casserole.* **Bottom left:** *Fiesta Kitchen Kraft patterns; Red, Yellow, Light Green, and Cobalt Blue Refrigerator Jars with lids, stacked.* **Middle:** *Fiesta Kitchen Kraft patterns; Red, Yellow, Cobalt Blue, and Light Green Salt & Pepper Shakers.* **Second down on right:** *Fiesta Kitchen Kraft–Light Green pattern; Pitcher with lid.* **Bottom middle:** *Fiesta Kitchen Kraft–Red; Ball Jar.* **Third down on right:** *Typical Fiesta Kitchen Kraft backstamp.* **Bottom right:** *Fiesta Kitchen Kraft patterns; Light Green Pie Server, Yellow Salad Fork, and Cobalt Blue Salad Spoon.*

Homer Laughlin

Kitchen Kraft Piece Type List

From Homer Laughlin Literature with Confirmed Actual Pieces

Bowl, Handy Andy, 8½ W x 3 H inches fits in a stand and has a metal lid
Bowl, Mixing Large, 10¼ inches
Bowl, Mixing Medium, 8½ inches
Bowl, Mixing Small, 6½ inches
Casserole, Large with lid, 8⅝ inches
Casserole, Medium with lid, 8 inches
Casserole, Promotional with lid Royal, 8 inches
Casserole, Small with lid, 4⅝ inches

Fork, Salad, 9⅞ inches
Jar, Ball Large with lid, 7½ inches
Jar, Ball Medium with lid, 6¼ inches
Jar, Ball Small with lid, 4¾ inches
Jar, Refrigerator with lid, 2⅜ inches
Pie Server, 9⅝ inches
Pitcher, Large Open, 6¼ inches
Pitcher, Large with lid, 6¼ inches
Pitcher, Medium with lid, 6 inches
Plate, 6 inches

Plate, 9 inches
Plate, Cake, 10⅞ inches
Plate, Pie, 9⅝ inches
Plate, Pie Royal, 10¼ inches
Platter, Oval Royal, 13 inches
Salt & Pepper Set, 2⅞ inches
Spoon, Salad, 8¾ inches
Teapot with lid

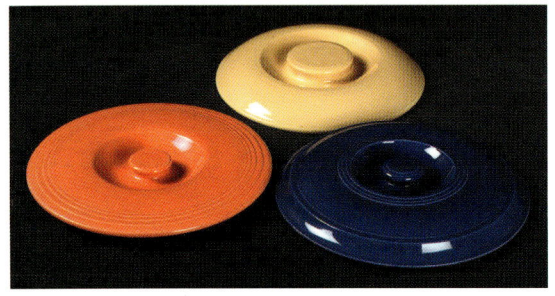

Top left: *KK343 pattern, Medium Covered Casserole, and Pie Plate.* **Bottom left:** *Fiesta–Red pattern; Mixing Bowl Lid (flat). Fiesta Kitchen Kraft patterns; Yellow Casserole Lid, and Cobalt Blue Promotional Casserole Lid.* **Top right:** *Fiesta Kitchen Kraft–Red pattern; Promotional Covered Casserole.* **Bottom right:** *Magazine advertisement; China, Glass & Lamps, April 1938.*

Kitchen Kraft Shape

Fiesta Kitchen Kraft–Ivory
Pitcher Shown
No Trim

Fiesta Kitchen Kraft–Yellow
Covered Casserole Shown
No Trim

Fiesta Kitchen Kraft–Light Green
Refrigerator Jar Shown
No Trim

Fiesta Kitchen Kraft–Cobalt Blue
Individual Casserole Shown
No Trim

Fiesta Kitchen Kraft–Red
Ball Jar Shown
No Trim

HLC1213
Cake Plate Shown
No Trim

HLC981
Cake Plate Shown
Platinum Band
No Trim

KK343
Pie Plate Shown
Gold Band
No Trim

KK303
No Trim

HLC1839
Cake Plate Shown
No Trim

KK334
No Trim

Sun Porch
Cake Plate Shown
No Trim

Mexicana
Pie Plate Shown
Red Band
No Trim

Mexicana
Pitcher Shown
Blue Band
No Trim

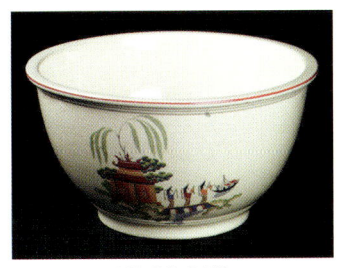

HLC1953
Mixing Bowl Shown
Red Trim

HLC1084
Cake Plate Shown
Platinum Band
No Trim

Kitchen Kraft Shape

Rhythm Rose
by Household Institute
Cake Plate Shown
No Trim

HLC3104
Handy Andy Bowl Shown
No Trim

HLC2173
Mixing Bowl Shown
Platinum Trim

KK350
No Trim

Priscilla
by Household Institute
Cake Plate Shown
Gold Band, No Trim

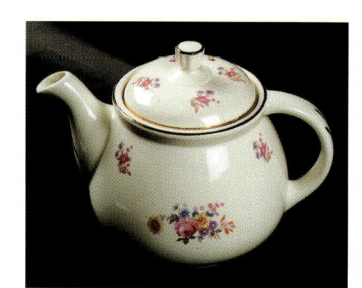

N1581
Teapot Shown
Gold Trim

HLC419
Cake Plate Shown
Platinum Trim

DK3
Cake Plate Shown
No Trim

DB13
Cake Plate Shown
No Trim

DK1
Cake Plate Shown
No Trim

MAJ4
Cake Plate Shown
Green Trim

HLC2179
Pie Server Shown
No Trim

298

Kraft

Piece Types

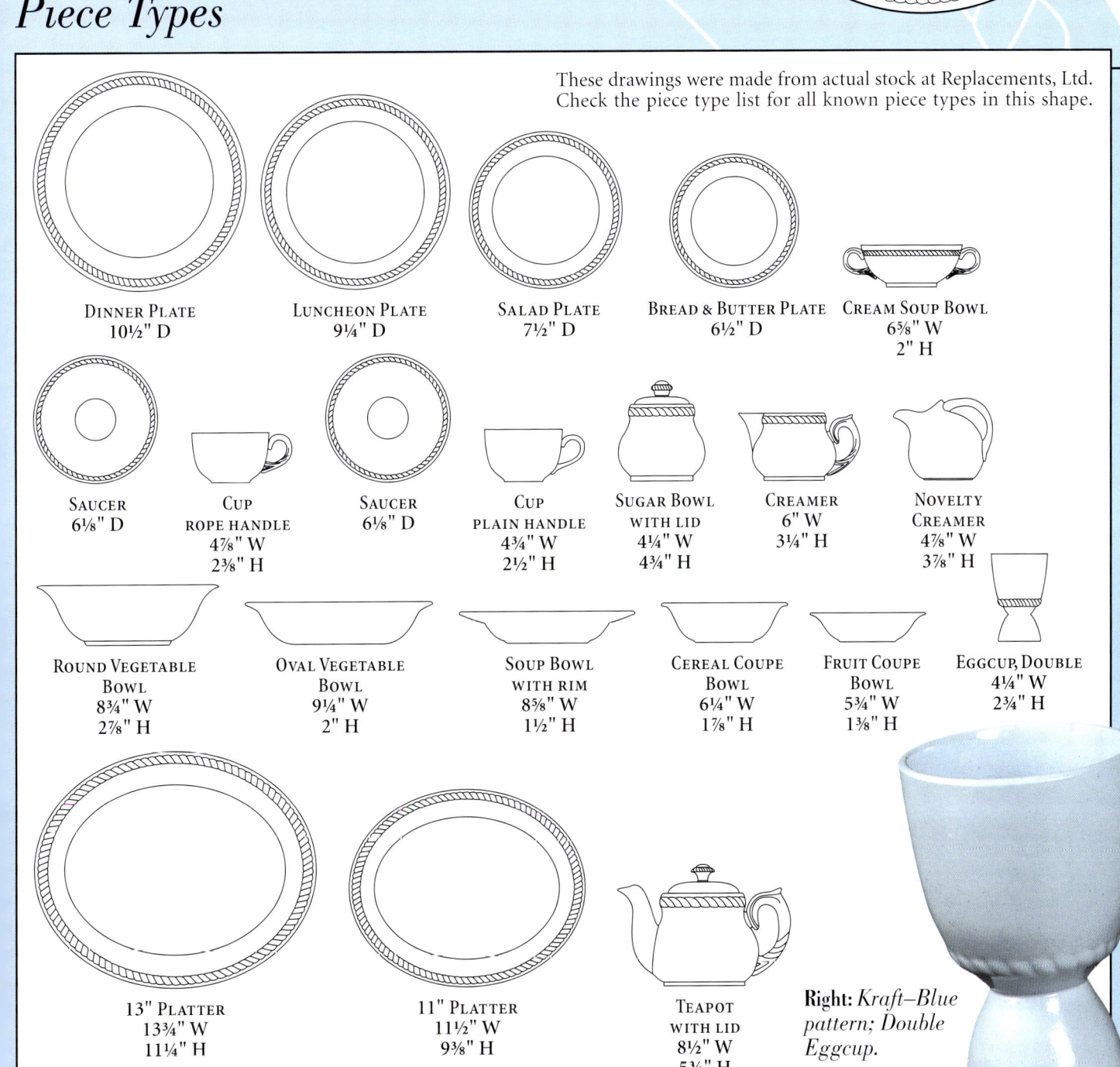

These drawings were made from actual stock at Replacements, Ltd. Check the piece type list for all known piece types in this shape.

Dinner Plate
10½" D

Luncheon Plate
9¼" D

Salad Plate
7½" D

Bread & Butter Plate
6½" D

Cream Soup Bowl
6⅝" W
2" H

Saucer
6⅛" D

Cup
ROPE HANDLE
4⅞" W
2⅜" H

Saucer
6⅛" D

Cup
PLAIN HANDLE
4¾" W
2½" H

Sugar Bowl
WITH LID
4¼" W
4¾" H

Creamer
6" W
3¼" H

Novelty Creamer
4⅞" W
3⅞" H

Round Vegetable Bowl
8¾" W
2⅞" H

Oval Vegetable Bowl
9¼" W
2" H

Soup Bowl
WITH RIM
8⅝" W
1½" H

Cereal Coupe Bowl
6¼" W
1⅞" H

Fruit Coupe Bowl
5¾" W
1⅜" H

Eggcup, Double
4¼" W
2¾" H

13" Platter
13¾" W
11¼" H

11" Platter
11½" W
9⅜" H

Teapot
WITH LID
8½" W
5¾" H

Right: *Kraft–Blue pattern; Double Eggcup.*

Homer Laughlin

KRAFT
1937 – 1940's

The Kraft shape has an embossed rope border. Like the Skytone and Suntone lines on the Jubilee shape, colored clay was used to create contrast on pieces. Because the color was in the clay, instead of painted on, the color was more permanent and created a vibrant contrast. Blue and white were the most popular colors used. Later, a new line of Kraft called Peasant Ware was introduced. This line featured a neutral colored clay body with stylized, handpainted decorations.

Collectors Note: One style of Tea Cups and the Novelty Creamer do not have the rope motif.

Top right: Kraft–Blue pattern; typical Kraft backstamp. **Top left:** Kraft–Blue pattern; Cup & Saucer Set, Dinner Plate, Luncheon Plate, Salad Plate, Bread & Butter Plate, Creamer, and Sugar Bowl with lid. **Second down on right:** Kraft–Blue pattern; Cup with plain handle on left, and Cup with rope handle on right. **Third down on right:** Kraft–Blue pattern; Cream Soup Bowl, Cereal Bowl, and Fruit Bowl. **Middle left:** Kraft–Blue pattern; Oval Vegetable Bowl, Oval Platter, and Novelty Creamer. **Middle:** GCM101 pattern; Round Vegetable Bowl, and Oval Platter. **Bottom left:** GCM101 pattern; Cup & Saucer Set, Soup Bowl with rim, and Cereal Bowl. **Bottom middle:** GCM101 pattern; Cup & Saucer Set, Dinner Plate, Salad Plate, and Bread & Butter Plate.

Kraft Shape

Kraft Piece Type List
From Homer Laughlin Literature with Confirmed Actual Pieces

Bowl, Cereal Coupe, 6¼ inches
Bowl, Cream Soup, 6⅝ inches
Bowl, Fruit Coupe, 5¾ inches
Bowl, Soup with rim, 8⅝ inches
Bowl, Vegetable Oval, 9¼ inches
Bowl, Vegetable Round, 8¾ inches
Creamer
Creamer, Novelty

Cup & Saucer Set, plain handle
　Cup, 2½ inches
　Saucer, 6⅛ inches
Cup & Saucer Set, rope handle
　Cup, 2⅜ inches
　Saucer, 6⅛ inches
Eggcup, Double
Plate, Bread & Butter, 6½ inches

Plate, Dinner, 10½ inches
Plate, Luncheon, 9¼ inches
Plate, Salad, 7½ inches
Platter, Oval, 11½ inches
Platter, Oval, 13¾ inches
Sugar Bowl with lid
Teapot with lid

Top left: *Original drawing from the Homer Laughlin Factory.* **Top right:** *Kraft–Blue pattern; Factory literature.* **Bottom left:** *GCM101 pattern; Creamer, and Sugar Bowl with lid.* **Bottom right:** *Kraft–Blue pattern; Teapot with lid.*

301

Kraft Shape

Kraft–White No Trim	 **Kraft–Blue** No Trim	 **GCM101** Luncheon Plate Shown Platinum Trim	 **HLC2043** Platinum Trim
 **HLC1886** No Trim	 **HLC1882** No Trim	 **HLC1868** No Trim	 **HLC1885** No Trim
 **HLC1880** No Trim	 **HLC1870** Blue Trim	 **HLC1869** Orange Trim	 **HLC1881** No Trim
 **HLC1883** Blue Trim	 **HLC1874** Blue Trim	 **HLC1888** No Trim	 **HLC1884** No Trim

Kraft Shape

HLC1889 *No Trim*	**HLC1483** *Blue Trim*	**HLC1887** *No Trim*	**HLC1871** *No Trim*
HLC1890 *No Trim*	**HLC1873** *No Trim*	**HLC1210** *No Trim*	**HLC1711** *No Trim*
HLC1482 *No Trim*	**Historical America–Blue** *No Trim*	**Historical America–Red** *No Trim*	**American Subjects–Red** *No Trim*
American Subjects–Blue *No Trim*			

Tea Rose

Piece Types

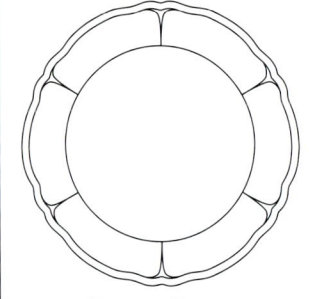

Dinner Plate

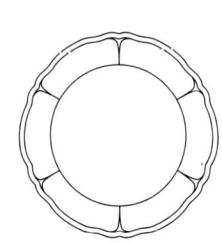

Bread & Butter Plate
6¾" D

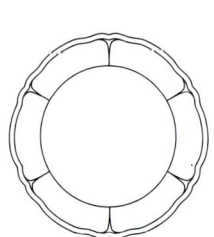

Cereal Bowl
6⅛" W
1¾" H

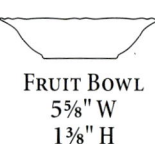

Fruit Bowl
5⅝" W
1⅜" H

These drawings were made from actual stock or literature at Replacements, Ltd. Check the piece type list for all known piece types in this shape.

Above: *Typical Tea Rose backstamp.*

Collectors Note: Tea Rose has a raised petal running to the well. Numerous look-a-likes have recessed "petal divisions."

TEA ROSE circa 1937

The Tea Rose line features a scalloped shaped plate composed of six equal panels. Comprised of graceful curves on its edge, a tracing of the outline would be similar to the more popular Virginia Rose line. According to Lois Lehner, Tea Rose was made by both Homer Laughlin and Taylor, Smith & Taylor for a retail promotion. The back mark found on the Tea Rose pattern is an outline of a rose intermingled with the words "Tea Rose" and "USA," usually with no other manufacturer symbol. Pieces of the Tea Rose line were found in the Homer Laughlin factory, as were artist drawings of the Tea Rose backstamp, further substantiating that Homer Laughlin made this line. Examples have been seen where both the Tea Rose mark and the Homer Laughlin mark were present.

Tea Rose Piece Type List

From Homer Laughlin Literature with Confirmed Actual Pieces

Bowl, Cereal (Oatmeal), 6⅛ inches
Bowl, Fruit, 5⅝ inches
Cup & Saucer Set
Plate, Bread & Butter, 6¾ inches
Plate, Dinner
Platter, Oval

Tea Rose Shape

HLC1627
No Trim

HLC1628
No Trim

R1521
No Trim

HLC2105
Bread & Butter Plate Shown
No Trim

Tea Rose
GO16
No Trim

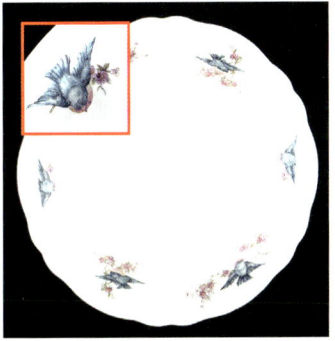

TR7
Cereal Bowl Shown
No Trim

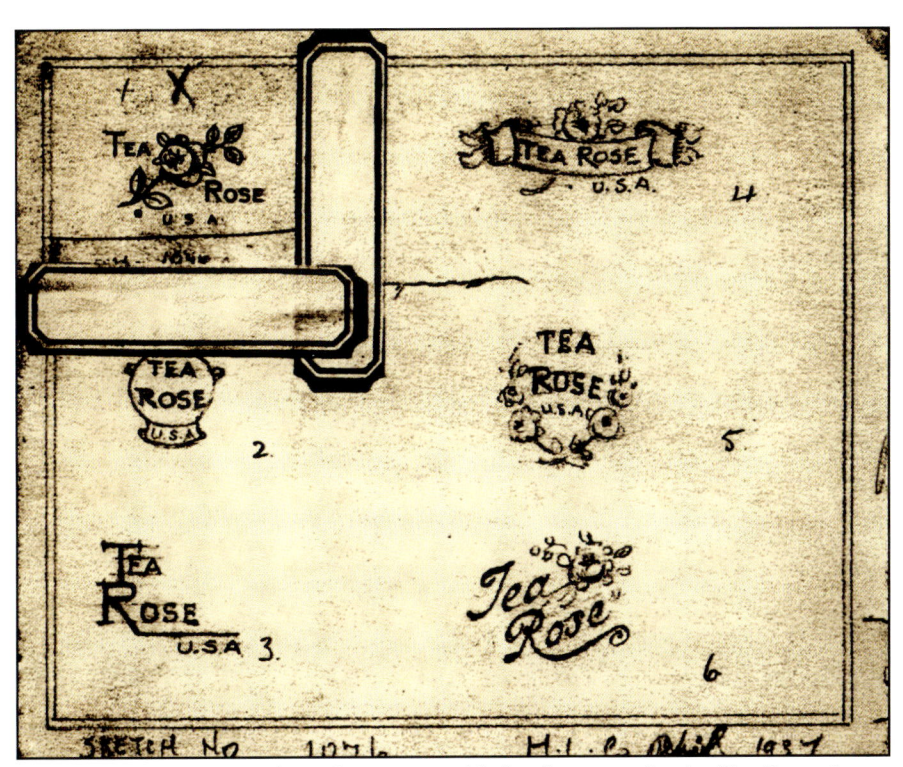

Above: *Original artwork exploring possible backstamps for the Tea Rose shape, found at the Homer Laughlin Factory. The backstamp used is framed and set apart with gummed labels.*

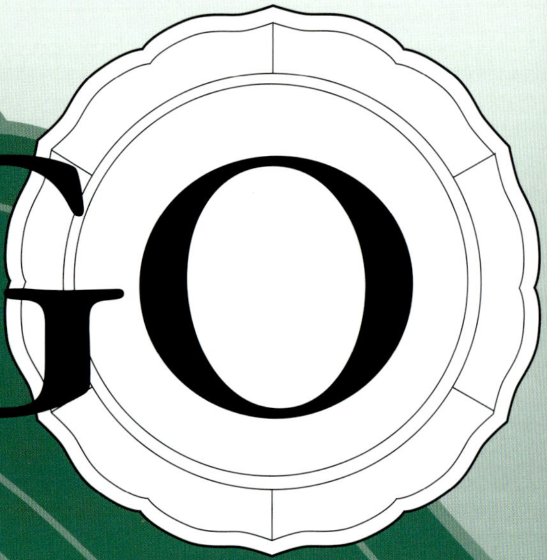

TANGO

Piece Types

These drawings were made from photographs, except the Salt & Pepper Set, which was drawn from actual stock at Replacements, Ltd. Check the piece type list for all known piece types in this shape.

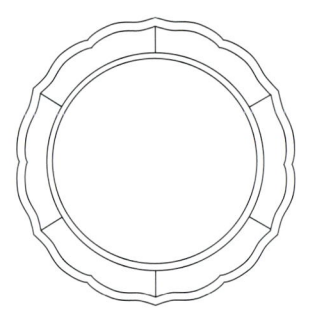

Dinner Plate
10" D

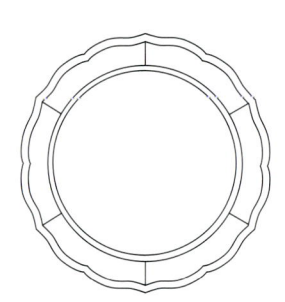

Luncheon Plate
9" D

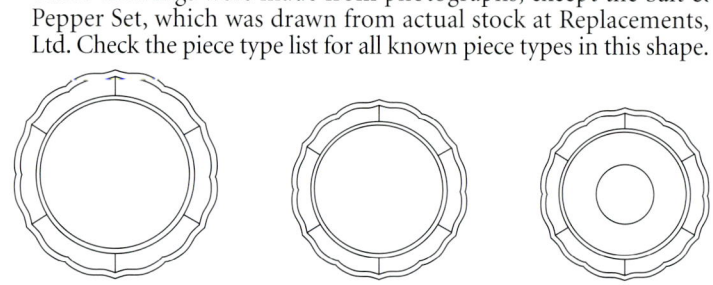

Salad Plate
7¼" D

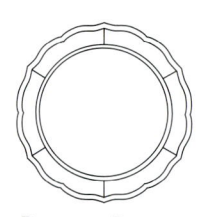

Bread & Butter Plate
6¼" D

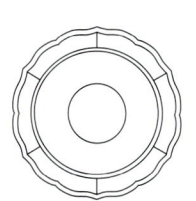

Saucer
6" D

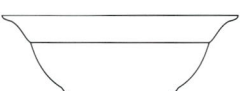

Round Vegetable Bowl
8½" W
2¾" H

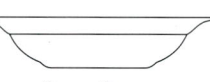

Soup Bowl with Rim
8½" W
1½" H

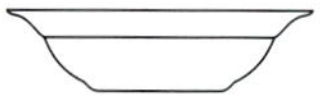

Fruit Bowl
5½" W
1⅜" H

Cup Curled Handle
4⅝" W
2½" H

Cup Plain Handle
4¾" W
2½" H

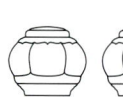

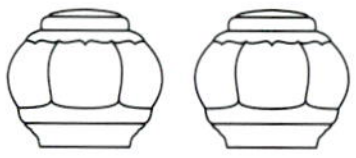

Salt & Pepper Set
2¾" W
2⅜" H

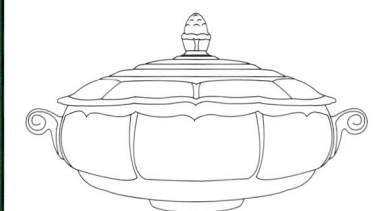

Round Covered Vegetable Bowl
10½" W x 5½" H

Sugar Bowl with Lid
6" W
4½" H

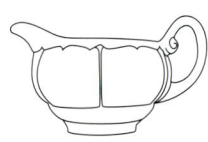

Creamer
6" W
3⅜" H

Right: Spruce Green pattern; Cup & Saucer Set.
Below: Spruce Green, Harlequin Yellow, Fiesta Red, Mauve Blue, and Maroon patterns; Salt & Pepper Sets.

Tango Shape

TANGO 1937 – 1941 (or later)

Tango is another of the Homer Laughlin solid color lines. Tango was produced in the bold colors: Mauve Blue, Spruce Green, Harlequin Yellow, Maroon, and Fiesta Red.

The Tango shape has a wide, petal-like border with broad panels and distinctive acorn-like finials. The authors of the Ohio River Pottery web site note the handles on pieces like the Tango covered casserole resemble the handles on Eggshell Nautilus shapes.

Tango patterns were probably produced to sell as premiums because they have no backstamps indicating Homer Laughlin was the manufacturer. Often Tango is not recognized or attributed to Homer Laughlin because of the lack of a backstamp.

Tango shaped shakers were used in other lines, which explains their appearance in other colors.

Harvey Duke reports that Homer Laughlin records suggest boldly colored Tango line demitasse cups and saucers were made using Republic shapes.

Top right: *Maroon Sugar Bowl with lid, Spruce Green Bread & Butter Plate, Mauve Blue Luncheon Plate, Harlequin Yellow Dinner Plate, Maroon Salad Plate, Fiesta Red Fruit Bowl, Spruce Green Creamer, and Fiesta Red Round Covered Vegetable Bowl.* **Second down on right:** *Harlequin Yellow Dinner Plate, Harlequin Yellow Luncheon Plate, Mauve Blue Salad Plate, and Fiesta Red Bread & Butter Plate.* **Third down on right:** *Mauve Blue Sugar Bowl with lid, and Maroon Creamer.* **Fourth down on right:** *Harlequin Yellow Fruit Bowl, Fiesta Red Round Vegetable Bowl, and Spruce Green Soup Bowl with rim.* **Fifth down on right:** *Mauve Blue Cup in revised style with plain handle, and Spruce Green Cup with original curled handle.* **Bottom left:** *Fiesta Red Round Covered Vegetable Bowl.* **Bottom right:** *Spruce Green Creamer, and Maroon Sugar Bowl with lid.*

Piece Type List
From Homer Laughlin Literature with Confirmed Actual Pieces

Bowl, Fruit, 5½ inches
Bowl, Soup with rim, 8½ inches
Bowl, Vegetable Oval, 9 inches
Bowl, Vegetable Round, 8½ inches
Bowl, Vegetable Round Covered, 10½ inches
Creamer

Cup & Saucer Set
   Cup with curled handle, 2½ inches
   Cup with plain handle, 2½ inches
   Saucer, 6 inches
Cup & Saucer Set, Demitasse (Republic)
Eggcup

Plate, Bread & Butter, 6¼ inches
Plate, Dinner, 10 inches
Plate, Luncheon, 9 inches
Plate, Salad, 7¼ inches
Platter, Oval, 11¾ inches
Salt & Pepper Set
Sugar Bowl with lid

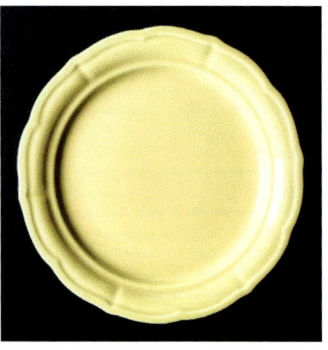

Tango Shape

Tango–Harlequin Yellow *No Trim*	**Tango–Mauve Blue** *No Trim*	**Tango–Spruce Green** *No Trim*	**Tango–Fiesta Red** *No Trim*
Tango–Maroon *No Trim*	**HLC1914** *No Trim*		

Above: *Postcards of various Homer Laughlin Factory buildings.*

308

Eggshell Dinnerware

EGGSHELL DINNERWARE 1937

The quest for lightweight, strong crazeproof china is almost as old as the art of pottery itself. Homer Laughlin invested years of research and experimentation into creating such a product line and was marketing it to the world by 1937. Eggshell lines proved successful for many years to follow.

The name of the new body material, "Eggshell," attempted to convey how thin, lightweight and durable the product was. A period Homer Laughlin advertisement illustrated with weighing scales that a single luncheon plate in eggshell was 4 ounces lighter than its competition! Tests of dropping steel balls on plates were performed to prove the durability of the newly engineered material. Eggshell was a winner. The Eggshell glaze was crazeproof, meaning patterns would not get an unsightly web of miniscule cracks that would become visible as the glaze and clay expanded and contracted over time.

Eggshell lines soared in popularity when the flow of china to the United States was reduced, and eventually stopped, due to the events of World War II. A box of Noritake plates, that was shipped from New York in the 1940's, remains at the Homer Laughlin Factory with the original manufacturer's labels still intact. When the availability of Noritake products ceased, Homer Laughlin used Eggshell Georgian and Nautilus shapes to create the formal floral patterns that were reminiscent of Noritake.

Eggshell lines were created on Andover, Georgian, Nautilus, Swing and Theme shapes. Formal dining was less popular after the war and casual Ironstone and handmade looking patterns began to be more in vogue. The Eggshell lines ceased to be profitable and disappeared from production.

Top right: *Magazine advertisement introducing the new Eggshell process and showing how much lighter it is; China, Glass & Lamps, January 1937.*
Bottom right: *Pamphlet from the Factory introducing the Eggshell process.*

EGGSHELL NAUTILUS

Piece Types

These drawings were made from actual stock at Replacements, Ltd. Check the piece type list for all known piece types in this shape.

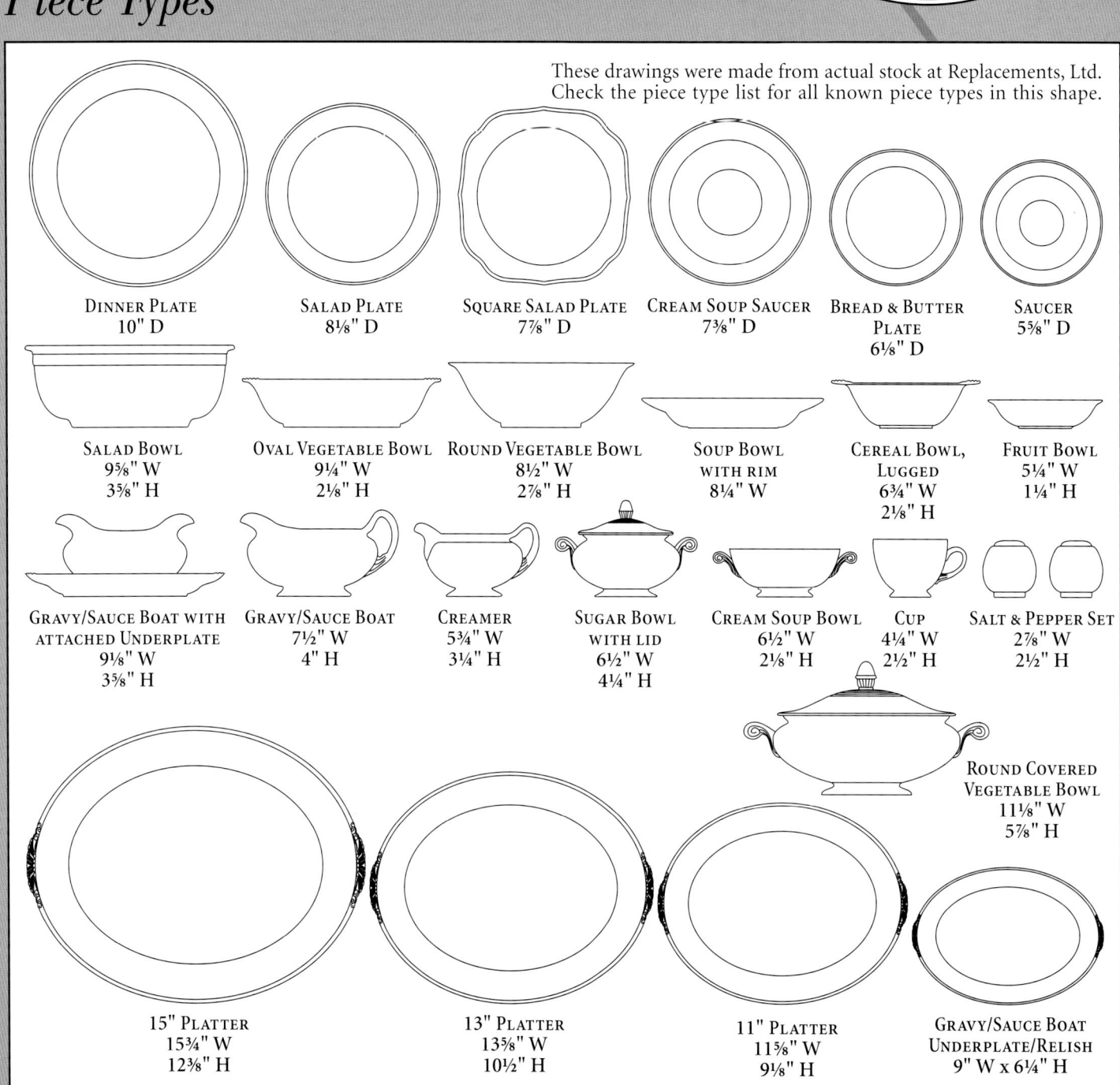

Dinner Plate 10" D	**Salad Plate** 8⅛" D	**Square Salad Plate** 7⅞" D	**Cream Soup Saucer** 7⅜" D	**Bread & Butter Plate** 6⅛" D	**Saucer** 5⅝" D
Salad Bowl 9⅝" W 3⅝" H	**Oval Vegetable Bowl** 9¼" W 2⅛" H	**Round Vegetable Bowl** 8½" W 2⅞" H	**Soup Bowl with Rim** 8¼" W	**Cereal Bowl, Lugged** 6¾" W 2⅛" H	**Fruit Bowl** 5¼" W 1¼" H
Gravy/Sauce Boat with attached Underplate 9⅛" W 3⅝" H	**Gravy/Sauce Boat** 7½" W 4" H	**Creamer** 5¾" W 3¼" H	**Sugar Bowl with Lid** 6½" W 4¼" H	**Cream Soup Bowl** 6½" W 2⅛" H	**Cup** 4¼" W 2½" H	**Salt & Pepper Set** 2⅞" W 2½" H

Round Covered Vegetable Bowl 11⅛" W 5⅞" H

15" Platter 15¾" W 12⅜" H

13" Platter 13⅝" W 10½" H

11" Platter 11⅝" W 9⅛" H

Gravy/Sauce Boat Underplate/Relish 9" W x 6¼" H

Eggshell Nautilus Shape

EGGSHELL NAUTILUS 1937 – 1955 or later

Homer Laughlin developed a new process for making dinnerware that was thinner and stronger than the dinnerware they had previously produced. Shapes and lines created using this new process were called "Eggshell." The Nautilus shape was the first shape produced using the Eggshell process: "Announcing a new light-weight ware by Homer Laughlin… for the present only our Nautilus shape is being offered in this new ware" (*Crockery, Glass & Lamps,* January 1937).

In 1937, ads for new patterns like Della Robbia (*Crockery, Glass & Lamps,* August 1937) and Starflower (*Crockery, Glass & Lamps,* June 1937) continued to attest to the new line's popularity. The *Homer Laughlin Pound Sterling Price Book of 1937* featured Eggshell Nautilus shapes with 121 different decorations/patterns.

Crockery, Glass & Lamps, February 1939 (review of Pittsburgh show): "Also new — a varied assortment of formal floral designs on ivory borders on the 'Nautilus shape,' formal decorations with rims in underglazed red or pale blue interrupted with gold medallions holding small floral clusters, and floral decals in the centers."

We first found Montgomery Ward offering Eggshell Nautilus in its 1938-39 Fall & Winter Catalog with the "new pattern" Daisy Field. Montgomery Ward also offered Rochelle, Aristocrat, and Dresden on Eggshell Nautilus in its 1942-43 Fall & Winter Catalog. By 1944, three patterns had grown to five and Aristocrat, Dresden, Bristol, Coronet, and Gardenia were available in the Spring & Summer Catalog.

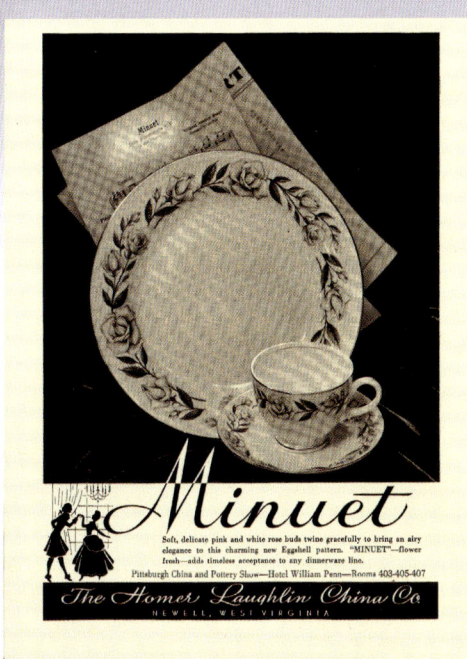

Top left: *Minuet pattern;* Crockery and Glass Journal, *1951.* **Top middle:** *Starflower pattern;* Crockery, Glass & Lamps, *1937.* **Top right:** *Della Robbia pattern;* Crockery, Glass & Lamps, *1937.* **Bottom left:** *Bristol pattern;* Montgomery Ward, *1944.* **Bottom middle:** *Dresden pattern;* Montgomery Ward, *1943.*

Homer Laughlin

Top left: *Ferndale pattern; Two Oval Platters, Round Covered Vegetable Bowl, and Oval Vegetable Bowl.* **Top right:** *Ferndale pattern; Dinner Plate, Square Salad Plate, Salad Plate, Round Vegetable Bowl, Lugged Cereal Bowl, Cup & Saucer Set, Fruit Bowl, and Cream Soup Bowl.* **Middle left:** *Ferndale pattern; Gravy/Sauce Boat, Sugar Bowl with lid, and Creamer.* **Middle right:** *Ferndale pattern; Round Vegetable Bowl, Soup Bowl with rim, Lugged Cereal Bowl, Cereal Bowl, Fruit Bowl, and Cream Soup Bowl.* **Bottom left:** *HLC2107 pattern; Dinner Plate, Soup Bowl with rim, Cup, Fruit Bowl, and Bread & Butter Plate.* **Bottom right:** *N1583 pattern; Round Covered Vegetable Bowl.*

Eggshell Nautilus Shape

Top left: *Typical Eggshell Nautilus backstamp.* **Top right:** *Apple Blossom pattern; Cup & Saucer Set, and Demitasse Cup & Saucer Set.* **Bottom:** *HLC1944 pattern; Gravy/Sauce Boat with unattached Underplate.*

Eggshell Nautilus Piece Type List

From Homer Laughlin Literature with Confirmed Actual Pieces

Bowl, Cereal Lugged, 6¾ inches
Bowl, Cream Soup & Saucer Set
   Bowl, 6½ inches
   Saucer, 7⅜ inches
Bowl, Fruit, 5¼ inches
Bowl, Salad, 9⅝ inches
Bowl, Soup with rim, 8¼ inches
Bowl, Vegetable Oval, 9¼ inches
Bowl, Vegetable Round, 8½ inches
Bowl, Vegetable Round Covered, 11⅛ inches

Creamer
Cup & Saucer Set
   Cup, 2½ inches
   Saucer, 5⅝ inches
Cup & Saucer Set, Demitasse (Swing Shape)
Gravy/Sauce Boat
Gravy/Sauce Boat with attached Underplate
Gravy/Sauce Boat/Underplate/Relish, 9 inches

Plate, Bread & Butter, 6⅛ inches
Plate, Dinner, 10 inches
Plate, Salad, 8⅛ inches
Plate, Salad Square, 7⅞ inches
Platter, Oval, 11⅝ inches
Platter, Oval, 13⅜ inches
Platter, Oval, 15¾ inches
Salt & Pepper Set (Swing Shape)
Sugar Bowl with lid
Teapot with lid

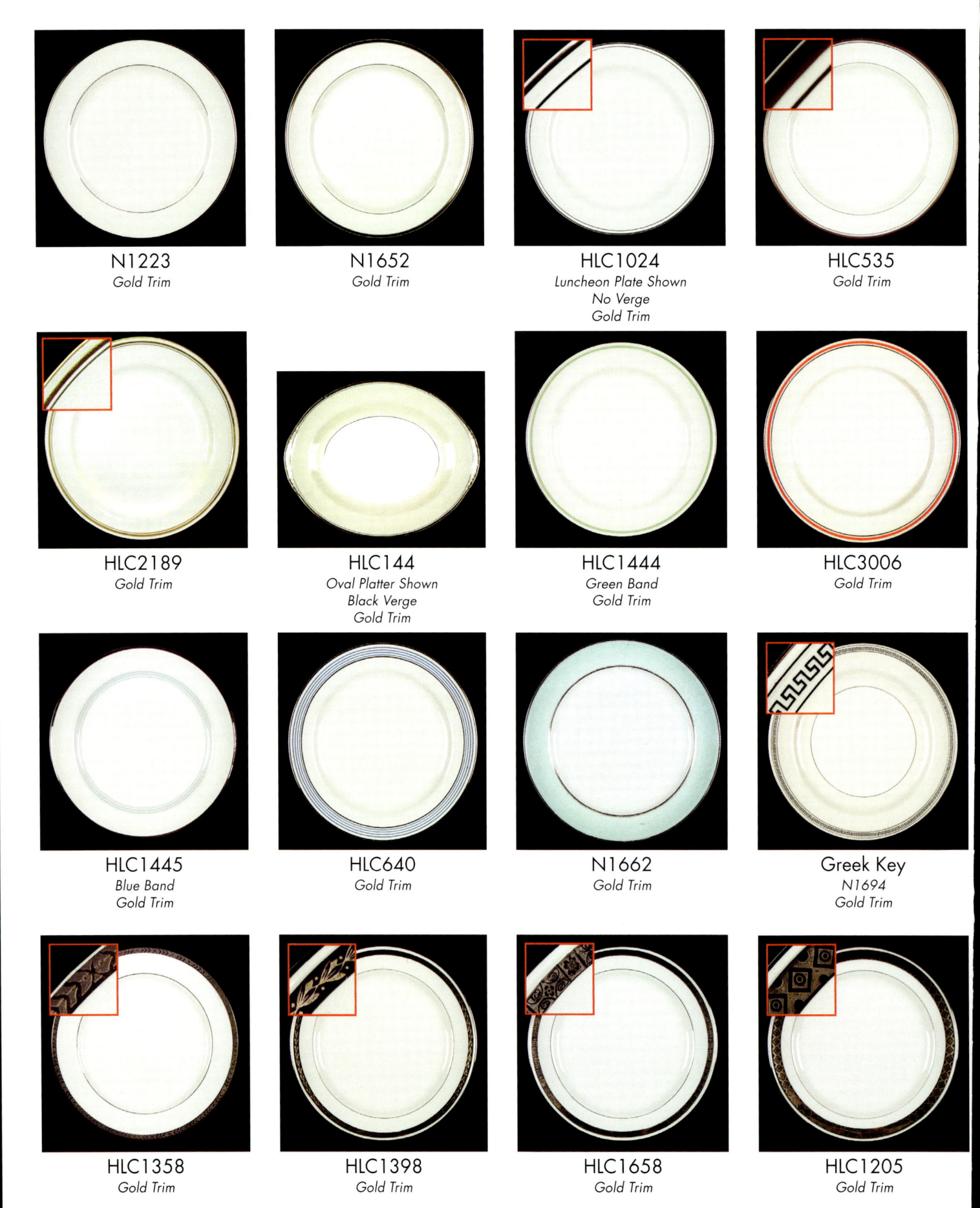

Eggshell Nautilus Shape (Gold Trim, Band or Gold Filigree)

N1223 *Gold Trim*	**N1652** *Gold Trim*	**HLC1024** *Luncheon Plate Shown* *No Verge* *Gold Trim*	**HLC535** *Gold Trim*
HLC2189 *Gold Trim*	**HLC144** *Oval Platter Shown* *Black Verge* *Gold Trim*	**HLC1444** *Green Band* *Gold Trim*	**HLC3006** *Gold Trim*
HLC1445 *Blue Band* *Gold Trim*	**HLC640** *Gold Trim*	**N1662** *Gold Trim*	**Greek Key** *N1694* *Gold Trim*
HLC1358 *Gold Trim*	**HLC1398** *Gold Trim*	**HLC1658** *Gold Trim*	**HLC1205** *Gold Trim*

Eggshell Nautilus Shape (Gold Trim, Band or Gold Filigree)

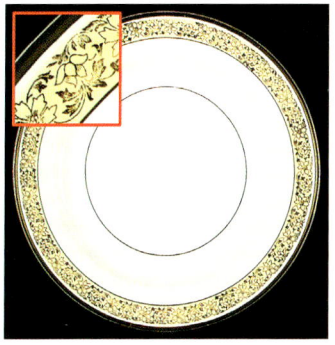

HLC175 *Gold Trim*	 **HLC1921** *No Trim*	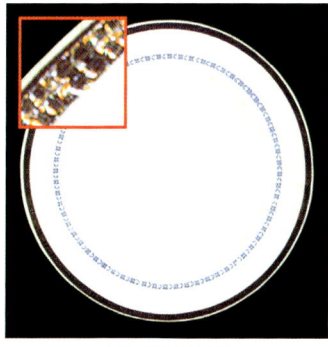 **HLC1757** *Gold Trim*	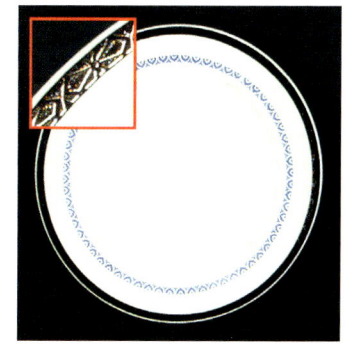 **HLC1922** *No Trim*
 **HLC1744** *Green Design* *No Trim*	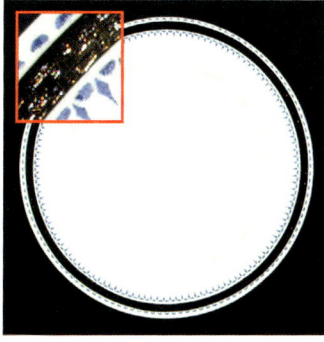 **HLC1923** *No Trim*	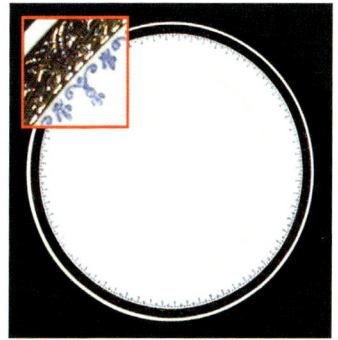 **HLC1745** *No Trim*	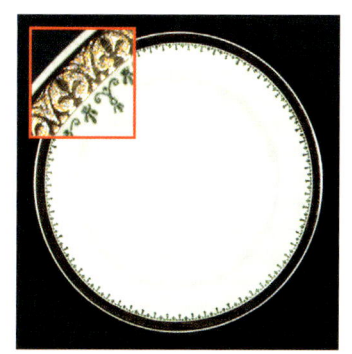 **HLC1768** *Green Scrolls* *No Trim*
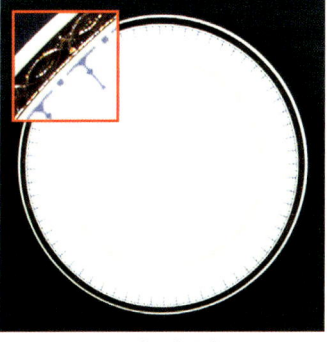 **HLC1360** *No Trim*	 **HLC1903** *No Trim*	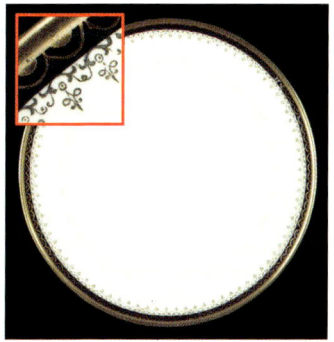 **N1617** *Blue Band* *Gold Trim*	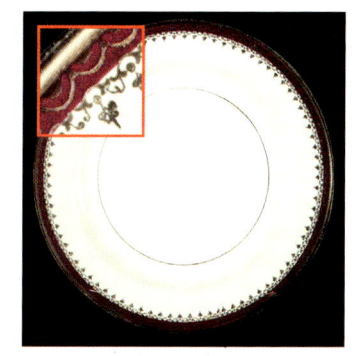 **N1642** *Gold Trim*
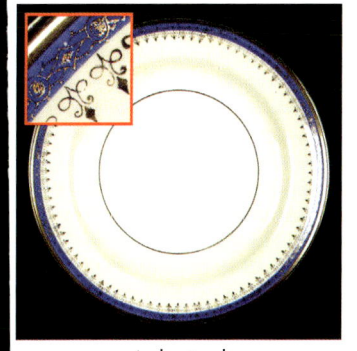 **Admiral** *N1708* *Gold Trim*	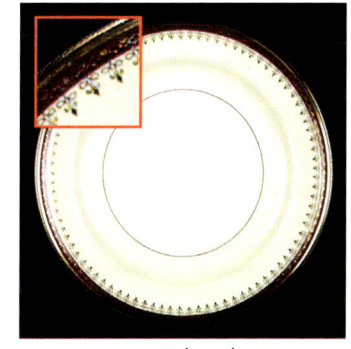 **Cardinal** *N1653* *Gold Trim*	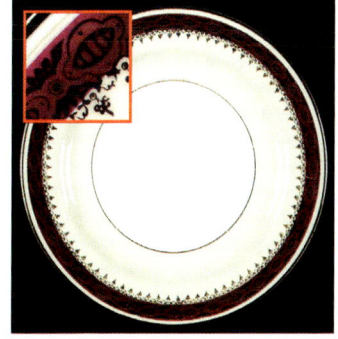 **HLC556** *Gold Trim*	 **HLC544** *Luncheon Plate Shown* *Gold Trim*

Eggshell Nautilus Shape (Gold Trim, Band or Gold Filigree)

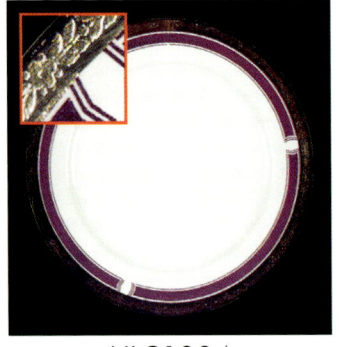

HLC1204 Gold Trim	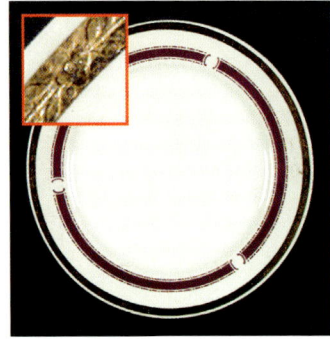 **HLC1361** No Trim	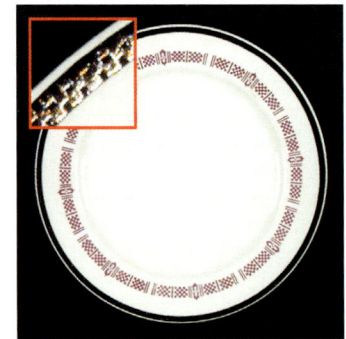 **HLC1904** No Trim	 **HLC1232** No Trim
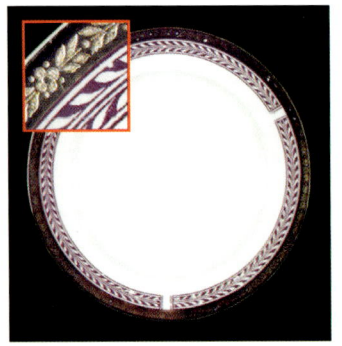 **HLC1740** Gold Trim	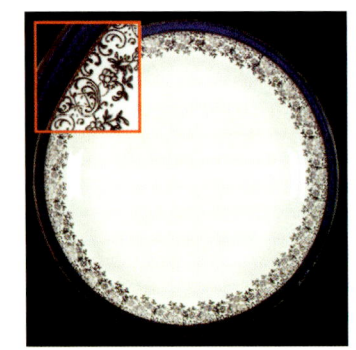 **HLC452** Gold Trim	 **HLC799** Bread & Butter Plate Shown Gold Trim	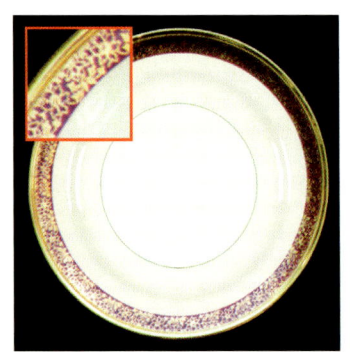 **N1654** Gold Trim
 **HLC1767** No Trim	 **HLC584** Gold Trim	 **N1711** Gold Trim	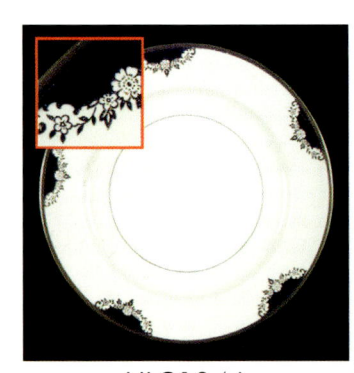 **HLC1246** Gold Trim
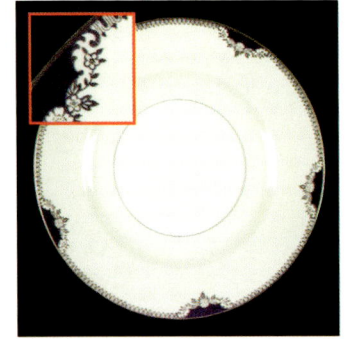 **HLC1253** Gold Trim	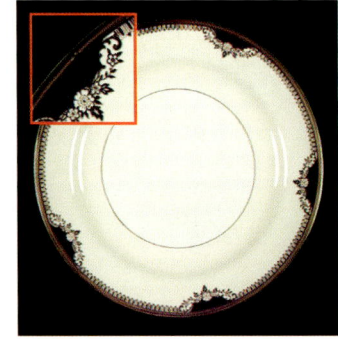 **HLC1448** Gold Trim	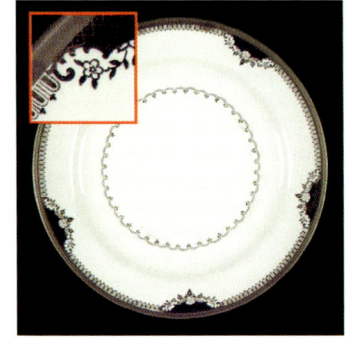 **HLC1252** Gold Trim	 **HLC1248** Gold Trim

Eggshell Nautilus Shape (Gold Trim, Band or Gold Filigree)

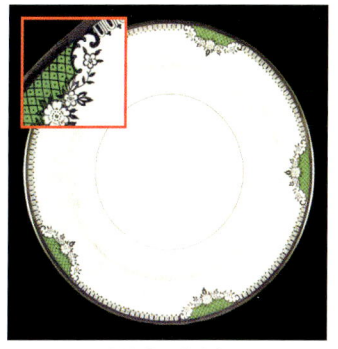

HLC1242
Gold Trim

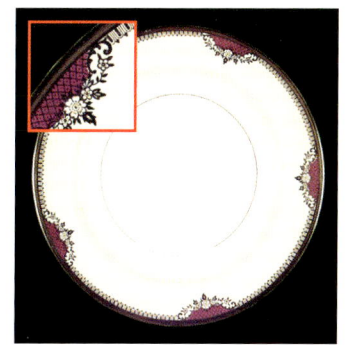

HLC1447
Gold Trim

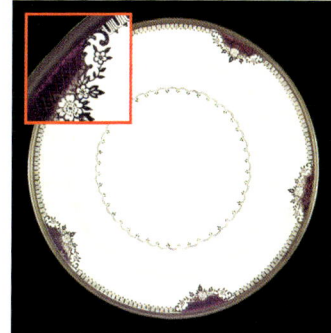

HLC1243
Gold Trim

HLC1250
Gold Trim

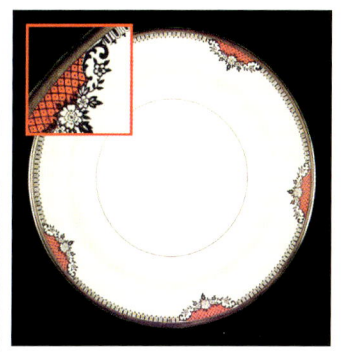

HLC1449
Gold Trim

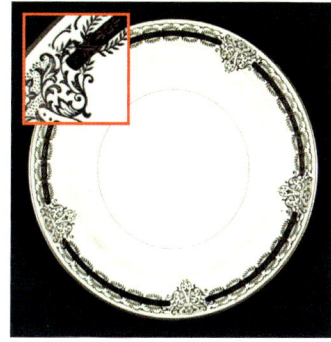

HLC1249
Gold Trim

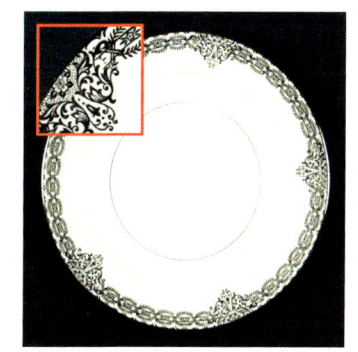

HLC1651
Gold Trim

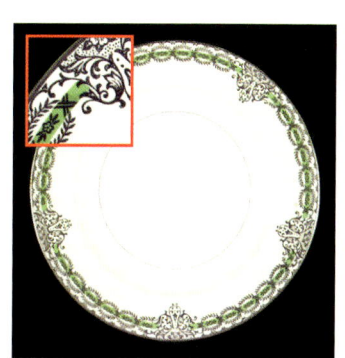

HLC1251
Gold Trim

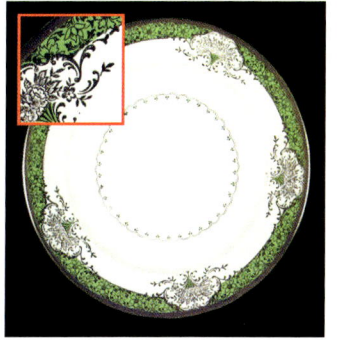

HLC1241
Gold Trim

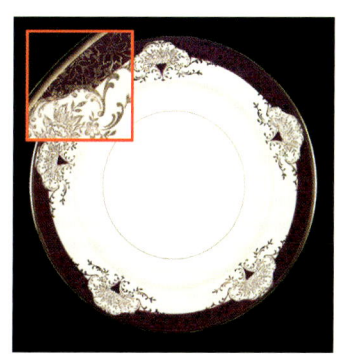

HLC1414
Gold Trim

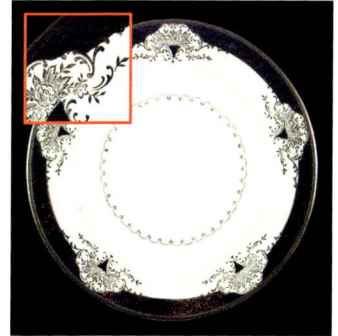

HLC1244
Gold Trim

HLC1399
Gold Trim

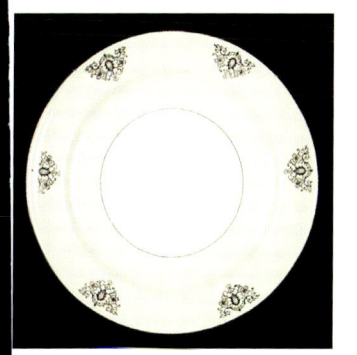

HLC901
Gold Trim

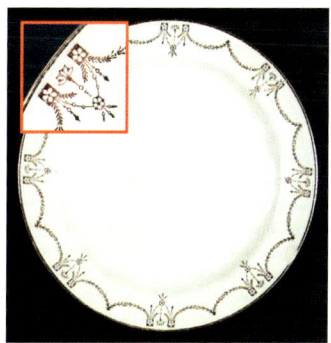

HLC2102
Luncheon Plate Shown
Gold Trim

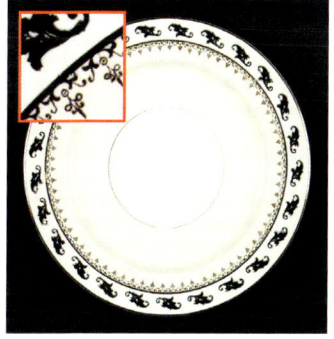

HLC1413
Gold Trim

HLC74
Salad Plate Shown
Gold Trim

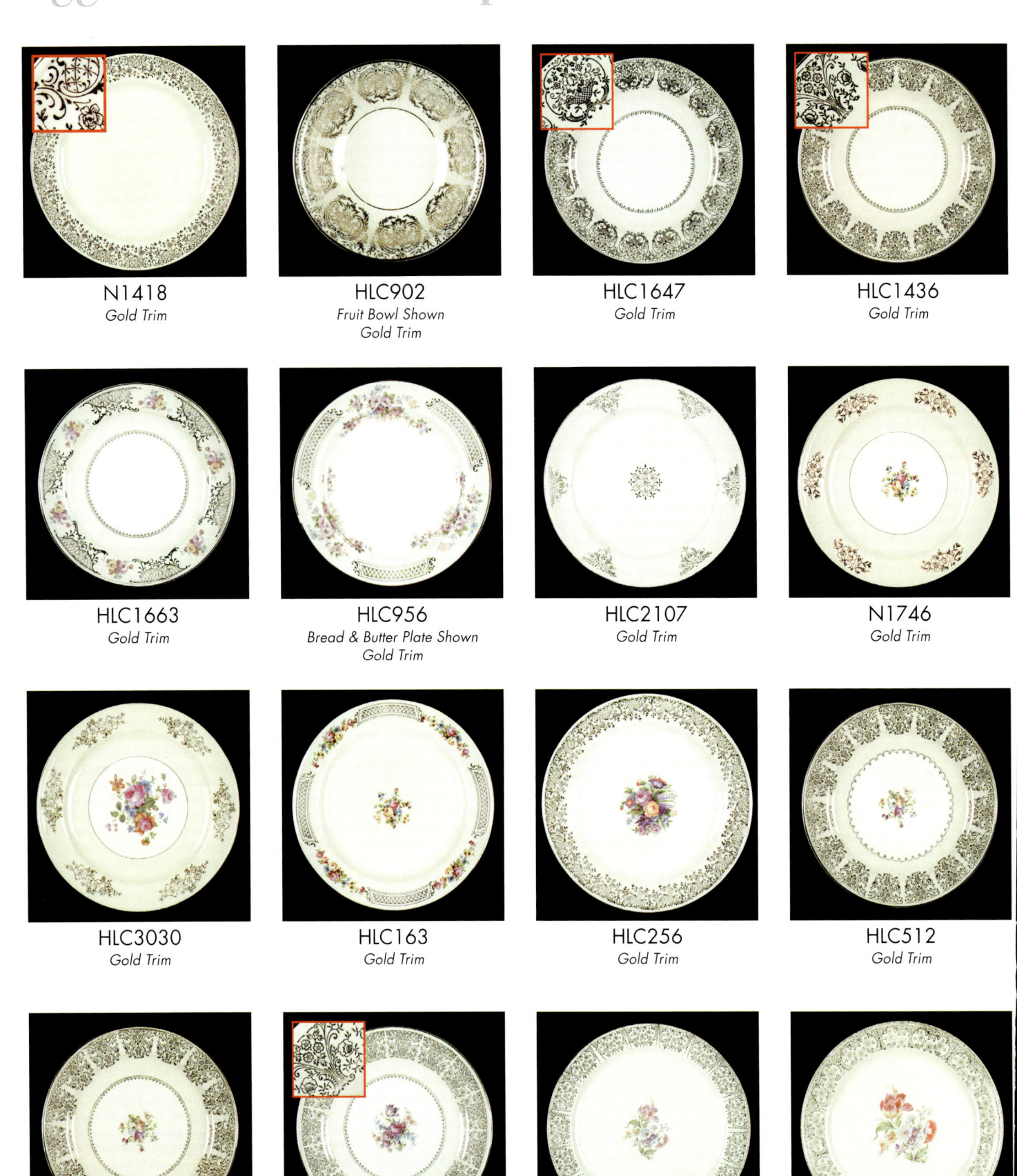

Eggshell Nautilus Shape (Gold Trim, Band or Gold Filigree)

N1418 *Gold Trim*	**HLC902** *Fruit Bowl Shown Gold Trim*	**HLC1647** *Gold Trim*	**HLC1436** *Gold Trim*
HLC1663 *Gold Trim*	**HLC956** *Bread & Butter Plate Shown Gold Trim*	**HLC2107** *Gold Trim*	**N1746** *Gold Trim*
HLC3030 *Gold Trim*	**HLC163** *Gold Trim*	**HLC256** *Gold Trim*	**HLC512** *Gold Trim*
HLC1703 *Gold Trim*	**HLC1650** *Gold Trim*	**HLC514G** *Chop Plate Shown Gold Trim*	**HLC514** *No Trim*

318

Eggshell Nautilus Shape (Gold Trim, Band or Gold Filigree)

HLC483
Luncheon Plate Shown
No Trim

HLC1406
No Trim

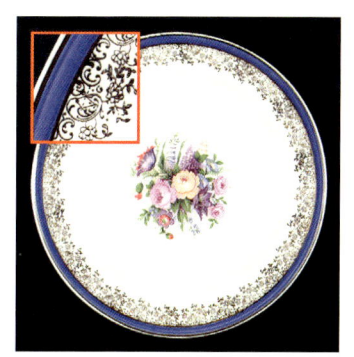

HLC986
Gold Trim

HLC755
Gold Trim

HLC1656
Gold Trim

HLC1214
Gold Trim

HLC1653
Gold Trim

HLC1395
Gold Trim

HLC1397
Gold Trim

HLC1396
Gold Trim

HLC522
Gold Trim

HLC1152
Gold Trim

HLC561
Gold Trim

HLC717
Gold Trim

HLC1195
Creamer Shown
Gold Trim

Eggshell Nautilus Shape (Floral Patterns with Gold Trim)

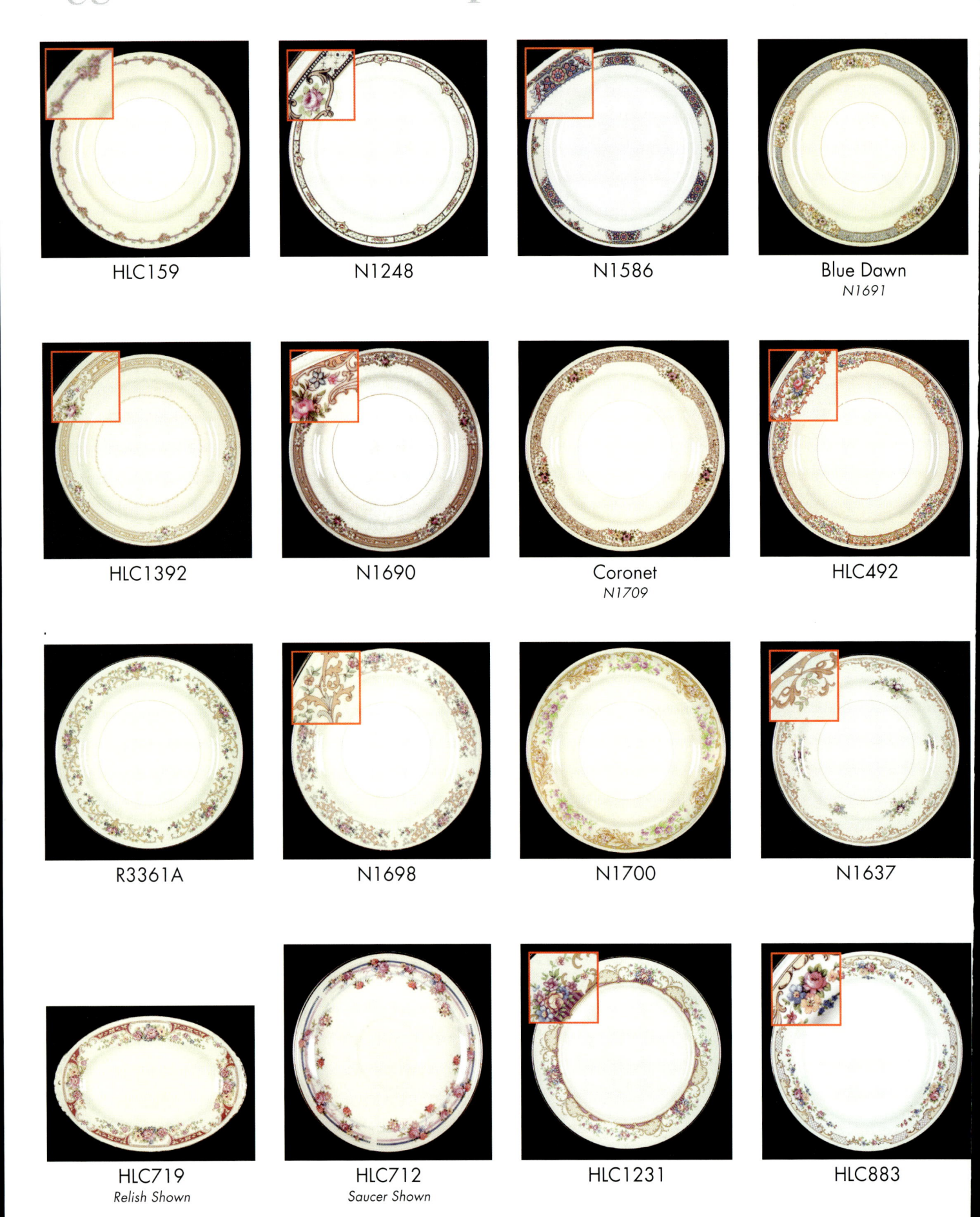

HLC159	N1248	N1586	Blue Dawn *N1691*
HLC1392	N1690	Coronet *N1709*	HLC492
R3361A	N1698	N1700	N1637
HLC719 *Relish Shown*	HLC712 *Saucer Shown*	HLC1231	HLC883

320

Eggshell Nautilus Shape (Floral Patterns with Gold Trim)

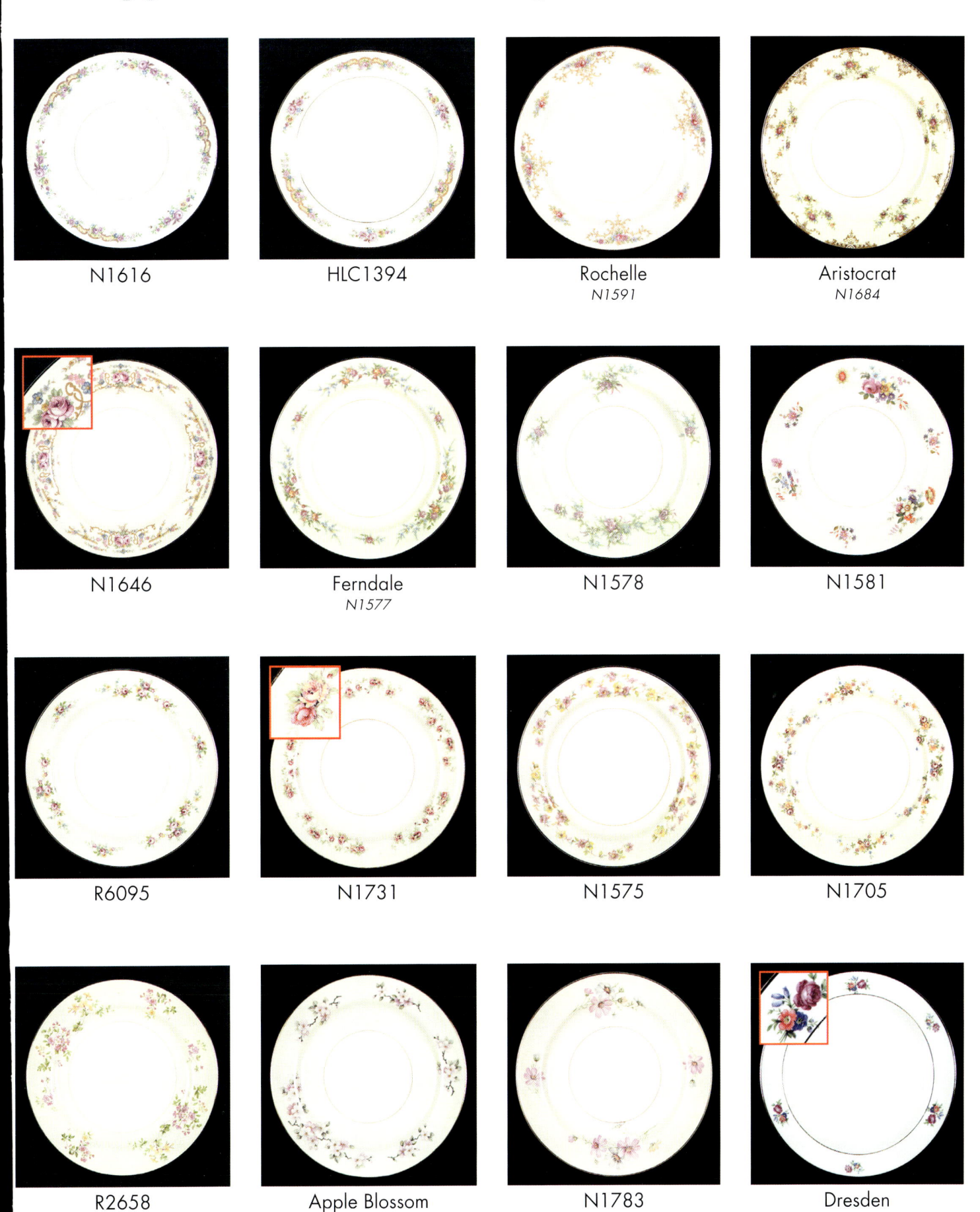

N1616	HLC1394	Rochelle *N1591*	Aristocrat *N1684*
N1646	Ferndale *N1577*	N1578	N1581
R6095	N1731	N1575	N1705
R2658	Apple Blossom *N1670*	N1783	Dresden *CP14* *by Cunningham & Pickett* *Luncheon Plate Shown*

321

Eggshell Nautilus Shape (Floral Patterns with Gold Trim)

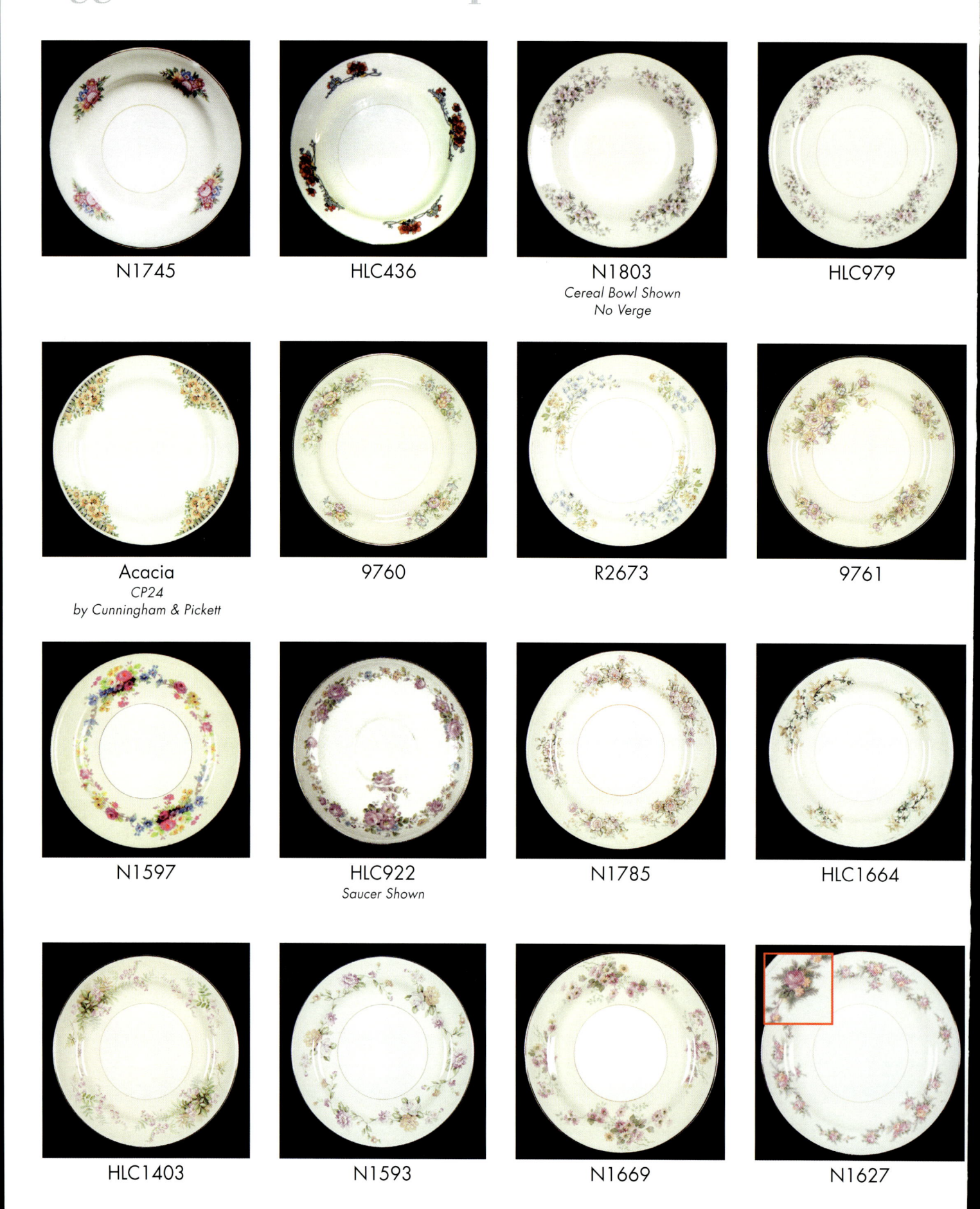

N1745	HLC436	N1803 *Cereal Bowl Shown No Verge*	HLC979
Acacia *CP24 by Cunningham & Pickett*	9760	R2673	9761
N1597	HLC922 *Saucer Shown*	N1785	HLC1664
HLC1403	N1593	N1669	N1627

322

Eggshell Nautilus Shape (Floral Patterns with Gold Trim)

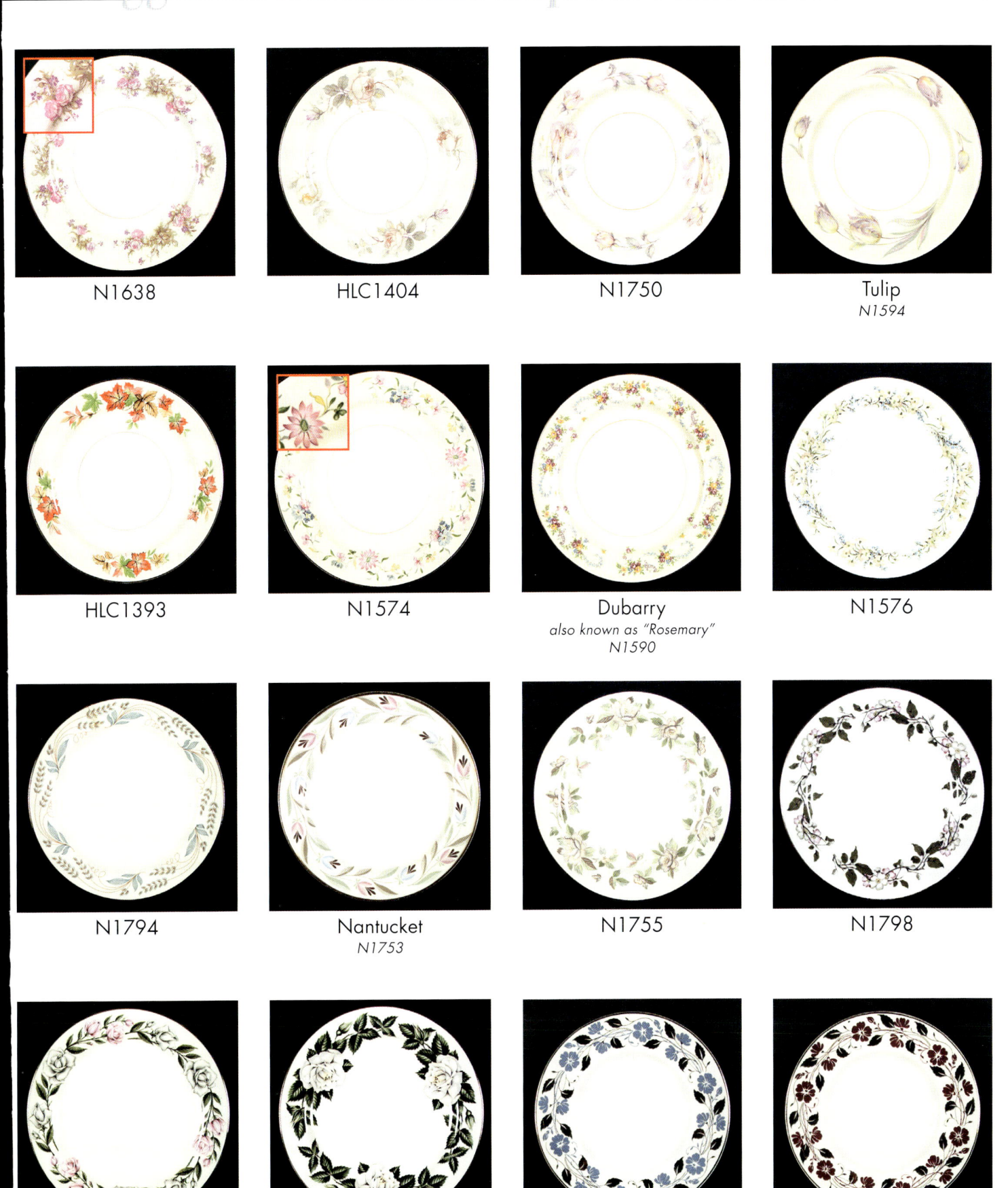

N1638	HLC1404	N1750	Tulip N1594
HLC1393	N1574	Dubarry also known as "Rosemary" N1590	N1576
N1794	Nantucket N1753	N1755	N1798
Minuet N1811	Nassau MW180	HLC1776	HLC1777

323

Eggshell Nautilus Shape (Floral Patterns with Gold Trim)

V2843	N1697	HLC1400￼Blue Band	N1732￼Gray Band
HLC1401￼Gray Band	N1580￼Pink Band	HLC784￼Blue Band	HLC1064￼Pink Band
HLC81￼Blue Band	HLC347￼Blue Band	HLC2007￼Green Verge	Belles Fleurs
N1769￼Pink Band	N1402￼No Verge	N1474￼Soup Bowl Shown	N1583

Eggshell Nautilus Shape (Floral Patterns with Gold Trim)

| HLC401 | N1405 | R8326C | Orchard
N1773 |

| Autumn | N1489 | HLC969 | Garland
CP5
by Cunningham & Pickett |

| HLC849 | N1838 | N1699 | Dresden
N1679 |

| Priscilla
N1639
by Household Institute | Gardenia
VM101 | HLC507 | N1807
Oval Platter Shown |

325

Eggshell Nautilus Shape (Floral Patterns with Gold Trim)

Bristol	HLC1187	B1316	HLC1271
VM8			

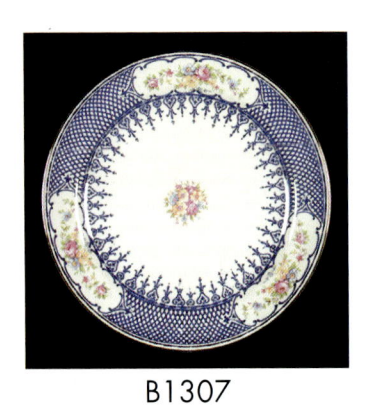

B1307

Eggshell Nautilus Shape (Platinum, Other Trim or No Trim)

N1221	N1219	N1439	N1539
Platinum Trim	*Platinum Trim*	*Platinum Trim*	*Platinum Trim*

Eggshell Nautilus Shape (Platinum, Other Trim or No Trim)

N1622 Platinum Trim	**N1675** Salad Plate Shown No Trim	**HLC2192** No Trim	**HLC1910** No Trim
HLC884 No Trim	**N1829** Platinum Trim	**HLC1405** No Trim	**HLC1225** No Trim
HLC1224 No Trim	**HLC1273** No Trim	**HLC1272** No Trim	**R3061A** No Trim
HLC1760 No Trim	**R2702** No Trim	**HLC1832** Yellow Trim	**HLC1866** Yellow Trim

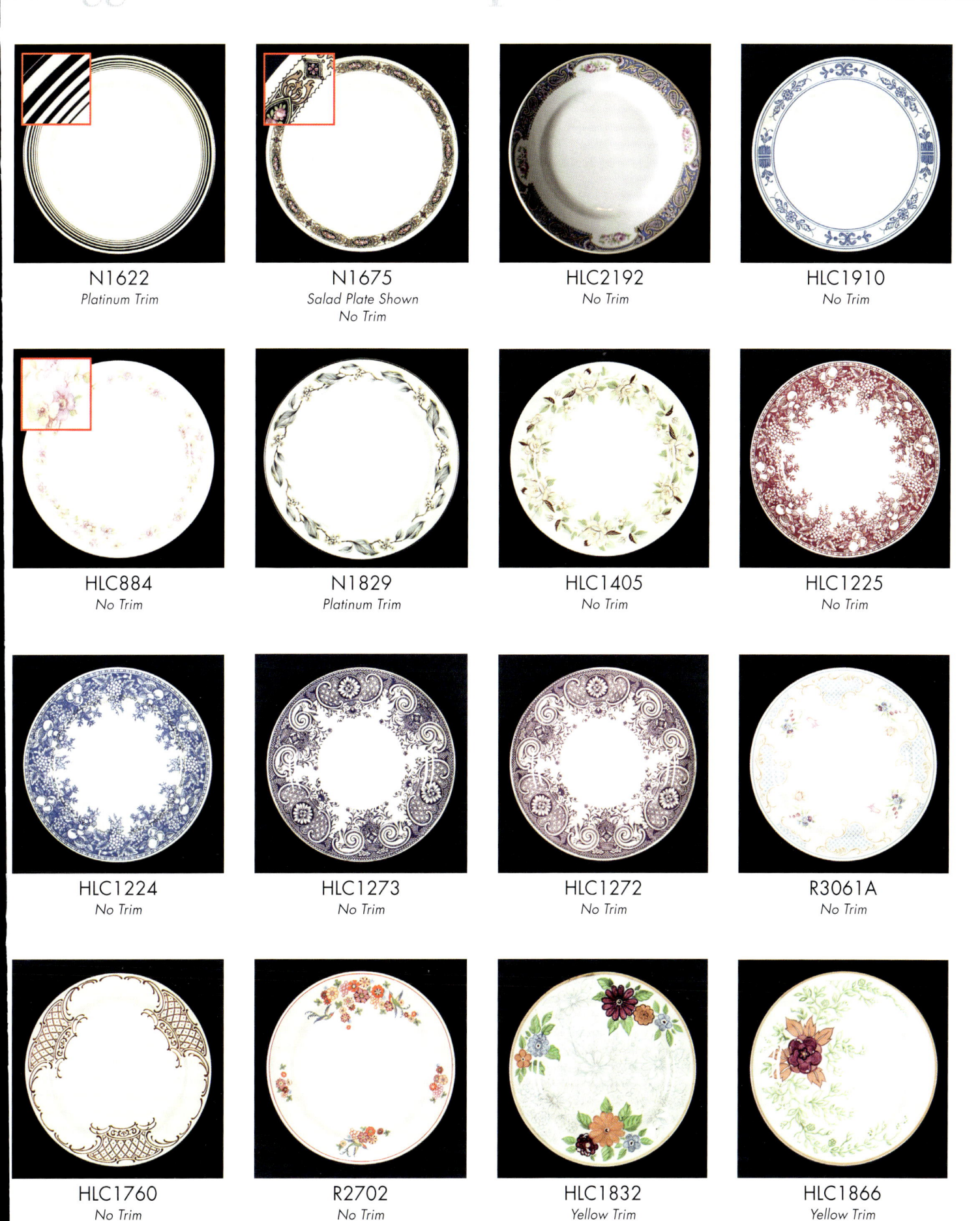

Eggshell Nautilus Shape (Platinum, Other Trim or No Trim)

HLC1092 No Trim	**HLC1944** No Trim	**N1481** Red Trim	**N1525** Blue Band No Trim
N1504 Blue Band No Trim	**Mexicana** N1524 Blue Band No Trim	**Colonial Kitchen** Red Band No Trim	**Colonial Kitchen** Red Trim
R2346 Blue Band No Trim	**N1470** Blue Band No Trim	**HLC1792** Bread & Butter Plate Shown Red Band No Trim	**HLC2014** Red Verge No Trim
HLC943 Red Trim	**N1580N** No Trim	**HLC1563** No Trim	**Lily Of The Valley** N1733 Green Band Platinum Trim

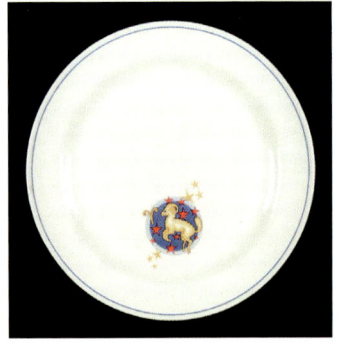

328

Eggshell Nautilus Shape (Platinum, Other Trim or No Trim)

HLC1876 Yellow Trim	**HLC1878** Yellow Trim	**HLC425** No Trim	**N1585** Luncheon Plate Shown Platinum Band No Trim
HLC3120 Blue Band No Trim	**HLC2118** Blue Trim	**N1458** Platinum Trim	**HLC1402** No Trim
Magnolia Gray Band No Trim	**N1775** Gray Band No Trim	**HLC1409** No Trim	**HLC759** Gray Band No Trim
R5431 Black Band Green Trim	**HLC999** Blue Band No Trim	**HLC720** Soup Bowl Shown Gray Band No Trim	**HLC1031** Chop Plate Shown Red Trim

Eggshell Nautilus Shape (Platinum, Other Trim or No Trim)

R5763
Blue Trim

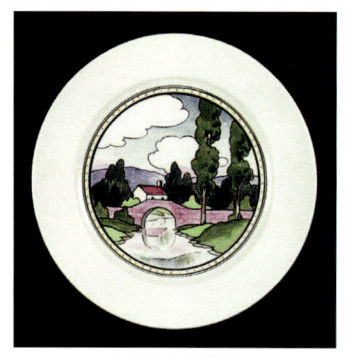

HLC1907
No Trim

HLC1838
No Trim

HLC1858
No Trim

HLC1796
No Trim

HLC1407
No Trim

HLC1526
Oval Platter Shown
No Trim

HLC1646
No Trim

HLC1598
No Trim

Della Robia
Bread & Butter Plate Shown
No Trim

R3274A
No Trim

HLC1230
No Trim

Saint Clement
Yellow Trim

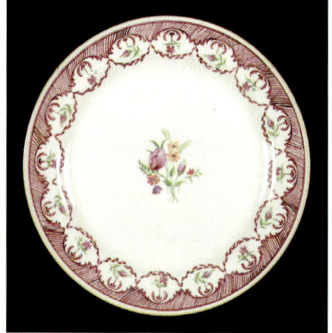

Les Islettes
2690
Yellow Trim

Bordeaux
2689
Mustard Trim

HLC1847
Yellow Trim

Eggshell Nautilus Shape (Platinum, Other Trim or No Trim)

HLC1872 Yellow Trim	**HLC1553** Yellow Trim	**Aprey** 2721 No Trim	**HLC1829** No Trim
HLC1908 No Trim	**La Rochelle** No Trim	**HLC1719** No Trim	**HLC1268** No Trim
HLC1417 No Trim	**R3318A** Mustard Trim	**R3311A** No Trim	**HLC1730** No Trim
Sinceny No Trim	**HLC1830** Yellow Trim	**HLC1865** Yellow Trim	**HLC1863** Yellow Trim

Eggshell Nautilus Shape (Platinum, Other Trim or No Trim)

HLC1849	HLC1828	HLC1827	HLC1848
Yellow Trim	Yellow Trim	Orange Trim	Yellow Trim

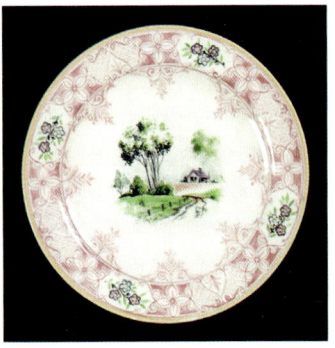

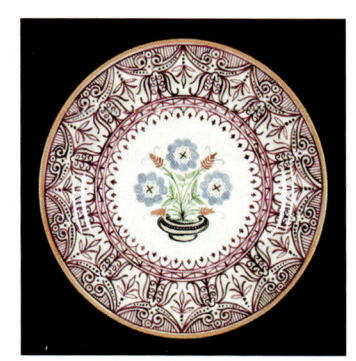

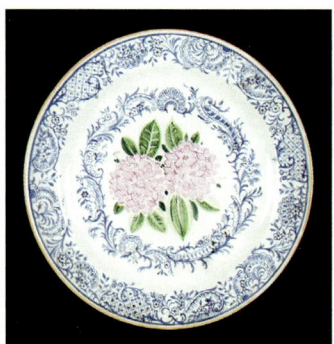

HLC1901	HLC1857	HLC1854	HLC1853
Yellow Trim	Yellow Trim	Yellow Trim	Orange Trim

HLC1862	HLC1900	State Flower Series	State Flower Series
Yellow Trim	Yellow Trim	2545 Multi-Motif (West Virginia) Yellow Trim	2545 Multi-Motif (Alaska & Ohio) Yellow Trim

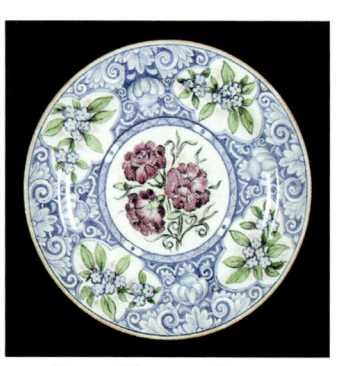

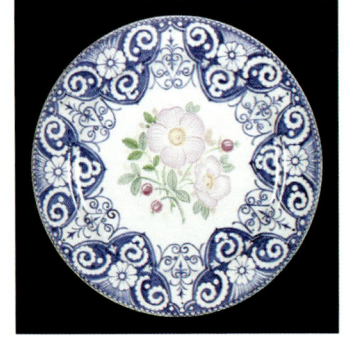

State Flowers Series	HLC1902	Lille	R3341A
2545 Multi-Motif (Georgia) Yellow Trim	Yellow Trim	Yellow Trim	No Trim

332

Eggshell Nautilus Shape (Platinum, Other Trim or No Trim)

HLC1864
No Trim

HLC1264
No Trim

HLC1226
No Trim

HLC1723
No Trim

HLC1722
No Trim

HLC1227
No Trim

Famous Old Ships–Red
Floral Border
Multi-Motif
No Trim

Famous Old Ships–Red
Shell Border
Multi-Motif
No Trim

Famous Old Ships–Blue
Shell Border
Multi-Motif
No Trim

Famous Old Ships–Mulberry
Shell Border
Multi-Motif
No Trim

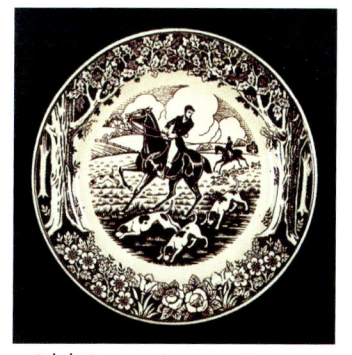

Old Sport Scene–Brown
Multi-Motif
No Trim

HLC1228
No Trim

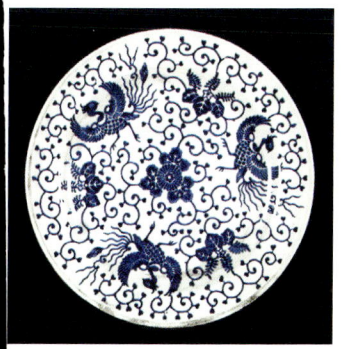

HLC1229
No Trim

HLC1265
No Trim

Eggshell Nautilus Shape with Eggshell Cavalier Hollowware

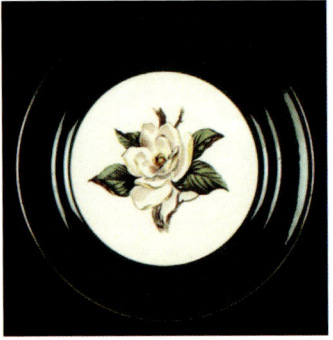

Jaderose
by Lifetime China
Gold Trim

Burgundy
by Lifetime China
Gold Trim

Nautilus Shape with Charm House, Eggshell Nautilus & Rhythm Hollowware

Lady Stratford
Gold Trim

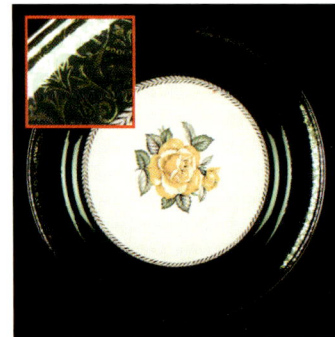

Lady Greenbriar
AS1
Gold Trim

Rhythm Shape with Eggshell Cavalier & Eggshell Nautilus Hollowware

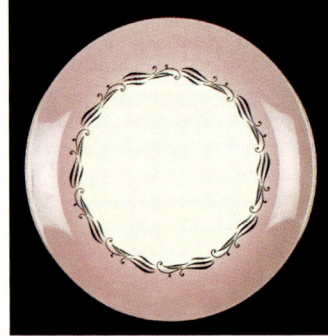

Sunrise–Pink
by Cunningham & Pickett
Gold Trim

Gold Crown
by Lifetime China
Gold Trim

Lynnwood
by Century Service Corp.
Platinum Trim

Autumn Gold
by Century Service Corp.
Gold Trim

Pink Radiance
No Trim

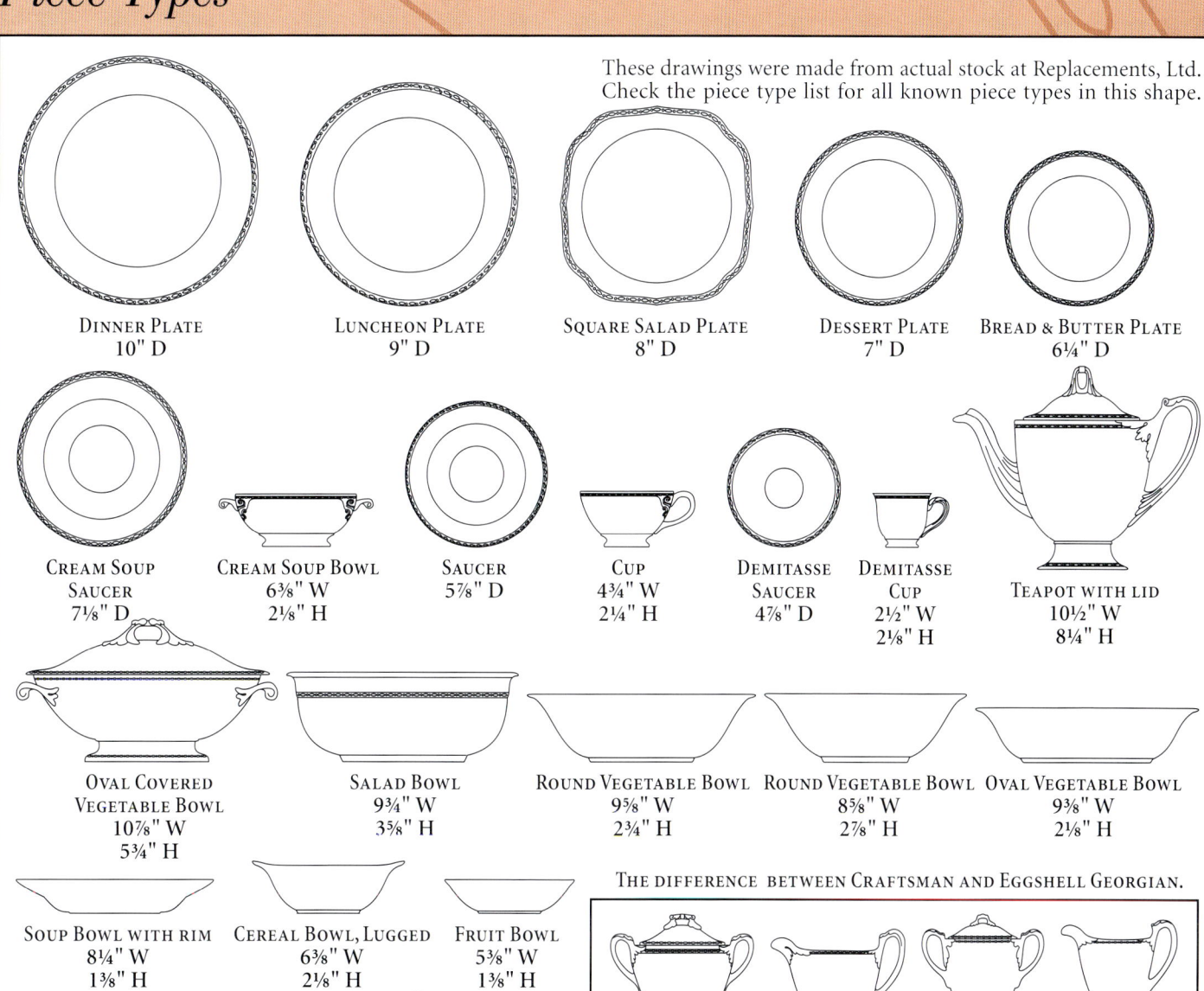

EGGSHELL GEORGIAN

Piece Types

These drawings were made from actual stock at Replacements, Ltd. Check the piece type list for all known piece types in this shape.

Dinner Plate 10" D	**Luncheon Plate** 9" D	**Square Salad Plate** 8" D	**Dessert Plate** 7" D	**Bread & Butter Plate** 6¼" D

Cream Soup Saucer 7⅛" D	**Cream Soup Bowl** 6⅜" W 2⅛" H	**Saucer** 5⅞" D	**Cup** 4¾" W 2¼" H	**Demitasse Saucer** 4⅞" D	**Demitasse Cup** 2½" W 2⅛" H	**Teapot with lid** 10½" W 8¼" H

Oval Covered Vegetable Bowl 10⅞" W 5¾" H	**Salad Bowl** 9¾" W 3⅝" H	**Round Vegetable Bowl** 9⅝" W 2¾" H	**Round Vegetable Bowl** 8⅝" W 2⅞" H	**Oval Vegetable Bowl** 9⅜" W 2⅛" H

Soup Bowl with rim 8¼" W 1⅜" H	**Cereal Bowl, Lugged** 6⅜" W 2⅛" H	**Fruit Bowl** 5⅜" W 1⅜" H

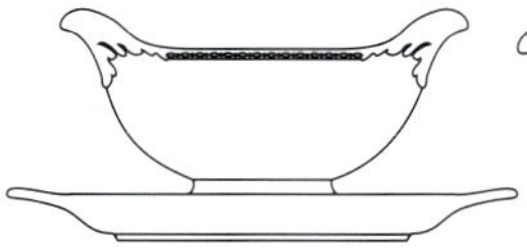

The difference between Craftsman and Eggshell Georgian.

Gravy/Sauce Boat with attached Underplate 9¼" W x 4⅛" H	**Gravy/Sauce Boat** 8¼" W x 4¼" H	**Salt & Pepper Set** 2" W 3⅝" H

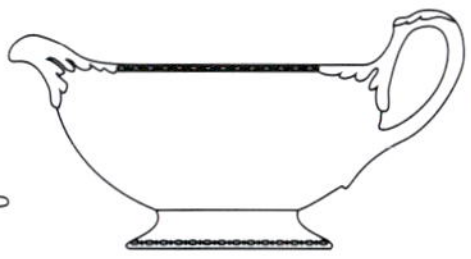

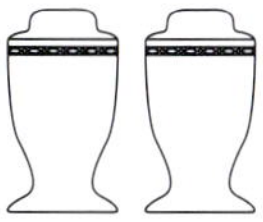

Sugar Bowl with lid 6" W x 5" H **Eggshell Georgian**	**Creamer** 5⅝" W 4⅜" H **Eggshell Georgian**	**Sugar Bowl with lid** 5¼" W x 5⅛" H **Craftsman**	**Creamer** 5" W 4⅞" H **Craftsman**

Homer Laughlin

EGGSHELL GEORGIAN   1937 – 1959 or later

In the *Homer Laughlin Pound Sterling Price Booklet of 1937*, we found the first mention of the Georgian shaped lines. They were offered that year with 70 decorations/patterns.

Reporting on a display at the Vanderbilt Hotel, *China, Glass & Lamps*, July 1940, wrote: "A large group of 50 decorations of the new and good-looking 'Georgian Eggshell' shape in dinnerware, with its delicate embossment at the edge line and its footed hollow pieces. Among the patterns are bands of coin gold over the embossment, maroon shoulder bands against ivory; gold scrolls and floral borders, most of them conventional styles so much in demand by the general public."

Frederick Rhead wrote in his journal, December 29, 1940, a passage titled "style data on Homer Laughlin Georgian Eggshell Tableware." It reads as follows:

> "The shape is typically English and styled after the beautiful formal silver tableware made during the reign of the four George's between the years 1714-1820… the shape properly belongs to this period and would style perfectly with the furniture of Chippendale and… others. The patterns G-3313; G-3315; G-3316 and G-3324 are styled after the fine hand painted wares of this period while G-3327 leans more to the early French porcelain decorations."

At the height of World War II, traditional china from Europe and Asia were not available and the opportunities to market a line like Eggshell Georgian seemed unlimited. By 1942-43, Montgomery Ward offered Viceroy, Monarch, Formal, and Cashmere on Eggshell Georgian in the Fall-Winter selection. The 1944 and 1945 Spring & Summer catalogs offered Cashmere, Viceroy, Monarch, Kingston, and Rambler Rose.

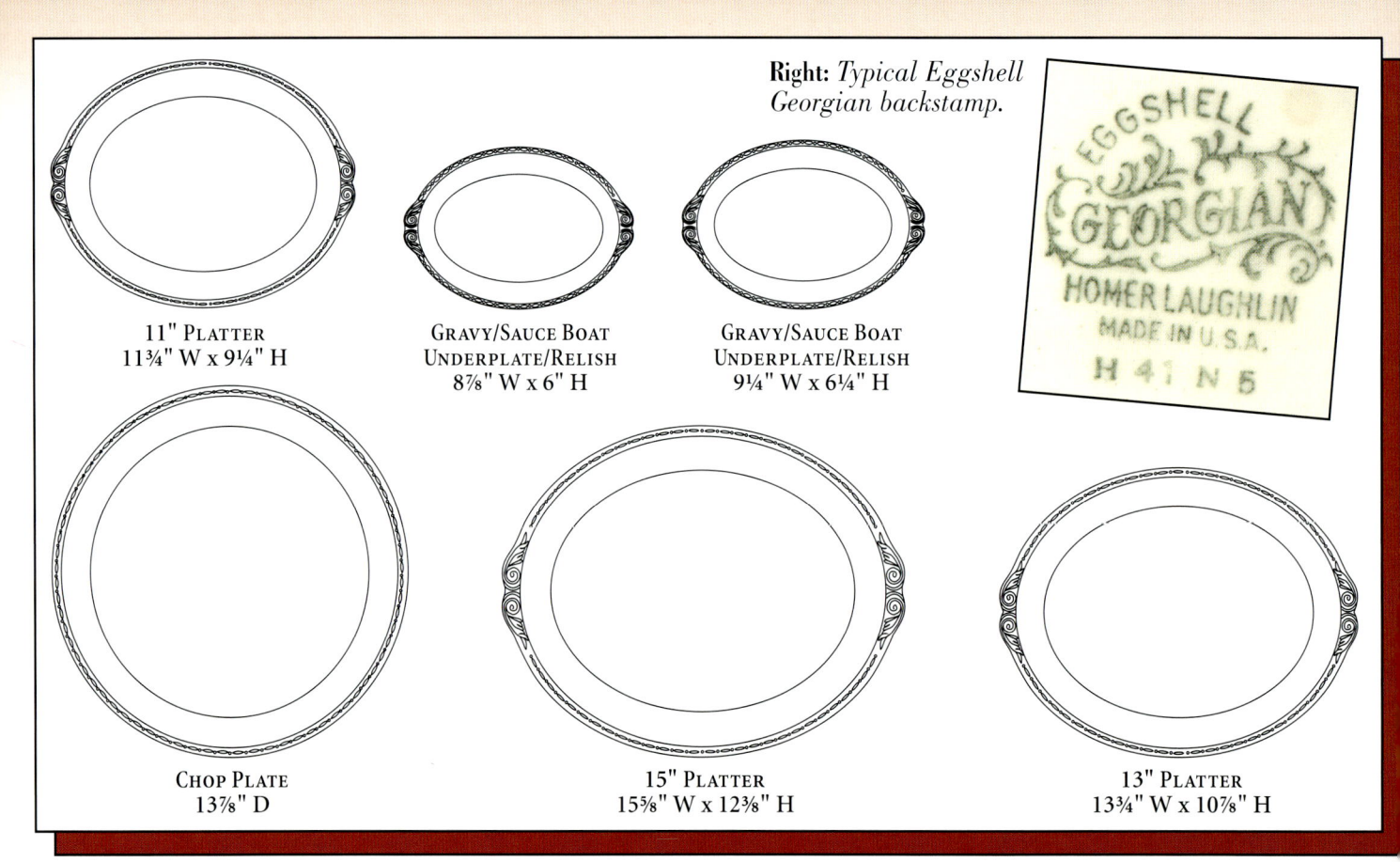

Right: *Typical Eggshell Georgian backstamp.*

11" Platter
11¾" W x 9¼" H

Gravy/Sauce Boat Underplate/Relish
8⅞" W x 6" H

Gravy/Sauce Boat Underplate/Relish
9¼" W x 6¼" H

Chop Plate
13⅞" D

15" Platter
15⅜" W x 12⅜" H

13" Platter
13¾" W x 10⅞" H

Eggshell Georgian Shape

Top left: *Viceroy pattern; Montgomery Ward Catalog, 1943 Spring & Summer.*
Top right: *Cashmere pattern; Montgomery Ward Catalog, 1945-1946 Fall & Winter.*
Middle left: *Marilyn and Countess patterns; Sears, Roebuck & Co. Catalog, 1943-44 Fall & Winter.*
Middle right: *Monarch pattern; Montgomery Ward Catalog, 1944 Spring & Summer.*
Bottom left: *Rambler Rose pattern; Montgomery Ward Catalog, 1944 Spring & Summer.*
Bottom Right: *Kingston pattern; Montgomery Ward Catalog, 1945-1946 Fall & Winter.*

Homer Laughlin

Top left: *Countess* pattern; Two Oval Platters, Oval Covered Vegetable Bowl, Gravy/Sauce Boat, Fruit Bowl, and Oval Vegetable Bowl.
Top right: *Cashmere* pattern; Dinner Plate, Salad Plate, and Cup & Saucer Set.
Middle left: *Kingston* pattern; Square Salad Plate, Sugar Bowl with lid, Creamer, Gravy/Sauce Boat with unattached Underplate.
Middle right: *Cotillion* pattern; Gravy/Sauce Boat, Dinner Plate, Dessert Plate, Cup & Saucer Set, and Gravy/Sauce Boat Underplate/Relish.
Bottom left: *HLC236* pattern; Soup Bowl with rim, Square Salad Plate, Dinner Plate, Fruit Bowl, Oval Vegetable Bowl, and Creamer.

Eggshell Georgian Shape

Eggshell Georgian Piece Type List

From 1933 Homer Laughlin Catalog and Confirmed Actual Pieces

Bowl, Cereal Lugged, 6⅜ inches
Bowl, Cream Soup & Saucer Set
  Bowl, 6⅜ inches
  Saucer, 7⅛ inches
Bowl, Fruit, 5⅜ inches
Bowl, Salad, 9¾ inches
Bowl, Soup with rim
Bowl, Vegetable Oval (Baker), 9⅜ inches
Bowl, Vegetable Oval (Baker), 10 inches*
Bowl, Vegetable Oval Covered, 10⅞ inches
Bowl, Vegetable Round (Nappy), 8⅝ inches
Bowl, Vegetable Round (Nappy), 9⅝ inches
Creamer
Cup & Saucer Set
  Cup, 2¼ inches
  Saucer, 5⅞ inches
Cup & Saucer Set, Demitasse
  Cup, 2⅜ inches
  Saucer, 4⅞ inches
Gravy/Sauce Boat
Gravy/Sauce Boat with attached Underplate (Fast Stand)
Gravy/Sauce Boat Underplate/Relish, 8⅞ inches
Gravy/Sauce Boat Underplate/Relish, 9¼ inches
Plate, 8 inches*
Plate, Bread & Butter, 6¼ inches
Plate, Chop, 13⅞ inches
Plate, Dessert, 7 inches
Plate, Dinner, 10 inches
Plate, Luncheon, 9 inches
Plate, Salad Square, 8 inches
Platter, 11¾ inches
Platter, 13¾ inches
Platter, 15⅝ inches
Salt & Pepper Set
Sugar Bowl with lid
Teapot with lid
*Reported but not confirmed.

Top right: *G3370 pattern; Teapot with lid.* **Top left:** *G3370 pattern; Demitasse Cup & Saucer Set.* **Bottom left:** *G3370 pattern; Salad Bowl.* **Bottom right:** *Chatham pattern; Square Salad Plate, Dinner Plate, Oval Platter, Cup & Saucer Set, Gravy/Sauce Boat with unattached Underplate, Round Vegetable Bowl, Fruit Bowl, and Soup Bowl with rim.*

Eggshell Georgian Shape (Gold Trim or Gold Band/Design)

G3343 Gold Trim	 **HLC1677** Gold Trim	 **Viceroy** G3330, G3571 Gold Trim	 **G3486** Gold Trim
 **G3324** No Trim	 **HLC1678** Gold Trim	 **HLC1681** Gold Trim	 **HLC516** Gold Trim
 **HLC1440** Gold Trim	 **G3332** No Trim	 **R3568** Gold Trim	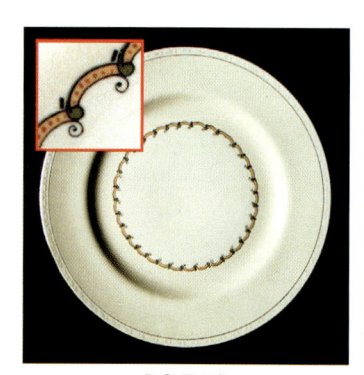 **R3569** Gold Trim
 **HLC219** No Trim	 **HLC1680** Gold Trim	 **HLC1439** Gold Trim	 **HLC1000** Gold Trim

Eggshell Georgian Shape (Gold Trim or Gold Band/Design)

G3386 Round Vegetable Bowl Shown *Gold Trim*	**HLC1661** *Gold Trim*	**HLC2119** *Gold Trim*	**HLC133** *Gold Trim*
Monarch *Gold Trim*	**Monarch** *Gold Trim*	**HLC240** *Gold Trim*	**HLC426** *Gold Trim*
HLC478 *Gold Trim*	**HLC2164** *Gold Trim*	**G3353** *Gold Trim*	**HLC867** *Gold Trim*
G3407 *Gold Trim*	**G3434** *Gold Trim*	**G142** *Gold Trim*	**Briarcliffe** G3385 *Gold Trim*

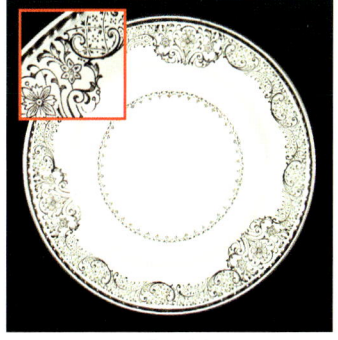

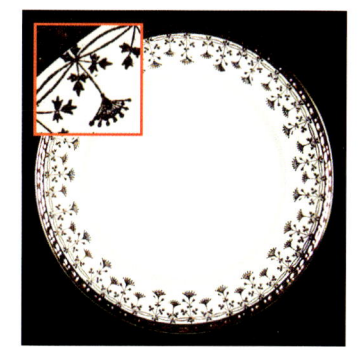

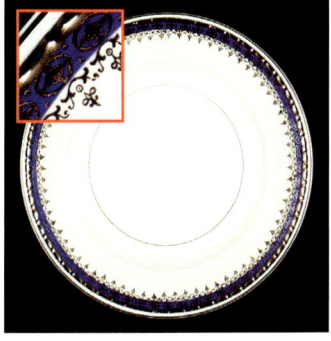

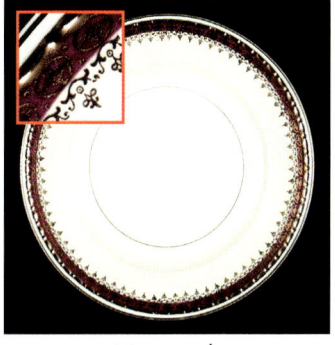

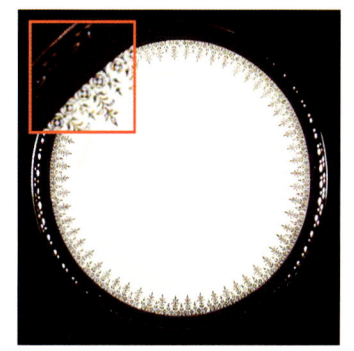

Eggshell Georgian Shape (Gold Trim or Gold Band/Design)

HLC1267 Gold Trim	**G138** Gold Trim	**HLC1442** Gold Trim	**HLC1049** Gold Trim
HLC1441 Gold Trim	**G3852** Gold Trim	**B3563A** Gold Trim	**Belmont** G177, G3400 Gold Trim
HLC760 Fruit Bowl Shown Gold Trim	**G3497** Oval Vegetable Bowl Shown Gold Trim	**HLC3004** Gold Trim	**Cashmere** G3391 also a Style House pattern Gold Trim
Countess G3432 Gold Trim	**G3523** Gold Trim	**HLC880** Gold Trim	**G3380** Gold Trim

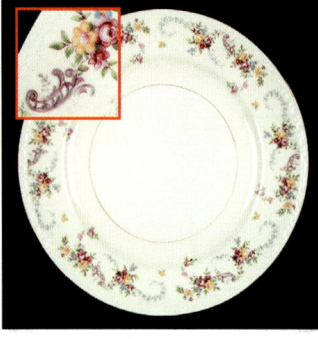

Eggshell Georgian Shape (Gold Trim or Gold Band/Design)

G3516 *Gold Trim*	**HLC376** *Gold Trim*	**G3351/G3444** *Gold Trim*	**G3381** *Gold Trim*
April G3535 *Gold Trim*	**Greenbriar** G3499 *Gold Trim*	**HLC407** *Gold Trim*	**HLC191** *Bread & Butter Plate Shown* *Gold Trim*
G3443 *Gold Trim*	**R1629** *Gold Trim*	**HLC372** *Gold Trim*	**G3303** *Gold Trim*
Cotillion G3517 *Gold Trim*	**G93** *Gold Trim*	**Forget-Me-Not** VM108 *Gold Trim*	**HLC605** *Gold Band* *No Trim*

343

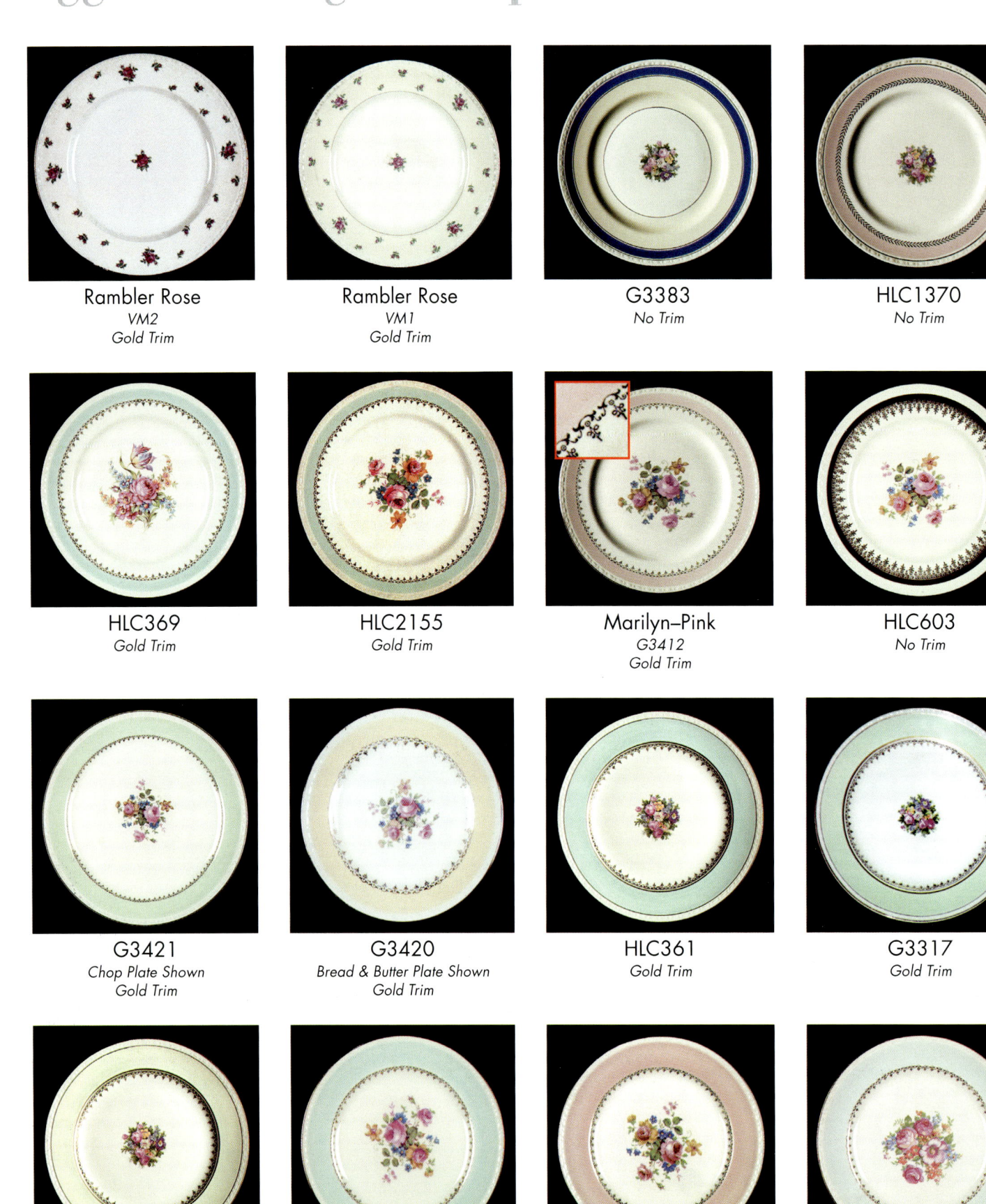

Eggshell Georgian Shape (Gold Trim or Gold Band/Design)

Rambler Rose VM2 Gold Trim	**Rambler Rose** VM1 Gold Trim	**G3383** No Trim	**HLC1370** No Trim
HLC369 Gold Trim	**HLC2155** Gold Trim	**Marilyn–Pink** G3412 Gold Trim	**HLC603** No Trim
G3421 Chop Plate Shown Gold Trim	**G3420** Bread & Butter Plate Shown Gold Trim	**HLC361** Gold Trim	**G3317** Gold Trim
G3315 Gold Trim	**Marilyn–Blue** G3419 Gold Trim	**Marilyn–Pink** G3418 Gold Trim	**HLC223** Gold Trim

Eggshell Georgian Shape (Gold Trim or Gold Band/Design)

Chateau *G3468* Gold Trim	 **G3467** Gold Trim	 **G3439** Gold Trim	 **HLC2090** Gold Trim
 **HLC180** Gold Trim	 **Arcadia** *G3522* Gold Trim	 **Chatham** *SR114* Gold Trim	 **HLC474** Gold Trim
 **HLC1645** Gold Trim	 **DP296B** Gold Trim	 **DP296A** Gold Trim	 **R3605A** Gold Trim
 **G3401** Gold Trim	 **G3369** Gold Trim	 **HLC562** Gold Trim	 **R6109** Gold Trim

Eggshell Georgian Shape (Gold Trim or Gold Band/Design)

HLC479 *Gold Trim*	**G3356** *Gold Trim*	**R6105** *Gold Trim*	**English Regency** *G3357* *Gold Trim*
R6102 *Gold Trim*	**HLC742** *Luncheon Plate Shown* *Gold Trim*	**R6106** *Gold Trim*	**HLC248** *Gold Trim*
HLC2095 *Gold Trim*	**HLC791** *Gold Trim*	**G3525** *Gold Trim*	**Calirose** *Gold Trim*
HLC130 *Bread & Butter Plate Shown* *Gold Trim*	**HLC1688** *No Trim*	**G3378** *No Trim*	**HLC757** *Gold Trim*

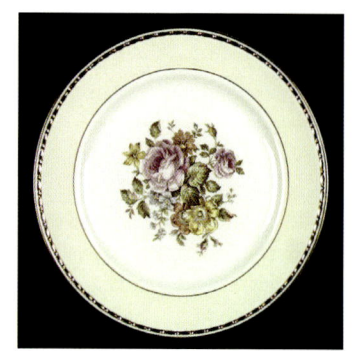

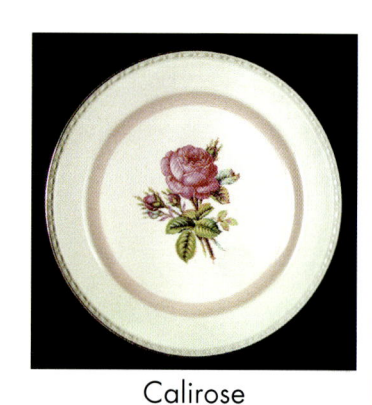

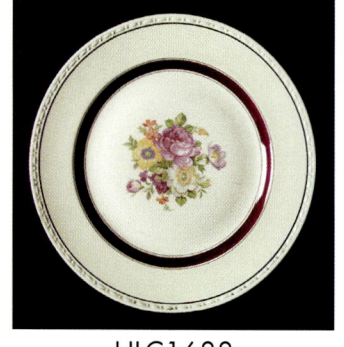

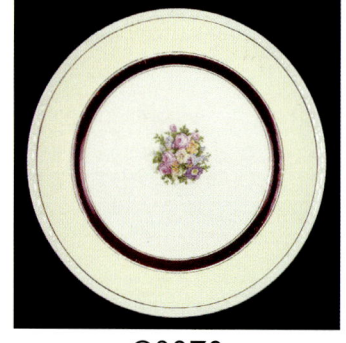

Eggshell Georgian Shape (Gold Trim or Gold Band/Design)

G3388 *Gold Trim*	**HLC1644** *Gold Trim*	**HLC480** *Bread & Butter Plate Shown* *Gold Trim*	**G3384** *Gold Trim*
R6111 *Gold Trim*	**Kingston** *G3459* *Gold Trim*	**HLC1367** *Gold Trim*	**G3320** *Gold Trim*
HLC197 *Gold Trim*	**R8617** *Gold Trim*	**HLC1026** *Soup Bowl Shown* *Gold Trim*	**G3453** *Square Salad Plate Shown* *Gold Trim*
G3549 *Gold Trim*	**HLC1845** *Gold Trim*	**G3535** *SR115* *Gold Trim*	**HLC1033** *No Trim*

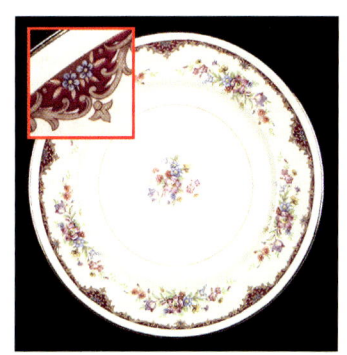

347

Eggshell Georgian Shape (Gold Trim or Gold Band/Design)

G3528 *Gold Trim*	**V2750** *Gold Trim*	**HLC1687** *Gold Trim*	**G3436** *Gold Trim*
R3656A *Gold Band No Trim*	**HLC1004** *No Verge Gold Trim*	**Bombay** *G3461 Gold Trim*	**Bristol** *Gold Trim*
HLC236 *Gold Trim*	**LEZ2** *by Le Noir Pitcher Shown Gold Trim*	**LEZ3** *by Le Noir Teapot Shown Gold Trim*	**LEZ1** *by Le Noir Square Salad Plate Shown Gold Trim*
HLC82 *Bread & Butter Plate Shown Gold Trim*	**HLC1708** *Gold Trim*	**HLC1521** *Gold Trim*	**HLC135** *Gold Trim*

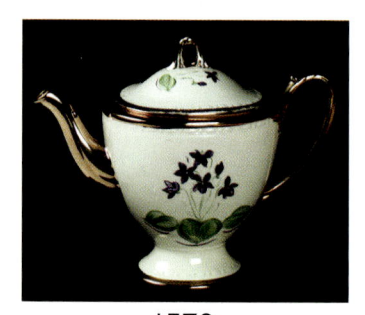

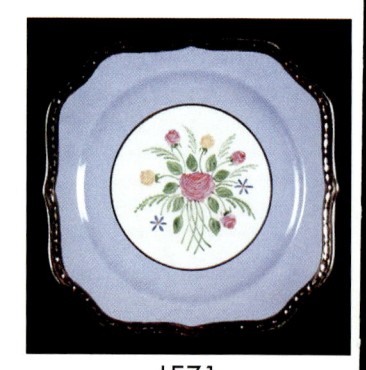

Eggshell Georgian Shape (Gold Trim or Gold Band/Design)

HLC804
Gold Trim

HLC485
Gold Trim

ATA5
by Atlas China
Bread & Butter Plate Shown
Gold Trim

HLC1135
Square Salad Plate Shown
Gold Trim

HLC3106
Gold Trim

HLC586
Gold Trim

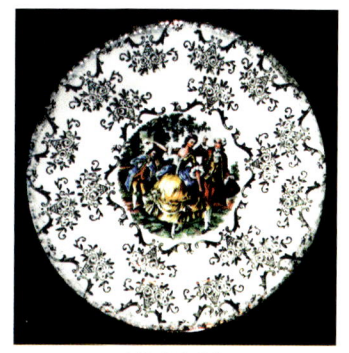

HLC638
Gold Trim

HLC2135
Oval Platter Shown
No Trim

HLC777
Bread & Butter Plate Shown
Gold Trim

HLC2158
Gold Trim

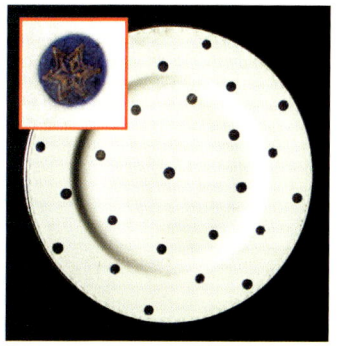

HLC1675
Gold Trim

Eggshell Georgian Shape (No Trim, Platinum or Other Trim)

Eggshell Georgian *No Trim*	HLC1541 *No Trim*	HLC1565 *No Trim*	HLC1635 *No Trim*
HLC1542 *No Trim*	HLC1633 *No Trim*	HLC1634 *No Trim*	HLC1543 *No Trim*
HLC134 *Platinum Trim*	HLC1606 *Red Trim*	HLC1438 *Green Trim*	HLC1676 *Platinum Trim*
HLC696 *No Trim*	HLC1679 *No Trim*	HLC1478 *No Trim*	HLC251 *Bread & Butter Plate Shown* *No Trim*

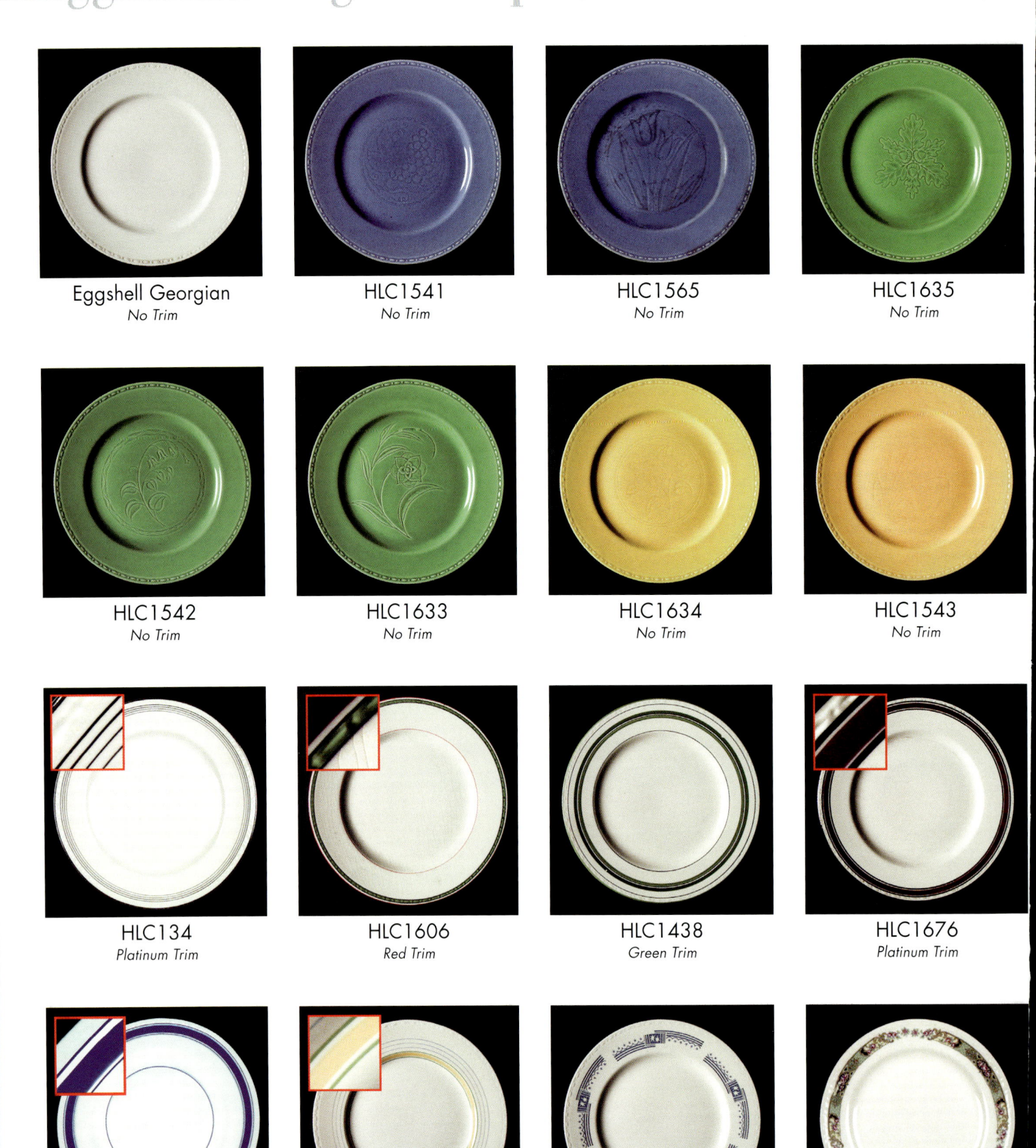

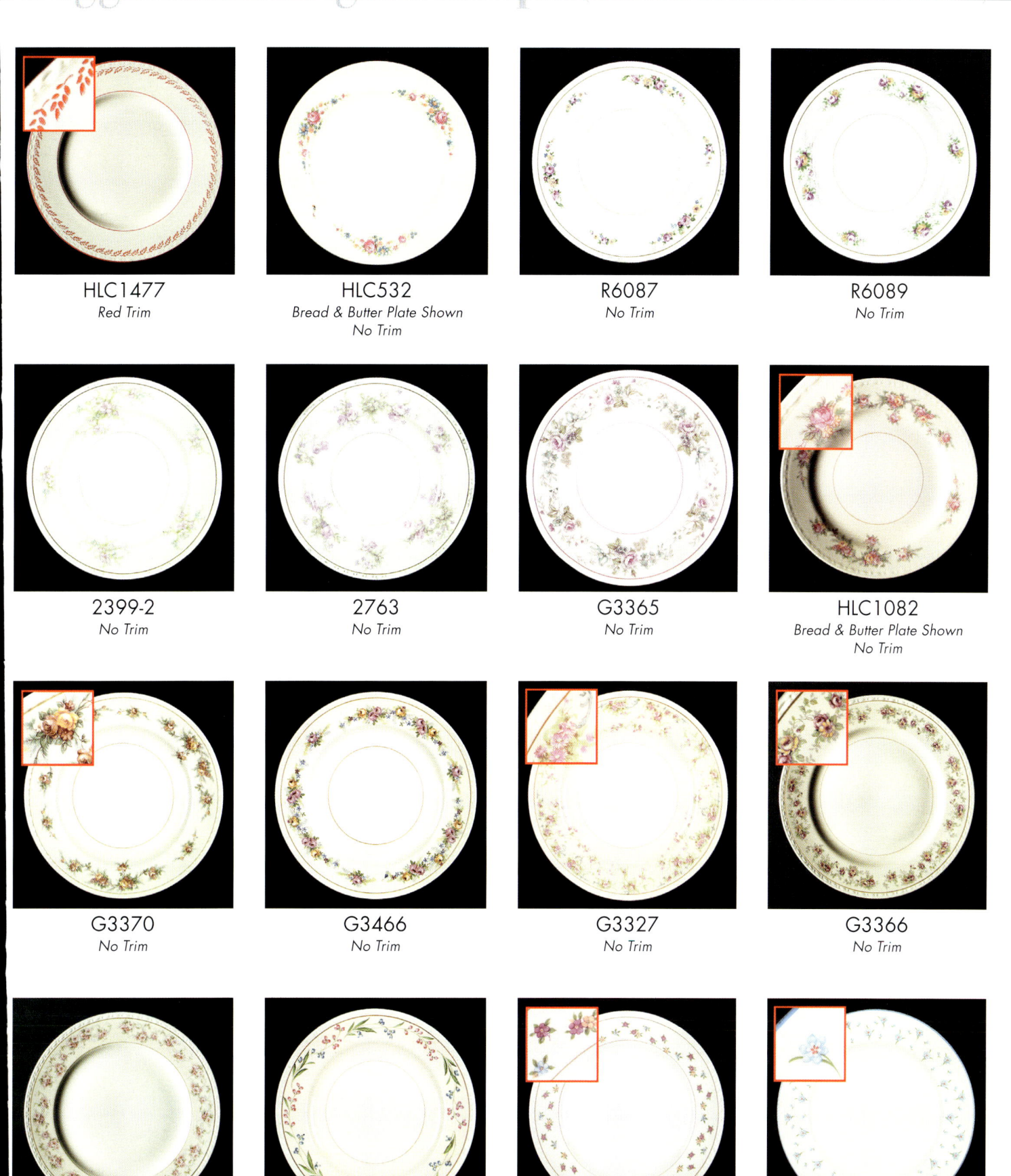

Eggshell Georgian Shape (No Trim, Platinum or Other Trim)

HLC1477 Red Trim	**HLC532** Bread & Butter Plate Shown No Trim	**R6087** No Trim	**R6089** No Trim
2399-2 No Trim	**2763** No Trim	**G3365** No Trim	**HLC1082** Bread & Butter Plate Shown No Trim
G3370 No Trim	**G3466** No Trim	**G3327** No Trim	**G3366** No Trim
2309 No Trim	**HLC374** No Trim	**Moselle** G3302 No Trim	**Forget-Me-Not** Blue Trim

Eggshell Georgian Shape (No Trim, Platinum or Other Trim)

G3304 No Trim	**G3335** Bread & Butter Plate Shown Mustard Trim	**HLC1369** No Trim	**HLC1993** Cup Shown No Trim
G3318 No Trim	**G3371** No Trim	**Norway Rose** by Cunningham & Pickett Platinum Trim	**G3331** No Trim
HLC2177 No Trim	**R3603A** No Trim	**R3606A** No Trim	**R3610A** No Trim
G3518 No Trim	**HLC1437** No Trim	**HLC994** No Trim	**HLC261** No Trim

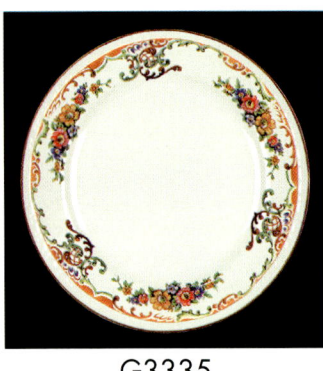

Eggshell Georgian Shape (No Trim, Platinum or Other Trim)

HLC993
No Trim

HLC252
Oval Platter Shown
No Trim

HLC359
No Trim

HLC2066
No Trim

HLC1682
No Trim

HLC1689
Black Trim

R1387
Blue Trim

R1531
Yellow Trim

R1419D
Green Trim

Right: *Countess, Belmont, and Marilyn patterns; Sears, Roebuck & Co. Catalog, 1943 Spring & Summer.*

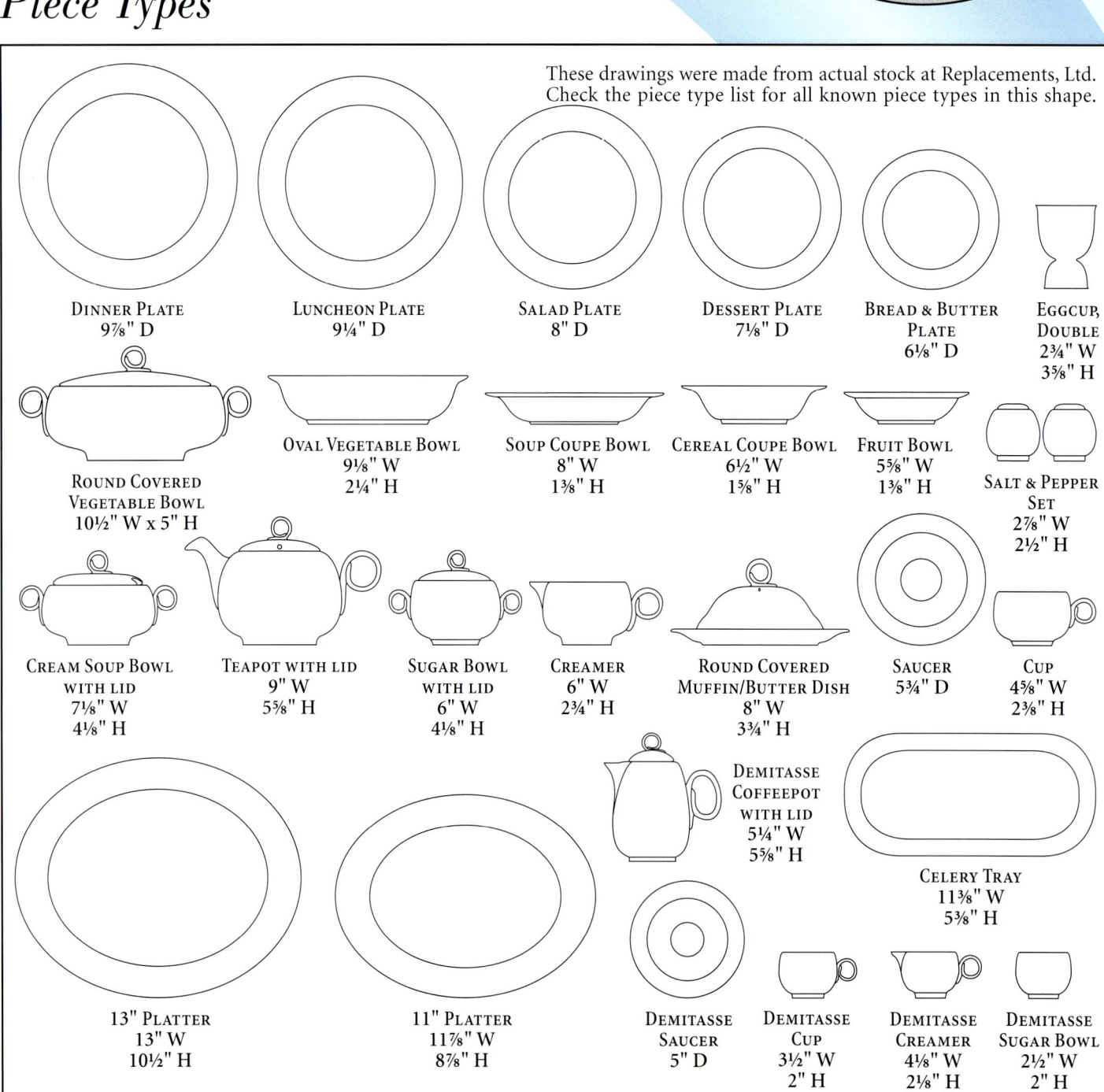

SWING Eggshell

Piece Types

These drawings were made from actual stock at Replacements, Ltd. Check the piece type list for all known piece types in this shape.

Dinner Plate	9⅞" D
Luncheon Plate	9¼" D
Salad Plate	8" D
Dessert Plate	7⅛" D
Bread & Butter Plate	6⅛" D
Eggcup, Double	2¾" W, 3⅝" H
Round Covered Vegetable Bowl	10½" W x 5" H
Oval Vegetable Bowl	9⅛" W, 2¼" H
Soup Coupe Bowl	8" W, 1⅜" H
Cereal Coupe Bowl	6½" W, 1⅝" H
Fruit Bowl	5⅝" W, 1⅜" H
Salt & Pepper Set	2⅞" W, 2½" H
Cream Soup Bowl with Lid	7⅛" W, 4⅛" H
Teapot with Lid	9" W, 5⅝" H
Sugar Bowl with Lid	6" W, 4⅛" H
Creamer	6" W, 2¾" H
Round Covered Muffin/Butter Dish	8" W, 3¾" H
Saucer	5¾" D
Cup	4⅝" W, 2⅜" H
Demitasse Coffeepot with Lid	5¼" W, 5⅝" H
Celery Tray	11⅜" W, 5⅜" H
13" Platter	13" W, 10½" H
11" Platter	11⅞" W, 8⅞" H
Demitasse Saucer	5" D
Demitasse Cup	3½" W, 2" H
Demitasse Creamer	4⅛" W, 2⅛" H
Demitasse Sugar Bowl	2½" W, 2" H

Eggshell Swing Shape

EGGSHELL SWING
1938 – 1948 or later

As early as February 1938, full-page Homer Laughlin ads in *Crockery, Glass & Lamps* proclaimed Eggshell Swing to be the "hit of the season." Eggshell Swing was also featured in a March ad and by July of that year was described as the "new tableware style created by Homer Laughlin Designers" in another full-page advertisement.

Swing, one of the specially engineered, strong, thin "eggshell" lines, has graceful ring handles and finials.

"Organdy pastels, soft tones of pink, blue, yellow and green — with pink selling exceptionally well — on the swing eggshell shape — handles in color contrasting with the item," said *Crockery, Glass & Lamps*, July 1938, reporting on the New York Show. Swing ring handles may be made of colored clay, instead of painted. This is like the Jubilee shaped lines of Skytone, Suntone or Kraft, but reversed. Swing pieces have white bodies with colored handles and finials. Examples of contrasting color handles and variations of color are numerous in the Swing line.

One of the most popular swing patterns was featured in *Crockery, Glass & Lamps*, February 1939, in a review of the Pittsburgh Show. It was noted: "Also new — colorful and informal design called the 'Colonial Kitchen' finished with a yellow rim, on the Swing shape."

Organdy Pastels

Top right: *Organdy Pastels, Blue pattern; Demitasse Cup & Saucer Set, and Demitasse Coffeepot with lid.*
Middle left: *Organdy Pastels patterns Green, Blue, Yellow, and Pink; Bread & Butter Plate, Dinner Plate, Luncheon Plate, Cup & Saucer Set, Sugar Bowl with lid, Creamer, Demitasse Cup, Demitasse Sugar Open, and Demitasse Creamer.* **Middle right:** *Organdy Pastels patterns Green, Yellow, Pink, and Blue; Bread & Butter Plates.* **Bottom right:** *Organdy Pastels patterns Green, Blue, Yellow, and Pink; Cup & Saucer Sets.*

Homer Laughlin

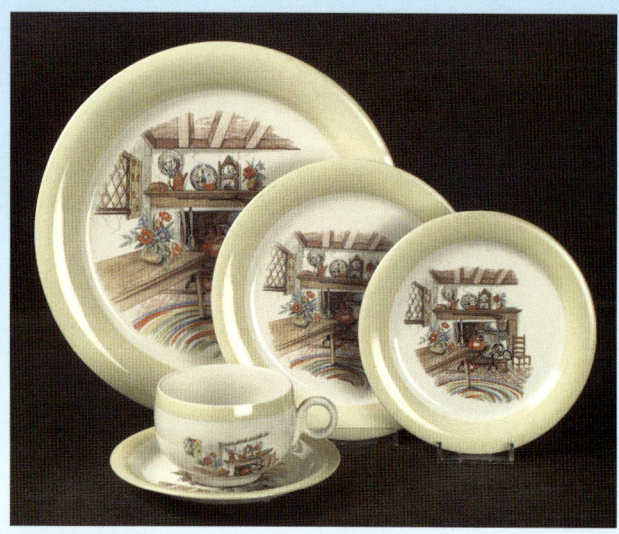

Top left: *Chinese Buddha pattern; Dinner Plate, Bread & Butter Plate, Cup & Saucer Set, Creamer, and Sugar Bowl with lid.* **Bottom left:** *Chinese Buddha pattern; Cream Soup Bowl without lid, Oval Platter, Soup Bowl, and Fruit Bowl.* **Top right:** *Colonial Kitchen pattern; Dinner Plate, Salad Plate, Bread & Butter Plate, and Cup & Saucer Set.* **Second down on right:** *Colonial Kitchen pattern; Cream Soup Bowl without lid, Oval Platter, and Round Covered Vegetable Bowl.* **Third down on right:** *Colonial Kitchen pattern; Creamer, and Sugar Bowl without lid.* **Bottom right:** *Colonial Kitchen pattern; Oval Vegetable Bowl, Soup Bowl, and Fruit Bowl.*

Eggshell Swing Shape

Eggshell Swing Piece Type List
From Homer Laughlin Catalog with Confirmed Actual Pieces

Bowl, Cereal Coupe, 6½ inches
Bowl, Cream Soup with lid
Bowl, Fruit, 5⅝ inches
Bowl, Soup Coupe, 8 inches
Bowl, Vegetable Oval, 9⅛ inches
Bowl, Vegetable Round Covered, 10½ inches
Coffeepot with lid, Demitasse
Creamer
Creamer, Demitasse

Cup & Saucer Set
  Cup, 2⅜ inches
  Saucer, 5¾ inches
Cup & Saucer Set, Demitasse
  Cup, 2 inches
  Saucer, 5 inches
Eggcup, Double, 3⅝ inches
Muffin/Butter Dish, Round Covered
Plate, Bread & Butter, 6⅛ inches
Plate, Dessert, 7⅛ inches

Plate, Dinner, 9⅞ inches
Plate, Luncheon, 9¼ inches
Plate, Salad, 8 inches
Platter, Oval, 11⅞ inches
Platter, Oval, 13 inches
Salt & Pepper Set
Sugar Bowl Open, Demitasse
Sugar Bowl with lid
Teapot with lid
Tray, Celery, 11⅜ inches

Collectors Note: Swing salt & pepper shakers were used with several other lines.

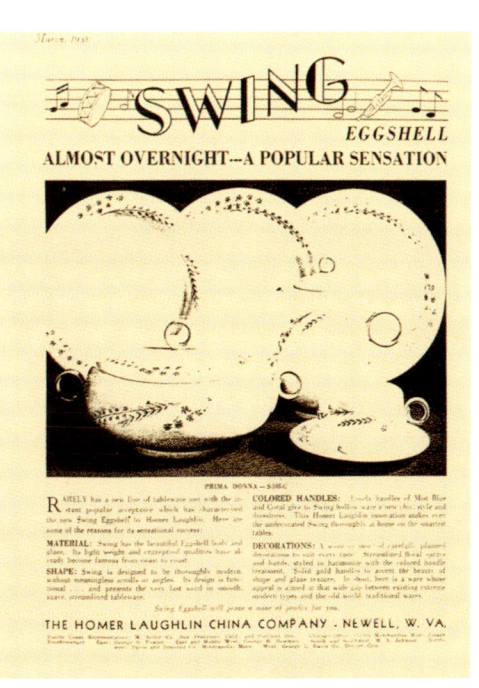

Top left: *Typical Eggshell Swing backstamps.* **Top middle:** *Lily Of The Valley pattern; Double Eggcup.* **Top right:** *Moss Rose pattern; Covered Muffin/Butter Dish, Demitasse Creamer, and Demitasse Sugar Bowl.* **Bottom left:** *Organdy Pastels pattern; Crockery, Glass & Lamps, February 1938.* **Bottom middle:** *Prima Donna pattern; Crockery, Glass & Lamps, March 1938.* **Bottom right:** *Crockery, Glass & Lamps, July 1938.*

Eggshell Swing Shape

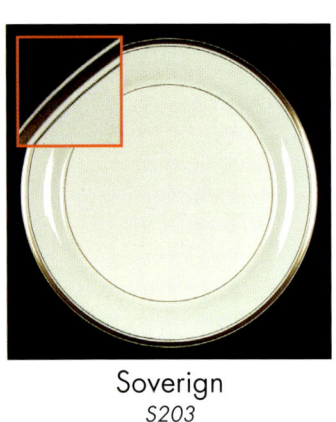

Soverign *S203* Gold Trim	**S187** No Trim	**S222** No Trim	**HLC1506** No Trim
HLC1507 Light Green Bands No Trim	**HLC1508** No Trim	**A2868** No Trim	**HLC679** Bread & Butter Plate Shown Orange Trim
6978 No Trim	**1180** No Trim	**1091** No Trim	**HLC1505** No Trim
Organdy–Pink No Trim	**Organdy–Blue** Bread & Butter Plate Shown No Trim	**Organdy–Green** Bread & Butter Plate Shown No Trim	**Organdy–Yellow** Salad Plate Shown No Trim

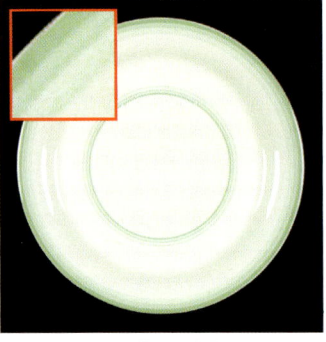

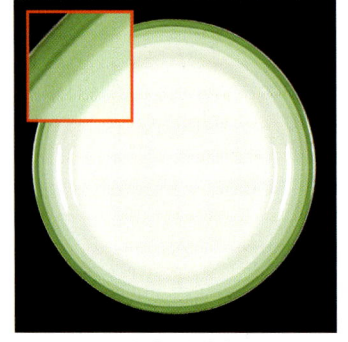

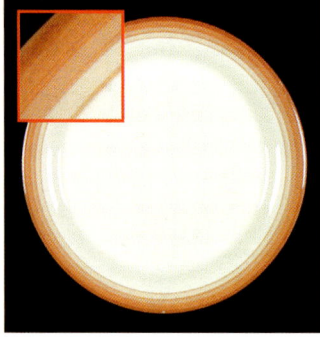

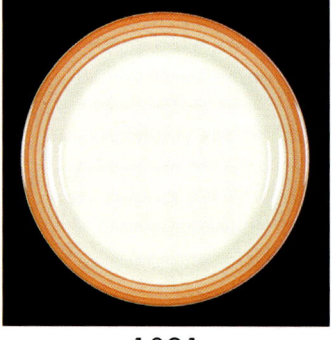

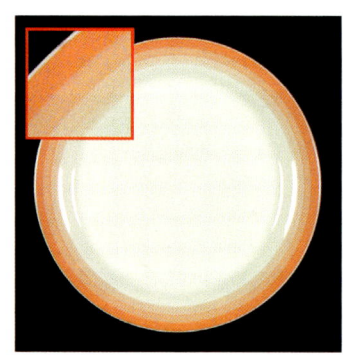

Eggshell Swing Shape

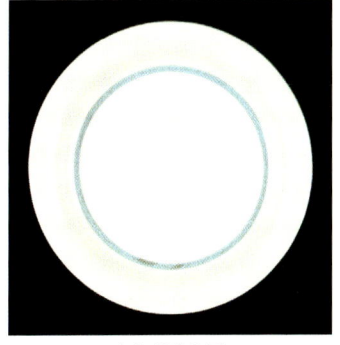

HLC837 Saucer Shown No Trim	**S240** Salad Plate Shown Gold Trim	**HLC894** Gold Trim	**HLC1517** Black Band Gold Trim
R8559 No Trim	**R8545** No Trim	**HLC1702** Gold Trim	**S326** Gold Trim
R2466 Gold Trim	**R8534** No Trim	**R8538** No Trim	**R8525** No Trim
R8553 No Trim	**HLC504** No Trim	**Colonial Kitchen** S178, S179 No Trim	**S329** No Trim

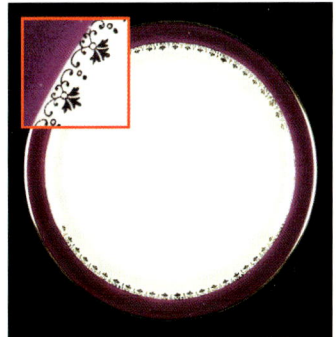

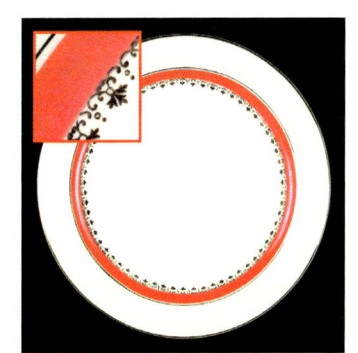

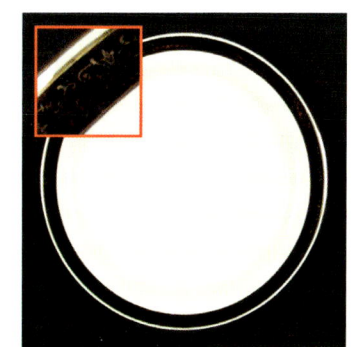

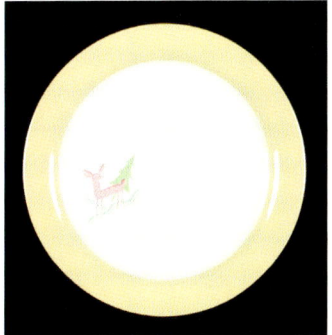

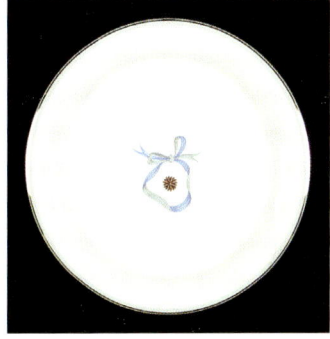

Eggshell Swing Shape

Conchita S129 No Trim	**Mexicana** No Trim	**Hacienda** Bread & Butter Plate Shown No Trim	**Chinese Porcelains** No Trim
HLC2117 Saucer Shown No Trim	**Chinese Buddha** S152P No Trim	**The China Lady** S108 No Trim	**Pueblo** S102 Multi-Motif No Trim
HLC1118 Fruit Bowl Shown No Trim	**HLC1388** No Trim	**Chinese Three** No Trim	**Chinese Princess** No Trim
Organdy Pastels No Trim	**Chinese Willow** S1465 No Trim	**Big Apple** S126 No Trim	**S112** No Trim

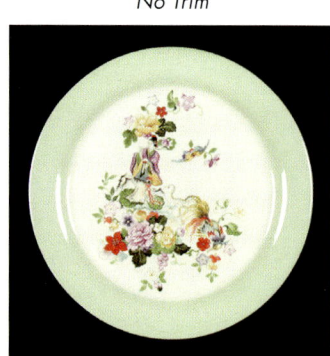

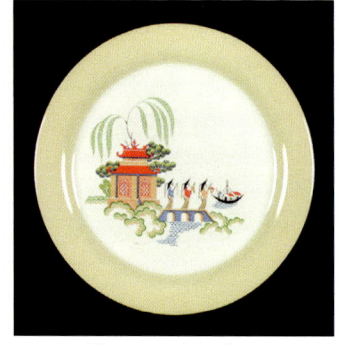

Eggshell Swing Shape

International
S149P
No Trim

R8563
No Trim

S212
Platinum Trim

Doll's House
S113
No Trim

R2534
No Trim

R2522
No Trim

R2639
No Trim

R2541
No Trim

Dubarry
CP133, by Cunningham & Pickett
Salad Plate Shown
No Trim

Dubarry
by Cunningham & Pickett
Salad Plate Shown
Green Trim

R8556
No Trim

HLC1453
No Trim

HLC775
No Trim

Moss Rose
S163, S191G
No Trim

Avon
by Cunningham & Pickett
Salad Plate Shown
Gold Trim

HLC609
No Trim

Eggshell Swing Shape

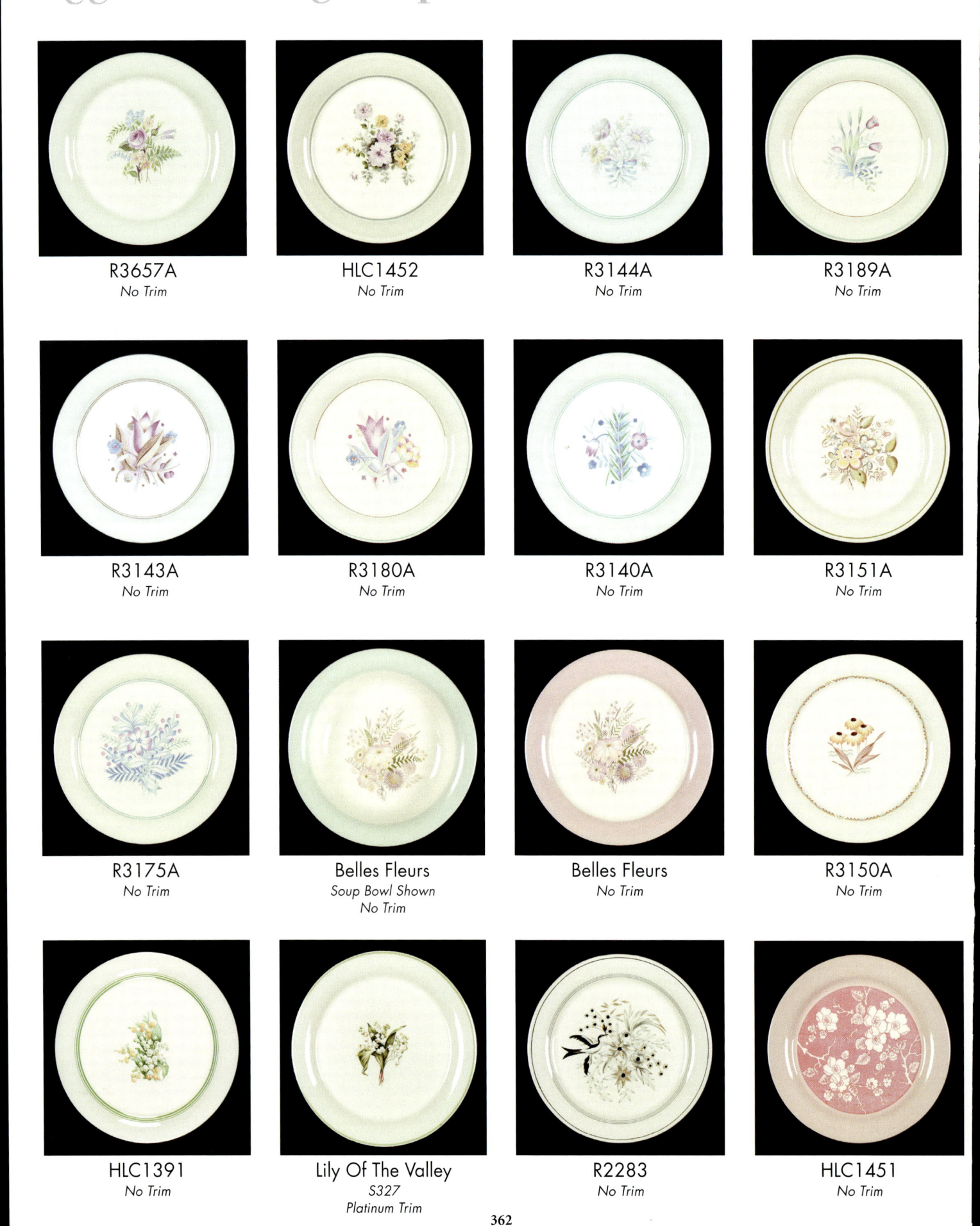

R3657A No Trim	HLC1452 No Trim	R3144A No Trim	R3189A No Trim
R3143A No Trim	R3180A No Trim	R3140A No Trim	R3151A No Trim
R3175A No Trim	Belles Fleurs Soup Bowl Shown No Trim	Belles Fleurs No Trim	R3150A No Trim
HLC1391 No Trim	Lily Of The Valley S327 Platinum Trim	R2283 No Trim	HLC1451 No Trim

Eggshell Swing Shape

R3273A
No Trim

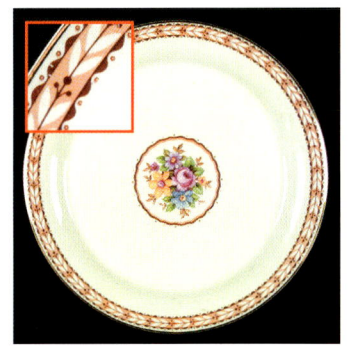

Autocrat
Gold Trim

R4642
No Trim

HLC2169
Demitasse Cup & Saucer Set Shown
Gold Trim

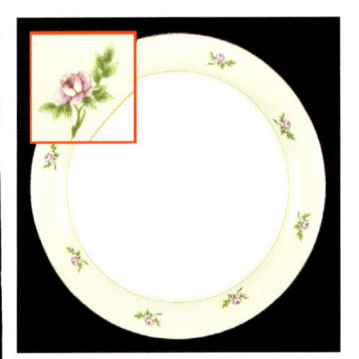

HLC961
Gold Trim

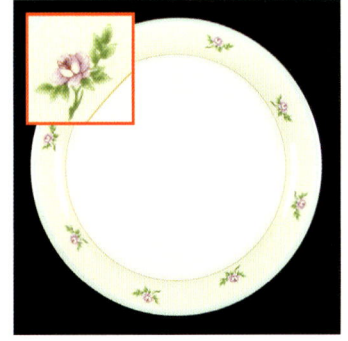

S181
Blue Band
No Trim

CUP1
by Cunningham & Pickett
Salad Plate Shown
Gold Trim

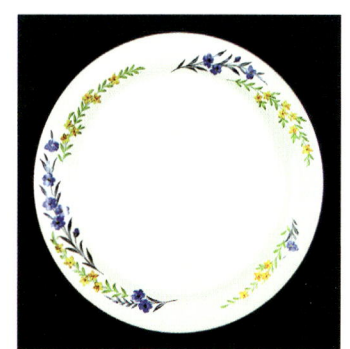

Blue Flax
S128C
No Trim

Alameda
S131C
Salad Plate Shown
No Trim

HLC1261
Tan Trim

HLC1262
No Trim

HLC1516
Black Trim

R2499
No Trim

363

Eggshell Swing Shape (Variations)

HLC1389
No Trim

HLC1274
No Trim

HLC1281
No Trim

HLC1279
No Trim

HLC1280
No Trim

HLC1282
No Trim

HLC1638
No Trim

Cretonne Pattern

Like a breath from a country garden, this new pattern, ringed with its decoration of flowers in varied hues, is utterly delightful. It will give a touch of spring to your table setting the year 'round. Of course it savors, too, of the popular floral designs of cretonne. A thought—imagine its effect in a cozy little breakfast nook, hung with floral cretonne drapes! Ivory body enhances the display and a blue line increases its effectiveness. Made of finest semi-porcelain.

Size of Set	32-pc. Set	54-pc. Set
Number	1757	1759
Coupon Price	$13.00	$24.00
Cash Price	6.50	12.00
Mlg. wt.	20 lbs.	35 lbs.

Left: *Cretonne pattern; Larkin ad, 1939.*

Eggshell Theme

Piece Types

These drawings were made from actual stock at Replacements, Ltd. Check the piece type list for all known piece types in this shape.

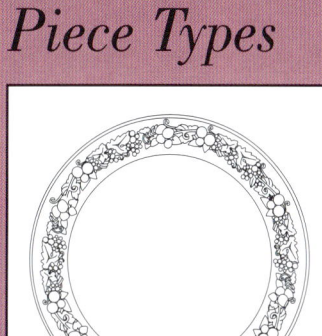

Dinner Plate
9⅞" D

Luncheon Plate
9¼" D

Salad Plate
8⅛" D

Square Salad Plate
8" D

Dessert Plate
7¼" D

Bread & Butter Plate
6⅛" D

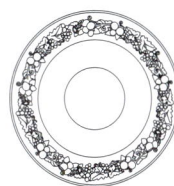

Saucer
6" D

Cup
4½" W
2⅜" H

Demitasse Saucer
5¼" D

Demitasse Cup
3¾" W
1⅞" H

Cream Soup Saucer
7⅛" D

Cream Soup Bowl
6½" W
2" H

Gravy Boat with attached Underplate, missing lid
9¼" W
3" H

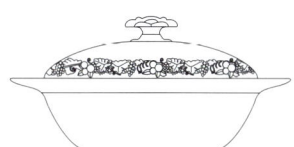

Round Covered Vegetable Bowl
9⅞" W
4⅞" H

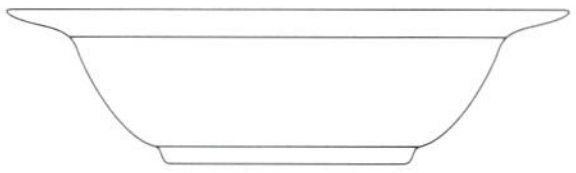

Round Vegetable Bowl
9⅞" W
2⅝" H

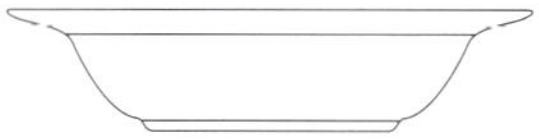

Oval Vegetable Bowl
9¼" W
2" H

Soup Bowl with Rim
8¼" W
1½" H

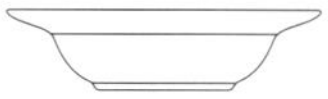

Fruit Bowl with Rim
5⅝" W
2⅜" H

Gravy/Sauce Boat
7⅞" W
3⅝" H

Sugar Bowl with lid
6¼" W
4¼" H

Creamer
6½" W
3½" H

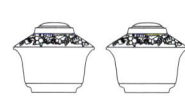

Salt & Pepper Set
2⅞" W
2⅜" H

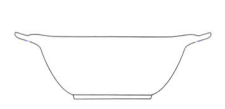

Cereal Bowl, Lugged
7" W
2¼" H

Cereal Bowl, Lugged Top

365

Homer Laughlin

EGGSHELL THEME   1939 – until after 1945

A full-page ad appeared in the trade journals, in January 1940, illustrating a new pattern and line. The announcement in bold caption was: "Theme... a stunning new tableware in the old tradition. For the first time in the history of American pottery making, a domestic factory offers to the public a table service designed and modeled in the finest traditional manner..."

China, Glass and Lamps, in July 1940, stated: "New (on display at the Vanderbilt) was a group of decorations on the 'Theme' shape — six of them, in all, including center flora and shoulder designs, finished with gold edge lines." The embossed border was fun and attractive, yet any added decoration complimented the border very well. This was the start of production of many patterns on this shape. Montgomery Ward offered six patterns on this shape alone in 1944 and 1945.

You will find many examples of "commemorative" plates on this shape. Most likely these were not decorated by Homer Laughlin china, rather the plates were bought by smaller decorating shops and completed as they had orders. Churches often commissioned and bought these decorative plates. Commemorative plates themselves may or may not have the Eggshell Theme mark.

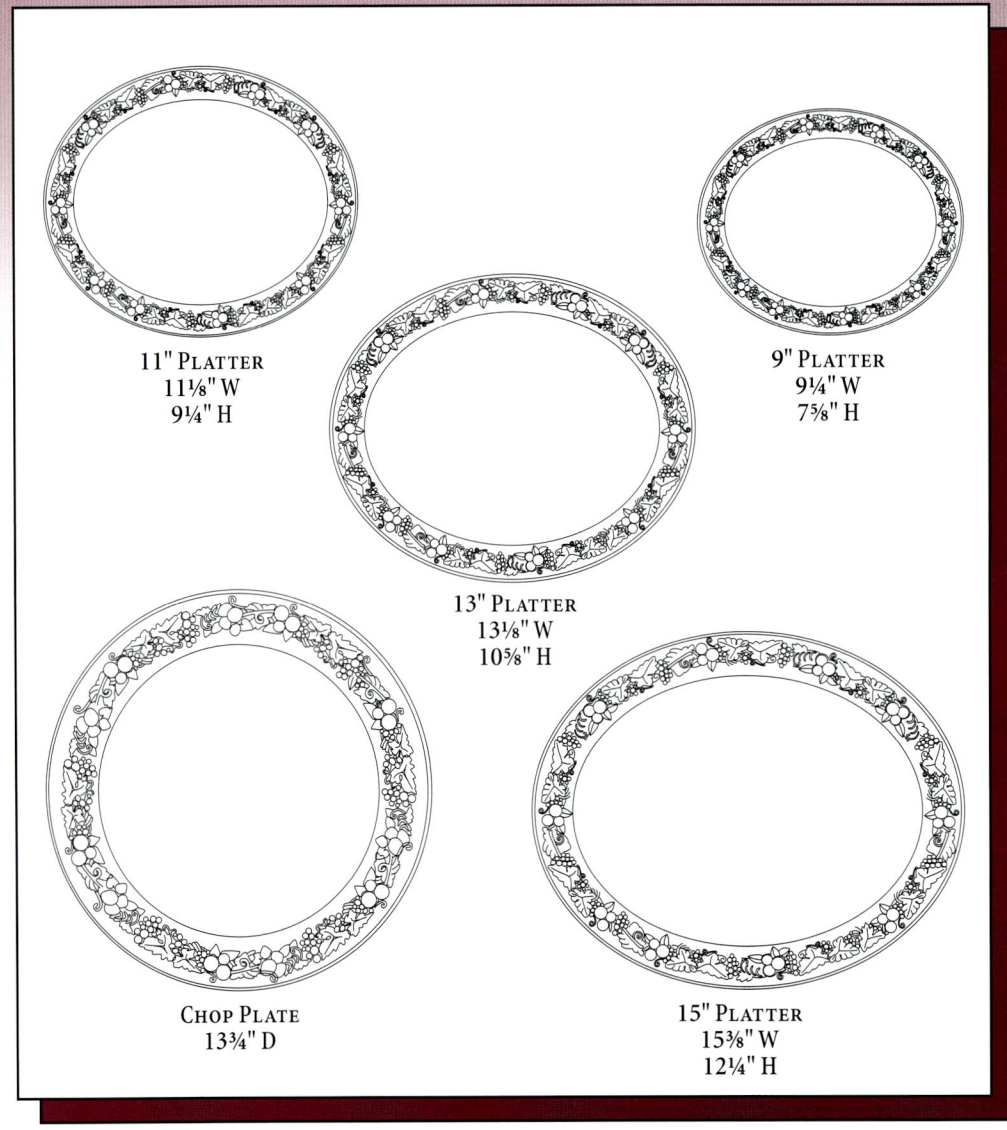

11" Platter
11⅛" W
9¼" H

9" Platter
9¼" W
7⅝" H

13" Platter
13⅛" W
10⅝" H

Chop Plate
13¾" D

15" Platter
15⅜" W
12¼" H

A less common Eggshell Theme backstamp.

The most common Eggshell Theme backstamp.

Eggshell Theme Shape

Top left: *TH6 pattern;* Round Covered Vegetable Bowl.
Top right: *TH6 pattern;* Oval Platter, Dinner Plate, Round Covered Vegetable Bowl, and Cup & Saucer Set. **Middle left:** *TH14 pattern;* Oval Platter, Fruit Bowl with rim, Cup & Saucer Set, and Soup Bowl with rim. **Middle right:** *TH11 pattern;* Oval Platter, Dinner Plate, Soup Bowl with rim, Gravy/Sauce Boat, and Salad Plate. **Bottom right:** *TH14 pattern;* Sugar Bowl with lid, and Creamer.

Homer Laughlin

Eggshell Theme Piece Type List

From Homer laughlin Literature with Confirmed Actual Pieces

Bowl, Cereal Lugged, 7 inches
Bowl, Cream Soup & Saucer Set
   Bowl, 2 inches
   Saucer, 7⅛ inches
Bowl, Fruit with rim, 5⅝ inches
Bowl, Soup with rim, 8¼ inches
Bowl, Vegetable Oval, 9¼ inches
Bowl, Vegetable Round, 9⅞ inches
Bowl, Vegetable Round Covered,
   9⅞ inches
Creamer

Cup & Saucer Set
   Cup, 2⅜ inches
   Saucer, 6 inches
Cup & Saucer Set, Demitasse
   Cup, 1⅞ inches
   Saucer, 5¼ inches
Gravy/Sauce Boat with attached
   Underplate and lid
Plate, Bread & Butter, 6⅛ inches
Plate, Chop, 13¾ inches
Plate, Dessert, 7¼ inches

Plate, Dinner, 9⅞ inches
Plate, Luncheon, 9¼ inches
Plate, Salad, 8⅛ inches
Plate, Salad Square, 8 inches
Platter, 9¼ inches
Platter, 11⅛ inches
Platter, 13⅛ inches
Platter, 15⅜ inches
Salt & Pepper Set
Sugar Bowl with lid
Teapot with lid

Top left: *Regency pattern; Montgomery Ward Catalog, 1944.* **Top right:** *TH11 pattern; Salt & Pepper Set.* **Bottom:** *Theme pattern; Demitasse Cup & Saucer Set, and Cup & Saucer Set.*

Eggshell Theme Shape

Theme *No Trim*	**HLC937** *Gold Trim*	**9205** *No Trim*	**HLC1668** *No Trim*
HLC1632 *No Trim*	**HLC1734** *Yellow Verge* *No Trim*	**HLC1667** *Gold Verge* *No Trim*	**HLC2013** *Gold Verge* *No Trim*
HLC1736 *Pink Verge* *No Trim*	**HLC1735** *Green Verge* *No Trim*	**HLC1737** *Blue Verge* *No Trim*	**HLC147** *No Trim*
HLC1733 *Gold Verge* *No Trim*	**HLC1572** *No Trim*	**HLC1573** *No Trim*	**TH14** *Gold Design* *No Trim*

Eggshell Theme Shape

TH14P Platinum Design No Trim	**TH21** No Trim	**TH10** No Trim	**R3029A** No Trim
TH20 No Trim	**HLC1149** Salad Plate Shown Gold Trim	**HLC734** Chop Plate Shown Gold Trim	**HLC212** Salad Plate Shown Gold Trim
HLC311 No Trim	**R8585** No Trim	**R8586** No Trim	**R3651A** No Trim
R6108 No Trim	**R3122A** No Trim	**TH5** No Trim	**R3044A** No Trim

Eggshell Theme Shape

TH1 *No Trim*	DP2285 *No Trim*	R4980 *No Trim*	HLC1825 *No Trim*
R6101 *No Trim*	R6104 *No Trim*	TH26 *No Trim*	HLC1826 *No Trim*
TH34 *No Trim*	TH6 *No Trim*	TH11 *No Trim*	R6107 *No Trim*
TH19 *No Trim*	TH24 *No Trim*	HLC2064 *No Trim*	R3131A *No Trim*

Eggshell Theme Shape

R6073
No Trim

R3269A
No Trim

Surrey
TH17
No Trim

HLC1053
No Trim

Regency
No Trim

Above: *Wrapped ware at the Homer Laughlin Factory.*

372

Eggshell Andover

Piece Types

These drawings were made from actual stock or literature at Replacements, Ltd. Check the piece type list for all known piece types in this shape.

- Dinner Plate — 9⅞" D
- Bread & Butter Plate — 6⅛" D
- Saucer — 5¾" D
- Cup — 5" W, 2⅜" H
- Round Covered Vegetable Bowl — 10¾" W x 5½" H
- Teapot with lid — 9" W, 5⅝" H
- Sugar Bowl with lid — 5¾" W, 4⅜" H
- Creamer — 5⅛" W, 3¼" H
- Cream Soup Bowl
- Cereal Coupe Bowl — 5" W, 1⅝" H
- Soup Bowl with rim — 8" W, 1½" H
- Celery Tray
- Platter — 12⅞" W, 10⅜" H

Top: *Typical Eggshell Andover backstamp.*
Left: *HLC2195 pattern; Teapot with lid.*

Homer Laughlin

EGGSHELL ANDOVER   1940 – 1942 or later

This shape, made of the then new, thin and durable eggshell body, was created expressly for use with the coordinating Carson Wishmaker line of products for the home. The idea was to make diverse products with a similar decorating theme. The Andover hollowware utilizes some new distinctive shapes mixed with Eggshell Swing shapes to create a whole new shape, a practice Homer Laughlin began to do frequently.

Eggshell Andover Piece Type List

From Homer Laughlin Literature with Confirmed Actual Pieces

Bowl, Cereal Coupe, 5 inches
Bowl, Cream Soup
Bowl, Soup with rim, 8 inches
Bowl, Vegetable Round Covered, 10¾ inches

Creamer
Cup & Saucer Set
Cup, 2⅜ inches
Saucer, 5¾ inches
Plate, Bread & Butter, 6⅛ inches

Plate, Dinner, 9⅞ inches
Platter, Oval, 12⅞ inches
Sugar Bowl with lid
Teapot with lid
Tray, Celery

Top left: *HLC2195 pattern; Bread & Butter Plate, Dinner Plate, Oval Platter, Teapot with lid, and Cup & Saucer Set.*
Top right: *HLC2195 pattern; Round Covered Vegetable Bowl, Cereal Bowl, and Soup Bowl with rim.*

HLC2195
Gold Trim

Andover Gold
*Sugar & Creamer Shown
All Gold*

Cavalier Eggshell

Piece Types

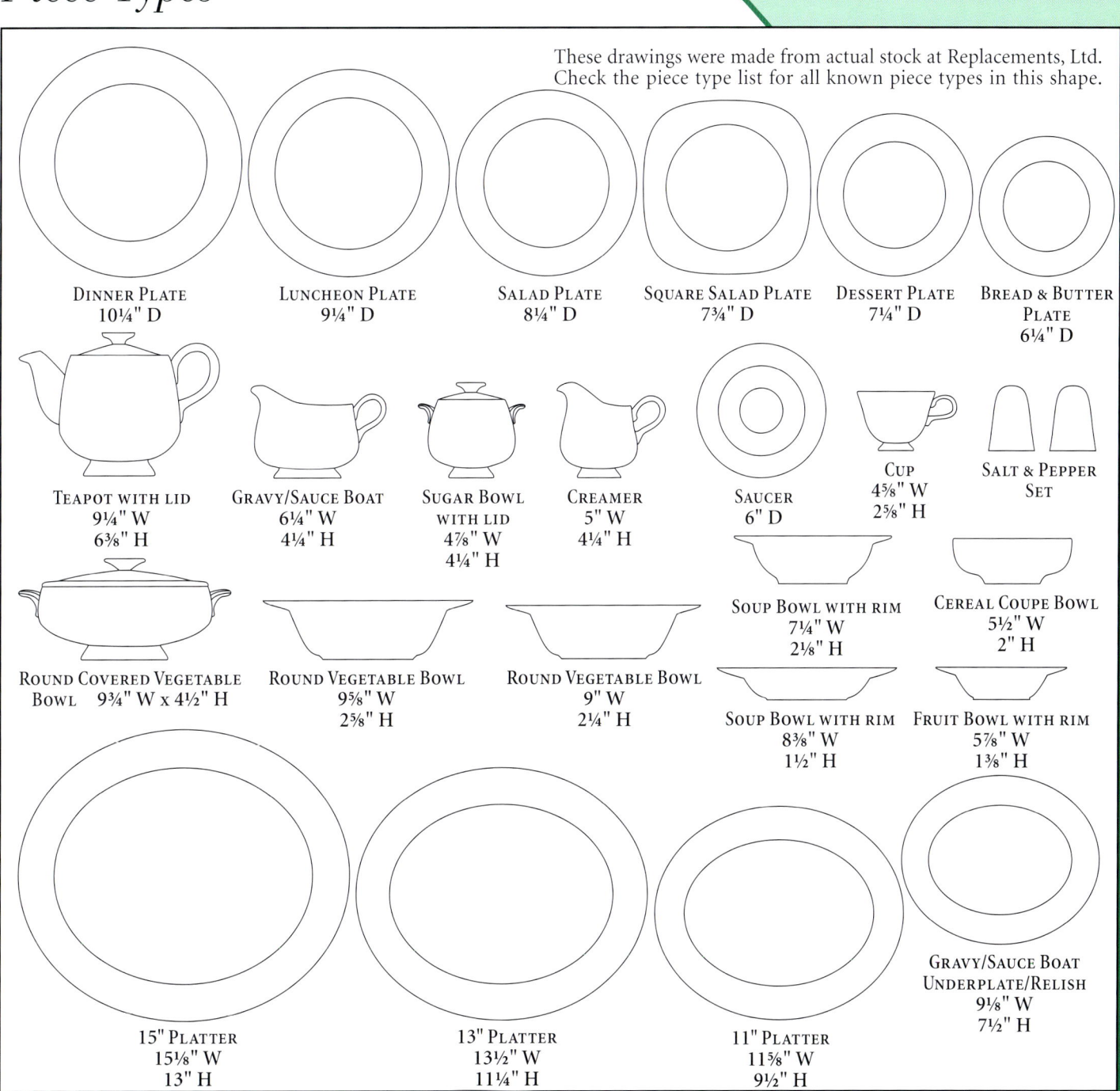

These drawings were made from actual stock at Replacements, Ltd. Check the piece type list for all known piece types in this shape.

Dinner Plate
10¼" D

Luncheon Plate
9¼" D

Salad Plate
8¼" D

Square Salad Plate
7¾" D

Dessert Plate
7¼" D

Bread & Butter Plate
6¼" D

Teapot with lid
9¼" W
6⅜" H

Gravy/Sauce Boat
6¼" W
4¼" H

Sugar Bowl with lid
4⅞" W
4¼" H

Creamer
5" W
4¼" H

Saucer
6" D

Cup
4⅝" W
2⅝" H

Salt & Pepper Set

Round Covered Vegetable Bowl 9¾" W x 4½" H

Round Vegetable Bowl
9⅝" W
2⅝" H

Round Vegetable Bowl
9" W
2¼" H

Soup Bowl with rim
7¼" W
2⅛" H

Cereal Coupe Bowl
5½" W
2" H

Soup Bowl with rim
8⅜" W
1½" H

Fruit Bowl with rim
5⅞" W
1⅜" H

15" Platter
15⅛" W
13" H

13" Platter
13½" W
11¼" H

11" Platter
11⅝" W
9½" H

Gravy/Sauce Boat Underplate/Relish
9⅛" W
7½" H

Homer Laughlin

EGGSHELL CAVALIER 1953 – 1966 or later

Eggshell Cavalier was introduced in 1953, according to Homer Laughlin dinnerware researcher Jo Cunningham, and was the product of designer Don Schreckengost. Ads for patterns on the Eggshell Cavalier shape appeared in the *Crockery & Glass Journal* in 1956 and 1957. *The Red Book Directory of 1966* listed Cavalier with overglaze decorations as a line being offered by Homer Laughlin, "The World's Largest Pottery." It was likely produced after that year, but no additional information has been found. A common decoration on many Eggshell Cavalier patterns is a solid color band covering the rim of the plate, sometimes framing a design in the center. Turquoise, pink, and green bands, accented by platinum trim, were most often utilized for this line. Eggshell Cavalier was used for a number of patterns made by Homer Laughlin exclusively for other distributors. These patterns may bear the distributors' mark, along with a Homer Laughlin mark, or some combination of both backstamps.

Left: *Melody in Blue, Romance in Blue,* and *South Wind* patterns; Crockery & Glass Journal, *January, 1959.* **Top right:** *Typical Eggshell Cavalier backstamp.* **Middle right:** *HLC634 pattern; Dinner Plate, Square Salad Plate, Gravy/Sauce Boat, Cup, and Sugar Bowl with lid.* **Bottom right:** *HLC634 pattern; Cereal Bowl with rim, and Soup Bowl with rim.*

Eggshell Cavalier Shape

Top left: *Crinoline* pattern; Crockery & Glass Journal, *1953*. **Top right:** Barclay, South Wind, Lupine, Persian Garden, back of Romance in Blue, Romance in Blue, Berkshire, Spring Song, and Triumph; Homer Laughlin pamphlets promoting Eggshell Cavalier patterns.

Homer Laughlin

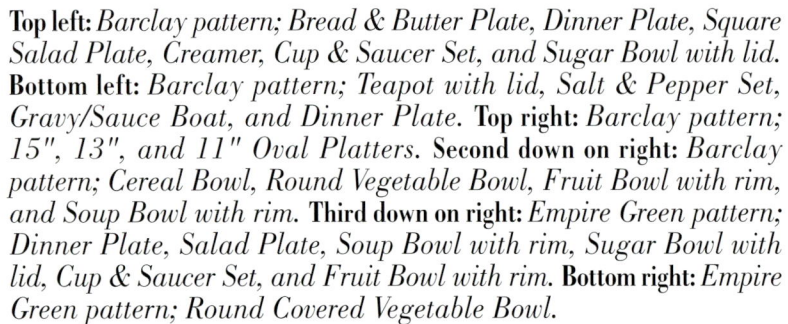

Top left: *Barclay pattern;* Bread & Butter Plate, Dinner Plate, Square Salad Plate, Creamer, Cup & Saucer Set, and Sugar Bowl with lid. **Bottom left:** *Barclay pattern;* Teapot with lid, Salt & Pepper Set, Gravy/Sauce Boat, and Dinner Plate. **Top right:** *Barclay pattern;* 15", 13", and 11" Oval Platters. **Second down on right:** *Barclay pattern;* Cereal Bowl, Round Vegetable Bowl, Fruit Bowl with rim, and Soup Bowl with rim. **Third down on right:** *Empire Green pattern;* Dinner Plate, Salad Plate, Soup Bowl with rim, Sugar Bowl with lid, Cup & Saucer Set, and Fruit Bowl with rim. **Bottom right:** *Empire Green pattern;* Round Covered Vegetable Bowl.

Eggshell Cavalier Shape

Eggshell Cavalier Piece Type List

From Homer Laughlin Literature with Confirmed Actual Pieces

Bowl, Cereal Coupe, 5½ inches
Bowl, Fruit with rim, 5⅞ inches
Bowl, Soup with rim, 7¼ inches
Bowl, Soup with rim, 8⅜ inches
Bowl, Vegetable Round, 9 inches
Bowl, Vegetable Round, 9⅝ inches
Bowl, Vegetable Round Covered, 9¾ inches
Creamer

Cup & Saucer Set
    Cup, 2⅝ inches
    Saucer, 6 inches
Cup & Saucer Set, Demitasse
Gravy/Sauce Boat
Gravy/Sauce Boat Underplate/Relish, 9⅛ inches
Plate, Bread & Butter, 6¼ inches
Plate, Dessert, 7¼ inches
Plate, Dinner, 10¼ inches

Plate, Luncheon, 9¼ inches
Plate, Salad, 8¼ inches
Plate, Salad Square, 7¾ inches
Platter, 11⅝ inches
Platter, 13½ inches
Platter, 15⅛ inches
Salt & Pepper Set
Sugar Bowl with lid
Teapot with lid

Top right: *HLC226 pattern; Teapot.* **Above left:** *CV125 pattern; Salad Plate, Dinner Plate, Oval Platter, Sugar Bowl with lid, Creamer, Cup & Saucer Set, Fruit Bowl, and Round Vegetable Bowl.*

Collectors Note: There are some service plates included in the rows of patterns that follow this page. Some of these service plates were made before Eggshell Cavalier was actually released and they have no dinnerware to match them. Since they have the same decorative treatment, design elements, and feel as Eggshell Cavalier, we have included them here.

Eggshell Cavalier Shape

CV135
Platinum Trim

Somerset
*CV87
Platinum Trim*

CV72
*Green Verge
Platinum Trim*

HLC1334
No Trim

CV73
*Round Vegetable Bowl Shown
Platinum Trim*

CV125
Platinum Trim

CV126
Platinum Trim

HLC1208
No Trim

HLC1772
No Trim

HLC549
Platinum Trim

Golden Harvest
*by Cunningham & Pickett
Gold Trim*

CV99
Gold Trim

Athena
*B1439
Gold Trim*

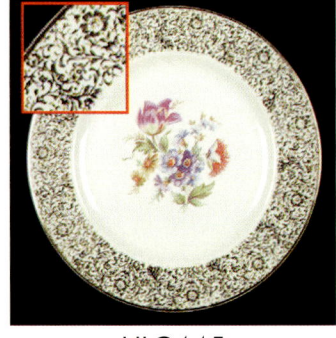

Princess
*H5259
by Cunningham & Pickett
Gold Trim*

HLC445
*Salad Plate Shown
Gold Trim*

HLC201
Gold Trim

380

Eggshell Cavalier Shape

HLC1911 *Round Vegetable Bowl Shown* *No Trim*	 **HLC1233** *No Trim*	 **CV138** *Platinum Trim*	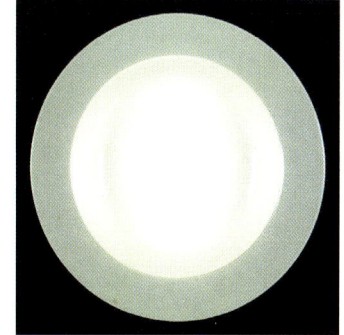 **HLC945** *Soup Bowl Shown* *No Trim*
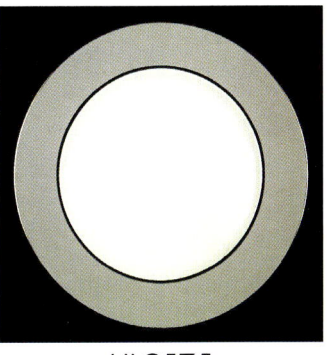 **HLC575** *Platinum Trim*	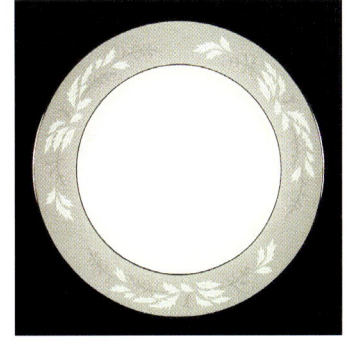 **HLC339** *Platinum Trim*	 **CV74** *Platinum Trim*	 **HLC226** *Platinum Trim*
 **Brittany Rose** *B1427* *Gold Trim*	 **Brittany Rose** *Platinum Trim*	 **Gray Dawn** *CV4* *Platinum Trim*	 **Gray Dawn** *by Lifetime China* *Platinum Trim*
 **Empire Grey** *Platinum Trim*	 **CV17** *Platinum Trim*	 **Crinoline** *CV5* *Platinum Trim*	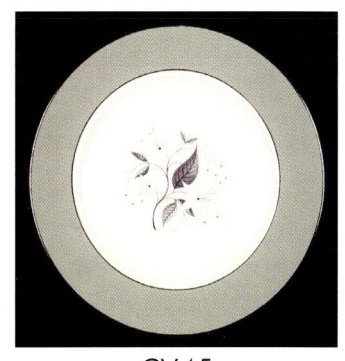 **CV45** *Platinum Trim*

Eggshell Cavalier Shape

CV20GR *Gold Trim*	**Concerto** *CV21* *Platinum Trim*	**Lily Of The Valley** *CV3* *Gold Trim*	**HLC1707** *Gold Trim*
HLC751 *Bread & Butter Plate Shown* *Platinum Trim*	**HLC1106** *Bread & Butter Plate Shown* *Gold Trim*	**HLC634** *No Trim*	**HLC411** *Brown Trim*
Turquoise Melody *CV63* *Platinum Trim*	**HLC2116** *Platinum Trim*	**Romance** *CV67* *Platinum Trim*	**CV116** *Platinum Trim*
HLC497 *Platinum Trim*	**LTC12** *by Lifetime China* *Platinum Trim*	**HLC3036** *Platinum Trim*	**CV69** *Gold Trim*

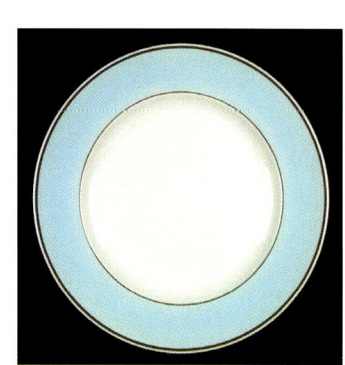

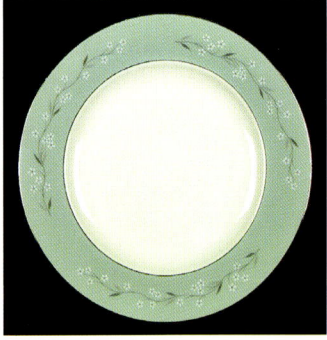

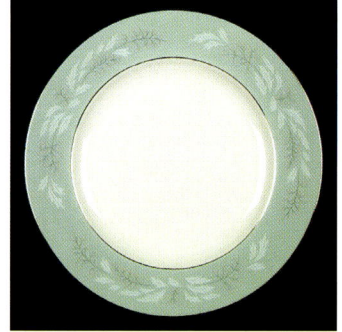

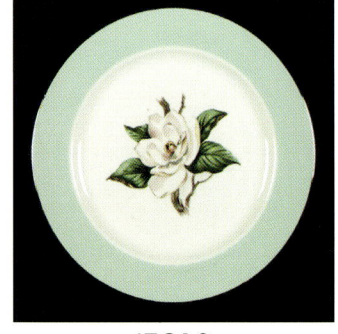

Eggshell Cavalier Shape

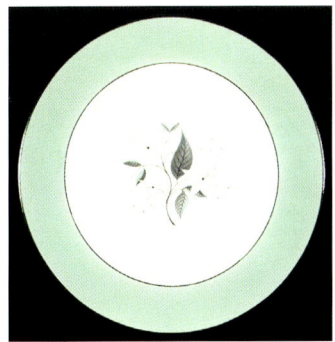

Dianne/Spring Song
CV49
Platinum Trim

Blue Lace
by Sevron China
Platinum Trim

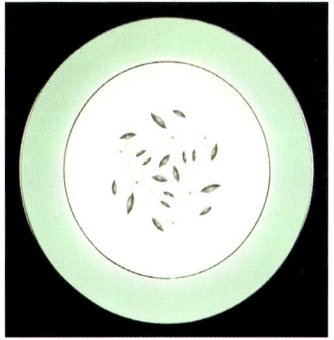

CV55
Platinum Trim

Triumph
CV52
Platinum Trim

Avalon
CV59
Platinum Trim

HLC1095
Platinum Trim

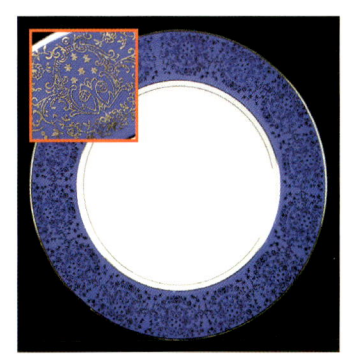

HLC344
Service Plate Shown
Gold Trim

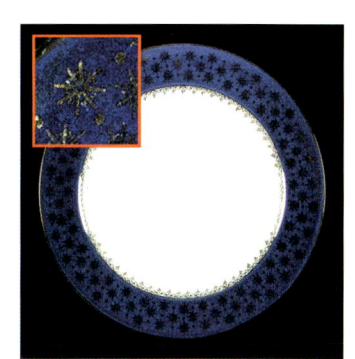

HLC1731
Service Plate Shown
Gold Trim

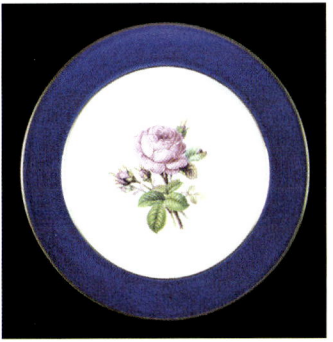

HLC1235
Gold Trim

SP2
Service Plate Shown
Gold Trim

IGS2
Service Plate Shown
Gold Trim

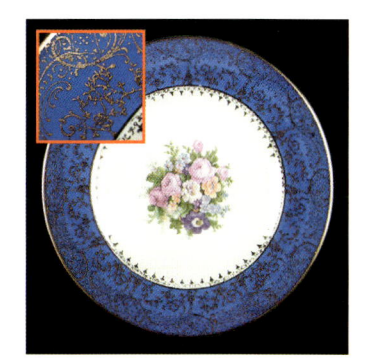

ATA2
by Atlas China Co.
Gold Trim

HLC1421
Service Plate Shown
Gold Trim

B1344
Gold Trim

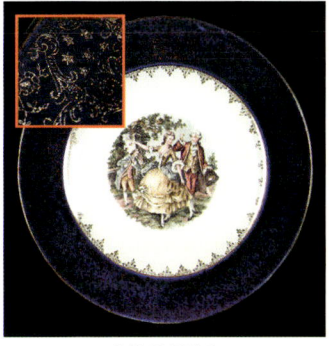

HLC579
Gold Trim

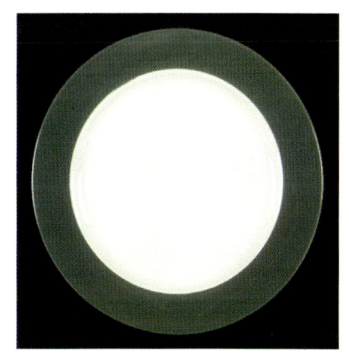

HLC965
No Trim

Eggshell Cavalier Shape

Lexington
Platinum Trim

Teal Green
by Century Service Corp.
No Floral Center
Gold Trim

Teal Green
by Century Service Corp.
Floral Center
Gold Trim

Emerald
by Century Service Corp.
Gold Trim

CV22
Platinum Trim

HLC238
Platinum Trim

HLC519
Platinum Trim

Cameo
by Lifetime China
Gold Trim

JCP141
Gold Trim

AS9
Gold Trim

Empire Green
CSC15
by Century Service Corp.
Gold Trim

HLC658
Gold Trim

Lupine
CV14
Platinum Trim

CV20
Gold Trim

CV54
Gold Trim

Berkshire
CV15
Gold Trim

Eggshell Cavalier Shape

CV1
Platinum Trim

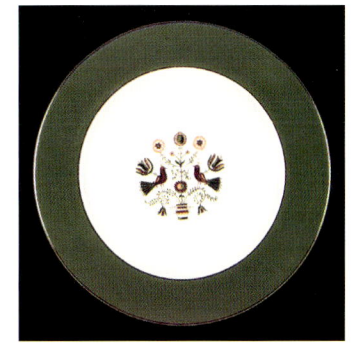

Persian Garden
CV28
Platinum Trim

HLC727
Oval Platter Shown
Gold Trim

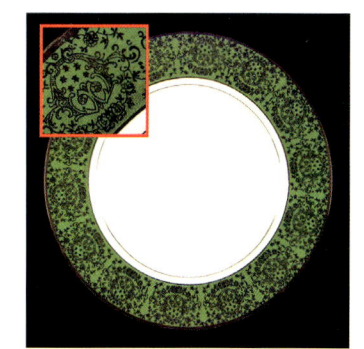

W136
Gold Trim

HLC1424
Service Plate Shown
Gold Trim

SP13
Service Plate Shown
Gold Trim

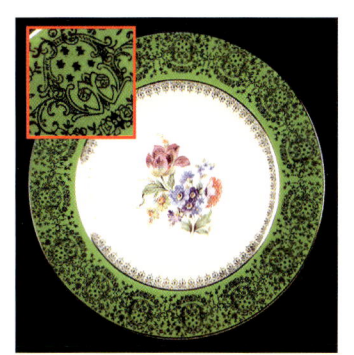

CPS1
Service Plate Shown
Gold Trim

HLC1420
Service Plate Shown
Gold Trim

PGC8
Service Plate Shown
Gold Trim

HLC728
Gold Trim

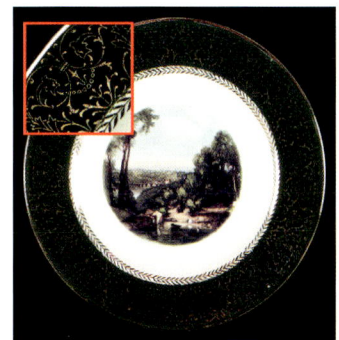

8266
Multi-Motif
Gold Trim

8266
Multi-Motif
Gold Trim

8266
Multi-Motif
Gold Trim

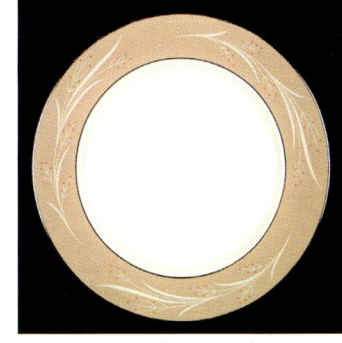

South Wind
CV75
Platinum Trim

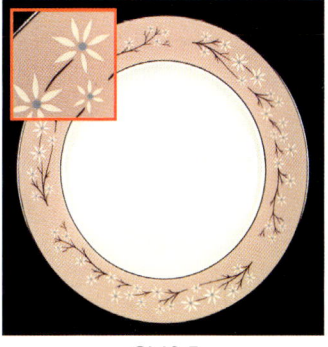

CV85
Platinum Trim

CV122
Gold Trim

385

Eggshell Cavalier Shape

CV78 *Platinum Trim*	**HLC70** *Bread & Butter Plate Shown Platinum Trim*	**HLC489** *No Trim*	**Pink Laurel** *Gold Trim*
Pink Melody *CV62.2 Bread & Butter Plate Shown Platinum Trim*	**Glenwood** *Gold Trim*	**Pink Rose** *by Lifetime China Platinum Trim*	**6507A** *Gold Trim*
Fair Lady *CV81 by Sevron China Gold Trim*	**HLC1912** *Round Vegetable Bowl Shown No Trim*	**B1415NT** *No Trim*	**B1415** *Platinum Trim*
Springtime *CV32 Platinum Trim*	**Barclay** *CV39 Platinum Trim*	**HLC467** *No Trim*	**HLC506** *Platinum Trim*

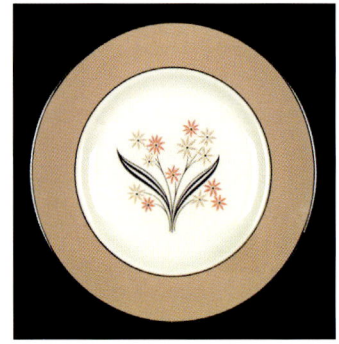

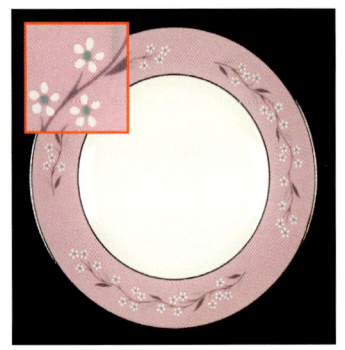

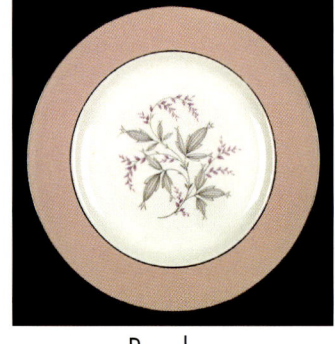

Eggshell Cavalier Shape

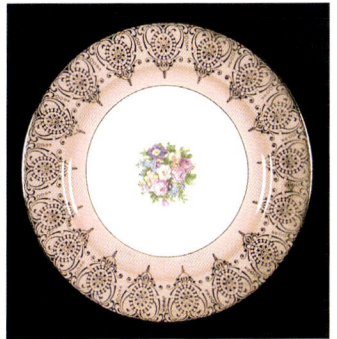

HLC1613
Gold Trim

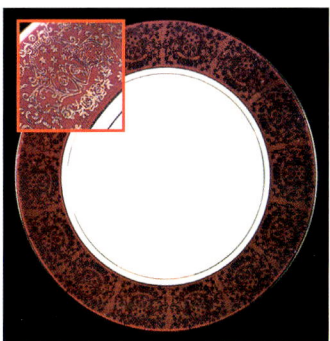

HLC2045
Service Plate Shown
Gold Trim

Regal Red
by Century Service Corp.
No Floral Center
Gold Trim

Regal Red
by Century Service Corp.
Floral Center
Gold Trim

Margaret Rose-Maroon
MW185
Gold Trim

HLC246
Gold Trim

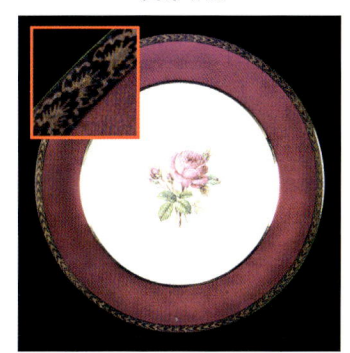

HLC1423
Service Plate Shown
Gold Trim

HLC1422
Service Plate Shown
Gold Trim

HLC1418
Service Plate Shown
Gold Trim

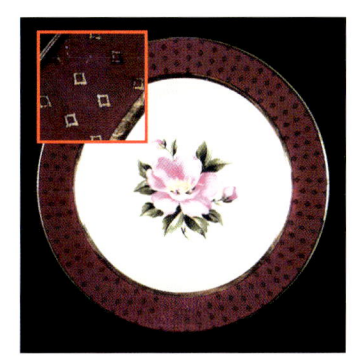

HLC644
Fruit Bowl Shown
Gold Trim

SP8
Service Plate Shown
Gold Trim

HLC1529
Service Plate Shown
Gold Trim

SP5
Service Plate Shown
Gold Trim

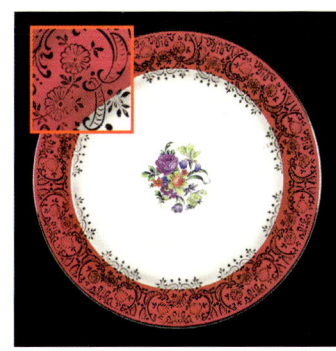

HLC430
Gold Trim

HLC1738
Service Plate Shown
Gold Trim

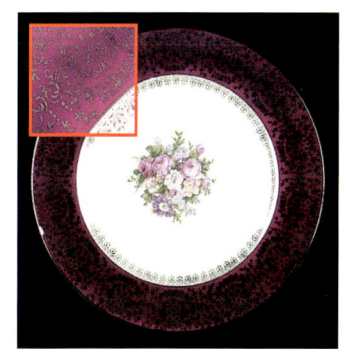

SP22
Service Plate Shown
Gold Trim

Eggshell Cavalier Shape

CPS2
Service Plate Shown
Gold Trim

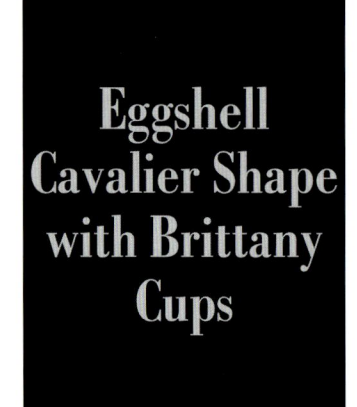

Eggshell Cavalier Shape with Brittany Cups

Imperial
by Lifetime China
Gold Trim

HLC342
Platinum Trim

Eggshell Nautilus Shape with Eggshell Cavalier Hollowware

Jaderose
by Lifetime China
Gold Trim

Burgundy
by Lifetime China
Gold Trim

Rhythm Shape with Eggshell Cavalier Hollowware

HLC26
Platinum Trim

Royal Harvest
RY255
Gold Trim

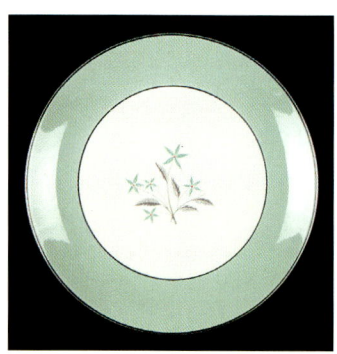

HLC723
Platinum Trim

W159
Platinum Trim

Baroness
by Century Service Corp.
Platinum Trim

Danube
CP203
by Cunningham & Pickett
Platinum Trim

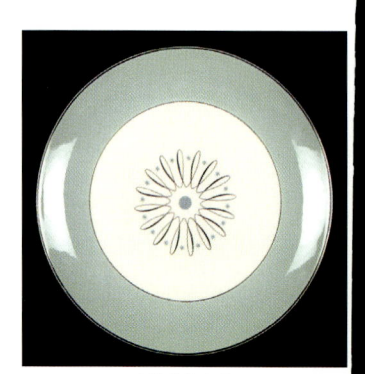

HLS302
Platinum Trim

Rhythm Shape with Eggshell Cavalier Hollowware

HLC592
Gold Trim

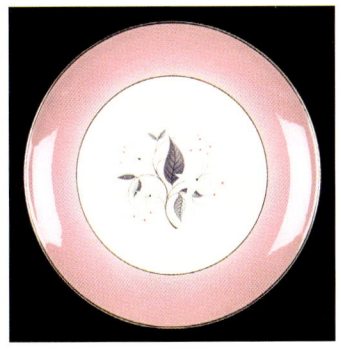

HLS301
Platinum Trim

Empress
by Century Service Corp.
Platinum Trim

Rhythm Shape with Eggshell Cavalier & Eggshell Nautilus Hollowware

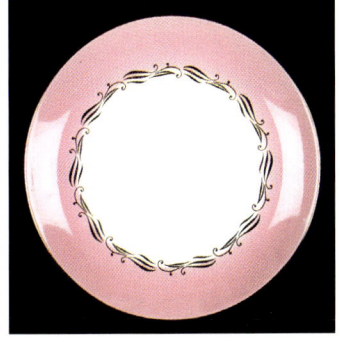

Sunrise–Pink
by Cunningham & Pickett
Gold Trim

Gold Crown
by Lifetime China
Gold Trim

Lynnwood
by Century Service Corp.
Platinum Trim

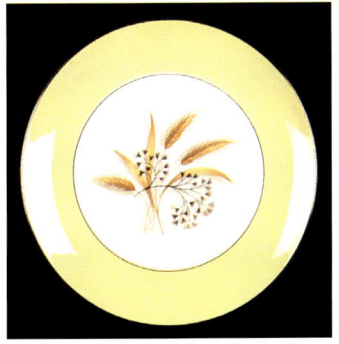

Autumn Gold
by Century Service Corp.
Gold Trim

Pink Radiance
No Trim

Right: *Painting platinum trim on pattern HLC549.*

389

CARNIVAL

Piece Types

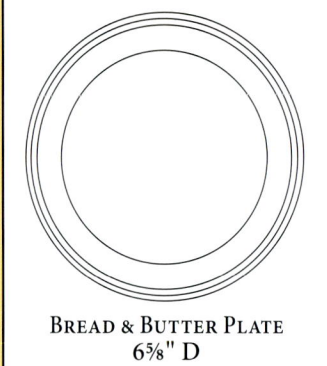

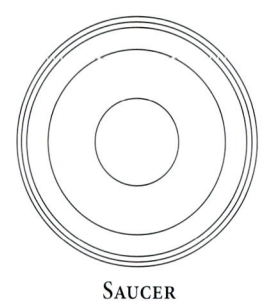

These drawings were made from actual stock at Replacements, Ltd. Check the piece type list for all known piece types in this shape.

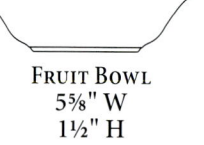

Bread & Butter Plate
6⅝" D

Saucer
5¾" D

Cup
4½" W
2½" H

Cereal Bowl
6⅛" W
2" H

Fruit Bowl
5⅝" W
1½" H

Above: *Mother's Carnival Oats boxes, by The Quaker Oats Company, that contained Carnival pieces.* **Right:** *Harlequin Yellow, Forest Green, and Turquoise Bread & Butter Plates, Gray Fruit Bowl, Light Green Cereal Bowl, Ivory Cup, and Cobalt Blue Saucer.*

Carnival Shape

CARNIVAL circa 1938 – 1950's

Carnival was one of several Homer Laughlin lines made expressly for one client. It was a bold, solid colored line produced for the Quaker Oats Company as a premium in Carnival brand Mother's Oats. Carnival is often hard to identify, or is overlooked, because it has no backstamp.

The nine colors of Carnival are: Red, Gray, Cobalt Blue, Turquoise, Fiesta Yellow, Harlequin Yellow, Ivory, Forest Green, and Light Green. While we have not confirmed specific production dates, the glaze colors utilized suggest two periods of color production. Early colors include: Red, Cobalt Blue, Light Green, Ivory, Turquoise, and both Harlequin Yellow and Fiesta Yellow; all colors utilized on Fiesta beginning in the 1930's. Carnival can also be found in Forest Green and Gray, which were not known to be used in the Homer Laughlin color pallet until 1951. Art for a backstamp (which was never used), found at the factory, suggests production of Carnival at least as late as 1954.

Left: *Fiesta Yellow (left), and Harlequin Yellow (right) Bread & Butter Plates.* **Right:** *Gray Cereal Bowl, Bread & Butter Plate, Fruit Bowl, and Cup & Saucer Set.* **Bottom:** *Photograph of the south front of Homer Laughlin's Plant No. 4.*

Carnival Piece Type List

From Homer Laughlin Literature with Confirmed Actual Pieces

Bowl, Cereal, 6⅛ inches
Bowl, Fruit, 5⅝ inches

Cup & Saucer Set
Cup, 2½ inches
Saucer, 5¾ inches

Plate, Bread & Butter, 6⅝ inches

South Front of Plant No. 4, Homer Laughlin China Co., Newell, W. Va.

391

Carnival Shape

Carnival–Ivory
Bread & Butter Plate Shown
No Trim

Carnival–Harlequin Yellow
Bread & Butter Plate Shown
No Trim

Carnival–Fiesta Yellow
Bread & Butter Plate Shown
No Trim

Carnival–Fiesta Red
Bread & Butter Plate Shown
No Trim

Carnival–Gray
Bread & Butter Plate Shown
No Trim

Carnival–Turquoise
Bread & Butter Plate Shown
No Trim

Carnival–Cobalt Blue
Bread & Butter Plate Shown
No Trim

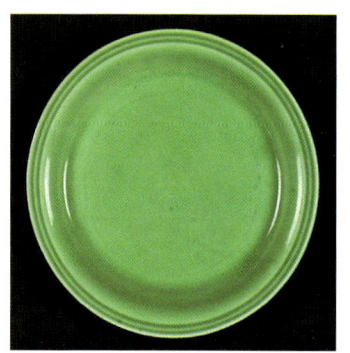

Carnival–Light Green
Bread & Butter Plate Shown
No Trim

Carnival–Forest Green
Bread & Butter Plate Shown
No Trim

Right: *Applying handles to cups.*

Modern Farmer

Piece Types

These drawings were made from actual stock or literature at Replacements, Ltd. Check the piece type list for all known piece types in this shape.

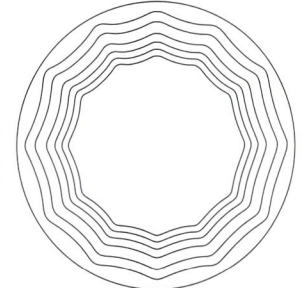

Dinner Plate
9" D

Creamer
4⅞" W
3⅛" H

Sugar Bowl with lid
5½" W
3½" H

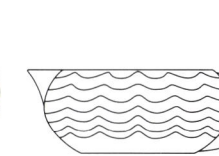

Gravy/Sauce Boat
7⅜" W
2½" H

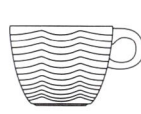

Cup
James River Potteries Style

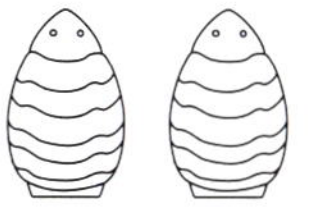

Salt & Pepper Set
James River Potteries Style

Cup
Homer Laughlin Style

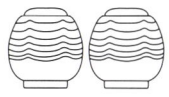

Salt & Pepper Set
Homer Laughlin Style

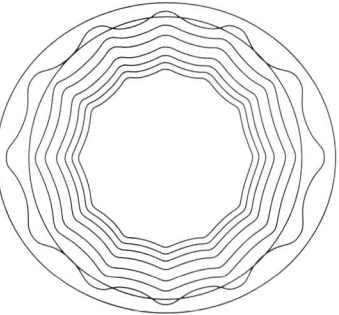

11" Platter
10⅞" W
9⅝" H

13" Platter
13¼" W
11¾" H

Collectors Note: Notice the difference between the cup handles made by Homer Laughlin and James River Potteries above. The salt & pepper set made by Homer Laughlin is similar to the Swing shape, and the one made by James River Potteries is pointed.

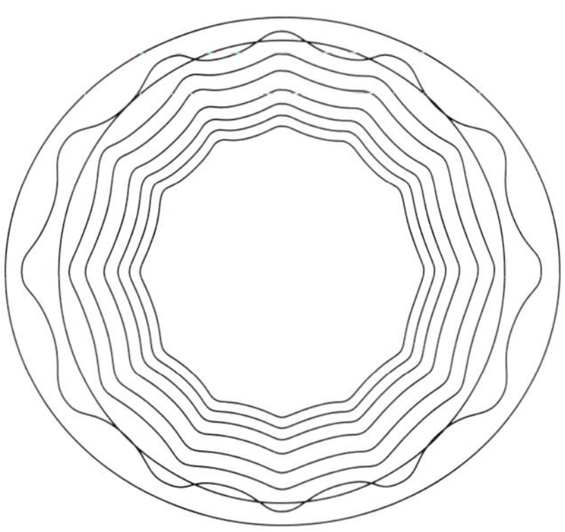

Above: Gascon pattern; 13" Oval Platter, 11" Oval Platter, Creamer, Sugar Bowl without lid, and Gravy/Sauce Boat. **Left:** Modern Farmer patterns; Red, Yellow, Light Green, and Rose. Photo taken at the Homer Laughlin Factory.

Homer Laughlin

MODERN FARMER
circa 1939 – 43 or later

The Modern Farmer shape was first produced as the Cascade line by the James River Potteries. This firm, located in Hopewell, Virginia employed 175 people. When James River ceased production of the shape a short time after its inception, circa 1939, it was continued by Homer Laughlin to fill orders for Sears who had been promoting the line. The Homer Laughlin produced pieces are predominately marked with the common Homer Laughlin company mark of the period, whereas the James River pieces can be found marked with that company's backstamp (Jo Cunningham, *Homer Laughlin China 1940s & 1950s*). Some of the piece types from the original production were modified by Homer Laughlin. The James River cup has a ring handle and the Homer Laughlin cup has an oval handle. Homer Laughlin shakers are similar to Swing shaped shakers, whereas James River shakers are pine cone shaped, as in the Sears illustration shown below.

Modern Farmer shaped patterns appear in the Sears catalogs from Fall & Winter, 1939-40, through Spring & Summer, 1943. It appears that James River Potteries ceased production prior to May 1940, indicating that most of the Modern Farmer may have been produced by Homer Laughlin.

Modern Farmer Piece Type List
From Homer Laughlin Literature with Confirmed Actual Pieces

Bowl, Cereal	Creamer	Plate, Salad, 7 inches
Bowl, Fruit, 5¼ inches	Cup & Saucer Set	Platter, Oval, 10⅞ inches
Bowl, Soup, 7½ inches	Gravy/Sauce Boat	Platter, Oval, 13¼ inches
Bowl, Vegetable Oval, 9½ inches	Gravy/Sauce Boat Underplate/Relish	Salt & Pepper Set
Bowl, Vegetable Round	Plate, Bread & Butter, 6 inches	Sugar Bowl with lid
Bowl, Vegetable Round Covered	Plate, Dinner, 9 inches	

Top right: *Cascade pattern; Dinner Plate, Bowl, Sugar Bowl with lid, Creamer, and Cup & Saucer Set. This set was originally made by James River Potteries, with later production by Homer Laughlin.* **Left:** *Gascon pattern; Sears, Roebuck & Co., Spring & Summer, 1943.* **Right:** *Breton pattern; Sears, Roebuck & Co., Fall & Winter, 1939-1940. This set was made by James River Potteries, but Homer Laughlin also made this pattern.*

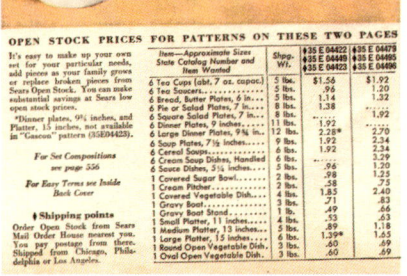

Modern Farmer Shape

Modern Farmer–White
No Trim

Modern Farmer–Yellow
No Trim

Modern Farmer–Light Green
No Trim

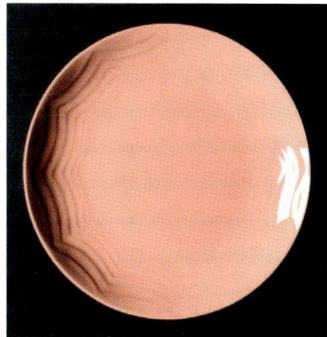

Modern Farmer–Rose
No Trim

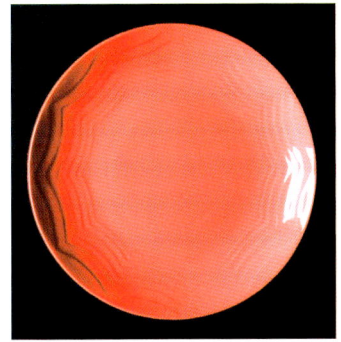

Modern Farmer–Red
No Trim

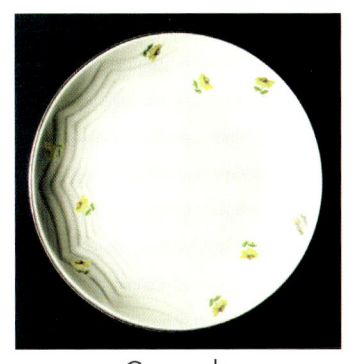

Cascade
Gold Trim

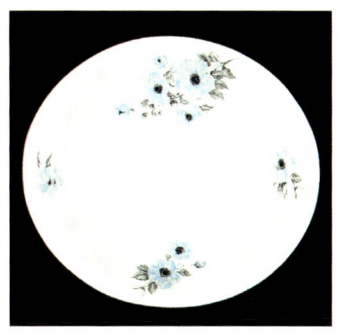

Gascon
Oval Platter Shown
No Trim

Breton
No Trim

HLC1605
No Trim

Right: *Aerial photograph of the Homer Laughlin Factory.*

Serenade

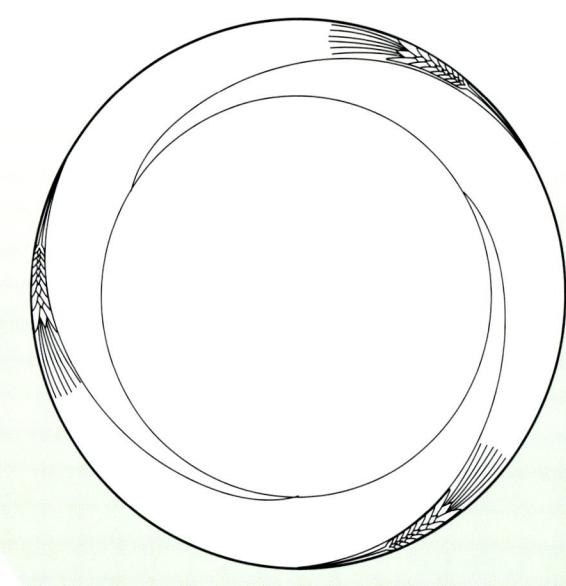

Piece Types

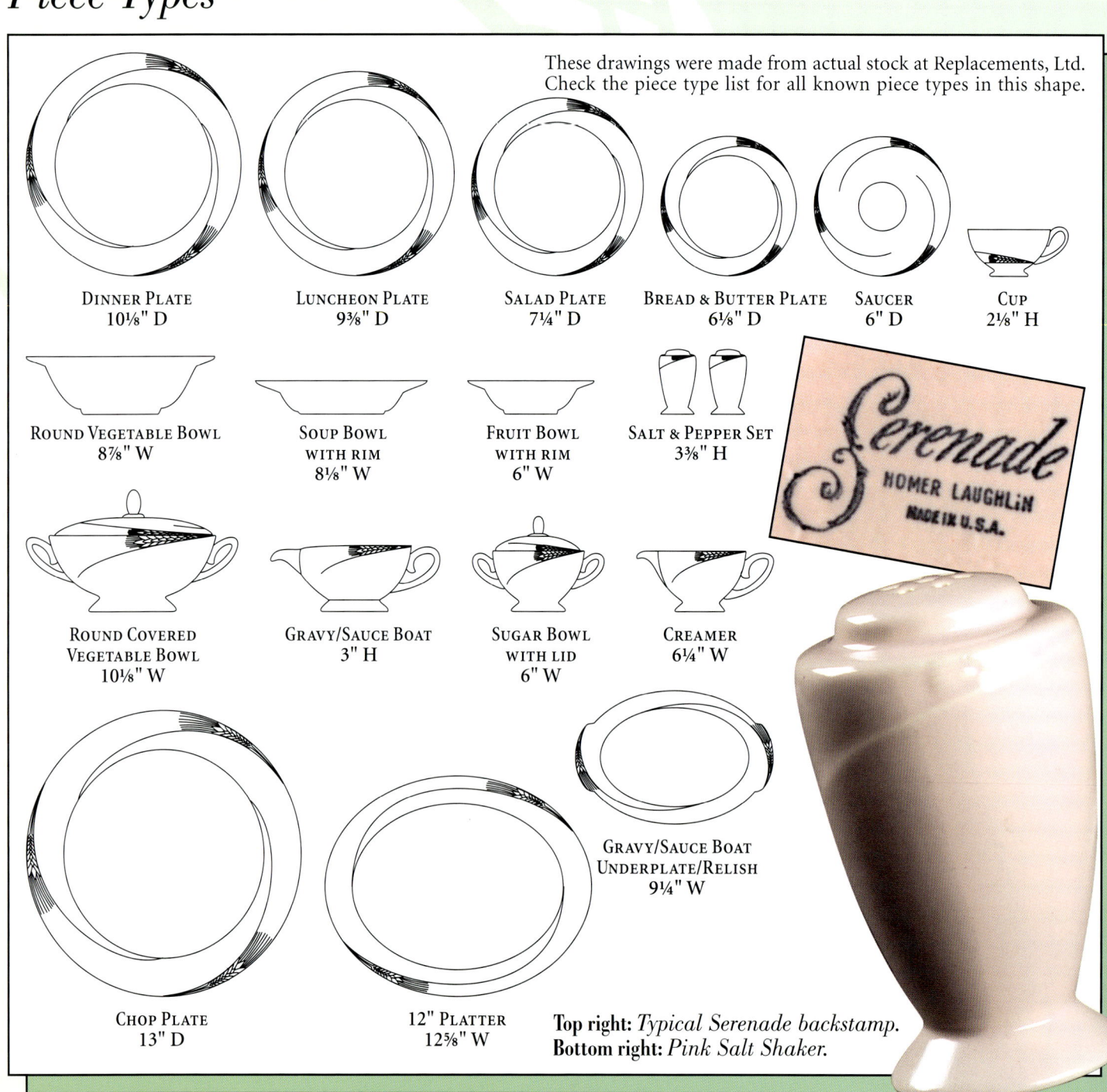

These drawings were made from actual stock at Replacements, Ltd. Check the piece type list for all known piece types in this shape.

- **Dinner Plate** 10⅛" D
- **Luncheon Plate** 9⅜" D
- **Salad Plate** 7¼" D
- **Bread & Butter Plate** 6⅛" D
- **Saucer** 6" D
- **Cup** 2⅛" H
- **Round Vegetable Bowl** 8⅞" W
- **Soup Bowl with rim** 8⅛" W
- **Fruit Bowl with rim** 6" W
- **Salt & Pepper Set** 3⅜" H
- **Round Covered Vegetable Bowl** 10⅛" W
- **Gravy/Sauce Boat** 3" H
- **Sugar Bowl with lid** 6" W
- **Creamer** 6¼" W
- **Chop Plate** 13" D
- **12" Platter** 12⅝" W
- **Gravy/Sauce Boat Underplate/Relish** 9¼" W

Top right: *Typical Serenade backstamp.*
Bottom right: *Pink Salt Shaker.*

396

Serenade Shape

SERENADE 1939 – 1942

"Serenade… the tableware of the year" proclaimed *Crockery, Glass & Lamps* in June 1939. Such fanfare raised expectations for a best selling line, but indications are that the results were less than anticipated. It is no coincidence that the pastel colored Lu-ray Pastels of competitor Taylor, Smith & Taylor had hit the market a short time before and had been doing quite well. Homer Laughlin was attempting to be competitive. "Serenade, a new shape in matte pastel colors, with gracefully whorled rim carrying a stylized wheat embossment, footed hollowware and lug handles. Serenade appears in blue, pink, green, and yellow, and its merchandizing setup is the same as that for 'Fiesta,' but priced about 25 percent less. A 20 piece set can be retailed for $3.40." (*Crockery, Glass & Lamps*, February 1939). The line was short-lived, despite early acclaim, and probably ceased production in 1942.

Left: *Advertisement featuring Serenade,* Crockery, Glass & Lamps, *1939.* **Top right:** *Yellow, Green, Blue, and Pink Dinner Plates, Blue Sugar Bowl with lid, Pink Creamer, Yellow Cup, and Green Saucer.* **Middle right:** *Yellow Chop Plate, Green Salad Plate, Blue Bread & Butter Plate, and Pink Cup & Saucer Set.* **Bottom right:** *Blue, Pink, Green, and Yellow Soup Bowls with rims.*

397

Homer Laughlin

Top left: Green Round Covered Vegetable Bowl, Soup Bowl with rim, and Gravy/Sauce Boat. **Top right:** Pink Round Covered Vegetable Bowl, Gravy/Sauce Boat Underplate/Relish, and Salt & Pepper Set. **Middle left:** Blue Fruit Bowl, Soup Bowl with rim, Bread & Butter Plate, Dinner Plate, Round Vegetable Bowl, Gravy/Sauce Boat, and Sugar Bowl with lid. **Middle right:** Yellow Chop Plate, Oval Platter, Round Vegetable Bowl, Creamer, and Round Covered Vegetable Bowl. **Bottom left:** Yellow Salt & Pepper Set, Dinner Plate, Luncheon Plate, Salad Plate, Bread & Butter Plate, Creamer, and Cup & Saucer Set. **Bottom right:** Green Round Vegetable Bowl, Chop Plate, Oval Platter, Round Covered Vegetable Bowl, Fruit Bowl, and Soup Bowl with rim.

Serenade Shape

Serenade Piece Type List

From Homer Laughlin Literature with Confirmed Actual Pieces

Bowl, Fruit, 6 inches
Bowl, Soup with rim, 8⅛ inches
Bowl, Vegetable Round, 8⅞ inches
Bowl, Vegetable Round Covered, 10⅛ inches
Creamer
Cup & Saucer Set
    Cup, 2⅛ inches
    Saucer, 6 inches
Gravy/Sauce Boat
Gravy/Sauce Boat Underplate/Relish, 9¼ inches
Plate, Bread & Butter, 6⅛ inches
Plate, Chop, 13 inches
Plate, Dinner, 10⅛ inches
Plate, Luncheon, 9⅜ inches
Plate, Salad, 7¼ inches
Platter, 12⅝ inches
Salt & Pepper Set
Sugar Bowl with lid

Top left: *Pink Sugar Bowl with lid, and Creamer.* **Top right:** *Yellow Round Vegetable Bowl, Fruit Bowl with rim, and Soup Bowl with rim.* **Middle left:** *Yellow Dinner Plate, Blue Luncheon Plate, Pink Salad Plate, and Green Bread & Butter Plate.* **Middle right:** *Blue Round Covered Vegetable Bowl, Chop Plate, Oval Platter, Salt & Pepper Set, and Cup & Saucer Set.*

Serenade–Pink
No Trim

Serenade–Blue
No Trim

Serenade–Green
No Trim

Serenade–Yellow
No Trim

Piccadilly

Piece Types

These drawings were made from actual stock at Replacements, Ltd. Check the piece type list for all known piece types in this shape.

Dinner Plate
10⅛" D

Luncheon Plate
9⅛" D

Salad Plate
8¼" D

Dessert Plate
7¼" D

Bread & Butter Plate
6¼" D

Soup Bowl with rim
8⅛" W

Fruit Bowl with rim
5⅞" W

Sugar Bowl with lid
6" W

Creamer
5⅞" W
2⅞" H

Saucer
5" W

Cup
2½" H

13" Platter
13½" W

11" Platter
11¾" W

Gravy/Sauce Boat Underplate/Relish
9⅛" W

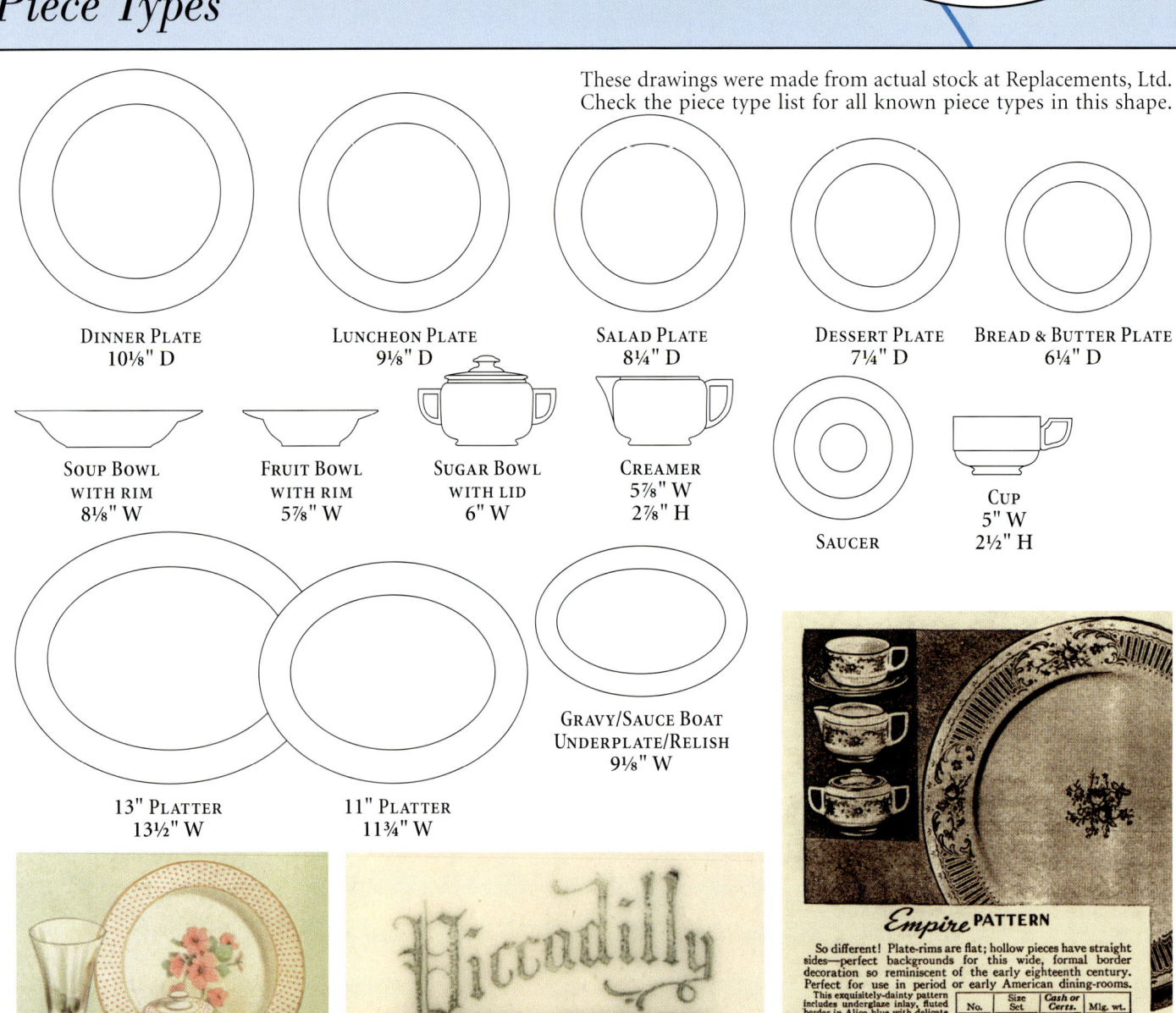

Left: *Mary Anne* pattern; Sears, Roebuck & Co. Catalog, 1948. **Middle:** Typical *Piccadilly* backstamp. **Right:** *Empire* pattern; Larkin Catalog, 1940.

Piccadilly Shape

PICCADILLY
1940 – 1948 or later

The Piccadilly shape is very easily confused with Homer Laughlin's Brittany shape. Both shapes utilized the same Brittany flatware, but Piccadilly introduced new hollowware forms. The flat tops and solid, flanged finials of Piccadilly are a departure from the slightly domed and open handled forms of Brittany. To make identification even more difficult, similar decorations were applied to both shapes. While Brittany was popular and had a long production run, Piccadilly was short-lived.

China, Glass & Lamps noted in 1940, "Piccadilly, a new dinnerware shape with plain, rather wide-brim plates, square handles — decorated with 12 new patterns, underglaze borders with inlaid decals." Sears offered the Mary Anne pattern in 1948.

Piccadilly are usually white, decal decorated patterns. Piccadilly pieces have a distinctive backstamp on larger shapes.

Top left: Temp Pica pattern; Dinner Plate, Oval Platter, Cup & Saucer Set, Fruit Bowl, and Soup Bowl with rim. *Top right:* B1315 and Temp Pica patterns; B1315 Cup (left) is Brittany Shape and Temp Pica Cup (right) is Piccadilly Shape. *Bottom right:* Temp Pica pattern; Sugar Bowl with lid, and Creamer.

Piccadilly Piece Type List
From Homer Laughlin Literature with Confirmed Actual Pieces

Bowl, Fruit with rim, 5⅞ inches
Bowl, Soup with rim, 8⅛ inches
Bowl, Vegetable Round Covered
Creamer
Cup & Saucer Set
  Cup, 2½ inches

Gravy/Sauce Boat Underplate/Relish, 9⅛ inches
Plate, Bread & Butter, 6¼ inches
Plate, Dessert, 7¼ inches
Plate, Dinner, 10⅛ inches
Plate, Luncheon, 9⅛ inches

Plate, Salad, 8¼ inches
Platter, Oval, 11¾ inches
Platter, Oval, 13½ inches
Sugar Bowl with lid

Piccadilly Shape

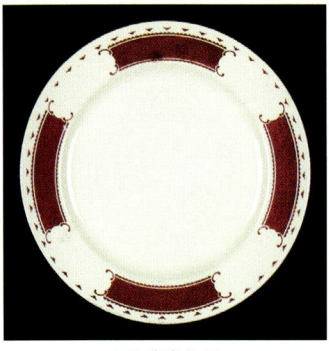

HLC917
No Trim

Oakleaf
P523
No Trim

P526
Saucer Shown
No Trim

P527
No Trim

Empire–Pink
Gold Trim

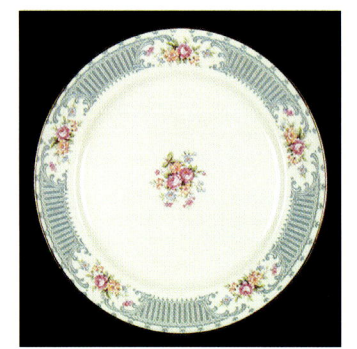

Empire–Blue
P511
Gold Trim

Temp Pica
280, P513
Gold Trim

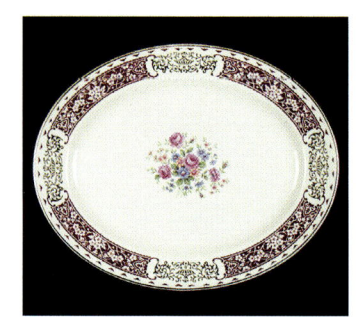

HLC2067
Oval Platter Shown
Gold Trim

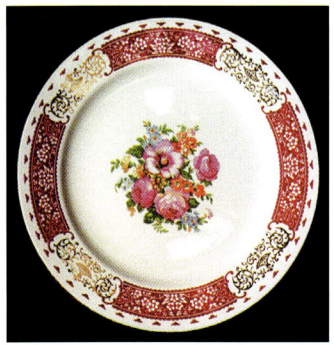

Royal Maroon
P516
Gold Trim

HLC290
No Trim

Mary Anne
Gold Trim

Rope Edge

ROPE EDGE
circa 1941

Rope Edge, a name we have given this shape, is similar to the Kraft shape. The difference between the shapes is that Rope Edge flatware is coupe shaped and Kraft flatware is rim shaped. Rope Edge was designed especially for Sears, Roebuck & Co. in 1941. Some reports say it was never put into production; however, Replacements, Ltd. and our customers have found Rope Edge patterns in the market, proving patterns are out there. The "Fruit Skin Glazes" were created, at the request of Sears, to produce another solid colored line that would rival the popularity of Fiesta. Most, but not all, of the images in this chapter are from the Homer Laughlin Factory.

Right: *Rope Edge patterns; Pieces with "Fruit Skin Glazes," Berry Bowl, Cereal Bowl, Salad Plate, Cup & Saucer Set, Dinner Plate, and Sugar Bowl with lid.*

Rope Edge Piece Type List
From Frederick Rhead's Modeling Log

Bowl, Berry
Bowl, Cereal
Bowl, Cream Soup with lid & Saucer
Bowl, Fruit
Bowl, Salad
Bowl, Vegetable Oval
Bowl, Vegetable Oval, Covered
Bowl, Vegetable Oval, Divided
Bowl, Vegetable Oval, Straight Sides

Bowl, Vegetable Round
Creamer
Cup & Saucer Set
 (pedestal foot cup)
Cup & Saucer Set
 (vertical grooves on foot of cup)
Cup & Saucer Set, Demitasse
Plate, Bread & Butter
Plate, Dessert

Plate, Dinner
Plate, Luncheon
Plate, Salad
Platter, Tree
Teapot with lid
Tray, Cracker
Tray, Dish
Tray, Relish Square

Rope Edge Shape

HLC1713
Green Band & Rope
Green Trim

HLC1716
Cream Band & Rope
Green Trim

HLC1811
Yellow Band, White Rope
Green Trim

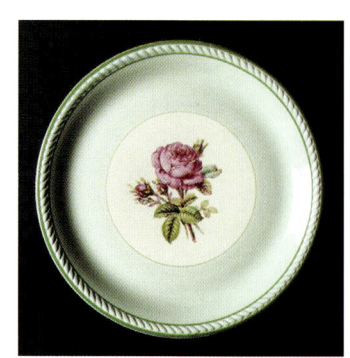

HLC1340
Blue Band & Rope
Green Trim

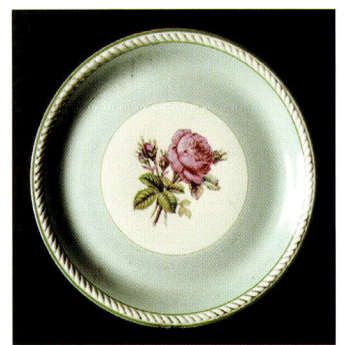

HLC1823
Blue Band, White Rope
Green Trim

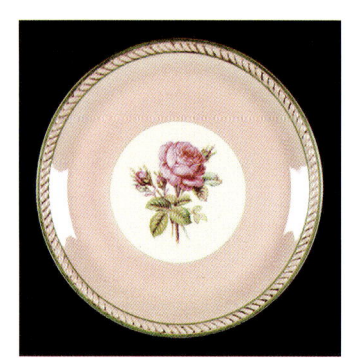

HLC1717
Pink Band & Rope
Green Trim

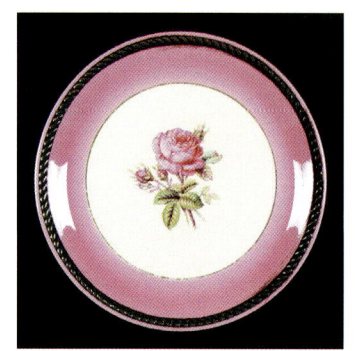

HLC1714
Pink Band, Green Rope
No Trim

R6096
Gold Trim

R6100
Black Trim

R6110
Black Trim

HLC1485
No Trim

HLC1809
No Trim

HLC1814
No Trim

HLC1820
No Trim

HLC1822
No Trim

HLC1815
No Trim

Rope Edge Shape

HLC1824 No Trim	HLC1808 No Trim	HLC1812 No Trim	HLC1819 No Trim
HLC1813 No Trim	HLC1810 No Trim	HLC1817 No Trim	HLC1816 No Trim
HLC1715 No Trim	HLC1818 No Trim	HLC1821 No Trim	HLC1490 No Trim
HLC1491 No Trim	HLC1489 No Trim	HLC1801 No Trim	HLC1800 No Trim

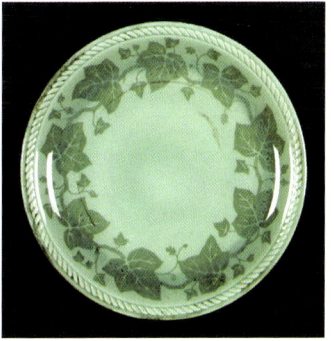

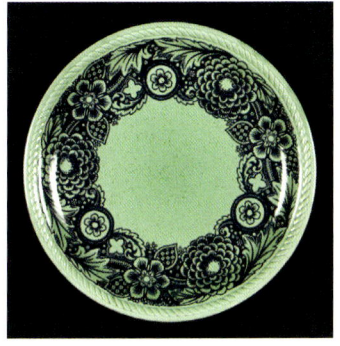

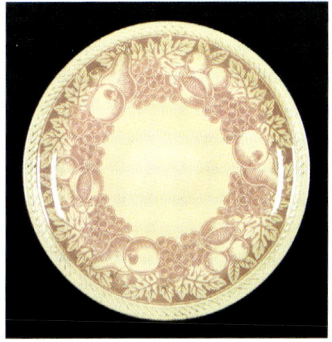

Rope Edge Shape

HLC1499 *No Trim*	 **HLC1802** *No Trim*	 **HLC1788** *No Trim*	 **HLC1488** *No Trim*
 **HLC1493** *No Trim*	 **HLC1492** *No Trim*	 **HLC1803** *No Trim*	 **HLC1807** *No Trim*
 **HLC1806** *No Trim*	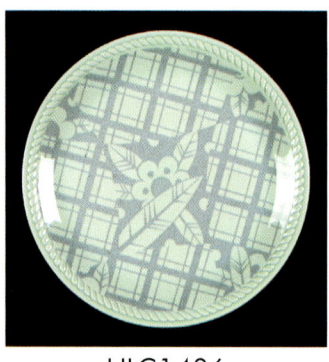 **HLC1486** *No Trim*	 **HLC1805** *No Trim*	 **HLC1804** *No Trim*
 **HLC1487** *No Trim*	 **HLC1498** *No Trim*	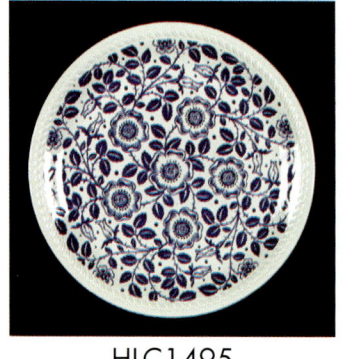 **HLC1495** *No Trim*	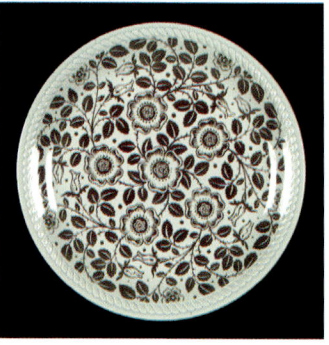 **HLC1494** *No Trim*

Rope Edge Shape

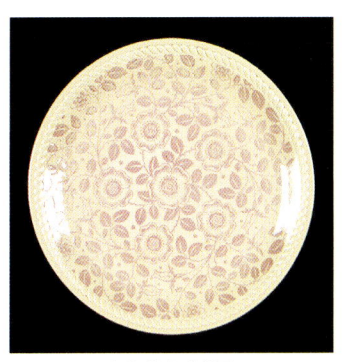

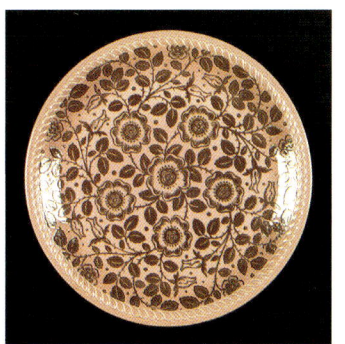

HLC1497
No Trim

HLC1496
No Trim

Above: *Photograph of worker sanding cup handles at the Homer Laughlin Factory.*

LIBERTY

Piece Types

These drawings were made from actual stock at Replacements, Ltd. Check the piece type list for all known piece types in this shape.

Dinner Plate
10" D

Luncheon Plate
9⅛" D

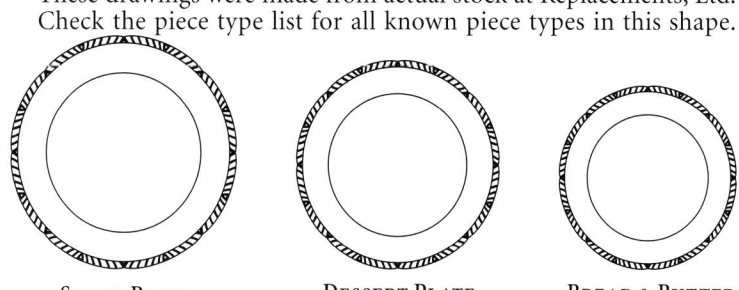

Salad Plate
8¼" D

Dessert Plate
7⅜" D

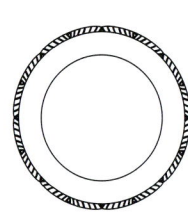

Bread & Butter Plate
6¼" D

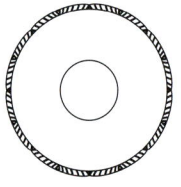

Saucer
6⅛" D

Cup
4½" W
2¾" H

Sugar Bowl with lid
4⅝" W x 5⅝" H

Creamer
5⅝" W
3⅜" H

Gravy/Sauce Boat
8⅝" W
3¾" H

Round Covered Vegetable Bowl
10⅜" W
5⅝" H

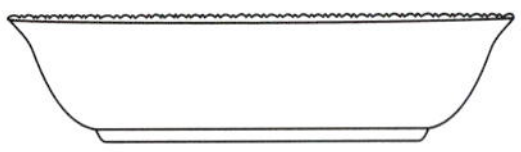

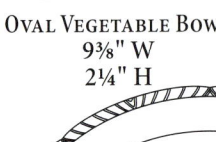

Oval Vegetable Bowl
9⅜" W
2¼" H

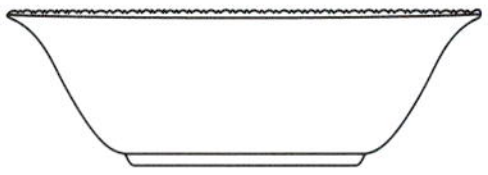

Round Vegetable Bowl
8¾" W
2¾" H

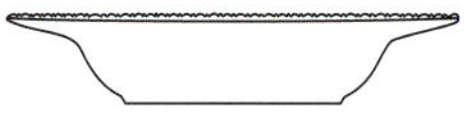

Soup Bowl with rim
8¼" W
1⅝" H

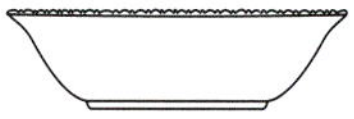

Cereal Coupe Bowl
6¼" W
1¾" H

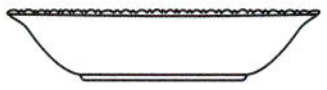

Fruit Bowl
5¾" W
1¼" H

Teapot with lid
10¼" W
7⅞" H

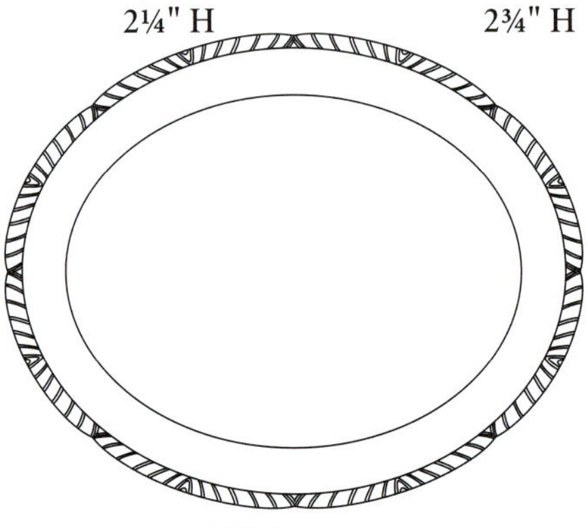

15" Platter
15⅜" W
12⅛" H

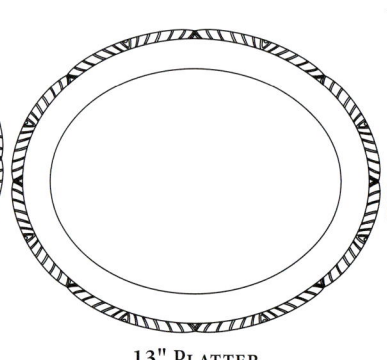

13" Platter
13⅝" W
10¾" H

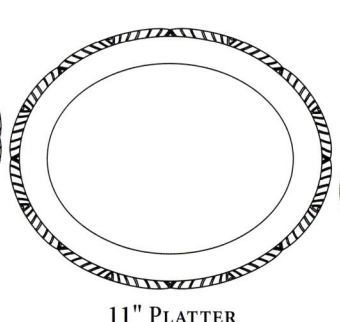

11" Platter
11¾" W
9¼" H

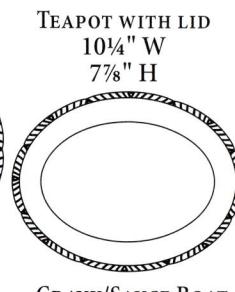

Gravy/Sauce Boat Underplate/Relish
8½" W x 6⅜" H

408

Liberty Shape

LIBERTY
1942 – 1954 or later

Homer Laughlin's Liberty shape has an edge treatment that imitates gadrooning. Adapted from metal working, and used to create decorative elements for china and glass, gadrooned edges have repeating small pearls or bumps. Liberty was a re-design of the earlier Homer Laughlin Newell shape, according to factory historian Jack Welch. Liberty and Newell can easily be confused at first glance, but the hollowware is distinct, and the shapes are quite different upon inspection.

Liberty decorated patterns include Historical America for Woolworth and patterns for Sears, Roebuck & Co. Liberty first appears in the Sears Catalog in 1943 with the Tulip Time pattern, and remained as a catalog offering as late as 1954, when the Windsor Rose pattern was featured. Liberty has a traditional Homer Laughlin backstamp that does not mention the shape or pattern. Historical America is an exception to this backstamp rule, look further into this chapter to learn more.

Left: *Monticello pattern; Original Liberty ad from the Homer Laughlin Factory.*
Right: *Tulip Time pattern; Sears, Roebuck & Co. Catalog, 1943.*

Homer Laughlin

HISTORICAL AMERICA

The Historical America pattern is featured on the Liberty shape. Produced exclusively for F. W. Woolworth, it was introduced in 1942 and discontinued circa 1952 (Lehner), or 1939 to 1958 according to Harvey Duke. Historical America has an elaborate backstamp stating: "Picture reproduced from original painting by Joseph Boggs Beale." Each piece in the line has a different scene and can be found in the more common red (pattern W449), or blue (pattern W342).

Historical America

Bowl, Cereal	Traveling By Old Stage Coach… 1847
Bowl, Fruit	Lincoln as a Rail Splitter. 1834
Bowl, Soup with rim	Ponce De Leon Discovers Florida. 1512
Bowl, Vegetable Oval	Lincoln's Gettysburg Address… 1863
Bowl, Vegetable Round	The Pony Express. 1860
Bowl, Vegetable Round Covered	Franklin's Experiment. 1752
Creamer	The Star Spangled Banner Francis Scott Key. 1814
Cup	Franklin's Experiment. 1752
Gravy/Sauce Boat	Lincoln's Gettysburg Address… 1863
Plate, Bread & Butter	Paul Revere Crossing Bridge into Medford Town… 1775
Plate, Dessert, 7⅜ inches	The First Tone from The Liberty Bell… 1753
Plate, Dinner, 10 inches	Gen. Washington Taking Command of the Army. 1775
Plate, Luncheon, 9⅛ inches	Betsy Ross Showing the First Flag… 1777
Plate, Salad, 8¼ inches	Purchase of Manhattan Island. 1626
Platter, 11¾ inches	The First Steamboat The Clermont. 1807
Platter, 13⅝ inches	The First Thanksgiving. 1621
Saucer	Arrival of The Mayflower. 1607
Sugar Bowl with lid	Barbara Fritchie. 1862
Teapot with lid	The Pony Express. 1860

Top left: *Original drawing copied from the Beale print.* **Top right:** *Historical America–Red pattern; Dinner Plate.* **Middle right:** *Cover of the* Beale Portfolio of Prints *with Rhead's name and the date 1941 at the top.* **Bottom right:** *One of the Beale prints that Rhead used as a reference for Historical America.*

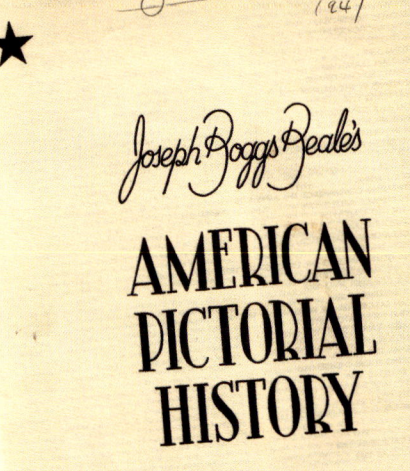

Liberty Shape

LIBERTY TEAPOT   DR. NO. 3609   MAR 1, 1943   6" DEEP PLATE OR 6" PLATE CENTER
SUGAR COVER BORDER   CREAM HANDLE

All pictured are the Historical America–Red pattern. **Top left:** Original watercolor proposal for teapot with Ponce De Leon image, from the factory. **Top right:** Teapot with lid as produced; note decoration changes from original art shown at left to a design featuring the Pony Express. **Middle right:** Original decals with notes, from the factory. **Bottom left:** Cereal Bowl, Round Vegetable Bowl, and Cup & Saucer Set. **Bottom right:** Typical Historical America backstamp.

Homer Laughlin

CURRIER & IVES

A decal pattern using classic American Currier & Ives imagery was produced on the Liberty shape. Two adaptations of this same decal were produced. The Sun Gold pattern has an elaborate border of gold filigree. The other has a blue border and is called Blue Heaven.

Top right: *Blue Heaven pattern; Round Covered Vegetable Bowl.* **Middle left:** *Sun Gold pattern; Dinner Plate, Oval Platter, Cup & Saucer Set, and Salad Plate.* **Middle right:** *Blue Heaven pattern; Dinner Plate, Oval Platter, Gravy/Sauce Boat with unattached Underplate, Fruit Bowl, and Soup Bowl with rim.* **Bottom left:** *Detail of Lady Esther silverplate fork from Queen Esther Silver.* **Bottom middle:** *Queen Esther pattern; backstamp.* **Bottom right:** *Queen Esther pattern; Salad Plate, Dinner Plate, Cup & Saucer Set, Liquor Cocktail glassware, and Lady Esther silverplate flatware from Queen Esther Silver.*

Homer Laughlin

Liberty Piece Type List

From Homer Laughlin Literature with Confirmed Actual Pieces

- Bowl, Cereal Coupe, 6¼ inches
- Bowl, Cranberry
- Bowl, Fruit, 5¾ inches
- Bowl, Soup with rim, 8¼ inches
- Bowl, Vegetable Oval, 9⅜ inches
- Bowl, Vegetable Round, 8¾ inches
- Bowl, Vegetable Round Covered, 10⅜ inches
- Creamer
- Cup & Saucer Set
  - Cup, 2¾ inches
  - Saucer, 6⅛ inches
- Gravy/Sauce Boat
- Gravy/Sauce Boat Underplate/Relish, 8½ inches
- Plate, Bread & Butter, 6¼ inches
- Plate, Dessert, 7⅜ inches
- Plate, Dinner, 10 inches
- Plate, Luncheon, 9⅛ inches
- Plate, Salad, 8¼ inches
- Platter, Oval, 11¾ inches
- Platter, Oval, 13⅝ inches
- Platter, Oval, 15⅝ inches
- Sugar Bowl with lid
- Teapot with lid

Above left: *Original factory design drawing for the Liberty Sugar Bowl with lid.* **Top right:** *Dogwood pattern; Creamer, and Sugar Bowl with lid.* **Bottom right:** *Original drawing of the Liberty Creamer.*

Liberty Shape

HLC3024
No Trim

PEA6
by Pearl China
Gold Trim

HLC990
Gold Trim

HLC2139
Oval Platter Shown
Red Trim

HLC2104
Soup Bowl Shown
No Trim

HLC466
Luncheon Plate Shown
Gold Trim

HLC39
Gold Trim

W146
Gold Trim

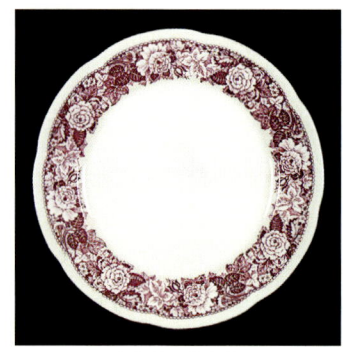

HLC582
Salad Plate Shown
No Trim

HLC465
No Trim

HLC680
Bread & Butter Plate Shown
Gold Trim

HLC1980
No Trim

HLC1012
Gold Trim

I42
No Trim

HLC557
Bread & Butter Plate Shown
Gold Trim

HLC578
No Trim

Liberty Shape

R3682
Gold Trim

9739A
No Trim

R3691A
No Trim

HLC593
Luncheon Plate Shown
No Trim

478
Bread & Butter Plate Shown
No Trim

HLC307
Salad Plate Shown
No Trim

W442
No Trim

4685
No Trim

HLC441
Gold Trim

Dogwood
L613
Gold Trim

W246
Gold Trim

R3683A
No Trim

L615
Gold Trim

L630
Gold Trim

HLC1974
No Trim

HLC1972
No Trim

415

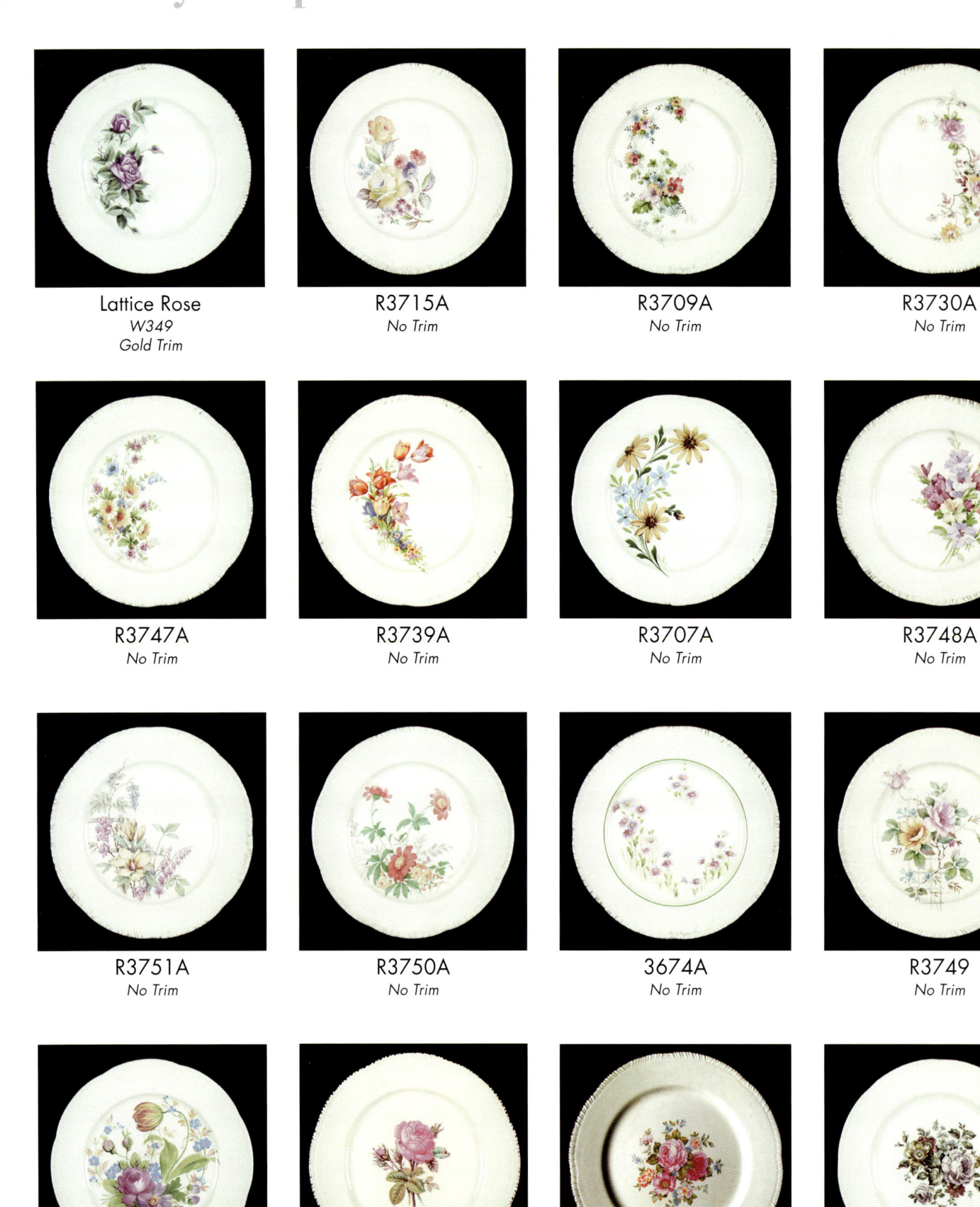

Liberty Shape

Lattice Rose W349 Gold Trim	**R3715A** No Trim	**R3709A** No Trim	**R3730A** No Trim
R3747A No Trim	**R3739A** No Trim	**R3707A** No Trim	**R3748A** No Trim
R3751A No Trim	**R3750A** No Trim	**3674A** No Trim	**R3749** No Trim
HLC1971 No Trim	**Calirose** by Cunningham & Pickett Gold Trim	**HLC1201** Gold Trim	**HLC1977** No Trim

Liberty Shape

Stratford
by Cunningham & Pickett
Gold Trim

L611
Gold Trim

HLC1202
No Trim

Greenbriar
by Cunningham & Pickett
Gold Trim

HLC984
Gold Trim

HLC280
Gold Trim

Windsor Rose
L633
Platinum Trim

Magnolia
Gold Trim

HLC631
Gold Trim

1830
No Trim

HLC77
Multi-Motif
Gold Trim

Currier & Ives
Multi-Motif
Gold Trim

HLC553
Salad Plate Shown
No Trim

Colonial Kitchen
Gold Trim

Colonial Kitchen
No Trim

L612
Gold Trim

Liberty Shape

HLC661
Salad Plate Shown
Platinum Trim

HLC423
Gold Trim

Queen Esther
SS28
Gold Trim

Apple Blossom
Gold Trim

HLC1976
No Trim

Golden Rose
Gold Trim

HLC521
No Trim

HLC911
Soup Bowl Shown
Gold Trim

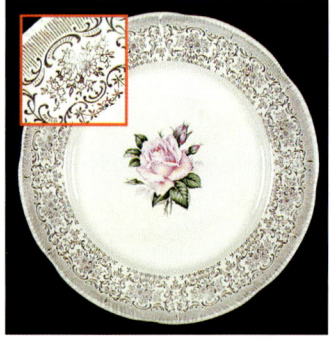

HLC2084
No Trim

HLC947
Soup Bowl Shown
No Trim

HLC1221
No Trim

HLC2133
Gold Trim

HLC1126
Bread & Butter Plate Shown
No Trim

HLC259
Gold Trim

L621
Gold Trim

HLC2123
Gold Trim

Liberty Shape

Monticello
Gold Trim

HLC2042
Gold Trim

HLC114
Bread & Butter Plate Shown
Gold Trim

HLC87
Bread & Butter Plate Shown
Gold Trim

HLC189
Gold Trim

HLC367
No Trim

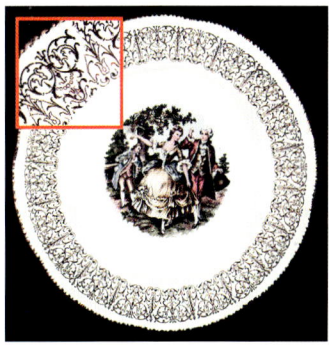

HLC2176
Gold Trim

HLC542
No Trim

HLC357
Multi-Motif
Gold Trim

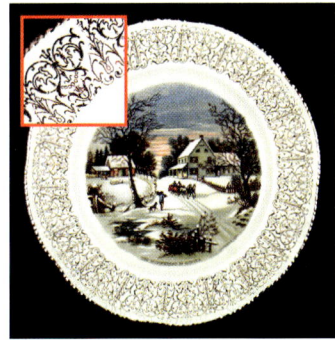

Sun Gold
Gold Trim

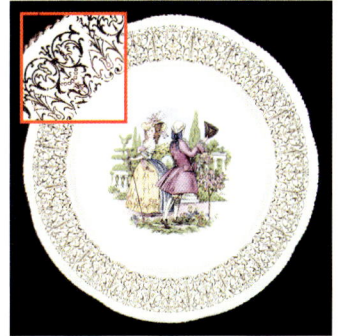

HLC490
Multi-Motif
Gold Trim

HLC1022
Bread & Butter Plate Shown
Gold Trim

Historical America–Blue
Multi-Motif
No Trim

Historical America–Red
Multi-Motif
No Trim

Pastoral

Piece Types

These drawings were made from actual stock at Replacements, Ltd. Check the piece type list for all known piece types in this shape.

Bread & Butter Plate	Saucer	Cup	Cereal Bowl	Fruit Bowl
6⅝" D	5⅞" D	4¾" W, 2⅜" H	6⅜" W, 1⅝" H	5⅞" W, 1⅜" H

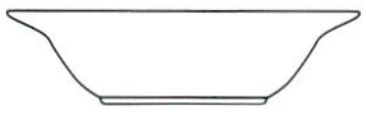

Wild Rose pattern; Cup & Saucer Set, Fruit Bowl, Bread & Butter Plate, and Cereal Bowl.

Pastoral Shape

PASTORAL circa 1944 – 1958

Pastoral, Harvest, and Wild Rose are patterns that were made by Homer Laughlin for the Mother's Oats company as premiums. The backstamps for these patterns include the pattern name. Pastoral was produced by Homer Laughlin and Taylor, Smith & Taylor for Mother's Oats. Both the Homer Laughlin version and Taylor, Smith & Taylor version identify the manufacturer as part of the backstamp. Wild Rose and Harvest were also produced by Royal China. Royal China backstamps are black.

Collectors Note: Pastoral is a multi-motif pattern, meaning each of the six piece types will have a different scene.

Top left: *Original drawing for Pastoral from the Homer Laughlin Factory.* **Top right:** *Pastoral pattern; Cup & Saucer Set, Fruit Bowl, Bread & Butter Plate, and Cereal Bowl.* **Bottom left:** *Harvest pattern; Cup & Saucer Set, Fruit Bowl, Bread & Butter Plate, and Cereal Bowl.* **Bottom right:** *Harvest pattern; The left plate was made by Homer Laughlin and the right plate was made by Royal China.*

Homer Laughlin

Pastoral Piece Type Lists
Harvest Pattern

From Homer Laughlin Literature with Confirmed Actual Pieces

Bowl, Cereal, 6⅜ inches
Bowl, Fruit, 5⅞ inches
Cup & Saucer Set
   Cup, 2⅜ inches
   Saucer, 5⅞ inches
Plate, Bread & Butter, 6⅝ inches

Above: Harvest backstamps. Left: Homer Laughlin. Right: Royal China.

Wild Rose Pattern

From Homer Laughlin Literature with Confirmed Actual Pieces

Bowl, Cereal, 6⅜ inches
Bowl, Fruit, 5⅞ inches
Bowl, Soup with rim, 9 inches
Bowl, Vegetable, 9 inches
Creamer
Cup & Saucer Set
   Cup, 2⅜ inches
   Saucer, 5⅞ inches
Gravy/Sauce Boat with attached
   Underplate, handleless
Plate, Bread & Butter, 6⅝ inches
Plate, Chop, 12 inches
Plate, Dinner
Plate, Luncheon, 9⅛ inches
Platter, Lugged
Sugar Bowl with lid

Above: Wild Rose backstamps. Left: Homer Laughlin. Right: Royal China.

Pastoral Pattern

From Homer Laughlin Literature with Confirmed Actual Pieces

Bowl, Cereal, 6⅜ inches
Bowl, Fruit, 5⅞ inches
Cup & Saucer Set
   Cup, 2⅜ inches
   Saucer, 5⅞ inches
Plate, Bread & Butter, 6⅝ inches
Plate, Luncheon, 9⅛ inches

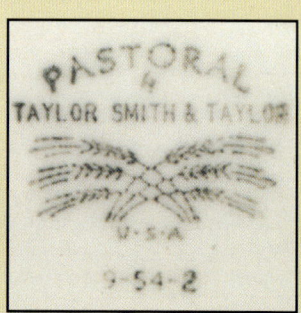

Above: Pastoral backstamps. Left: Homer Laughlin. Right: Taylor, Smith & Taylor.

Pastoral Shape

Wild Rose
Bread & Butter Plate Shown
No Trim

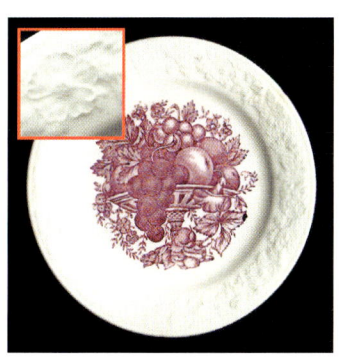

Harvest
Bread & Butter Plate Shown
No Trim

Pastoral
Luncheon Plate Shown
No Trim

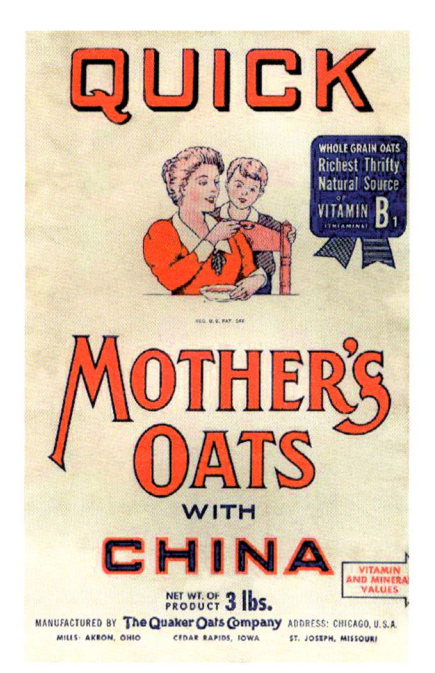

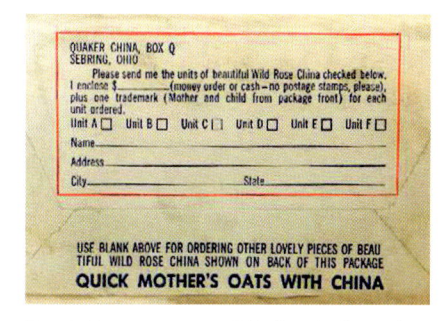

Top left and above: *Mother's Oats box containing Wild Rose china pattern.*
Bottom left: *Mother's Oats box containing Pastoral china pattern.*
Bottom right: *Multi-motif images on Pastoral china.*

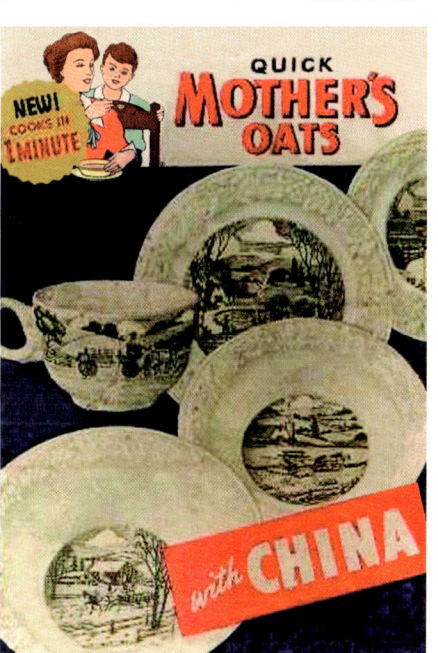

423

Jubilee

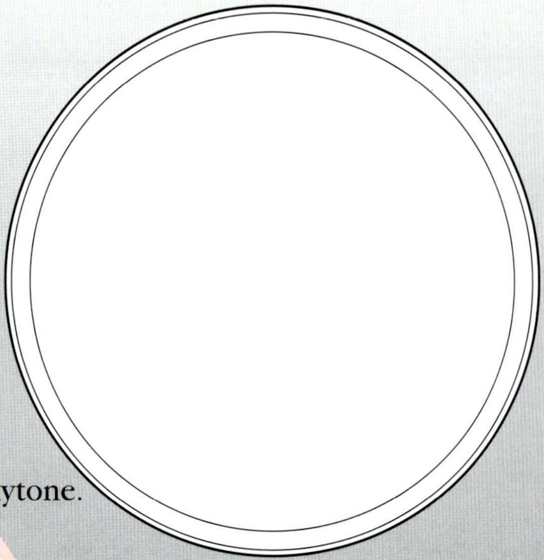

Lines with the same shape as Jubilee are Debutante, Suntone, and Skytone.

Piece Types

These drawings were made from actual stock or literature at Replacements, Ltd. Check the piece type list for all known piece types in this shape.

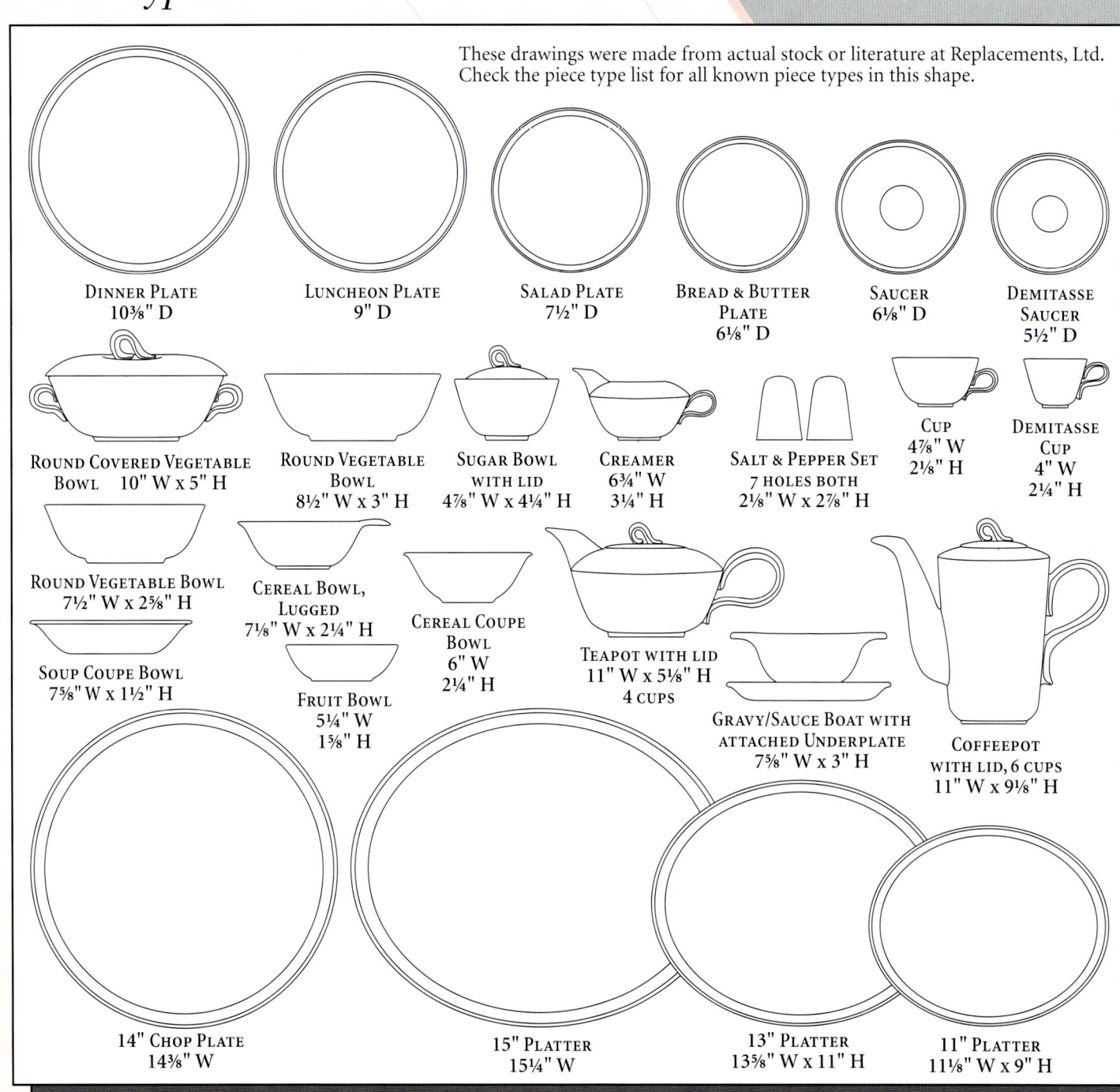

Dinner Plate 10⅜" D

Luncheon Plate 9" D

Salad Plate 7½" D

Bread & Butter Plate 6⅛" D

Saucer 6⅛" D

Demitasse Saucer 5½" D

Round Covered Vegetable Bowl 10" W x 5" H

Round Vegetable Bowl 8½" W x 3" H

Sugar Bowl with lid 4⅞" W x 4¼" H

Creamer 6¾" W 3¼" H

Salt & Pepper Set 7 holes both 2⅛" W x 2⅞" H

Cup 4⅞" W 2⅛" H

Demitasse Cup 4" W 2¼" H

Round Vegetable Bowl 7½" W x 2⅝" H

Cereal Bowl, Lugged 7⅛" W x 2¼" H

Cereal Coupe Bowl 6" W 2¼" H

Teapot with lid 11" W x 5⅛" H 4 cups

Gravy/Sauce Boat with attached Underplate 7⅝" W x 3" H

Coffeepot with lid, 6 cups 11" W x 9⅛" H

Soup Coupe Bowl 7⅝" W x 1½" H

Fruit Bowl 5¼" W 1⅝" H

14" Chop Plate 14⅜" W

15" Platter 15¼" W

13" Platter 13⅝" W x 11" H

11" Platter 11⅛" W x 9" H

Shape – Jubilee
line – Jubilee

JUBILEE 1948

To help celebrate the 75th anniversary of the Homer Laughlin China Company, the factory introduced a new shape in 1948, aptly named Jubilee. The pieces in this line were made in solid colors. Homer Laughlin was competing with other manufacturers, who would be introducing similar solid-colored patterns during the prosperous post-war years. The Jubilee colors introduced were: Celadon Green, Shell Pink, Mist Gray, and Cream "Foam" Beige. Pieces have a distinctive backstamp declaring them to be "Jubilee." This "modern" shape gives us plates with large eating surfaces rounding up to a slight rim.

Top left: *Typical Jubilee backstamp.* **Above:** *Jubilee pamphlet, both sides showing piece types and colors. Retail pamphlet from the Homer Laughlin Factory.*

Homer Laughlin

Jubilee

the new dinnerware sensation

● The Homer Laughlin China Company—creator of Fiesta, Eggshell, Riviera and other famous dinnerware—proudly presents its crowning achievement, Jubilee. Here is the supreme expression of seventy-five years of ceramic craftsmanship; one of the finest lines ever created by American designers and craftsmen.

Jubilee will be obtainable in four beautiful, delicate color tones: Celadon Green, Mist Gray, Foam Beige, Shell Pink. It has the charm, richness and personality of fine china. It is unique in the soft depth and loveliness of its glaze; unmatched in its graceful, flowing lines.

THE HOMER LAUGHLIN CHINA COMPANY
Newell — West Virginia

CROCKERY & GLASS JOURNAL for July.

Left: Three concept drawings for advertisements before the line was named Jubilee. These three drawings were found at the Homer Laughlin Factory.
Top right: Jubilee advertisement; Crockery & Glass Journal, *July 1948.*

426

Shape – Jubilee
line – Jubilee

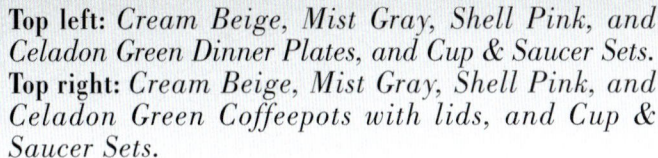

Top left: *Cream Beige, Mist Gray, Shell Pink, and Celadon Green Dinner Plates, and Cup & Saucer Sets.*
Top right: *Cream Beige, Mist Gray, Shell Pink, and Celadon Green Coffeepots with lids, and Cup & Saucer Sets.*
Middle left: *Shell Pink Cereal Bowl, Round Vegetable Bowl, Soup Coupe Bowl, and Fruit Bowl.*
Second down on right: *Celadon Green Creamer, Cream Beige Bread & Butter Plate, Shell Pink Dinner Plate, Mist Gray Sugar Bowl with lid, Cream Beige Cup & Saucer Set, Mist Gray Luncheon Plate, Celadon Green Salad Plate, and Shell Pink Demitasse Cup & Saucer Set.*
Third down on right: *Celadon Green Teapot with lid, Shell Pink Coffeepot with lid, Mist Gray Sugar Bowl with lid, Mist Gray Creamer, and Cream Beige Salt & Pepper Set.*
Bottom left: *Shell Pink Dinner Plate, Mist Gray Luncheon Plate, Celadon Green Salad Plate, and Cream Beige Bread & Butter Plate.*
Bottom middle: *Cream Beige Cup & Saucer Set, Dinner Plate, Luncheon Plate, Salad Plate, and Bread & Butter Plate.*
Bottom right: *Celadon Green Covered Vegetable Bowl, and Gravy/Sauce Boat with attached Underplate.*

Debutante

DEBUTANTE
1951

In 1951, a new line was advertised using the Jubilee shape. "Debutante" ads began appearing in consumer catalogs like Sears and Montgomery Ward and the *Crockery & Glass Journal*. Where the Jubilee patterns were solid colors, Debutante patterns were on a white body and were largely decorated with bold floral decals.

Above: Hawaii pattern; *Crockery & Glass Journal, May 1951*. *Top right:* Original engraving for an ad for Gray Laurel found at the Homer Laughlin Factory. *Bottom:* Pamphlet for the Flame Flower pattern in the Debutante Line found at the Homer Laughlin Factory. *Right:* Typical Debutante backstamp.

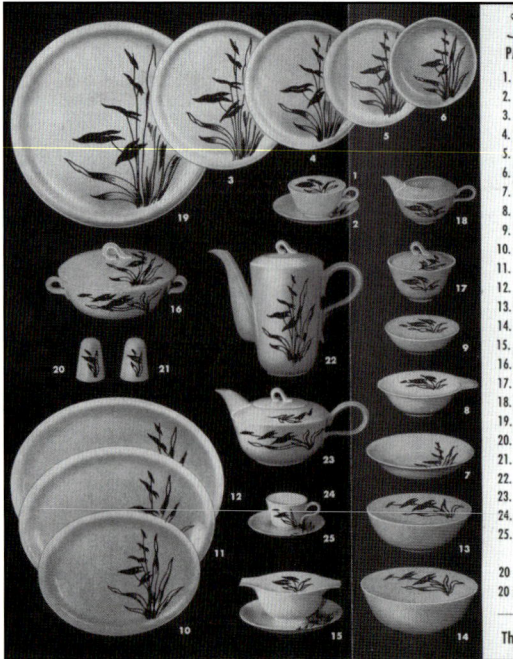

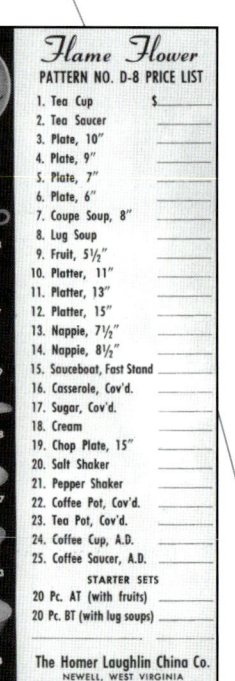

Gray Laurel — Debutante

Homer Laughlin presents its newest, smartly styled line of exciting dinnerware, created to meet the demand of modern America.

The subtle beauty of a graceful shape and a new "Snow White" glaze combine with fresh, new, colorful, decorative treatments to bring charm to the table of the most discriminating hostess. GRAY LAUREL in soft silvery gray with crisp accents in dubonnet is one of many new available patterns, moderately priced.

The Homer Laughlin China Co.
NEWELL, WEST VIRGINIA

Hawaii

Exquisite simplicity and elegance is reflected by this young spirited DEBUTANTE pattern—gracefully brushed in deep forest green leaves to silhouette the soft wine purple details of a tropical flower.

The Homer Laughlin China Co.
NEWELL, WEST VIRGINIA
CROCKERY & GLASS JOURNAL for May 1951

Flame Flower by Homer Laughlin

Flame Flower PATTERN NO. D-8 PRICE LIST

1. Tea Cup
2. Tea Saucer
3. Plate, 10"
4. Plate, 9"
5. Plate, 7"
6. Plate, 6"
7. Coupe Soup, 8"
8. Lug Soup
9. Fruit, 5½"
10. Platter, 11"
11. Platter, 13"
12. Platter, 15"
13. Nappie, 7½"
14. Nappie, 8½"
15. Sauceboat, Fast Stand
16. Casserole, Cov'd.
17. Sugar, Cov'd.
18. Cream
19. Chop Plate, 15"
20. Salt Shaker
21. Pepper Shaker
22. Coffee Pot, Cov'd.
23. Tea Pot, Cov'd.
24. Coffee Cup, A.D.
25. Coffee Saucer, A.D.

STARTER SETS
20 Pc. AT (with fruits)
20 Pc. BT (with lug soups)

The Homer Laughlin China Co.
NEWELL, WEST VIRGINIA

Shape – Jubilee
line – Debutante

Top left: *MW181 pattern; Sugar Bowl with lid, Fruit Bowl, and Round Vegetable Bowl.* **Top right:** *MW181 pattern; Dinner Plate, and Cup & Saucer Set.* **Middle left:** *D1 pattern; Dinner Plate, Cup & Saucer Set, and Bread & Butter Plate.* **Middle right:** *D1 pattern; Oval Platter, Creamer, and Sugar Bowl with lid.* **Bottom left:** *JCP131 pattern; Gravy/Sauce Boat with attached Underplate.* **Bottom middle:** *JCP131 pattern; Oval Platter, Dinner Plate, Fruit Bowl, and Salt & Pepper Set.* **Bottom right:** *JCP131 pattern; Sugar Bowl with lid, and Creamer.*

Skytone

SKYTONE — 1951

Skytone was also introduced on the Jubilee shape around 1951. The Skytone line features a sky blue body with contrasting white handles. Many different patterns were produced in the Skytone line, most with a center decoration and accented with platinum trim. This line is seen in advertisements as late as 1958.

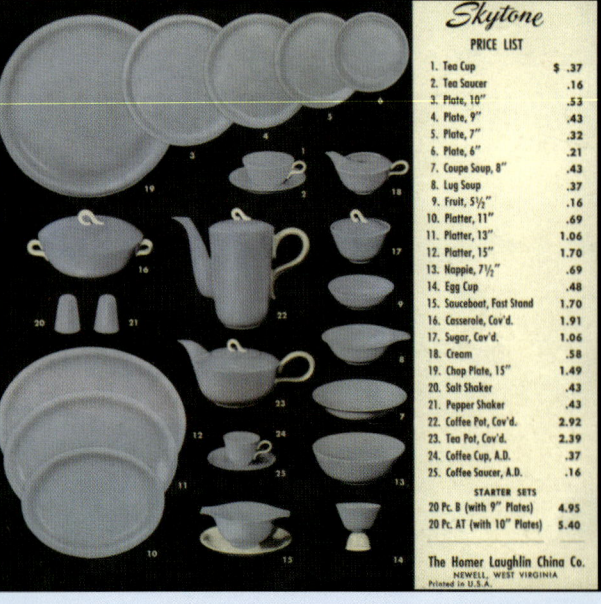

AMERICA'S NEWEST DINNERWARE CREATION

By blending subtle sky-blue color with the clays for permanence and uniformity, and accenting with snow-white handles for charm and elegance, Homer Laughlin presents "SKYTONE," styled to enhance any table.

Very moderately priced.

THE HOMER LAUGHLIN CHINA CO.
NEWELL, WEST VIRGINIA

CROCKERY & GLASS JOURNAL for March 5, 1951

Skytone PRICE LIST

#	Item	Price
1.	Tea Cup	$ .37
2.	Tea Saucer	.16
3.	Plate, 10"	.53
4.	Plate, 9"	.43
5.	Plate, 7"	.32
6.	Plate, 6"	.21
7.	Coupe Soup, 8"	.43
8.	Lug Soup	.37
9.	Fruit, 5½"	.16
10.	Platter, 11"	.69
11.	Platter, 13"	1.06
12.	Platter, 15"	1.70
13.	Nappie, 7½"	.69
14.	Egg Cup	.48
15.	Sauceboat, Fast Stand	1.70
16.	Casserole, Cov'd.	1.91
17.	Sugar, Cov'd.	1.06
18.	Cream	.58
19.	Chop Plate, 15"	1.49
20.	Salt Shaker	.43
21.	Pepper Shaker	.43
22.	Coffee Pot, Cov'd.	2.92
23.	Tea Pot, Cov'd.	2.39
24.	Coffee Cup, A.D.	.37
25.	Coffee Saucer, A.D.	.16

STARTER SETS
20 Pc. B (with 9" Plates) ... 4.95
20 Pc. AT (with 10" Plates) ... 5.40

The Homer Laughlin China Co.
NEWELL, WEST VIRGINIA
Printed in U.S.A.

NEW Bluemont

THE HOMER LAUGHLIN CHINA COMPANY

BLUEMONT . . . The ever popular light blue Skytone ware gains fresh appeal with the dainty pink and white blossoms and graceful stem treatment of this lovely pattern. White handles and platinum trim lines are added to furnish the correct finishing touch. Pattern No. HLS 205
THE HOMER LAUGHLIN CHINA COMPANY, NEWELL, W. VA.

- BREAD & BUTTER PLATE 6" - .35
- PIE PLATE 7" - .45
- LUNCHEON PLATE 9" - .75
- DINNER PLATE 10" - .85
- TEA CUP - .55
- TEA SAUCER - .35
- CREAM - 1.05
- TEA POT COV'D. - 2.75
- SUGAR, COV'D. - 2.00
- COUPE SOUP 8" - .60
- SALT - .75
- LUG SOUP - .55
- ROUND VEGETABLE DISH, 8½" - 1.05
- PEPPER - .75
- FRUIT, 5¼" - .30
- OVAL PLATTER 13¼" - 1.65
- OVAL PLATTER 11¼" - .90
- FAST-STAND SAUCE BOAT - 3.00

Top right: *Skytone advertisement; Crockery & Glass Journal, March 1951.*
Left: *Pamphlet for Skytone found at the Homer Laughlin Factory.*
Above: *Bluemont pattern; Pamphlet found at the Homer Laughlin Factory.*

430

Shape – Jubilee
line – Skytone

Top left: *Stardust pattern; Dinner Plate, Salad Plate, Bread & Butter Plate, and Cup & Saucer Set.* **Top right:** *Stardust pattern; Teapot with lid, Coffeepot with lid, Cup & Saucer Set, Creamer, and Sugar Bowl with lid.* **Middle left:** *Stardust pattern; Round Covered Vegetable Bowl.* **Middle right:** *Typical Skytone backstamp.* **Bottom left:** *Skytone Blue pattern; Gravy/Sauce Boat with attached Underplate.* **Bottom right:** *Stardust pattern; Gravy/Sauce Boat with attached Underplate.*

Suntone

SUNTONE 1951

Suntone, another line using the Jubilee shape, was featured in advertisements in 1951. Suntone is a description of the pattern, a solid terra cotta color. The only decoration is the contrasting white handles of the cups and accessory pieces.

Top right: *Suntone advertisement;* Crockery & Glass Journal, *1951.*
Below: *Pamphlet for Suntone found at the Homer Laughlin Factory.*

Suntone advertisement

ONCE in a blue moon a star is born—that is what happened when HOMER LAUGHLIN'S skilled craftsmen refined nature's own clays and blended them to create beautiful "SUNTONE"—America's newest dinnerware. The rich red-brown colored body is complemented by striking accents of snowy-white handles—producing a product of elegance and charm to thrill every hostess.

VERY MODERATELY PRICED

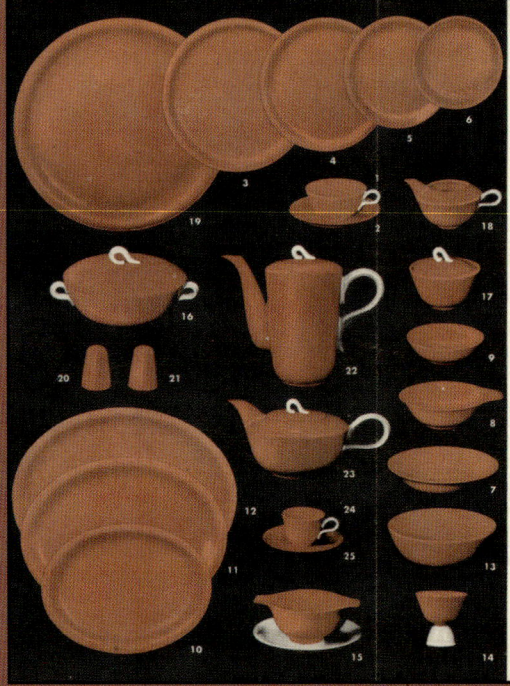

The Homer Laughlin China Co.
NEWELL, WEST VIRGINIA

Suntone by Homer Laughlin

Suntone Price List

1.	Tea Cup	$ .35
2.	Tea Saucer	.15
3.	Plate, 10"	.50
4.	Plate, 9"	.40
5.	Plate, 7"	.30
6.	Plate, 6"	.20
7.	Coupe Soup, 8"	.40
8.	Lug Soup	.35
9.	Fruit, 5½"	.15
10.	Platter, 11"	.65
11.	Platter, 13"	1.00
12.	Platter, 15"	1.60
13.	Nappie, 7½"	.65
14.	Egg Cup	.45
15.	Sauceboat, Fast Stand	1.60
16.	Casserole, Cov'd.	1.80
17.	Sugar, Cov'd.	1.00
18.	Cream	.55
19.	Chop Plate, 15"	1.40
20.	Salt Shaker	.40
21.	Pepper Shaker	.40
22.	Coffee Pot, Cov'd.	2.75
23.	Tea Pot, Cov'd.	2.25
24.	Coffee Cup, A.D.	.35
25.	Coffee Saucer, A.D.	.15
	STARTER SETS	
	20 Pc. B (with 9" Plates)	4.95
	20 Pc. AT (with 10" Plates)	5.40

The Homer Laughlin China Co.
NEWELL, WEST VIRGINIA

Shape – Jubilee
line – Suntone

Top right: *Salt & Pepper Set, and Creamer.* Top right: *Dinner Plate, Bread & Butter Plate, and Cup & Saucer Set.* Bottom left: *Lugged Cereal Bowl.* Bottom Right: *Typical Suntone backstamp.*

Jubilee Piece Type List

From Homer Laughlin Literature With Confirmed Actual Pieces

Bowl, Cereal, 6 inches
Bowl, Cereal Lugged, 7⅛ inches
Bowl, Fruit, 5¼ inches
Bowl, Soup Coupe, 7⅜ inches
Bowl, Vegetable Round, 7½ inches
Bowl, Vegetable Round, 8½ inches
Bowl, Vegetable Round, 9 inches
Bowl, Vegetable Round, 10 inches
Bowl, Vegetable Round Covered
 (Casserole), 10 inches
Coffeepot with lid

Creamer
Cup & Saucer Set
 Cup, 2⅛ inches
 Saucer, 6⅛ inches
Cup & Saucer Set, Demitasse
 Cup, 2¼ inches
 Saucer, 5½ inches
Eggcup, Double
Gravy/Sauce Boat
 with attached Underplate
Plate, Bread & Butter, 6⅛ inches

Plate, Chop, 14⅜ inches
Plate, Dinner, 10⅜ inches
Plate, Luncheon, 9 inches
Plate, Salad, 7½ inches
Platter Oval, 11⅛ inches
Platter Oval, 13⅜ inches
Platter Oval, 15¼ inches
Salt & Pepper Set
Sugar Bowl with lid
Teapot with lid

Jubilee Shape

Jubilee Line

Mist Gray
No Trim

Celadon Green
No Trim

Cream "Foam" Beige
No Trim

Debutante Line

Shell Pink
No Trim

Gray Laurel
No Trim

HLC1625
No Trim

HLC570
No Trim

HLC1191
No Trim

Dogwood
No Trim

MW181
Luncheon Plate Shown
No Trim

HLC1623
No Trim

Wild Grapes
No Trim

D10
Gray Band
No Trim

D16
No Trim

Jubilee Shape

D11 *Platinum Trim*	**HLC1631** *No Trim*	**Hawaii** *D17* *No Trim*	**D1** *No Trim*
D18 *No Trim*	**RCP25** *Gray Band* *No Trim*	**RCP27** *Yellow Band* *No Trim*	**D14** *No Trim*
Flame Flower *No Trim*	**JCP131** *No Trim*	**D2** *No Trim*	**HLC371** *No Trim*

Skytone Line

Skytone *No Trim*	**Narcissus** *Platinum Trim*	**HG2** *Round Vegetable Bowl Shown* *Platinum Trim*

435

Jubilee Shape

Blue Mist
Platinum Trim

Stardust
HLS180
Platinum Trim

Bluemont
HLS205
Platinum Trim

Sequence
Platinum Trim

Suntone Line

HLC663
Oval Platter Shown
Gold Trim

Suntone
No Trim

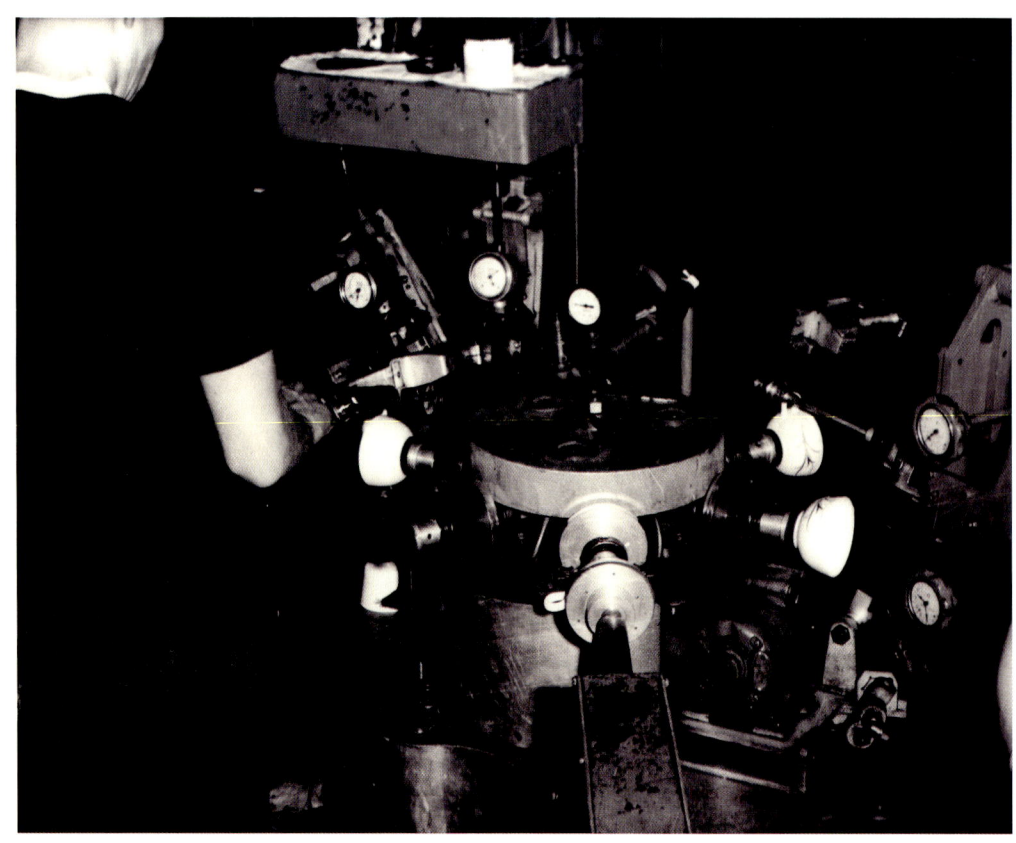

Above: *Worker at the Homer Laughlin Factory.*

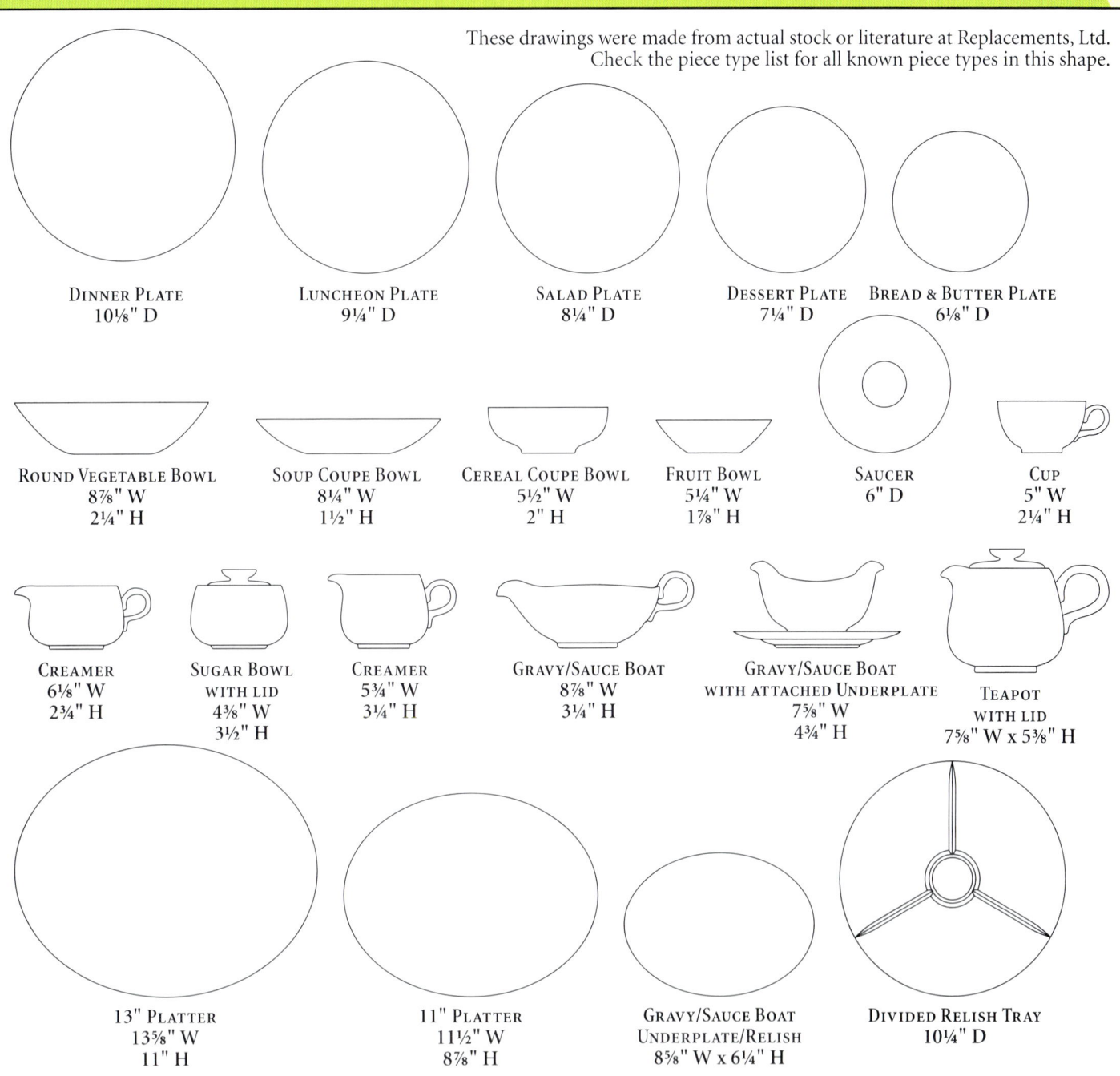

Rhythm

Piece Types

These drawings were made from actual stock or literature at Replacements, Ltd. Check the piece type list for all known piece types in this shape.

Dinner Plate
10⅛" D

Luncheon Plate
9¼" D

Salad Plate
8¼" D

Dessert Plate
7¼" D

Bread & Butter Plate
6⅛" D

Round Vegetable Bowl
8⅞" W
2¼" H

Soup Coupe Bowl
8¼" W
1½" H

Cereal Coupe Bowl
5½" W
2" H

Fruit Bowl
5¼" W
1⅞" H

Saucer
6" D

Cup
5" W
2¼" H

Creamer
6⅛" W
2¾" H

Sugar Bowl with Lid
4⅜" W
3½" H

Creamer
5¾" W
3¼" H

Gravy/Sauce Boat
8⅞" W
3¼" H

Gravy/Sauce Boat with attached Underplate
7⅝" W
4¾" H

Teapot with Lid
7⅝" W x 5⅜" H

13" Platter
13⅝" W
11" H

11" Platter
11½" W
8⅞" H

Gravy/Sauce Boat Underplate/Relish
8⅝" W x 6¼" H

Divided Relish Tray
10¼" D

437

Homer Laughlin

RHYTHM
1949 – 1966 or later

    Homer Laughlin produced Rhythm as a solid color line and with decal decorations. The solid colors utilized for Rhythm include: Burgundy, Gray, Chartreuse, Dark Green, and Harlequin Yellow. Undecorated white pieces are reported. In 1951, *Crockery & Glass Journal* ran an ad for American Provincial on the Rhythm shape, this was the earliest promotion for the shape we found.

    A January 1953 ad in *China, Glass & Lamps* featured a pattern named Trellis on the Rhythm shape. Montgomery Ward picked up the line in 1956 and offered Rhythm patterns through 1961. John Plain, a wholesale dealer, offered Rhythm patterns beginning in 1957, and Bennett Wholesale Catalogs included Rhythm patterns from 1958 through 1962. White Flower was a Rhythm pattern sold exclusively to J.J. Newberry. In 1966, the *China, Glass & Tableware Red Book Directory* ad for Homer Laughlin notes: "Overglaze Decorated Cavalier and Rhythm shapes," indicating the shape was in use through at least 1966. Rhythm patterns bear the distinctive Rhythm backstamp, except on smaller pieces.

    Rhythm flatware and bowls were used for several other shapes during the 60's, including Bristol, Charm House, Duratone, Fashion, Orbit, the Serenade Line, Studio, and Vogue.

Left: Homer Laughlin Factory retail brochures, left to right: Cascade, Frolic, Golden Wheat, and Sun Valley patterns.

Left: Typical Rhythm backstamp.
Right: RY308 pattern; Three Tier Server.

Pitcher/Jug	Three Tier Server	Two Tier Server
10" W	9¼" W	9¼" W
7¼" H	13½" H	10" H

Rhythm Shape

AMERICAN PROVINCIAL...Pennsylvania Dutch pattern with a cheery point of view that's welcome any time, any place. You'll love the bright gaiety of the quaint, stylized figures and flowers in definite shades of red, black, deep blue and green (plus a dash of chartreuse) on white semi-porcelain. Contents of sets on page 536.

708-727	C1050	23-pc. Set (service for 4).....$15.25
708-735	C1595	35-pc. Set (service for 6).....22.95
708-743	C2450	53-pc. Set (service for 8).....34.95

Top: American Provincial pattern; Homer Laughlin retail brochure. **Middle left:** American Provincial pattern; John Plain Catalog, 1956-1957. **Middle right:** American Provincial pattern; Oval Platter, Dinner Plate, Oval Platter, and Creamer. **Bottom right:** American Provincial pattern; Dinner Plate, Bread & Butter Plate, Salad Plate, Cereal Coupe Bowl, Fruit Bowl, Soup Coupe Bowl, and Cup & Saucer Set.

Homer Laughlin

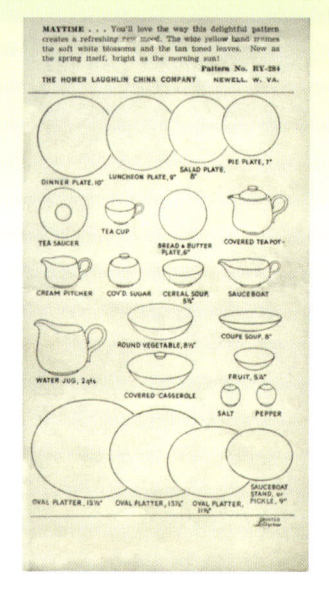

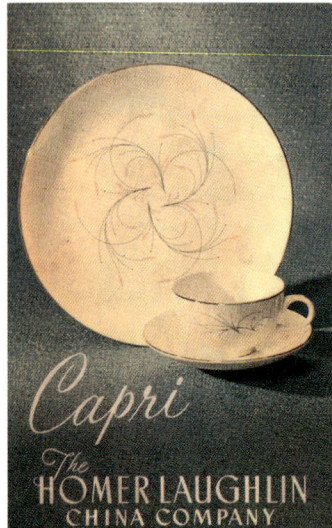

Top: *White Flower* pattern; Homer Laughlin retail brochure outside and inside. **Middle left:** *Maytime* pattern; Homer Laughlin retail brochure outside and inside. **Middle:** *Bordeaux* pattern; Crockery & Glass Journal *advertisement*. **Middle right:** *Rubaiyat* pattern; Crockery & Glass Journal *advertisement*. **Bottom left:** *Capri* pattern; Homer Laughlin retail brochure outside. **Bottom middle:** *Frolic* pattern; John Plain Catalog, 1956-1957.

Rhythm Shape

Top left: *Rhythm patterns; Gray Oval Platter, Yellow Dinner Plate, Burgundy Round Vegetable Bowl, Chartreuse Salad Plate, Gray Cereal Coupe Bowl, Yellow Cup & Saucer Set, Forest Green Fruit Bowl, and Chartreuse Sugar Bowl with lid.* **Middle left:** *Rhythm patterns; Gray, Forest Green, and Yellow Divided Relish Trays.* **Bottom left:** *Rhythm patterns; Burgundy Salad Plate, Forest Green Dinner Plate, Chartreuse Platter, Gray Creamer, Burgundy Gravy/Sauce Boat, and Yellow Soup Coupe Bowl.* **Top right:** *Original ad mock-up.* **Middle right:** *Forest Green Creamer, 2⅞" high.* **Bottom right:** *Forest Green Creamer, 3¼" high.*

Homer Laughlin

Rhythm Piece Type List

From Homer Laughlin Literature with Confirmed Actual Pieces

Bowl, Cereal Coupe, 5½ inches
Bowl, Fruit, 5¼ inches
Bowl, Soup Coupe, 8¼ inches
Bowl, Vegetable Round, 8⅞ inches
Bowl, Vegetable Round Covered
Creamer, 2¾ inches
Creamer, 3¼ inches
Cup & Saucer Set
   Cup, 2¼ inches
   Saucer, 6 inches
Gravy/Sauce Boat
Gravy/Sauce Boat Underplate/Relish,
   8⅜ inches
Gravy/Sauce Boat with attached
   Underplate
Pitcher/Jug, Water, 2 qt.
Plate, Bread & Butter, 6⅛ inches
Plate, Dessert, 7¼ inches
Plate, Dinner, 10⅛ inches
Plate, Luncheon, 9¼ inches
Plate, Salad, 8¼ inches
Platter, Oval, 11½ inches
Platter, Oval, 13⅜ inches
Platter, Oval, 15½ inches
Salt & Pepper Set (Swing shape)
Server, Three Tier, 13½ inches
Server, Two Tier, 10 inches
Sugar Bowl with lid
Teapot with lid
Tray, Relish Divided, 10¼ inches

Top right: *RY135 pattern; Pitcher/Jug.* **Bottom left:** *Pink Magnolia pattern; Dinner Plate, Salad Plate, Bread & Butter Plate, and Cup & Saucer Set.* **Bottom right:** *Pink Magnolia pattern; Three Oval Platters, Sugar Bowl with lid, Creamer, and Gravy/Sauce Boat with attached Underplate.*

Rhythm Shape

Rhythm–White *No Trim*	 **Rhythm–Gray** *No Trim*	 **Rhythm–Green (Chartreuse)** *No Trim*	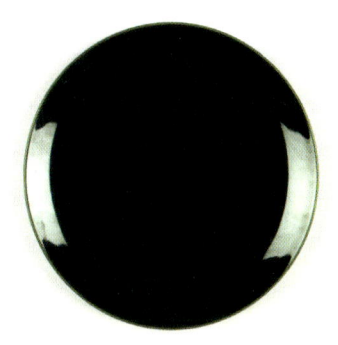 **Rhythm–Forest Green** *No Trim*
 **Rhythm–Burgundy** *No Trim*	 **Rhythm–Yellow** *No Trim*	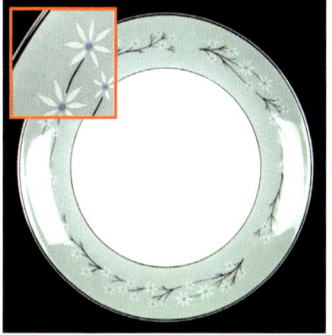 **Starflower** *RY346* *Platinum Trim*	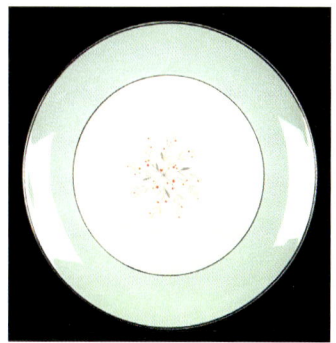 **JJ167** *Platinum Trim*
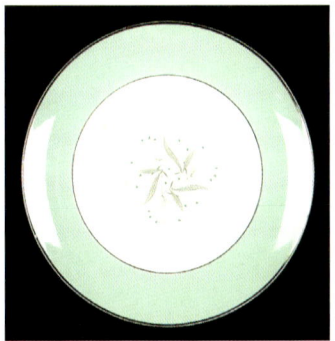 **RY308** *Platinum Trim*	 **HLC115** *Platinum Trim*	 **Sunrise** *No Trim*	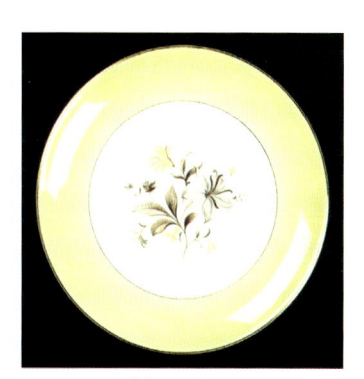 **Maytime** *RY284* *Platinum Trim*
 **RY288** *Gold Trim*	 **Provincial** *MW190* *Platinum Trim*	 **Colonial Kitchen** *No Trim*	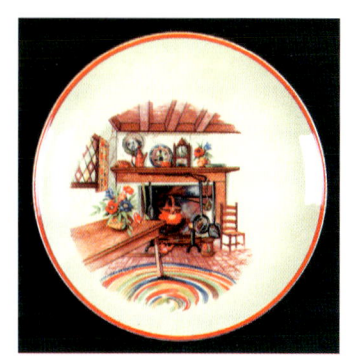 **Colonial Kitchen** *Red Trim*

Rhythm Shape

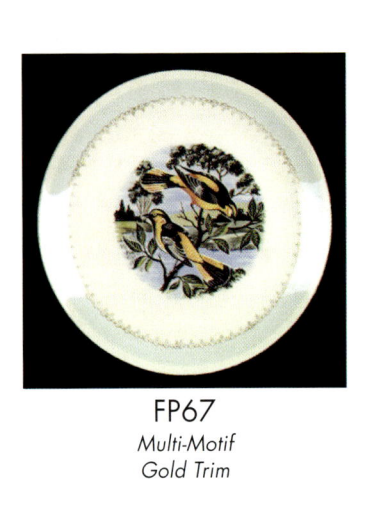

FP67
Multi-Motif
Gold Trim

Currier & Ives
FP160
Multi-Motif
Gold Trim

Melody
by Cunningham & Pickett
No Trim

Golden Wheat
by Century Service Corp.
No Trim

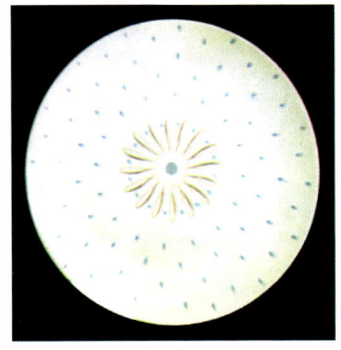

Frolic
No Trim

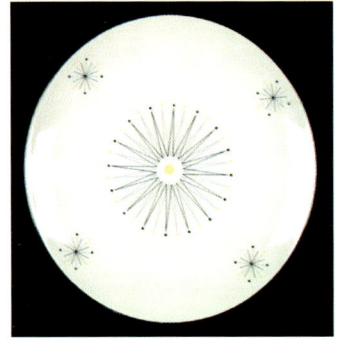

Sun Valley
Platinum Trim

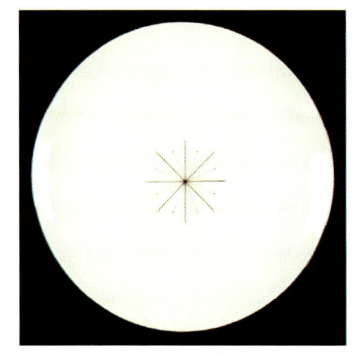

Modern Star
Q22
Platinum Trim

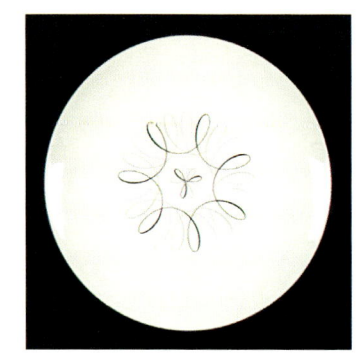

RY251
No Trim

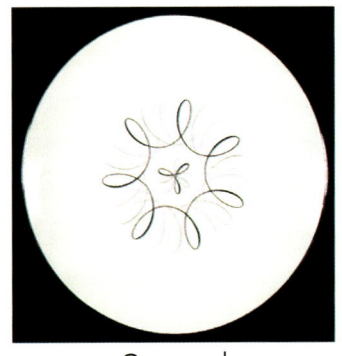

Carousel
by Sevron China
Platinum Trim

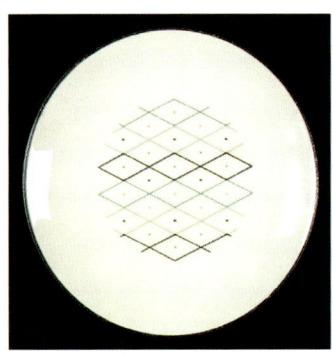

Fifth Avenue
Bread & Butter Plate Shown
Platinum Trim

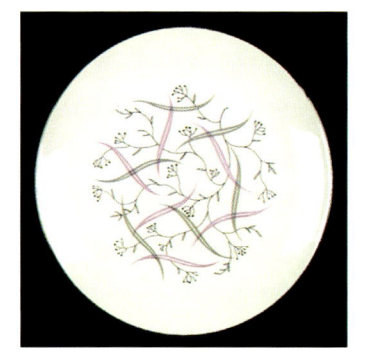

Allegro
RY194
Platinum Trim

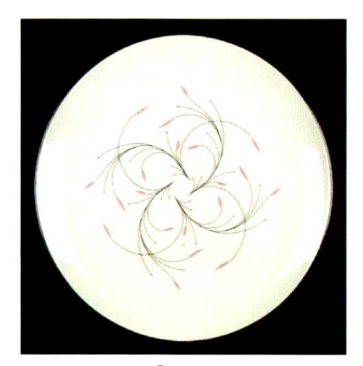

Capri
RY172
Platinum Trim

Cascade
Gold Trim

RY184
Platinum Trim

HLC526
Platinum Trim

RY307PT
Platinum Trim

Rhythm Shape

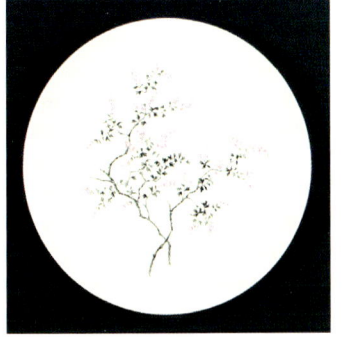

RY307 *No Trim*	**RY330** *Round Vegetable Bowl Shown* *Platinum Trim*	**HLC1062** *Gold Trim*	**RY252** *Platinum Trim*
HLC996 *Platinum Trim*	**RY217** *Platinum Trim*	**RY316** *Platinum Trim*	**HLC263** *Platinum Trim*
Golden Wheat *RY225* *Gold Trim*	**RY365** *Platinum Trim*	**RY366** *Platinum Trim*	**RY322** *Gold Trim*
Lotus Hai *RY135* *Platinum Trim*	**Bali Flower** *RY171* *Bread & Butter Plate Shown* *Platinum Trim*	**Pink Magnolia** *RY122* *Gold Trim*	**HLC781** *Gold Trim*

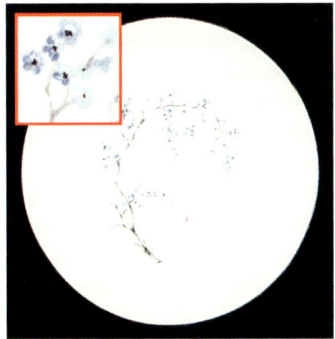

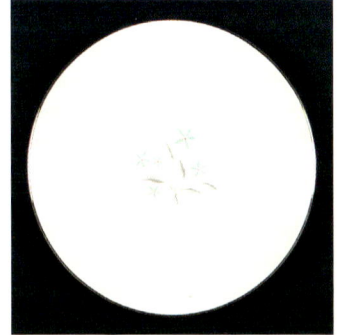

445

Rhythm Shape

Wheat Spray
CP171, by Cunningham & Pickett
also called "Harvest Gold"
Gold Trim

Hawaii
RY163
Platinum Trim

RY191
Platinum Trim

HLC970
Gold Trim

RY170
Gold Trim

Dubarry
Green Trim

Dubarry
CP133
by Cunningham & Pickett
No Trim

Sweet Pea
RY190
Platinum Trim

Sweet Pea
W350
No Trim

RY153
Platinum Trim

Bordeaux
Platinum Trim

HLC676
Platinum Trim

RY168
Gold Trim

London
RY175
Platinum Trim

Red Apple
JJ150
Green Trim

HLC78
Platinum Trim

Rhythm Shape

White Flower
JJ152
No Trim

Autumn
RY159
Platinum Trim

RY204
Platinum Trim

W152
No Trim

Dogwood
Gold Trim

RY209
Gold Trim

RY102
Oval Platter Shown
Gold Trim

RY203
Soup Bowl Shown
Platinum Trim

Rhythm Rose
by Household Institute
No Trim

W251
No Trim

American Provincial
Multi-Motif
Gold Trim

American Provincial
RY104
Multi-Motif
No Trim

FP222
Gold Trim

HLC957
Oval Platter Shown
Gold Trim

Rhythm Shape with Unknown Hollowware

HLC1123
Fruit Bowl Shown
Platinum Trim

HLC1329
Platinum Trim

HLC1330
No Trim

HLC2138
Salad Plate Shown
Platinum Trim

HLC1305
Platinum Trim

HLC1317
No Trim

Royal Harvest
RY255
No Trim

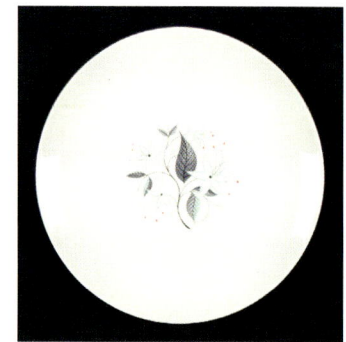

HLC1302
No Trim

HLC2199
Oval Platter Shown
No Trim

HLC1008
Gold Trim

HLC73
Platinum Trim

HLC580
Gold Trim

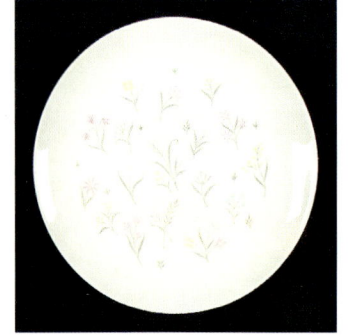

HLC1312
No Trim

HLC1318
Platinum Trim

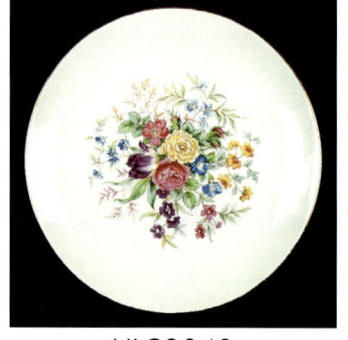

HLC2048
Gold Trim

HLC459
Platinum Trim

Rhythm Shape with Unknown Hollowware

HLC2055
Salad Plate Shown
Multi-Motif
Gold Trim

HLC1316
No Trim

HLC1844
Multi-Motif
Platinum Trim

HLC1879
Gold Trim

HLC1179
Soup Bowl Shown
Platinum Trim

FP221
Multi-Motif
Blue Band
Platinum Trim

HLC1207
Multi-Motif
No Trim

HLC1315
No Trim

HLC629
Gold Trim

GCM99
No Trim

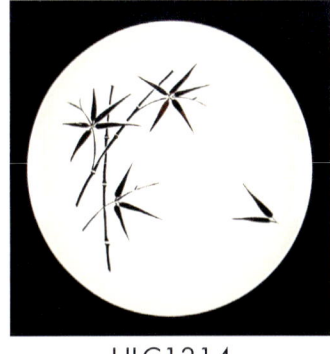

HLC1314
No Trim

HLC1234
No Trim

Fantasy
254
Bread & Butter Plate Shown
Gold Trim

HLC938
Round Vegetable Bowl Shown
Platinum Trim

HLC440
No Trim

HLC2200
Gold Trim

Rhythm Shape with Unknown Hollowware

HLC1238
No Trim

HLC1954
Bread & Butter Plate Shown
Gold Trim

HLC1342
No Trim

Woodland
254
Bread & Butter Plate Shown
Gold Trim

HLC1589
Gold Trim

HLC627
Platinum Trim

HLC312
Gold Trim

HLC1310
Gold Trim

HLC2005
Gold Trim

HLC2142
No Trim

HLC1331
No Trim

HLC3449
Salad Plate Shown
Gold Trim

HLC1332
No Trim

HLC1474
No Trim

HLC2129
No Trim

HLC1190
Oval Platter Shown
Platinum Trim

450

Rhythm Shape with Unknown Hollowware

HLC1328
No Trim

HLC806
Platinum Trim

HLC200
Soup Bowl Shown
Gold Trim

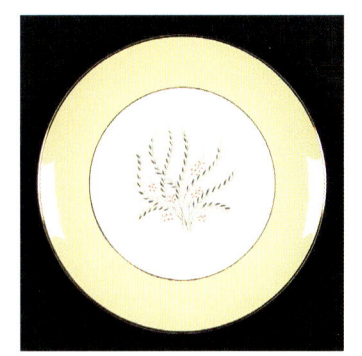

HLS304
Gold Trim

HLC1311
No Trim

HLC186
Platinum Trim

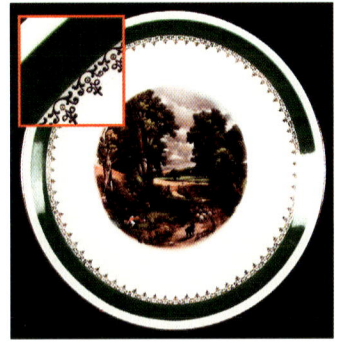

FP122
Green Band
Gold Trim

HLC1313
No Trim

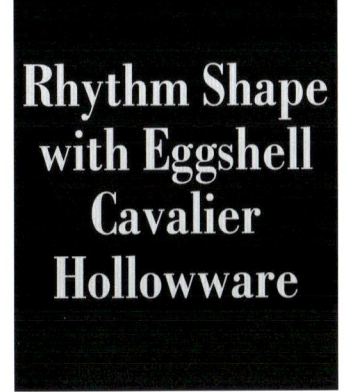

Rhythm Shape with Eggshell Cavalier Hollowware

HLC26
Platinum Trim

Royal Harvest
RY255
Gold Trim

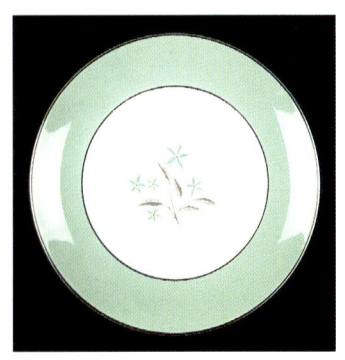

HLC723
Platinum Trim

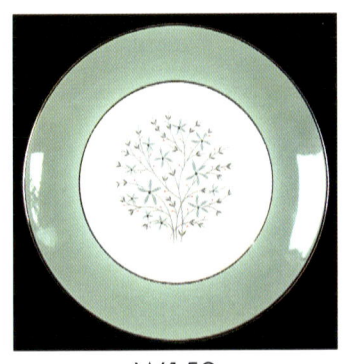

W159
Platinum Trim

Baroness
by Century Service Corp.
Platinum Trim

Danube
CP203
by Cunningham & Pickett
Platinum Trim

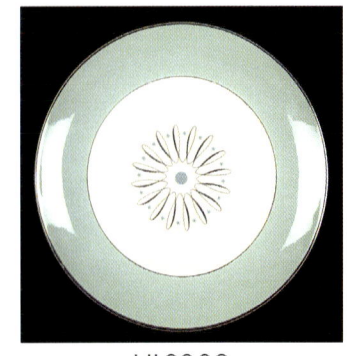

HLS302
Platinum Trim

Rhythm Shape with Eggshell Cavalier Hollowware

HLC592
Gold Trim

HLS301
Platinum Trim

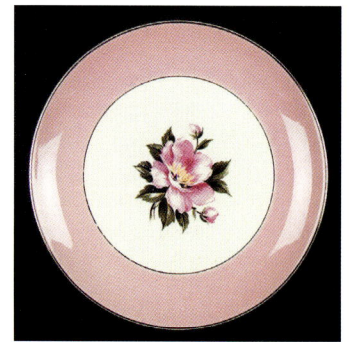

Empress
by Century Service Corp.
Platinum Trim

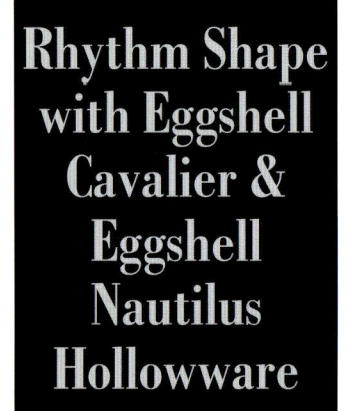

Rhythm Shape with Eggshell Cavalier & Eggshell Nautilus Hollowware

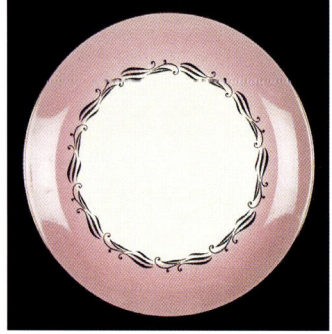

Sunrise–Pink
by Cunningham & Pickett
Gold Trim

Gold Crown
by Lifetime China
Gold Trim

Lynnwood
by Century Service Corp.
Platinum Trim

Autumn Gold
by Century Service Corp.
Gold Trim

Pink Radiance
No Trim

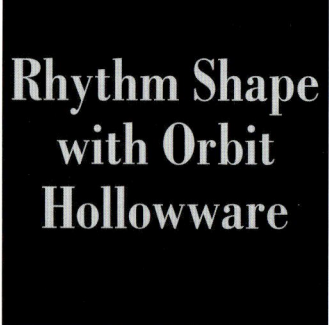

Rhythm Shape with Orbit Hollowware

Everglade
No Trim

Orient
Serenade Line
No Trim

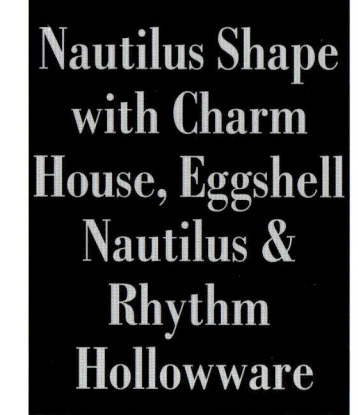

Nautilus Shape with Charm House, Eggshell Nautilus & Rhythm Hollowware

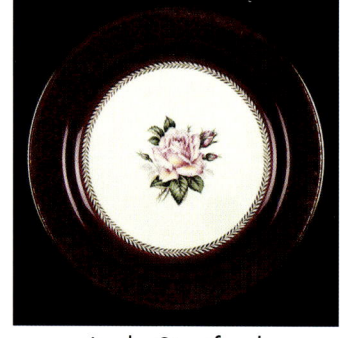

Lady Stratford
Gold Trim

Lady Greenbriar
AS1
Gold Trim

Charm House

Piece Types

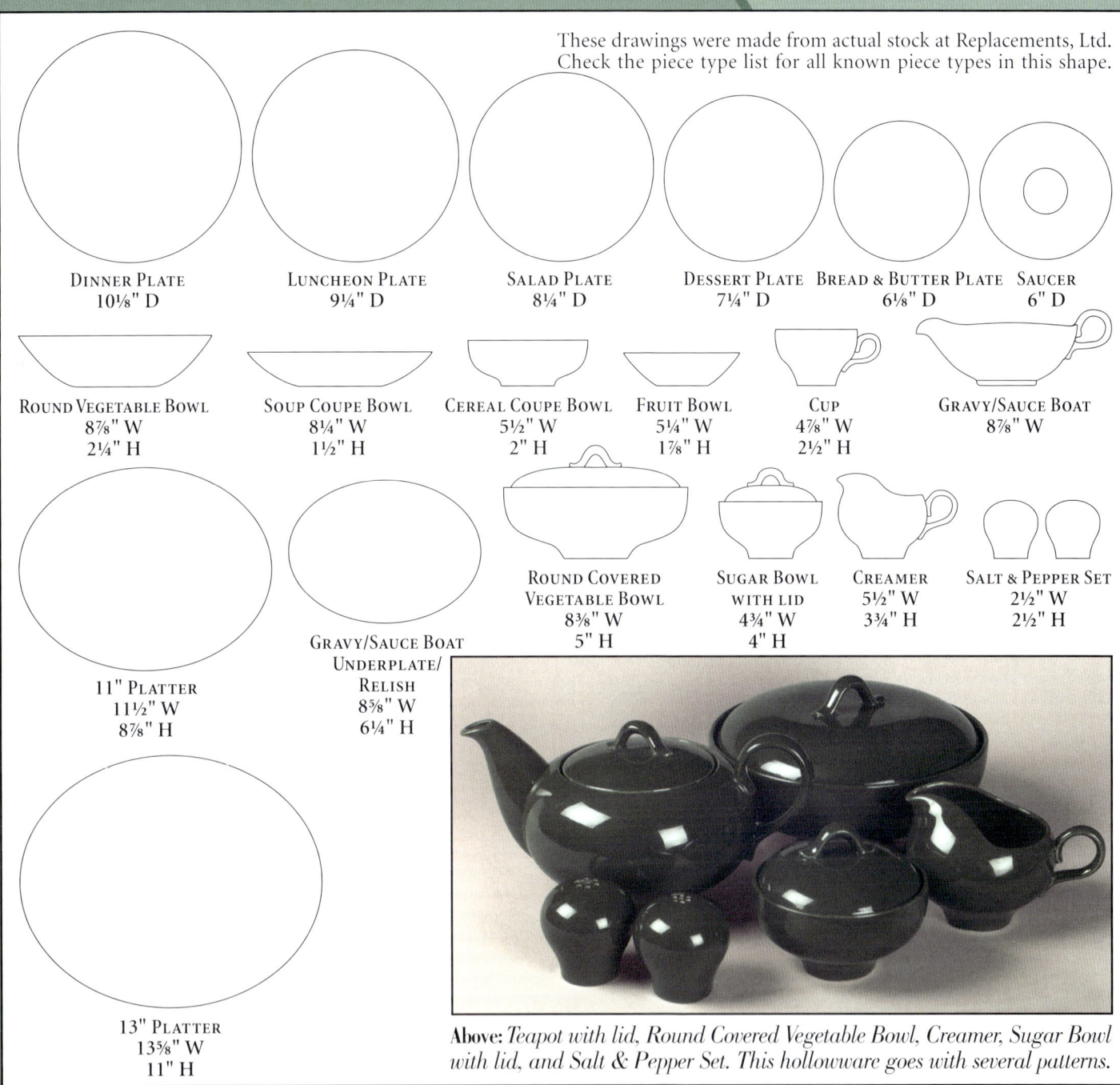

These drawings were made from actual stock at Replacements, Ltd. Check the piece type list for all known piece types in this shape.

Dinner Plate
10⅛" D

Luncheon Plate
9¼" D

Salad Plate
8¼" D

Dessert Plate
7¼" D

Bread & Butter Plate
6⅛" D

Saucer
6" D

Round Vegetable Bowl
8⅞" W
2¼" H

Soup Coupe Bowl
8¼" W
1½" H

Cereal Coupe Bowl
5½" W
2" H

Fruit Bowl
5¼" W
1⅞" H

Cup
4⅞" W
2½" H

Gravy/Sauce Boat
8⅞" W

11" Platter
11½" W
8⅞" H

Gravy/Sauce Boat Underplate/Relish
8⅝" W
6¼" H

Round Covered Vegetable Bowl
8⅜" W
5" H

Sugar Bowl with Lid
4¾" W
4" H

Creamer
5½" W
3¾" H

Salt & Pepper Set
2½" W
2½" H

13" Platter
13⅝" W
11" H

Above: *Teapot with lid, Round Covered Vegetable Bowl, Creamer, Sugar Bowl with lid, and Salt & Pepper Set. This hollowware goes with several patterns.*

Homer Laughlin

CHARM HOUSE   circa 1952 – 1958 or later

Charm House was a revision and extension of the existing Rhythm line. It retained the coupe shaped flatware of Rhythm, or less commonly, other flatware, and introduced new hollowware shapes. This hollowware is what distinguishes a Charm House shaped pattern.

Charm House patterns supplement existing flat plate shapes with new, bold, solid colored or printed hollowware in the distinctly Charm House shapes. This mixing of plate shapes with hollowware makes identification and classification within this book challenging.

Remember: Charm House is a line of hollowware (serving pieces) using various lines of flatware (plates).

To complicate this more, there is not a Charm House backstamp. Instead, Charm House shaped patterns are usually marked Rhythm or Dura-Print. Dura-Print identifies the printing process of decorating and not the shape. It is a common backstamp used with other shapes as well.

The first print notice of Charm House we discovered was a *China, Glass & Lamps* ad, August 1952, where the Desert Lily pattern was featured. We found Sears selling Charm House shaped lines in 1954 and 1955. Montgomery Ward offered Charm House patterns from 1955-1958, and John Plain, a wholesale firm, offered Charm House patterns in 1957.

The Applique line uses Charm House hollowware. Again, Applique refers to a line based on the process used to decorate it and not the shape, pattern, or such. Applique does not use Rhythm flatware, it uses Brittany. Applique pieces bear a generic Homer Laughlin backstamp.

DESERT LILY...semi-porcelain in simple, modern shapes. Chartreuse and forest green, splashed with warm desert red and dark brown, make a lovely raised enameled lily pattern on ivory ground. Cups, bowls, sugar and creamer in solid chartreuse. Desert Lily presents such a friendly invitation to dine. Contents of sets on page 536.
708-164 C885 23-pc. Set (service for 4) $13.25
708-172 C1350 35-pc. Set (service for 6) 19.25
708-180 C2060 53-pc. Set (service for 8) 29.50

Above: *Flyers for Charm House patterns; Calico, Ming Glory, Dogwood, Lotus Hai, Lyric, and Something Blue.* **Top middle:** *Typical Dura-Print backstamp.* **Middle:** *Salt & Pepper Set.* **Top right:** *Desert Lily pattern; John Plain Catalog, 1957.*

Charm House Shape
Applique Line

Dundee Plaid—lovely to look at—delightful to own! This beautifully styled dinnerware in gay green and brown underglaze Dura-Print, accented by solid green hollow ware, lends a special charm to casual dining!

PRICE LIST

ITEM	PER PIECE
Tea Cups	$ .45
Tea Saucers	.20
Plates, 10¾"	.65
Plates, 9¼"	.55
Plates, 7¼"	.35
Plates, 6¼"	.30
Coupes, 8¼"	.55
Cereal Soups	.50
Fruits, 5¼"	.20
Nappies, 8¾"	.85
Dishes, 11¾"	.85
Dishes, 13½"	1.35
Sugars, Cov'd	1.35
Creams	.80
Sauceboats, Regular	1.35
Pickles	.80
Salts	.65
Peppers	.65
Teapots, Cov'd	2.15
Casseroles, Cov'd	2.65

Top left: *Highland Plaid (Green and Black)* pattern; Coupe Cereal Bowl, Dinner Plate, Bread & Butter Plate, and Cup & Saucer Set. **Top middle:** *Desert Lily* pattern; Coupe Cereal Bowl, Dinner Plate, Bread & Butter Plate, and Cup & Saucer Set. **Top right:** *Highland Plaid (Brown and Green)* pattern; Coupe Cereal Bowl, Dinner Plate, Bread & Butter Plate, and Cup & Saucer Set. **Middle left:** *Chanticleer* pattern; Coupe Cereal Bowl, Dinner Plate, Bread & Butter Plate, and Cup & Saucer Set. **Bottom left:** *Wheat, Americana* pattern; Coupe Cereal Bowl, Dinner Plate, Bread & Butter Plate, and Cup & Saucer Set. **Middle and right:** Factory pamphlet, Dundee Plaid Pattern; Sugar Bowl with lid, Dinner Plate, Cup & Saucer Set, and Creamer. **Bottom right:** Teapot with lid.

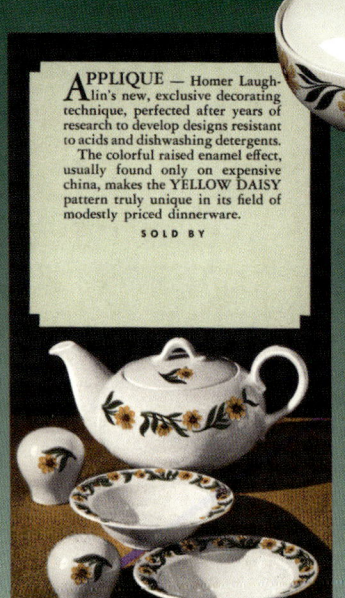

Homer Laughlin

Applique Yellow Daisy Price List — Oct. 6, 1953

Item	Per Piece
Tea Cups	$ .50
Tea Saucers	.20
Plates 10"	.65
Plates 9"	.55
Plates 7¼"	.35
Plates 6¼"	.30
Rim Soups 8¼"	.50
Fruits 5¾"	.25
Oatmeals 6¼"	.50
Nappies 9"	.90
Platters 15½"	2.40
Platters 13½"	1.40
Platters 11½"	.90
Sugars, Covered	1.40
Creams	.80
Sauceboats, Regular	1.35
Pickles 9"	.80
Casseroles, Covered	2.65
Tea Pots, Covered	2.25
Salts	.65
Peppers	.65

THE HOMER LAUGHLIN CHINA CO.
NEWELL, WEST VIRGINIA

Top left: *Yellow Daisy pattern, Applique Line; Retail pamphlet cover and back. Note the description of "Applique" as a decorating process.* **Top middle:** *Yellow Daisy pattern, Applique Line; Sugar Bowl with lid, and Creamer.* **Top right:** *Yellow Daisy pattern, Applique Line; Three Oval Platters, Round Covered Vegetable Bowl, Gravy/Sauce Boat with unattached Underplate, and Salt & Pepper Set.* **Bottom left:** *Yellow Daisy pattern, Applique Line; Pamphlet inside.* **Middle right:** *Yellow Daisy pattern, Applique Line; Soup Bowl with Rim, Round Vegetable Bowl, and Fruit Bowl.* **Bottom right:** *Yellow Daisy pattern, Applique Line; Luncheon Plate, Salad Plate, Cup & Saucer Set, and Bread & Butter Plate.*

Charm House Shape
Applique Line

Charm House Piece Type List
From Homer Laughlin Literature with Confirmed Actual Pieces

Bowl, Cereal, 5½ inches	Cup & Saucer Set	Plate, Luncheon Coupe, 9¼ inches
Bowl, Fruit, 5¼ inches	Cup, 2½ inches	Plate, Salad Coupe, 8¼ inches
Bowl, Soup Coupe, 8¼ inches	Saucer, 6 inches	Platter, Oval 11½ inches
Bowl, Vegetable Round, 8⅞ inches	Gravy/Sauce Boat	Platter, Oval 13⅝ inches
Bowl, Vegetable Round Covered, 8⅜ inches	Gravy/Sauce Boat Underplate/Relish, 8⅝ inches	Platter, Oval 15½ inches*
Creamer	Plate, Bread & Butter Coupe, 6⅛ inches	Salt & Pepper Set
	Plate, Dessert Coupe, 7¼ inches	Sugar Bowl with lid
	Plate, Dinner Coupe, 10⅛ inches	Teapot with lid
		*Reported but not confirmed.

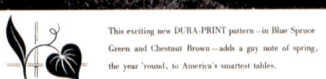

Top left: *Trellis pattern; Magazine advertisement.* **Top right:** *Desert Lily pattern; Magazine advertisement.* **Bottom left:** *Yellow Daisy pattern, Applique Line; Crockery & Glass Journal, July 1948.* **Bottom middle:** *Highland Plaid pattern; Magazine advertisement.* **Bottom right:** *Highland Plaid pattern; Backstamp.* "Plaids are the historic designs of the Scottish Highland clans, each having its distinctive tartan. Modern styling translates these ancient patterns into today's smartest decor."

Charm House Shape

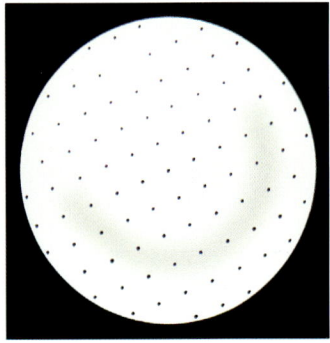

Confetti
also known as "Polka-Print"
Black Dots
No Trim

Pink Magnolia
CH100
Gold Trim

Desert Lily
RY117
No Trim

Wheat (Americana)
No Trim

Malay
No Trim

Chanticleer
also known as "Daybreak"
No Trim

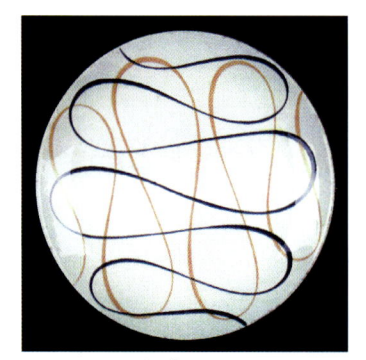

Calypso
No Trim

Highland Plaid
Brown/Yellow
Round Vegetable Bowl Shown
No Trim

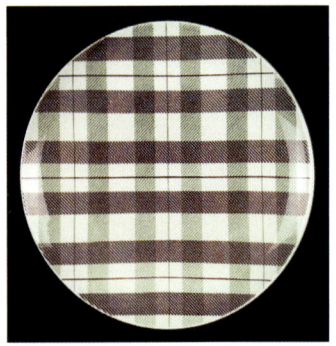

Highland Plaid
Green/Brown
No Trim

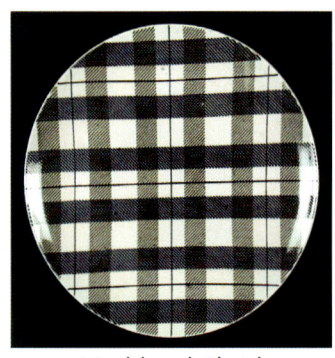

Highland Plaid
Green/Black
No Trim

Applique Line

HLC1353
No Trim

HLC2008
No Trim

HLC1335
No Trim

Buttercup
No Trim

Yellow Daisy
Luncheon Plate Shown
No Trim

Charm House Shape

Orange Blossom
Gray Band
No Trim

HLC1432
No Trim

Strawberry
No Trim

HLC1428
No Trim

Cherry Valley
No Trim

HLC1426
No Trim

Plaid
A105
No Trim

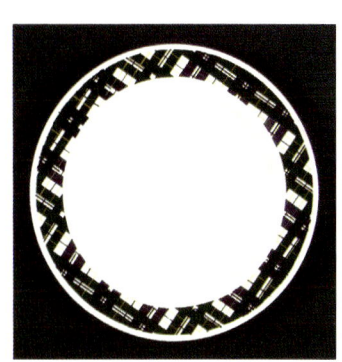

HLC1425
No Trim

Charm House Shape with Triumph Hollowware

HLC551
No Trim

Aster
No Trim

Orchard
No Trim

Nautilus Shape with Charm House, Eggshell Nautilus & Rhythm Hollowware

Lady Stratford
Gold Trim

Lady Greenbriar
AS1
Gold Trim

459

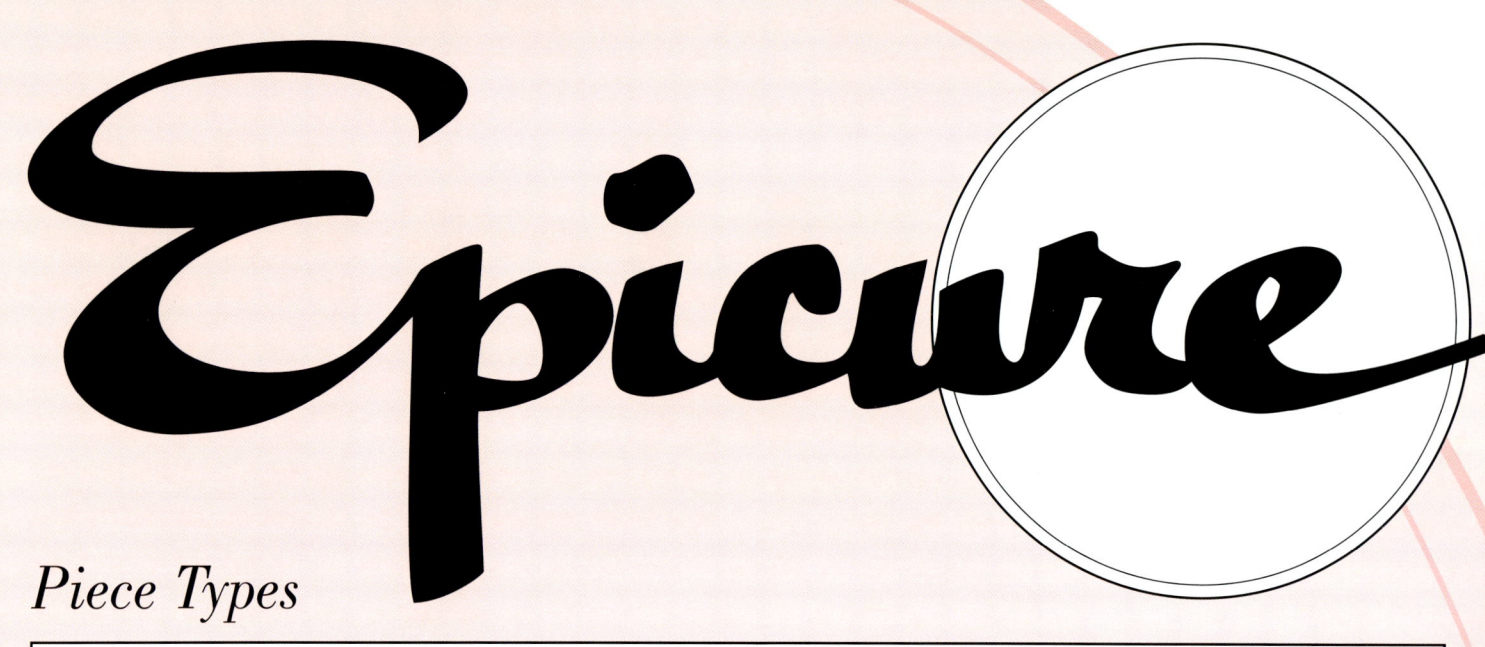

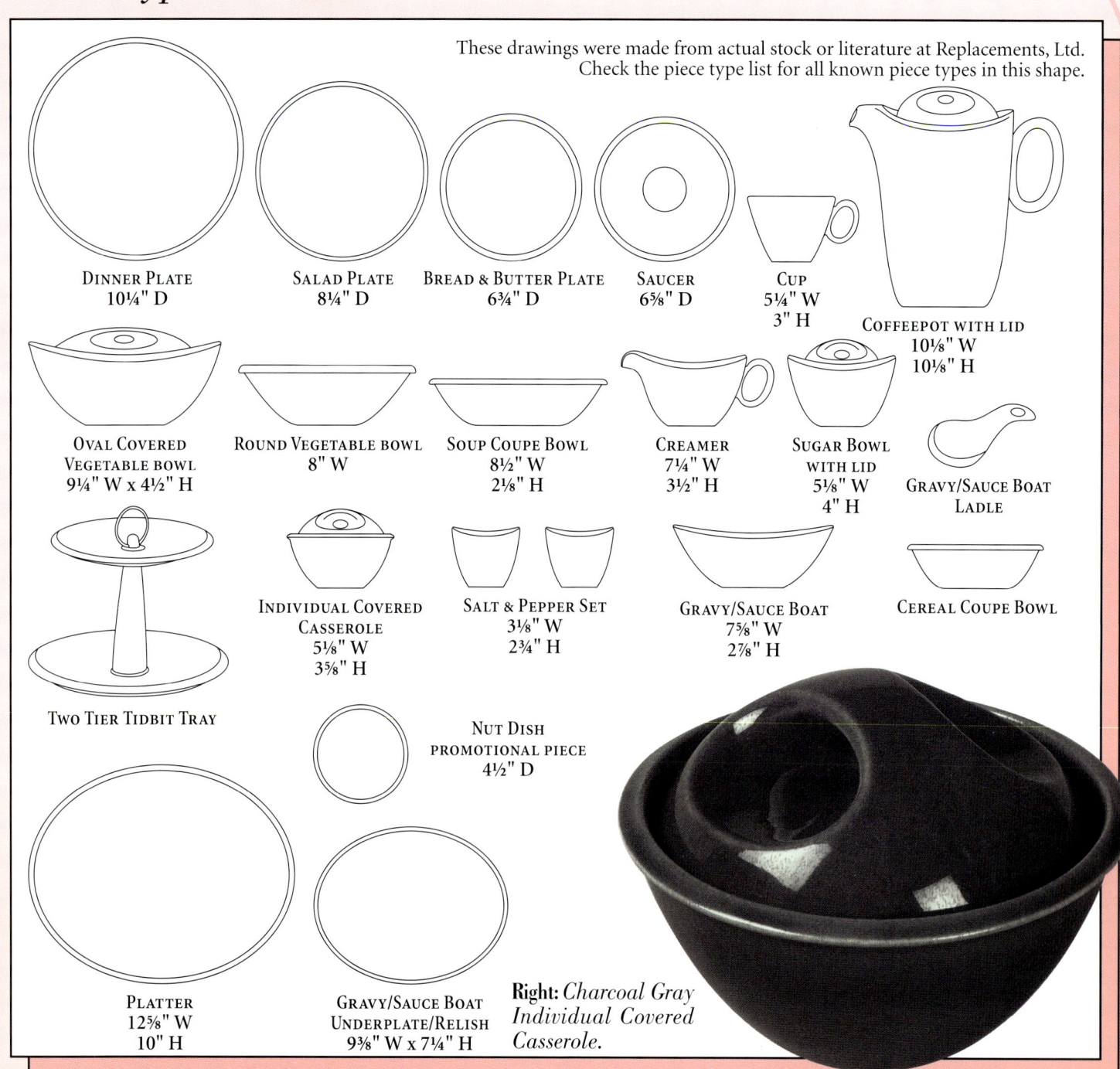

Epicure

Piece Types

These drawings were made from actual stock or literature at Replacements, Ltd. Check the piece type list for all known piece types in this shape.

Dinner Plate 10¼" D

Salad Plate 8¼" D

Bread & Butter Plate 6¾" D

Saucer 6⅝" D

Cup 5¼" W 3" H

Coffeepot with lid 10⅛" W 10⅛" H

Oval Covered Vegetable bowl 9¼" W x 4½" H

Round Vegetable bowl 8" W

Soup Coupe Bowl 8½" W 2⅛" H

Creamer 7¼" W 3½" H

Sugar Bowl with lid 5⅛" W 4" H

Gravy/Sauce Boat Ladle

Two Tier Tidbit Tray

Individual Covered Casserole 5⅛" W 3⅝" H

Salt & Pepper Set 3⅛" W 2¾" H

Gravy/Sauce Boat 7⅝" W 2⅞" H

Cereal Coupe Bowl

Nut Dish promotional piece 4½" D

Platter 12⅝" W 10" H

Gravy/Sauce Boat Underplate/Relish 9⅜" W x 7¼" H

Right: *Charcoal Gray Individual Covered Casserole.*

Epicure Shape

EPICURE   circa 1955

Epicure is one of the boldly "modern" lines created at Homer Laughlin. The designer of the line and creator of some of the original advertisement art was Don Schreckengost. Authors have suggested production for Epicure began as early as 1953, but all pieces we viewed were stamped 1955. The April 1955 *Crockery & Glass Journal* features a Homer Laughlin ad introducing "Epicure." The extensive ad campaign for Epicure indicates Homer Laughlin had great expectations for the line. A professional ad firm handled the promotion of the line, seemingly with little success. The limited production period, indicated by backstamps, and the limited availability of pieces suggest it did not fare as well as anticipated.

With the dated backstamps found and the trade journal quote as our information, we suggest, as have other authors, that Epicure was introduced and primarily produced in 1955. Reports of Epicure with a 1960's backstamp appear in print.

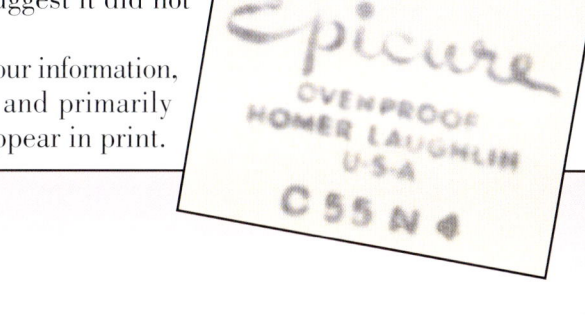

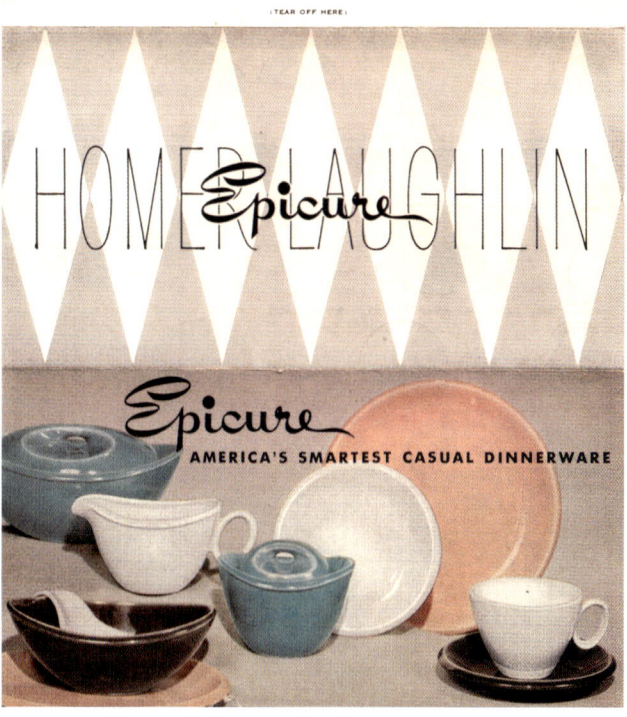

Top right: *Typical Epicure backstamp.*
Left: *Epicure Order Form.*
Bottom right: *Epicure Order Form.*

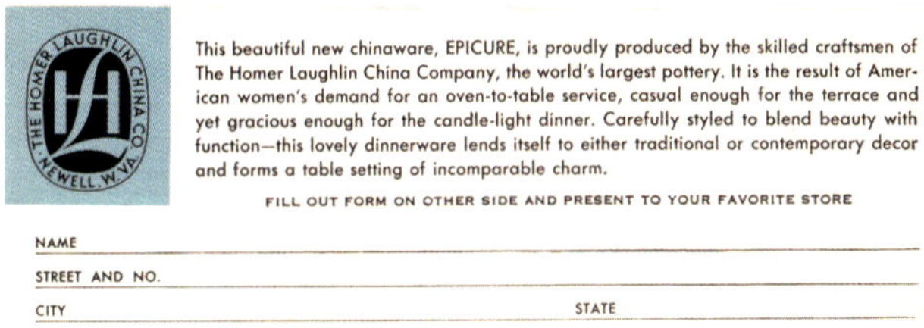

461

Homer Laughlin

Top left: Turquoise Blue Dinner Plate, Dawn Pink Oval Platter, Charcoal Gray Sugar Bowl with lid, Dawn Pink Cup & Saucer Set, and Snow White Creamer. **Top right:** Ladies Home Journal *advertisement*. **Middle left:** Snow White Sugar Bowl with lid, Dawn Pink Oval Covered Vegetable Bowl, and Charcoal Gray Individual Covered Casserole. **Bottom left:** Dawn Pink Oval Vegetable Bowl, Snow White Dinner Plate, Charcoal Gray Bread & Butter Plate, Turquoise Blue Salad Plate, Dawn Pink Fruit Bowl, Turquoise Blue Salt, and Snow White Pepper. **Bottom right:** Turquoise Blue Gravy/Sauce Boat with unattached Underplate.

Epicure Shape

Epicure Piece Type List

From Homer Laughlin Literature with Confirmed Actual Pieces

Ashtray
Bowl, Cereal Coupe
Bowl, Soup Coupe, 8½ inches
Bowl, Vegetable Oval Covered, 9¼ inches
Bowl, Vegetable Round, 8 inches
Casserole Covered, Individual
Coffeepot with lid, 10⅛ inches

Creamer
Cup & Saucer Set
   Cup, 3 inches
   Saucer, 6⅝ inches
Gravy/Sauce Boat
Gravy/Sauce Boat Underplate/Relish, 9⅜ inches
Ladle, Gravy/Sauce Boat

Nut Dish, 4½ inches
Plate, Bread & Butter, 6¾ inches
Plate, Dinner, 10¼ inches
Plate, Salad, 8¼ inches
Platter, 12⅝ inches
Salt & Pepper Set
Sugar Bowl with lid
Tray, Tidbit Two Tier

Top left: *Original Epicure ad drawing from the Homer Laughlin Factory.*
Top right: *Dawn Pink Coffeepot with lid.* **Bottom left:** *Turquoise Blue, Dawn Pink, Snow White, and Charcoal Gray Salt & Pepper Sets.*

Epicure Shape

Epicure–Snow White
No Trim

Epicure–Dawn Pink
No Trim

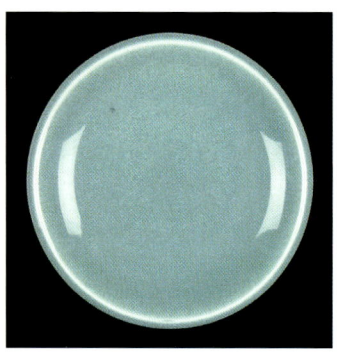

Epicure–Turquoise Blue
Bread & Butter Plate Shown
No Trim

Epicure–Charcoal Gray
No Trim

Epicure

Homer Laughlin's newest and smartest dinnerware for casual dining! Its superb styling with textured glazes in charming colors of Dawn Pink, Snow White, Charcoal Gray and Turquoise Blue creates an incomparable table setting. Sturdy . . . Multi-purpose . . . Ovenproof . . . Meeting America's demand for function and beauty at modest prices.

Full color National advertising starting in May issues of leading consumer magazines will bring pre-sold customers to your store.

Plan now to meet the demand with EPICURE — The most salesworthy dinnerware 1955 will see.

The Homer Laughlin China Co.
NEWELL, WEST VIRGINIA

CROCKERY & GLASS JOURNAL for March 4, 1955

Above: *Epicure ad,* Crockery & Glass Journal, *March 4, 1955.*

Studio

Piece Types

These drawings were made from actual stock or literature at Replacements, Ltd. Check the piece type list for all known piece types in this shape.

Dinner Plate
10⅛" D

Luncheon Plate
9¼" D

Salad Plate
8¼" D

Dessert Plate
7¼" D

Bread & Butter Plate
6¼" D

Round Vegetable Bowl
8¾" W
2⅜" H

Cereal Bowl
6⅜" W
1⅝" W

Fruit Bowl
5¼" W
1½" H

Creamer

Sugar Bowl with Lid

Saucer
6" D

Cup
4⅜" W
2⅞" H

13" Platter
13⅝" W
11" H

Left: *Unknown patterns photographed at the Homer Laughlin Factory.* **Right:** *HLC2229 pattern; Dinner Plate, Bread & Butter Plate, Cup & Saucer Set, and Fruit Bowl.*

Homer Laughlin

STUDIO circa 1957

Studio was created in the late 1950's to extend the usefulness of existing Rhythm flatware shapes. Studio accomplished this by offering new hollowware shapes that were decorated and marketed in sets utilizing existing flatware. A number, but not all, of the Studio patterns used solid, single color glaze on the interior of hollowware pieces.

Left: *Blue Horizon* pattern; Crockery & Glass Journal, 1958.
Right: *Pink Magnolia* pattern; Crockery & Glass Journal, 1957.

Studio Piece Type List

From Homer Laughlin Literature with Confirmed Actual Pieces

Bowl, Cereal, 6⅜ inches	Cup & Saucer Set	Plate, Dinner, 10⅛ inches
Bowl, Fruit, 5¼ inches	Cup, 2⅞ inches	Plate, Luncheon, 9¼ inches
Bowl, Vegetable Round, 8¾ inches	Saucer, 6 inches	Plate, Salad, 8¼ inches
Creamer	Plate, Bread & Butter, 6¼ inches	Platter, Oval, 13⅜ inches
	Plate, Dessert, 7¼ inches	Sugar Bowl with lid

Studio Shape

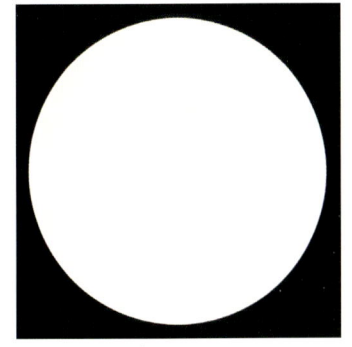

Blue Star
Luncheon Plate Shown
No Trim

Tulip Wreath
No Trim

HLC2229
No Trim

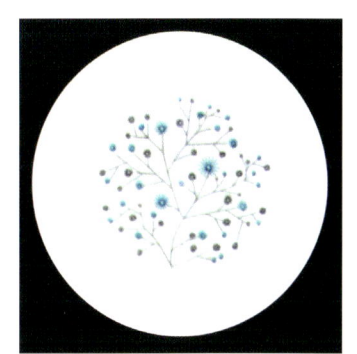

Paradise
No Trim

Pink Magnolia
No Trim

Rose Garden
No Trim

HLC1239
No Trim

HLC1988
No Trim

Above left: *Woman screen printing the Pink Magnolia pattern at the Homer Laughlin Factory.*
Right: *Color-Tone, a printing process, was used on several Studio patterns, China, Glass & Tableware, May 1960.*

Color-Tone... STOPS THE SHOW

A NEW HIGH IN DINNERWARE ACHIEVEMENT...

Color-Tone belies its popular pricing. An exclusive new decorative technique achieves a new fidelity of color sharpness. Buyers at the China and Glass Show acclaimed Color-Tone as the line for 1960. Order now for early shipment.

EASTERN SALES AND DISPLAY ROOM: SUITE 2000, 212 FIFTH AVE., NEW YORK 10, N.Y. — BERNARD MENGE
CHICAGO SALES OFFICE: ROOM 916, LaSALLE-WACKER BLDG., 221 NO. LaSALLE ST., CHICAGO 1, ILL. — N. W. MacDONALD

The Homer Laughlin China Co.
NEWELL, WEST VIRGINIA

Fashion

Piece Types

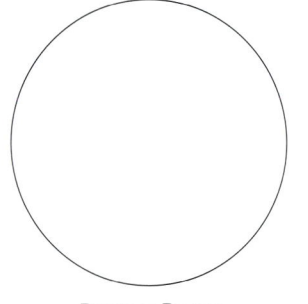

Dinner Plate 10⅛" D

Cup 4½" W, 2⅞" W

Sugar Bowl with lid 4¼" W, 4" H

Creamer 5¼" W, 4" H

These drawings were made from actual stock at Replacements, Ltd. Check the piece type list for all known piece types in this shape.

Right: *Autumn Song pattern; Cup & Saucer Set, Soup Coupe Bowl, Dinner Plate, Bread & Butter Plate, Creamer, Fruit Bowl, and Sugar Bowl with lid.*

FASHION — circa 1958

Fashion is a line of hollowware created to supplement existing Homer Laughlin flatware. It appears the line was sold exclusively to the Alliance China Company. Authors Jo Cunningham and Darlene Nossaman suggest it was first sold in 1958. A Don Schreckengost design, Fashion embodies the simplified shape and form of the earlier Epicure line.

Autumn Song
Gold Trim

Autumn Song
Soup Bowl Shown
Platinum Trim

Fairfield
by Cunningham & Pickett
Gold Trim

Triumph

Piece Types

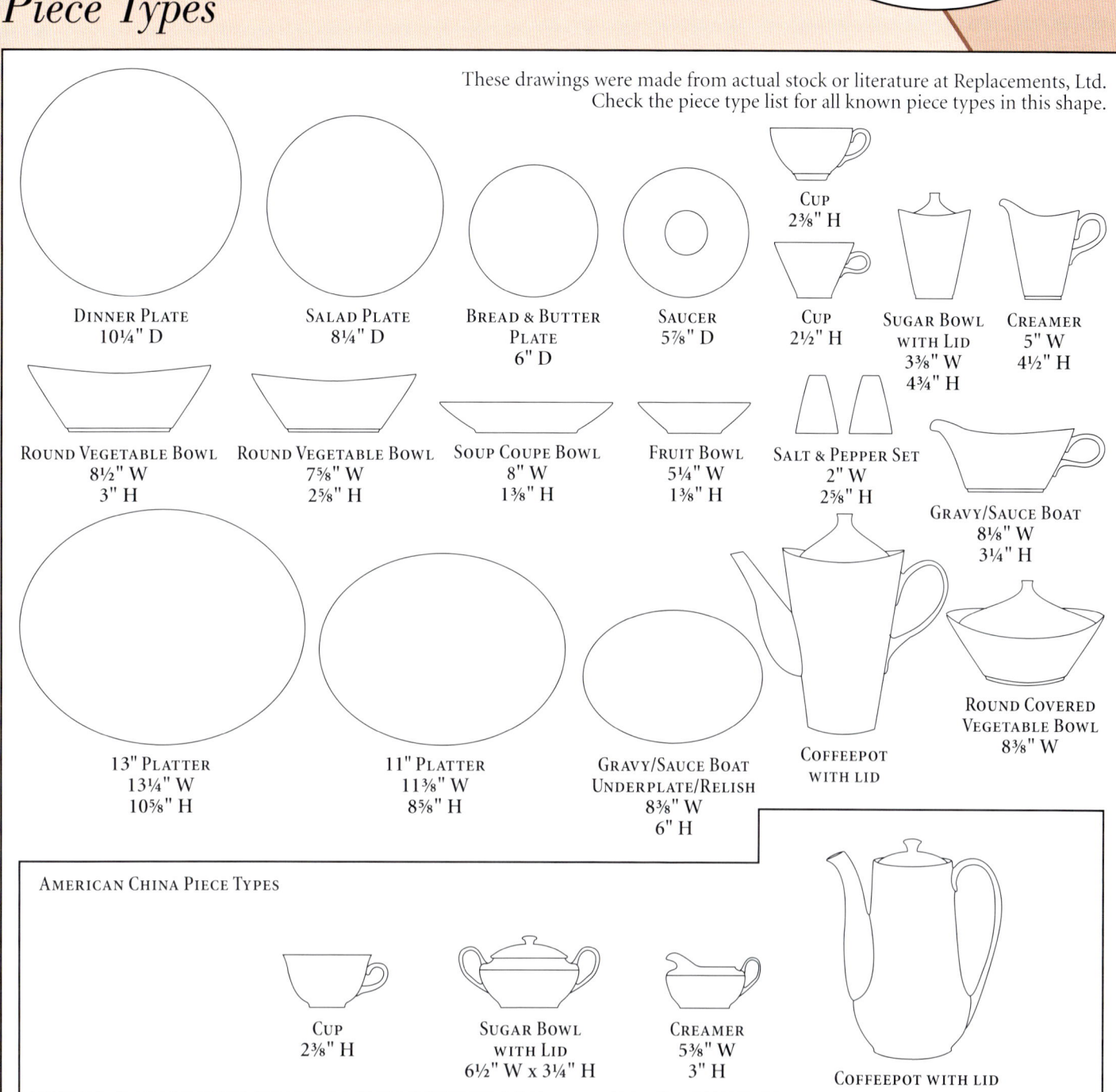

These drawings were made from actual stock or literature at Replacements, Ltd. Check the piece type list for all known piece types in this shape.

Dinner Plate 10¼" D	Salad Plate 8¼" D	Bread & Butter Plate 6" D	Saucer 5⅞" D	Cup 2⅜" H / Cup 2½" H	Sugar Bowl with Lid 3⅜" W 4¾" H	Creamer 5" W 4½" H
Round Vegetable Bowl 8½" W 3" H	Round Vegetable Bowl 7⅝" W 2⅝" H	Soup Coupe Bowl 8" W 1⅜" H	Fruit Bowl 5¼" W 1⅜" H	Salt & Pepper Set 2" W 2⅝" H	Gravy/Sauce Boat 8⅛" W 3¼" H	
13" Platter 13¼" W 10⅝" H	11" Platter 11⅜" W 8⅝" H	Gravy/Sauce Boat Underplate/Relish 8⅜" W 6" H	Coffeepot with lid	Round Covered Vegetable Bowl 8⅜" W		

American China Piece Types

Cup 2⅜" H	Sugar Bowl with Lid 6½" W x 3¼" H	Creamer 5⅜" W 3" H	Coffeepot with lid

469

Homer Laughlin

TRIUMPH

1959 – 1966 or later

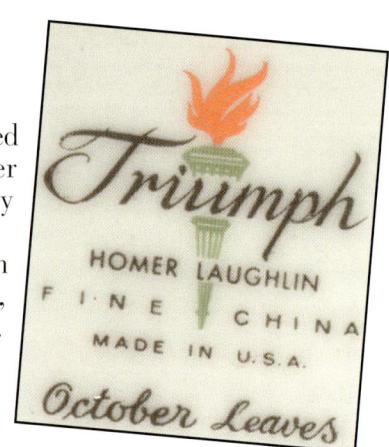

Homer Laughlin registered the name Triumph on September 4, 1959 and claimed they had used it since June 1959 (Lehner). The shape was designed by Homer Laughlin art director Don Schreckengost. Coupe shaped plates paired with gently contoured hollowware gave the shape a strong yet simple appearance.

Homer Laughlin advertised a variety of patterns on the Triumph shape in *China, Glass and Lamps* during 1959. The April issue featured Spring Rose, August featured Woodland, and September promoted the October Leaves pattern. The Montgomery Ward catalog offered Triumph shaped lines in 1959 and 1960. Bennett Brothers, Inc., a wholesale company, included Triumph lines in their catalogs from 1961 through 1965. Triumph was promoted in the May 15, 1966 company ad in *China, Glass & Tablewares, Red Book Issue* and was described as "Triumph China for home use."

Homer Laughlin actually created two sets of shapes that were marked with the Triumph backstamp. Along with the regular dinnerware line, a new set of hollowware shapes was created for the "American China" line, produced in the early 1960's. Ads featuring patterns on both sets of shapes, with and without decorations, have been found.

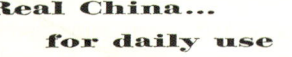

Above left: *Snow White pattern; China, Glass & Tablewares, February 1959.* **Top right:** *Typical Triumph backstamp.* **Above right:** *October Leaves, Woodland, Snow White, Spring Rose, and Linda patterns; Crockery & Glass Journal, July 1960.*

Triumph Shape

Top left: Spring Rose pattern; Bread & Butter Plate, Dinner Plate, and Cup & Saucer Set. **Top right:** Spring Rose pattern; 11" Oval Platter, 13" Oval Platter, Round Vegetable Bowl, Gravy/Sauce Boat Underplate/Relish, Gravy/Sauce Boat, Round Vegetable Bowl, Fruit Bowl, Salt & Pepper Set, and Soup Coupe Bowl. **Middle left:** Spring Rose pattern; Sugar Bowl with lid, and Creamer. **Bottom right:** Spring Rose pattern; Crockery and Glass Journal, April 1959. **Bottom left:** Order form for Triumph.

USE THIS TRIUMPH ORDER FORM

No. of Pieces	Price Each	No. of Pieces	Price Each
		Coffee Pot and Cover	7.65
Tea Cup	1.20	A. D. Coffee Cup	1.00
Tea Saucer	.70	A. D. Coffee Saucer	.60
Dinner Plate 10"	1.60	Salt	1.50
Salad Plate 8"	1.10	Pepper	1.50
Bread and Butter Plate 6"	.80	**Special Set Prices**	
Coupe Soup 8"	1.20	16 Piece "B" Starter Set includes	
Fruit - Dessert 5¼"	.75	4 each: Dinner Plates, Bread & Butter	
Platter, Large 13⅛"	3.50	Plates, Cups & Saucers	12.95
Platter, Medium 11¼"	2.50	(Open Stock Value $17.20)	
Vegetable Dish 8¼"	2.50	45 Piece TE Set for 8 includes	
Vegetable Dish 7¾"	2.10	8 each: Dinner Plates, Bread & Butter	
Sugar and Cover	3.30	Plates, Cups, Saucers, Soups	
Creamer	2.30	1 each: Sugar with Cover, Creamer	
Sauceboat	2.80	Round Vegetable Dish 8¼" and	
Pickle - Relish Dish	2.10	Platter 13⅛"	42.95
Casserole and Cover	8.50	(Open Stock Value $55.60)	

☐ Charge   ☐ C. O. D.   ☐ Payment Enclosed

Name
Address

SPRING ROSE...
A NEW *Triumph China* PATTERN

Real China...for daily use

Spring Rose is fresh as today's relaxed living. Soft pink and gray on a swan-white background, with platinum bands, this fine TRIUMPH pattern is truly *living china*.

The TRIUMPH shape and craftsmanship bring the graciousness of beautiful American china to today's informal living. Combining Old World charm with New World simplicity, the sculptural theme compliments both the traditional and contemporary setting. Delicately-bodied for high translucency, yet fully oven-proof and chip resistant. Popularly-priced and guaranteed open stock.

EASTERN SALES AND DISPLAY ROOM: SUITE 2000, 212 FIFTH AVE., NEW YORK 10, N. Y. BERNARD MENGE
CHICAGO SALES OFFICE: ROOM 916, LaSALLE-WACKER BLDG., 221 NO. LaSALLE ST., CHICAGO 1, ILL. N. W. MacDONALD

The Homer Laughlin China Co.
NEWELL, WEST VIRGINIA

CROCKERY & GLASS JOURNAL for April, 1959

Homer Laughlin

Top left: *Moselle pattern; Dinner Plate, Luncheon Plate, Salad Plate, Round Vegetable Bowl, Soup Large Coupe Bowl, Cup & Saucer Set, Soup Coupe Bowl, and Fruit Bowl.* **Top right:** *Snow White pattern; Dinner Plate, Luncheon Plate, Bread & Butter Plate, and "American China" Cup & Saucer Set.* **Middle left:** *Moselle pattern; 13" Oval Platter, 11" Oval Platter, "American China" Gravy/Sauce Boat, "American China" Sugar Bowl with lid, and "American China" Creamer.* **Middle right:** *Snow White pattern; "American China" Teapot with lid.* **Bottom left:** *Snow White pattern; "American China" Cup.* **Bottom middle:** *Moselle pattern; Cup.* **Bottom right:** *Moselle pattern; Cup.*

Triumph Shape

Triumph Piece Type List

From Homer Laughlin Literature with Confirmed Actual Pieces

Bowl, Fruit, 5¼ inches
Bowl, Soup Coupe, 8 inches
Bowl, Vegetable Round, 7⅜ inches
Bowl, Vegetable Round, 8½ inches
Bowl, Vegetable Round Covered, 8⅜ inches
Coffeepot with lid (2 styles)
Creamer (2 styles)

Cup & Saucer Set
 Cup (3 styles)
 Saucer, 5⅞ inches
Cup & Saucer, Demitasse
Gravy/Sauce Boat
Gravy/Sauce Boat Underplate/Relish, 8⅜ inches
Plate, Bread & Butter, 6 inches

Plate, Dinner, 10¼ inches
Plate, Salad, 8¼ inches
Platter, 11⅜ inches
Platter, 13¼ inches
Salt & Pepper Set
Sugar Bowl with lid (2 styles)

Above left: *Woodland* pattern; *Crockery & Glass Journal, July 1959*. **Top right:** *Woodland* pattern; Dinner Plate, Salad Plate, Gravy/Sauce Boat, Sugar Bowl with lid, Creamer, Bread & Butter Plate, and Cup & Saucer Set. **Bottom right:** *Woodland* pattern; 13" Oval Platter, 11" Oval Platter, Two Round Vegetable Bowls, Salt & Pepper Set, Soup Coupe Bowl, and Fruit Bowl.

Triumph Shape

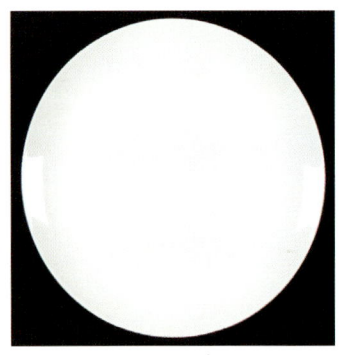

Snow White
No Trim

Moselle
Platinum Trim

October Leaves
Gold Trim

October Leaves
TR6
Gold Trim

Woodland
Platinum Trim

HLC1304
Platinum Trim

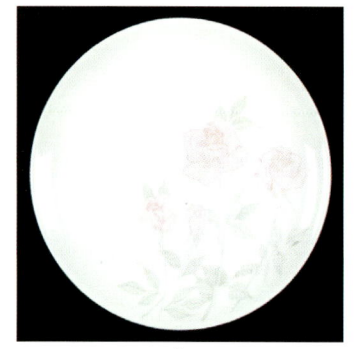

Pastel Rose
TR21
No Trim

HLC1336
No Trim

Plume
Gold Trim

Spring Rose
TR1
Platinum Trim

HLC1583
Gold Trim

Cynthia
Platinum Trim

Linda
TR7
Platinum Trim

Charm House Shape with Triumph Hollowware

HLC551
No Trim

Aster
No Trim

Orchard
No Trim

Alliance

Piece Types

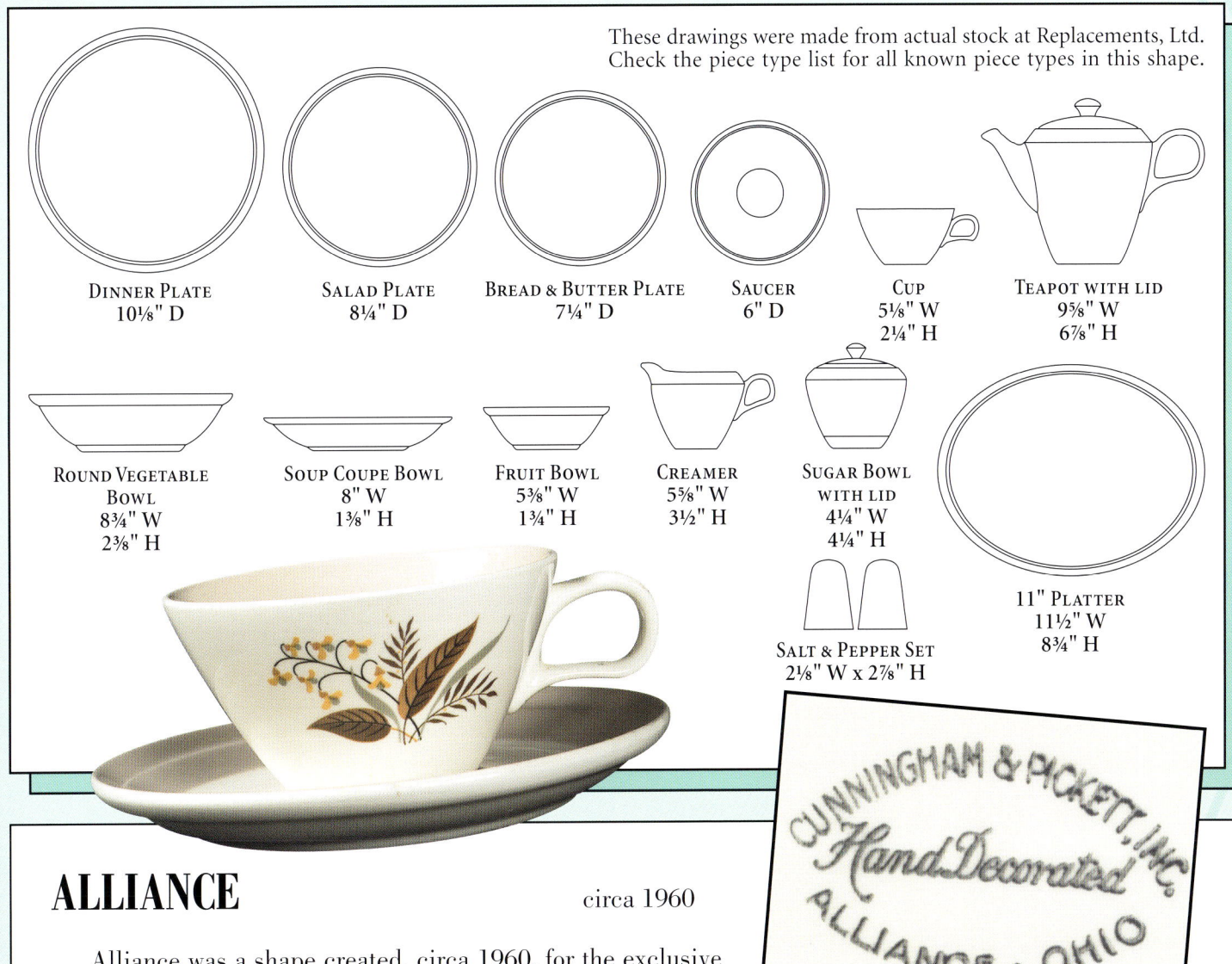

These drawings were made from actual stock at Replacements, Ltd. Check the piece type list for all known piece types in this shape.

Dinner Plate	10⅛" D
Salad Plate	8¼" D
Bread & Butter Plate	7¼" D
Saucer	6" D
Cup	5⅛" W, 2¼" H
Teapot with lid	9⅝" W, 6⅞" H
Round Vegetable Bowl	8¾" W, 2⅜" H
Soup Coupe Bowl	8" W, 1⅜" H
Fruit Bowl	5⅜" W, 1¾" H
Creamer	5⅝" W, 3½" H
Sugar Bowl with lid	4¼" W, 4¼" H
11" Platter	11½" W, 8¾" H
Salt & Pepper Set	2⅛" W x 2⅞" H

ALLIANCE   circa 1960

Alliance was a shape created, circa 1960, for the exclusive use of Cunningham & Pickett, Inc. Alliance was the Ohio town where the firm was located and the name of one of several subdivisions of Cunningham & Pickett (Alliance China). Few patterns have been identified to date on this shape. All patterns bear the Cunningham & Pickett backstamp, which includes the town, state and pattern name.

Left: *Vogue* pattern; Cup & Saucer Set. **Right:** *Dixie Rose* pattern; Typical Alliance backstamp.

Homer Laughlin

Alliance Piece Type List

From Homer Laughlin Literature with Confirmed Actual Pieces

Ashtray*
Bowl, Fruit, 5⅜ inches
Bowl, Soup Coupe, 8 inches
Bowl, Vegetable Round, 8¾ inches
Bowl, Vegetable Round Covered*
Coffeepot with lid
Creamer

Cup & Saucer Set
Cup, 2¼ inches
Saucer, 6 inches
Gravy/Sauce Boat*
Plate, Bread & Butter, 7¼ inches
Plate, Dinner, 10⅛ inches
Plate, Luncheon*

Plate, Salad, 8¼ inches
Platter, Oval, 11½ inches
Platter, Oval, 13 inches*
Salt & Pepper Set (Jubilee Shape)
Sugar Bowl with lid
Teapot with lid
*Reported but not confirmed.

Avalon
by Cunningham & Pickett
Mint Band
No Trim

Dixie Rose
by Cunningham & Pickett
Pink Band
No Trim

Vogue
by Cunningham & Pickett
Tan Band
No Trim

Top left: Avalon pattern; Teapot with lid, Oval Platter, Creamer, and Sugar Bowl with lid. Top right: Avalon pattern; Dinner Plate, Salad Plate, and Cup & Saucer Set. Bottom left: Vogue pattern; Soup Coupe Bowl, Round Vegetable Bowl, and Fruit Bowl. Bottom right: Dixie Rose pattern; Soup Coupe Bowl, Dinner Plate, Salad Plate, Cup & Saucer Set, and Cereal Bowl.

Dover

Piece Types

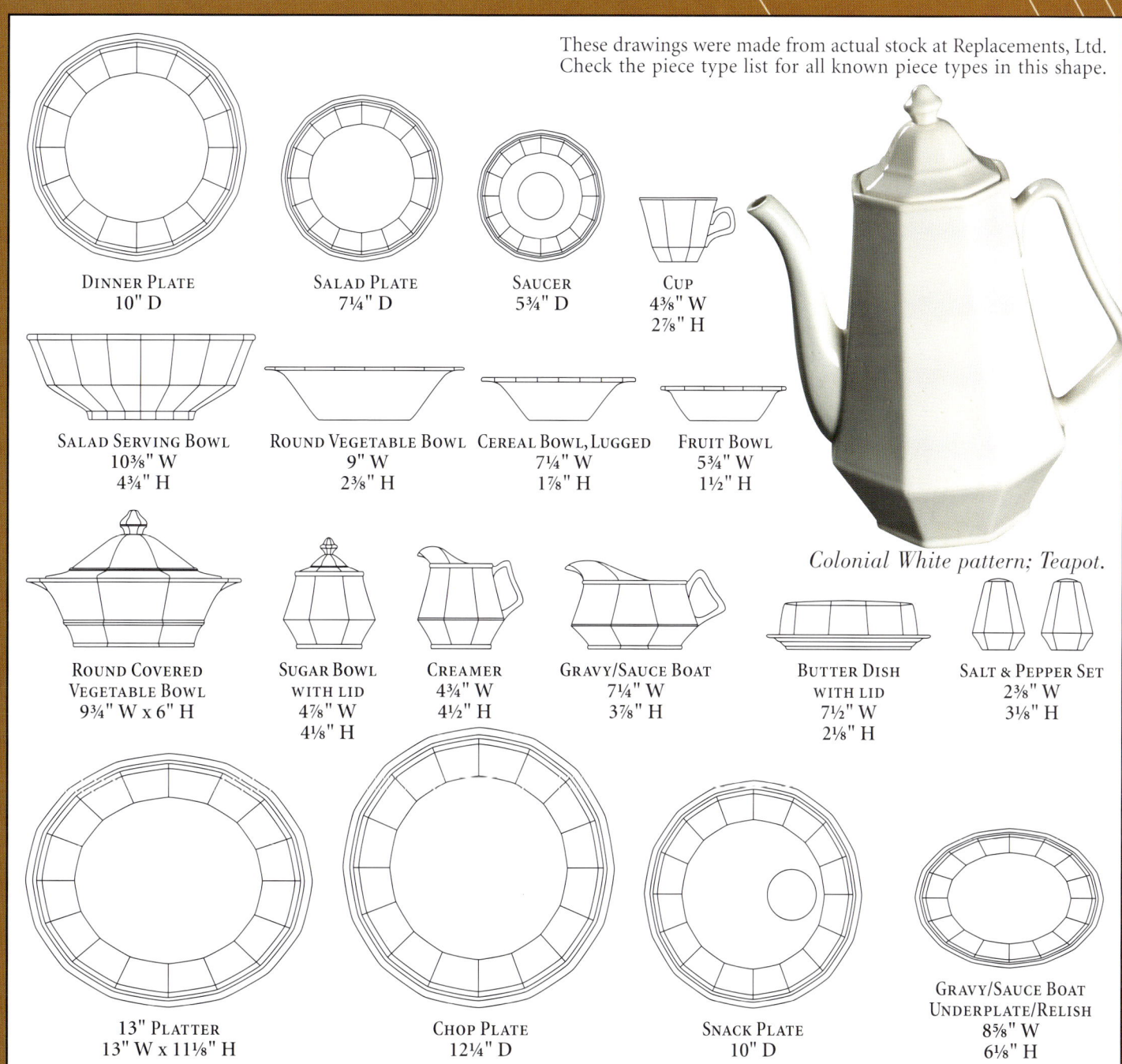

These drawings were made from actual stock at Replacements, Ltd. Check the piece type list for all known piece types in this shape.

Dinner Plate
10" D

Salad Plate
7¼" D

Saucer
5¾" D

Cup
4⅜" W
2⅞" H

Salad Serving Bowl
10⅜" W
4¾" H

Round Vegetable Bowl
9" W
2⅜" H

Cereal Bowl, Lugged
7¼" W
1⅞" H

Fruit Bowl
5¾" W
1½" H

Colonial White pattern; Teapot.

Round Covered Vegetable Bowl
9¾" W x 6" H

Sugar Bowl with lid
4⅞" W
4⅛" H

Creamer
4¾" W
4½" H

Gravy/Sauce Boat
7¼" W
3⅞" H

Butter Dish with lid
7½" W
2⅛" H

Salt & Pepper Set
2⅜" W
3⅛" H

13" Platter
13" W x 11⅛" H

Chop Plate
12¼" D

Snack Plate
10" D

Gravy/Sauce Boat Underplate/Relish
8⅝" W
6⅛" H

Homer Laughlin

DOVER
late 1960's – early 1980's

The Dover shape was created in the late 1960's, when interest in American Colonial designs was popular. It was produced throughout the 1970's and into the early 1980's. The most popular pattern on this multi-sided form was Colonial White, an undecorated white pattern. Homer Laughlin assigned numbers to most Dover patterns; a letter code and number for the specific pattern decoration. Most patterns have the designation CW for Colonial White, and not D for Dover. The interest in the 1976 American Bicentennial helped sales of Dover patterns remain strong through the 1970's. Many Bicentennial Commemoratives were produced on the shape. Amber/brown and green glazed Dover patterns were also produced to coordinate with the harvest gold and avocado colors used in kitchens of the period. The shape was used to make china marketed by others and may have backstamps by other manufacturers or none at all.

Top left: *Colonial White pattern; Gravy/Sauce Boat with unattached Underplate, Coffeepot with lid, Creamer, and Sugar Bowl with lid.* **Top middle:** *Colonial White pattern; Lugged Cereal Bowl, Dinner Plate, Salad Plate, Fruit Bowl, and Cup.* **Top right:** *Bayberry pattern; Cup & Saucer Set, Dinner Plate, and Gravy/Sauce Boat with unattached Underplate.* **Bottom right:** *Colonial White pattern; Salad Serving Bowl, Salt & Pepper Set, and Round Covered Vegetable Bowl.* **Bottom left:** *Colonial White pattern; Butter Dish with lid.*

Dover Piece Type List
From Homer Laughlin Literature with Confirmed Actual Pieces

Bowl, Cereal Lugged, 7¼ inches
Bowl, Fruit, 5¾ inches
Bowl, Salad Serving, 10⅜ inches
Bowl, Soup
Bowl, Vegetable Round Covered, 9¾ inches
Butter Dish with lid, 7½ inches
Coffeepot with lid
Creamer

Cup & Saucer Set
Cup, 2⅞ inches
Saucer, 5¾ inches
Gravy/Sauce Boat
Gravy/Sauce Boat Underplate/Relish, 8⅝ inches
Plate, Bread & Butter
Plate, Chop, 12¼ inches
Plate, Dinner, 10 inches

Plate, Salad, 7¼ inches
Plate, Snack, 10 inches
Platter, Oval, 13 inches
Sugar Bowl with lid
Teapot with lid
Tureen, two handles with Notched Lid and Ladle

Dover Shape

Colonial White *No Trim*	**Revere** *D101* *Trim Unknown*	**HLC124** *No Trim*	**HLC732** *Salad Plate Shown* *No Trim*
HLC624 *No Trim*	**Homespun** *No Trim*	**HLC2146** *No Trim*	**HLC701** *No Trim*
HLC1920 *No Trim*	**HLC156** *No Trim*	**Bayberry** *CW105* *No Trim*	**Madrid** *No Trim*
Milano Gold *No Trim*	**Milano Green** *No Trim*	**All Seasons** *CW120* *No Trim*	**Strawberries** *No Trim*

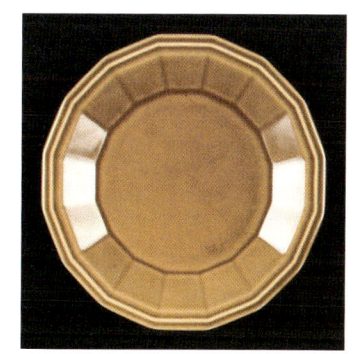

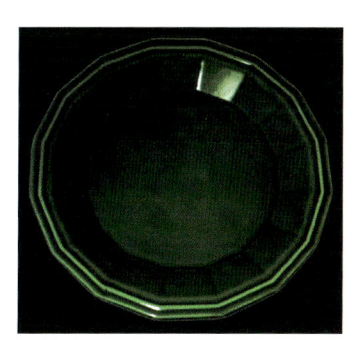

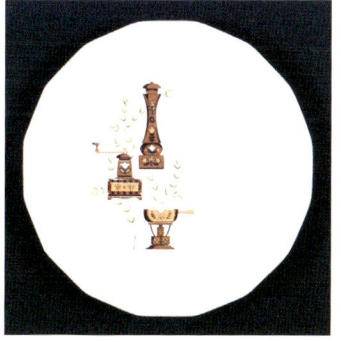

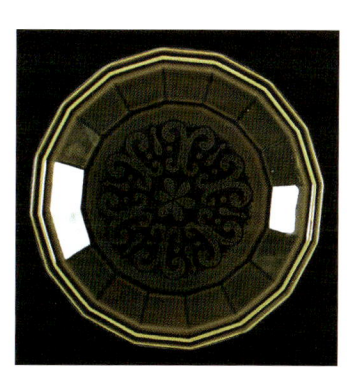

Dover Shape

Gingham
CW119
No Trim

Country Life
CW108
No Trim

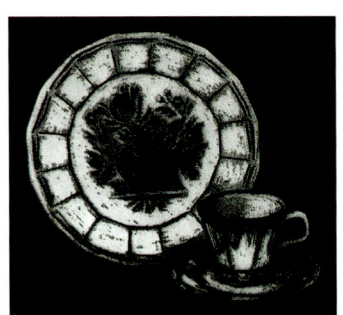

Floribunda
CW128
No Trim

CW114
No Trim

Mary Lloyd
CW131
No Trim

Dover Rose
Brown Band
No Trim

Autumn Gold
No Trim

Above: *Jepcor advertisement featuring several 1960's shapes.*

Duratone

Piece Types

Dinner Plate 10⅛" D

Sugar Bowl with lid 4¼" W 4" H

Creamer 5⅜" W 3½" H

Cup 4½" W 2¾" H

These drawings were made from actual stock at Replacements, Ltd. Check the piece type list for all known piece types in this shape.

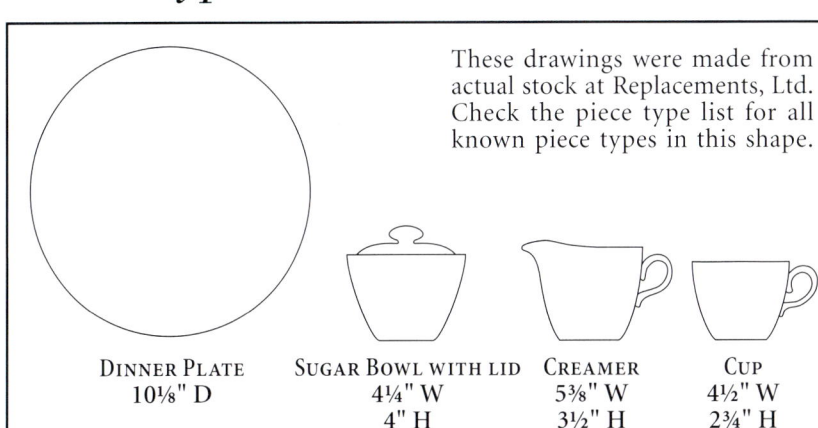

THE HOMER LAUGHLIN CHINA COMPANY. "Buttercup" is a cheerful new pattern of flowers in an underglaze decal used with a new "fade-off" color technique. A 45-piece set retails for $19.95; coffee pot and warmer retail for $5.95.

DURATONE — 1960

Duratone is a printing process and also the name of a line of hollowware shapes created to demonstrate the process. Rhythm flatware is used with Duratone hollowware.

Top middle: *Typical Duratone backstamp.* **Top right:** *Buttercup pattern; China, Glass & Tablewares, February 1961.* **Right:** *Buttercup pattern; Bennett Brothers Catalog, 1963.*

Buttercup
also known as "Primula"
Yellow Edge, No Trim

Royal Joci
Gold Trim

Black Eyed Susan
RU-505
Bread & Butter Plate Shown
Gray Edge, No Trim

HLC628
Cereal Bowl Shown
Blue Edge
No Trim

Spring Garden
Blue Band
No Trim

Saxon

Piece Types

These drawings were made from actual stock at Replacements, Ltd. Check the piece type list for all known piece types in this shape.

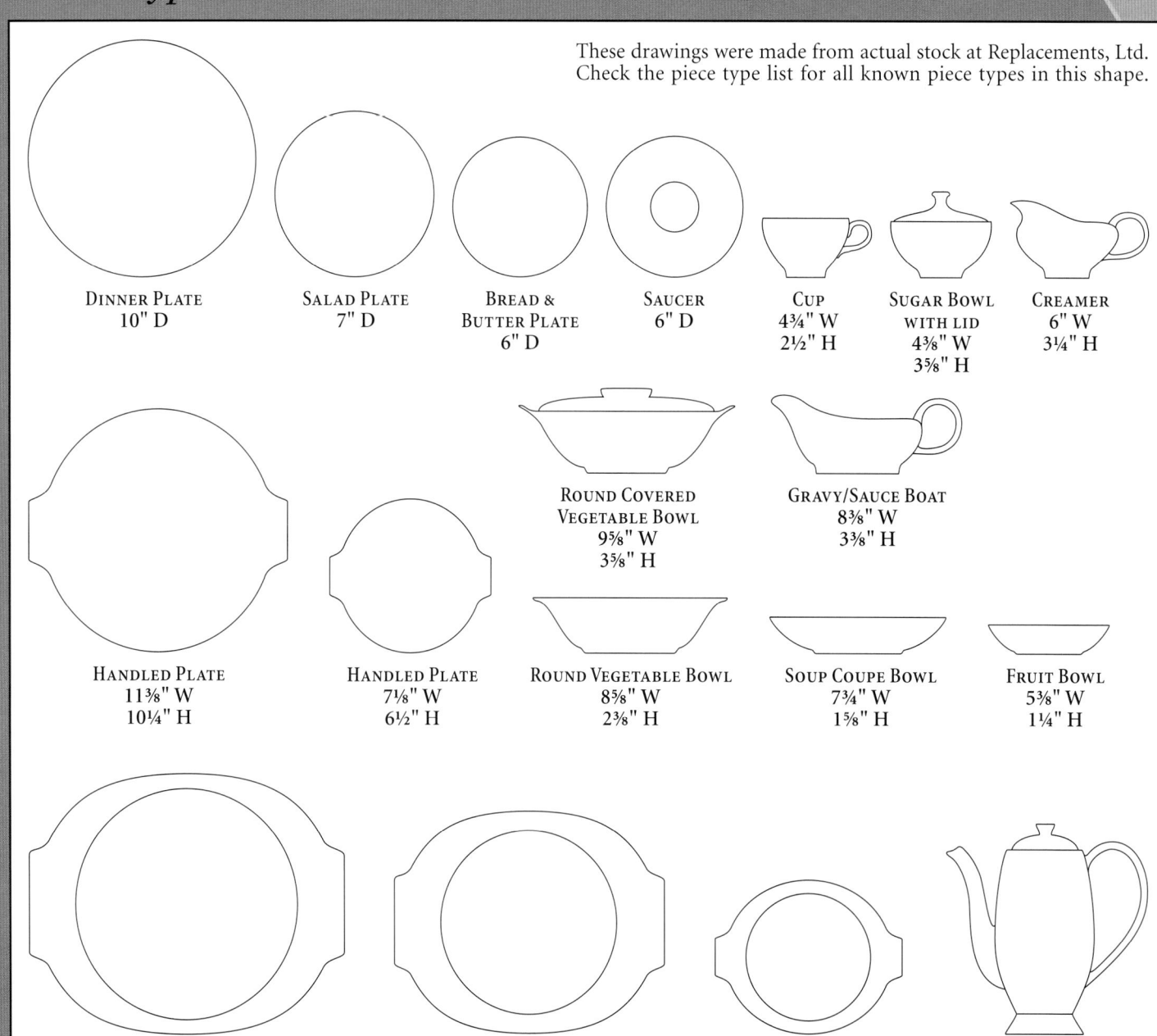

Dinner Plate 10" D	Salad Plate 7" D	Bread & Butter Plate 6" D	Saucer 6" D	Cup 4¾" W 2½" H	Sugar Bowl with lid 4⅜" W 3⅝" H	Creamer 6" W 3¼" H
Handled Plate 11⅜" W 10¼" H	Handled Plate 7⅛" W 6½" H	Round Covered Vegetable Bowl 9⅝" W 3⅝" H	Round Vegetable Bowl 8⅝" W 2⅜" H	Gravy/Sauce Boat 8⅜" W 3⅜" H	Soup Coupe Bowl 7¾" W 1⅝" H	Fruit Bowl 5⅜" W 1¼" H
Handled Platter 13⅞" W 11" H	Handled Platter 11⅞" W 9⅜" H	Handled Platter 8⅛" W 6½" H	Coffeepot with lid 8⅞" W 9" H			

Saxon Shape

SAXON   circa 1960's

Saxon is one of several Homer Laughlin shapes, created in the 1960's era, that was made for a single customer. Other authors have reported the shape used existing flatware borrowed from other shapes. We found Saxon to have its own distinctive shape for both flatware and hollowware. The plates and flat pieces have distinctly more abrupt and sharper curves where the rim plunges into the well. This is visually distinguishable from Rhythm or other similar coupe shapes. Saxon hollowware has large, looping handles. Small Saxon pieces bear no backstamp, while all of the other pieces we viewed had Cunningham & Pickett backstamps.

Top left: *Sunglow pattern; Cup & Saucer Set, Handled Plate, and Coffeepot with lid.* **Top middle:** *Sunglow pattern; Dinner Plate, Salad Plate, Creamer, Sugar Bowl with lid, and Gravy/Sauce Boat.* **Top right:** *Sunglow pattern; Round Covered Vegetable Bowl, Handled Platters, and Handled Plate.* **Middle left:** *Goldcrest pattern; Soup Coupe Bowl, Round Vegetable Bowl, and Fruit Bowl.* **Middle:** *Regal pattern; Round Covered Vegetable Bowl.* **Middle right:** *Sunglow pattern; Typical Saxon backstamp.* **Bottom left:** *Regal pattern; Gravy/Sauce Boat.* **Bottom right:** *Goldcrest pattern; Coffeepot with lid.*

Saxon Piece Type List
From Homer Laughlin Literature with Confirmed Actual Pieces

- Bowl, Fruit, 5⅜ inches
- Bowl, Soup Coupe, 7¾ inches
- Bowl, Vegetable Round, 8⅝ inches
- Bowl, Vegetable Round Covered
- Coffeepot with lid
- Creamer
- Cup & Saucer Set
- Cup, 2½ inches
- Saucer, 6 inches
- Gravy/Sauce Boat
- Plate, Bread & Butter, 6 inches
- Plate, Dinner, 10 inches
- Plate, Handled, 7⅛ inches
- Plate, Handled, 11⅜ inches
- Plate, Salad, 7 inches
- Platter, Handled, 8⅛ inches
- Platter, Handled, 11⅞ inches
- Platter, Handled, 13⅞ inches
- Salt & Pepper Set
- Sugar Bowl with lid

Saxon Shape

Regal
by Alliance
Platinum Trim

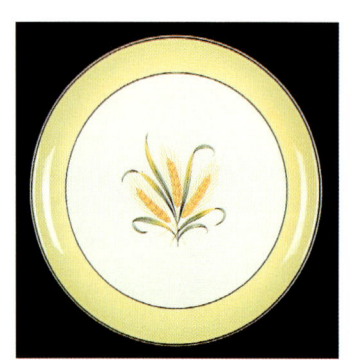

Goldcrest
by Alliance
Gold Trim

Sunglow
by Cunningham & Pickett
Gold Trim

CUP3
by Cunningham & Pickett
Gold Trim

Above: *Photograph from the Homer Laughlin Factory.*

Vogue

Piece Types

These drawings were made from actual stock at Replacements, Ltd. Check the piece type list for all known piece types in this shape.

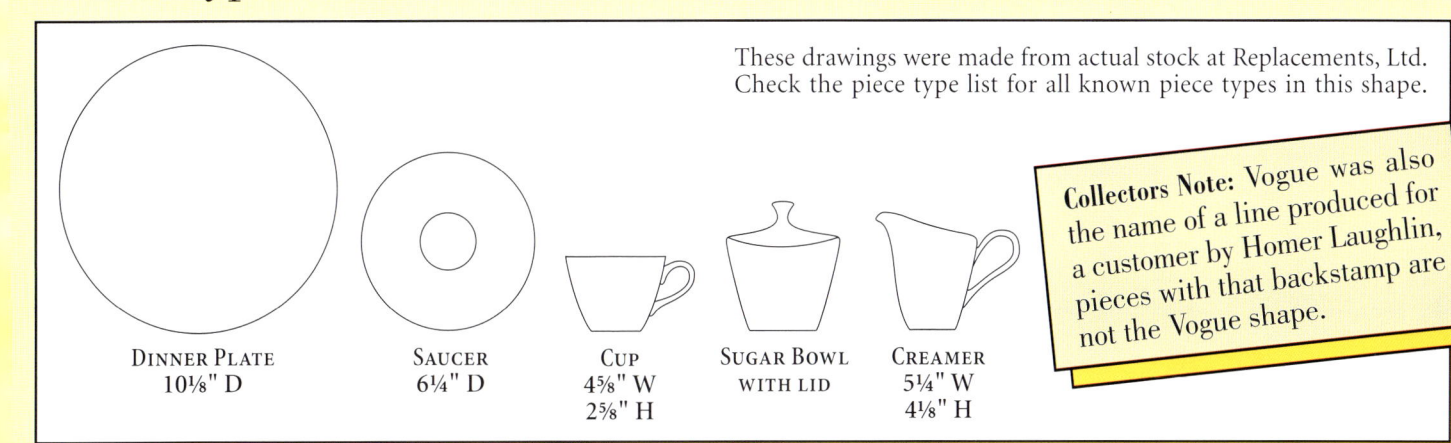

- Dinner Plate 10⅛" D
- Saucer 6¼" D
- Cup 4⅝" W 2⅝" H
- Sugar Bowl with lid
- Creamer 5¼" W 4⅛" H

Collectors Note: Vogue was also the name of a line produced for a customer by Homer Laughlin, pieces with that backstamp are not the Vogue shape.

VOGUE   1963 – 1966 or later

Vogue was introduced in 1963 and produced for F. W. Woolworth stores. It is a line of modern shapes with looping pronounced handles and curving, fluid lines. Several Homer Laughlin backstamps contain the word Vogue, but they are not related to this shape. Color Harmony Dinnerware is the backstamp found on Vogue shapes from Homer Laughlin. Ads for the Vogue shape have been found as late as 1966.

Left: *Blue Duchess* pattern; Creamer, Oval Platter, Dinner Plate, Cereal Bowl, Lugged Bowl, and Cup & Saucer Set. **Middle:** *Apache* pattern; Dinner Plate, Creamer, Sugar Bowl with lid, and Cup & Saucer Set. **Right:** *Typical Vogue backstamp.*

Vogue Shape

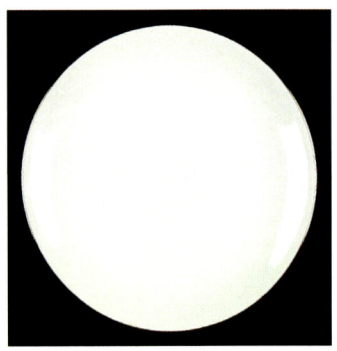

HLC126
Platinum Trim

HLC1303
Gold Trim

Blue Duchess
C-305
Blue Band
No Trim

HLC1994
Yellow Band
No Trim

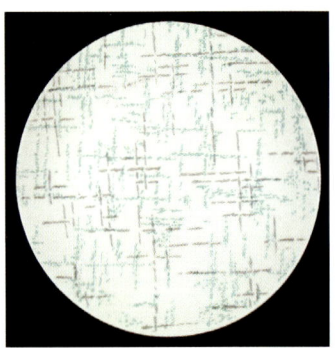

HLC431
Blue & Gray Design
No Trim

Apache
No Trim

R6263A
No Trim

E343
No Trim

Homestead
C325
No Trim

Right: *Workers at the Homer Laughlin Factory.*

Orbit

Piece Types

These drawings were made from actual stock at Replacements, Ltd. Check the piece type list for all known piece types in this shape.

Dinner Plate	Saucer	Cup	Sugar Bowl with lid	Creamer
10⅛" D	5⅞" D	4¼" W, 3" H	3⅛" W, 4⅝" H	4⅝" W, 4¼" H

ORBIT — circa 1964 – 1968 or later

Homer Laughlin's ad in the May 15th, 1966 *Red Book Directory* issue of *China, Glass & Tablewares* notes the "new Orbit shape." Orbit shaped patterns have white flatware with color decorations. Orbit hollowware shapes were produced in bold solid colors that complimented the flatware decorations.

The only Orbit pattern found in catalogs is the Maplewood pattern, which was offered in a Bennett Brothers Wholesale Catalog. It appeared from 1964-68.

Left: *HLC2240 pattern; Coffeepot with lid, Chop Plate, Cup & Saucer Set, and Salt & Pepper Set.* **Middle:** *HLC2240 pattern; Butter Dish with lid, Lugged Cereal Bowl, Dinner Plate, Salad Plate, Creamer, and Sugar Bowl with lid.* **Right:** *Orient pattern; Sugar Bowl with lid, and Creamer.*

Orbit Shape

Maplewood
No Trim

HLC2240
No Trim

Trent
No Trim

Fashion
No Trim

Rhythm Shape with Orbit Hollowware

Everglade
No Trim

Orbit
Serenade Line
No Trim

Above: *Workers applying decals to china at the Homer Laughlin Factory.*

488

Victoria

Piece Types

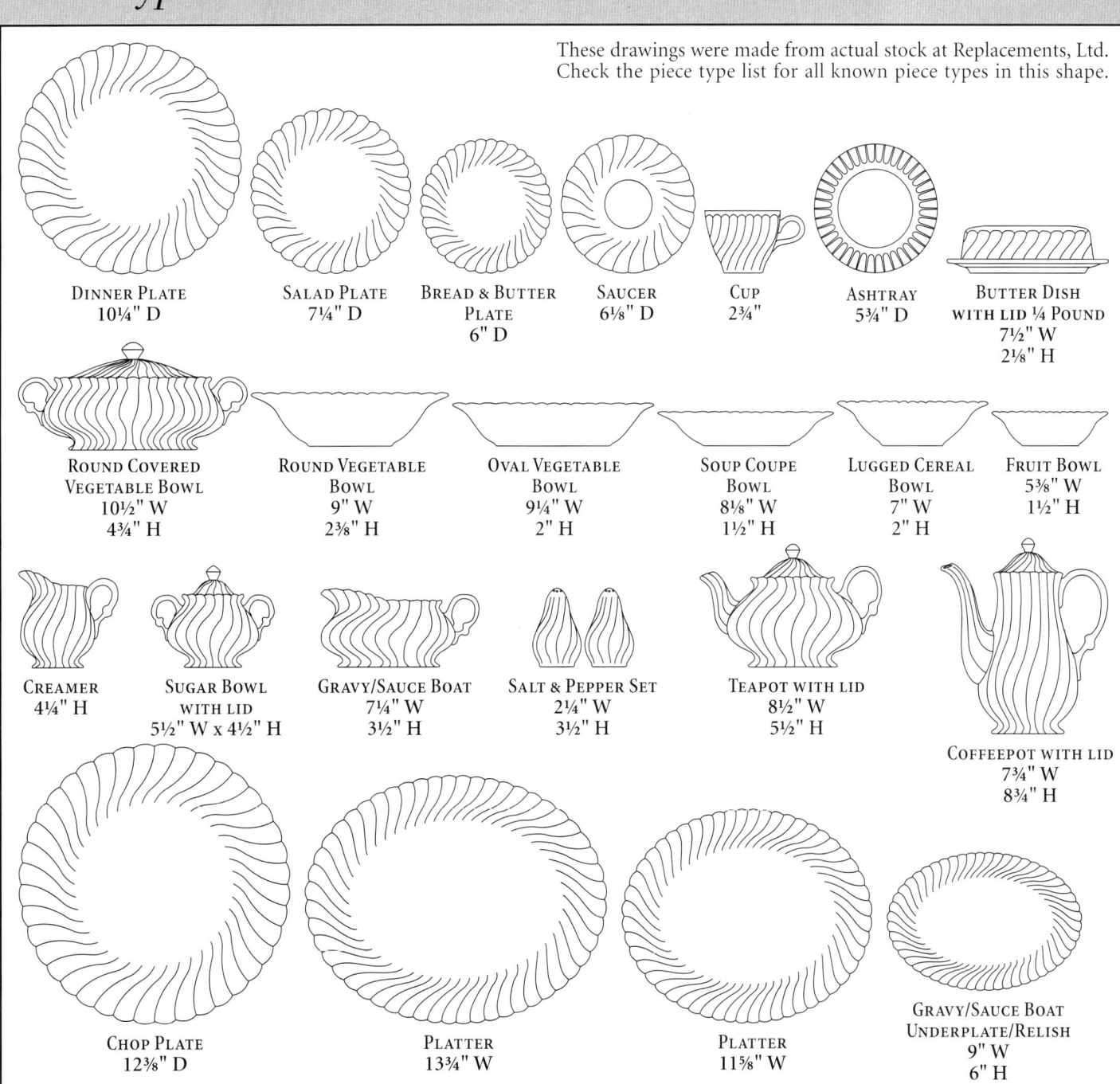

These drawings were made from actual stock at Replacements, Ltd. Check the piece type list for all known piece types in this shape.

Dinner Plate	10¼" D
Salad Plate	7¼" D
Bread & Butter Plate	6" D
Saucer	6⅛" D
Cup	2¾"
Ashtray	5¾" D
Butter Dish with lid ¼ Pound	7½" W, 2⅛" H
Round Covered Vegetable Bowl	10½" W, 4¾" H
Round Vegetable Bowl	9" W, 2⅜" H
Oval Vegetable Bowl	9¼" W, 2" H
Soup Coupe Bowl	8⅛" W, 1½" H
Lugged Cereal Bowl	7" W, 2" H
Fruit Bowl	5⅜" W, 1½" H
Creamer	4¼" H
Sugar Bowl with lid	5½" W x 4½" H
Gravy/Sauce Boat	7¼" W, 3½" H
Salt & Pepper Set	2¼" W, 3½" H
Teapot with lid	8½" W, 5½" H
Coffeepot with lid	7¾" W, 8¾" H
Chop Plate	12⅜" D
Platter	13¾" W
Platter	11⅝" W
Gravy/Sauce Boat Underplate/Relish	9" W, 6" H

Homer Laughlin

VICTORIA   1965 – 1968 or later

In the US Potters Association Annual Report for 1965 we read: "Homer Laughlin China Company introduced their new Victoria shape in early 1965 consisting of 23 items. This is a fluted swirl shape with softened rim in a semi-opaque snowhite glaze. While most of the production has been in the plain white, several overglaze decal patterns and silver treatments were introduced."

The Bennett wholesale catalog included three patterns on the Victoria shape between 1966 and 1968. Homer Laughlin produced patterns on the Victoria shape for distribution by Sheffield.

Top left: *Bone White pattern; Lugged Cereal Bowl, Oval Vegetable Bowl, and Ashtray.*
Middle left: *Bone White pattern; Soup Coupe Bowl, Round Vegetable Bowl, and Fruit Bowl.*
Bottom left: *Bone White pattern; Teapot with lid.*
Top right: *Bone White pattern; Round Covered Vegetable Bowl, Oval Platter, Chop Plate, Salt & Pepper Set, and Covered Butter Dish.*
Bottom right: *Bone White pattern; Gravy/Sauce Boat with unattached Underplate, and Coffeepot with lid.*
Middle: *Bone White pattern; backstamp.*

Victoria Shape

Victoria Piece Type List
From Homer Laughlin Literature with Confirmed Actual Pieces

Ashtray, 5¾ inches
Bowl, Cereal Lugged, 7 inches
Bowl, Fruit, 5⅜ inches
Bowl, Soup Coupe, 8⅛ inches
Bowl, Vegetable Oval, 9¼ inches
Bowl, Vegetable Round, 9 inches
Bowl, Vegetable Round Covered, 10½ inches
Butter Dish with lid, ¼ pound

Coffeepot with lid
Creamer
Cup & Saucer Set
  Cup, 2¾ inches
  Saucer, 6⅛ inches
Gravy/Sauce Boat
Gravy/Sauce Boat Underplate/Relish, 9 inches
Plate, Bread & Butter, 6 inches

Plate, Chop, 12⅜ inches
Plate, Dinner, 10¼ inches
Plate, Salad, 7¼ inches
Platter, 11⅝ inches
Platter, 13¾ inches
Salt & Pepper Set
Sugar Bowl with lid
Teapot with lid

Top left: *Photograph from the Homer Laughlin Factory of the Bone White pattern.* **Top right:** *Arcadia pattern; Dinner Plate, Salad Plate, and Cup & Saucer Set.* **Bottom left:** *Arcadia pattern; Soup Coupe Bowl, Oval Platter, and Round Vegetable Bowl.* **Bottom right:** *Silver Swirl pattern; Sugar Bowl with lid, and Creamer.*

Victoria Shape

Bone White *by Sheffield* No Trim	**SH6** *by Sheffield* Tan Specks No Trim	**Silver Swirl** Platinum Trim	**Arcadia** V100 Platinum Trim
V112 Platinum Trim	**HLC1794** Silver Wheat Gold Trim	**Rosedale** V131 No Trim	**Royal Rose** V125 No Trim
V111 No Trim	**V118** No Trim	**Lady Eleanor** V117 No Trim	**Rosebud** No Trim
Fairhaven V107 No Trim	**Rambling Rose** V126 No Trim		

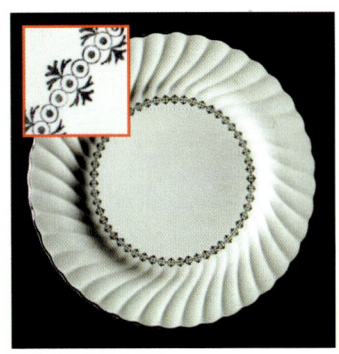

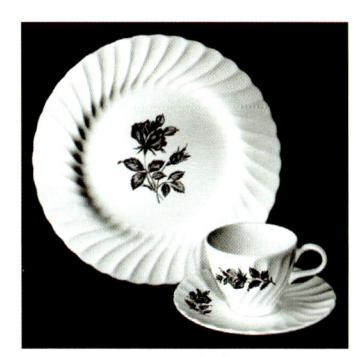

492

Granada

Piece Types

These drawings were made from actual stock at Replacements, Ltd. Check the piece type list for all known piece types in this shape.

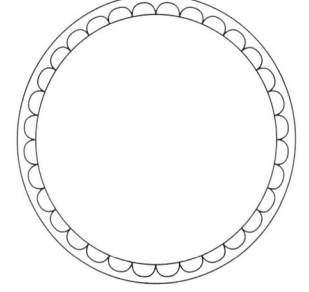

Dinner Plate 10⅛" D	**Salad Plate** 7⅛" D	**Bread & Butter Plate** 6¼" D	**Saucer** 5¾" D	**Cup** 4⅜" W 3" H	**Individual Soup Server, Open** 5" W 2⅝" H
Round Vegetable Bowl 9" W 2¼" H	**Round Vegetable Bowl** 8" W 2⅛" H	**Soup Bowl with rim** 8¼" W 1½" H	**Cereal Bowl with rim** 6¾" W 2⅞" H	**Fruit Bowl with rim** 7" W 1½" H	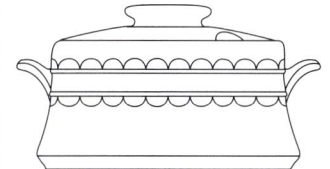
Tureen with lid 11" W 5¾" H	**Round Covered Vegetable Bowl** 9⅜" W 4½" H	**Butter Dish with lid** 7⅝" W 2⅛" H	**Gravy/Sauce Boat** 6¼" W 3½" H	**Gravy/Sauce Boat Underplate/Relish** 8⅞" W 6⅛" H	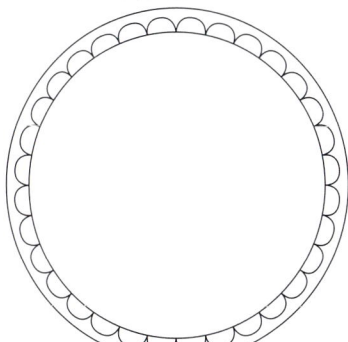
Chop Plate 12⅜" W	**Coffeepot with lid** 6⅛" W 10" H	**Sugar Bowl with lid** 3¾" W 3¾" H	**Creamer** 4⅜" W 4⅜" H	**Salt & Pepper Set** 2¼" W 3⅜" H	**Teapot with lid** 7¾" W 6¼" H

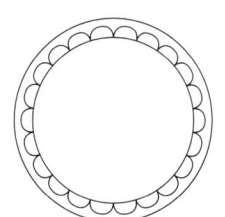

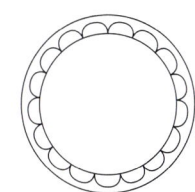

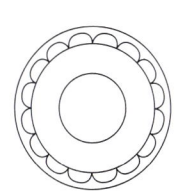

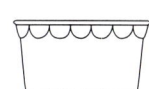

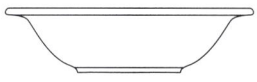

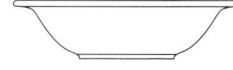

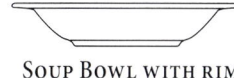

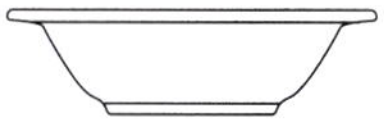

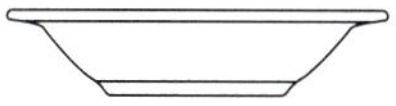

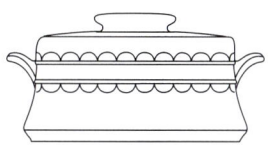

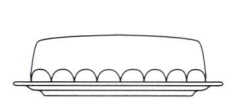

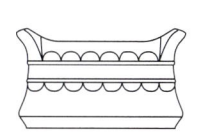

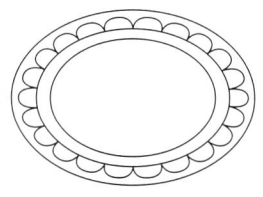

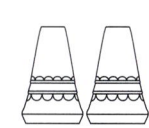

Homer Laughlin

GRANADA circa 1966 – 1970's

Granada is a casual ironstone line. It was introduced in the mid 1960's and frequently used colored glazes that were popular during that time — shades to match harvest gold and avocado green kitchens. Granada shapes were utilized to make patterns for other distributors, so they may be found with backstamps saying Coventry, Sheffield, Jepcor, and others. All pieces in this line have petal-like embossing; some near the edge, others in double rows mid-object.

Collectors Note: Golden Harvest's glaze varies from shades of brown to green.

45 PIECE SERVICE FOR EIGHT
- 8 Dinner Plates
- 8 Cups
- 8 Saucers
- 8 Salad Plates
- 1 Covered Sugar Bowl
- 8 Soup/Cereal Bowls
- 1 Vegetable Bowl
- 1 Buffet Platter
- 1 Creamer

FASHION FLOWER SR-119 American Made Ironstone

Refrigerator Freezer-Safe   Oven-Proof

JEPCOR LIFETIME GUARANTEE: Any piece bearing the JEPCOR trademark refrigerator/freezer-safe, oven-proof, detergent-proof, in normal, everyday...

Left: *Fashion Flower pattern; Advertisement from the Factory.* **Top right:** *Golden Harvest pattern; Teapot with lid.* **Bottom right:** *Golden Harvest pattern; Gravy/Sauce Boat with unattached Underplate, Cup & Saucer Set, and Coffeepot with lid.*

Granada Shape

Granada Piece Type List

From Homer Laughlin Literature with Confirmed Actual Pieces

Ashtray
Bowl, Cereal with rim, 6¾ inches
Bowl, Fruit, 7 inches
Bowl, Soup with rim, 8¼ inches
Bowl, Soup Server Individual, Open, 5 inches
Bowl, Vegetable Round, 8 inches
Bowl, Vegetable Round, 9 inches
Bowl, Vegetable Round Covered
Butter Dish with lid

Coffeepot with lid
Creamer
Cup & Saucer Set
   Cup, 3 inches
   Saucer, 5¾ inches
Gravy/Sauce Boat
Gravy/Sauce Boat Underplate/Relish, 8⅞ inches
Plate, Bread & Butter, 6¼ inches
Plate, Chop, 12⅜ inches

Plate, Dinner, 10⅛ inches
Plate, Salad, 7⅛ inches
Salt & Pepper Set
Sugar Bowl with lid
Teapot with lid
Tray, Serving with handle, 12½ inches
Tureen with lid

Top left: *Golden Harvest pattern; Bread & Butter Plate, Chop Plate, Dinner Plate, Creamer, Sugar Bowl with lid, Round Covered Vegetable Bowl, Salt Shaker, and Butter Dish with lid.* **Top right:** *Garden pattern; Cereal Bowl with rim, Chop Plate, Dinner Plate, Bread & Butter Plate, Cup & Saucer Set, Sugar Bowl with lid, and Creamer.* **Bottom left:** *Golden Harvest pattern; Soup Bowl with rim, Round Vegetable Bowl, Fruit Bowl with rim, Individual Soup Server, and Cereal Bowl with rim.*

Granada Shape

Granada–White	**Granada–Green** *by Sheffield* *No Trim*	**Sorrento** *No Trim*	**Fashion Flower** *No Trim*
HLC282 *No Trim*	**Garden** *No Trim*	**HLC341** *No Trim*	**Golden Harvest** *SR118* *No Trim*
Sonesta *SR108* *Salad Plate Shown* *No Trim*	**Gold Cortez** *No Trim*	**Castilian** *by Coventry* *No Trim*	**Del Rio** *SR100* *No Trim*
Fantasy *No Trim*	**Mystique** *SR120* *No Trim*		

Regency

Piece Types

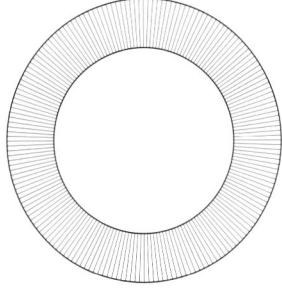

These drawings were made from actual stock at Replacements, Ltd. Check the piece type list for all known piece types in this shape.

Dinner Plate 10⅛" D

Creamer 4⅞" W, 3¾" H

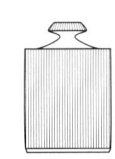

Sugar Bowl with lid 3¼" W, 4⅝" H

Cup 4" W, 2⅞" H

REGENCY   circa 1966

The Regency shape has a tight ribbed edge design on both flat pieces and hollowware. The hollowware pieces were produced in solid colors to coordinate with the more decorated flat pieces. This line had a limited distribution and was mainly produced for other customers. You'll find Sheffield backstamps on Regency patterns.

Bottom left: *Serenade pattern; Two Round Vegetable Bowls, Lugged Cereal Bowl, Fruit Bowl, and Soup Bowl.* **Bottom right:** *Serenade pattern; Dinner Plate, Salad Plate, Sugar Bowl with lid, Creamer, Cup & Saucer Set, and Ashtray.*

Homer Laughlin

Top left: *Serenade pattern; Round Covered Vegetable Bowl, Chop Plate, Oval Platter, Gravy/Sauce Boat with unattached Underplate, and Salt & Pepper Set.* **Top right:** *Malibu pattern; Round Vegetable Bowl, Oval Platter, Dinner Plate, Salad Plate, Sugar Bowl with lid, Creamer, Cup & Saucer Set, Soup Bowl, and Fruit Bowl.*

Regency Piece Type List

From Homer Laughlin Literature with Confirmed Actual Pieces

Ashtray	Creamer	Plate, Dinner, 10⅛ inches
Bowl, Cereal Lugged	Cup & Saucer Set	Platter, Oval
Bowl, Fruit	Cup, 2⅞ inches	Salt & Pepper Set
Bowl, Soup	Gravy/Sauce Boat	Sugar Bowl with lid
Bowl, Vegetable Round	Gravy/Sauce Boat Underplate/Relish	
Bowl, Vegetable Round Covered	Plate, Chop	

Serenade
by Sheffield
No Trim

1959
No Trim

Malibu
No Trim

Bristol

Piece Types

These drawings were made from actual stock or literature at Replacements, Ltd. Check the piece type list for all known piece types in this shape.

- Dinner Plate
- Cup
- Sugar Bowl with Lid
- Creamer

BRISTOL   1970's

Bristol was a line of hollowware developed to supplement already available flatware shapes. Images from the factory show a creamer, sugar bowl with lid, and cup only. While images of patterns suggest some marketing was invested in the line, we have yet to hold a physical piece of Homer Laughlin Bristol in our hands! From the images in our possession, the only flatware we've seen to date is a coupe shaped dinner plate, which we believe to be the Rhythm shape.

Springtime
No Trim

Sunflower
No Trim

Dawn
No Trim

Marigold
No Trim

Bristol Shape

Ginja
No Trim

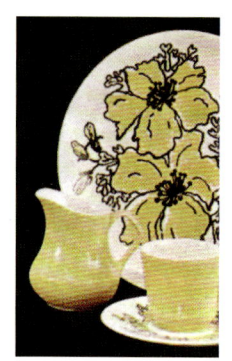

Amy
No Trim

Quilt
No Trim

Poppy
No Trim

Shamrock
No Trim

Needlepoint
No Trim

Floral Garden
No Trim

Melody
No Trim

Left: *A train in front of the Homer Laughlin Factory.* **Right:** *Potentiometer Pyrometers Advertisement, proudly stating that Homer Laughlin used their equipment, The Clay Worker.*

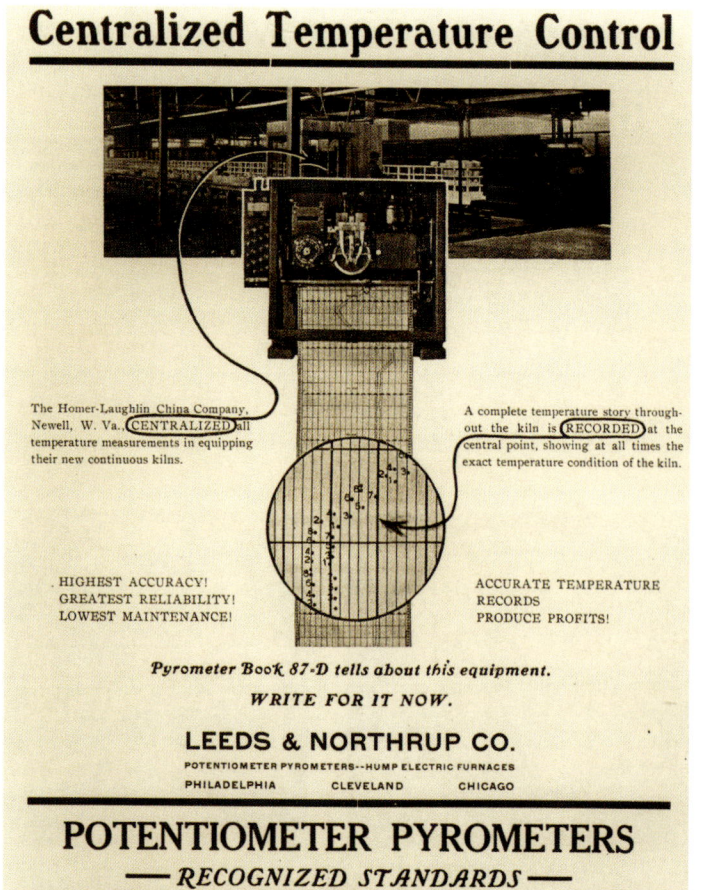

Hearthside

Piece Types

These drawings were made from actual stock or literature at Replacements, Ltd. Check the piece type list for all known piece types in this shape.

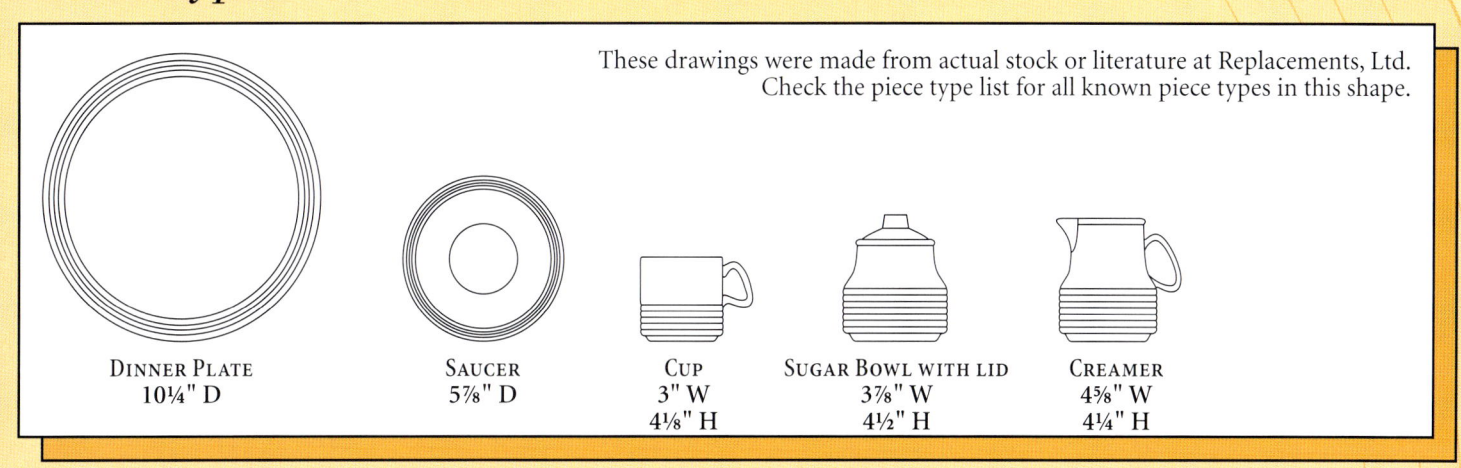

| Dinner Plate 10¼" D | Saucer 5⅞" D | Cup 3" W 4⅛" H | Sugar Bowl with lid 3⅞" W 4½" H | Creamer 4⅝" W 4¼" H |

HEARTHSIDE — early 1970's

Hearthside is a flat rimmed, modern shape featuring ringed grooves on the rims of flatware and banding on the lower body of hollowware. Other authors report it was designed by Vincent Broomhall, when he served as Homer Laughlin's art director. Hearthside illustrations from factory records feature a diversity of patterns.

Left: *Gold Glade pattern; Sugar Bowl with lid, and Creamer.* **Right:** *Gold Glade pattern; Salad Plate, Dinner Plate, and Cup & Saucer Set.*

Hearthside Shape

HLC863 *No Trim*	**HLC725** *No Trim*	**Sun Drops** *HS263* *No Trim*	**Garden Song** *HS216* *No Trim*
Daybreak *No Trim*	**Delightful** *by Andre Ponche* *No Trim*	**Fresh 'N Green** *HS241* *No Trim*	**HLC188** *No Trim*
Nutmeg *No Trim*	**Lucy** *Brown Band* *No Trim*	**HLC1091** *No Trim*	**Rock Garden** *No Trim*
Wheat *No Trim*	**HLC678** *No Trim*	**HLC278** *No Trim*	**Aztec** *No Trim*

Hearthside Shape

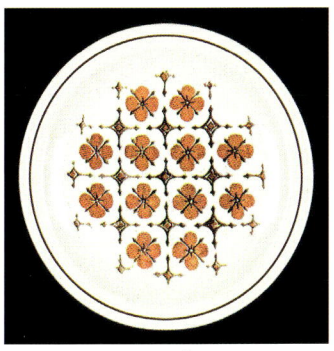

Petals HS240 No Trim	**Round 'N Round** No Trim	**Kaleidoscope** No Trim	**Sierra** by Sheffield No Trim
Gold Glade No Trim	**Banded Cortez** No Trim	**Waves** No Trim	**Contemporary** No Trim
Paradise No Trim	**Fleur** No Trim	**Green Glade** No Trim	**New Fiesta** No Trim
Stitchery No Trim	**HLC939** Multi-Motif No Trim	**Desert Flower** No Trim	**Barcellona** No Trim

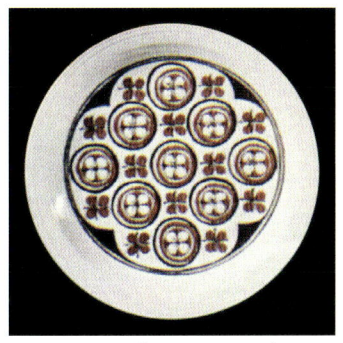

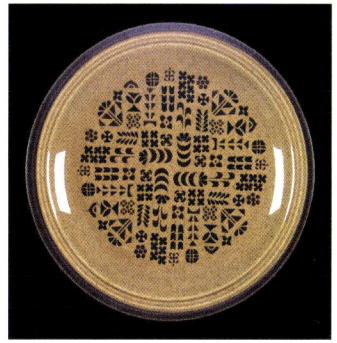

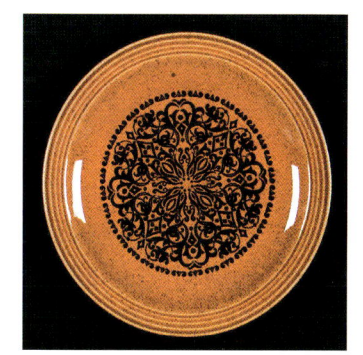

Hearthside Shape

Gold Capri *No Trim*	**Navajo** *No Trim*	**Raindrops** *No Trim*	**Palma** *No Trim*
Apollo *No Trim*	**Butterscotch** *No Trim*	**Irish Spring** *HS268* *No Trim*	**Treasure** *No Trim*
Floral Jubilee *HS270* *No Trim*	**Harvest** *No Trim*	**Heavenly** *No Trim*	**Joy** *No Trim*
Birds *No Trim*	**Old Orchard** *No Trim*	**More Fleur** *No Trim*	**New Paradise** *No Trim*

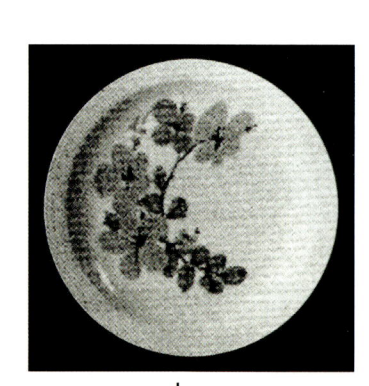

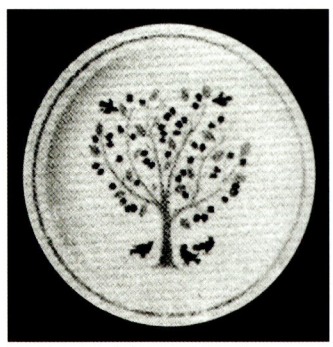

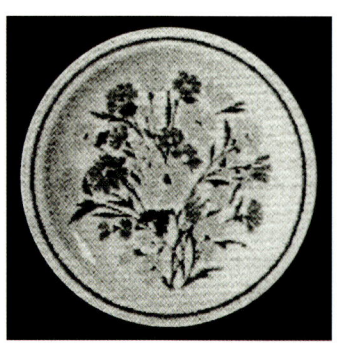

Hearthside Shape

Country Road
HS234
No Trim

HLC3132
No Trim

Pimlico
HS207
No Trim

Dimension
HS204
No Trim

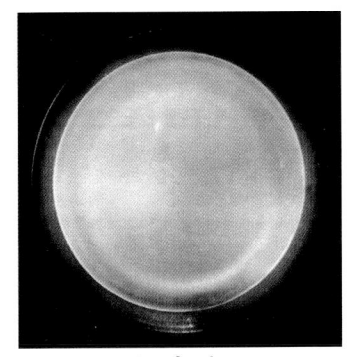

Surfside
No Trim

Spindrift
HS271
No Trim

Above left and right: *Screen printing plates at the Homer Laughlin Factory.*

International

Piece Types

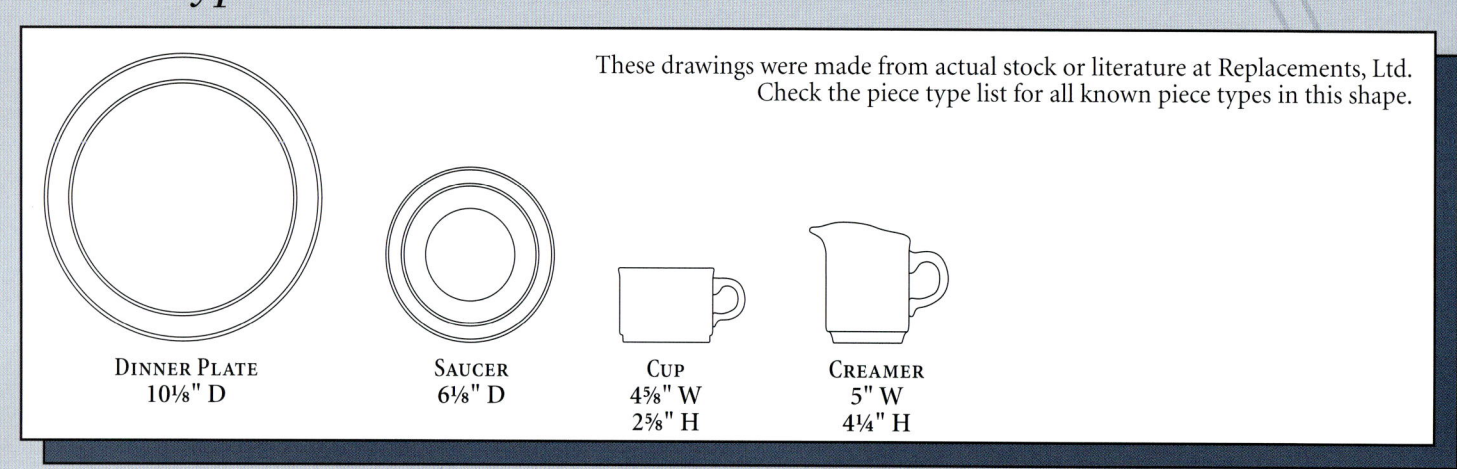

These drawings were made from actual stock or literature at Replacements, Ltd. Check the piece type list for all known piece types in this shape.

Dinner Plate	Saucer	Cup	Creamer
10⅛" D	6⅛" D	4⅝" W, 2⅝" H	5" W, 4¼" H

INTERNATIONAL — 1970's

Featuring a flat rim with relief circles in the clay, the International shape was a statement in 1970's modernism. Produced in white with various decorations, or in designs where the colored glazes and band of color were the decoration, it embodied straight forward design and equally simple motifs. Marketing for the patterns often referred to them as Ironstone dinnerware, a popular type of dinnerware in the 1970's. The designer for this shape is reported to have been Dennis Newbury.

Left: HLC29 pattern; Cup & Saucer Set. **Right:** Country Manor pattern; Creamer, Dinner Plate, Salad Plate, and Cup & Saucer Set.

International Shape

HLC29 *No Trim*	**HLC462** *No Trim*	**HLC350** *Brown Band* *No Trim*	**Mountain Meadow 2** *Rust & Brown Bands* *No Trim*
HLC671 *Brown & Blue Bands* *No Trim*	**HLC273** *No Trim*	**HLC461** *No Trim*	**Country Manor** *No Trim*
HLC846 *No Trim*	**HLC740** *Brown Band* *No Trim*	**HLC980** *No Trim*	**HLC228** *No Trim*
HLC207 *No Trim*	**Mountain Meadow** *No Trim*	**HLC909** *No Trim*	**HLC653** *No Trim*

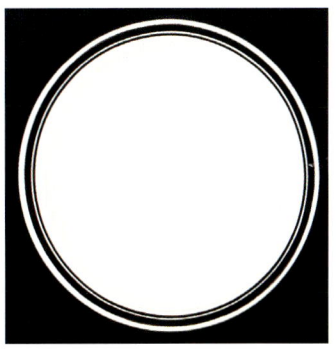

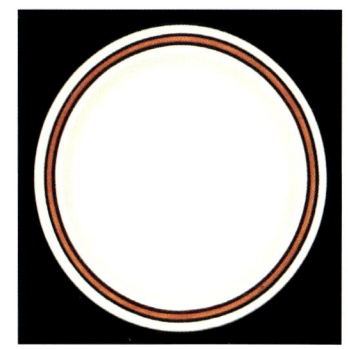

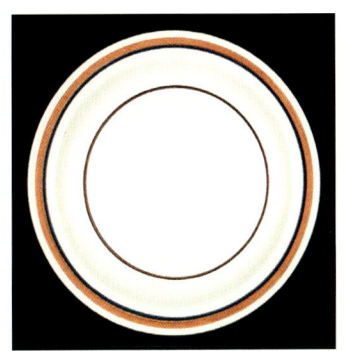

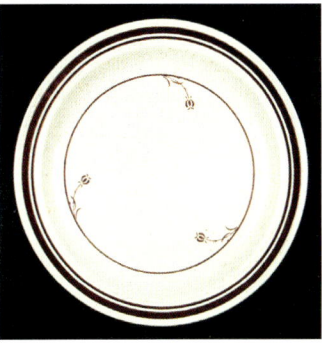

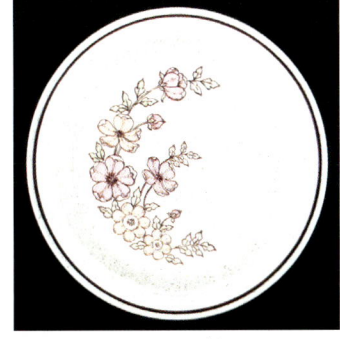

International Shape

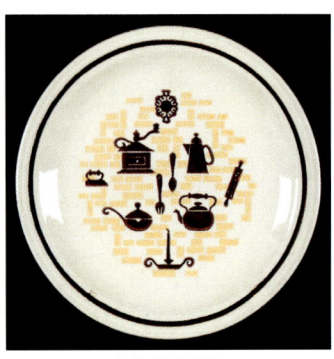

HLC253
No Trim

HLC803
No Trim

HLC1083
Salad Plate Shown
No Trim

Cross Stitch
No Trim

PFD1
by Pacific Flyway Designs
Tan Trim

PFD2
by Pacific Flyway Designs
Tan Trim

PFD3
by Pacific Flyway Designs
Tan Trim

Cannes
No Trim

International Shape with Challenger Hollowware

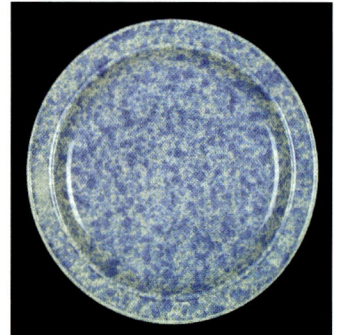

Splatter–Blue
No Trim

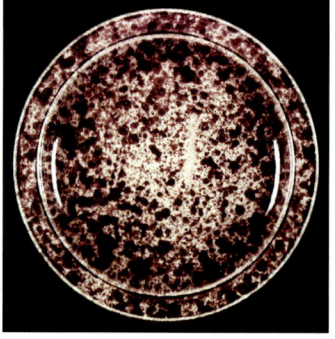

Splatter–Brown
No Trim

Challenger

Piece Types

These drawings were made from actual stock at Replacements, Ltd. Check the piece type list for all known piece types in this shape.

- **Dinner Plate** 10⅜" D
- **Salad Plate** 7½" D
- **Saucer** 6⅜" D
- **Cup** 4⅞" W 2½" H
- **Sugar Bowl with lid** 4" W 2¾" H
- **Creamer** 5⅜" W 3" H
- **Round Vegetable Bowl** 9" W 2¼" H
- **Cereal Bowl** 5⅞" W 2" H
- **Chop Plate** 12⅜" D

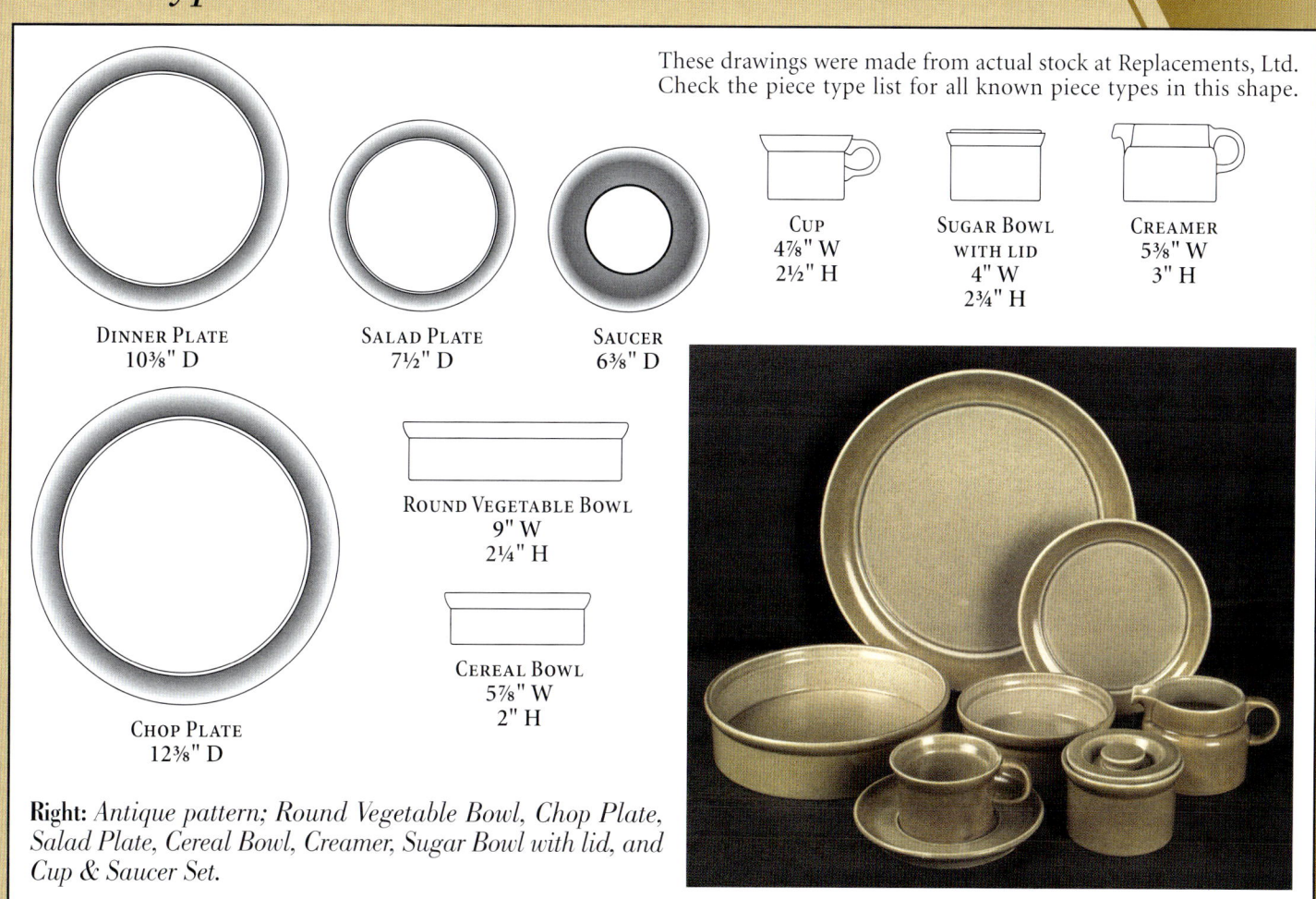

Right: *Antique pattern; Round Vegetable Bowl, Chop Plate, Salad Plate, Cereal Bowl, Creamer, Sugar Bowl with lid, and Cup & Saucer Set.*

Collectors Note: Several of the Challenger forms have an impressed "MADE IN THE USA" on their bases, generally an uncommon practice at Homer Laughlin.

CHALLENGER
circa 1974

The Challenger line of shapes was created for Block China based on their designs. The shape must have met with less than desired success as the line was sold to Jepcor International. Original Homer Laughlin promotional photos and copy describe the earthtone line as "new and exciting." Its shape, particularly the hollowware forms, are in the design vocabulary of the 1970's — stark and modern in form.

Homer Laughlin

Challenger Piece Type List

From Homer Laughlin Literature with Confirmed Actual Pieces

Bowl, Cereal, 5⅞ inches
Bowl, Vegetable Round, 9 inches
Coffeepot with lid
Creamer

Cup & Saucer Set
Cup, 2½ inches
Saucer, 6⅜ inches
Plate, Chop, 12⅜ inches

Plate, Dinner, 10⅜ inches
Plate, Salad, 7½ inches
Sugar Bowl with lid

HLC300
No Trim

Antique
H114
by Jepcor
No Trim

HLC230
Bread & Butter Plate Shown
No Trim

HLC229
No Trim

Goldenrod
CH150
by Jepcor
No Trim

April Flowers
CH108, also known as "Springtime"
by Jepcor
No Trim

Gingersnap
CH151
by Jepcor
No Trim

Woodstock
CH152
by Jepcor
No Trim

JEP1
by Jepcor
No Trim

International Shape with Challenger Hollowware

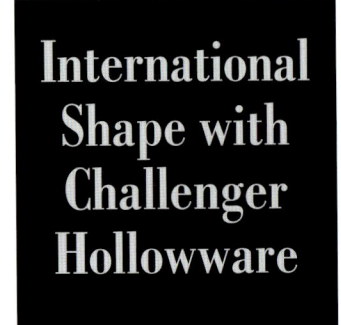

Splatter–Blue
No Trim

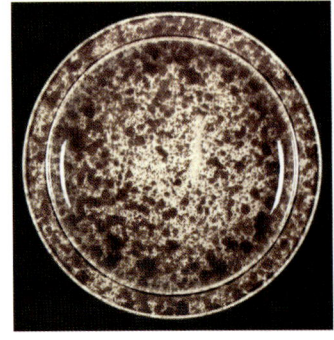

Splatter–Brown
No Trim

TABLEFAIR

Piece Types

These drawings were made from actual stock at Replacements, Ltd. Check the piece type list for all known piece types in this shape.

Dinner Plate 10⅛" D

Saucer 6⅛" D

Cup 4¾" W 2¾" H

Sugar Bowl with lid 4" W 4" H

Creamer 5⅜" W 4" H

Collectors Note: Tablefair round covered vegetable bowls and cups have an impressed USA or MADE IN THE USA on their bases.

TABLEFAIR circa 1980's

Tablefair is a 1980's continuation of the practice of creating a short line of new hollowware shapes, that coupled with an existing line of flatware shapes, created a new look and line of shapes. Tablefair hollowware is straight sided with rings near the base form. This ringed design complimented earlier shapes of Harlequin flatware which had rings on the rim. Harlequin flatware was used for the Tablefair line. Noteworthy is the predominance of Tablefair patterns using the then popular speckled glazes.

Tablefair Piece Type List

From Homer Laughlin Literature with Confirmed Actual Pieces

Bowl, Cereal
Bowl, Fruit
Bowl, Vegetable Round
Bowl, Vegetable Round Covered
Butter Dish with lid
Creamer

Cup & Saucer Set
Cup, 2¾ inches
Saucer, 6⅛ inches
Gravy/Sauce Boat
Mug
Plate, Bread & Butter

Plate, Chop
Plate, Dinner, 10⅛ inches
Plate, Salad
Salt & Pepper Set
Sugar Bowl with lid
Teapot with lid

Homer Laughlin

Country Sage
No Trim

Suzanne
No Trim

HLC505
No Trim

HLC287
No Trim

HLC218
No Trim

Top left: *HLC287 pattern; Dinner Plate. Country Sage pattern; Butter Dish with lid, Mug, and Salad Plate.* **Top right:** *Country Sage pattern; Cup & Saucer Set, Teapot with lid, and Chop Plate. HLC218 pattern; Dinner Plate, and Salad Plate.* **Bottom left:** *Country Sage pattern; Sugar Bowl with lid, and Creamer.* **Bottom second from left:** *Country Sage pattern; Salt & Pepper Set.* **Bottom third from left:** *Country Sage pattern; Round Covered Vegetable Bowl.* **Bottom right:** *Country Sage pattern; Fruit Bowl, Dinner Plate, Round Vegetable Bowl, and Gravy/Sauce Boat.*

MIXED SHAPES

Some patterns produced by Homer Laughlin used multiple shapes from different lines. The teapot may be one shape, the plates another, and the cups yet a third. While this was not a rare occurrence, mixing shapes was also not common. It seems that Homer Laughlin rarely mixed shapes for their own patterns, but when creating patterns for other customers, like the numerous Cunningham & Picket type companies, the attitude seems to have been "give the buyer what they want." The results are patterns that mix shapes with a common and unifying decoration. You will find these patterns listed in each of the different shapes in which the pattern was produced.

Top left: *Lady Greenbriar* pattern; Round Covered Vegetable Bowl, and Two Oval Platters. **Top right:** *Royal Harvest* pattern; Salad Plate, Oval Platter, Dinner Plate, Creamer, Gravy/Sauce Boat, Teapot with lid, Round Covered Vegetable Bowl, Fruit Bowl, Cup & Saucer, and Juice and Old Fashion glassware. **Middle left:** *Lady Greenbriar* pattern; Gravy/Sauce Boat with unattached Underplate, Dinner Plate, Salad Plate, Bread & Butter Plate, Sugar Bowl with lid, Soup Bowl with rim, and Fruit Bowl. **Middle right:** *HLC551* pattern; Round Vegetable Bowl, Sugar Bowl with lid, Creamer, and Cup. **Bottom left:** *Lady Greenbriar* pattern; Teapot with lid, Round Vegetable Bowl, and Cup & Saucer Set. **Bottom right:** *HLC551* pattern; Dinner Plate, Salad Plate, and Cup & Saucer Set.

Unknown Shapes or Lines

The following patterns were made on shapes or lines that are presently unknown to the authors.
We have included them in this section in order to add to the record of patterns produced by Homer Laughlin.

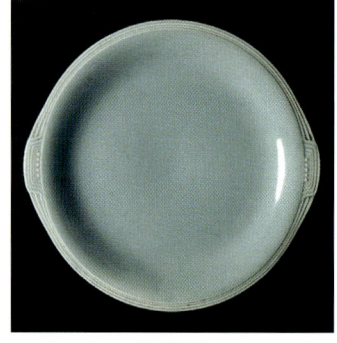

Coupe Shape

2809
Cake Plate Shown
No Trim

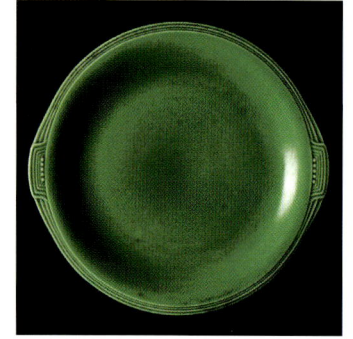

HLC1539
Cake Plate Shown
No Trim

HLC1538
Cake Plate Shown
No Trim

HLC1540
Cake Plate Shown
No Trim

Colorama–Terra Cotta
No Trim

HLC3099
No Trim

HLC1338
No Trim

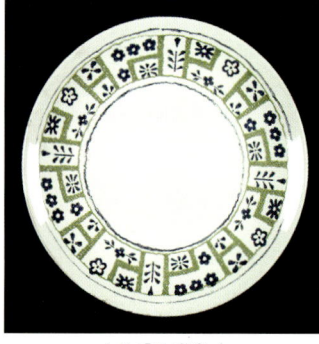

HLC1985
No Trim

HLC1984
No Trim

HLC782
No Trim

Moss Rose
Gold Trim

Royal Maytime
No Trim

Embassy
by Cunningham & Pickett
No Trim

HLC1435
No Trim

HLC1215
Platinum Trim

Unknown Shapes or Lines

Coupe Shape continued

HLC208
No Trim

Viking
by Cunningham & Pickett
Fruit Bowl Shown
Gold Trim

Windemere
C320
Platinum Trim

HLC933
Oval Platter Shown
No Trim

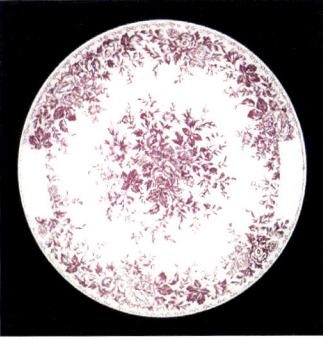

HLC935
No Trim

HLC1584
No Trim

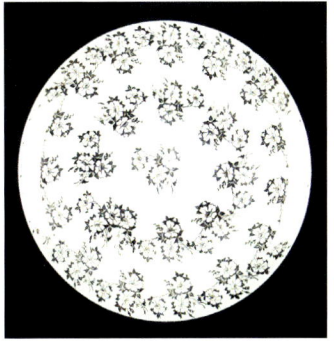

HLC983
No Trim

HLC1434
No Trim

Paisley
by Mikasa
No Trim

Scottsdale
1970
by Mikasa
No Trim

HLC1032
Salad Plate Shown
No Trim

HLC446
No Trim

HLC1308
No Trim

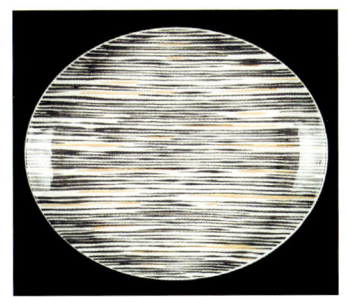

HLC602
Oval Platter Shown
No Trim

HLC1339
No Trim

HLC1158
No Trim

Unknown Shapes or Lines

Coupe Shape continued

R3080A
Yellow Trim

Honey Bunch
C442
No Trim

Patchwork
C420
No Trim

Norway
E339
No Trim

Patchwork
E421
No Trim

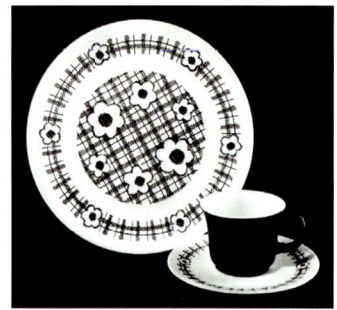

Plaid
E419
No Trim

Crescendo
No Trim

Rim Shape (Smooth)

HLC1564
No Trim

2617
No Trim

1392
No Trim

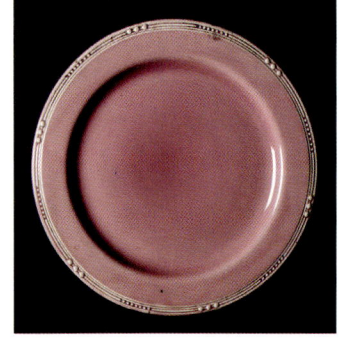

2642
No Trim

2647
No Trim

HLC1617
No Trim

3480
No Trim

516

Unknown Shapes or Lines

Rim Shape (Smooth) continued

HLC1533 No Trim	**HLC1545** No Trim	**HLC1558** Blue No Trim	**HLC1608** Cobalt Blue No Trim
2345 No Trim	**HLC1546** No Trim	**HLC1547** No Trim	**HLC1549** No Trim
HLC1548 No Trim	**2317** No Trim	**HLC1618** No Trim	**HLC1580** No Trim
X5 Bread & Butter Plate Shown Blue Trim	**R5012** Bread & Butter Plate Shown Blue Trim	**R5011** Bread & Butter Plate Shown Blue Trim	**HLC3028** Saucer Shown Gold Trim

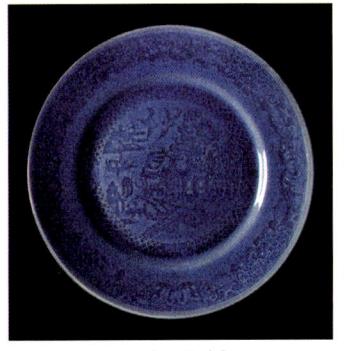

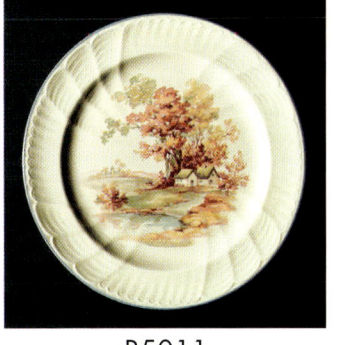

517

Unknown Shapes or Lines

Rim Shape (Smooth) continued

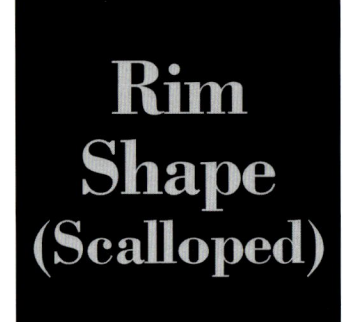

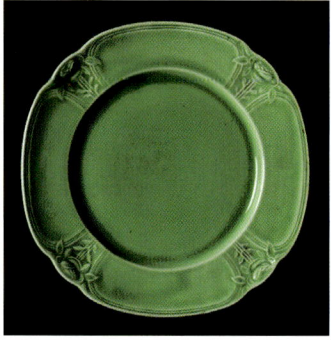

HLC2239	10034	10023	7103-3
Gold Trim	Green Trim	Green Trim	Green Trim

Rim Shape (Scalloped)

HLC1579	HLC1537	HLC1550
No Trim	No Trim	No Trim

HLC1544	HLC1607	R1524	4336
Brown Trim	No Trim	No Trim	Yellow Trim

HOM4313	HLC1206	G646	HLC1531
Yellow Trim	Red Trim	Green Band No Trim	Black Band No Trim

518

Unknown Shapes or Lines

Rim Shape (Scalloped) continued

HLC1601
No Trim

G559
No Trim

HLC1602
No Trim

HLC1603
No Trim

HLC1570
No Trim

R1177
No Trim

Right: *Worker applying decal to plate at the Homer Laughlin Factory.*

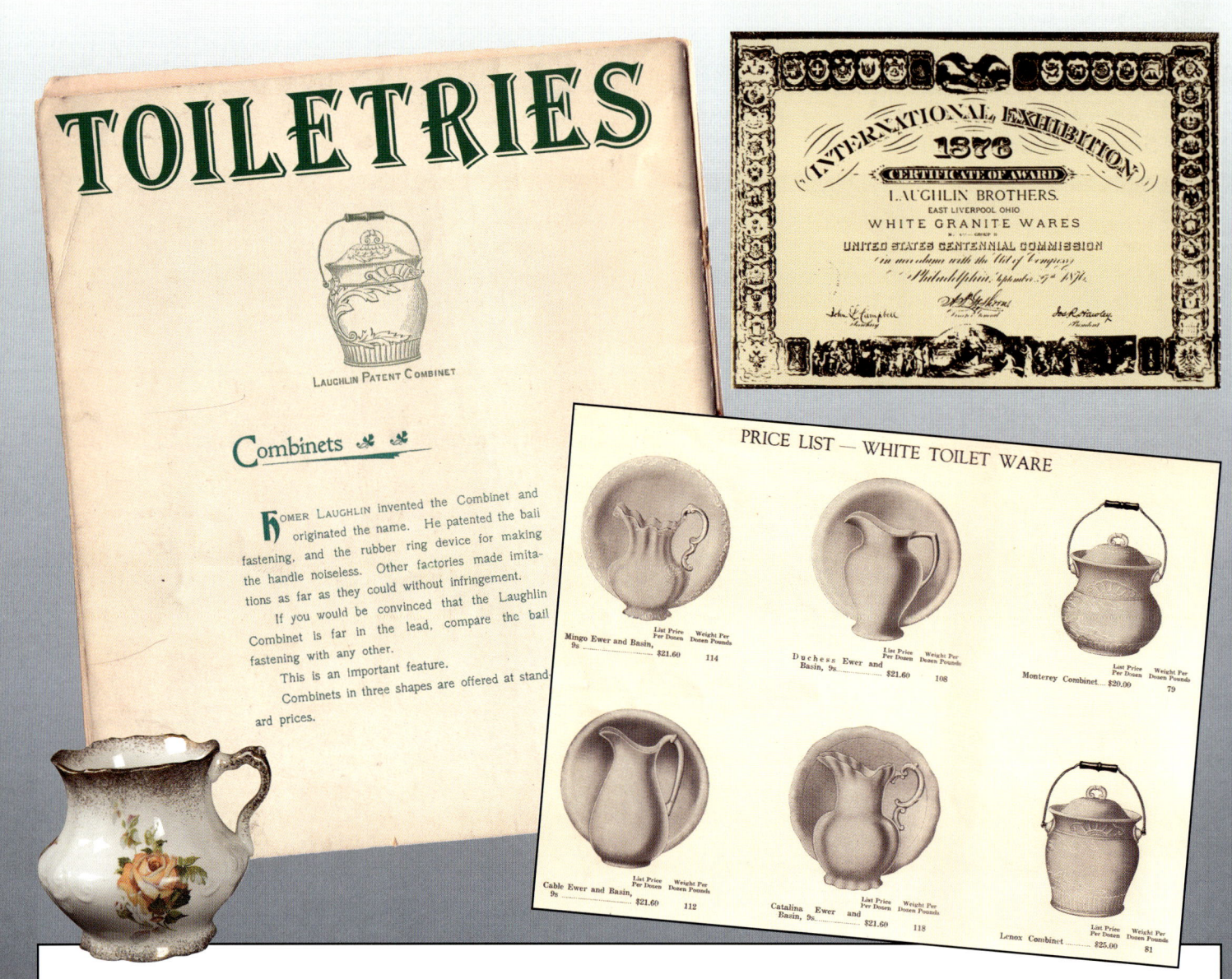

TOILETRIES   late 1800's – 1925 or later

Many names for lines and shapes have been tossed about in telling the Homer Laughlin story. Some of those were lines that included only "toiletries." In the Victorian world of the late 1800's and into the early 1900's, indoor plumbing, running water, and bathrooms were still uncommon in many places. What served in those places was a set of china to serve personal hygiene needs. Few of us today can imagine such sets as a necessary part of daily life. They were!

A traditional toiletry set usually consisted of six to twelve pieces. Among these were a pitcher and washbowl, which Homer Laughlin dramatically called Ewers and Basins in many company catalogs. The covered chamber pot and much less elegantly named "slop jar," were the equivalent of the toilet. Human waste was deposited directly into these often-fancy Victorian marvels and disposed of in the morning. Homer Laughlin devised a combination slop jar and chamber pot called, not surprisingly, "the Combinet." These were staples produced at the factory for many years. Other toiletry set pieces include: a brush vase to hold toothbrushes, mugs, a covered soap container, and a "mouth ewer" for drinking water. Today these objects may seem fanciful or even disgusting, but they were necessities for daily life a century ago. As late as 1925, numerous choices in toilet sets appeared in the Sears catalog.

Several toiletry lines were produced by Homer Laughlin. These lines included sets that were named and decorated. These should not be confused with lines of tableware! Toiletry lines include the shapes Lenox, Duchess, Mingo, Catalina, Cable, Monterey, Wyoming, Arno, and Superba. These known Homer Laughlin toilet sets are included in this section — there may be others.

Top left: *Lenox Combinet shown in a factory booklet.* **Top right:** *1876 International Exhibition of Philadelphia award given to the Laughlin Brothers for best White Granite Wares.* **Bottom left:** *Mingo Shape, Handled Mug.* **Bottom Right:** *Factory literature showing Ewer and Basin Sets in Mingo, Duchess, Monterey, Cable, Catalina, and Lenox shapes.*

Toiletries

Homer Laughlin Catalog of Toiletry Shapes. **Top left:** *Wyoming Toiletry Set.* **Top right:** *Superba Toiletry Set.* **Middle left:** *Mingo Toiletry Set.* **Middle right:** *Catalina Toiletry Set.* **Bottom left:** *Bridal Toiletry Set.* **Bottom right:** *Duchess Toiletry Set.*

Homer Laughlin

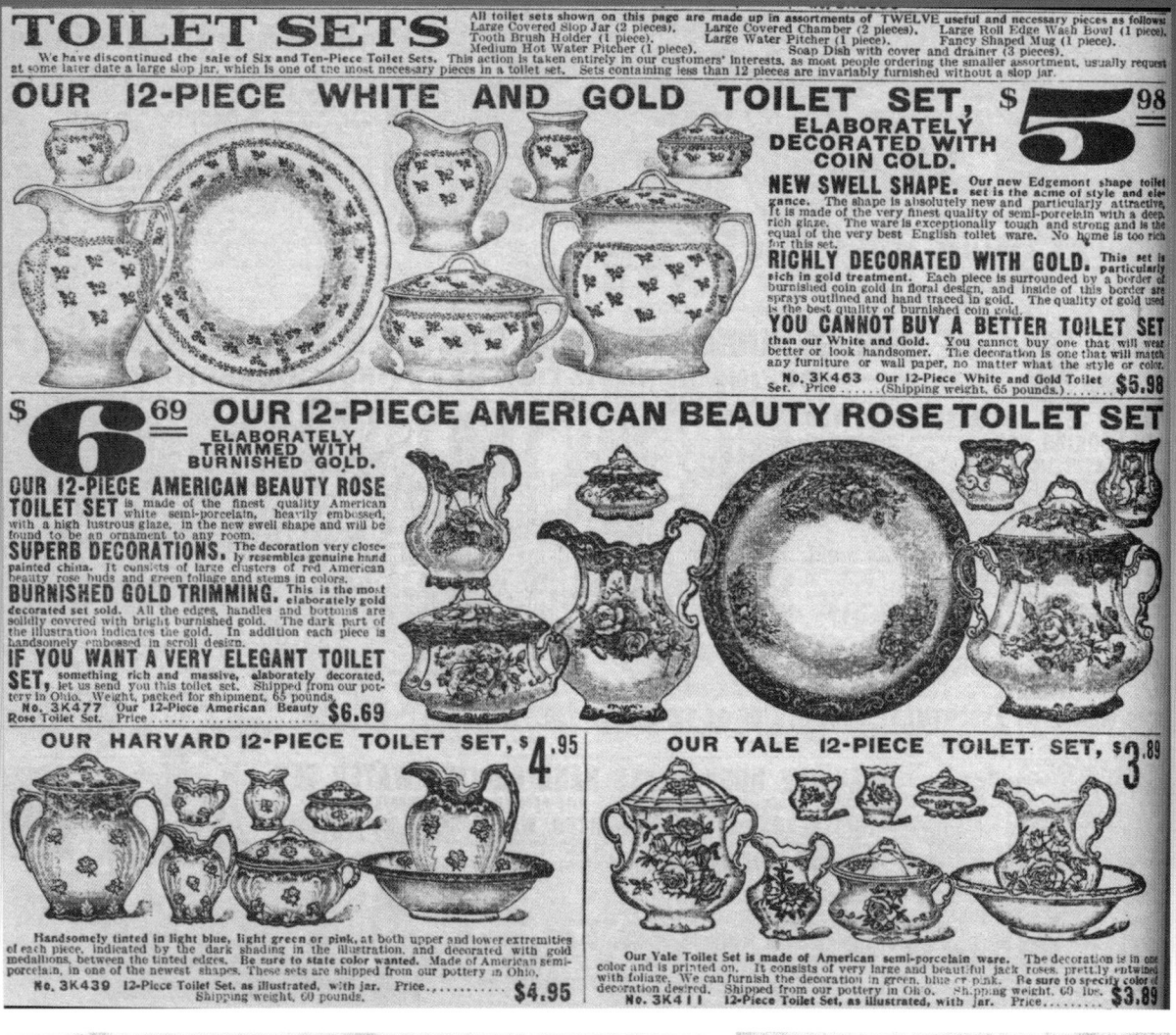

Above: *Toiletry Sets, Sears, Roebuck & Co. Catalog, 1908. Top ad: White and Gold pattern; Duchess shape. Middle ad: American Beauty Rose pattern; Mingo shape. Bottom left ad: Harvard pattern; unknown shape. Bottom right ad: Yale pattern; Mingo shape.* **Bottom left:** *Factory literature showing Arno Toiletry Set.* **Bottom right:** *Factory literature showing Superba Toiletry Set.*

CHILDREN'S WARE

CHILDREN'S WARE

Homer Laughlin has created china specifically for children since at least the 1930's. Most children's ware was initially a premium for cereal or food products. Early examples include decorations on the Empress shape. An early creation was the Little Orphan Annie mug for an Ovaltine drink promotion. Found at the factory are examples of a child's line created with decorations titled "Jungle Sam." To date, no examples of Jungle Sam have been reported on the market, indicating these may have never moved into actual production. Tom Thumb was a line of decorations on children's pieces, reportedly a premium for Ralston Purina's whole wheat cereal.

Dick Tracy appears on a child's set utilizing the Ovaltine mug, a Century plate, and a bowl made for Purina. A shape called "I Go Here" was created for the International Silver Company and produced by both Homer Laughlin and Salem China Co. The manufacturer's name will appear as part of the backstamp. Most recently a set of "My First Fiesta®" has been marketed as a toy set for children.

These photographs are from the Homer Laughlin Factory. **Top:** *Animal embossed bowls with Art glazes.* **Bottom left:** *Alphabet divided plates and embossed bowls for children.* **Bottom right:** *Jungle Sam on elephant embossed plates and bowls for children.*

Homer Laughlin

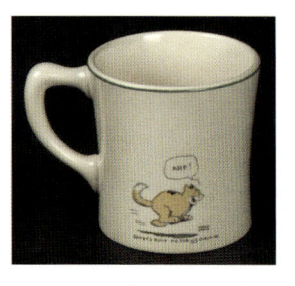

Top left: *Tongue Twister Tableware* pattern; backstamp. **Top second from left:** *Tongue Twister Tableware* pattern; photographed at the Homer Laughlin Factory. **Top third from left:** *Alice in Wonderland Tableware* pattern; Children's Mug photographed at the Factory. **Top right:** *Alice in Wonderland Tableware* pattern; backstamp. **Second row left:** "I Go Here" plate with a steamboat decal made for International Silver Co. **Second row middle:** "I Go Here" plate with a Betsy McCall decal made for International Silver Co. **Second row right:** "I Go Here" Betsy McCall plate backstamp. **Third row left:** Dick Tracy Child's Plate, Tom Thumb Bowl, and Betsy Ross Mug, photographed at the Factory. **Third row middle:** *Tom Thumb* pattern, Bowl photographed at the Factory. **Third row right:** *Tom Thumb* pattern; inside Bowl, photographed at the Factory. **Fourth row right:** *Tea Party* pattern; Children's Set. **Fifth row right:** *Little Orphan Annie* Ovaltine Mug with Annie on one side and Sandy on the other side.

Giftware

Some of the most intriguing and least known products Homer Laughlin made are not dinnerware lines and do not easily fit into recognized Homer Laughlin categories. To provide an introduction and superficial overview, we gathered images of some of the wonderful and endlessly diverse products made by this immense company over the decades. From art glazes to unrecognized forms, use these images to challenge yourself to see beyond the known lines and decorations. There is indeed a wealth of unexpected, generally unrecognized Homer Laughlin China out there awaiting you!

MIXING BOWL SET OF GREEN GLAZED PORCELAIN

The beauty of these new mixing bowls will make 'em a joy to use. They are of heavy, high-grade, glazed porcelain in a charming light green with their attractiveness further increased by the appletree design in bold relief. A heavy roll edge makes them easy to hold. The set consists of five bowls, 5, 6, 7, 8 and 9 in. diameter at top.

1g. 7 lbs. 2866 $2.50 Pur. or With Cpns.

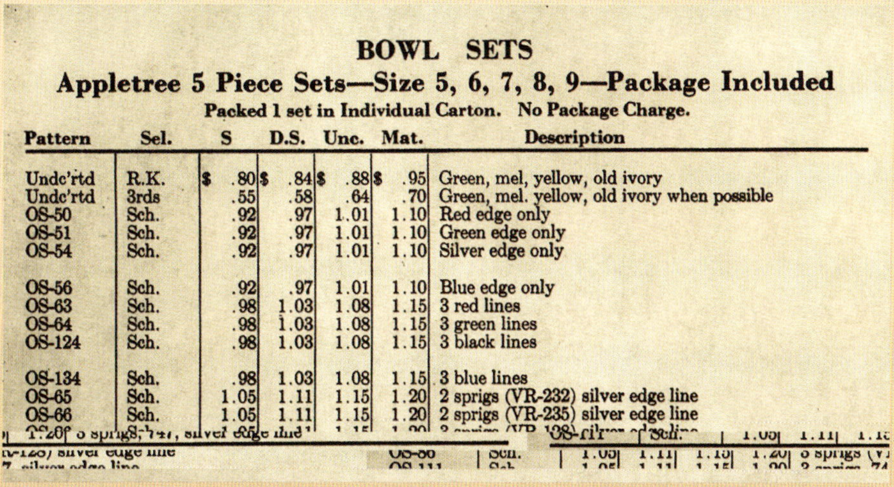

BOWL SETS
Appletree 5 Piece Sets—Size 5, 6, 7, 8, 9—Package Included
Packed 1 set in Individual Carton. No Package Charge.

Pattern	Sel.	S	D.S.	Unc.	Mat.	Description
Undc'rtd	R.K.	$ .80	$ .84	$ .88	$ .95	Green, mel, yellow, old ivory
Undc'rtd	3rds	.55	.58	.64	.70	Green, mel, yellow, old ivory when possible
OS-50	Sch.	.92	.97	1.01	1.10	Red edge only
OS-51	Sch.	.92	.97	1.01	1.10	Green edge only
OS-54	Sch.	.92	.97	1.01	1.10	Silver edge only
OS-56	Sch.	.92	.97	1.01	1.10	Blue edge only
OS-63	Sch.	.98	1.03	1.08	1.15	3 red lines
OS-64	Sch.	.98	1.03	1.08	1.15	3 green lines
OS-124	Sch.	.98	1.03	1.08	1.15	3 black lines
OS-134	Sch.	.98	1.03	1.08	1.15	3 blue lines
OS-65	Sch.	1.05	1.11	1.15	1.20	2 sprigs (VR-232) silver edge line
OS-66	Sch.	1.05	1.11	1.15	1.20	2 sprigs (VR-235) silver edge line

Appletree bowls were a popular premium in the 1930's era. Incorrectly dubbed Orange Tree by collectors, these bowls were sold in stacking sets of 5, 4, & 3 bowls. Colors produced were green, yellow, and ivory. Ivory can be found plain, or decorated with color bands and decals. **Top left:** *Appletree bowls in the most commonly found color which the factory called green.* **Top middle:** *Shown here are two bowls found at the Homer Laughlin Factory. The one on the right is the Homer Laughlin Appletree bowl, the bowl on the left is a clearly marked Japanese version. The unanswered question; Who copied whom? The designs are nearly identical.* **Top right:** *Appletree bowl backstamps.* **Middle left:** *Appletree bowls advertisement, Larkin Catalog #109.* **Middle right:** *Appletree bowls listed in the 1937 Pound Sterling Price Book.* **Bottom:** *Melon Yellow Appletree Bowls shown in all five sizes, photographed at the Homer Laughlin Factory.*

525

Homer Laughlin

Top left: Tom & Jerry sets were popular in the first half of the 20th century and made in several shapes and decorations by Homer Laughlin. **Middle left:** Currant pattern; Chocolate Set made around 1906. **Bottom left:** Typical Art China backstamp found on the Chocolate Set. **Right:** Jewel Tea Bowls from top to bottom: Virginia Rose Shape, Pennsylvania Shape, Orange Border Shape, and New York Shape. Several other shapes and styles were made.

Giftware

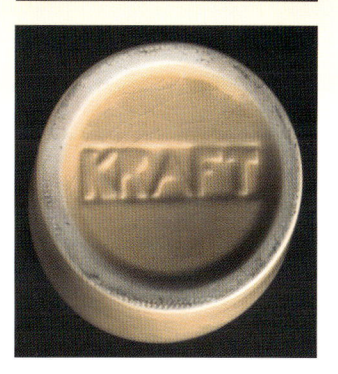

These photographs are from the Homer Laughlin Factory. **Top left:** *Open Rose decal on a creamer or milk pitcher that does not appear as part of a dinnerware pattern and was likely produced for use as a premium; based on the decoration, probably a Jewel Tea item.* **Top middle:** *Open Rose decal on a very large bowl, sold as a Jewel Tea premium.* **Top right:** *This vase was produced in the 1930's as a Jewel Tea premium.* **Middle left:** *Large stock pot sized containers. The left combination shows the pie pan lid removed revealing a divided double boiler type cooking tray. It is unknown if this piece was produced commercially, but examples in several colors exist at the Factory. Right foreground is an individual casserole, included for scale. The individual casserole and left pieces are in pumpkin, the assembled piece is undecorated cream.* **Middle right:** *Small, thick walled pot was produced for Kraft as a cheese container.* **Bottom left:** *Unverified cups & saucers. The Factory collection includes extensive Homer Laughlin pieces as well as pottery products from around the world, largely amassed by Frederick Rhead for design studies.* **Bottom right:** *Two wonderful cookie jars and matching plates.*

Homer Laughlin

Top left: *Juno pattern; Art China Berry Bowls from the early 1900's.* **Top right:** *A Kitchen Kraft pitcher handpainted and signed by a Wells family member.* **Second down on left:** *From the Homer Laughlin Factory comes these two wonderful Wells shaped and decorated pitchers. The cartoon-like caricatures that are the center of the daisies are clearly meant to be recognizable as individuals and the piece was likely for a special promotion, meeting or other presentation. Who these gentlemen are would be a great riddle to solve, providing insight into the origins of the piece and event it commemorated.* **Third row on left:** "When touring the Homer Laughlin Factory, a tour offered daily on weekdays, one is presented with a souvenir plate. A neat collectible and memento of any visit to the "World's Largest Pottery." **The following are commemorative plates, some made by other companies, using Homer Laughlin blanks.: Third row second from left:** *North Carolina, Souvenir Plate.* **Third row third from left:** *Radium Springs, Albany, Georgia.* **Third right:** *1957 Skytone Calendar Plate.* **Bottom left:** *1954 Fiesta Calendar Plate.* **Bottom second from left:** *Jamestown, Virginia, Souvenir Plate.* **Bottom third from left:** *Bellmont Methodist Church, Burlington, North Carolina.* **Bottom right:** *California Centennial Souvenir Plate.*

World's Fairs & Expositions

WORLD'S FAIRS & EXPOSITIONS

Fairs and other Expositions have long been showcases for industrial excellence. Homer Laughlin participated in the 1876 International Exhibition in Philadelphia, the 1893 Colombian Exposition in Chicago, the 1939 New York World's Fair, and the 1939 Golden Gate International Exposition in San Francisco.

The 1876 Exhibition was in celebration of the United States Centennial. A certificate from this event notes the success of the Laughlin brother's award-winning White Granite Ware. The Homer Laughlin Company would have only been a few years old at the time. In Chicago in 1893, Homer Laughlin won three awards for their wares.

The 1939 New York World's Fair was a conscious effort to shift away from the economic depression of the 1930's and toward the future and Modernism. The Homer Laughlin China Co. joined Edwin M. Knowles China Co., Hall China Co., Cronin China Co., Paden City Pottery, and the National Brotherhood of Operative Potters to build and staff an operating kiln, mural, and exhibit in New York. Demonstrations were given at the working potters wheels at the Fair. Many souvenirs were made, including the multicolored, decal decorated, service plates which feature the ball-like Parisphere and pointed Trylon, symbols of the Fair. These exist with both 1939 and 1940 dates. George and Martha Washington pitchers and individual creamers were available. Other souvenir plates include two single color glazed examples of the potter at work, "the artist decorating the vase" and "the potter at his wheel." Ashtrays embossed with the four seasons, Zodiac cup & saucer sets, and hand-thrown vases were also made. The Homer Laughlin collection included a yellow vase, inscribed with the signature, "Arthur Wells." Another piece in the collection from this venture, seen on the following page, is a small orb with an inscribed base representing the Parisphere, one of the modernistic symbols of the Fair.

A plate for the Golden Gate International Exposition, also held in 1939 (perhaps to attract visitors to the west coast in competition with the popular east coast World's Fair) is strikingly similar in appearance. Also shown is an ashtray with a similar treatment. The extent of Homer Laughlin's participation in San Francisco is not known.

Top right: *The American Potter World's Fair plate "Thrower at Wheel;" from the Joint Exhibit of Capital and Labor, 1939.* **Middle right:** *The American Potter World's Fair plate "Artist at Wheel;" from the Joint Exhibit of Capital and Labor, 1939.* **Bottom right:** *The American Potter World's Fair plate "Thrower at Wheel;" backstamp.*

Homer Laughlin

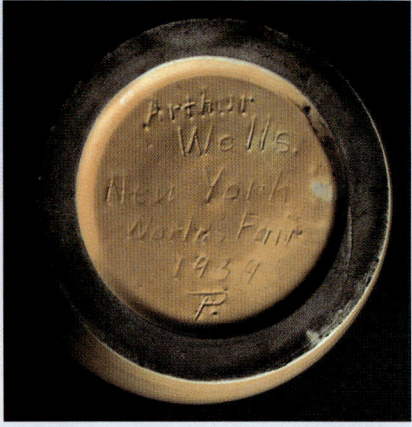

Top left and middle: *Novelties from the 1939 New York World's Fair. Small Blue Orb, representing the Parisphere. Yellow Vase, signed by Arthur Wells. These pieces were photographed at the Homer Laughlin Factory.* **Top right:** *Vases from the 1939 New York World's Fair.* **Middle left:** *George Washington Pitchers, photographed at the Factory.* **Middle:** *George and Martha Washington Pitchers, from the 1939 New York World's Fair.* **Middle right:** *George Washington Pitcher backstamp.* **Bottom left, top plate:** *1939 New York World's Fair.* **Bottom left, middle plate:** *1940 New York World's Fair.* **Bottom left, bottom plate:** *1939 Golden Gate International Exposition, San Francisco Bay.* **Bottom middle:** *1939 Golden Gate International Exposition, San Francisco Bay; Ashtray.* **Bottom right:** *1939 New York World's Fair, original drawing from the Factory.*

American Potters Repeat Dramatic Exhibit at N. Y. World's Fair

Five Potters and National Brotherhood Continue Sponsorship

In the Home Furnishings Building at the New York World's Fair for 1940 will be housed, substantially in the same form as last season, the working exhibit of the American pottery industry.

As will be recalled by most World's Fair visitors, the potters exhibit consists of a complete working miniature kiln which produces authentic pieces of American dinnerware continuously during the Fair season.

It is approached by the visitor across a semi-circular glass enclosed case in which are shown products which contribute to the manufacture of the dinnerware being shaped and fired in the kiln.

The sponsoring group of potters will be the same this year as last, namely, Homer Laughlin China Co., Edwin M. Knowles China Co., Hall China Co., Cronin China Co., and Paden City Pottery Co.

The committee in charge of the exhibit is again acting under the chairmanship of Arthur A. Wells of the Homer Laughlin China Co., and includes F. B. Lawrence of Edwin M. Knowles, M. C. Sondles of Paden City Pottery, W. J. Hocking of the Hall China Co., Kress Cronin of the Cronin China Co., and W. H. Locke-Anderson of Edwin M. Knowles China Co.

One of the most interesting and effective displays in the entire World's Fair exhibit area, this pottery display is particularly significant because it represents an alliance between the employer and employee in the pottery industry, and represents the result of common contributions from both factors.

The National Brotherhood of Operative Potters, in the A. F. of L. union unit, under the presidency of James M. Duffy, contributed thousands of dollars last year and again this year from their "strike" fund, and the balance of the funds is contributed equally between the five potteries involved.

The mural which acts as a background for the working exhibit depicts this alliance dramatically and was painted by Charles Murphy. It stresses the 40 years of successful collective bargaining in this industry, which is, as available records show, unique in the American employer-employee relation.

It is also significant that in 1840 the American pottery industry had its beginnings in East Liverpool, Ohio, and that this exhibit for two successful seasons celebrates that hundred-year history.

The visitor to this pottery exhibit gets perhaps the most comprehensive view of the American dinnerware industry at work than could ever be made possible under a single roof. The complete workings from the raw clay through the jiggering, or hand-turning, firing, decorating, glazing, are all easily visible. Also, all the mineral products and various contributers to the clay formulae are lined up in correct order in front of the main working exhibit. CROCKERY AND GLASS JOURNAL is included as a contributory agent to the functioning of the industry, in these smaller exhibit cases.

Arthur A. Wells, Chairman of the committee in charge of the potters exhibit at the Fair.

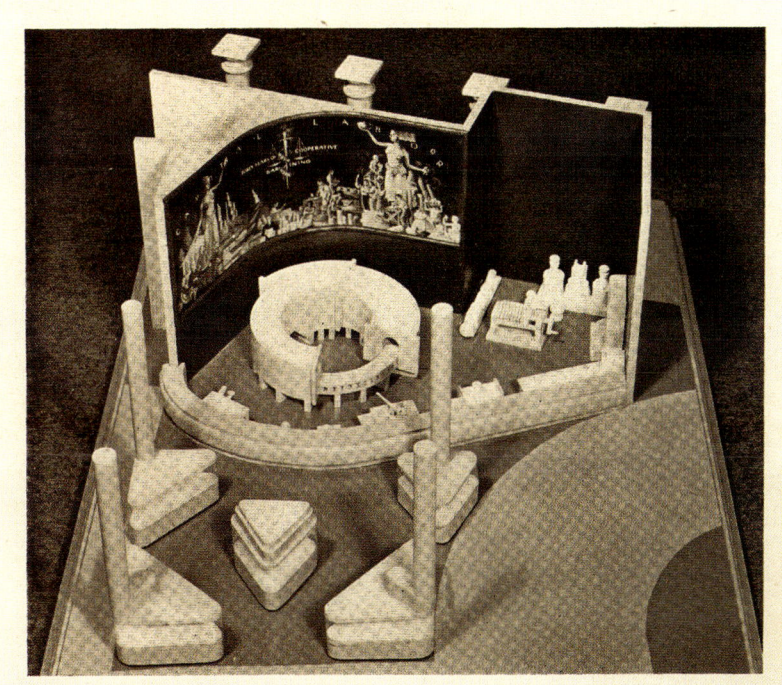

Miniature model of the actual potters exhibit in the Home Furnishings Building at the N. Y. World's Fair.

Homer Laughlin

Capital and Labor United

This is the theme of the mural to be used as the background for the American Potter's exhibit at the N. Y. World's Fair. Here we see the artists at work in the number six plant of the Homer Laughlin China Company. Left to right: William H. Blair, the assisting artist; Charles Murphy, the artist and designer of the mural and William Gill, attendant.

CHARLES MURPHY
The Artist Behind The Pottery Mural Brush

All images from Pottery, Glass & Brass Salesman *magazine article on The Potters Exhibit at the 1939 New York World's Fair.* **Top left:** *Charles Murphy painting the mural.* **Top right:** *Charles Murphy.* **Bottom:** *Mural.*

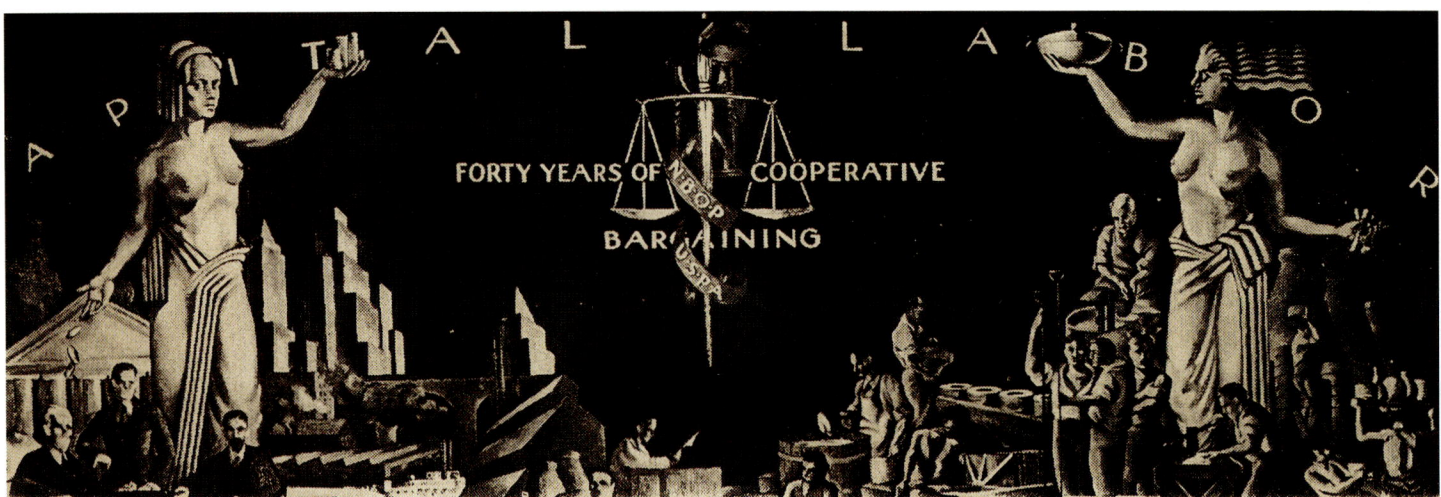

532

Mexican Decals

MEXICAN DECALS

"A touch of Old Mexico! The quaintness and gaiety that give ware from south of the Rio Grande its charm is caught in this pattern. The decoration, with a Mexican pottery motif, permits full display of the warm colors, and is effectively framed by a red line. Even the shape is distinctive! Made of finest semi-porcelain, with an ivory body, it has a 'Velvet' glaze that is soft and lovely to the touch and the eye. It's smart in every detail, and such a change." — *Larkin China Catalog*

HOMER LAUGHLIN
Mexicana
..the Pattern that Started a Vogue

WHEN this Homer Laughlin pattern was first exhibited last July at the House Furnishing Show, it was an instant smash hit. Its popularity has grown steadily ever since . . . and retailers have found it a constant and dependable source of profit. It started the vogue for the Mexican motif in crockery decoration which has since swept the country.

And small wonder! For this Mexicana pattern is smart, colorful and attractive. It embodies the old-world atmosphere of Mexico with the modern verve and personality which is so appealing to American housewives. Applied to the pleasing, beautifully designed Homer Laughlin shapes, it presents a best-seller of the first order.

C228

CENTURY MEXICANA . . . C. 228. A tableware that offers the beauty of shape and pattern which constitutes a fast-seller and a sure profit-maker. Century Mexicana will dress up a table so that every meal becomes an occasion.

KITCHEN KRAFT MEXICANA . . . K.K. 324. Here is a delightful kitchen ware that catches the eye and opens the customer's pocketbook. For baking and table use, for refrigerator and kitchen cabinet storage.

KK324

Two of these Homer Laughlin lines are shown on this page . . . the Kitchen Kraft Mexicana and the Century Mexicana. We urge you to take advantage of the wide popularity this pattern has built up . . . and get your share of Mexicana profits.

THE HOMER LAUGHLIN CHINA COMPANY - NEWELL, W. VA.

Pacific Coast Representative: M. Seller Co., San Francisco, Calif., and Portland, Ore. Chicago Office: 15-104 Merchandise Mart. Joseph Feuchtwanger. East: George B. Fowler. East and Middle West: George H. Bowman. South and Southwest: M. A. Johnson. Northwest: Davis and Braisted Co., Minneapolis, Minn. West: George L. Davis Co., Denver, Colo.

Top right: *Unknown magazine advertisement, May 1938.* **Top left:** *Mexicana pattern; Teapot with lid.* **Middle right:** *Mexicana pattern; Covered Vegetable Bowl.* **Bottom:** *Daisy Chain pie plate, Kitchen Kraft Mixing Bowl, and Casserole Bowl with lid, all with Mexicana decals.*

533

Mexican Decals

Here are a few of the popular 1930's – 1940's era Mexican decal patterns. These are popular with collectors and fun to mix and match.

Mexicana
Century Shape
Red Band

Mexicana
Eggshell Nautilus Shape
Blue Band

Mexicana
Eggshell Swing Shape
Red Band

Mexicana
Virginia Rose Shape
No Trim

Maxicana
Yellowstone Shape
Red Trim

Maxicana
Republic Shape
Gold Band

Conchita
Century Shape
Red Band

Conchita
Eggshell Swing Shape
Red Band

Hacienda
Eggshell Swing Shape
Red Band

Hacienda
Century Shape
Red Band

Hacienda
Eggshell Nautilus Shape
Red Band

R4703
Nautilus Shape
Red Band

Pueblo
Eggshell Swing Shape
Red Band

R2526
Nautilus Shape
Red Band

HLC1118
Eggshell Swing Shape
Fruit Bowl Shown
Red Band

HLC1880
Kraft Shape
No Trim

HOW TO READ HLC BACKSTAMPS

There are four distinct periods of Homer Laughlin dated backstamps. This information is based on data from the company, as organized and filtered by several authors. The contributions of Gerald DeBolt are beneficial in understanding how to read Homer Laughlin dated backstamps.

Before 1910 there is no effort to include date or manufacturing information in the backstamp.

1910-1919
the *first digit* designates the month

the *second digit* is the year within that decade

the *final digit* designates the factory

Thus:
5 4 N
5th month (May) – 1914 – HLC factory N

7 2 N
7th month (July) – 1912 – HLC factory N
1 7 N
1st month (January) – 1917 – HLC factory N

1920-1921

In this slightly revised version, *two digits* indicate the year within this 1920s decade. Thus:
12 20 N
12th month (December) – 1920 – HLC factory N
5 20 N
5th month (May) – 1920 – HLC factory N

1922-1929
For these seven years, a letter has been designated to replace the numeric expression for the month. A to M (the letter "I" was not used) are the corresponding months of the year, with a single digit following to designate the year within this 1920s decade. The factory designation is last.

Thus:
E 6 N is 5th month (May), 1926, HLC factory N
H 7 L is 8th month (August), 1927, HLC factory L
C 2 N7 is 3rd month (March), 1922, HLC factory N-7

Beginning in **1930**, Homer Laughlin's backstamp dating system expanded beyond a system that differed by the decade. Many post-1930 backstamps do not have dating information. When post-1930 pieces are dated they have a simple, straight forward two digit year designation. Thus:
M (letter "I" not used) 57 N-6
12th month (Dec.) – 1957 – HLC factory N-6
D 45 N5
4th month (April) – 1945 – HLC factory N-5
F 35 N5
6th month (June) – 1935 – HLC factory N-5

Homer Laughlin

Books
Ayars, Walter. *Larkin China*. Sulphur Springs, TX: Echo Publishing, 1990.
Cunningham, Jo. *The Collector's Encyclopedia of American Dinnerware*. Paducah KY: Schroeder Publishing, Collector Books, 1982.
Cunningham, Jo. *Homer Laughlin China; 1940s & 1950s*. Atglen, PA: Schiffer Publishing, 2000.
Cunningham, Jo. *Homer Laughlin China: A Giant Among Dishes, 1873–1939*. Atglen, PA: Schiffer Publishing, 1998.
Cunningham, Jo., and Darlene Nossaman. *Homer Laughlin China: Guide to Shapes and Patterns*. Atglen, PA: Schiffer Publishing, 2002.
DeBolt, Gerald. *DeBolt's Dictionary of American Pottery Marks: Whiteware and Porcelain*. Paducah KY: Schroeder Publishing, Collector Books, 1994.
Duke, Harvey. *The Official Price Guide to Pottery and Porcelain*. 8th ed. New York, NY: House of Collectibles, 1995.
Gonzalez, Mark. *An Overview of Homer Laughlin Dinnerware*. Gas City, IN: L-W Book Sales, 2002.
Gonzalez, Mark. *Collecting Fiesta, Lu-Ray & Other Colorware*. Gas City, IN: L-W Book Sales, 2000.
Homer Laughlin Collectors Association. *Fiesta, Harlequin, & Kitchen Kraft Dinnerwares*. Atglen, PA: Schiffer Publishing, 2000.
Huxford, Bob & Sharon Huxford. *Collector's Encyclopedia of Fiesta: Plus Harlequin, Riviera, and Kitchen Kraft*. 8th ed. Paducah, KY: Schroeder Publishing, Collector Books,1998.
Jasper, Joanne. *The Collector's Encyclopedia of Homer Laughlin China: Reference and Value Guide*. Paducah, KY: Schroeder Publishing, Collector Books, 1993.
Jasper, Joanne. *Turn of the Century American Dinnerware: 1880s to 1920s*. Paducah, KY: Schroeder Publishing, Collector Books, 1996.
Lehner, Lois. *Lehner's Encyclopedia of U.S. Marks on Pottery, Porcelain, & Clay*. Paducah KY: Schroeder Publishing, Collector Books, 1988.
Racheter, Richard G. *Collector's Guide to Homer Laughlin's Virginia Rose: Identification & Values*. Paducah KY: Schroeder Publishing, Collector Books, 1997.
Snyder, Jeffrey B. *Fiesta: The Homer Laughlin China Company's Colorful Dinnerware*. 3rd ed. Atglen, PA: Schiffer Publishing, 2000.

Magazines
Century Magazine
China, Glass and Decorative Accessories, 1947-1954.
China, Glass & Tablewares, 1956-1975.
The Clay Worker
Crockery and Glass Journal, 1936-1961.
Crockery (or China), Glass & Lamps, 1927-1953.
The Dish: The Publication of the Homer Laughlin China Collectors Association
Glass and Pottery World, 1908.
Good Housekeeping Magazine, 1913, 1914.
Guide For the Bride, 1955.
Holland's The Magazine of the South, 1930.
Ladies Home Journal
The Laughlin Eagle
McClure's Magazine
The Potter
Pottery, Glass & Brass Salesman, 1925-1939.

Catalogs
American Beauty, 1899.
Betty Crocker
Bloomingdale's
Blue Book of Quality Merchandise. Bennett Brothers, Inc., 1958-1968.
Butler Brothers, 1925, 1935.
Catalog and Price List Plain White Ware, 1929.
The China Book, 1912.
Condensed Price List Plain White Wares all Shapes and Weights, 1910.
Decorated Dinnerware Pound Sterling Price List, 1937.
Decorated Wares, Descriptions and Prices, 1916.
Good Housekeeping
Homer Laughlin
Hotel Sterling Book Price Scales Applying to Double Thick Hotel Wares, 1920.
House of 1776
JCPenney
John Plain, 1957.
Larkin, 1925-1940.
Montgomery Ward, 1930-1963.
Red Book Directory of 1966
Sears, Roebuck & Co., 1908-1964.
Sterling Book Price Scales Decorated Ware,
    Special Set Compositions, Standard White Ware List, 1949.
Table of Weights and Measures Fine White Earthenware, 1911.

Websites
Betty Crocker, www.bettycrocker.com
Circa '36 Fiestaware, www.pcis.net/geocat/
Ebay, www.ebay.com
Fiesta Fanatic, www.fiestafanatic.com
Fiesta Fast, www.fiestafast.com
Fiestaware Mega China, www.megachina.com
Go Fiesta!, www.tc.umn.edu/~mutc0003/INDEX.htm
Homer Laughlin China Co., www.hlchina.com
JCPenney, www1.jcpenney.com
Macys, www.macys.com
The Missing Piece, www.missing-piece.com
Ohio River Pottery, www.ohioriverpottery.com
Robbins Nest, www.robbinsnest.com
Virtual Tour of Homer Laughlin, http://members.aol.com/hlfiesta/tour/

Worker at the Homer Laughlin Factory.

About the Authors

BOB PAGE was born April 19, 1945 and grew up working the fields of his family's small tobacco farm in Ruffin, North Carolina. He attended the University of North Carolina at Chapel Hill and graduated with a degree in business and a major in accounting. After two years in the U.S. Army, he obtained his CPA certificate and worked in public accounting for eight years. In 1978, he took a position as an auditor for the State of North Carolina.

In March of 1981, Bob left his accounting career forever to form Replacements, Ltd. He and his company have received extensive publicity and public recognition. Awards include: The North Carolina Excellence Award presented by Governor James Martin; North Carolina Small Businessman of the Year; a ranking of #81 in Inc. magazine's annual list of America's fastest-growing privately-held companies (1986); North Carolina Person of the Week from UNC Center for Public Television; and 1991 Retail Entrepreneur of the Year for the State of North Carolina. In 1998, Bob received the National Partnership for Progress Award from the U.S. Postmaster General. Bob is involved in numerous charitable endeavors in North Carolina as well as the nation and is also a tireless advocate for the rights of gay and lesbian individuals. Bob was named one of America's Top 25 "Out" Executives in 1999. He also won the Human Rights Campaign's Torch Award in 1996.

Bob, Owen, Dale, and Ryan
Photography: Donna Pickerel, School Pictures, Inc.

DALE FREDERIKSEN was born June 15, 1962 in Pontiac, Michigan and attended Waterford Township High School. In 1980, Dale moved to Chattanooga, Tennessee to attend Tennessee Temple University, graduating in 1984 with a BS degree in secondary education. He taught junior and senior high mathematics for three years in Kansas City, Kansas, returning to Chattanooga in 1987 to teach mathematics and to coach volleyball at Ooltewah Middle School.

In 1989, he joined the staff of Replacements, Ltd. as an inventory purchasing agent and is currently involved in the creation and production of various china, crystal and silver identification guides. Dale enjoys researching and discovering patterns that have previously been undocumented, along with spending time with his partner Bob and their twin boys — Owen and Ryan.

DEAN SIX was born February 23, 1956, in West Virginia. He studied history and literature at West Virginia University, later taking a Doctorate of Juris Prudence degree. He practiced law and later worked for the American Friends Service Committee (Quakers) before joining Replacements, Ltd. in 1998.

Dean has written and lectured widely on American Glass organizations. He was one of the founders of the West Virginia Museum of American Glass and is active in a number of national glass organziations. Dean divides his work time between Replacements, Ltd. in North Carolina and several small businesses he owns in West Virginia.

THE HISTORY OF REPLACEMENTS, LTD.

The World's Largest Retailer of Old and New China, Crystal, Silver and Collectibles

The Replacements, Ltd. Museum

One of Replacements' collectibles showcases

Inside the 225,000 sq. ft. warehouse

Our careful inspection of china

An overhead view of Replacements, Ltd.

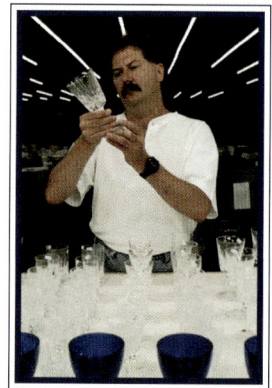

Our careful inspection of crystal

In 1981, Bob Page, an accountant-turned-flea-marketer, founded Replacements, Ltd. Since then, the company's growth and success can only be described as phenomenal.

Today, Replacements, Ltd. locates hard-to-find pieces in over 180,000 patterns — some of which have not been produced for more than 100 years. Now serving more than 5 million customers, with an inventory of 9.5 million pieces, they mail and e-mail up to 800,000 inventory listings weekly to customers seeking additional pieces in their patterns.

The concept for Replacements, Ltd. originated in the late 1970's when Page, then an auditor for the state of North Carolina, started spending his weekends combing flea markets buying china and crystal. Before long, he was filling requests from customers to find pieces they could not locate. "I was buying and selling pieces primarily as a diversion," Page explains. "Back when I was an auditor,

no one was ever happy to see me. And, quite frankly, I wasn't thrilled about being there either."

Page began placing small ads in shelter publications and started building a file of potential customers. Soon, his inventory outgrew his attic, where he had been storing the pieces, and it was time to make a change. "I reached the point where I was spending more time with dishes than auditing," Page says. "I'd be up until one or two o'clock in the morning. Finally, I took the big step — I quit my auditing job and hired one part-time assistant. Today I'm having so much fun, I often have to remind myself what day of the week it is!"

Replacements, Ltd. continued to grow quickly. In fact, in 1986, Inc. magazine ranked Replacements, Ltd. 81st on its list of fastest-growing independently-owned companies in the U.S. "Our growth has been incredible," says Page, who was named 1991 North Carolina

A view of Replacements' 12,000 square foot Showroom.

Entrepreneur of the Year. "I had no idea of the potential when I started out."

Providing high-quality merchandise and the highest possible levels of customer service are the cornerstones of the business, resulting in a shopping experience unparalleled in today's marketplace. Page also attributes much of the success of Replacements, Ltd. to a network of about 1,000 dedicated suppliers from all around the U.S. The company currently employs more than 550 people in an expanded 225,000 square foot facility (the size of four football fields).

Another major contributor to the company's fast growth and top-level customer service is the extensive computer system used to keep track of the inventory. This state-of-the-art system also stores customer files, including requests for specific pieces in their patterns. It is maintained by a full-time staff of 20 people and is constantly upgraded to ensure customers receive the information they desire quickly and accurately.

For those who are unsure of the name and/or manufacturer of their patterns, Replacements, Ltd. also offers a free pattern identification service. In addition, numerous books and publications focusing on pattern identification have been published by Replacements, Ltd. for both suppliers and individuals.

Replacements, Ltd. receives countless phone calls and letters from its many satisfied customers. Some need to replace broken or lost items while others want to supplement the sets they have had for years. A constant in the varied subjects customers write about is their long and fruitless search — a search that ended when they learned what Replacements, Ltd. could offer. "Since many patterns are family heirlooms that have been handed down from generation to generation, most customers are sentimental about replacing broken or missing pieces," Page says. "It's a great feeling to help our customers replace pieces in their patterns and to be able to see their satisfaction. Like our logo says — We Replace the Irreplaceable."

Another growing area that Replacements, Ltd. has developed for its customers is the collectibles market. The company now offers a wide range of collectibles from companies such as Bing and Grondahl, Royal Copenhagen, Boehm, Hummel, Lladro and many more. "It was a natural progression of our business," says Page, "and something our customers had been requesting."

The Replacements, Ltd. Showroom and Museum in Greensboro, NC is a 12,000 square-foot retail facility located in front of the massive warehouse. It is decorated with late 19th century hand-carved showcases, 20-foot ceilings and classic chandeliers. Inside, one can view an incredibly varied selection of merchandise — from figurines, mugs and ornaments to the china, crystal and silver that made the company famous.

The fascinating Replacements, Ltd. Museum, adjacent to the retail Showroom, is the home for over 2,000 rare and unusual pieces that Page has collected over the years. It includes a special section dedicated to one of Page's first loves — early 20th century glass from companies such as Tiffin, Fostoria, Heisey, Imperial and Cambridge.

Some of the 50,000 shelves which hold over 9.5 million pieces of inventory.

For More Information

- Call 1-800-REPLACE (1-800-737-5223) from 8 am to midnight, Eastern Time, 7 days a week).
- Write to: 1089 Knox Road
  PO Box 26029
  Greensboro, NC 27420
- Fax: 336-697-3100
- Internet: www.replacements.com
- Visit the Replacements, Ltd. Showroom and Museum, at exit 132 off I-85/40 in Greensboro, NC. The Showroom and Museum are open 7 days a week, from 9 am to 8 pm.

From the Industry Experts...
Tableware Reference Guides

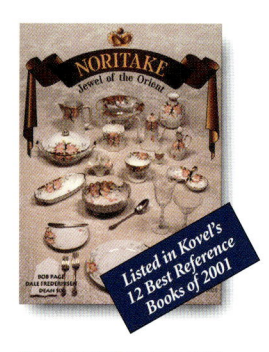

Noritake
Jewel of the Orient
Over 3,000 pattern images in full color, beautifully organized for identification. Includes price guide, company history, and special sections featuring Azalea, Tree in the Meadow, and 175.
Hardcover, 315 pages. ISBN: 1-889977-11-X

Listed in Kovel's 12 Best Reference Books of 2001

Suggested Retail $29.95 **Our Price $27.95**

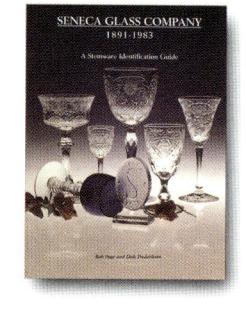

Seneca Glass Company: 1891-1983
Includes information on over 1,200 different stems and patterns, along with a history of the Seneca Glass Company by West Virginia glass authority Dean Six.
Hardbound, 132 pages.

Suggested Retail $24.95 **Our Price $22.95**

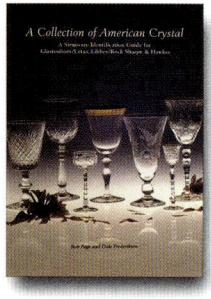

A Collection of American Crystal
Includes descriptions of crystal by Glastonbury/Lotus, Libbey/Rock Sharpe and the TG Hawkes glass companies. Over 1,000 patterns and 200 stems.
Hardbound, 140 pages.

Suggested Retail $24.95 **Our Price $22.95**

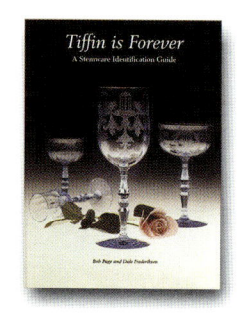

Tiffin is Forever
This helpful guide includes comprehensive, detailed illustrations of over 2,700 stems and patterns of Tiffin Glass. A must for the glass enthusiast or collector.
Hardbound, 175 pages.

Suggested Retail $29.95 **Our Price $27.95**

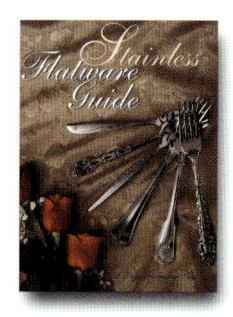

Stainless Flatware Guide
More than 5,000 stainless patterns from over 100 manufacturers. Over 700 pages of highly detailed, digitally-captured images organized by shape and style.
Softbound, 798 pages. ISBN: 1-57432-067-X

Suggested Retail $39.95 **Our Price $27.95**

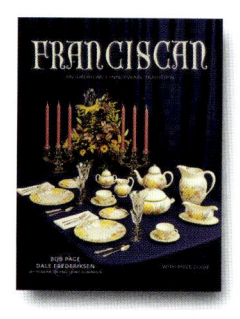

Franciscan – An American Dinnerware Tradition
The foremost comprehensive book on Franciscan dinnerware. Full color, beautifully designed for identification. Includes company history and price guide!
Hardcover, 272 pages. ISBN: 1-889977-70-1

Suggested Retail $29.95 **Our Price $27.95**

China Identification Kits and Guides

Suggested Retail $59.95 **Our Price: $49.95**

China Identification Kits
Each kit features full color and black & white digital images of dinner plates from various companies. Quickly identify patterns with no markings or other patterns which are difficult of identify due to multiple shapes, etc. Looseleaf, page count will vary by kit.

KIT #1
Denby, Easterling, Flintridge, Gorham, Johann Haviland, Longchamp, Royal Jackson, Royal Tettau, and Syracuse.

KIT #2
Adams, Arabia, Crown Ducal, Franconia, Gold Castle, Midwinter, Pfaltzgraff, and Winfield.

KIT #3
Corning, Dansk, Independence, Iroquois, Lefton, and Nikko.

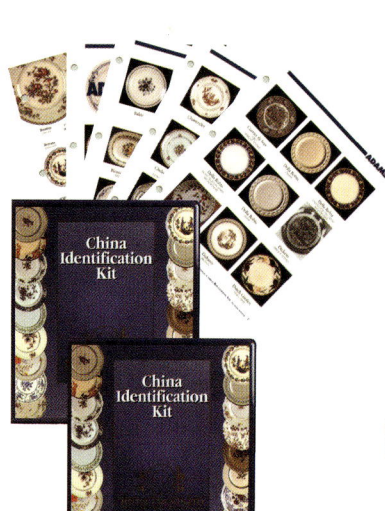

TO ORDER: CALL 1-800-REPLACE (1-800-737-5223)
OUTSIDE USA: (1-336-697-3000)

Suggested Retail $59.95 **Our Price: $39.95**

China Identification Guides
Each guide features full color and black & white digital images of dinner plates from various companies. Each manufacturer is organized by shape and style. Quickly identify patterns with no markings or other patterns which are difficult due to multiple shapes, etc. We've also included brief histories of each manufacturer.

Guide #1
Heinrich, Hutschenreuther, and Rosenthal.
Softbound, 119 pages. ISBN: 1-57432-131-5

Guide #2
Edwin M. Knowles, Salem, and Taylor, Smith & Taylor.
Softbound, 144 pages. ISBN: 1-889977-06-3

Guide #3
Canonsburg, Cronin, Crooksville, Cunningham & Pickett, French Saxon, Leigh Potters, Mt. Clemens Pottery, Paden City Pottery, Pope Gosser, Sebring Pottery, Stetson, Universal China, and W. S. George.
Softbound 213 pages. ISBN: 1-889977-08-X

Guide #4
Altrohlau, Epiag, Jean Pouyat, Paul Müller, Schumann, and Wm. Guerin.
Softbound 163 pages. ISBN: 1-889977-09-8

Guide #5
Bawo & Dotter, Charles Ahrenfeldt, Tirschenreuth, and Tressemann & Vogt. Softbound 187 pages.
ISBN: 1-889977-10-1

Guide #6
Arcadian, Harker, Limoges (American), Princess, Royal, Shenango, Steubenville, and Warwick. Softbound 197 pages.
ISBN: 1-889977-12-8

Numbered Patterns

30	13, 105, 107
135	127
149	55
254	449, 450
280	402
397	127
478	415
487	46
533	125
585	131
586	131
704RG	131
718DP	130
718DPBR	130
863	57
1091	358
1107	33
1107A	46
1108	58
1121RG	159
1140	45
1180	358
1180C	146
1200	79
1203	76
1392	516
1400	79
1544	116
1695	274
1699	59
1830	417
1959	498
1970	515
2039	124
2309	351
2317	517
2337-A	291
2337A	291
2345	517
2399-2	351
2545	332
2617	516
2642	516
2647	516
2689	330
2690	330
2692	271
2721	331
2763	351
2809	514
3017	58
3480	516
3674A	416
4113	131
4304	59
4336	518
4523	128
4591J	274
4592A	280
4592D	274
4592E	279
4595	279
4685	415
4740A	126
4740B	126
4740D	126
4740E	126
4740H	126
4764	40
4806	58
4807	40
4812B	150
4862	86
5801	86
6001	86
6201	57
6402	277
6507A	386
6830	57
6865	57
6978	358
7090	100
7103-2	98
7103-3	98, 518
8266	385
8487A	126
9205	369
9739A	415
9760	322
9761	322
9950	46
9952	46
9983	46
10023	518
10034	518
71002	118

A

A105	459
A335	107
A740	176
A2868	358
A3220A	276
Aaron, Charles I.	8, 9
Aaron, Louis I.	8, 9
Aaron, Marcus	8, 9
Aaron, Marcus II	9
Aaron, Marcus L.	9
Acacia CP24	322
Admiral N1708	315
AJS26	106
Alameda S131C	363
Alice In Wonderland Tableware	524
All Seasons CW120	479
Allegro RY194	444
Alliance (Shape)	16, 475-476
Alliance China Company	468, 475, 483
Amberstone	211, 219, 220, 221, 234
American Beauty (Shape)	25, 34-37
American Beauty Rose (Shape)	522
American China	469, 470, 472
American Provincial	438-439, 447
American Provincial RY104	447
American Subjects–Blue	273, 303
American Subjects–Red	303
Americana–Currier & Ives	238, 244, 245-249
Amsterdam	252, 258
Amy	500
Anchor (Shape)	30
Andover Gold	374
Angelus, The	45
Angelus, The (Shape)	27, 41-47
Angelus, The Plain White	43
Antique H114	509, 510
Antique–Burnt Orange	162
Antique Orleans	161
Apache	485, 486
Apollo	504
Apple Blossom	418
Apple Blossom N1670	313, 321
Appletree	525
Applique (Line)	18, 455-459
Aprey 2721	331
April G3535	343
April Flowers CH108	510
Arbutus Floral	39
Arbutus Green	40
Arcadia G3522	345
Arcadia V100	491, 492
Aristocrat N1684	311, 321
Armand (Ovenserve Shape)	192
Armand (Virginia Rose Shape) Gold Trim, No Trim, Platinum Trim, VR235	170, 176
Arno (Shape)	520, 522
AS1	259, 452, 334, 459
AS9	384
Aster	459, 474
Atlas China	349, 383
Athena B1439	380
Aurelia G13	204
Autocrat	363
Autumn	325
Autumn Gold	334, 389, 452, 480
Autumn RY159	447
Autumn Ivory	102, 103
Autumn Song (Gold Trim)	468
Autumn Song (Platinum Trim)	468
Avalon	476
Avalon CV59	383
Avon	90, 361
AX5	46
AX26	45
AX27	45
AX30	45
AX32	45
AX37	46
AX55	45
AX56	45
AX57	45
AX59	45
AX60	45
AX63	46
AX85	45
AX86	45
AX107	43, 47
Ayars, Walter	134, 214, 294
Aztec	502

B

B4S	58
B1141	291
B1307	326
B1307NV	279
B1307P	275
B1308	274
B1309	277
B1310	279
B1312	277
B1312L	275
B1314	276
B1315	274, 401
B1316	276, 326
B1318	276
B1319	277
B1320	278

(B-C) *Homer Laughlin Index*

B1323 ... 262, 278
B1326 ... 278
B1335 ... 278
B1339 ... 276
B1340 ... 276
B1344 ... 383
B1345 ... 262, 278
B1346 ... 279
B1347 ... 275
B1348 ... 278
B1350 ... 277
B1354 ... 279
B1355 ... 277
B1409 ... 274
B1415 ... 386
B1415NT ... 386
B1427 ... 381
B1439 ... 380
B1447 ... 274
B1472 ... 271
B2001 ... 266
B2428 ... 275
B3563A ... 342
Bali Flower RY171 ... 445
Banded Cortez ... 503
Barcellona ... 503
Barclay CV39 ... 377, 378, 386
Baroness ... 388, 451
Bayberry CW105 ... 478, 479
BB7 ... 80
Beale, Joseph Boggs ... 410
Belles Fleurs ... 324, 362
Belmont ... 353
Belmont G177, G3400 ... 342
Bennett Brothers ... 438, 470, 481
Bennett Brothers Catalog ... 481, 487, 490
Berkshire CV15 ... 377, 384
Big Apple S126 ... 360
Birds ... 504
Black Eyed Susan RU-505 ... 481
Block China ... 509
Blue Bells ... 195
Blue Bonnet VR420 ... 180
Blue Dawn N1691 ... 320
Blue Duchess C-305 ... 485, 486
Blue Fantasy ... 238, 244
Blue Flax S128C ... 363
Blue Heaven ... 412
Blue Horizon ... 466
Blue Lace ... 383
Blue Mist ... 436
Blue Star ... 467
Blue Willow ... 238, 239-243, 244
Bluemont HLS205 ... 430, 436
Bombay G3461 ... 348
Bone White ... 490, 491, 492
Bordeaux ... 440, 446
Bordeaux 2689 ... 330
Bouquet ... 257
Bouquet W137 ... 170, 175
Breton ... 394-395
Briar Rose ... 133, 135, 146
Briarcliffe G3385 ... 341
Bridal (Shape) ... 521
Bright Gold Band ... 62
Bristol (Shape) ... 15, 438, 499-500
Bristol ... 348
Bristol VM8 ... 311, 326
Brittany (Shape) ... 18, 240, 241, 246
    260-280, 388, 401, 454
Brittany Rose
    Gold Trim B1427, Platinum Trim ... 381
Broomhall, Vincent ... 501
BT1 ... 57
Burgundy ... 334, 388
Butler Brothers ... 62, 82, 92, 93, 133, 134
    169, 172, 185, 197, 198, 205
Butler Brothers BB7 ... 80
Buttercup (Charm House, Applique) ... 458
Buttercup (Duratone Shape) ... 481
Butterscotch ... 504

C

C-305 ... 486
C3 ... 146
C6 ... 147
C7 ... 145
C8 ... 136, 148
C14 ... 145
C15 ... 145
C17 ... 146
C21 ... 148
C23 ... 148
C24 ... 135, 148
C28 ... 147
C29 ... 147
C33 ... 136, 147
C41 ... 147
C43 ... 145
C45 ... 148
C48 ... 143
C56 ... 142
C57 ... 142
C58 ... 142
C59 ... 142
C61 ... 147
C64 ... 144
C65 ... 144
C71 ... 143
C72 ... 143
C73 ... 144
C77 ... 147
C79 ... 147
C82 ... 146
C84 ... 146
C87 ... 143
C94 ... 143
C95 ... 148
C96 ... 145
C97 ... 148
C99 ... 144
C101 ... 143
C106 ... 145
C107 ... 146
C108 ... 147
C110 ... 146
C114 ... 145
C116 ... 146
C121 ... 147
C124 ... 147
C129 ... 147
C132 ... 148
C183 ... 143
C202 ... 147
C203 ... 148
C204 ... 147
C205 ... 146
C206 ... 147
C207 ... 146
C320 ... 515
C325 ... 486
C420 ... 516
C442 ... 516
C8213 ... 267
Cable (Shape) ... 30, 31, 169, 520
CAC6 ... 143
CAC24 ... 151
CAC55 ... 144
CAC84 ... 106
CAC186 ... 175
Calender Plates ... 211
Calico ... 454
Calirose ... 346, 416
Calypso ... 458
Cameo ... 384
Cannes ... 508
Capri RY172 ... 440, 444
Cardinal ... 257
Cardinal N1653 ... 315
Cardinal N211 ... 257
Carnival (Shape) ... 17, 390-392
Carnival–Cobalt Blue ... 392
Carnival–Fiesta Red ... 392
Carnival–Fiesta Yellow ... 392
Carnival–Forest Green ... 392
Carnival–Gray ... 392
Carnival–Harlequin Yellow ... 392
Carnival–Ivory ... 392
Carnival–Light Green ... 392
Carnival–Turquoise ... 392
Carousel ... 444
Carson Wishmaker ... 374
Cascade (Modern Farmer Shape) ... 394-395
Cascade (Rhythm Shape) ... 438, 444
Cashmere G3391 ... 336, 337, 338, 342
Castilian ... 234, 496
Casualtone ... 211, 220
Catalina (Shape) ... 520, 521
CC5 ... 87
CC8 ... 87
Celadon Green ... 434
Century (Shape) ... 6, 7, 24, 121
    132-148, 523, 534
Century ... 82
Century Service Corp. ... 270, 334, 384
    387, 388, 389, 444, 451, 452
Century's Three Daisies ... 183
Century's Three Daisies VR261 ... 183
Century's Three Daisies VR421 ... 174
CH5 ... 195
CH31 ... 194, 195
CH100 ... 458
CH108 ... 510
CH150 ... 510
CH151 ... 510
CH152 ... 510
Challenger (Shape) ... 21, 508, 509-510
Chanticleer ... 455, 458
Charm House (Shape) ... 14, 259, 334, 438, 452,
    453-459, 474
Chartreuse ... 204
Chateau G3468 ... 345
Chatham SR114 ... 339, 345
Chelsea (Shape) ... 27, 194-195
Cherry Valley ... 459
Cheyenne R4937 ... 255
China, Glass and Decorative Accessories ... 8
    185, 293

Homer Laughlin Index (C–D)

China, Glass & Lamps 102, 103, 167, 293, 296, 309, 336, 366, 401, 438, 454, 470
China, Glass & Tablewares 261, 262, 438, 467, 470, 481, 487
China & Glass Journal 206
China Book, The 49, 51, 72, 73
China Lady, The S108 360
Chinese Buddha S152P 356, 360
Chinese Porcelains 360
Chinese Princess 360
Chinese Three 360
Chinese Willow S1465 360
Chintz 257
Clair de Lune 154, 156
Clay Worker, The 11, 12, 500
Clive B1316 .... 261, 276
CO-564 207
CO57 208
CO58 208
CO63 208
CO109 208
CO110 208
CO118 209
CO532 209
CO553 209
CO574 208
CO604 208
Colonial 255
Colonial (Shape) 27, 38-40
Colonial Kitchen 29
Colonial Kitchen (Eggshell Nautilus Shape) Red Band, Red Trim 328
Colonial Kitchen 178, S179 (Eggshell Swing Shape) 355, 356, 359
Colonial Kitchen (Liberty Shape) Gold Trim, No Trim 417
Colonial Kitchen (Republic Shape) 90
Colonial Kitchen (Rhythm Shape) No Trim, Red Trim 443
Colonial Kitchen (Virginia Rose Shape) .. 170, 181
Colonial White 478, 479
Colonial–Blue B1335 278
Colonial–Pink B1339 276
Color Harmony Dinnerware 485
Colorama–Terra Cotta 514
Color-Tone 467
Columbia Exposition 529
Columbine 144
Columbines VR232 175
Concerto CV21 382
Conchita 144, 534
Conchita S129 .... 360, 534
Confetti 458
Constellation–Black, The 273
Constellation–Blue, The 273
Contemporary 503
Coronation Rose 257
Coronet (Shape) 27, 205-209
Coronet N1709 .... 311, 320
Cotillion G3517 .... 338, 343
Countess 338, 353
Countess G3432 342
Country Life CW108 480
Country Manor 506, 507
Country Road HS234 505
Coventry 211, 220, 494, 496
CP5 325
CP14 .... 255, 321
CP24 322

CP95 181
CP133 .... 361, 446
CP171 446
CP203 .... 388, 451
CPS1 385
CPS2 388
Craftsman (Shape) 20, 201-204
Cream "Foam" Beige 434
Crescendo 516
Cretonne 364
Crinoline CV5 .... 377, 381
Crocker, Betty 228
Crockery and Glass Journal 13, 121, 133, 202, 311, 376, 377, 426, 428, 430, 438, 440, 457, 461, 464, 466, 470, 471, 473, 531
Crockery, Glass & Lamps 114, 261, 311, 355, 357, 397
Cronin China Co. 529
Cross Stitch 508
CSC15 384
Cunningham & Pickett 90, 181, 200, 255, 256, 257, 321, 322, 325, 334, 352, 361, 363, 380, 388, 389, 416, 417, 444, 446, 451, 452, 475, 476, 483, 484, 513, 514, 515
Cunningham, Jo 376, 394, 468
Currant 526
Currier & Ives (Americana) 238, 245-249
Currier & Ives (Liberty Shape) 412, 417
Currier & Ives–Green (Nautilus Shape) 258
Currier & Ives FP160 (Rhythm Shape) 444
CV1 385
CV3 382
CV4 381
CV5 381
CV14 384
CV15 384
CV17 381
CV20 384
CV20GR 382
CV21 382
CV22 384
CV28 385
CV32 386
CV39 386
CV45 381
CV49 383
CV52 383
CV54 384
CV55 .... 280, 383
CV59 383
CV62.2 386
CV67 382
CV69 382
CV72 380
CV73 380
CV74 381
CV75 385
CV78 386
CV81 386
CV85 385
CV87 380
CV99 380
CV116 382
CV122 385
CV125 .... 379, 380
CV126 380
CV135 380
CV138 381
CW105 479

CW108 480
CW114 480
CW119 480
CW120 479
CW128 480
CW131 480
Cynthia 204, 474

D

D1 .... 429, 435
D2 435
D10 434
D11 435
D14 435
D16 434
D17 435
D18 435
D101 479
D533 125
D5626 272
Daisy Chain 185, 191
Daisy Field 311
Danube (Shape) 30
Danube CP203 .... 388, 451
Darcy K8124 .... 92, 98
Dawn 499
Daybreak (Charm House Shape) 458
Daybreak (Hearthside Shape) 502
DB13 298
Debolt, Gerald 535
Debutante 424, 428-429
Del Rio SR100 496
Delightful 502
Della Robbia 311, 330
Desert Flower 503
Desert Lily RY117 .... 454, 455, 457, 458
Dianne 383
Dimension HS204 505
Diplomat 261
Dixie Rose 475, 476
DK1 298
DK3 298
Dogwood (Charm House Shape) 454
Dogwood (Jubilee Shape) 434
Dogwood L613 (Liberty Shape) 413, 415
Dogwood (Rhythm Shape) 447
Doll's House S113 361
Double Gold Band 173
Dover (Shape) 24, 477-480
Dover Rose 480
DP1625 200
DP2285 371
DP296A 345
DP296B 345
Dresden 171, 183
Dresden CP14 .... 255, 321
Dresden N1679 .... 311, 325
DS626 266
Dubarry (Eggshell Swing Shape) Green Trim, No Trim (CP133) 361
Dubarry (Rhythm Shape) Green Trim, No Trim (CP133) 446
Dubarry N1590 323
Dubarry P133 361
Duchess (Shape) 520, 521, 522
Duke, Harvey 82, 133, 161, 164, 167, 307, 410
Dundee Plaid 455
Dura-Print 454
Duratone (Shape) 15, 438, 481

(E–G) Homer Laughlin Index

E

E155	58
E187	64
E272	64
E339	516
E343	486
E419	516
E421	516
E481	108
E783	86
E1315M	97
E2002	64
E2202	64
E2301	66
E2513	66
E2706	64
E2806	66
E3006	65
E3406	64
E3806	65
E3903	64
E4102	64
E4613	66
E4713	66
E4904	62, 67
E5203	64
E7104	66
E7113	66
E7413	66
E7504B	66
E7505	65
E7603	66
E8115	65
E8703	62, 66
Early America	251, 254
Early American Homes	246
Early Shapes	30-33
Echo	270
Eggshell	309
Eggshell Andover (Shape)	17, 309, 373-374
Eggshell Cavalier (Shape)	19, 280, 375-389, 438, 451
Eggshell Georgian (Shape)	20, 202, 335-353, 309, 334
Eggshell Georgian	350
Eggshell Nautilus (Shape)	20, 251, 259, 307, 309, 310-334, 388, 389, 452, 459, 534
Eggshell Nautilus	20
Eggshell Swing (Shape)	17, 309, 354-364, 374, 393, 394, 534
Eggshell Swing (Shape, Variations)	364
Eggshell Swing	169
Eggshell Theme (Shape)	23, 309, 365-372
Elaine	204
Embassy	514
Emerald	384
Empire Green CSC15	378, 384
Empire Grey	381
Empire–Blue P511	400, 402
Empire–Pink	402
Empress (Shape)	7, 19, 61-67, 72, 239, 240, 242, 246, 523
Empress	389, 452
Engdus, The	46
English Garden	136, 148
English Regency G3357	346
English Scenes–Brown	269
Epicure (Shape)	16, 460-464, 468
Epicure–Charcoal Gray	464
Epicure–Dawn Pink	464
Epicure–Snow White	464
Epicure–Turquoise Blue	464
Everglade	452, 488
Exmoor G177	66

F

F107	234
F108	234
Fair Lady CV81	386
Fairfield	468
Fairhaven V107	492
Famous Old Ships–Blue (Shell Border)	333
Famous Old Ships–Mulberry (Shell Border)	333
Famous Old Ships–Red (Floral Border)	333
Famous Old Ships–Red (Shell Border)	333
Fantasy (Willow Shape)	244
Fantasy	496
Fantasy 254	449
Fashion (Shape)	15, 438, 468
Fashion	488
Fashion Flower	494, 496
FC125	258
Ferndale N1577	312, 321
Fiesta (Shape)	6, 7, 12, 13, 21, 210-237, 282, 397, 403, 528
Fiesta, Children's	211, 228
Fiesta, Ironstone	211, 212, 221
Fiesta, New	211, 222-227
Fiesta, New with Decals	211, 228
Fiesta, Old	211, 215-217, 221
Fiesta, Old with Decals	211
Fiesta, Original	211, 215-217, 219
Fiesta, Vintage	211, 215-217
Fiesta, with Stripes	211
Fiesta–Antique Gold Ironstone	232
Fiesta–Apricot Newer	232
Fiesta–Black Newer	234
Fiesta–Chartreuse Newer	233
Fiesta–Chartreuse Older	233
Fiesta–Christmas	234
Fiesta–Cinnabar (Maroon) Newer	233
Fiesta–Cobalt Blue Newer	233
Fiesta–Cobalt Blue Older	233
Fiesta–Forest Green Older	233
Fiesta–Gray Older	232
Fiesta–Ivory (Cream) Older	232
Fiesta–Juniper Newer	233
Fiesta–Light Green Older	233
Fiesta–Lilac Newer	233
Fiesta–Loony Tunes (Turquoise)	234
Fiesta–Loony Tunes (Yellow)	234
Fiesta–Loony Tunes Christmas	234
Fiesta–Mango Red (Orange) Ironstone	233
Fiesta–Medium Green Older	233
Fiesta–Pearl Gray Newer	232
Fiesta–Periwinkle Blue Newer	232
Fiesta–Persimmon Newer	232
Fiesta–Plum Newer	233
Fiesta–Red (Orange) Older	296, 233
Fiesta–Red Stripe (Yellow)	234
Fiesta–Rose Newer	232
Fiesta–Rose Older	232
Fiesta–Sapphire Blue Newer	233
Fiesta–Scooby Doo (Sea Mist Green)	234
Fiesta–Sea Mist Green Newer	232
Fiesta–Shamrock Green Newer	233
Fiesta–Sunflower Newer	232
Fiesta–Turf Green Ironstone	233
Fiesta–Turquoise Newer	232
Fiesta–Turquoise Older	232
Fiesta–White Newer	232
Fiesta–Yellow Newer	232
Fiesta–Yellow Older	232
Fiesta Ensemble	141, 211, 229
Fiesta Casuals (Line)	211, 218
Fiesta Go-Alongs	211, 229
Fiesta Harmony (Line)	211
Fiesta Kitchen Kraft (Line)	211, 293, 295
Fiesta Kitchen Kraft–Cobalt Blue	295-297
Fiesta Kitchen Kraft–Ivory	297
Fiesta Kitchen Kraft–Light Green	295, 297
Fiesta Kitchen Kraft–Red	295-297
Fiesta Kitchen Kraft–Yellow	295-297
Fiesta Mates (Line)	211
Fifth Avenue	444
Flame Flower	428, 435
Fleur	503
Flight Of The Swallows	121, 128
Floral Basket	67
Floral Garden	500
Floral Jubilee HS270	504
Floral Medallions	205
Florence	261, 262
Floribunda CW128	480
Flowers And Filigrees VR231	182
Flowers Of The Dell	121
Fluffy Rose 1 VR128	168, 169, 172, 179, 190
Fluffy Rose 2 VR178	172, 179
Fluffy Rose 5	172, 179
Flying Bluebird	66, 67
Forget-Me-Not	351
Forget-Me-Not VM108	343
Formal (Craftsman)	202-204
Formal (Eggshell Georgian)	336
Fostoria	133
FP67	444
FP122	451
FP160	444
FP221	449
FP222	447
Fresh 'N Green HS241	502
Frolic	438, 440, 444
Fruit Skin Glazes	403
FW2	127
FW12	129
FW13	125
FW14	124
FW115	276

G

G-302	73
G-1305	73
G-1601	73
G-1705	73
G-3313	336
G-3315	336
G-3316	336
G-3324	336
G-3327	336
G13	204
G22	204
G93	343
G118	100
G138	342
G142	341

G150	204	
G177	66, 342	
G190	100	
G220	76	
G270	79	
G271	77	
G275	79	
G278	79	
G286	75	
G291	76	
G295	76	
G300	75	
G312	75	
G559	519	
G646	518	
G1100	58	
G1106	78	
G1201	76	
G1206	78	
G1300	79	
G1301	75	
G1401	77	
G1402	75	
G1506	78	
G1600	75	
G1700	79	
G1701	75	
G2003	74, 77	
G2103	77	
G2106	79	
G2203	76	
G2301	79	
G2303	77	
G2406	77	
G2503	77	
G2601	77	
G2606	75	
G2701	77	
G2801	76	
G2802	75	
G3302	351	
G3303	343	
G3303G	76	
G3304	352	
G3315	344	
G3317	344	
G3318	352	
G3320	347	
G3324	340	
G3327	351	
G3330	340	
G3331	352	
G3332	340	
G3335	352	
G3343	340	
G3351	343	
G3353	341	
G3356	346	
G3357	346	
G3365	351	
G3366	351	
G3369	345	
G3370	339, 351	
G3371	352	
G3378	346	
G3380	342	
G3381	343	
G3383	344	
G3384	347	

G3385	341
G3386	341
G3388	347
G3391	342
G3400	342
G3401	345
G3407	341
G3412	344
G3418	344
G3419	344
G3420	344
G3421	344
G3432	342
G3434	341
G3436	348
G3439	345
G3443	343
G3444	343
G3453	347
G3459	347
G3461	348
G3466	351
G3467	345
G3468	345
G3486	340
G3497	342
G3499	343
G3516	343
G3517	343
G3518	352
G3522	345
G3523	342
G3525	346
G3528	348
G3535	343, 347
G3549	347
G3571	340
G3803	75
G3805	78
G3852	342
G3905	78
G4003	76
G4103	76
G4105	78
G4205	78
G4605	78
G4805	78
Garden	495, 496
Garden Ring VR104	175
Garden Song HS216	502
Gardenia	200
Gardenia VM101	311, 325
Garland	93
Garland C45, C132	148
Garland CP5	325
Gascon	393-395
GCM99	449
GCM101	300-302
Geisha (Shape)	39
Geisse, Jope	211
Genesee (Shape)	19, 69, 71-80
GH1500	57
Gingersnap CH151	510
Gingham CW119	480
Ginja	500
Glass and Pottery World	42, 49, 51
Glenwood	386
GO16	305
Gobelin	202, 204

Gold Bowknot	93
Gold Band (Empress Shape)	62, 64
Gold Band (Kwaker Shape)	93
Gold Border	122
Gold Capri	504
Gold Cortez	496
Gold Crown	334, 389, 452
Gold Glade	501, 503
Gold Rose VR115	173
Gold Stripe	121, 122
Goldcrest	483, 484
Goldenrod CH150	510
Golden Gate (Shape)	30, 31, 33, 39
Golden Gate International Exposition	529, 530
Golden Harvest	380
Golden Harvest SR118	494, 495, 496
Golden Rose (Liberty Shape)	418
Golden Rose (Republic Shape)	86
Golden Rose (Yellowstone Shape)	105, 107
Golden Rose 2 (Virginia Rose Shape)	181
Golden Wheat	438, 444
Golden Wheat RY225	445
Good Housekeeping Magazine	62, 71
Country Sage	512
Granada (Shape)	22, 493-496
Granada–Green	496
Granada–White	496
Gray Dawn	381
Gray Dawn CV4	381
Gray Laurel	428, 434
Greek Key N1694	314
Green Glade	503
Greenbriar	417
Greenbriar G3499	343

H

H27	55
H107	58
H110	56
H111	52, 53, 56
H114	510
H129	56
H135	53, 59
H149	55
H150	55
H151	55
H152	55
H153	55
H154	55
H157	55
H158	55
H159	55
H160	55
H216	56
H225	56
H230	56
H232	55
H314	56
H315	57
H420	58
H1804	60
H1851	127
H2100	57
H2400	57
H2500	57
H3000	58
H4101	56
H5259	380
H7213	58

(H-K) Homer Laughlin Index

Hacienda (Century Shape) ... 144, 534
Hacienda (Eggshell Swing Shape) ... 360, 534
Hacienda N363 (Nautilus Shape) ... 254, 534
Hall China Co. ... 529
Hankscraft ... 229
Harlequin (Shape) ... 21, 281-291, 511
Harlequin–Chartreuse ... 290
Harlequin–Coral Newer ... 290
Harlequin–Forest Green ... 290
Harlequin–Gray ... 290
Harlequin–Light Green ... 290
Harlequin–Maroon ... 290
Harlequin–Mauve Blue ... 290
Harlequin–Medium Green ... 290
Harlequin–Medium Green Newer ... 290
Harlequin–Red ... 290
Harlequin–Rose ... 290
Harlequin–Spruce Green ... 290
Harlequin–Turquoise ... 290
Harlequin–Turquoise Newer ... 290
Harlequin–Yellow ... 290
Harlequin–Yellow Newer ... 290
Harvard (Shape) ... 522
Harvest (Pastoral Shape) ... 421-423
Harvest ... 504
Harvest Gold ... 446
Haviland ... 82
Hawaii D17 ... 428, 435
Hawaii RY163 ... 446
Hawaiian Daisy F108 ... 218, 234
Hawthorn ... 114, 118, 119
Head Of Class VR101 ... 178
Hearthside (Shape) ... 20, 501-505
Heavenly ... 504
Heirloom ... 257
Hemlock B2001 ... 261, 266
HG2 ... 435
Highland Plaid ... 457
Highland Plaid (Brown/Yellow) ... 458
Highland Plaid (Green/Black) ... 455, 458
Highland Plaid (Green/Brown) ... 455, 458
Historical America ... 246, 409
Historical America (Kraft Shape)
Blue, Red ... 303
Historical America (Liberty Shape)
Blue, Red ... 410, 411, 419
HLS8 ... 279
HLS9 ... 277
HLS52 ... 87
HLS53 ... 87
HLS180 ... 436
HLS205 ... 436
HLS301 ... 389, 452
HLS302 ... 388, 451
HLS304 ... 451
Hollands, The Magazine of the South ... 110, 112
HOM4313 ... 518
Homer Laughlin China 1940s & 1950s ... 394
Homespun ... 479
Homestead C325 ... 486
Honey Bunch C442 ... 516
Household Institute ... 90, 294, 298, 325, 447
HR20 ... 97
HS204 ... 505
HS207 ... 505
HS216 ... 502
HS234 ... 505
HS240 ... 503
HS241 ... 502
HS263 ... 502
HS268 ... 504
HS270 ... 504
HS271 ... 505
HUC2 ... 131
Hudson (Shape) ... 7, 25, 42, 48-60

I

I42 ... 414
IGS2 ... 383
I Go Here ... 523, 524
Imperial ... 280, 388
Imperial Faience ... 42
International (Shape) ... 21, 506-508, 510
International S149P ... 361
International Silver Company ... 523, 524
Irish Spring HS268 ... 504

J

J2 ... 157
J3 ... 158
J4 ... 158
J5 ... 158
J6 ... 158
J7 ... 159
J9 ... 158
J11 ... 157
J14 ... 157
J27 ... 157
J30 ... 158
J36 ... 159
J37 ... 158
J41 ... 158
J43 ... 159
J44 ... 158
J62 ... 155, 158
J102 ... 157
J105 ... 158
J106 ... 158
J112 ... 157
J113 ... 157
J115 ... 157
J116 ... 157
J117 ... 157
J123 ... 157
J201 ... 158
J202 ... 157
J205 ... 157
J207 ... 159
J208 ... 157
J209 ... 158
J212 ... 158
J213 ... 155, 159
J214 ... 157
J224 ... 158
Jade (Shape) ... 23, 121, 133, 153-159, 156, 169
Jaderose ... 388, 334
James River Potteries ... 393-394
J. C. Penney ... 246
JCP86 ... 277
JCP131 ... 429, 435
JCP141 ... 384
Jean ... 82, 83, 84, 88
Jepcor International ... 480, 494, 509, 510
Jewel Tea ... 526, 527
JJ45 ... 104, 107
JJ50 ... 146
JJ59 ... 167, 168, 169, 176
JJ63 ... 96
JJ150 ... 256, 446
JJ152 ... 447
JJ167 ... 443
JJ647 ... 95
John Plain ... 438, 454
John Plain Catalog ... 439, 440, 454
Joy ... 504
Juanita ... 141
Jubilee (Shape) ... 16, 300, 355, 424-436
June Rose ... 206
Jungle Sam ... 523
Juno ... 528

K

K 5315 M ... 92
K 5615 M ... 92
K05 ... 33
K14 ... 99
K16 ... 70
K24 ... 59
K26 ... 76
K35 ... 79
K61 ... 94, 95
K93 ... 90
K655 ... 97
K657 ... 97
K671-7 ... 98
K913 ... 79
K1013 ... 80
K1027 ... 95
K1077M ... 96
K1377M ... 97
K1413 ... 78
K1477M ... 98
K1877M ... 97
K2253 ... 96
K2277M ... 97
K2413 ... 100
K2713 ... 99
K3177M ... 95
K3314 ... 79
K3377 ... 97
K3443 ... 99
K3477M ... 97
K3577M ... 96
K3623 ... 99
K3677M ... 98
K4124 ... 99
K4315M ... 96
K4424 ... 96
K4513 ... 99
K4613 ... 99
K5602 ... 95
K5677M ... 95
K5713 ... 99
K5913 ... 98
K6137 ... 98
K6177M ... 95
K6877 ... 96
K6906 ... 95
K7077M ... 97
K7254 ... 98
K7313 ... 99
K7517 ... 98
K7673 ... 58
K7673N ... 70
K7817 ... 97
K7877 ... 96
K8077M ... 97

Homer Laughlin Index (K–N)

K8124 98
K8177M 97
K8317 96
K8415 95
K8477 95
K8623 99
K8655 98
K8677 96
K8723 99
K8904B 99
K8917M 98
K9104B 98
K9177M 96
K9277M 96
K9477 96
K9504 98
K9577M 99
Kaleidoscope 503
KD5 111
Kenmore 195
King Charles (Shape) 30, 32, 33
Kingston G3459 .... 336, 337, 338, 347
Kitchen Kraft (Shape) 19, 169, 211
292-298, 528
KK303 297
KK334 297
KK343 .... 296, 297
KK350 298
Knowles, Edwin M. China Co. 529
Kraft 527
Kraft (Shape) 22, 299-303, 355, 403, 534
Kraft–Blue 299-302
Kraft–White 302
Kress, S. H. 72
Kwaker (Shape) 7, 18, 72, 91-100, 242

L

L611 417
L612 417
L613 415
L615 415
L621 418
L630 415
L633 417
La Rochelle 331
Ladies Home Journal, The 11, 62, 102
Lady Alice 261, 276
Lady Eleanor V117 492
Lady Esther 412
Lady Greenbriar AS1 .... 259, 334, 452, 459, 513
Lady Stratford 259, 334, 452, 459
Larkin 112, 114, 119, 134, 170, 184, 185
195, 206, 214, 294, 400, 525, 533
Lattice Rose W349 416
Laughlin, Homer 8
Laughlin, Shakespeare 8
Laughlin International 261
Lehner's Encyclopedia of U. S. Marks on Pottery, Porcelain & Clay 202
Lehner, Lois 202, 304, 410, 470
Le Noir 348
Lenox (Shape) 520
Les Islettes 2690 330
Lexington 384
LFF1 127
Liberty (Shape) 24, 114, 408-419
Lifetime China 280, 334, 381, 382, 384
386, 388, 389, 452
Lille 332
Lily Of The Valley CV3 382
Lily Of The Valley N1733 328
Lily Of The Valley S327 .... 357, 362
Linda TR7 .... 470, 474
Little Orphan Annie 523, 524
Liza VR351 176
LK1 96
London RY175 446
Lotus Hai 454
Lotus Hai RY135 .... 442, 445
Louis XVI (Shape) 30
Louise R5766, VR390 .... 172, 177
LTC12 382
Lu-ray Pastels (Taylor, Smith & Taylor) 397
Lucy 502
Lupine CV14 .... 377, 384
Lynnwood 334, 389, 452
Lyric 454

M

M1 57
M6S 57
M90 199
M100 199
M114 199
M137 199
M156 200
M177 199
M201 200
M203 .... 197, 199
M207 .... 197, 199
M208 199
M211 200
M212 200
M212V 183
M217 199
Madrid 479
Magnolia 329, 417, 256
MAJ4 298
Majestic 33
Majestic W538 .... 261, 263, 276
Majestic W638 279
Malay 458
Malibu 498
Maple Leaf R9524 90
Maplewood 487, 488
Margaret Rose-Maroon MW185 387
Marigold (Shape) 26, 196-200
Marigold 499
Marilyn–Blue G3419 344
Marilyn–Pink G3412 344
Marilyn–Pink G3418 .... 337, 344, 353
Mary Anne 400, 402
Mary Lloyd CW131 480
Matte Gold Band 62, 67
Maude VR108 174
MAW4 124
Maxicana (HLC3105) 534
Maxicana W440 .... 108, 534
Mayfair (Fostoria) 133
Maytime RY284 .... 440, 443
McCall, Betsy 524
McClure's Magazine 37
Meadow Goldenrod VR411 179
Mega China 228
Melody (Bristol Shape) 500
Melody 444
Melody In Blue 376
Mexicana (Century Shape) 134, 144, 533, 534
Mexicana (Daisy Chain Shape) 191, 193, 533
Mexicana N1524 (Eggshell Nautilus Shape) 328, 534
Mexicana (Eggshell Swing Shape) 360, 534
Mexicana (Kitchen Kraft Shape)
Blue Band, Red Band 297, 533
Mexicana (Virginia Rose Shape) 534
Mikasa 515
Milano Gold 479
Milano Green 479
Ming Glory 454
Mingo (Shape) 520, 521, 522
Minuet N1811 .... 311, 323
Mist Gray 434
ML4 257
Modern Farmer (Shape) 22, 393-395
Modern Farmer–Light Green 395
Modern Farmer–Red 395
Modern Farmer–Rose 395
Modern Farmer–White 395
Modern Farmer–Yellow 395
Modern Laurel 122, 127
Modern Star Q22 444
Monarch 336, 337, 341
Monterey (Shape) 520
Montgomery Ward 42, 121, 122, 133
135, 167, 185, 190, 203, 206, 206, 240, 241,
244, 246, 251, 261, 311, 336, 337, 366, 368,
428, 438, 454, 470
Monticello 409, 419
More Fleur 504
Moselle 472, 474
Moselle G3302 351
Moss Rose 514
Moss Rose S163, S191G 357, 361
Mother's Oats 110, 112, 390-391, 421, 423
Mountain Meadow 507
Mountain Meadow 2 507
MS22 143
MS41 143
MS43 143
MS69 143
MS146 144
MW67 127
MW180 323
MW181 .... 429, 434
MW185 387
MW190 443
My First Fiesta 523
Mystique SR120 496

N

N80 117
N164 70
N199 70
N200 256
N201 199
N211 257
N212 70
N213 70
N224 70
N277 254
N291 256
N300 255
N301 255
N318 256
N334 257
N363 254
N388 255

(N-O) Homer Laughlin Index

Entry	Page
N419	257
N428	257
N429	257
N552	70
N1219	326
N1221	326
N1223	314
N1248	320
N1402	324
N1405	325
N1418	318
N1439	326
N1458	329
N1470	328
N1474	324
N1481	328
N1489	325
N1504	328
N1524	328
N1525	328
N1539	326
N1574	323
N1575	321
N1576	323
N1577	321
N1578	321
N1580	324
N1580N	328
N1581	293, 298, 321
N1583	312, 324
N1585	329
N1586	320
N1590	323
N1591	321
N1593	322
N1594	323
N1597	322
N1616	321
N1617	315
N1622	327
N1627	322
N1637	320
N1638	323
N1639	325
N1642	315
N1646	321
N1652	314
N1653	315
N1654	316
N1662	314
N1669	322
N1670	321
N1675	327
N1679	325
N1684	321
N1690	320
N1691	320
N1694	314
N1697	324
N1698	320
N1699	325
N1700	320
N1705	321
N1708	315
N1709	320
N1711	316
N1728	118
N1731	321
N1732	324
N1733	328
N1745	322
N1746	318
N1750	323
N1753	323
N1755	323
N1769	324
N1773	325
N1775	329
N1783	321
N1785	322
N1794	323
N1798	323
N1803	322
N1807	325
N1811	323
N1829	327
N1838	325
N2023	114, 115, 119
N2123	117
N2124	117
N2228	118
N2423	117
N2628	116
N2723	116
N2728	116
N2823	119
N2928	117
N3023	118
N3123	118
N3128	114, 116
N3328	116
N3628	119
N3923	118
N3928	118
N3943	117
N4143	117
N5202	116
N5428	118
N5728	118
N6528	117
N6828	117
N6928	117
N7028	117
N7128	117
N7415	116
N7615	116
N7715	116
N8228	118
Nantucket N1753	323
Narcissus	435
Nassau MW180	323
Nasturtium K8904B	99
National Brotherhood of Operative Potters	529
Nautilus (Shape)	20, 211, 250-259, 309, 452, 459, 534
Navajo	504
Needlepoint	500
Neville K2253	93, 94, 96
New Fiesta	503
New Paradise	504
New York (Shape)	526
New York World's Fair	523, 530
Newberry, J. J.	167, 207, 438
Newbury, Dennis	506
Newell (Shape)	24, 110, 113-119, 409
Newell	251, 258
Niagara (Shape)	25, 68-70
Noritake	309
Norway E339	516
Norway Rose	352
Nosegay VR423	170, 179
Nossaman, Darlene	468
Nutmeg	502

O

Entry	Page
O10	162
O12	161, 162
O16	163
O19	162
O25	162
O27	162
O28	163
O31	162
O32	162
O34	162
O35	162
O37	163
O39	163
O43	162
O45	162
O52	163
O56	163
O60	162
O63	162
O65	163
O79	163
Oakleaf P523	402
October Leaves	470, 474
October Leaves TR6	474
Ohio	146
Old English Scene	144
Old Orchard	504
Old Roman (Shape)	28, 164-165
Old Sport Scene–Brown	333
OR47	165
OR51	165
OR52	165
OR53	165
OR54	165
OR55	165
OR58	165
OR65	165
OR72	165
OR73	165
OR78	165
Orange Blossom	459
Orange Border (Shape)	526
Orbit (Shape)	16, 18, 438, 452, 487-488
Orbit	488
Orchard	459, 474
Orchard N1773	325
Organdy Pastels	355, 357, 360
Organdy–Blue	355, 358
Organdy–Green	355, 358
Organdy–Pink	355, 358
Organdy–Yellow	355, 358
Orient (Orbit Shape)	487
Orient (Rhythm Shape)	452
Orleans (Shape)	28, 121, 149, 160-163
OS81	192
Ovaltine	523, 524
OvenServe (Shape)	23, 161, 169, 184-193, 293
OvenServe–Brown	192
OvenServe–Cream	192
OvenServe–Pink	192
OvenServe–Pumpkin	192
OvenServe–Turquoise	192

Homer Laughlin Index (O–R)

OvenServe–Yellow 192
Ovide (Shape) 39

P

P511 402
P513 402
P516 402
P523 402
P526 402
P527 402
Pacific Flyway Designs 508
Paden City Pottery 529
Paisley 515
Palma 504
Paradise 467, 503
Pastel Rose TR21 474
Pastel Wood Rose VRD220 178
Pastoral (Shape) 23, 420-423
Pastoral 421-423
Patchwork C420 516
Patchwork E421 516
Patrician 170, 172
Patterson, H. W. 9
Peacock backstamp 121, 122, 154
Pearl China 145, 146, 204, 414
Peasant Ware 300
Pennsylvania (Shape) 526
Persian Garden CV28 .... 377, 385
Persian Rose 92
Petals HS240 503
Petipoint 200
Petipoint CP95 181
PG10 89
PGC8 385
Philadelphia International Exhibition 529
Piccadilly (Shape) 18, 400-402
Pimlico HS207 505
Pink Laurel 386
Pink Magnolia 466, 467
Pink Magnolia CH100 458
Pink Magnolia RY122 .... 442, 445
Pink Melody CV62.2 386
Pink Moss Rose E4904 62
Pink Print 206, 209
Pink Radiance 389, 334, 452
Pink Rose 386
Pink Willow 238, 240, 243
PK16 76
Plaid A105 459
Plaid E419 516
Plain, John 438
Platinum Wreath CO109 .... 205, 206, 208
Plume 474
Polka-Print 458
Ponche, Andre 502
Poppy 500
Pottery, Glass & Brass Salesman, The 13, 49
62, 92, 102, 114, 115, 197, 202, 532
Premium Stone China 30
Presidential 92
Prima Donna 357
Primula 481
Primuline 204
Princess H5259 380
Priscilla N1639 (Eggshell Nautilus Shape) 325
Priscilla (Kitchen Kraft Shape) 294, 298
Priscilla (Republic Shape) 90
Provincial MW190 443
Pueblo S102 .... 360, 534

Q

Q22 444
QO10 .... 110, 111
Quaker Oats 185, 194, 390-391
Queen Esther SS28 .... 412, 418
Queen Esther Silver 412
Quilt 500

R

R135 88
R1177 519
R1275 146
R1294 90
R1334 88
R1387 353
R1419D 353
R1521 305
R1524 518
R1531 353
R1629 343
R1804 1/2 88
R1808 209
R1810 209
R2134A 254
R2134B 254
R2140A 254
R2140B 254
R2168 256
R2256 176
R2283 362
R2346 328
R2466 359
R2499 363
R2519 255
R2522 361
R2526 .... 254, 534
R2534 361
R2541 361
R2639 361
R2658 321
R2673 322
R2700 86
R2702 327
R2734 89
R3029A 370
R3044A 370
R3061A 327
R3080A 516
R3102 85
R3122A 370
R3131A 371
R3140A 362
R3143A 362
R3144A 362
R3150A 362
R3151A 362
R3175A 362
R3180A 362
R3189A 362
R3202 85
R3234 89
R3235A 277
R3269A 372
R3273A 363
R3274A 330
R3300 86
R3302 85
R3311A 331
R3318A 331
R3341A 332
R3361A 320
R3378A 88
R3381A 88
R3382A 88
R3402 85
R3423A 279
R3435A 269
R3442A 279
R3446A 269
R3448A 272
R3449A 272
R3453A 269
R3455A 272
R3459A 273
R3482A 268
R3483A 272
R3486A 268
R3488A 268
R3492A 278
R3495A 278
R3496A 278
R3499A 278
R3514A 279
R3518A 279
R3521A 276
R3543 89
R3562A 269
R3568 340
R3569 340
R3597A 269
R3603A 352
R3605A 345
R3606A 352
R3610A 352
R3624 87
R3651A 370
R3656A 348
R3657A 362
R3682 415
R3683A 415
R3691A 415
R3707A 416
R3709A 416
R3715A 416
R3730A 416
R3734 150
R3739A 416
R3747A 416
R3748A 416
R3749 416
R3750A 416
R3751A 416
R4343 89
R4642 363
R4703 .... 254, 534
R4806 85
R4901 86
R4937 255
R4938 255
R4939 255
R4941 255
R4980 371
R5001 85
R5006 85
R5011 517
R5012 517
R5101 85
R5106 85

(R-S) Homer Laughlin Index

R5206 85	Regency 368, 372	RV27 150
R5306 85	Republic (Shape) 25, 72, 81-90, 307, 534	RV28 150
R5334 88	Republic 82, 85	RV31 150
R5411 127	Revere D101 479	RV34 150
R5431 329	RG4508 128	RV36 151
R5671 178	RGC24 128	RV39 151
R5745 177	Rhead, Frederick 114, 121, 149, 211	RV41 151
R5763 330	336, 403, 410, 527	RV43 151
R5766 177	Rhythm (Shape) 14, 240, 259, 334, 388, 389	RV44 150
R5904 88	437-452, 454, 459, 466, 481, 483, 487, 499	RV45 150
R6059 278	Rhythm Rose (Kitchen Kraft Shape) 294, 298	RV46 152
R6073 372	Rhythm Rose (Rhythm Shape) 447	RV47 151
R6087 351	Rhythm–Burgundy 443	RV48 151
R6089 351	Rhythm–Forest Green 443	RV49 150
R6095 321	Rhythm–Gray 443	RV50 151
R6096 404	Rhythm–Green (Chartreuse) 443	RV52 151
R6100 404	Rhythm–White 443	RV1043 150
R6101 371	Rhythm–Yellow 443	RV1143 150
R6102 346	Riviera (Line) 9, 137-141, 156, 229	RV1343 150
R6104 371	Riviera–Ivory 142	RV9233 150
R6105 346	Riviera–Light Green 142	RV9533 150
R6106 346	Riviera–Mauve Blue 142	RY102 447
R6107 371	Riviera–Pumpkin 142	RY104 447
R6108 370	Riviera–Red 142	RY117 458
R6109 345	Riviera–Yellow 142	RY122 445
R6110 404	Rochelle N1591 .... 311, 321	RY135 .... 442, 445
R6111 347	Rock Garden 502	RY153 446
R6263A 486	Rococo (Shape) 26, 30-33, 39	RY159 447
R6401 86	Romance CV67 382	RY163 446
R8204 89	Romance, The 154, 158	RY168 446
R8290A 275	Romance In Blue 376, 377	RY170 446
R8326C 325	Rope Edge (Shape) 17, 403-407	RY171 445
R8333 152	Rose & Lattice (Empress Shape) 63, 65, 67	RY172 444
R8412 269	Rose & Lattice (Kwaker Shape) 94, 96	RY175 446
R8525 359	Rose Fantasy 238, 244	RY184 444
R8533 151	Rose Garden 467	RY190 446
R8534 359	Rose Garland 92	RY191 446
R8538 359	Rose Medallion C114 145	RY194 444
R8545 359	Rose Melody VR109 174	RY203 447
R8553 359	Rosebud 492	RY204 447
R8556 361	Rosebud Wreath 251	RY209 447
R8559 359	Rosedale V131 492	RY217 445
R8563 361	Rosemary (Eggshell Nautilus Shape) 323	RY225 445
R8585 370	Rosemary (Ravenna Shape) 152	RY251 444
R8586 370	Rosewood 98	RY252 445
R8617 347	Rosewood B1314 276	RY255 .... 388, 448, 451
R8733 151	Rosewood K9504 98	RY284 443
R9524 90	Ross, Betsy 524	RY288 443
R152588 273	Rouen 2692 271	RY307 445
Racheter, Richard 167	Round 'N Round 503	RY307PT 444
Raindrops 504	Royal China 421-422	RY308 .... 438, 443
Ralston Purina 523	Royal Gold 145	RY316 445
Rambler Rose VM1 344	Royal Harvest RY255 .... 388, 448, 451, 513	RY322 445
Rambler Rose VM2 .... 336, 337, 344	Royal Joci 481	RY330 445
Rambling Rose V126 492	Royal Maroon P516 402	RY346 443
Ranson (Shape, Haviland) 82	Royal Maytime 514	RY365 445
Ravenna (Shape) 28, 149-152, 161	Royal Metal Manufacturing Co. 185, 229, 293	RY366 445
RAY1 79	Royal Rose V125 492	
RAY2 76	RU-505 481	**S**
RCP25 435	Rubaiyat 440	
RCP27 435	RV3 152	S102 360
Red Apple JJ150 (Nautilus Shape) 252, 256	RV4 152	S108 360
Red Apple JJ150 (Rhythm Shape) 446	RV5 151	S112 360
Red Beauty (No Trim, Platinum Trim) 178	RV7 151	S113 361
Red Book Directory, The 376	RV12 150	S126 360
Red Ring 173	RV19 151	S128C 363
Regal 483, 484	RV20 151	S129 360
Regal Red 387	RV23 151	S131C 363
Regency (Shape) 22, 497-498	RV25 150	S1465 360
		S149P 361

550

Homer Laughlin Index (S–V)

S152P 360
S163 361
S178 359
S179 359
S181 363
S187 358
S191G 361
S203 358
S212 361
S222 358
S240 359
S326 359
S327 362
S329 359
Saint Clement 330
Salem China Company 523
Saxon (Shape) 16, 482-484
Schreckengost, Don 376, 461, 468, 470
Scottsdale 1970 515
Sears, Roebuck & Co. 31, 35, 39, 42, 43, 49,
    50, 62, 67, 82, 92, 93, 103, 115, 149, 152,
    154, 167, 170, 172, 241, 251, 261, 337, 394,
    400, 401, 403, 409, 428, 454, 520, 522
Seller, M. 185
Seneca (Shape) 25, 30-33
Sequence 436
Serenade (Line) 438, 452
Serenade (Regency Shape) 497, 498
Serenade (Shape) 22, 396-399
Serenade–Blue 397-399
Serenade–Green 397-399
Serenade–Pink 396-399
Serenade–Yellow 397-399
Sevron China 383, 386, 444
SH6 492
Shakespeare (Shape) 30, 33
Shakespeare Country–Blue 261, 263, 273
Shamrock (Bristol Shape) 500
Shamrock (Brittany Shape) 261
Sheffield 211, 219, 490, 492, 494
    496, 497, 498, 503
Sheffield Dresden 167
Shell Pink 434
Shrewsbury, The 277
Sienna 204
Sierra 503
Silver Rose VR124 173
Silver Scrolls VR172 173
Silver Swirl 491, 492
Sinceny 331
Skytone 300, 355, 424, 430-431, 435
Snow White 470, 472, 474
Somerset CV87 380
Something Blue 454
Sonesta SR108 496
Song of Spring 118
Sorrento 496
South Of France VR387 175
South Wind CV75 .... 376, 377, 385
Soverign S203 358
SP2 383
SP5 387
SP8 387
SP13 385
SP22 387
Sperry & Hutchinson 72
Spindrift HS271 505
Splatter–Blue 508, 510
Splatter–Brown 508, 510

Spring Garden 481
Spring Rose TR1 .... 470, 471, 474
Spring Song CV49 .... 377, 383
Spring Wreath 89
Springtime (Bristol Shape) 499
Springtime (Challenger Shape) 510
Springtime (Ravenna Shape) 152
Springtime CV32 386
Springtime W245 (Marigold Shape) 200
Springtime W245 (Virginia Rose Shape) 183
SR100 496
SR108 496
SR114 345
SR115 347
SR118 496
SR120 496
SS28 418
Stardust HLS180 .... 431, 436
Starflower 311
Starflower RY346 443
State Flower Series 2545 (Alaska & Ohio) 332
State Flower Series 2545 (West Virginia) 332
State Flowers Series 2545 (Georgia) 332
Stitchery 503
Stratford 417
Strawberries 479
Strawberry 459
Studio (Shape) 15, 438, 465-467
Sturbridge 273
Style House 342
Sugar Pine 261, 262
Sun Drops HS263 502
Sun Gold 412, 419
Sun Porch 294, 297
Sun Valley 438, 444
Sunflower 499
Sunglow 483, 484
Sunrise 443
Sunrise–Pink 334, 389, 452
Suntone 300, 355, 424, 432-433, 436
Superba 520, 521, 522
Surfside 505
Surrey TH17 372
Susan 89
Suzanne 512
Sweet Pea RY190 446
Sweet Pea W350 446
Sylvan 272

T

T2 111
T24 111
T26 111
T27 111
T35 111
T46 112
T48 112
T50 112
T7 111
T91 111
T92 111
T93 111
T95 112
T8028 111
Tablefair (Shape) 21, 511-512
Tango (Shape) 26, 306-308
Tango–Fiesta Red 308
Tango–Harlequin Yellow 308
Tango–Maroon 308

Tango–Mauve Blue 308
Tango–Spruce Green 308
Taylor, Smith & Taylor 185, 189, 194
    304, 397, 421-422
Tea Party 524
Tea Rose (Shape) 26, 304-305
Tea Rose GO16 305
Teal Green 384
Temp Pica 280, P513 .... 401, 402
TH1 371
TH5 370
TH6 .... 367, 371
TH10 370
TH11 .... 367, 368, 371
TH14 .... 367, 369
TH14P 370
TH17 372
TH19 371
TH20 370
TH21 370
TH24 371
TH26 371
TH34 371
Theme 368, 369
Tom & Jerry 526
Tom Thumb 523, 524
Tongue Twister Tableware 524
TR1 474
TR6 474
TR7 .... 305, 474
TR21 474
Tracy, Dick 133, 523, 524
Treasure 504
Trellis (Shape) 27, 110-112
Trellis (Charm House Shape) 457
Trellis (Rhythm Shape) 438
Trent 488
Triumph (Shape) 14, 459, 469-474
Triumph CV52 .... 377, 383
True Love 262
TS2 144
Tulip N1594 323
Tulip Time 409
Tulip Wreath 467
Tulips In A Basket 167, 180
Tulips In A Basket VR396 180
Tulips In A Basket VR412 180
Turquoise Melody CV63 382

U

Unknown Shapes & Lines 514-519

V

V100 492
V107 492
V111 492
V112 492
V117 492
V118 492
V125 492
V126 492
V131 492
V2750 348
V2843 324
V2903 89
Vandemere 93
Vellum 121, 133, 154
Vellum Ware 134
Viceroy G3330, G3571 .... 336, 337, 340

(V-W) Homer Laughlin Index

Victor (Shape) 30
Victoria (Shape) 24, 489-492
Viking 515
Virginia Rose (Shape) 6, 26, 29, 121, 149
    156, 166-183, 194, 304, 526, 534
VM1 344
VM2 344
VM8 326
VM101 325
VM108 343
Vogue (Shape) 15, 438, 485-486
Vogue 475, 476
VR101 178
VR104 175
VR105 182
VR106 182
VR107 175
VR108 174
VR109 174
VR114 173
VR115 173
VR118 174
VR119 175
VR120 173
VR121 173
VR122 173
VR124 173
VR128 .... 167, 169, 179
VR132 178
VR133 179
VR134 177
VR135 177
VR136 182
VR138 174
VR141 176
VR142 177
VR143 179
VR151 177
VR152 176
VR153 174
VR155 178
VR162 176
VR172 173
VR175 177
VR178 179
VR194 182
VR205 182
VR231 182
VR232 175
VR233 178
VR261 183
VR266 177
VR269 177
VR316 175
VR320 174
VR351 .... 169, 176
VR387 175
VR390 177
VR396 180
VR398 180
VR411 179
VR412 180
VR420 180
VR421 174
VR431 175
VR437 175
VRD220 178

W

W-138 253
W3S 57
W4S 58
W5S 58
W7S 47
W9S 47
W11 77
W30 60
W33 77
W35 59
W101 129
W102 127
W104 128
W106 128
W113 77
W1133 128
W114 60
W117 75
W122 88
W127 .... 13, 102, 105, 107
W132 .... 104, 105, 107
W134 .... 198, 199
W136 385
W137 175
W138A 255
W141 266
W142 163
W146 414
W150 256
W152 447
W159 .... 388, 451
W213 76
W215 77
W226 127
W232 .... 160, 162
W239 255
W245 .... 183, 2003
W246 415
W251 447
W342 410
W349 416
W350 446
W426 .... 102, 104, 106
W428 102
W442 415
W449 410
W530 65
W538 276
W613 78
W617 85
W638 279
W713 78
W813 80
W817 59
W1726 90
W1970 125
W2133 129
W2333 131
W2338 130
W2533 130
W2543 128
W2633 129
W2643 129
W2733 130
W2833 130
W2943 129
W3133 130
W3733 129

W3924 126
W4033 129
W4224 126
W4324 125
W4633 129
W4743 124
W4923 130
W4970 125
W5033 129
W5270 125
W5333 131
W5433 129
W5502 124
W5670 125
W5833 124
W5923 128
W6023 130
W6033 127
W6123 130
W6170 125
W6180M 125
W6223 129
W6233 128
W6333 128
W6433 127
W6470 125
W6580M 125
W6733 128
W6780M 126
W6833 125
W6933 127
W7080M 126
W7133 129
W7506 124
W7633 130
W7733 128
W7806 124
W7923 130
W7933 128
W8033 127
W8377 125
W8423 129
W8523 128
W8743 127
W8923 129
W8970 127
W8980 126
W9123 129
W9223 130
W9423 128
W9480M 125
W9570 125
W9823 129
W9980M 126
W42930 116
Wally 131
Warner Brothers 228
Water Lily VR398 180
Waves 503
Wayside 90
Welch, Jack 10, 114, 167, 409
Wells (Shape) 17, 120-131, 154, 239
    240, 241, 242, 243, 528
Wells, Joseph III 5
Wells, Joseph M. 9
Wells, Joseph M. III 9
Wells, W. E. 8
Wells, William E. 9
Wells Art Glaze 121, 122

Homer Laughlin Index **(W–Unidentified Patterns)**

Wells Art Glaze–Blue 124
Wells Art Glaze–Green 123, 124
Wells Art Glaze–Peach 123, 124
Wells Art Glaze–Red 123, 124
Wells Art Glaze–Rust 122, 124
Wells Art Glaze–Yellow 124
WHC1 258
Wheat 502
Wheat (Americana) 455, 458
Wheat Spray CP171 446
White and Gold 49, 82
White Flower JJ152 ..... 438, 440, 447
White Granite Ware 520, 529
Wild Grapes 434
Wild Pink Rose VR233 178
Wild Rose 420-423
Wild Rose 1 VR269 177
Wild Rose Y220 107
Willow (Shape) 19, 238-249
Wilshire House 219, 220
Wind-Blown 152
Windemere C320 515
Windsor Rose L633 ..... 409, 417
WMS3 57
Wood Violet Gold Stippled 35
Woodland 470, 473, 474
Woodland 254 450
Woodland Gold 173
Woodstock 510
Woolworth, (F. W.) 8, 102, 246, 282, 286, 409, 410, 485
World's Fairs & Expositions 529-532
Wyoming (Shape) 520, 521

X

X2S 58
X5 517
XN6 117

Y

Y14 ..... 104, 106
Y24 106
Y40 106
Y43 ..... 105, 107
Y137 106
Y137G 107
Y162 106
Y219 106
Y220 107
Y222 108
Y795 106
Yale (Shape) 522
Yellow Carnation F107 ..... 218, 234
Yellow Daisy 456-458
Yellowstone (Shape) 13, 23, 101-109, 534

Unidentified Patterns

ATA2 383
ATA5 349
CUP1 363
CUP3 484
HLC26 ..... 388, 451
HLC29 ..... 506, 507
HLC39 414
HLC54 94
HLC56 88
HLC60 182
HLC70 386
HLC73 448
HLC74 317
HLC77 417
HLC78 446
HLC81 324
HLC82 348
HLC85 270
HLC87 419
HLC89 88
HLC103 179
HLC104 209
HLC106 95
HLC107 272
HLC109 ..... 262, 267
HLC110 ..... 83, 89
HLC114 419
HLC115 443
HLC116 89
HLC117 274
HLC124 479
HLC125 183
HLC126 486
HLC128 87
HLC130 346
HLC132 142
HLC133 341
HLC134 350
HLC135 348
HLC142 87
HLC144 314
HLC147 369
HLC151 108
HLC152 106
HLC155 181
HLC156 479
HLC158 89
HLC159 320
HLC161 183
HLC163 318
HLC172 87
HLC175 315
HLC176 65
HLC179 157
HLC180 345
HLC181 108
HLC182 146
HLC183 256
HLC186 451
HLC188 502
HLC189 419
HLC190 108
HLC191 343
HLC196 77
HLC197 347
HLC200 451
HLC201 380
HLC204 256
HLC205 80
HLC207 507
HLC208 515
HLC212 370
HLC218 512
HLC219 340
HLC223 344
HLC226 ..... 379, 381
HLC228 507
HLC229 510
HLC230 510
HLC233 276
HLC235 64
HLC236 ..... 338, 348
HLC238 384
HLC240 341
HLC243 273
HLC245 89
HLC246 387
HLC247 208
HLC248 346
HLC251 350
HLC252 353
HLC253 508
HLC256 318
HLC258 272
HLC259 418
HLC261 352
HLC263 445
HLC273 507
HLC276 178
HLC278 502
HLC280 417
HLC282 496
HLC287 512
HLC290 402
HLC292 80
HLC300 510
HLC307 415
HLC310 90
HLC311 370
HLC312 450
HLC336 ..... 134, 146
HLC339 381
HLC341 496
HLC342 ..... 280, 388
HLC343 86
HLC344 383
HLC347 324
HLC350 507
HLC352 177
HLC353 264
HLC357 419
HLC358 95
HLC359 353
HLC361 344
HLC364 109
HLC367 419
HLC368 268
HLC369 344
HLC371 435
HLC372 343
HLC374 351
HLC375 107
HLC376 343
HLC399 180
HLC401 325
HLC407 343
HLC411 382
HLC418 266
HLC419 298
HLC420 ..... 104, 106
HLC423 418
HLC425 329
HLC426 341
HLC430 387
HLC431 486
HLC435 90
HLC436 322
HLC438 80
HLC440 449

(Unidentified Patterns) *Homer Laughlin Index*

HLC441 415	HLC579 383	HLC742 346
HLC445 380	HLC580 448	HLC743 55
HLC446 515	HLC582 414	HLC746 67
HLC448 258	HLC584 316	HLC749 59
HLC449 46	HLC586 349	HLC751 382
HLC450 173	HLC592 .... 389, 452	HLC755 319
HLC452 316	HLC593 415	HLC756 257
HLC455 66	HLC594 192	HLC757 346
HLC459 448	HLC595 106	HLC759 329
HLC461 507	HLC600 59	HLC760 342
HLC462 507	HLC602 515	HLC770 174
HLC465 414	HLC603 344	HLC775 361
HLC466 414	HLC605 343	HLC776 131
HLC467 386	HLC609 361	HLC777 349
HLC468 87	HLC614 95	HLC779 97
HLC470 87	HLC615 95	HLC781 445
HLC471 199	HLC619 265	HLC782 514
HLC473 258	HLC621 40	HLC783 181
HLC474 345	HLC622 258	HLC784 324
HLC477 78	HLC624 479	HLC785 87
HLC478 341	HLC625 257	HLC786 111
HLC479 346	HLC627 450	HLC787 276
HLC480 347	HLC628 481	HLC791 346
HLC483 319	HLC629 449	HLC799 316
HLC485 349	HLC631 417	HLC801 96
HLC489 386	HLC634 .... 376, 382	HLC803 508
HLC490 419	HLC638 349	HLC804 349
HLC491 157	HLC639 182	HLC806 451
HLC492 320	HLC640 314	HLC809 88
HLC495 145	HLC644 387	HLC812 95
HLC497 382	HLC653 507	HLC836 108
HLC498 65	HLC655 173	HLC837 359
HLC503 204	HLC658 384	HLC846 507
HLC504 359	HLC661 418	HLC848 40
HLC505 512	HLC663 436	HLC849 325
HLC506 386	HLC664 183	HLC850 86
HLC507 325	HLC668 183	HLC851 45
HLC510 65	HLC671 507	HLC856 90
HLC512 318	HLC673 270	HLC858 267
HLC514 318	HLC674 .... 111, 112	HLC860 272
HLC514G 318	HLC675 177	HLC863 502
HLC516 340	HLC676 446	HLC866 200
HLC518 108	HLC678 502	HLC867 341
HLC519 384	HLC679 358	HLC868 117
HLC521 418	HLC680 414	HLC874 87
HLC522 319	HLC689 46	HLC877 108
HLC524 88	HLC694 143	HLC878 59
HLC526 444	HLC696 350	HLC880 342
HLC532 351	HLC697 108	HLC883 320
HLC534 276	HLC701 479	HLC884 327
HLC535 314	HLC702 107	HLC886 77
HLC541 .... 155, 159	HLC704 177	HLC887 59
HLC542 419	HLC707 204	HLC890 99
HLC544 315	HLC712 320	HLC892 148
HLC545 276	HLC717 319	HLC894 359
HLC549 .... 380, 389	HLC718 145	HLC895 .... 134, 142
HLC551 .... 459, 474, 513	HLC719 320	HLC896 .... 185, 192
HLC553 417	HLC720 329	HLC897 181
HLC556 315	HLC722 130	HLC899 59
HLC557 414	HLC723 .... 388, 451	HLC901 317
HLC558 55	HLC724 145	HLC902 318
HLC561 319	HLC725 502	HLC905 65
HLC562 345	HLC726 65	HLC906 204
HLC564 60	HLC727 385	HLC907 256
HLC569 145	HLC728 385	HLC909 507
HLC570 434	HLC732 479	HLC910 256
HLC575 381	HLC734 370	HLC911 418
HLC576 106	HLC735 99	HLC916 60
HLC578 414	HLC740 507	HLC917 402

Homer Laughlin Index (Unidentified Patterns)

HLC922 ... 322	HLC1053 ... 372	HLC1207 ... 449
HLC923 ... 142	HLC1060 ... 269	HLC1208 ... 380
HLC925 ... 255	HLC1062 ... 445	HLC1210 ... 303
HLC933 ... 515	HLC1063 ... 89	HLC1213 ... 297
HLC935 ... 515	HLC1064 ... 324	HLC1214 ... 319
HLC937 ... 369	HLC1069 ... 46	HLC1215 ... 514
HLC938 ... 449	HLC1071 ... 145	HLC1217 ... 266
HLC939 ... 503	HLC1072 ... 78	HLC1218 ... 270
HLC943 ... 328	HLC1073 ... 182	HLC1219 ... 270
HLC945 ... 381	HLC1081 ... 268	HLC1221 ... 418
HLC947 ... 418	HLC1082 ... 351	HLC1222 ... 33
HLC949 ... 208	HLC1083 ... 508	HLC1223 ... 264
HLC950 ... 59	HLC1084 ... 297	HLC1224 ... 327
HLC953 ... 252, 256	HLC1089 ... 272	HLC1225 ... 327
HLC956 ... 318	HLC1090 ... 114, 118	HLC1226 ... 333
HLC957 ... 447	HLC1091 ... 502	HLC1227 ... 333
HLC959 ... 56	HLC1092 ... 328	HLC1228 ... 333
HLC960 ... 60	HLC1095 ... 383	HLC1229 ... 333
HLC961 ... 363	HLC1098 ... 275	HLC1230 ... 330
HLC965 ... 383	HLC1100 ... 59	HLC1231 ... 320
HLC968 ... 204	HLC1102 ... 276	HLC1232 ... 316
HLC969 ... 325	HLC1104 ... 119	HLC1233 ... 381
HLC970 ... 446	HLC1106 ... 382	HLC1234 ... 449
HLC972 ... 275	HLC1107 ... 76	HLC1235 ... 383
HLC973 ... 142	HLC1109 ... 80	HLC1237 ... 257
HLC977 ... 183	HLC1110 ... 60	HLC1238 ... 450
HLC979 ... 322	HLC1111 ... 270	HLC1239 ... 467
HLC980 ... 507	HLC1112 ... 85	HLC1240 ... 271
HLC981 ... 297	HLC1116 ... 106	HLC1241 ... 317
HLC983 ... 515	HLC1117 ... 268	HLC1242 ... 317
HLC984 ... 417	HLC1118 ... 360, 534	HLC1243 ... 317
HLC986 ... 319	HLC1121 ... 175	HLC1244 ... 317
HLC987 ... 181	HLC1123 ... 448	HLC1246 ... 316
HLC989 ... 58	HLC1125 ... 144	HLC1247 ... 144
HLC990 ... 414	HLC1126 ... 418	HLC1248 ... 316
HLC991 ... 86	HLC1134 ... 108	HLC1249 ... 317
HLC993 ... 353	HLC1135 ... 349	HLC1250 ... 317
HLC994 ... 352	HLC1137 ... 100	HLC1251 ... 317
HLC996 ... 445	HLC1142 ... 176	HLC1252 ... 316
HLC997 ... 40	HLC1143 ... 45	HLC1253 ... 316
HLC999 ... 329	HLC1144 ... 148	HLC1255 ... 256
HLC1000 ... 340	HLC1149 ... 370	HLC1257 ... 278
HLC1001 ... 183	HLC1152 ... 319	HLC1258 ... 267
HLC1004 ... 348	HLC1155 ... 181	HLC1259 ... 56
HLC1008 ... 448	HLC1157 ... 152	HLC1261 ... 363
HLC1012 ... 414	HLC1158 ... 515	HLC1262 ... 363
HLC1014 ... 151	HLC1174 ... 208	HLC1263 ... 56
HLC1015 ... 56	HLC1175 ... 74, 80	HLC1264 ... 333
HLC1016 ... 65	HLC1176 ... 62, 64	HLC1265 ... 333
HLC1018 ... 175	HLC1178 ... 258	HLC1266 ... 107
HLC1019 ... 206, 209	HLC1179 ... 449	HLC1267 ... 342
HLC1020 ... 107	HLC1180 ... 142	HLC1268 ... 331
HLC1022 ... 419	HLC1186 ... 56	HLC1269 ... 80
HLC1024 ... 314	HLC1187 ... 326	HLC1270 ... 80
HLC1026 ... 347	HLC1188 ... 59	HLC1271 ... 326
HLC1029 ... 46	HLC1189 ... 173	HLC1272 ... 327
HLC1031 ... 329	HLC1190 ... 450	HLC1273 ... 327
HLC1032 ... 515	HLC1191 ... 434	HLC1274 ... 364
HLC1033 ... 347	HLC1193 ... 86	HLC1275 ... 47
HLC1034 ... 208	HLC1195 ... 319	HLC1276 ... 193
HLC1037 ... 173	HLC1197 ... 30	HLC1277 ... 192
HLC1042 ... 45	HLC1198 ... 174	HLC1278 ... 188, 192
HLC1044 ... 188, 193	HLC1199 ... 60	HLC1279 ... 364
HLC1046 ... 80	HLC1201 ... 416	HLC1280 ... 364
HLC1047 ... 57	HLC1202 ... 417	HLC1281 ... 364
HLC1048 ... 126	HLC1203 ... 273	HLC1282 ... 364
HLC1049 ... 342	HLC1204 ... 316	HLC1284 ... 100
HLC1051 ... 208	HLC1205 ... 314	HLC1287 ... 234
HLC1052 ... 208	HLC1206 ... 518	HLC1299 ... 69, 70

(Unidentified Patterns) *Homer Laughlin Index*

HLC1300 267	HLC1382 57	HLC1464 126
HLC1301 266	HLC1383 268	HLC1465 273
HLC1302 448	HLC1384 99	HLC1467 264
HLC1303 486	HLC1385 256	HLC1468 264
HLC1304 474	HLC1387 268	HLC1469 265
HLC1305 448	HLC1388 360	HLC1470 264
HLC1308 515	HLC1389 364	HLC1471 269
HLC1310 450	HLC1391 362	HLC1472 265
HLC1311 451	HLC1392 320	HLC1473 270
HLC1312 448	HLC1393 323	HLC1474 450
HLC1313 451	HLC1394 321	HLC1475 272
HLC1314 449	HLC1395 319	HLC1476 265
HLC1315 449	HLC1396 319	HLC1477 351
HLC1316 449	HLC1397 319	HLC1478 350
HLC1317 448	HLC1398 314	HLC1479 267
HLC1318 448	HLC1399 317	HLC1480 272
HLC1319 265	HLC1400 324	HLC1481 267
HLC1320 265	HLC1401 324	HLC1482 303
HLC1321 264	HLC1402 329	HLC1483 303
HLC1322 264	HLC1403 322	HLC1485 404
HLC1323 265	HLC1404 323	HLC1486 406
HLC1324 268	HLC1405 327	HLC1487 406
HLC1325 264	HLC1406 319	HLC1488 406
HLC1326 266	HLC1407 330	HLC1489 405
HLC1327 266	HLC1408 265	HLC1490 405
HLC1328 451	HLC1409 329	HLC1491 405
HLC1329 448	HLC1410 275	HLC1492 406
HLC1330 448	HLC1411 97	HLC1493 406
HLC1331 450	HLC1412 97	HLC1494 406
HLC1332 450	HLC1413 317	HLC1495 406
HLC1334 380	HLC1414 317	HLC1496 407
HLC1335 458	HLC1415 269	HLC1497 407
HLC1336 474	HLC1416 271	HLC1498 406
HLC1337 266	HLC1417 331	HLC1499 406
HLC1338 514	HLC1418 387	HLC1501 256
HLC1339 515	HLC1419 265	HLC1502 89
HLC1340 404	HLC1420 385	HLC1504 145
HLC1342 450	HLC1421 383	HLC1505 358
HLC1345 .... 5, 127	HLC1422 387	HLC1506 358
HLC1346 256	HLC1423 387	HLC1507 358
HLC1347 258	HLC1424 385	HLC1508 358
HLC1350 279	HLC1425 459	HLC1509 79
HLC1351 278	HLC1426 459	HLC1510 40
HLC1352 270	HLC1428 459	HLC1512 130
HLC1353 458	HLC1432 459	HLC1516 363
HLC1354 274	HLC1434 515	HLC1517 359
HLC1355 75	HLC1435 514	HLC1520 274
HLC1356 258	HLC1436 318	HLC1521 348
HLC1357 255	HLC1437 352	HLC1522 78
HLC1358 314	HLC1438 350	HLC1523 46
HLC1359 98	HLC1439 340	HLC1526 330
HLC1360 315	HLC1440 340	HLC1528 .... 30, 33
HLC1361 316	HLC1441 342	HLC1529 387
HLC1362 255	HLC1442 342	HLC1531 518
HLC1363 126	HLC1443 267	HLC1533 517
HLC1364 180	HLC1444 314	HLC1534 291
HLC1366 258	HLC1445 314	HLC1537 518
HLC1367 347	HLC1447 317	HLC1538 514
HLC1368 257	HLC1448 316	HLC1539 514
HLC1369 352	HLC1449 317	HLC1540 514
HLC1370 344	HLC1450 76	HLC1541 350
HLC1371 106	HLC1451 362	HLC1542 350
HLC1373 177	HLC1452 362	HLC1543 350
HLC1376 268	HLC1453 361	HLC1544 518
HLC1377 47	HLC1454 267	HLC1545 517
HLC1378 267	HLC1455 265	HLC1546 517
HLC1379 266	HLC1457 257	HLC1547 517
HLC1380 56	HLC1462 278	HLC1548 517
HLC1381 56	HLC1463 126	HLC1549 517

Homer Laughlin Index (Unidentified Patterns)

Pattern	Page	Pattern	Page	Pattern	Page
HLC1550	518	HLC1653	319	HLC1739	274
HLC1553	331	HLC1654	258	HLC1740	316
HLC1558	517	HLC1656	319	HLC1741	268
HLC1559	124	HLC1658	314	HLC1743	274
HLC1560	124	HLC1661	341	HLC1744	315
HLC1563	328	HLC1663	318	HLC1745	315
HLC1564	516	HLC1664	322	HLC1746	271
HLC1565	350	HLC1665	86	HLC1747	277
HLC1569	267	HLC1667	369	HLC1748	277
HLC1570	519	HLC1668	369	HLC1749	274
HLC1572	369	HLC1670	86	HLC1750	275
HLC1573	369	HLC1671	75	HLC1751	267
HLC1579	518	HLC1672	78	HLC1752	279
HLC1580	517	HLC1673	75	HLC1753	274
HLC1582	275	HLC1674	75	HLC1754	274
HLC1583	474	HLC1675	349	HLC1755	274
HLC1584	515	HLC1676	350	HLC1756	272
HLC1585	268	HLC1677	340	HLC1757	315
HLC1587	270	HLC1678	340	HLC1758	267
HLC1588	275	HLC1679	350	HLC1759	264
HLC1589	450	HLC1680	340	HLC1760	327
HLC1592	271	HLC1681	340	HLC1761	267
HLC1593	272	HLC1682	353	HLC1762	278
HLC1597	271	HLC1683	208	HLC1763	126
HLC1598	330	HLC1686	264	HLC1764	277
HLC1599	176	HLC1687	348	HLC1765	278
HLC1600	195	HLC1688	346	HLC1766	269
HLC1601	519	HLC1689	353	HLC1767	316
HLC1602	519	HLC1691	77	HLC1768	315
HLC1603	519	HLC1692	47	HLC1769	265
HLC1605	395	HLC1693	208	HLC1770	277
HLC1606	350	HLC1695	268	HLC1771	143
HLC1607	518	HLC1696	266	HLC1772	380
HLC1608	517	HLC1697	271	HLC1773	277
HLC1609	291	HLC1699	268	HLC1774	270
HLC1610	291	HLC1700	254	HLC1775	277
HLC1611	291	HLC1701	265	HLC1776	323
HLC1612	291	HLC1702	359	HLC1777	323
HLC1613	387	HLC1703	318	HLC1778	276
HLC1614	269	HLC1704	268	HLC1779	275
HLC1615	269	HLC1705	265	HLC1780	279
HLC1616	265	HLC1707	382	HLC1781	143
HLC1617	516	HLC1708	348	HLC1782	89
HLC1618	517	HLC1710	270	HLC1783	131
HLC1620	254	HLC1711	303	HLC1784	131
HLC1621	254	HLC1713	404	HLC1785	131
HLC1622	254	HLC1714	404	HLC1786	131
HLC1623	434	HLC1715	405	HLC1787	131
HLC1625	434	HLC1716	404	HLC1788	406
HLC1627	305	HLC1717	404	HLC1791	130
HLC1628	305	HLC1718	275	HLC1792	328
HLC1629	147	HLC1719	331	HLC1794	492
HLC1631	435	HLC1721	279	HLC1795	46
HLC1632	369	HLC1722	333	HLC1796	330
HLC1633	350	HLC1723	333	HLC1798	269
HLC1634	350	HLC1724	270	HLC1800	405
HLC1635	350	HLC1725	270	HLC1801	405
HLC1636	33	HLC1726	265	HLC1802	406
HLC1638	364	HLC1727	275	HLC1803	406
HLC1639	117	HLC1728	275	HLC1804	406
HLC1642	267	HLC1729	275	HLC1805	406
HLC1643	270	HLC1730	331	HLC1806	406
HLC1644	347	HLC1731	383	HLC1807	406
HLC1645	345	HLC1733	369	HLC1808	405
HLC1646	330	HLC1734	369	HLC1809	404
HLC1647	318	HLC1735	369	HLC1810	405
HLC1648	258	HLC1736	369	HLC1811	404
HLC1650	318	HLC1737	369	HLC1812	405
HLC1651	317	HLC1738	387	HLC1813	405

(Unidentified Patterns) *Homer Laughlin Index*

HLC1814 404	HLC1890 303	HLC1975 159
HLC1815 404	HLC1891 87	HLC1976 418
HLC1816 405	HLC1892 87	HLC1977 416
HLC1817 405	HLC1893 87	HLC1978 111
HLC1818 405	HLC1894 200	HLC1979 157
HLC1819 405	HLC1895 199	HLC1980 414
HLC1820 404	HLC1896 208	HLC1984 514
HLC1821 405	HLC1897 165	HLC1985 514
HLC1822 404	HLC1898 165	HLC1987 234
HLC1823 404	HLC1899 165	HLC1988 467
HLC1824 405	HLC1900 332	HLC1989 291
HLC1825 371	HLC1901 332	HLC1990 254
HLC1826 371	HLC1902 332	HLC1991 254
HLC1827 332	HLC1903 315	HLC1993 352
HLC1828 332	HLC1904 316	HLC1994 486
HLC1829 331	HLC1907 330	HLC1996 195
HLC1830 331	HLC1908 331	HLC1997 118
HLC1832 327	HLC1909 277	HLC1998 .... 207, 209
HLC1835 47	HLC1910 327	HLC2003 182
HLC1836 46	HLC1911 381	HLC2004 117
HLC1837 264	HLC1912 386	HLC2005 450
HLC1838 330	HLC1914 308	HLC2006 182
HLC1839 297	HLC1919 269	HLC2007 324
HLC1840 59	HLC1920 479	HLC2008 458
HLC1841 58	HLC1921 315	HLC2010 181
HLC1842 57	HLC1922 315	HLC2012 291
HLC1844 449	HLC1923 315	HLC2013 369
HLC1845 347	HLC1927 266	HLC2014 328
HLC1847 330	HLC1928 267	HLC2015 64
HLC1848 332	HLC1930 271	HLC2017 64
HLC1849 332	HLC1932 271	HLC2018 192
HLC1851 33	HLC1933 271	HLC2019 112
HLC1852 60	HLC1934 271	HLC2020 37
HLC1853 332	HLC1935 273	HLC2021 147
HLC1854 332	HLC1936 269	HLC2022 88
HLC1855 264	HLC1937 264	HLC2023 199
HLC1856 271	HLC1938 272	HLC2025 90
HLC1857 332	HLC1939 264	HLC2027 108
HLC1858 330	HLC1940 270	HLC2029 40
HLC1859 291	HLC1942 264	HLC2035 60
HLC1860 291	HLC1944 .... 313, 328	HLC2036 182
HLC1861 273	HLC1945 266	HLC2037 108
HLC1862 332	HLC1946 271	HLC2038 164
HLC1863 331	HLC1947 271	HLC2039 180
HLC1864 333	HLC1948 271	HLC2040 144
HLC1865 331	HLC1949 265	HLC2042 419
HLC1866 327	HLC1950 165	HLC2043 302
HLC1867 112	HLC1951 116	HLC2044 86
HLC1868 302	HLC1952 116	HLC2045 387
HLC1869 302	HLC1953 297	HLC2048 448
HLC1870 302	HLC1954 450	HLC2049 270
HLC1871 303	HLC1955 266	HLC2054 56
HLC1872 331	HLC1956 272	HLC2055 449
HLC1873 303	HLC1957 268	HLC2064 371
HLC1874 302	HLC1958 264	HLC2066 353
HLC1875 266	HLC1960 .... 63, 65	HLC2067 402
HLC1876 329	HLC1961 174	HLC2069 64
HLC1878 329	HLC1962 176	HLC2070 60
HLC1879 449	HLC1963 174	HLC2075 64
HLC1880 .... 302, 534	HLC1964 182	HLC2078 .... 110, 111
HLC1881 302	HLC1965 178	HLC2081 209
HLC1882 302	HLC1966 116	HLC2084 418
HLC1883 302	HLC1967 116	HLC2085 108
HLC1884 302	HLC1968 119	HLC2090 345
HLC1885 302	HLC1969 116	HLC2091 158
HLC1886 302	HLC1971 416	HLC2095 346
HLC1887 303	HLC1972 415	HLC2099 70
HLC1888 302	HLC1973 182	HLC2100 58
HLC1889 303	HLC1974 415	HLC2101 177

Homer Laughlin Index (Unidentified Patterns)

HLC2102 317	HLC3002 79	HLC3097 255
HLC2104 414	HLC3003 65	HLC3099 514
HLC2105 305	HLC3004 342	HLC3100 192
HLC2107 .... 312, 318	HLC3006 314	HLC3101 192
HLC2108 66	HLC3010 173	HLC3103 159
HLC2110 107	HLC3011 179	HLC3104 298
HLC2112 37	HLC3012 234	HLC3105 90
HLC2116 382	HLC3013 79	HLC3106 349
HLC2117 360	HLC3014 .... 63, 65	HLC3107 107
HLC2118 329	HLC3015 262	HLC3110 87
HLC2119 341	HLC3016 107	HLC3112 .... 52, 55
HLC2120 .... 39, 40	HLC3017 192	HLC3118 85
HLC2121 183	HLC3019 258	HLC3120 329
HLC2123 418	HLC3022 258	HLC3132 505
HLC2124 145	HLC3023 108	HLC3447 88
HLC2125 66	HLC3024 414	HLC3448 40
HLC2126 142	HLC3026 .... 197, 199	HLC3449 450
HLC2128 145	HLC3028 517	HLC3452 118
HLC2129 450	HLC3029 70	JEP1 510
HLC2131 145	HLC3030 318	LEZ1 348
HLC2132 65	HLC3031 180	LEZ2 348
HLC2133 418	HLC3032 180	LEZ3 348
HLC2134 144	HLC3033 181	PEA6 414
HLC2135 349	HLC3034 181	PFD1 508
HLC2138 448	HLC3035 180	PFD2 508
HLC2139 414	HLC3036 382	PFD3 508
HLC2140 75	HLC3037 182	
HLC2142 450	HLC3038 178	
HLC2146 479	HLC3039 174	
HLC2150 179	HLC3040 182	
HLC2151 176	HLC3041 179	
HLC2152 175	HLC3042 181	
HLC2153 176	HLC3043 .... 198, 199	
HLC2154 181	HLC3044 177	
HLC2155 344	HLC3045 183	
HLC2157 .... 69, 70	HLC3046 180	
HLC2158 349	HLC3047 173	
HLC2160 254	HLC3048 180	
HLC2161 165	HLC3049 174	
HLC2163 178	HLC3050 175	
HLC2164 341	HLC3052 181	
HLC2165 204	HLC3053 174	
HLC2169 363	HLC3054 180	
HLC2171 95	HLC3056 178	
HLC2173 298	HLC3057 180	
HLC2176 419	HLC3059 179	
HLC2177 352	HLC3060 178	
HLC2178 85	HLC3061 178	
HLC2179 298	HLC3062 175	
HLC2181 163	HLC3063 174	
HLC2182 180	HLC3066 179	
HLC2183 47	HLC3067 183	
HLC2186 178	HLC3068 179	
HLC2189 314	HLC3070 183	
HLC2190 59	HLC3071 183	
HLC2192 327	HLC3072 181	
HLC2195 373-374	HLC3074 174	
HLC2197 146	HLC3075 176	
HLC2198 143	HLC3076 179	
HLC2199 448	HLC3077 177	
HLC2200 449	HLC3078 175	
HLC2206 118	HLC3079 179	
HLC2229 .... 465, 467	HLC3080 108	
HLC2239 518	HLC3081 200	
HLC2240 .... 487, 488	HLC3083 181	
HLC2250 72	HLC3086 148	
HLC2254 .... 136, 148	HLC3088 234	
HLC3000 266	HLC3092 162	
HLC3001 193	HLC3095 107	

559